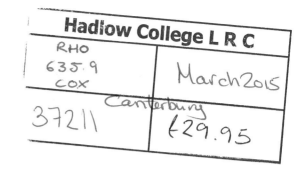
RHODODENDRONS & AZALEAS
A COLOUR GUIDE

Kenneth Cox

THE CROWOOD PRESS

First published in 2005 by
The Crowood Press Ltd
Ramsbury, Marlborough
Wiltshire SN8 2HR

www.crowood.com

This impression 2012

British Library Cataloguing-in-Publication Data
A catalogue record for this book is available from the British Library.

ISBN 978 1 86126 784 9

DEDICATION
TO JANE

Typeface used: ITC Franklin Gothic.

Typeset and designed by
D & N Publishing
Hungerford, Berkshire.

Printed and bound in India by Replika Press Pvt. Ltd.

CONTENTS

ACKNOWLEDGEMENTS

This book could not have been written without the wealth of knowledge passed on from my father Peter Cox, who is also a great checker of manuscripts; I do the same checking for his books. My wife Jane, with years of publishing experience, is my unofficial agent and is also an excellent editor, more on the stylistic stuff, but I must really thank her too for putting up with all the long hours I have been at work on my computer while the children were screaming. This book has been a mammoth research project: looking into what plants are available, sifting through endless catalogues, websites and books. But most of all, it has been about asking questions to rhododendron growers in the furthest corners of the globe: I have corresponded with growers in Chile and Brazil, as well as in more obvious growing regions. Huge numbers of people have helped out with information and evaluations, which have gone into this book. None more so than Dr Alan Leslie at the RHS at Wisley, who is guardian of the Rhododendron Register. He has been patiently answering questions on obscure hybrids for the last year and finally produced his magnum opus in time for me to check the whole book against the new register, which you can now buy in print.

The following people, a veritable Who's Who of rhododendron and azalea experts, provided me with valuable information, much of which went straight into the book, especially forthright comments. UK: Dr David Chamberlain, Will Murch, Chris Fairweather, Chris Callard, Cameron Fleming, Gerald Dixon, George Argent, Dave Mitchell (for allowing me to photograph vireyas at RBGE), John Hammond, Gerald Dixon, David Millais, and many of our customers over the years, too many to list here. USA and Canada: Al Campbell, John Weagle, Chris Watson, Ken Gibson, Steve Hootman, Hank Schannen, Ron Rabideau and Jerry van de Sande from Rarefind, Warner Brack, George Woodard, Bill Steele, Kathy Van Veen, Howard Klein, Paul Molinari, Bill Moyles, Bob Stelloh, Parker Smith, Tadeusz Dauksza, W. Spohn, W. Sweeny, Dick Chaikin, Peter Schick and Vincent Lynch, Dr Harold Sweetman, Dick Cavender, Paul James, Sonia Nelson, Maarten Van Der Giessen, Buddy Lee, William Miller, Dave Hammond, Whitney Berry and PDSI, Sally and John Perkins, Jim Barlup, Annie and Ellie Sather, Harold Greer, Warren Berg, June Sinclair, H. Edward Reiley, Herb Spady, Steve Krebbs, L. Clarence Towe, Don Voss, Don Hyatt, Sonoma Nursery. Australia: Ken Gillanders (for lots of useful information on Australian rhododendrons), Graham Snell, Barry Davidson, Camellia Grove Nursery. New Zealand: Denis Hughes, Tony and Lyn Blythe, John Kenyon, Richard Currie, Kathryn Millar. Holland: Tijs Huisman. Belgium: Henrick Van Oost. Germany: Holger and Mrs Hans Hachmann, Hartwig Schepker, Wolfgang Reich. Finland: Peter Tigerstedt, Kristian Theqvist, Lennarth Jonsson. Latvia: Prof Rihards Kondratovičs.

The following people kindly lent me excellent pictures for use in this book: Dan Krabill, Don Voss, Don Hyatt, Mike Creel, Earl Sommerville, Martin van der Giessen, J. Coleman, Ron Rabideau, John Weagle, Henrick Van Oost, Peter Cox, Patricia Cox, Matt Heasman, Keith Rushforth, PDSI (Encore Azaleas), Richard Currie (Vireyas), H. Helm.

R. ORBICULARE LEAVES.

INTRODUCTION

With around 900 species, the genus *Rhododendron* is one of the largest and most varied in the plant kingdom. Rhododendrons can be found growing wild from the Arctic to the equator and from sea level to over 5,000m in the Himalaya. For most people, the word rhododendron conjures up a vision of the large-flowered hybrids that line the driveways of large country-houses and estates but, in fact, many rhododendrons don't look like this at all. Some alpine species have tiny leaves and carpet the ground in low mounds, while other species are giant trees with leaves up to 1m in length. Another part of the genus encompasses the spectacular tropical *Vireya* rhododendrons found in Indonesia and neighbouring areas. And to make things a little more confusing, azaleas were merged into the genus *Rhododendron* over 100 years ago.

My family has been long associated with rhododendron collecting and growing. Just after the First World War, my grandfather, Euan Cox, was looking for an excuse to postpone returning to Dundee in Scotland to run the family jute-business. A chance meeting with the then well-known plant-hunter Reginald Farrer resulted in an invitation to go on an adventure to Burma. The 1919 expedition was to be Farrer's last, as he died in the field in 1920. Knowing virtually nothing about plants before he went on this expedition, Euan arrived back with considerable knowledge and a large quantity of exciting seed to distribute. Some of the resulting seedlings were planted at Glendoick, in Eastern Scotland, the Cox family home. Euan never went plant-hunting again, though he spent the rest of his life in gardening-related activities, editing horticultural publications, writing gardening columns and books and, in the process, enthusing my father, with whom he started a rhododendron nursery at Glendoick in 1953. My father, Peter Cox V.M.H., is himself a nurseryman, plant-hunter, author and rhododendron hybridizer and I had only two choices: to run away, or carry on the family tradition.

R. CALOSTROTUM AND *R. WARDII* NEAR POME, SOUTH-EAST TIBET.

WILD RHODODENDRONS AND HOW THEY CAME TO BE CULTIVATED

It is impossible to say exactly how many rhododendron species there are. The figure of 900 is often bandied about, but the number goes up and down, a bit like stocks and shares, as species are described and 'sunk' by rival botanists. Man-made rhododendron hybrids have been raised over the last 200 years and there are now approximately 25,000 registered cultivars, most of which are probably still in existence somewhere. This book covers all the temperate and many of the tropical rhododendron and azalea species in cultivation, and the 3,000 or so most commercially important man-made cultivars.

Rhododendrons belong to the family Ericaceae, which also includes the heathers, *Kalmia*, *Enkianthus*, *Gaultheria*, blueberries and cranberries; almost all the members of this family require acidic soil and a fair amount of moisture. Rhododendrons are found throughout much of the northern hemisphere, extending into the southern hemisphere through the Malay peninsula and the Indonesian islands, with two species on mountains in northern Australia. The distribution of temperate rhododendrons – the kind commonly grown as garden plants in parts of the world with cold winters – centres on China and the Himalaya. There are several species native to Europe, while most of the deciduous azalea species come from North America. There are no species native to South America or Africa. The European species, such as the alpine *R. ferrugineum* and the sweetly scented pontic azalea *R. luteum*, have long been cultivated in gardens and are referred to in both horticultural and medicinal literature of the sixteenth and seventeenth centuries. Several American azalea species were introduced to Europe in the seventeenth and eighteenth centuries and by 1800 there were around twelve species in garden cultivation in Europe, including the infamous *R. ponticum*, now an invasive weed in parts of the British Isles. It wasn't long before hybridizers got to work on the raw material, trying to improve flower size and colour. From 1810–1840 a range of hardy azalea hybrids known as 'The Ghents' were developed, as well as the first so-called hardy hybrid rhododendrons

such as 'Cunningham's White' and 'Nobleanum'. You can still buy many of these early hybrids today. The mid-nineteenth century also saw the Golden Age of the newly developed glasshouses and conservatories, constructed on an ever more lavish scale to house the newly introduced tropical plants. One of the most popular groups of plants was the tropical 'Vireya' rhododendron species and the numerous hybrids soon created from them.

The number of cultivated species of rhododendron more than doubled in the 1850s, with the new discoveries from Joseph Hooker's expedition to Sikkim. He collected forty-five species, most new to science, many of which proved their garden value and which would, in turn, be used to breed an ever larger range of hybrids. The Hooker Himalayan species included the blood-red *R. thomsonii* with rounded leaves and fine peeling bark, the tall and vigorous *R. griffithianum* with massive scented white flowers and the magnificent *R. falconeri* with large furry leaves and enormous trusses of cream. Gardeners marvelled at these flowering trees, the like of which had never been seen before. Soon rhododendrons were the 'must-have' plant and the newest varieties commanded considerable prices. No self-respecting country house was complete without beds of them incorporated into drive sides and parkland landscapes.

The first two decades of the twentieth century were the peak years of plant-hunting in China and the Himalaya. Following in the footsteps of French missionaries-turned-botanists in China, such as Père David and Abbé Delavay, Ernest Wilson's first expedition to Hubei province in 1899 introduced *Rhododendron auriculatum*, *R. maculiferum* and *R. sutchuenense*. He returned

to China in 1903–4 and was followed by George Forrest in Yunnan in 1904, Frank Kingdon Ward in 1911 and Joseph Rock in 1920. These plant hunters sent back specimens and seeds of thousands of species of plants, including several hundred species of rhododendron. The pressed specimens would be pounced on by eager botanists at the herbaria at the British Museum, Edinburgh, Kew or the Arnold Arboretum in Boston, who described scores of new species in the obligatory botanical Latin. Keen gardeners, usually those with great estates and plenty of labour, grew the seeds on a huge scale – though, with virtually no idea what conditions these new plants required, many seed batches never reached maturity. After returning from his one and only plant-hunting expedition, my grandfather Euan Cox edited the magazine *New Flora and Silva*, which documented these exciting new plant introductions and their qualities or failings, describing the first time many plant species were grown in gardens. This was the era of the woodland garden and great gardens, such as Caerhays and Exbury, were laid out, with their owners competing for awards at the exclusive gentleman's club that was The Rhododendron Society. Some of the recently introduced species, such as *R. griersonianum* and *R. wardii*, soon proved to be excellent parents and many new hybrids of all shapes and sizes were created. Some of the all-time classic hybrids, such as 'Loderi', 'Fabia', 'Vanessa' and 'Lady Chamberlain', were created at this time. The introduction of *R. yakushimanum*, a compact, hardy, easily grown species from Japan, in the early 1930s proved, in time, to be the most important hybridizing parent of all: breeders in the U.K., Germany and North America raised 'Yak' hybrids, a range of

RHODODENDRON LEAVES SHOWING THE RANGE OF SHAPES, COLOURS AND TEXTURES.

GLENDOICK BIRDS: A RANGE OF DWARF HYBRID RHODODENDRONS FROM THE AUTHOR'S NURSERY.

TRADITIONAL LANDSCAPE USE OF RHODODENDRONS, DRUMLANRIG CASTLE, SCOTLAND.

low-growing, compact and hardy plants with showy flowers of many different shades. At Glendoick, my father, Peter Cox, began hybridizing very dwarf species of rhododendron in the late 1950s, raising the now well-known bird hybrids such as 'Curlew' and 'Ptarmigan'. I began making crosses of my own in the 1980s and the breeding programme continues to this day, now concentrating on coloured foliage. Since the 1950s, North America and Germany have taken over as key areas for hybridizing new hardy rhododendrons, while in Australia and New Zealand hundreds of spectacular tender Vireya hybrids have been raised.

China, Burma and many of the other key rhododendron countries closed their doors to foreigners during the 1950s, 1960s and 1970s. Only a handful of new rhododendron species were introduced during this period. These included my parents' discovery *R. coxianum* from N.E. India, the wonderful *R. pachysanthum* from Taiwan and several species of Vireyas from Borneo and New Guinea. China re-opened its borders to plant hunters in 1980–81 and my father, who had waited thirty years for the chance, was on the first major expedition back into the stomping ground of his plant-hunting heroes from the early part of the twentieth century. The Sino-British Expedition to the Cang Shan (SBEC) in Yunnan was the first of many that have explored and re-explored this extraordinarily plant-rich region of the world. Since 1981, many new plant species have been introduced to the West, including several new species of rhododendron. Among the most important introductions of the last few years are the giant *R. sinofalconeri* with yellow flowers and large leaves, the red species from the Yunnan/Sichuan border *R. ochraceum* and the neat deep-pink dwarf species *R. dendrocharis*. I have led several expeditions to south-east Tibet and the Indian state of Arunachal Pradesh during the last few years, in some cases into completely virgin territory for plant hunters, introducing several species for the first time, such as *R. bulu*, *R. dignabile* and *R. trilectorum*. You might well think that all the species of rhododendron had been discovered by now, but I discovered two species new to science in 2001 in Arunachal Pradesh, near the India-Tibet border, and I'm sure that there are more out there. In fact, new species and subspecies are still being named and there are several desirable species that we only know from photographs and which have never been introduced to the West.

RHODODENDRONS AND AZALEAS: WHAT IS THE DIFFERENCE?

Rhododendrons and azaleas were once two separate genera, but taxonomists merged them into a single genus *Rhododendron*. Most people can see that rhododendrons and azaleas look a bit different and there are some taxonomic characters that separate them: most azaleas have five stamens and most rhododendrons have ten or more. Azaleas never have scales on their leaves and the hairs on the leaves differ from those found on rhododendrons. Rhododendrons cannot normally be hybridized with azaleas, though there are a few examples, called azaleodendrons. It turns out that the two main groups of azaleas, the Japanese or evergreens and the deciduous azaleas, are probably more distantly related to one another than they are to the typical rhododendrons and no one has ever managed to cross the evergreen and deciduous groups, as far as I know. From a gardening point of view it is true to say that the azaleas are more versatile than rhododendrons in some ways. Some deciduous azaleas, such as the Northern Lights series of hybrids, are extremely hardy and, as they lose their leaves, can survive extreme winter cold, while many evergreen azaleas are heat and humidity tolerant and can also make excellent houseplants.

RHODODENDRONS IN THE WILD

There are few sights in the plant world to equal rhododendrons in full flower in their native mountains. The greatest concentration of rhododendron species, around 300–400, is found in an area from Nepal, Bhutan and Burma, north and east through S.E. Tibet into Yunnan and Sichuan provinces in China. Here mighty rivers, the Tsangpo, the Salween, the Mekong and the Yangtze, flow though deep gorges at altitudes of up to 2,700–3000m (9,000–10,000ft) while, on either side, mountain ranges climb to 7,500m (25,000ft) or more. Wherever the rainfall is high enough for rich forest, there are usually rhododendrons to be found. The river valleys are often hot and dry, but a little further up the mountain sides the rhododendrons begin. At the lower altitudes, in deep lush forest, epiphytic species can be found (which grow on other plants and mossy logs) and large-leaved species, such as the magnificent *R. sinogrande* with leaves up to 1m in length. A little higher up, rhododendrons often form the dominant forest: in Nepal the red *R. arboreum* turns the hillsides a dazzling shade of crimson in March and April. Elsewhere species such as *R. phaeochrysum*, *R. oreotrephes* and *R. uvariifolium* form a dense understorey beneath the *Picea* and *Abies*. A little higher still and the trees

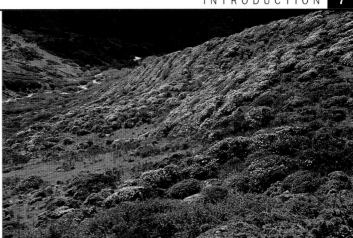

R. PRIMULIFLORUM **AND** *R. AGANNIPHUM* **IN TSARI, TIBET.**

start to thin. Here shrubby species, such as *R. campylocarpum* or *R. roxieanum*, may be the dominant vegetation at and above the treeline. Higher still, the leaves get smaller and the species become lower growing. Here on the windswept moorland you might find Frank Kingdon Ward's 'Scarlet Runner', *R. forrestii*, with its bright waxy flowers often opening up soon after the leaves emerge from the melting snow, or one of the small blue-purple Lapponica species, such as *R. fastigiatum*. It is possible to find 20–30 species on a single mountainside in some of the richer areas and the rhododendrons are usually accompanied by *Primula*, *Meconopsis*, *Diapensia*, *Clematis*, *Deutzia*, *Sorbus*, orchids and many other common garden-plants. If the flowers were not enough, the rhododendrons grow in some of the world's most dramatic scenery. Forget any photographs you have seen. Nothing prepares you for the vastness of the Himalayan and Chinese mountains until you are looking at 3–4,000m (10–13,000ft) of mountain towering above you when you are actually already standing at 3,000m, (10,000ft) yourself. Short of breath but triumphant, you can sit at the top of a mountain pass, surrounded by snow-covered peaks, with the largest natural flower gardens you will ever see spread out in all directions around you. Hunting for rhododendrons in the wild is addictive and exhilarating, but usually exhausting. At the end of each expedition I feel a simultaneous sense of never-again weariness and where-shall-we-go-next expectation.

My first serious rhododendron collecting took place on mountains in Java, Indonesia, where towering bushes of *R. javanicum*, with the brightest orange flowers I had ever seen, tempted me to look for seed. I was astonished to find that shaking the 3m-high bush caused the seed to float slowly towards the ground, strands of it catching in my hair. Vireya rhododendron seed looks rather stringy but, on close inspection, the seed turns out to have a fin or tail, rather like that of a sycamore seed, which enables the seed to float on the breeze and lodge on the mossy branches of trees where it can germinate and grow. Many rhododendrons are epiphytes, growing high up in the branches of trees in forests where the floor is too dark for them to flourish. In 1992, I joined one of my father's collecting expeditions to learn how it is done and since then I have led expeditions almost every year in search of wild rhododendrons. Perhaps the most impressive display of them I have seen was in the sacred valley of Tsari, south-east Tibet. Here hillsides were covered in several species of rhododendron: sweetly pink *R. aganniphum* and daphne-flowered cream *R. primuliflorum* surrounded by drifts of the virtually unknown pale-yellow form of *R. phaeochrysum* and, everyone's favourite, rich yellow *R. wardii*, bordered by fast-flowing cataracts of ice-cold snow-melt through primula-filled yak pastures, everything in full flower and framed by jagged snow-topped peaks.

Plant hunter and prolific author Frank Kingdon Ward is probably the finest describer of wild rhododendrons. Here he describes the 'rhododendron fairyland' of the Doshong La in south-east Tibet, a place I have visited three times myself:

> The Valley, flanked by grey cliffs, roofed by grey skies, with the white snowfields above, spouting water which splashed and gurgled in a dozen babbling becks; and everywhere the rocks swamped under a tidal wave of tense colours which gleam and glow in leagues of breaking light. The colours leap at you as you climb the moraine: Scarlet Runner dripping in blood red rivers from the ledges…choppy sulphur seas breaking from a long, low surf of pink…

RIDDLE OF THE TSANGPO GORGES

CULTIVATING RHODODENDRONS

The basic requirements of rhododendrons are:

1. **Acid soil** (*see* below).
2. **Moisture *and* air to the roots in the growing season**.
   Rhododendrons are shallow-rooted and not very drought-tolerant. They can withstand a few days of wilting, but much beyond this, most will desiccate and not recover. Rhododendron roots need a constant supply of oxygen and for this soil needs to be open and friable. Heavy, clay soils are dense with very little air and this is not suitable for rhododendrons. Waterlogged or heavy soil and high temperature is a particularly lethal combination.
3. **Temperatures**.
   Most rhododendrons suffer or die in extremes of heat or cold; areas with very cold winters or very hot and dry summers make rhododendron growing very difficult or impossible. The limit for cold hardiness is about –30 to –34°C (–22 to –29°F) (USDA zone 4). Outside the China–Himalaya region, the best rhododendron growing areas are found not too far from the sea.

SOILS: ACID OR ALKALINE?

Acidity in soil is measured by the pH scale. Neutral is pH 7 (neither acid nor alkaline). Lower numbers are acid and higher numbers are alkaline. Most rhododendrons enjoy a pH of between 4 and 6 – ideally between 4.5 and 5.5. On chalky or limey soils or where water is very hard rhododendrons grow very poorly or not at all. The reasons for this are complex but, essentially, soil pH affects the availability to the plant of elements, such as iron, and the health of micro-organisms, both essential to rhododendron growth. In addition, in alkaline soils rhododendrons appear to poison themselves by taking up too much calcium, hindering photosynthesis. Some rhododendrons actually grow on dolomitic limestone in the wild but, on closer inspection, their roots are usually in a layer of acidic leaf-litter on top of the limestone – the high rainfall ensures that the water is constantly replaced. I have seen plenty of examples of very chlorotic (sick) plants on limestone in the wild, where the roots have come into contact with the rock itself. Soil pH can be ascertained, either professionally or with a soil test kit or meter, which can be purchased from a garden centre. Ensure that soil samples are taken from several sites in the garden, as pH can vary considerably even within a small area. Alternatively and more simply, you can work out what the soil of your area is like by looking in other people's gardens. Rhododendrons (including azaleas) and other members of the family Ericaceae, such as heathers, are an indicator of acid soil, as are blue Hortensia hydrangeas. Conversely, a lack of acid-loving plants in the area and hard water (which doesn't lather) in the taps are two very obvious clues to alkalinity. A few words to neighbouring gardeners will soon give you all the information you need.

If the soil is found to be alkaline, the next thing to find out is whether it is artificially (and therefore temporarily) alkaline. Both farmers and vegetable gardeners often lime their soil routinely to increase yield; in this case, the lime will be washed out over several years, the soil gradually becoming acid.

Sometimes the materials of house building and hard landscaping, such as rubble, cement and mortar, will result in pockets of alkaline soil. Chlorotic leaves (with yellow veining) are a good indicator. Removal of rubble/cement or similar and the addition of peat will usually solve the problem.

Neutral soil or artificially limed soil can be acidified by mixing in a percentage of peat. Alternatively, flowers of sulphur or ferrous sulphate can be applied. Ferrous sulphate can be sprinkled on the top of the soil, while sulphur is best dug through. To reduce an area of soil of 20sq m by one pH unit (from pH7 to pH6, for instance) requires approximately 1.5kg of ferrous sulphate. Light soils require less than heavy, clay soils. It takes a while for the acidification to take place and it advisable to retest the pH several months after application. Iron chelates (sequestrene) can be used to treat plants with iron-deficiency chlorosis caused by too high a pH. Sequestrene is often prescribed by so-called experts as a cure-all antibiotic for any yellow-leaved rhododendron. In my opinion, yellow leaves are more commonly caused by poor drainage, over-deep planting, starvation or drought rather than a soil pH/iron problem and the expensive sequestrene won't cure any of these problems.

You might be surprised to find that there are several varieties of rhododendron that can tolerate only slightly acid or near-neutral soil. These include the species *R. augustinii*, *rubiginosum*, *decorum*, *hirsutum*, *primuliflorum*, *sanguineum* ssp. *didymum*, *trichostomum*, *vernicosum* and the hybrids 'Cunningham's White' and 'Puncta'. An important recent breakthrough for near-neutral soils is the German INKARHO® rootstock. This selected rootstock grows well in pH 5.5–7 and popular hybrids are grafted onto it. It is also tolerant of relatively heavy soils, so it allows a larger range of cultivars to be grown in less than ideal conditions.

If your soil and water are actually alkaline (higher than pH7), probably the only solution, apart from moving house, is to grow rhododendrons in a raised bed that isolates the growing medium of the rhododendrons and other acid lovers from the natural garden soil. Beds are usually lined with heavy polythene or similar, and filled with acid topsoil from elsewhere or a compost made up from peat, bark and other acid organic matter, usually with some acid loam and grit added. It is most important to ensure good drainage. A flat, polythene-lined bed can all too easily become like a muddy swimming pool in wet weather, so where possible, the lining should be sloped so excess water can drain out the front, back or sides. Where this is not possible, fill the bottom layer of the bed with coarse, free-draining material such as coarse crushed rock, or gravel or even build small drains or soakaways. If possible the bed should be 30cm (12in) or more in depth, so that the roots are not in contact with the lining. The sides of the bed can be of any suitable materials: wood, bricks, peat blocks and so on. If tap water is alkaline, the bed must be watered with rainwater or artificially acidified water. Many people collect roof water in water butts for this purpose. To cut down on evaporation, it is well worth applying a mulch (*see* page 9).

WHAT IS MY SOIL STRUCTURE LIKE?

Having the right soil structure to grow rhododendrons is very important. Soil types are usually defined by the particle size they contain. Soils with the largest particle size are sands. These have excellent drainage, but poor retention of water and nutrients. At the other end of the scale are clays, which have microscopically small particles and have very good water and mineral retentive properties but are compacted and slow-draining, preventing aeration for the roots. Loams are made up of a combination of sand and clay and are the ideal basis for a growing medium for rhododendrons, being well aerated but moisture and nutrient retentive.

Clay soils do not crumble when squeezed and they are heavy and dense. The speed of drainage can easily be seen by digging a hole and filling it with water. Clay soils tend to have very slow drainage while, in sandy soils, the water drains away very quickly. Soils with poor drainage encourage the potentially lethal fungal disease Phytophthora. Certain rhododendron varieties are particularly sensitive (many species and most yellow hybrids for instance) and it is a severe problem in areas with hot summers, especially when combined with frequent artificial watering. Almost all soils are best improved artificially for optimum growing conditions for rhododendrons; heavy clay or very sandy soils will normally require the most work. Clay soils can be improved by the addition of larger particles. This can take the form of inert materials such as grit and perlite or, better, the use of organic matter such as leafmould and composted bark (*see* below). Clay should be worked in fairly dry conditions and compacted clay can be broken up with gypsum applications in winter and by exposure to frost. But it is usually better to build raised beds and garden *on* rather than *in* your clay; it saves a lot of backache working in your heavy soil, as well as being good for the plants. Sandy soils also benefit from the addition of organic matter and, in this case, peat can be added to the list as it has excellent moisture retention. A mulch to cut down evaporation is also useful on light or sandy soils.

LEAF CHLOROSIS IS A SURE SIGN OF POOR SOIL CONDITIONS.

ORGANIC MATTER: THE MAGIC INGREDIENT

There are lots of examples of organic matter: composted leaves (leafmould), bark, conifer needles or garden waste are some. This soil ameliorant has many functions: improving soil structure, maintaining the correct pH, adding nutrients and trace elements, and encouraging tiny beneficial fungi called mycorrhiza, which associate with the rhododendron roots. Only now are we starting to understand what role these microscopic organisms play: it seems that they aid nutrient absorption into the roots and also produce a substance (glomalin) that binds soil particles together, giving the soil the structure that rhododendrons need.

Rhododendrons benefit from thorough soil preparation. It is astonishing how many people are prepared to invest a lot of money in plants but are reluctant to spend anything on soil improvement. The healthiest rhododendrons I have seen live in soils rich in leafmould and conifer needles that have fallen year after year from the trees which shelter them. Partially rotted leafmould from the previous year's leaf-fall is an excellent planting medium, which, if you are lucky, may be available for nothing. Composted bark can be bought by the bag or by the lorry load. We make excellent organic matter at Glendoick by chipping conifer trimmings (from × *Cupressocyparis leylandii* hedges, for instance), mostly needles rather than sawdust, and letting them compost for a year. General garden compost or, on a larger scale, composted straw, general green-waste, sawdust, wood chippings, newspaper and other substances have also been used successfully. All these substances contribute to soil aeration and moisture retention, as well as providing nutrients as they rot down. There have been some disasters, however, and I do not recommend using large quantities of an untried source of organic matter until it has been tested on a small scale, especially if you are unsure of the source, exact ingredients or age of the material. In the case of bark, sawdust and woodchips, extra fertilizer is required, as these substances require large amounts of nitrogen to break down and, without added feeding, the soil can soon become nitrogen-starved. Ammonium sulphate, often used for this purpose, is a common and cheap fertilizer. In the process of breaking down the organic matter, it brings about greater acidity, which in turn provides a favourable pH for the micro-organisms essential for composting. Fresh organic matter can heat up to considerable temperatures when composting and should not be used until it has cooled down, which may take several months.

Sawdust can be a good organic medium but it can be a curse. In the Pacific Northwest of North America, the sawdust from Douglas fir seems to be of a consistent standard and is commonly and successfully used in huge quantities by nurserymen to raise field-grown rhododendrons. The downside of sawdust is that, over the years, it can rot down to a fine sludge with very poor drainage. It also seems to be a substance that encourages the dreaded root-rot *Phytophthora cinnamoni*. Outside the Pacific Northwest, I would only add a small percentage of sawdust to your soil mix due to the variability both of tree source and degree of composting (and therefore fertilizer requirement). Beware of lawn-mowings in your compost; ensure it is well mixed with other substances as, used on its own, it is too fine and will heat up to red hot as it breaks down. Do not use mowings at all if you have applied chemicals on your lawn. We find the ideal rhododendron growing medium is a combination of garden soil with a generous mixture of several of the previously described organic materials mixed into the planting area. Think about preparing an area large enough for the rootball of the future rather than just preparing a small hole large enough for the root at time of purchase. Individual holes with organic matter dug in are fine for large growing varieties, but smaller varieties may well benefit from having a whole bed made up for them as, in time, their roots can spread out into the whole area.

Recent research has revealed that organic matter has the added bonus of providing a suitable environment for bio-control agents (natural pesticides) in the soil. The way this works is very complex, but it appears that the organic matter encourages beneficial soil micro-organisms, which both attack harmful fungal diseases, such as phytopthora, and induce pest and disease resistance in the plant itself, through the production of antibiotics and plant growth-hormones. It seems likely that, in the future, as more and more pesticides are restricted or banned, bio-control agents and specially formulated organic matter will be used more and more to control pests and diseases. The fungus *Trichoderma* is already used in some parts of the world as a soil-mix additive, acting as a mycoparasite to reduce the effects of harmful fungi such as phythopthora.

PLANTING PROCEDURES

Rhododendrons are shallow-rooted plants and planting them too deep is a common cause of failure. The top of the rootball should be at the soil surface, or above it in areas of high rainfall. In heavier soils, loosen it up to a considerable depth below where the rootball will be, to ensure the root is not left sitting on a hard pan with poor drainage. Alternatively plant on top of the soil level, bringing in new compost as planting material. The classic advice given when planting most shrubs is to put fertilizer (such as bonemeal) at the bottom of the hole. This won't do any harm, but is largely a waste of time for rhododendrons because most feeding roots are on the outside and upper surface of the rootball. When planting any rhododendron, remove weeds and improve the soil in an area considerably larger than the current rootball, so that there is ample surrounding soil for the new roots to grow into. As they are so shallowly rooted, it is advisable to keep the area over the roots free of weeds and other competition for moisture. For the same reason, it is usually not a good idea to plant rhododendrons singly in holes cut into lawns, as the grass will soon cover the rootball, competing for nutrients and moisture.

When planting on steep slopes, especially in areas of low rainfall and on very well-drained soils, it may be necessary to terrace the slope somewhat, so that rainwater and artificial irrigation is allowed to collect and soak into the ground around the rootball. Conversely, where rainfall is very high or the ground is heavy clay, considerable success can be had by planting the rhododendrons on the soil surface itself and mounding up a compost high in organic matter around the plant for the roots to grow into. We have found this planting method to be essential in the high rainfall of our Argyll garden, but plants are vulnerable to drying out in their first few growing seasons.

PLANTING STAGES

Remove weeds (with weedkillers if necessary, see page 19) from the planting area.

Prepare the soil. This normally requires the addition of organic matter, as discussed previously, over an area wider and deeper than the rootball. Avoid working soil in wet weather if possible.

A dry rootball will repel water once it has been planted and the plant will languish or die, so ensure the rootball of the plant is moist right through. If very dry or potbound, soak in a bucket of water.

Do not plant the rhododendron too deep. Just cover the rootball and no more. Firm up the soil moderately but thoroughly around the roots, but do not compress the rootball itself. This just compacts the soil under the plant and impairs the drainage.

Unless the rootball and soil are already very wet, water in thoroughly.

It is often useful to mulch the area over the rootball.

MULCHING

Mulching involves putting a thin layer or barrier on top of the rootball of a plant or plants. It can be of many substances: chipped bark, woodchips, compost, grit, old newspaper, old carpets and more. Mulches have several benefits: reducing evaporation (lessening the need for watering), keeping the roots cool in hot weather and insulating them from frost in cold weather, and discouraging weeds. There can be disadvantages too: mulches can prevent the rain penetrating the soil and can tend to provide a hiding place for insects such as vine weevil. Roots sometimes grow up into the mulch, making them vulnerable to winter damage.

Different mulches have different attributes. Beech and oak leafmould are particularly good. Leafmould from sycamore, lime and horse chestnut are less suitable, as the resulting leafmould is slimy at first and powdery later – and can even be alkaline. There are many other materials that work. Old carpets are a favourite of the organic gardening fraternity but they are hardly something that comes readily to hand most of the time, they look dreadful and they don't allow water to penetrate. Keep them for your organic vegetables. Bark and woodchips are excellent for keeping down weeds but they take nitrogen out of the soil as they break down, so you may need to apply extra fertilizer. I do not recommend using these substances fresh, as they heat up when they begin to compost and may also release undesirable chemicals; let them compost for several months first. We have used layers of newspaper for mulching around small and fussy plants. Water it so it becomes soggy and plant through the paper. Then cover with a thin layer of bark or woodchips to improve the appearance. This is especially good for keeping down weeds for the first year when plants are very small and it cuts down on watering.

DEEP MULCH AT RARE FIND NURSERY, EAST U.S.A.

SUNBURN ON
RHODODENDRON LEAVES.

I should put in a word here about using peat as a mulch. Many garden-centre labels give the advice 'mulch with peat once a year'. Peat is a fine soil ameliorant, but 'never mulch with peat' is my slogan; it is worse than useless for this purpose. Peat has no nutrients, repels water and tends to dry to a fine powder that is liable to blow away. And if you asked germinating weeds what their favourite place to germinate might be…. Don't waste your money; peat has none of the qualities required of a mulch.

Finally, avoid the worst mulch of all. Fresh grass clippings are deadly. Whole collections have been killed by mulching with clippings, which heat up to red hot and kill the surface roots. If you use any grass, make sure it is well-composted and mixed with other things. Whichever mulch you choose, keep the layer fairly thin: if the rhododendron roots are buried too deep, the plants will suffer. University of Maryland research revealed a large number of rhododendrons and azaleas in private and public gardens were being killed by over-mulching.

SHADE

The advantages of good shade cover is the protection it offers from frost (especially in spring when flowers and growth are vulnerable), sunburn and heat. In very cold areas such as northern Europe and north-east North America, winter sun coupled with extreme cold can cause a great deal of damage, as the plant loses water to evaporation but cannot replace it because the ground is frozen. Shade can greatly reduce this damage. The disadvantages of too much shade can, however, be significant. Many shade trees are very demanding as regards moisture. Trees such as beech and sycamore are particularly greedy and rhododendrons growing under or near such trees invariably suffer from drought. Oak, larch, pines, spruce and fir are less greedy and let in more light. Heavy shade also causes spindly, straggly and sparse plants, which are often shy-flowering. How much shade rhododendrons require depends on the varieties you grow and where you live. In northern climates, such as Scotland and Scandinavia where summer sun is not intense, most varieties grow and flower best with little or no overhead shade. Here, I think you should always be able to see sky overhead above your plants. As you move south, filtered shade helps to avoid foliage sunburn, flowers quickly wilting, high soil-temperatures and drought. In eastern U.S.A. and other areas with high summer temperatures, most varieties require a considerable amount of shade. In the southern hemisphere the rule, of course, applies in reverse: rhododendrons in Tasmania and Dunedin need less shade than in Adelaide and Auckland further north. For the best of both worlds, try to obtain part-day sun: plenty of light in the morning, but shade in the afternoon, for example.

As a broad generalization, people tend to garden in too much shade. This may not be through choice; often there are restrictions and difficulties in

felling trees. It is worth bearing in mind, however, that it is always easier to fell trees before an area is planted, than when the plants are already growing. Existing trees will get larger and larger, their roots spreading further and further, so do consider doing some serious thinning before you plant up an area. Think hard about which trees to remove. Often a group of trees shelter one another and if you thin them out the remaining ones may blow down. Another option is to leave most of the trees but to limb them up (remove all or most of the lower branches). Too much shade also encourages fungal disease such as mildew. It is sometimes an eye-opener how much better rhododendrons grow after overhead shade is blown down: initial despair after devastating storms often gives way a few years later to comments such as 'it was the best thing that ever happened to the garden'.

In the various rhododendron-growing regions of the world, different trees have been found to be particularly good for shading rhododendrons. We have found oak, Scot's pine, larch, *Sorbus*, *Malus*, *Prunus* and small-leaved maples to be particularly good. *Sorbus* are especially valuable, as they bring colour into the garden in autumn when rhododendrons are at their least interesting. In North America, many of the native trees such as *Liquidamber*, *Nyssa*, dogwood, hemlock, redwood, pine, hickory and oak are all excellent subjects. Trees better avoided include Douglas fir, which is rather greedy and the constant shedding branches tend to damage plants growing beneath them, while *Juglans nigra* and some of its relatives secrete a chemical into the soil that inhibits the growth of many plants. In Australia, *Eucalyptus* species, such as *E. regnans*, and *Quercus coccinea* are successful while, in New Zealand, *Gleditsia* and alder are good. In semi-tropical areas, where vireyas can be grown outdoors, wonderful combinations of palms, tree ferns and other local vegetation can be made with the rhododendrons. If the rainfall is high enough, you may be able to plant the rhododendrons on mossy logs. Wherever you garden, the key is always to avoid greedy trees with shallow roots that will compete with those of the rhododendrons. Try to have the minimum canopy that will give you the protection you require. Some collectors (mostly in North America) have decided in favour of artificial shade and shelter for their species collections, constructing lathe houses with wooden or plastic strip. While not as ornamental as natural tree-cover, the fact that the shade is constant and that there is no competition from tree roots make this an attractive option to provide light or heavy shade and a degree of heat and frost protection.

As plants of open moorland, alpine rhododendron varieties should ideally be grown without tree branches overhead. Unfortunately, alpine varieties, with a few exceptions, are not heat-tolerant and particularly dislike having hot roots, so in areas with hot summers, part-day but not overhead shade is the best option. In Scotland, the only reason for providing alpine varieties with a little shade would be to protect the often early flowers from spring frosts.

WIND

Shelter from strong winds is important for many varieties of rhododendron. As a general rule, rhododendron varieties with the largest leaves and the earliest growth need the most shelter. Unsheltered large-leaved species can easily have their leaves broken at the petiole and can be completely defoliated. Many species have delicate new growth that is vulnerable to wind damage. It is important to ascertain the direction of the prevailing winds. In the U.K., for example, we get strong, rain-bearing south-westerly winds and cold, sometimes snow-bearing, easterlies. Both can be severely damaging. Buildings and walls do, of course, provide shelter but, as solid barriers, they also funnel and lift the wind, redirecting it to strike as hard in other directions. The best wind shelter is provided by permeable barriers, such as trees, shrubs or artificial materials, so that the velocity of the wind is reduced. Rhododendrons shelter one another very well and the tougher ones can always be planted as a barrier to protect less wind-tolerant varieties from the prevailing winds. Shelter may take some time to establish and become effective and, in the meantime, artificial shelter, such as plastic netting, may be used. In coastal gardens, shelter is often absolutely crucial to the success of the garden; ferocious winds laden with salt spray can severely damage many plants. In U.K. coastal gardens, such as Inverewe in Scotland, *Cupressus macrocarpa, Pinus muricata, Pinus radiata, Griselinia littoralis, Arbutus unedo, Escallonia, Olearia,* and many other trees and shrubs are used to create essential dense windbreaks. In colder areas, hardier trees and shrubs are required. In areas with severe winters, strong winds when the ground is frozen can cause severe desiccation of foliage and can defoliate and kill plants. Low-growing and alpine rhododendrons usually require little or no wind-protection (as long as it is not laden with salt spray), as many of them grow in full exposure on mountainsides in the wild.

FROST AND COLD

Rhododendrons vary greatly in cold hardiness. The very hardiest (often known as ironclads) can withstand −32°C (−26°F) or colder, while, in contrast, most of the tropical vireya varieties can withstand little or no frost. Snow, which covers many of the rhododendron species in winter in their native habitats, is an excellent protection from extremes of cold (though its weight can cause breakage) but, in cultivation, snow does not necessarily coincide with the coldest weather. While it is common policy to select only varieties of proven hardiness for the area you live in, few gardeners can resist attempting to grow one or two that are of borderline suitability. In this case, selection of site and clever use of shelter is very important. Even within a small garden, there are microclimates. South and west walls are amongst the warmest sites (in the northern hemisphere), while hollows and the bottom of slopes, where frost settles, are usually amongst the coldest places. Overhead shade provides a few degrees of protection from late frosts for flowers and emerging young growth.

Many people use forms of artificial protection, such as spun polypropelene fleece, for their more tender varieties. Beware of leaving such materials on when thawing occurs, as it can cause rotting of foliage; all materials used must allow air to circulate. The purpose of the artificial protection is as much to moderate temperature fluctuations as it is to protect the plant from extreme cold. In the Pacific Northwest, and even south into California, the most damaging weather is the occasional very sudden drops in temperature in autumn before plants have had time to harden off. Young plants are especially vulnerable to cold damage. A mature plant may well be able to re-sprout from the base, even after severe damage, whereas a young plant of the same variety might well be killed in the same conditions. At Glendoick, we use several materials to protect young plants from spring and early autumn frosts. Spun polypropylene (available in different widths and thicknesses) is lightweight but gives protection from a few degrees of frost. It is hard to anchor, gets heavy when wet and must be taken off if snow is forecast. Better are sheets of corrugated plastic (milky is best to diffuse the sun): these are about 3–5mm thick, act like double-glazing and the sheets can be bent over to make miniature hoophouses or cloches. These can be secured and will withstand rain, snow and wind. The only problem is that plants dry out underneath them. Some people use wicker baskets, which they place over individual plants overnight. These should come off in daylight hours unless it is still freezing. Others wrap stems or the whole plant in burlap or sacking, or

use conifer branches (including the Christmas tree!). Plants in the open are more vulnerable than ones in a sheltered site, so placing or moving borderline plants to the most favourable sites may reduce or eliminate the need for artificial protection.

Spring frosts (and, to some extent, early autumn frosts) are the bane of rhododendron gardeners in many parts of the world. Few rhododendrons have frost-resistant flowers or growth and few rhododendron growers have not experienced the forlorn sight of a specimen in full flower one day, reduced the following morning to a mountain of limp, soggy, grey-brown mush after an overnight frost. Overhead shade, good frost drainage or an artificial cover such as lightweight spun-polypropylene can all help prevent such disasters, but with severe frost there is very little that can be done. Commercial growers in some parts of the world use their sprinkler systems to keep the air moving and prevent frost damage. This can cause severe flooding and even a garden full of icicle-covered plants but it does work. Start the watering before the pipes freeze up. As well as flowers, new growth is often damaged or completely burnt off by frost. In the former case, it can be very unsightly with brown and wrinkled leaf ends. Such growth can be cut off. In the later case, growth will usually be replaced by a flush from lateral buds further down the branches. More damaging is bark-split, caused by the sap running in the stem freezing and splitting a branch open. Often the damage is not revealed immediately but the plant or part of the plant can collapse later in the growing season. Young plants, even hardy varieties, can easily be killed this way. Cold hardiness is partly an issue of acclimatization. It is not by any means determined simply by minimum temperatures. In addition to problems of bark-split outlined above, it is important to consider the role of summer heat in ripening wood to withstand the winter. Most evergreen azaleas fail to ripen wood in areas with cool summers, so the plants languish and die in winter temperatures that their hardiness rating indicates they should be able to withstand. The importance of summer heat was also brought home to me at Tromso in Norway, well inside the Arctic Circle, where the short growing season makes ripening of wood very difficult. When rhododendrons are planted between rocks, the additional heat generated by the sun heating the rocks greatly increases both the ripening of wood and the setting of flower buds. In cool climates, siting plants that need extra heat near south and west walls has the same effect.

HEAT

Rhododendrons have a love-hate relationship with heat. Summer heat in moderation is a good thing: it encourages bud set for next year's flowers and it ripens wood to withstand the winter. In Scotland, Scandinavia and Nova Scotia, for instance, many varieties of evergreen azalea grow very poorly, as lack of summer heat causes insufficiently ripened wood. Many so called 'hardy' varieties are not suitable for these growing conditions. But I suspect that, in more southerly climates, as many rhododendrons die from too much summer heat as from winter cold. It is much easier to protect plants from cold than it is from heat. Most rhododendron species simply cannot tolerate hot roots for extended periods of time. And where the temperature does not drop at night time, the problem is exacerbated.

Rhododendrons mostly come from mountainous areas where summer heat is moderated by monsoon rains and fairly constant cloud cover for much of the growing season. The further removed they are from this environment the harder it is to keep most of them happy. The exceptions are the eastern American rhododendron and azalea species and many of the evergreen azaleas. And it is no surprise that the majority of the most heat-tolerant varieties of rhododendron are derived from these species. To protect from heat, provision of shade is the most obvious solution: hottest soil temperatures are reached with direct sunlight on the rootball. Rhododendrons shade their own and their neighbours' roots well. Mulches and groundcover plants also help to keep the temperature down. Many eastern American gardens use ground-cover plants, such as *Tiarella,* to run over the rhododendron rootballs. But be careful: greedy and very dense groundcovers that will take all the moisture and nutrients from the soil will not co-exist with happy rhododendrons. Another option is to look at obtaining grafted plants. Grafting onto heat-tolerant rootstocks gives a degree of root heat-tolerance: this method is very commonly used in Germany, where most larger hybrids are grafted. It should be used much more widely, particularly in the Eastern U.S.A., using a heat and phytopthora-resistant rootstock. The plants would attract a premium price.

Having read this chapter, you may well feel daunted in finding the right conditions to grow rhododendrons. But they are good adaptable plants, not hard to please in most climates. If in doubt, choose varieties that are recommended for your particular climactic conditions. You will find these clearly marked in the 'Encyclopaedia of Rhododendron Varieties' (*see* pages 38–225).

FLOWER BUDS DESTROYED BY SPRING FROSTS AS THEY OPENED.

RHODODENDRONS IN THE LANDSCAPE

Given the right soil conditions – acidity, drainage and moisture – rhododendrons are quite accommodating, easily grown, low-maintenance plants. They require no routine pruning and little or no feeding. As most are evergreens, they can provide a year-round structure to the garden and their foliage can make a fine foil for other plants. In full flower, often almost hiding the leaves, few plants can equal rhododendrons for quantity of bloom, variety of colours from white to pink, red, purple, yellow and orange, and range of flower and truss shape, from rounded to hanging and tubular. With careful selection of varieties you can have rhododendrons in flower in midwinter, around Christmas in milder climates, such as the U.K., while, at th end of the season, you can still have rhododendrons in flower in late summer.

Rhododendrons are seldom successfully used formally in the garden. I have once or twice seen them trained as standards or clipped into hedges but they generally don't suit straight lines, order and regiment. Woodland gardening, rock gardens and peat gardens are all imitations of nature and are therefore essentially informal. The informality is also a boon in the amount of labour required for upkeep. Much of the weeding, pruning, clipping, edging and mowing that goes on in other sorts of garden should be less necessary, especially in the woodland garden. Evergreen azaleas are the best choice for shearing into shape, making bonsais, and training into standards.

I leave the vexed question of colour co-ordination to others. There are varieties and planting combination to suit every taste. I dislike certain multicoloured combinations and you will deduce some of my prejudices in the variety descriptions in the encyclopaedia section (pages 38–225) of this book. Mauve-lavenders do clash horribly with reds, a truth more or less universally acknowledged. But somebody out there probably loves the effect. The great thing about rhododendrons is that you can move them if you find a colour combination offensive. The depth of feeling inspired by colour is considerable: the otherwise calm and reasonable rhododendron author David Leach, in his classic *Rhododendrons of the World*, takes exception to one of my favourite rhododendron species thus:

> I advise all readers to turn their eyes from *R. niveum* in its usual dull purple form, which is one of the most degraded, poisonously bilious colours to be found on earth. An axe, not a woodland, is the remedy for its appalling hue.

THE ADDED ATTRACTIONS: FOLIAGE, BARK AND SCENT

While most of the larger hybrids have fairly standard green leaves, many of the species and some of the smaller hybrids have attractive and interesting foliage, giving year-round interest. Some have a leaf under-surface, and sometimes the upper surface too, covered in a layer of hairs known as indumentum, varying in colour from silver to white, fawn, rufous to dark brown. The indumentum is often particularly fine on the new growth as it unfurls. Fine examples include *R. bureavii*, with a thick reddish-brown layer on the leaf underside, and *R. pachysanthum*, whose indumentum changes colour from white to fawn to deep reddish-brown. Sometimes the foliage effect comes from the size of the leaf: those of *R. sinogrande* can be up to 1m (3ft) in length. In other cases it is the leaf shape: almost round in *R. williamsianum* and *R. orbiculare*, long and narrow in *R. makinoi* and *R. roxieanum*. Leaf colour also varies: grey-blue in some forms of *R. cinnabarinum* and *R. lepidostylum*, variegated in 'President Roosevelt', 'Molten Gold' and 'Girard's Hotshot Variegated', and red in cultivars such as 'Ever Red' and 'Elizabeth Red Foliage'.

The new growth of rhododendrons is very variable and often very showy, almost as good as a second flowering. Species with coloured new growth include forms of *R. keiskei*, *R. lutescens* (both red) and *R. decorum* and *R. williamsianum* (bronzy). Other species have showy red leaf-bud scales (which protect the resting buds through the winter) that are displayed as the new leaves unfurl. Good examples are *R. fortunei* and *R. falconeri*. Many species have outstanding peeling or smooth, coloured bark. Some of the finest include *R. thomsonii*, *R. faucium* and *R. hodgsonii*.

Scent is another desirable feature of many rhododendrons and azaleas, mostly in the paler shades: white, pink and yellow. The pigments that give deep-coloured flowers, especially in red and orange shades, appear to block the genes that produce scent. There are plenty of hardy scented varieties to choose from: species in section Fortunea and hybrids raised from them are often sweetly

ABOVE: **CONTRASTING FOLIAGE OF** *R. ORBICULARE* **AND** *R. FLINCKII.*
ABOVE RIGHT: **COLOURED RHODODENDRON FOLIAGE: 'MOLTEN GOLD', 'ELIZABETH RED' AND 'VIKING SILVER'.**
BELOW: **THE FINE, PEELING BARK OF** *R. THOMSONII.*
BELOW RIGHT: *R. AUSTRINUM*, **A FINE SCENTED AZALEA SPECIES FOR AREAS WITH WARM SUMMERS.**

A SELECTION OF SCENTED RHODODENDRONS AND AZALEAS

Hardiness ratings H0–9 (*see* page 34)

Hardy rhododendrons: (H4–8) *R. decorum, R. fortunei, R. auriculatum,* 'Loderi', 'Dexter's Spice', 'Dexter's Peppermint', 'Polar Bear', 'Wheatley'

Deciduous azaleas: (H5–8) *R. atlanticum, R. arborescens, R. luteum, R. occidentale,* 'Snowbird'

Maddenia and related (H2–3/4): 'Lady Alice Fitzwilliam', 'Bill Massey', 'Martha Wright', 'Virginia Stewart'

Vireyas: (H0) *R. jasminiflorum, R. konori, R. superbum,* 'Aravir', 'Gwenevere', 'Highland White Jade', 'Marshall Pierce Madison', 'Moonwood'

scented. So, too, are many of the deciduous azaleas species, such as *R. viscosum* and *R. luteum* and the many hybrids raised from them. If you garden in a mild climate – western Britain, California, much of New Zealand, for example – you can grow the many scented Maddenia species and hybrids outdoors. In colder climates these are grown indoors with the even more tender Vireyas, many of which are also strongly scented.

SPACING RHODODENDRONS OR HOW LONG IS A PIECE OF STRING?

Some gardens have huge old specimen plants growing out on their own, perhaps surrounded by lawn, with no competition from other plants or trees. The thriving plant has formed a perfect shape and is the envy of everyone who sees it. Such plants tend to be the exception, not the rule. Individual specimens are hard to establish, tending to be buffeted by wind, to dry out and to have weeds or grass

growing at their roots. Rhododendrons are sociable plants so, unless you are prepared to put in the extra work required, don't dot them around too much. Conversely, planting too densely is also to be avoided: there are many once fine collections now reduced to a few spindly branches competing for light, with the handful of flowers high up and far out of reach. Planting specimens close together for quick impact is fine if you are prepared to move them or thin them later but, in my experience, this is easier said than done. One garden in Ireland was initially so over-planted that the paths completely disappeared under the rhododendrons. The owner had to cut through the foliage and the resulting paths were then lined with ugly bare branches. In optimum conditions, rhododendrons live for a very long time – 100 years is not uncommon. Plant with one eye on posterity and you will not usually regret it. You can easily see how big a plant might get by looking at a rhododendron's annual growth: it will carry on growing outward and upward at this rate indefinitely, if it is happy.

The dimensions given in the main listings in this book are very approximate and apply to plants aged 10–20 years. The rainfall, amount of fertilizer used and length of growing season are all important factors. Often rhododendrons grow as wide as they do high and there is a limit to the pruning you can do with many of them. If you can spare the space, let the really large species grow into fully clothed, rounded specimens. With the small-leaved and dwarf varieties, letting them grow into one another fairly quickly is the best plan.

WHAT TO PLANT WITH RHODODENDRONS

The older I get, the more I dislike 'rhododendron gardens'. What I mean by this are gardens that contain little or nothing but rhododendrons. These gardens appeal to those who treat rhododendrons rather as if they were collecting stamps. I have no right to demand that anyone plant their garden in an aesthetically pleasing way but, given that it takes about the same amount of effort to look after an eye-pleasing garden as a non-pleasing one, I'd have though it worth thinking about. 'But I don't have enough space for the plants I have, I don't have room for anything else.' I know, I know; many people don't have the luxury of large gardens. Keen rhododendron people always have endless trays of need-to-be-transplanted seedlings lying in every nook and cranny till space can be found for them. However small your garden, bulbs and perennials, shade trees and climbers can be grown through, around and over your rhododendrons, to give you something to look at outside the main flowering time. The Rhododendron Species Botanic Garden, Tacoma, Washington, U.S.A. is now a fine garden, full of interesting plants. Twenty years ago, it was a stamp collection. I know which I prefer.

When you are selecting the best plants to grow with your rhododendrons, the golden rule here is to try to avoid too much competition for moisture. Competition can come either from below, in the case of greedy tree-roots, or from above, in the case of ground cover. As rhododendrons are moisture-loving and shallow-rooted, they will tend to lose the battle with greedy plants and their health will suffer unless you have very high rainfall, such as in western Scotland and around Bergen in Norway. For smaller trees consider both the ultimate size

FINE EXAMPLES OF PLANTING COMBINATIONS.

TOP LEFT: AZALEA WITH *ACER SHIRASAWANUM AUREUM* (HACHMANN NURSERY).

ABOVE: *CLEMATIS VITICELLA* WITH *R. BUREAVIOIDES*.

RIGHT: 'FANTASTICA' WITH *EUONYMOUS FORTUNEI*.

BELOW: *MECONOPSIS (SHELDONII)* LINGHOLM WITH *R. CAMPANULATUM* SSP. *AERUGINOSUM*.

LEFT: *R. QUINQUEFOLIUM* WITH *CORYDALIS CASHMERIANA.*

BELOW: *R. ROXIEANUM* UNDERPLANTED WITH *ERYTHRONIUM* AT GLENDOICK.

THE WOODLAND GARDEN

Woodland gardening, developed as a naturalistic style of planting, often up a valley with a stream running through it or around a pond or lake, has become the most popular way to display rhododendrons on the larger scale, especially in Britain. The development of this gardening style coincided with, and indeed was largely inspired by, the flood of new rhododendron species from the Himalaya and China from 1850 onwards. It soon became apparent that many other plants from the Sino-Himalayan region, such as camellias and magnolias, also suited this method of cultivation. The essential character of the woodland garden is the informal nature of the winding paths through both native and exotic trees, underplanted with rhododendrons and other shrubs, often with a layer of wild flowers, bulbs and other smaller plants carpeting the ground underneath. Using contours and bridges to provide paths at different levels allows plants and grouping of plants to be viewed from above and below. The steep slopes in Bodnant, North Wales and the bridges over the burn at Crarae, Scotland are good examples. Woodland conditions, with shelter and filtered shade, are essential for varieties of borderline hardiness; here at Glendoick, the most favourable sites allow us to grow *R. lindleyi* and *R. sinogrande*, which would not be hardy in the open. Woodland, especially if on a slope with frost drainage, allows protection from several degrees of frost and often will make the difference between frost damage to flowers and foliage, and escaping from it.

Although predominantly a British development, the woodland gardening style has also been used in other parts of the world with great effect. The University of British Columbia Botanic Garden's Asian garden is a good example, while Pukeiti in North Island, New Zealand is a spectacular native woodland filled with indigenous trees and tree ferns, interplanted with rhododendron species. Particularly fine there are tender rhododendrons such as *R. elliottii* and *R. protistum*, which thrive in the luxuriant shelter that grows in the high rainfall.

Obviously, few of us are lucky enough to be able to garden on the grand scale that woodland gardening implies: many of the great woodland gardens cover acres and can take hours to walk round. However, the basic tenets of woodland gardening – informality, shade and shelter, and plant associations – apply equally well in smaller gardens, and the most satisfactory displays of healthy rhododendrons in small and medium-sized gardens are often those which have adapted the aesthetics of the woodland garden landscape.

In Britain, the dominant feature of most woodland gardens is their rhododendrons, but certain other genera are fairly omnipresent too. The best larger shade-trees to associate with rhododendrons are discussed under shade and shelter. The ideal is a mixture of conifers and hardwoods. In our west of Scotland garden, Baravalla, the natural woodland is a mixture of beech, hazel and oak, with a few mature fir trees that seed themselves. At Glendoick, we have lost our dominant trees, the elms, from Dutch Elm Disease, leaving a mixture of larch, Douglas fir, sycamore and beech, with an undergrowth of *Sambucus nigra* (elder) and other plants.

In choosing trees to plant, consider the bark as well as the flowers, foliage and berries. *Betula utilis* and *B. jacquemonii* have fine reddish-brown and white peeling-bark, respectively. Other species with fine bark include *Prunus serrula*, *Acer griseum* and *A. hersii* and other snake-bark maples. Magnolias are another obvious choice. On the large scale in relatively mild climates, the massive growing *M. campbellii* and its relatives give a spectacular display in early spring. On a smaller scale you can use other species, such as the summer flowering *M. wilsonii*, and hybrids, such as 'Leonard Messel'. In eastern North America, many of the new, hybrid magnolias put on a spectacular display in the few weeks before the main rhododendron blooming-period. Magnolias are rather greedy feeders, so avoid planting rhododendrons directly underneath them in areas of low rainfall.

Camellias are another mainstay companion plant, especially in Cornish gardens. Here the rhododendrons are often companion plants to the endless, and to my taste rather monotonous, camellias, which look particularly uninteresting when not flowering. If you can obtain *Embothrium coccineum*, the fiery orange flowers of this South American native provide a fine contrast to the colours of the rhododendrons. *Pieris* thrive in considerable shade and there are now many different forms with red, pink or white flowers, red or bronze young-growth and some have variegated leaves. These and *Enkianthus* are both members of the Ericaceae, the same family as rhododendrons, and they enjoy similar growing conditions. As well as their attractive hanging flowers, *Enkianthus* have amongst the most spectacular autumn colour, with red, orange and yellow tones.

Hydrangea species and cultivars associate well with rhododendrons with summer and autumn flowering. Plants with good autumn colour include *Rhododendron luteum* (otherwise known as *Azalea pontica*), *Euonymous alatus*, Japanese Maples, Sassafras and many others. Berries can be provided by *Vaccinium*, *Gaultheria* (which now includes *Pernettya mucronata*), *Cotoneaster*,

and spread and the season of interest. As rhododendrons are predominantly plants of spring interest, autumn- and winter-interest plants are invaluable.

In moderate climates, such as the U.K. and the Pacific Northwest of North America, there is a huge range of choices for trees and shrubs. *Sorbus* species are particularly good, as they are not greedy feeders, provide filtered shade and have long-lasting berries of white, yellow, pink, orange, or red. *Eucryphia* is another fine choice: these have very showy white flowers in late-summer and early autumn. Japanese maples (*Acer palmatum* cultivars) act as a wonderful foil for the foliage of rhododendrons, and many have the bonus of autumn colour. Winter colour can be provided by *Mahonia*, winter jasmine, *Viburnum* and *Hammamelis*, as well as perennials and bulbs, such as hellebores, *Meconopsis*, lilies, *Narcissus* and snowdrops.

In severe climates use a mixture of native and hardy exotics. There are many Japanese and eastern North American natives, such as *Styrax*, *Hammamelis*, *Cercis*, *Amelanchier*, *Halesia* and *Stewartia*, which provide filtered shade, fine flowers and/or autumn colour and whose roots are not too greedy. Some of these only thrive in areas with hot summers. *Kalmia*, *Leucothoe*, *Vaccinium* and other Ericaceous plants enjoy similar soil conditions to rhododendrons and provide interest after the main period of rhododendron flowering.

RIGHT: **GLENDOICK WOODLAND GARDEN, 'THE DEN'.**

BELOW: **THE CLASSIC ENGLISH LANDSCAPE – STOURHEAD.**

Sorbus and many other trees and shrubs. North American natives such as *Styrax* and *Halesia* have showy flowers and provide dappled shade. Bamboos are often found in association with rhododendrons in the wild and can be used effectively in cultivation. The best are the taller-growing clump-forming types, such as *Arundinaria murieliae* (now *Thamnocalamus spathaceus*). Beware the very rampant, spreading species, such as the tall *Sasa palmata* and the low-growing *Arundinaria vagans* (now *Sasaella ramosa*). These need lots of space, though they can be kept in-bounds with artificial barriers in the soil. Most woodland gardens contain sites on the dry side for rhododendrons. These can be filled with shrubs such as *Ilex*, *Deutzia*, *Philadelphus*, *Viburnum*, *Ribes*, *Hypericum* and the like. All of these associate with rhododendrons in the wild, as do climbers such as *Schizandra* and *Clematis montana*.

In the large or smaller garden, rhododendrons also associate well with bulbs and herbaceous plants. Here the key is to use plants that are subtle rather than garish, to keep the 'natural' look of the planting. In the wild, rhododendrons are often associated with *Primula* and *Meconopsis* and they make ideal companion plants in areas with fairly cool summers. The easiest primulas to establish and naturalize are the candelabra types, such as *Primula japonica*, *P. helodoxa*, *P. bulleyana*, *P. poissoni* and so on. These tend to hybridize and produce seedlings of a huge range of colours. *Meconopsis*, particularly the blue poppies *M. betonicifolia*, *M. grandis* and their hybrids, prefer moist, cool woodland – they are a struggle in areas with summer heat and low rainfall. Some of the monocarpic varieties, such as the *M. napalensis* or *M. regia* hybrids, are more suited to hotter and drier conditions. Other fine companion plants include *Trillium*, *Erythronium*, *Helleborus*, *Cardiocrinum* and *Lilium*. Most woodland gardeners encourage wild flowers by avoiding mowing or scything until midsummer, when most of the flowers are over. At Glendoick we have many British native plants that thrive among the rhododendrons; these include *Meconopsis cambrica* (the Welsh poppy), species of *Pentaglottis* and *Digitalis* (foxgloves), as well as several varieties of ferns.

ABOVE: **PART OF THE WOODLAND GARDEN IN SPRING AT GLENDOICK: *TRACHYCARPUS* AND *RHODODENDRON*.**

RIGHT: **RHODODENDRON BANK AT THE PAGODA GARDEN, GLENDOICK.**

BELOW: **HACHMANN NURSERY, GERMANY.**

BELOW RIGHT: **A BED OF DWARF RHODODENDRON SPECIES AT GLENDOICK.**

A SMALLER SCALE: RHODODENDRON BORDERS

A border planted only with rhododendrons and azaleas tends to be monotonous outside the flowering season. Much better to plant at least a few key plants of similar vigour with summer flowers, autumn berries or colour, and bulbs and perennials to come up through and between the shrubs, making a winning combination. With dwarf and medium-sized growers, if you garden in a moderate climate, you can plant rhododendron-dominated borders that remain interesting all year round. I would tend to use plants with an ultimate height of up to 1.5–2m in height at the back, gradually sloping down to low-growing varieties at the front. In nature, rhododendrons and azaleas are usually found in clumps and colonies, sheltering and shading each other's roots. In the garden, imitate this by allowing the rhododendrons to grow into one another, forming an undulating carpet. On a larger scale or for quick impact, plant three or more of each variety so that they can form large clumps. We often do this with dwarf varieties grown from wild seed, so we can display the variation that a species can show.

Most people want as long and spectacular a flowering season as possible. In favourable climates, the year can begin in winter with *R. lapponicum* and *R. dauricum* and end with late-flowering evergreen azaleas such as *R. nakaharae* in June and July, with a more or less continuous display of flower. Flower shape, size and colour should also be considered. The rounded trusses of the 'Yak' hybrids are very different from the bells of the *R. williamsianum* hybrids, for instance. In frost pockets choose early flowering varieties, such as

'Ptarmigan' and 'Christmas Cheer', which open their flowers over a long period. This ensures that if flowers are spoiled by frost, more will open later. Most 'Yak' hybrids, as well as evergreen and deciduous azaleas, are late enough flowering to avoid spring-frost danger.

Always consider the importance of foliage when planning a rhododendron border. After all, flowers last only a few weeks whereas fine foliage is always on display. Choose a variety of leaf shapes, from the rounded and oval *R. williamsianum* and its hybrids, such as 'Gartendirektor Rieger', 'Linda' and 'Osmar', to those with narrow or long leaves, such as *R. roxieanum* and *R. elegantulum*. Leaf size is also important. The larger-leaved hybrids, such as 'Unique' and some of the 'Yaks', contrast well with those at the other end of the scale, such as the tiny *R. calostrotum* ssp. *keleticum* Radicans Group with some of the smallest and narrowest leaves of all. The texture of the leaf itself can provide interest. The hybrid 'Rubicon' has deeply ribbed, deep-green leaves, while the leaves of *R. thomsonii* are completely smooth and flat. Many dwarf and medium-sized species and a few hybrids have magnificent indumentum. This is usually on the leaf underside but in some species, such as *R. pachysanthum*, *R. pseudochrysanthum*, *R. yakushimanum* and several others, the silvery dusting on the upper leaf-surface persists all summer, giving a most attractive effect. In many other varieties the white, silver, fawn or brown indumentum on the upper leaf-surface is only temporary; a good example are the 'Yak' hybrids 'Hydon Dawn', 'Sneezy', 'Ken Janeck' and the like. Exploit the coloured foliage of *R. lepidostylum*, *R. fastigiatum* and *R. campanulatum* ssp. *aeruginosum* (glaucous-blue), 'Elizabeth Lockhart' and 'Elizabeth Red Foliage' (reddish purple), or 'Ponticum Variegatum' and 'Goldflimmer' (variegated). Many species have very showy new growth, giving a 'second flowering'. Some of the best include the bronzy and purplish new leaves of *R. williamsianum* and its hybrids and the red, young growth of forms of *R. keiskei* and *R. lutescens*. Good autumn colour can be provided by deciduous azaleas, such as *R. luteum*, which can be placed at the back of a border, or *R. dauricum*, *R. mucronulatum* and their hybrids, with leaves that turn to rich deep-reds, purples and mahogany before falling. Some varieties, including many evergreen azaleas, have reddish or bronzy winter colour.

PEAT BEDS AND ROCK GARDENS

Dwarf and alpine rhododendrons are often best displayed in a peat-bed or rock-garden situation. Here the alpine varieties are grown in an imitation of their wild state on moorland or rocky slopes. Such plantings should be out in the open, away from trees, allowing the dwarf plants to maintain their natural compact shape. Let the individual plants grow into one another, forming an undulating mat of foliage textures, leaving occasional patches of bare ground to plant bulbs and alpine perennials. Peat gardening may be unfashionable due to the recent controversy over the extraction of peat in lowland peatbogs, but the whole debate has been filled with misinformation. I often hear that 'peat is a non-renewable resource'. This is nonsense: live sphagnum peat can be grown and harvested in cycles, as it is in Scandinavia.

Peat beds are constructed by using a mix, predominantly of peat, usually with some of the existing soil, and often with added grit or other substances to ensure good drainage. The best rock and peat gardens have natural or artificial contours, imitating the mountain slopes where the plants grow wild. Often, levels are created using peat blocks that themselves become an excellent medium for spreading plants to root into. As well as dwarf rhododendrons, peat beds are ideal for dwarf Ericaceae such as *Phyllodoce* with pink or creamy-white bells, *Cassiope* with tiny white bells, *Kalmiopsis* and its hybrid × *Phylliopsis* with pink flowers, and dwarf *Gaultheria*, *Andromeda*, *Gaylussacia* and *Vaccinium*. Dwarf bulbs and alpines such as *Rhodohypoxis*, *Primula*, *Corydalis*, *Nomocharis*, *Fritillaria* and smaller ground orchids are all excellent choices. At Glendoick we have found by bitter experience that certain bulbs and perennials are too invasive and soon get out of control. For us these included *Muscari*, *Chionodoxa*, *Crocus* and bluebells, all of which are almost impossible to eradicate. In other climates, other plants might be equally troublesome.

In rock gardens, rhododendrons and dwarf azaleas can form a dominant part or just be scattered through a mixed planting of assorted alpines. Natural rock gardens on windswept Himalayan mountains can inspire garden-design ideas. Plants that require excellent drainage grow on scree, others which require more moisture grow in snowmelt. Some species prefer full exposure, while others prefer to grow in the lee of rocks that provide wind shelter and help to retain moisture. Imitate these habitats in gardens, using scree beds, planting next to rocks to protect new growth from prevailing winds and making use of moisture-retaining crevices to keep roots moist and cool.

CONTAINER GROWING

Rhododendrons in containers, whether outside or indoors, need a fairly free-draining and open but, at the same time, moisture-retentive compost. This is not a contradiction and is essential for healthy plants; rhododendrons cannot survive for long with dry roots but, equally, if the compost is too soggy and the water in the pot becomes stagnant, then chlorotic foliage and poor growth or

RIGHT: **AN UNDULATING BED OF MATURE DWARF RHODODENDRONS AT GLENDOICK.**

FAR RIGHT: **A TIERED PEAT-BED AT GLENDOICK, FILLED WITH DWARF RHODODENDRONS.**

even death through root-rot (*Phytophthora*) may result. A mixture of fairly coarse bark and fibrous peat, sometimes with added perlite, needles or woodchips is the ideal combination for container rhododendrons indoors or out. The first two substances, either singly or together, are used by most commercial growers of rhododendrons in containers. The easiest option for feeding containers is slow-release granules, lasting up to eighteen months, which can either be incorporated into the compost or clusters can be pushed into the soil of already containerized plants. Alternatively, granular or liquid feeding can be applied from late-spring to midsummer. Don't go on feeding too late or growth will continue at the expense of flower buds. Rhododendrons should not be over-potted. If anything, they grow and flower better if slightly pot-bound, as long as they are well fed and watered. Be wary of shallow pan-shaped pots: due to the physical properties of water in containers, all pots tend to have a soggy layer at the bottom and this layer should not come in contact with the rhododendron roots. All containers need adequate drainage holes and you may well need to make extra ones, especially for vireyas and Maddenia. I have seen excellent results growing rhododendrons in slices of tree-fern logs, which may be available in places such as Australia, New Zealand and similar mild climates, which imitates the wild habitat of epiphytic rhododendrons.

CONTAINERS OUTDOORS

Many of the saddest-looking rhododendrons I have seen were in containers outside townhouses – straggly, yellow- and brown-leaved sentinels expending the last months of their short lives pushing out the odd feeble flower, before expiring, unloved and abandoned. It is certainly possible to grow fine rhododendrons in containers, but only if you are prepared to maintain them properly. Most plants in containers require more attention than they would in the ground; they can easily get too hot or too cold, they need regular feeding and watering, and plants can become root-bound if not repotted. And weevils love containers. Rhododendrons can and do make excellent container plants and often containers are the best or only option for growing them: many people have no garden but have, perhaps, some hard space such as a patio, balcony or driveway. Others have gardens with alkaline or heavy clay soil. *R. williamsianum* and 'Yak' hybrids, with fine foliage and compact habit, are amongst the best choice as they look fine year-round and their silvery or bronzy new growth adds interest when flowers are over.

By all means put other plants in your containers with the rhododendrons, but avoid ground covers with greedy root-systems, such as heathers, which compete for moisture and nutrients. Bulbs, alpines and bedding plants can all be used successfully. Rhododendrons (especially evergreen azaleas) are one of the most popular subjects for bonsai. There are thousands of varieties of Satsuki and other azaleas bred in Japan for this purpose. Such varieties need winter protection in colder and more northern climates.

As with many other plants, the foliage of rhododendrons will tolerate much colder temperatures than the roots, as much as 5–10°C (10–20°F) of difference. In the ground the frost actually creates a layer of insulation, preventing the soil from getting as cold as the air above. Plants in containers do not have this insulation and the roots, usually pressed against the inside of the pot, are very vulnerable to being hard frozen, which can kill an otherwise hardy plant. If you can't bring your containers indoors in severest weather, then it is worth taking other precautions. Insulation with polystyrene, bubble-plastic, straw and so on will help. Placing all your containers 'pot thick' so they are all touching and then insulating the outside of the block, is a practice followed by nurserymen. Alternatively dig the container into the ground so that the surrounding soil insulates it. This also stops the container blowing over.

RHODODENDRONS INDOORS

Unless you live in the milder areas where rhododendrons are cultivated, western Britain or France, California, Australia or New Zealand, for example, the more tender rhododendrons need to be grown indoors, at least during the winter. Indica or tender azaleas are the only part of the genus *Rhododendron* that make good 'house' plants, as they can put up with the low light-levels and central heating of the home. Maddenia and Vireyas really need a greenhouse or conservatory with plenty of light, cool winter-temperatures and a fairly high humidity. Maddenia species and hybrid plants can be brought into the house in-flower and can stay in for a week or two, as long as they are kept fairly cool. Vireyas should only be brought in for a day or two, as the low light-levels and low humidity of the house, especially in winter, can be fatal. You'll find more information about Vireya cultivation on page 73.

The new greenhouse at Windsor Great Park, England, where the whole front can be opened in summer, gives the best of both worlds, with cool temperatures and good ventilation in summer and frost protection in winter. If expense were no object, this is the greenhouse I would have for my Maddenia and Vireyas.

MAINTENANCE AND HUSBANDRY

FERTILIZERS AND FEEDING

Rhododendrons are not greedy plants when it comes to fertilizer; indeed, if you follow the correct procedures in soil preparation, with well-drained moisture-retentive soil without competition from other plants, rhododendrons may need no feeding at all. Many fine rhododendron collections, not to mention the plants in their wild state, get by fine without any artificial feed. Vigour, good leaf-retention and deep-green foliage are the signs of a healthy plant that needs no added help. Short growth, a sparse appearance and pale or yellowish leaves all indicate an unhappy plant, which may be due to a need for fertilizer, but the symptoms may also point to poor drainage or drought. The golden rule with feeding rhododendrons is 'little and often' rather than a single large dose. Most evergreen and deciduous azaleas and most larger hybrids can take considerable amounts of fertilizer without any ill effects and some, such as 'Lem's Cameo' and some of its hybrids, seem to require extra-large doses to maintain healthy foliage. But you do need to be careful, as some dwarf varieties and many species are extremely sensitive and will suffer leaf-tip burn or worse if you overdo it. Some varieties prefer little or no fertilizer at all and young plants can be particularly sensitive.

Compound fertilizers contain three main ingredients: nitrogen, phosphorus and potassium. The ratio of the three is known as an NPK rating: for example, 5:5:5 signifies equal amounts of each. Nitrogen is essential for growth and flower-bud formation and is quickly used up in the soil, so needs to be replenished. It is this ingredient that causes leaf scorch, so it is important to be very careful with high-nitrogen fertilizers, such as those used on vegetables. Phosphorus promotes growth and the ripening of wood at the end of the season, so the plant can withstand the winter. Potassium (or potash) induces hardiness and disease resistance. At Glendoick, we use granular fertilizers with ratios of 5:7:10 and 10:5:10. Both seem to do the job. For liquid feeding, the concentration is usually higher in nitrogen: the ubiquitous Miracid/Miracle-Grow has an analysis of 30:10:10. There is nothing wrong with it, but it is rather expensive – you are paying for all that advertising. Most compound fertilizers also contain secondary and trace elements, which include calcium, sulphur, magnesium, iron and other substances essential for healthy plant development. These minerals are required in small to minute quantities; too much of some of them can be as harmful as too little. The trace elements usually occur naturally in garden soils in sufficient quantity and rarely need replenishing artificially, but they are useful for making composts for plants growing indoors and/or in containers.

Both organic and inorganic fertilizers can be used. Beware of farmyard manures; they can be extremely high in nitrogen and can, therefore, cause severe leaf-burn. This is especially true of poultry manure. Well-rotted cow manure is fine. Many of the substances used as mulches in parts of the world, such as pea straw and oilseed-rape straw, are naturally high in nitrogen and will feed as they break down. Other substances, such as bark and sawdust, have the reverse effect,

R. ROXIEANUM FOLIAGE WITH FERNS AT GLENDOICK.

taking nitrogen from the soil as they compost down. In such cases extra feeding may be required. Some of the traditional organic fertilizers, such as bonemeal, are not particularly recommended for rhododendrons, though they are unlikely to do any harm. Of the inorganic fertilizers, ammonium sulphate is undoubtedly the cheapest and most effective way to increase nitrogen in the soil. Yellow-leaved plants, suffering from nitrogen deficiency due to the breakdown of organic materials, such as bark and sawdust, respond very quickly and soon green up. Use small doses at first and ensure that the powdery fertilizer is not left on the foliage, as it tends to burn. It can be washed off with a hose if it sticks to the leaves. Organic favourites such as seaweed, cottonseed, alfalfa or soyabean meal are all good sources of nitrogen and are usually not too strong. On a large scale, though, this is an expensive way to feed. Chlorosis (when leaves turn yellow with just the veins remaining green) can be caused by drainage problems, soil pH or drought, as well as by mineral deficiency. Iron chelates or sequestrene are often recommended as the cure-all for chlorotic foliage. This will only be of benefit if the problem is one of a lack of available iron. As the iron chelates are relatively expensive, try a small amount on a few plants during the growing season to see if there is any improvement. It should take no more than a month to green up the leaves.

HOW AND WHEN TO FEED

The main feeder-roots of a rhododendron are near the soil surface and tend to be at the perimeter of the rootball, which is at or a little way inside the drip-line (the edge of the spread of foliage). It is, therefore, not usually worth putting fertilizer at the bottom of the hole (as is recommended for many other plants) and not worth scattering it around the trunk of older plants, as the feeder roots are further out. How much to put on depends on the strength of the fertilizer and the composition and temperature of the soil. A soil whose organic content is mainly bark or sawdust requires much more fertilizer than one that is predominantly peat or leafmould. Although some authorities recommend applying phosphate and potash outside the growing season, our own trials have shown no benefit from this. Wait until growth starts in spring and then feed with 2–3 small doses of compound fertilizer in the growing season. By midsummer, growth may be starting to slow down and flower buds starting to be set. If you continue fertilizing beyond this time, it tends to encourage leaves at the expense of flower buds and the resultant soft growth is vulnerable to early autumn frosts. This is especially important in severe climates, where new growth must have the maximum length of time to harden up before the onset of coldest midwinter temperatures.

For young plants, such as recently propagated material, as well as plants grown in pots or other containers, slow-release fertilizer or liquid feeding are often the safest and most convenient methods. Slow-release granules can last up to eighteen months and can be incorporated into the potting mix. These usually contain all three major elements as well as trace elements. Liquid foliar feeding is another excellent method, as the little and often philosophy allows careful monitoring of any signs of leaf-tip burn caused by too much nitrogen. Liquid-feeding mature plants outdoors is also possible.

WEEDS AND WEEDKILLERS

The shallow roots of rhododendrons cannot compete with vigorous weeds for moisture and greedy weeds should be removed. Hand weeding, hoeing and weedkillers can be used but it is also worth looking at planting strategies that will reduce the need for weeding. In the wild, rhododendrons usually grow in colonies, growing into one another, providing shelter from wind and sun and often preventing enough light reaching the ground for vigorous weeds to thrive. Often it is only moss that is found growing under dense canopies of rhododendrons in their native habitat. Particularly with dwarf and alpine rhododendrons, plant them in groups that will mat together and carpet the ground. Once this state begins to be achieved, the weeding required is minimal. Mulching is another method of reducing weed growth. When hand-pulling weeds and hoeing, bear in mind that the shallow roots are vulnerable to being exposed if soil is removed with the weed roots or to being cut by careless hoeing.

Weedkillers are either total or selective (kill everything or only specific plants) and are contact or systemic (penetrate the plant itself) or pre-emergence (prevent seed germinating). All have their place in rhododendron growing but environmental concerns should always be borne in mind before using them: some weedkillers can contaminate water with run-off. Legislation concerning their use by professional growers and amateurs varies greatly from country to country and rules are constantly changing, so check locally as to which chemicals are legal for amateurs and professionals.

Total weedkillers are used to clean up an area before planting and they kill or damage any plant that is sprayed. Glyphosate is now the total weedkiller most commonly used by professionals and amateurs, effective on most

R. VISCOSUM WITH SCOTCH CREEPER *TROPAEOLUM SPECIOSUM* CLIMBING THROUGH IT.

herbaceous weeds and some woody ones, including *R. ponticum*. It should be used when weeds are in full growth. The foliage of stubborn weeds with a waxy leaf surface, such as ivy, may need to be bruised before application. Planting of the area can commence 8–10 weeks after application. Another useful chemical is Gluphosinate, which kills weeds more quickly than Glyphosate. Sodium chlorate can be used to clear areas of weeds and it is very effective, but this weedkiller persists in the soil for up to two years or more and is very toxic. Don't use this in any area that you wish to use for planting in the near future. Its use will probably be restricted in the future.

Contact weedkillers quickly kill the top growth of most weeds but are quickly inactivated in the soil. Paraquat seems to be coming off the market in many countries, but diquat is still available in the U.K. These chemicals are usually harmless on woody trunks, so can be used right up to old, established rhododendrons. Damage occurs to anything green, including leaves and any stems and trunks that remain green from chlorophyll: maples are an example. Spray drift that touches rhododendrons causes unsightly black spotting on the foliage. Both are very quick acting and can even be applied during light rain. Used on paths, they encourage the growth of moss and are sometimes used deliberately for this purpose. An alternative contact-weedkiller is the gas flame-gun, which works by scorching the weeds. Obviously extreme care should be taken to avoid damaging precious plants.

Selective weedkillers are for use against difficult-to-eradicate weeds. One of the best is cycloxydim, which kills grass (including couch) but which is virtually harmless to most other cultivated plants, so may be sprayed among them. Another useful one is a combination of 2,4-D, Mecoprop-P and Dicamba, which is used for killing nettles, brambles and tree stumps. Most other selective weedkillers are developed for use on lawns.

Pre-emergence weedkillers are applied to clean soil and prevent germination of seed. They can be watered or applied as granules around growing plants. They generally have little effect on established weeds, so they are best applied after an area has been cleaned by other means. Some of them have proven to cause damage to rhododendrons, but we have found that propachlor, oxadiazon and propyzamide seldom cause damage, even to very young plants. Simazine is best on mature plants only; we have found it can damage young stock. This chemical now has very restricted use in Europe. It is advisable to wash foliage of rhododendrons after applying pre-emergence herbicides, in case there are any adverse effects. There are some rhododendron varieties (in Sect. Pogonanthum), for instance, which are sensitive to most of them, especially as young plants, so we avoid using them around these. We have found that specific weeds, such as groundsel, nettles and cleavers (Galium), are resistant to certain pre-emergence herbicides.

LEFT: **HOSTA AND RHODODENDRON COMBINATION.**

BELOW: **AN INSPIRING PAIRING OF *CAREX BUCHANANII* AND RHODODENDRON FOLIAGE.**

PINCHING AND PRUNING

It is another of the old myths about rhododendron cultivation that you cannot or should not pinch and prune rhododendrons to improve their shape. Nurserymen do it constantly to produce those symmetrical bushes that your local nursery or garden centre stocks and it is often worth doing this in the garden. Pinching is a preventative measure, while pruning is a cure. Pinching means removing the terminal or central growth-bud of a rhododendron as it elongates, to encourage multiple branching from lateral buds that form in the leaf axils of each whorl (circle at the branch end) of leaves. Pruning involves cutting a mature shoot or branch so that buds break and grow further down, hopefully improving the shape.

I'm not claiming that rhododendrons require pruning in the same way that, for instance, a rose does, on an annual basis. It is just a tool that can be used from time to time to improve the shape of your plants. Many of the alpine and dwarf varieties, such as 'Yak' hybrids, need little or no pruning to maintain a good shape, as long as they are grown in plenty of light. As soon as rhododendrons start to flower freely, most growth comes from lateral shoots from below the flower buds and, therefore, nature does its own pinching. When plants are young and before they start to flower freely, however, the simplest way to ensure a plant of good habit is to pinch out all the single, terminal buds as they elongate in the spring. Wait until this becomes easy to do: if you have to dig out the bud, then it is too early. I recommend this for vigorous dwarfs, subsection *Triflora* species and most larger hybrids. With species, many of the largest ones are, in essence, trees and they should be left to form a single trunk until they attain a substantial height. Others, such as the very vigorous *R. decorum*, are better pinched as a small plant to encourage bushiness. Spring frosts do a lot of natural pinching, with the central bud being frosted, leaving the later growth to come from below as multiple shoots.

There are several reasons why you may want to prune a bush. It may have been crowded out by other plants and become straggly. It may have been severely damaged by cold or wind, or had its first flush of growth frosted, causing unsightly, brown, distorted leaves. You may want to reduce it in size because it has got too big or because you want to move it. Perhaps the most common pruning tasks are when you want to rejuvenate an old collection that has become completely overgrown. Scaly-leaved rhododendrons and all azaleas can be pruned to any point on a branch or shoot and new growth will come from buds lower down. Maddenia and Vireyas grown indoors tend to get straggly if not hard pruned every few years. With larger-leaved, non-scaly varieties, you should cut back to a whorl of leaves.

Although it is possible to prune at any time of year, perhaps the most satisfactory time is straight after flowering. This gives time for production of new growth and for formation of flower buds the following year. Alternatively, prune in early spring, just as new growth is starting to elongate. When pruning, it is best to leave a substantial quantity of leaves: cutting back into too much old wood is

REGROWTH AFTER HARD PRUNING OF DECIDUOUS AZALEAS.

THE LACK OF DEADHEADING HAS INHIBITED NEW GROWTH.

risky. Among larger species and hybrids there is considerable variation in how well they respond to pruning. If you can cut back to a healthy whorl of leaves, one or some of the buds above each leaf stalk will almost certainly grow. It is when a more severe pruning is required, cutting back to a bare trunk, that results vary considerably. As a rough rule, those with a smooth bark, such as *R. thomsonii* and *R. barbatum*, as well as most of the large-leaved species, such as *R. sinogrande*, are reluctant to respond to being cut back to the trunk. One exception is the large-leaved *R. macabeanum*, which produces plenty of shoots from the base if cut back deliberately or by severe weather. Amongst the best responders to being severely cut back are *R. arboreum* and the ubiquitous *R. ponticum*. The latter's ability to regenerate is one of the reasons it is so hard to eradicate in areas where it has become a pest. This species was traditionally used as a rootstock for grafting cultivars and its extreme propensity to throw suckers has commonly overwhelmed whatever was grafted on top of it in old collections, incorrectly referred to as 'reverting'. Many *R. ponticum*-lined drives of stately homes in the U.K. were formerly plantings of hardy hybrids of various colours. This is important to bear in mind when trying to rejuvenate plantings that date back to the 1950s or earlier in the U.K. The characteristic purple flowers and dark-green, shiny, narrow leaves of *R. ponticum* should make it possible to identify which are the suckers. These should be wrenched off at the base of the stem. If you prune them off, they will just produce a whole cluster of shoots from below the cut. Since the 1950s grafting has fallen from favour, as cuttings and, more recently, micropropagation have become the major production techniques for rhododendrons (except in northern Europe where most cultivars are grafted on 'Cunningham's White' – fortunately far less prone to suckering).

DEADHEADING

Rhododendrons are not perpetual-flowering so deadheading does not prolong the flowering season as it does with some rose varieties, for instance. There are, however, sound arguments for doing at least some deadheading. Rhododendrons are a rather promiscuous lot and are very often cross-pollinated by insects. The resulting seed set can be large and unsightly but, more importantly, the seed set can inhibit vigorous new growth and therefore a good flowering season the following year. If you only have a few rhododendrons, deadhead them if you have time. If you have a large collection, then concentrate on those that set the most seed. Young plants, especially those bought and planted in flower, will definitely benefit. So will most larger-growing species that produce enormous, multiple-flowered trusses. Most popular hardy hybrids, 'Yak' hybrids, dwarfs and deciduous and evergreen azaleas seldom need deadheading and most will flower well every year whether deadheaded or not. One or two dwarfs such as *R. campylogynum* tend to produce large unsightly seed-heads held above the foliage, which are most easily removed with a pair of scissors. The technique when removing spent flower heads from larger species and hybrids is to break the truss off at the base, above the whorl of leaves with

your fingers. Be careful not to break off the emerging growth buds underneath. Take your time until you get the knack; it doesn't take long before you can do it very quickly. Deadheading can be a very sticky job with some varieties, due to secretions from the flower stalk and new growth.

MOVING RHODODENDRONS

Don't be frightened of moving rhododendrons. Because of their compact, fibrous rootballs, mature rhododendrons can be moved, even when they are very large, provided you can find the physical means to lift and transport. The U.K. National Species Rhododendron Collection at Windsor Great Park was established by moving the huge collection from Tower Court, several miles away. The majority of the plants, some of which were enormous, survived the move and many are living quite happily, many years later. We find that mature larger-leaved species and hybrids respond best to moving. Dwarf rhododendrons move less well and both evergreen and deciduous azaleas are often very slow to re-establish if moved as mature plants. The best time of year for such moving is generally in autumn, when rootballs are moist and the plants will have time to re-establish and send out roots into the surrounding soil in spring before the heat of the summer. The exception to this is in very cold areas such as eastern North America, where wind and frozen ground can easily desiccate newly planted specimen-plants. Spring may be a better choice in such areas. There are many reasons why a mature plant may need to be moved: the area may be crowded with plants too close together, all competing for light; a plant or plants may be expanding to block a path; or perhaps it may just look out of place with its surroundings. When moving a rhododendron try to keep as much width of rootball as possible; the youngest and most vigorous roots are usually at the outermost part of the root. Investigate with a spade until you find the healthy, most recent roots and dig round just outside this circle. The depth of rootball required is seldom much more than 30cm and usually considerably less. Beware of trying to keep too much root, as the weight of it (particularly when wet) may break the stem of the plant or cause the root to drop off. If the rootball you end up with seems on the small size – because a bit breaks off, for instance – it may be advisable to cut back the foliage quite hard. One way to move large plants is by making a sledge out of heavy-duty polythene or similar material and simply dragging the plant along on this. Good soil preparation for the new hole, careful planting (*see* page 9) and diligent watering in the first growing season are all crucial for good establishment. Also, plants may need staking and artificial wind protection to prevent rocking and allow successful establishment in the surrounding soil.

WATER/IRRIGATION

In the rhododendron-rich mountains of the Himalaya and China, typically there is a relatively dry period in spring when flowering occurs, followed by heavy monsoon rains during the main part of the growing season. Few of us are fortunate (or unfortunate!) enough to live in areas with such reliable summer rains and so we are forced to supplement our rainfall artificially. Rhododendron root-systems are shallow and compact and so, if the soil dries out, rhododendrons are one of the first plants to wilt. None will withstand sustained periods of drought but small-leaved species and evergreen azaleas and one or two larger-leaved species such as *R. macrophyllum* and *R. decorum* are able to tolerate fairly dry conditions, under trees for example. Conversely, ample moisture throughout the growing season is required to produce the spectacular large leaves on species such as *R. sinogrande*. Rhododendrons wilt and curl up their leaves when they are suffering from lack of water. Most varieties can withstand this for a few days without ill effects but it can stunt fresh growth.

Complexity of watering systems varies hugely, from a single can or hose for a small garden, to sophisticated and computer-controlled sprinkler-systems with pipes buried underground. Seep-hose and trickle irrigation, which slowly leak water from numerous holes or small pipes laid in or on the planting beds, are an excellent way of directing moisture to exactly where it is needed and it cuts down on wasted water. As a general rule it is better to give plants an occasional good soaking than a series of inadequate doses. Rhododendrons with good root-systems can survive a surprising amount of drought, though the stress this incurs may make them vulnerable to other problems such as honey fungus (*see* page 27). In very hot weather it is best to water in early morning or late at night to avoid burning of foliage. Excess water coupled with poor drainage and high temperature is a sure recipe for the lethal phytophthora root-rot (*see* page 26). Overhead watering of plants in bloom encourages petal blight, which can ruin the flowers (*see* page 27).

With recent changes in weather patterns, as well as huge increases in demand, water is becoming a more and more precious commodity and the threat of hosepipe bans hangs over many a rhododendron garden. There are various things that can be done to cut down on the amount of watering required. Autumn planting with plenty of moisture-retaining organic matter and good mulching are all well worth considering. In our experience tree roots rather than evaporation are the most common cause of dry soil. If greedy trees cannot be removed or are required for shade and shelter, it may be worth trying to isolate the rhododendron roots from the tree roots with barriers, such as thick polythene. We have found that beds lined with polythene to keep tree roots out, with a good mulch on top, seldom require watering, even in our south-facing garden with long periods of dry weather. In areas with alkaline soil, this method may be essential, as all watering will have to be done with collected rainwater. The fact that seep hoses and trickle hoses can be buried or hidden means that you can usually use them during hosepipe and sprinkler bans and as they are much less wasteful, they should be encouraged. Water quality is another concern. Los Angeles water seems to have been causing problems for Vireya growers, due to its chemical content, and all of us are at the mercy of water companies' chemical additives.

There are several advantages to cutting down watering in late-summer, even to the extent of stressing the plants a little. Plants that go on growing into the autumn are very vulnerable to damage, while those whose roots are allowed to dry out from August onwards are often better prepared for winter. It is, however, important to water dry plants thoroughly in late autumn, before the onset of winter, especially if you intend to move any of them. In all climates, cutting down on watering in late summer encourages the setting of flower buds for next season; nurserymen do this as a matter of course. Larger species flower at a much younger age in dry eastern Scotland than they do in the much wetter west, where they grow more lushly and vigorously.

LABELLING

It is a great pity how many fine rhododendron collections have been reduced in value by inadequate labelling. While species can usually be identified, hybrids and azaleas are often very difficult and, once the labels or records are lost, there is seldom any way of recovering all of the names. Over the years we have tried many different labelling methods. Embossed labels, such as those found in botanical gardens, are clear, large and last well but are very expensive. Probably the best cheap option we have tried is aluminium labels, written on in pencil. These are small and rather hard to find and they must be periodically loosened or relocated to avoid strangling the branch they are tied to. Plastic labels only last a few years and then become brittle. The writing of so-called indelible pens only seems to last for a year or two. Don't forget to record collector's numbers on labels and in records (*see* page 32). Whatever method you use, it is well worth keeping records as to when and where things are planted. Such lists and/or accompanying sketch maps have been invaluable to new owners of good collections. Recently people have been mapping with GPS (global positioning using satellites to pin-point position).

PESTS, DISEASES, PROBLEMS AND DISORDERS

Although the list of pests and diseases in this section is quite daunting, you will be relieved to know that only a handful of these are a problem in any given area. In areas with a moderate climate, the most likely-to-be-encountered pest is vine weevil, the most damaging disease is powdery mildew and the most irksome climatic problem is that of spring frosts. In regions where temperatures are more extreme, such as in eastern North America and parts of continental Europe, the problems encountered are more likely to include stem- and root-rots, and climatic problems such as sunburn and winter cold-damage. More plants are killed or damaged by poor soil preparation and lack of care in the first growing season than most of the other problems put together.

INSECT PESTS

Vine weevil. Black vine weevil (*Otiorhynchus sulcatus* and at least three other related species) is probably the most serious rhododendron pest. Its incidence is on the increase and it is notoriously difficult to control, especially for the amateur grower. The damage by vine weevil falls into two categories: that caused to foliage by adults and the more serious damage caused underground by larvae. The adult vine weevil is a flightless black insect about 1cm long, which is seldom seen as it feeds at night. It eats irregular notches in the margins of leaves – unlike caterpillars, which usually eat away whole portions of the leaf or make holes in it. This adult damage is seldom more than cosmetic and often tends to occur in shady conditions where the insects can shelter in the undergrowth or leaf litter during the day. A plant moved out into more light will often not be attacked. Alternatively a plant can be sprayed with a systemic insecticide. In North America the most popular chemical control is acephate (most commonly sold under the name Orthene), which is both contact and systemic, that is to say it kills insects it touches and it enters the leaves, rendering them poisonous when eaten (but apparently only for a period of three days). Another excellent chemical is Imidacloprid (sold as Provado in the U.K.), which can be used as a foliar spray or soil drench and will control adults and larvae. Contact insecticides such as fenitrothion, which kill by spraying the insect itself, are of limited use unless you are prepared to get up in the middle of the night to spray the feeding weevils. Adults tend to hatch out from May onwards and need to feed for several weeks before egg-laying can begin; the main reason for killing adults is to prevent them from laying the eggs that produce the much more damaging larvae. Spray the foliage of plants as soon as the characteristic notching is seen on the new growth of the rhododendron.

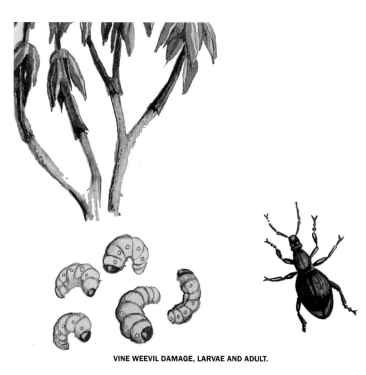

VINE WEEVIL DAMAGE, LARVAE AND ADULT.

DAMAGE BY ADULT VINE WEEVILS ON *R. PONTICUM*.

APHIDS ON NEW GROWTH.

Vine weevil larvae are white, 'C'- or croissant-shaped, 1–1.2cm long at maturity with a brownish head. One adult female can lay up to 200 eggs and a plant can be killed by the munching of a single larva. These hatch out from eggs laid around the stem of plants (usually in summer or autumn) and eat either the bark or the roots of the plant through late-summer, autumn and winter. The girdling (eating) of the bark around the stem at, or above and below, soil level, usually results in death, the plant collapsing quite quickly during the growing season but more slowly during the winter. This is the most common damage in containers. In the open ground the larvae tend to graze the fresh roots. On an older plant this is often only debilitating, unless there are larger numbers of larvae, but in small and young plants the root eating can be fatal. Many plant species are very vulnerable to vine weevil. Some of their favourites include yew, strawberries and primulas. Some people use such plants as indicators to show when weevils are active. Many of the older treatments for vine weevil, such as aldrin and dieldrin, have long since been withdrawn due to their toxicity while their replacements, fonophos and chlorpyriphos, are not generally available to amateur growers. Professionals can apply these substances as a drench or as tiny, green granules (SuSCon Green and Vinyl) incorporated into the potting or planting mix, giving slow-release protection for up to two years. Bifenthrin can also be used in this way. H. Edward Reiley reports that this can offer some protection for as long as 3–4 years. Imidacloprid is available to amateurs (as Provado, Merit and Marathon) and has proven to be very effective. Used as a drench, it is taken up by the plant and protects the roots and foliage from both adults and grubs for several months.

Also available are biological controls against larvae. These include *Steinernema* (eelworm) species and *Heterorhabditis*. These products are available mail order and arrive in a packet, and are mixed with lukewarm water and watered on. Most biological controls require a minimum temperature to breed and attack the weevil larvae, so are only effective in warm weather outdoors and are most effective in greenhouses and in containers, which is where the worst problems tend to occur. Compost must be moist in order that the nematode solution can penetrate the whole of the pot. The best time to apply is July–August, when soil temperatures are high and before larvae have had a chance to do too much damage. Adult vine weevils undoubtedly prefer to lay eggs in containers, and in greenhouses and frames, so concentrate your resources there. The fact that weevils are flightless means infestations usually start in localized areas and, provided these can be dealt with, the spread may be halted. I have read claims that some cultivars such as 'P.J.M.' are resistant to weevils. This is not borne out in my experience.

Aphids. Whitefly and greenfly can suddenly appear in large numbers on the underside of young leaves and on the stems, particularly in dry weather, sucking out the sap and causing puckered or wrinkled leaves. Vireyas seem particularly prone to attack. Spray with a contact insecticide or with a systemic such as imidacloprid. If you dislike using chemicals, soap concentrates such as 'Savona' or 'Safers' can be used. It may take several doses to clear the infestation. With both chemicals and soap sprays, it is important to target the insects on the leaf undersides. This requires a fine spray to allow the water droplets to adhere. There are also a number of biological controls, which are most effective under glass. These include *Aphidoletes* (midge) and *Aphideius* (predatory wasp).

Lacebug (*Stephanitis*) is a serious problem in some areas. There are two different species of these sap-sucking insects, one which attacks rhododendrons and the other azaleas. Lacebug damage on leaves causes a greyish or whitish leaf upper-surface with a discolouring on the lower surface. The effect is most severe on plants grown in full sun and in shade it may not be a problem, where there are more lacebug predators to keep them under control. Evergreen azaleas are worst affected in eastern North America. Chemical controls include imidacloprid, dimethoate (Cygon), or acephate (Orthene) and you can also use insecticidal soaps. Repeat the application every ten days until control is obtained. University of Maryland research indicates that some species and cultivars of azalea are resistant to lacebugs, examples include: 'Dream', 'Elsie Lee', 'Macrantha', 'Red Wing', *R. canescens* and *R. prunifolium*. Azaleas apparently particularly susceptible include: *R. alabamense*, *R. calendulaceum*, 'Mother's Day', 'Rosebud', 'Girard's Rose' and 'Hershey's Red'. I have recently read that *Stephanitis takeyai*, which attacks *Pieris*, may also affect rhododendrons.

LACEBUG DAMAGE.

CATERPILLAR DAMAGE.

THRIPS ON RHODODENDRONS IN NEW ZEALAND.

Caterpillars can be troublesome, munching holes in leaves and sometimes destroying expanding buds, leaving shredded new growth that usually has to be removed. We find that most damage is done to plants where the caterpillars drop from surrounding trees and shrubs, so cutting back undergrowth can halt the problem. If you cannot pick off and squash the offenders by hand, then use a chemical control such as derris or acephate (Orthene).

Scale is a small sap-sucking insect that leaves cottony or fluffy traces on the leaves and stems, and an unsightly black residue. H. Edward Reiley says that to identify them, look for a red liquid when you crush them. Spray with insecticide and use a winter-tar or paraffin-oil wash to prevent re-infection. Maple soft-body scale has become a serious problem in Philadelphia and Washington areas, particularly on evergreen azaleas. This scale resembles mealy bug. Azalea expert Bill Steele recommends a mixture of contact and systemic insecticide. An alternative is paraffinic or horticultural oil, which can be applied as a winter wash or when eggs hatch out.

Thrips is a problem in warm and dry climates such as California and parts of New Zealand. It is characterized by a silvery discoloration on the leaf upper-surface. Most of the standard insecticides and insecticidal soaps can be used. Locally, biological controls may also be available.

Other insect pests can be very troublesome, locally or regionally. Some eat roots, some munch leaves, suck sap or bore into the stems (stem borers, the larvae of moths). New Zealand seems to have a particularly fine selection of endemic nasties. Most of the chemicals listed for other insect pests are effective, though you may have to seek local advice.

WARM-BLOODED PESTS

Rhododendrons are toxic to many animals, which usually know not to eat them, but there are cases of sheep and cattle poisoning from time to time. Horses and cattle are more likely to cause breakage than to graze your plants; this and the soil compaction that they can cause means that is advisable to keep farm animals fenced from your rhododendrons. Birds can cause considerable damage, both in dust bathing and in looking for food, especially around small, newly planted stock. Indoors and in frames, mice and voles can be troublesome, especially in cold and snowy winters.

Deer and rabbits. Both these animals can cause great destruction in the rhododendron garden. Azaleas, both deciduous and evergreen, seem to be particularly palatable and certain species always seem to be the first to be attacked. American rabbits seem to be particularly keen on Satsuki azaleas, while we find Scottish rabbits less discerning, eating most evergreen azaleas and species deciduous azaleas such as *R. albrechtii*. When grazing is lush and there is plenty to eat, rhododendrons are often left well alone. The problems

usually occur when there is snow on the ground, especially when the ground is frozen solid. Often rhododendrons are one of the few evergreen plants that the deer and rabbits can easily reach and so considerable damage, such as the loss of leaf tips, branch tips or, more seriously, the stripping of the bark, may occur. Ideally fencing is the perfect option, but this is expensive, especially where deer are concerned. To fence effectively against rabbits, use netting at least 1m wide and bury 10–15cms in the ground to prevent them from digging underneath. In really severe infestations it may be necessary to poison rabbit warrens using sodium cyanide or similar gases. Such chemicals are potentially very dangerous and countries have strict regulations as to who is allowed to use them. An effective deer-fence needs to be 2m high for roe deer (the most common deer species in the U.K.) but may need to be higher where larger species of deer occur. In North America, where deer are often a plague, I saw effective use of single strand electric fences. Another deterrent is to use substances with animal-repellent properties. H. Edward Reiley describes his use of six beaten eggs added per gallon of water. There is now a product called 'Deer Away' sold in North America, which smells of rotten eggs bound into a latex polymer that allows it to stick to plants for up to three months. Some people swear by bundles of human hair (try your local hairdresser), while others obtain dung of predatory animals such as lions from their local zoo! Several commercial animal-repellents have been developed over the years. The most common is aluminium ammonium sulphate (sold under the name 'scoot', 'stay off', etc.). A substance called Bitrex is now available in North America. This is the bitterest substance known and it makes any plant painted with it inedible. You'll find their website on the internet. Another new substance is Plantskydd® Deer Repellent, which is an organic product that apparently contains a 'predator odour' which discourages animals. All, some or none of these might work in your area. As a last resort, someone will need to get a gun out, as the populations of deer and rabbits in some areas are far larger than the environment can sustain.

DISEASES

POWDERY MILDEW

Mildews occur on many plant genera and new strains and mutations occur from time to time. There are at least three different powdery mildews that attack the genus *Rhododendron*. One mildew occurs on deciduous azaleas, one on Vireyas and perhaps the most troublesome occurs on temperate rhododendron (as opposed to azalea) species and hybrids.

Rhododendron powdery mildew. (2–3 species) Although said to have been first reported in the 1960s, this disease did not start to cause problems until the early 1980s. Since then, it has become one of the major problems for rhododendron growers in moderate climates, such as the British Isles, western North America, Australia and New Zealand. Powdery mildew has not caused problems in places with high summer temperatures and/or cold winters, such as most of Germany, Sweden and eastern North America (except the most favourable coastal areas – I have seen it on Cape Cod). The symptoms are light, usually yellowish rings, circles or blotches on the upper leaf, which correspond on the leaf lower-surface with brown or grey patches of mycelium that may spread and cover the whole surface.

POWDERY MILDEW.

Severe infection causes premature leaf-drop and a plant can be defoliated. Only some species and cultivars are very susceptible to the problem, though if infection is allowed to increase unchecked, almost all varieties can be affected to some extent.

MILDEW-SUSCEPTIBLE VARIETIES: Species: R. *cinnabarinum*, R. *thomsonii*, and their relatives, R. *calostrotum* ssp. *riparioides*. Hybrids: most R. *cinnabarinum* hybrids such as 'Lady Chamberlain' and 'Lady Rosebery'; R. *thomsonii* hybrids, for example 'Cornish Cross', 'Naomi'; R. *griersonianum* hybrids such as 'Vanessa Pastel', 'Anna Rose Whitney', 'Elizabeth' and yellow hybrids containing R. *wardii* such as 'Virginia Richards', 'Golden Star' and so on. Semi-dwarfs such as 'Seta'.

The only sure way to control this disease is to spray with fungicides and this only works as a preventative and only as long as you spray. Fungicides that have proven reliable include bupirimate, propiconazole, myclobutanil and triadimefon (Bayleton). In some countries some of these are restricted to commercial use only. For organic gardeners, horticultural oils and neem oil are said to have some effect in controlling the disease. Products containing sulphur are also said to be effective but may burn foliage if temperatures exceed 29°C (84°F). There appear to be other promising chemical controls about to come onto the market.

Mildews mainly affect recently developed young growth; it will not usually spread onto old leaves, which means that the most effective time to spray is in late-spring and summer. The problem is that many smaller-leaved varieties produce new growth more or less continuously through the growing season and this requires a spraying programme every 3–4 weeks from late-spring to autumn. The disease spreads most quickly in dry, mild weather and in conditions of shade and of low air-circulation. Over-planted or mature, dense gardens are, therefore, often the worst affected and, of course, large plants are the hardest and most time-consuming to spray. There are several possible strategies to follow in dealing with this disease:

1. Spray all your plants several times a year. Of course, using large amounts of fungicide is a dangerous, unpleasant, time-consuming and expensive business. It is possible to keep everything disease free.
2. Identify and spray only the most susceptible varieties (such as those listed above). This should prevent obvious sources of infection building up in the garden and it may well cut down infection to other plants. Plants that can live happily with moderate levels of infection can be left to fend for themselves.
3. Let nature take its course. The most susceptible varieties such as 'Lady Chamberlain' and 'Elizabeth' will defoliate and probably die. Some varieties

will look semi-permanently under-clothed and sparse, with leaves hooching with unsightly disease. It may well be worth eliminating such varieties as a preventative measure and avoiding susceptible varieties when planting. Several very large public gardens with extensive rhododendron collections seldom, if ever, spray and, although some plants have been lost, the effect of the disease on the majority is largely cosmetic and most flower and grow freely. We have never sprayed in our Scottish west-coast garden and have only lost a few R. *cinnabarinum* from the disease.

Deciduous azalea mildew. Characterized by a silvery mycelium that develops on the upper and, sometimes, lower surface of the leaf from midsummer onwards. It occurs on wild populations of R. *occidentale* in western U.S.A. and on cultivated azaleas, mainly pale-flowered varieties containing R. *occidentale*, and R. *luteum*. Most azalea species and hybrids with orange and red flowers seem to be resistant. Apart from being unsightly, the disease, if unchecked, can cause early leaf-fall and therefore a general loss of vigour and decrease in flowering. Breeding non-susceptible varieties has been quite successful and many disease-resistant cultivars are available. For susceptible cultivars, spray with triadimefon or myclobutanil, monthly in severe outbreaks. Potassium-bicarbonate and sulphur-based fungicides are also effective in reducing the disease. This strain of mildew has recently spread to Europe.

Vireya mildew. This mildew also affects other parts of the family Ericaceae, such as *Gaultheria*. It is characterized by white patches on the young leaves, which often causes the leaves to become undersized or distorted. It can be controlled using the same fungicides as are used to treat rhododendron mildew.

RUSTS

Like the mildews, rusts are a group of constantly evolving fungi that attack many genera of plants. In wild populations, rusts are most commonly found on natural hybrids. There are several species of rust (up to thirteen have been reported), which attack rhododendrons in different parts of the world and have differing alternative hosts. Rusts usually have two hosts and the rust moves from one to the other as part of its life cycle, though apparently it can live for several years on one host. Rhododendron-rust alternative hosts include *Picea* and *Tsuga*, so it might be worth eliminating these two genera from the garden. Rust usually appears on the leaf underside and is characterized by the spores, which form an orange powdery covering. If left untreated the rust will cause black spotting on the upper surface of the leaf and infected leaves will usually drop off. As with mildew, a severe attack can defoliate and kill a plant, though this is rare except in the most susceptible varieties. Fungicides such as myclobutanil (Systhane) and triadimefon (Bayleton) are effective controls.

RUST-SUSCEPTIBLE VARIETIES: Mostly hybrids. R *cinnabarinum* hybrids such as 'Trewithen Orange'; R. *edgeworthii* hybrids such as 'Fragrantissimum';

RUST.

ABOVE: **RHODODENDRON LEAF HOPPER.**
RIGHT: **BUD BLAST, SHOWING SPORES.**

Azaleodendrons such as 'Martha Isaacson'; dwarf hybrids such as 'Anna Baldsiefen' and 'Arctic Tern'. Rusts seem to be affecting more varieties from year to year and we have recently found *R. occidentale* to be prone to infection.

BUD BLAST

This unsightly disease is characterized by flower buds that do not open but instead turn black and are covered with bristly black spores. This disease worst affects hybrids of *R. caucasicum* – examples include 'Boule de Neige' and 'Cunningham's White' – and is often spread by leaf hoppers, which are a particular problem in parts of northern Europe. I have seen hybrids in Germany and Holland with every bud black and covered with bristly spores. The only way to control it is to try to kill the leaf hoppers with an insecticide. In the U.K. we seldom find bud blast to be of such serious concern, as we don't appear to have a significant leaf hopper problem.

ROOT ROTS AND STEM DIEBACK

In hot climates, these diseases are undoubtedly the greatest cause of rhododendron death and have wiped out whole collections and thousands of plants of nursery stock. In climates with regular and sustained heat in summer, many varieties are so susceptible to these diseases that they cannot be grown.
Root rot/wilt. *Phytophthora cinnamoni* is a root disease that is usually fatal and often kills a plant extremely quickly. The symptoms are, usually, a sudden collapse during the growing season, usually of the whole plant or several plants in one area of the garden. Check the roots and cut into the stem of the plant. The disease is characterized by the roots turning a deep-brown colour (rather than white, as healthy growing-roots should be). If you scrape away the bark at ground level, you will find the cambium layer below the bark has been stained a dark reddish-brown colour. The disease is caused by inadequate drainage and warm or hot soil-temperatures. The combination of these is very often fatal to rhododendrons. It is most common in areas with hot summers but can occur anywhere if poor drainage is allowed to occur. *Phytophthora cinnamonii* is most active at a soil temperature of 20–22°C (68–72°F). Plants in containers are particularly susceptible, especially if watered overhead with sprinklers. To avoid the disease, ensure that the planting area is well prepared with coarse organic and inorganic matter to give free drainage and maintain aeration in the soil. Freshly composted bark has been shown to have some root-rot resistant properties and is the most popular medium for container growing in North America. Ensure that the soil where the rhododendrons are growing is not allowed to become compacted by people or animals walking over it. In warmer climates, growing in shade and mulching will help to keep the soil temperature down. In Germany, most varieties of rhododendron are grafted, which increases tolerance of poorly drained soils. In areas with heavy clay soils, the best practice is often to plant above soil level, either in raised beds or by mounding up the soil around the root of the plant.
SUSCEPTIBLE VARIETIES: Most members of subsection *Taliensia* (for example *R. phaeochrysum*), subsection *Neriiflora* (for example *R. dichroanthum*), and many other species such as *R. souliei* and *R. lanatum*. Most larger yellow hybrids (which are almost all derived from *R. wardii*), such as 'Hotei' and 'Goldkrone', are also susceptible, as are many of the smaller-leaved or alpine species and hybrids. Drought makes plants more susceptible. Most larger-growing hybrids (other than in yellow shades) and most azaleas are more heat tolerant and therefore less susceptible. A few cultivars such as 'Roseum Elegans', 'Rocket', 'Caroline', 'Besse Howells' and 'Cadis' are known to be particularly resistant to *Phytophthora*. Breeders could breed a whole range of resistant cultivars using these varieties.

Planting an infected plant in your garden can be the start of a major outbreak of disease. If you remove a plant which has died of this disease, dispose of the whole plant including all of the rootball. It is also prudent to remove the soil that surrounded the dead plant's rootball, as it will have many fungal spores in it. If a plant dies of phytophthora, there is little point replacing with the same or a similar variety without doing something to improve the drainage or decrease the soil temperature. There are several chemicals on the market, mostly not available to amateurs, which can be used as a drench to suppress phytophthora. These contain chemicals such as fosetyl-aluminium and metalaxyl (Aliette and Subdue). These should be used in conjunction with good hygiene and optimum planting conditions and it is important to remember that none of these fungicides will eradicate the fungus, just control it temporarily. Poor drainage and heat will eventually kill plants, even with added chemicals. A home test for phytophthora can be done by infecting a hard apple or pear by sticking some infected tissue into the fruit, then sealing up the lesion. Any infection will grow some dry mealy rot into the fruit in 5–6 days. I am grateful to Tony Blyth from New Zealand for supplying me with information on the use of *Trichoderma* fungi added to soil and container mixes to help combat rhododendron fungal root-diseases. In New Zealand many nurseryman use this in pellet form, added to potting mixes, which both reduces phytophthora and encourages more vigorous root growth. We are about to try it at Glendoick.
Stem dieback. (*Botryosphaeria* (canker), *Phytophthora cactorum*, *P. ramorum*.) These are serious diseases of rhododendrons, particularly in regions with considerable summer heat and/or humidity. They are characterized by the sudden wilting and death of a branch or part of a plant and tend to attack where plants have been physically damaged in some way. Check the inside of the wilted stem for diagnosis: it will normally have turned brown, usually with a dark reddish-brown core. The dead stem must be cut out well into green wood in the healthy part of the plant and the dead branch should be disposed of or burnt, but not composted. Ensure secateurs are sterilized using bleach or alcohol to avoid spreading the disease. Good hygiene, adequate air circulation and moderate use of fertilizer all help prevent the diseases. Drought stress increases susceptibility to the disease. *Botryosphaeria* can begin as leaf spot and go on to cause stem dieback. There is no effective chemical control for this disease. For phytophthora, fungicides such as mancozeb, metalaxyl and fosetyl-aluminium can be used. *Phytophthora ramorum* (Sudden Oak Death) is a recently described disease that has caused much worry. I suspect it has been around for many years and that scientists have only just recognized it as a separate species. The disease has been found on a wide variety of plants, including *Rhododendron*, *Camellia*, *Viburnum*, *Pieris*, *Kalmia* and *Taxus*, and the symptoms are similar to those of *Botryosphaeria* dieback. It can spread from rhododendrons onto other plants, which can be more seriously affected by it. Thought to be spread by water-splashing, its effects on rhododendrons are not very severe, causing limited stem dieback. This disease has, however, been widely publicized in the media in recent years and has caused widespread panic in the plant world, as it attacks and kills members of the oak family, such as *Lithocarpus* in western North America. In much of Europe and North America outbreaks of this disease are required to be notified to

PHYTOPHTHORA STEM DIEBACK.

agricultural authorities and infected plants are destroyed. I suspect that, over time, this will be perceived as just another fungal disease, particularly prevalent in mild and warm areas, such as California and Cornwall, England, and with which we will just have to learn to live. Most of the chemicals that suppress other dieback diseases will also be effective on *P. ramorum*. There are said to be two different strains: apparently the one in Europe is not the same as the one in the U.S.A. At the time of writing there are restrictions in the commercial movement of rhododendrons from areas where the disease is present.

HONEY FUNGUS (*ARMILLARIA*)

This fungus can attack and kill rhododendrons in the woodland garden or areas where tree stumps are prevalent. There are many species of honey fungus or *Armillaria*, which occur in different parts of the world, most of which feed exclusively on decaying matter. Several species, unfortunately, are also able to colonize and weaken or kill living plants and rhododendrons are particularly susceptible. Sometimes sending up conspicuous fruiting bodies, the main part of the fungus lives underground, sending out vigorous rhizomorphs (commonly known as bootlaces), which colonize both dead and living tree and plant roots. Gardens with lots of old tree-stumps in the ground are at most risk. Of course, one can glibly recommend that all tree roots be removed, but this is impossible with the enormous root-systems of mature broad-leaf trees such as elm, beech or sycamore. Digging out a dead plant killed by honey fungus will usually reveal the tell-tale black bootlaces that have run through the rootball and into the stem, virtually strangling it in severe cases. Symptoms vary from yellowing of leaves, poor leaf retention, poor growth length, partial dieback of branches on the plant, or sudden total collapse. Often a last-gasp attempt to flower heavily will be made. There is little doubt that stressed plants (by water logging, drought, etc.) are more susceptible to the fungus. Certain species, such as *R. lacteum*, most of subsection *Taliensia* and many in subsection *Neriiflora*, are particularly at risk, while many hybrids seem to be able to withstand having the fungus in their roots, though it can reduce their vigour.

To prevent the fungus occurring, it is advisable to remove the roots of trees wherever possible. There is very little else you can do about *Armillaria*, apart from using artificial barriers to keep it from spreading. The fungus usually remains close to the surface, seldom deeper than 30–45cm in lighter soils, though it is said to go deeper in clay soils, so heavy duty plastic and other materials can be used to make impermeable barriers rather like underground walls. Alternatively, plants can have an underground wall made in a circle around the rootball. Raised beds with a solid lining are another solution, but ensure there is adequate drainage: try to construct on a slope if possible. We have tried using permeable membranes but the fungus appears to be able to penetrate these. There are various phenolic compounds which kill honey fungus. These are expensive and they can only be safely used around mature plants. The fungus will usually return if there is infection nearby. There is some hope that *Trichoderma* fungi can be used to reduce *Armillaria* infection.

PETAL BLIGHT (*OVULINIA*)

This fungal disease is one of the most upsetting diseases, as it ruins the flowers you have waited so long to enjoy. It has long been associated mainly with warmer parts of the rhododendron-growing world, such as south and eastern U.S.A., and is particularly troublesome on evergreen azaleas. Unfortunately the disease is spreading and is now a serious problem in much of North America, parts of Europe and Australia: indeed it has significantly reduced the popularity of azaleas in some areas. Infected flowers first exhibit small spots, which appear water-soaked. These rapidly enlarge, turning the petals into a slimy grey mass that sinks limply onto the leaves below. It can even strike before the flowers open. It takes 2–3 days for the flowers to be completely ruined and a whole bush or group of plants can quickly be affected. The destroyed petals dry-stick to the foliage and white patches that turn to black fruiting bodies are produced, which will infect the following year's flowers. The disease usually occurs during moist weather at flowering time, especially if accompanied by warmth and poor air-circulation. Watering overhead so that it wets the flowers is to be avoided if possible. If you have an infected plant brought in from another source, it is well worth removing all blooms immediately so that the spores cannot be spread. If you have a large amount of infection, it may be necessary to spray with a fungicide containing myclobutanil, triadimefon (Bayleton) or benomyl, from when buds start to show colour and then at weekly intervals until the flowers go over. Keeping the foliage and especially the flowers as dry as possible is the best way to avoid the disease. Another chemical that has proven very useful is terraclor, which is applied as a solution on the ground under rhododendrons and azaleas: this is taken up via the roots and suppresses the disease. *Botrytis* (mould) can cause very similar

PETAL BLIGHT.

symptoms; it differs in the absence of black fruiting bodies. I hope that petal-blight-resistant cultivars may be bred in the future. This disease is a terrible curse that seriously affects the viability of rhododendron gardening in some areas.

LEAF GALL

This unsightly fungal disease is characterized by green, pink or red swellings on the leaves and shoots. It is found on wild populations of some species and also found in gardens on some species and hybrids, and especially on evergreen/Japanese azaleas and *R. ferrugineum* and its hybrids. The diseased part should be picked off and destroyed: the problem usually occurs only once a season with the main flush of new growth. Many of the fungicides used to control mildew and rust also seem to have an effect in reducing this disease. Many authorities claim that galls are spread by an insect, but I have never seen any firm evidence for this.

AZALEA GALLS.

COLD, SUN AND
WEATHER-RELATED PROBLEMS

Spring frosts are undoubtedly the single most frustrating weather problem rhododendron growers have to put up with in many areas. Few rhododendrons have frost-resistant flowers or growth and all too often those long-admired buds are just about to open, or have just opened, when a few degrees of frost turns everything to a brown mush. This problem is, perhaps, most extreme in the maritime climate of the British Isles, where mild winters can bring plants into flower and growth as early as February and March and then see the return of frost in April or May. Site tender and vulnerable plants with care: frost flows downwards, with hollows such as river beds particularly vulnerable, while surrounding higher ground may escape. Shelter from trees will also moderate the temperature a degree or two, which is often the difference between damage and being virtually unscathed. A few early-flowering varieties, such as *R. lapponicum* and *R. hippophaeoides*, have frost-resistant flowers, while one or two others, including the very popular 'Ptarmigan' and 'Christmas Cheer', open their flowers in batches over a long period, so that if one flush of flowers is frosted another one follows on. You can, of course, put artificial protection over plants with early flowers and growth. The problem is that the best protection is afforded by covering but not touching the plants and this is often hard to achieve. Use woven material rather than polythene or plastic if possible: old sacks and sheets, spun polypropylene (sold specifically for this purpose) and bubble polythene are all effective. Try to keep the material dry, as the weight of wet cloth can cause damage and wet material is a less effective frost-protectant. Covers are often blown off and we expend much energy at Glendoick trying to attach covers that stay on. Having the flowers frosted does no long-term damage to the plant. Even when growth is badly damaged – brown, wrinkled or puckered – the damage is mainly cosmetic and the plant will usually recover well, putting on a second flush of growth later. If the leaves are badly distorted they can usually be pruned off and the growth will be replaced from lateral buds. More serious and long-term damage can be caused by bark-split, when sap running in the stem is frozen, bursting the outer layer of bark. Often the plant looks healthy for a few months and then the split branch will die off. Young plants can be killed outright from bark-split. Small plants of species, such as *R. yunnanense* and certain forms of

BARK-SPLIT ON *R. MACABEANUM.*

R. augustinii, are particularly vulnerable; they become tougher and more resistant with age. Sometimes the wound will heal up but, if not, you may have to prune back to below where the split occurred. Bark-split is usually caused by spring frosts but can also be caused in autumn in late-growing varieties, such as those with *R. griersonianum* and *R. auriculatum* blood, 'Vanessa Pastel' and 'Polar Bear' for instance.

Cold damage is usually seen in browned, brittle foliage, not to mention brown and dead flower-buds. Even the hardiest varieties can be severely damaged by a combination of frozen ground with sun and/or wind. This causes severe foliage desiccation and can defoliate a plant. Prudent use of shade and shelter is the way to alleviate this. Most of us are tempted to grow plants of borderline hardiness, making use of the most favourable, sheltered sites in the garden. In an extreme winter, which seems to occur less often these days, substantial damage, such as loss of flower buds and browned foliage, may occur. In colder parts of continental Europe and much of the eastern states of the U.S.A. and Canada, the majority of rhododendrons simply are not hardy enough to survive the winter temperatures, so the choice of which varieties to grow is crucial. The hardiest varieties, known as 'ironclads', number an increasingly large range, bred to withstand –32°C (–26°F). The early crosses in

FAR LEFT: **FROST DAMAGE ON YOUNG GROWTH.**

LEFT: **LICHENS ON AZALEAS.**

this group were made in Europe, especially by the Waterers in England, but there are many hybridizers, such as David Leach in the eastern U.S.A., who have greatly increased the range of flower colours available. Gardeners in extreme climates often go to extraordinary lengths to provide extra shelter to bring plants though the winter.

Wind damage is manifest in leaves broken at the petiole and ragged or brown-edged leaves. Further details can be found in the sections on shelter and wind (*see* page 10). Sunburn is common after hot summers in many regions. Mild sunburn turns leaves bright yellow, while a more severe attack will burn the leaves to a crisp. This issue is dealt with in greater detail under 'shade' (*see* page 10). Lichens often form on old, straggly specimens, particularly when they have few leaves and are lacking in vigour. Evergreen and deciduous azaleas seem particularly prone. You can scrub the lichen off, but often it is a sign of poor soil conditions, lack of fertilizer or old age and it can best be dealt with by rejuvenating the plants by pruning and fertilizer or by throwing them out and starting again. Lichen tends to grow on weak plants rather than causing the weakness.

WHY DOES MY RHODODENDRON HAVE YELLOW LEAVES?

Old leaves naturally turn yellow before dropping off; this is nothing to worry about. However, if the current year's leaves are yellow, it is a sure sign the plant is not happy. This can be caused by a number of different factors (or a combination of them). If the whole leaf is yellow, the cause is usually sunburn or starvation. If yellowing is more pronounced on the blade of the leaf, with greener veins (chlorosis), the cause is more likely to be mineral (too much or too little) or incorrect pH. The following can cause yellow leaves:

■ Poor drainage from heavy or compacted soil (*see* pages 8–9). This may lead to death from phytophthora.
■ Drought through lack or rain or watering, or from competition from tree roots (*see* page 10).
■ Plant is planted too deep. The top of the rootball should be just below the surface of the soil.
■ Nitrogen deficiency. The plant is starving. This can be easily remedied by feeding (*see* page 18).
■ Mineral deficiency (*see* page 18).
■ Soil pH is too high/alkaline. Test the pH (*see* page 10). A few varieties like a near-neutral soil and benefit from an application of dolomitic limestone (*see* the list of varieties for near-neutral soil, page 8).

WHY DOES MY RHODODENDRON NOT FLOWER?

1. Flower buds form but do not open. Frost/cold is the most likely cause, either in early autumn before buds have had time to harden off, in midwinter by the hardest frosts of the year, or by spring frosts when the buds are swelling and about to open. Certain varieties, such as *R. pemakoense*, have very frost-vulnerable swelling buds, while many species in subsection *Maddenia* have over-wintering buds that are easily destroyed, even by quite mild frosts. A variety that always gets its buds frosted, unless it has very fine foliage, may not be worth space in your garden. If the dead buds are covered with spore-laden black bristles, you have bud blast (*see* page 26).
2. No (or few) flower buds are formed. Too much shade is one of the commonest causes. The more light you can give a plant, the more likely it is to flower, so there is a subtle trade-off between the need for shade to protect from sunburn and the need for light.

Many varieties of rhododendron take several years to flower. This particularly applies to the large-leaved species, such as *R. sinogrande* and some of the species in subsection *Taliensia*. Some of the well-known older hybrids, such as 'Loderi' and 'Crest', need to be reach the age of 5–7 years before they flower freely. One or two species, such as the infamous *R. pronum*, hardly ever flower in cultivation at all. Thankfully, this species is mainly grown for its foliage. Many species do not flower well every year: especially after a heavy flowering season, many will take a rest.

Rhododendrons flower in order to reproduce. A contented, well-fed, well-watered, well-shaded plant may not feel any need to reproduce and therefore to flower, as it perceives no threat to its survival. The moral of this is not to be too kind to your plants: a little stress does no harm at all. Do not feed after midsummer, as this encourages growth at the expense of flowers. Nurserymen cut down watering in late summer to encourage plants to set buds. If all else including threats fails, then try a bit of root pruning. You can even lift a plant and replace it in its hole.

PROPAGATION

Rhododendrons and azaleas are not one of the easier genera to propagate: seed is small, seedlings are slow-growing and cuttings generally take several months to root, even in heated propagators. With a little care and attention, however, it is possible to have very successful results and many amateur rhododendron enthusiasts are very successful at propagating their plants. Propagation falls into two main categories, sexual or asexual/vegetative. The crucial difference is that from sexual reproduction (seed) the offspring are all genetically unique individuals and are not identical to the parent, while the asexual/vegetative methods (cuttings, layers, grafts) produce plants genetically identical to the parent. All named varieties and selected clones must be produced by vegetative means. For the majority of rhododendrons, seeds and cuttings are the methods of propagation used. The other propagation methods, grafting and tissue culture, tend to be for professionals and keenest amateurs only.

SEED

This method is used to raise species from wild or garden seed and for creating new hybrids. It cannot be used to reproduce a named hybrid: seedlings of 'Pink Pearl' are not 'Pink Pearl' and probably will not look anything like it. Rhododendrons are notoriously promiscuous; this means that in a garden they will be cross-pollinated by insects flying from one plant to another and the seed-grown offspring will almost always be hybridized, unless there is no compatible plant flowering at the same time in the vicinity. If you want to grow species from garden seed or make deliberate hybrids, you have to make controlled pollinations so that insects do not get involved. This involves removing the corolla (petals) and stamens of the flower of the female parent before it opens, then waiting for stigma to ripen (it becomes sticky) and then applying pollen from the stamens of the other (male) parent to the ripened stigma. Pollen can be stored in a fridge for several weeks, can be frozen and thawed and can be sent through the mail, so the male parent does not have to be flowering near by or at the same time. Do not forget to label the pollinated flower and record it, so that you can find the seed capsules in the autumn. If you want to try seed raising, seed packets of both hybrids and species are available from rhododendron society seed exchanges. Wild collected seed is always the most exciting and, from time to time, completely new species are introduced. Such seed often has a collector's number, recording when, where and by whom the seed was collected. Keep the collector's number on the plant label or record to document its origins (*see* page 32).

Rhododendron seed takes 3–7 months to ripen and is, therefore, harvested in the autumn/winter following pollination the previous spring. When ripe, the seed capsules are swollen and turning brown. Try to collect them just before they split.

SEED CAPSULES: THE LARGER HAVE SET SEED, THE SMALLER NOT.

If capsules are collected on the green side, place them in a dry place, such as on a windowsill, and the capsules will dry and split within a few days or weeks. The seed is fairly small and the seeds should be separated from the capsules and chaff, as this will go mouldy if sown. Dry seed can be stored in envelopes in the fridge, in an airtight container, until you are ready to sow. Seed should be sown in pans or trays containing moist, but not soaking, peat or clean, living (but not dried) sphagnum moss. Sow seed thinly onto the surface. We find covering pans with perforated polythene keeps the humidity up but lets air circulate. Germination usually takes 2–3 weeks if the temperature is 15–20°C (59–68°F), which can be under lights or in a propagator in wintertime. In a cold-frame, germination is much slower and will probably not take place until the spring. All watering of seed pans should be done by soaking from below, to avoid encouraging mould on the foliage. Once seed has germinated it needs sufficient light (but not direct sunlight) to keep plants strong and compact. Inadequate light causes weak, etiolated (drawn) seedlings. When large enough to handle, prick out the seedlings into trays in peat-based compost. Be very careful with feeding at this stage, as seedlings, especially dwarfs and species, are very sensitive to fertilizer. Use slow-release or dilute liquid feed. Usually, young seedlings are best over-wintered under cover, in a cold-frame or greenhouse. Small seedlings are vulnerable to botrytis (mould) and other pests and diseases.

VEGETATIVE METHODS OF PROPAGATION: GETTING IDENTICAL OFFSPRING

LAYERING

This is a good method to obtain a few new plants. It involves bending side branches of a plant into the surrounding soil so that they make roots. In moist climates, it often happens naturally. After 1–3 years (depending on the variety, soil preparation and rainfall) the rooted shoot can then be cut from the mother plant and moved elsewhere. Tree-like varieties, such as *R. arboreum* and *R. griffithianum*, are unlikely to have suitable branches to layer. It is usually advisable to improve the soil where the layers will be made, by adding organic matter. In moist climates you can layer into pots or trays placed around the growing plant. This avoids root disturbance when the layers are cut. With dwarf varieties shoots can be anchored with rocks and stones. With larger varieties layers are usually held in place with stakes, large rocks or wire. Bend the

branch or shoot into the surrounding soil (prepared if necessary) and anchor it so that the end of the shoot is as near upright as possible. Many layers can be made from a single dwarf specimen: we have sometimes layered the entire plant. To encourage root-production in larger varieties it is advisable to cut a thin layer of bark off the underside of the branch or shoot where it is to be anchored into the ground. Once a good root system has formed, the plant can then be severed from the mother and transplanted. Ensure the layers are well watered before moving them. The disadvantage of layered plants is that they usually have a rather obvious bend in the stem. Judicious pruning can usually result in an acceptable plant. Some people have had success with air-layering, where roots are encouraged to form into a bag of moss, wrapped round the branch, with the bark wounded to encourage callousing. It might be fun to try, but it is not a method I have ever used.

CUTTINGS

Rhododendrons and azaleas vary greatly in the ease in which they root from cuttings. Evergreen azaleas and most dwarf rhododendrons are relatively easy, while many deciduous species and larger hybrids are rather slow and tricky to root. Some varieties refuse to root at all and these have to be grafted. The easiest way to root rhododendrons is under polythene in a box, tray, pots or modules, or in a propagator – ensure these are well cleaned before use. Small mist systems can give excellent results, but require more looking after. Bottom heat is advisable but not essential; without it, cuttings take longer to root. Cuttings root best with bottom heat of 15–20°C (59–70°F). In December and January, we reduce heat to about 10°C (50°F), as Scottish light levels are very low. Further south this may not be necessary. Timing of taking cuttings is important: they should be taken when sufficiently hardened-up to be flexible and springy when subjected to a bit of bending. This tends to be from late-summer onwards. Dwarfs and evergreen azaleas should be cut to 2.5–5cm or so, larger varieties can be up to 10cm long. Remove leaves to leave a single circle of 4–7 leaves at the top of a cutting. Leaves that are shaded by other leaves tend to rot in the rooting bed. With longer-leaved varieties, you can reduce the leaf length by 30–40 per cent (chop off the end) to save space.

The most satisfactory rooting-media tend to be 50–60 per cent peat and 40–50 per cent perlite, grit or other substance to keep the compost open. Rooting hormones are useful to speed up the rooting process. With larger varieties, it also helps to cut a thin slice off the side of the part of the cutting to be inserted in the soil. Compost should be moist but not wet; over-wet compost causes rotting. Cover the cuttings with a propagator lid, polythene sheet or a polythene bag, making it more or less airtight so that the humidity is maintained. The leaves must not dry out or wilt: they need plenty of light but must be shaded from direct sunlight. Check over the cuttings regularly and remove dead cuttings and leaves to avoid the spread of disease. Cuttings with roots often start to sprout new growth and put up resistance when tugged. Once a reasonable root system has formed, roughly the same size as the foliage on the cutting, remove from heat and harden off by covering with slit polythene, or shading.

Transplant rooted cuttings into a peat-based compost: you can add composted bark, perlite, leaf-mould or conifer needles and some slow-release fertilizer. Rooted cuttings are best grown with some protection for most of their first growing season. We plant out our cuttings in late summer, or you can pot them up.

The other propagation methods, grafting and tissue culture, tend to be for professionals and keenest amateurs only. Consult the further reading list for sources of information on these methods.

SEEDLINGS IN TRAYS, AROUND SIX MONTHS OLD.

SEEDLINGS IN A COLD-FRAME, AFTER THE SECOND GROWING SEASON.

LEFT: **HOW TO PREPARE A CUTTING.**

ABOVE: **CUTTINGS NEWLY TAKEN, TO BE ROOTED UNDER POLYTHENE.**

ABOVE RIGHT: **CUTTINGS ROOTED AND READY FOR TRANSPLANTING.**

A RIOT OF COLOUR IN MAY AT HACHMANN NURSERY, GERMANY.

BUYING AND COLLECTING RHODODENDRONS

With around 900 species and over 25,000 named hybrids, it can be hard work to decide what you want and to track the varieties down. You'll be lucky if your local garden centre stocks more than a handful of common varieties and then probably only in spring, at flowering time. For species and more unusual hybrids you will have to go to one of the many specialist nurseries, some of which offer between 500–1,000 different varieties. Many offer a mail order service and some will export. The RHS Plantfinder (in book form or on the internet) and its European equivalent have made it easier to track down rarities.

Rhododendrons are one of the more challenging genera to grow well commercially: they take 2–3 years to reach a saleable size and they need careful handling. Traditionally, rhododendrons have been purchased bare-rooted from nurseries when dormant in autumn, winter and early spring and planted before the onset of new growth in the spring. This would be my choice if at all possible. These days, when most nursery stock is container grown, you may not be able to find bare-root stock. While there is no reason why a well-looked after, container-grown rhododendron should not thrive once planted in the garden, it pays to know what to avoid. Modern nursery practice involves a beauty treatment of forcing containerized plants as fast as possible to a saleable size using fertilizer, heat and artificial protection to ensure good budding and healthy foliage. The pot size is usually too small (to encourage budding and reduce transport costs) and such plants often take considerable time to recover when planted in the garden, especially if the plant is becoming root-bound in its pot. Rhododendron roots are shallow and spreading, while the pots they grow in are narrow and deep. I have often seen sad pot-bound rhododendrons planted in gardens where, several years later, the pot shape is still all too visible when the roots are inspected. Very little in the way of new roots have been put out into the surrounding soil, resulting in a corresponding lack of healthy new growth and few flower buds. Such 'plants-to-avoid' are usually found in garden-centres in August or September, looking forlorn and lonely, vainly hoping someone will take pity on them. The rootball will invariably have dried out and there may be roots coming out the drainage holes. Look out for signs of powdery mildew and other diseases.

Rhododendrons have compact, fibrous and shallow rootballs, so they can be planted and moved at any time of year. I have heard of American gardeners (admittedly with good irrigation systems) moving their plants around in full flower to ensure the best colour combinations. Having said this, there is no doubt that autumn planting ensures best establishment. The warmth of the soil allows a little root-growth before the onset of the severest weather and the winter rains wash soil well into contact with the rootball, which, in turn, allows new roots in early spring to penetrate the surrounding soil before growth starts above ground. This provides a degree of drought-resistance and ensures the best possible growth and bud set in the first growing season. The exception to this advice is in very severe climates, such as north-eastern U.S.A. and eastern Canada, and parts of northern Europe. Here it is probably preferable to plant in late spring, so that the plant has a full growing season in situ before having to brave the winter. Prepare the planting area in summer or early autumn, when weeds respond to weedkillers and the ground is dry enough to work easily without compacting the soil. If you are not yet ready to plant, you can cover the prepared area with polythene to keep heavy rain and weed seeds out.

GRAFTED RHODODENDRONS

Most rhododendrons and azaleas are produced from cuttings, with hard-to-propagate varieties produced by grafting and tissue-culture. Grafted rhododendrons have something of a bad reputation, largely due to the traditional use of *R. ponticum* as an understock until the 1950s. This species is so vigorous that it constantly sends up suckers that, if not removed, gradually take all the sap from the plant, eventually causing the variety grafted onto the rootstock to die off. Many old hybrid collections have now become dense plantings of *R. ponticum*, with the hybrids grafted on top lost long ago. Few nurseries graft onto *R. ponticum* these days: I only know of one nursery in Belgium, but if you buy a grafted plant, it is always worth enquiring what rootstock was used. If you don't get an answer, don't buy. Most nurseries now use 'Cunningham's White', 'County of York' and other rootstocks that throw far fewer suckers. Don't buy grafted plants less than two years old, as it takes this long to know whether the graft has taken or not. Avoid plants with an unnatural bulge where the union is, as this indicates incompatibility; in the long term, these usually fail. In Germany most larger hybrids are grafted, which makes them relatively expensive, but it does allow tolerance of less-than-ideal growing conditions. A new German rootstock called 'Inkarho' has been developed, which is tolerant of near neutral (but not alkaline) and heavier clay soils. There is no doubt that the careful testing of suitable rootstocks for different climates would allow plants to be grown more widely that struggle on their own roots. Some species, such as *R. lacteum*, *R. wightii* and *R. bhutanense*, are much

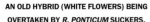

AN OLD HYBRID (WHITE FLOWERS) BEING
OVERTAKEN BY *R. PONTICUM* SUCKERS.

GLENDOICK HOUSE WITH DECIDUOUS AZALEAS.

longer-lived grafted than on their own roots and, likewise, most yellow hybrids require sharp drainage and often perform best when grafted. In hot climates many rhododendrons are killed by root problems such as phytophthora and grafting would certainly help to reduce this problem. I have never understood why gardeners in eastern North America don't graft. They would be able to grow a wider selection of varieties if they did.

MICROPROPAGATION OR TISSUE CULTURE

Many mass-produced garden-centre larger hybrids and deciduous azaleas these days are produced by tissue-culture. This involves inducing a cutting to produce tiny shoots in a test tube, which are cut up and rooted on agar gel. This technique has been widely used for over twenty years now and, as long as correct procedures have been followed, plants should turn out exactly as the parent but unfortunately, things can and all too often do go wrong. One common problem is unnaturally bushy plants with thin stems and smaller-than-normal leaves. These plants are in a suspended juvenility, caused by high rates of hormones, which they never grow out of. The resulting runts with thin stems, small leaves and undersized flowers are useless and should be returned to whoever supplied them for a refund. There were thousands of 'Crest' sold like this several years ago. Another major problem is misidentification: all varieties look the same in test tubes, and it only takes one careless labelling of a test tube…. There have been dozens of examples of huge batches of wrongly labelled plants from tissue culture labs widely distributed, only for the flowers to turn out the wrong colour. One particularly farcical episode concerned a German hybrid that was grafted onto 'Cunningham's White'. Instead of culturing the new variety, the nursery cultured the suckers from the rootstock instead and sent out thousands of Europe's commonest rhododendron to unsuspecting buyers. Perhaps the worst aspect of tissue culture is mass production: nurseries are able to produce almost infinite numbers of new and untested plants very fast. Fine if they turn out to be good. But what about those who purchased dogs such as 'Pink Petticoats' and 'Brigadoon'? To sum up, tissue culture is a good tool much abused.

SEED-RAISED PLANTS

Rhododendrons are extremely promiscuous: most of them will cross with whatever pollen the bees bring from the last plant they visited. This means that, in gardens, seed is almost certainly hybridized and you can only guess what the other parent might be. It is a waste of time, therefore, growing open-pollinated seed at all, except in the very rare circumstances when a species is unable to cross with any others: *R. schlippenbachii* and *R. albrechtii* are two examples. Rhododendron hybrids can never, never be reproduced from seed and must be vegetatively propagated: cuttings, layers, grafts or micropropagation (tissue culture). Of course, all new hybrids are created in the first place by mating two different species or hybrids, but all the resulting seedling offspring are unique and none are identical to their parents. Species, on the other hand, can be raised from seed and this is an excellent way to obtain moderately priced plants. But you must ensure that the seed was wild collected or, in the garden, hand or

control-pollinated, to ensure that the seed is not pollinated by insects. I know that some unscrupulous nurseries, especially in the Pacific Northwest of North America, still sell open-pollinated seedlings as 'species': this is dishonest and heart-breaking for the unsuspecting customers, many of whom have to wait years before their treasures flower with the wrong flower colour.

WHEN THE BUG BITES: BECOMING A RHODODENDRON COLLECTOR

You may not notice the exact moment when you become a full-blown rhodoholic. Perhaps someone will draw attention to the fact that there is no way your garden has room to accommodate all the little plants that are sitting around near the back door, let alone all the new hybrids you made this year, or the wild-collected seed you are raising, or the plants you bought at that convention, or those species that are far too tender for your garden. Eventually you just have to accept your addiction and most collectors join one of the many rhododendron societies worldwide, from North America to Europe, Japan, Australia, New Zealand and elsewhere. Collectors usually start growing some of the widely-available good-doer hybrids and gradually start to notice the qualities of species, especially in foliage and new growth. There is a degree of snobbery involved: species are considered by some to be the 'real thing'.

One of the most interesting facets of growing rhododendron species are collectors' numbers. Most of the early collectors, as well as many contemporary ones, collect wild seed under collector's number, where a number is assigned to the seed packet with notes on when and where the plant was collected, how large it was and what grew with it. Often a specimen of the plant is pressed and sent back to a botanic garden herbarium. As an example: K.W. 7724 was collected by Frank Kingdon Ward on his 1927–28 expedition to India, Tibet and Burma. In his field notes, he records it as, 'A forest tree with handsome foliage, truss with 12–18 flowers … it goes right to the summit where it forms forests … it should be hardy.' He records the location as Mt Javpo, Naga Hills, Assam, occurring from 8–10,000ft and he collected the seed on 1 December 1927. The seed from this collection was distributed far and wide, but wherever the plants have ended up, as long as the collection number was retained, the plant's origin can be traced. It turns out that K.W. 7724 was the first introduction of *R. macabeanum*, discovered by Sir George Watt forty years earlier. Armed with Kingdon Ward's field notes, my plant-collecting companion and director of the Rhododendron Species Botanic Garden, Steve Hootman, was able to go back to Mt Javpo in 2003 and relocate this species in the same spot where Ward had collected it.

Rhododendron species are quite widely available with collector's numbers, either propagated from garden-selected clones or as seedlings grown from recent expeditions to the wild. The latter are perhaps the most exciting, as each seedling is unique and you may be lucky enough to have one of the best. If you buy species with collector's numbers or grow them from wild seed, keep the collector's number on the label, so that the plant always carries its own coded identity card. The number can be decoded, with a bit of research, at a later date, allowing each plant to tell its own story and making a collection more interesting and complete. It is very gratifying for me as a collector to find plants with my numbers on them growing well in far-flung corners of the globe.

ENCYCLOPAEDIA OF RHODODENDRON VARIETIES

This section of the book contains over 4,300 of the most important varieties of rhododendrons and azaleas grown worldwide. It contains virtually all the non-Vireya species in cultivation and a selection of the most commercially important of the over 25,000 named cultivars. With the Vireyas, I have covered the most important and widely grown species and hybrids.

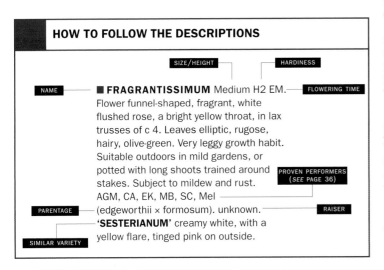

HOW TO FOLLOW THE DESCRIPTIONS

NAME — SIZE/HEIGHT — HARDINESS

■ **FRAGRANTISSIMUM** Medium H2 EM. — FLOWERING TIME
Flower funnel-shaped, fragrant, white flushed rose, a bright yellow throat, in lax trusses of c 4. Leaves elliptic, rugose, hairy, olive-green. Very leggy growth habit. Suitable outdoors in mild gardens, or potted with long shoots trained around stakes. Subject to mildew and rust. — PROVEN PERFORMERS (SEE PAGE 36)
AGM, CA, EK, MB, SC, Mel
PARENTAGE — (edgeworthii × formosum). unknown. — RAISER
SIMILAR VARIETY — 'SESTERIANUM' creamy white, with a yellow flare, tinged pink on outside.

SIZE/HEIGHT

Rhododendrons and azaleas can, in theory, go on growing indefinitely and so there is no ultimate size. Heights given are those attainable after 10–15 years. Most will eventually grow much bigger under ideal conditions and reach a considerable age. Plants in dry and cold climates grow more slowly than those in mild and wet climates with long growing seasons. Under each species or hybrid group heading, information on ultimate sizes is given.

Dwarf	to 40cm (1½ft) usually spreading, wider than high
Semi-dwarf	40–80cm (1½–3ft) often spreading wider than high
Low	80–135cm (3–4½ft) sometimes spreading wider than high
Medium	135–180cm (4½–6ft) considerably more with time
Tall	180cm and more (6ft+) much larger over time

HARDINESS RATINGS (see Table 1)

There are two main rating systems used for plants, both useful but also somewhat inadequate and misapplied. The USDA ratings are used in North America, sometimes in Europe and seldom in the U.K. In most cases the way the USDA ratings are mapped onto Europe is often very inaccurate: southern Denmark placed in zone 8 for example, where it should probably be in zone 5a. Most U.K. publications use the parochial and utterly inadequate rating system of H1 (tender)–H4 (hardy) promoted by the Royal Horticultural Society, which is not even sufficient for the U.K., let alone further afield. Royal Horticultural Society publications, widely sold internationally, are full of plants rated as H4

TABLE 1 HARDINESS RATINGS

RHS/COX RATINGS	USDA	DEGREES CELSIUS	DEGREES FAHRENHEIT	EXAMPLE AREAS
H9	4a	–31.7 to –34.4	–30 to –25	Minneapolis/St Paul, Minnesota. Finnish hybrids and Northern Lights azaleas.
H8	4b	–28.9 to –31.6	–25 to –20	Coldest parts of E. Europe and much of inland E. U.S.A. and Canada. Varieties known as 'ironclads'.
H7	5a	–26.2 to –28.8	–20 to –15	Colder parts of Germany and Scandinavia, New York, Nova Scotia, etc., much of Sweden, inland New England, Des Moines, Iowa; Illinois.
H6	5b	–23.4 to –26.1	–15 to –10	Columbia, Missouri; Mansfield, Pennsylvania.
H5	6a	–20.6 to –23.3	–10 to –5	Hardy anywhere in the U.K. and moderate parts of Europe such as Holland, S. Sweden, coastal Denmark, favourable parts of Germany, etc., moderate parts of N.E. U.S.A. and E. Canada.
H4	6b	–17.8 to –20.5	–5 to 0	Hardy in all but coldest parts of Pacific Northwest and U.K., coastal France and N. Italy, around Bergen (Norway) and mildest parts of N.E. U.S.A. such as Cape Cod.
H3	7a	–15.0 to –17.7	0 to 5	Hardy in a sheltered site in most of U.K., coastal France and N. Italy and Pacific Northwest gardens, but may be damaged in severest winters. Often early into flower and growth.
H2	7b	–12.3 to –14.9	5 to 10	Hardy outdoors in milder parts of U.K., such as Cornwall and Argyll; S. Ireland; most of California; Vancouver Island, Canada; most of New Zealand; Tasmania.
H1	8a	+9.5 to +12.2	10 to 15	Greenhouse culture, except for milder areas such as most of California, mildest western U.K. gardens.
H1	8b	+6.7 to +9.4	15 to 20	
	9a	+3.9 to +6.6	20 to 25	Houston, Texas; St Augustine, Florida.
	9b	+1.2 to +3.8	25 to 30	Brownsville, Texas; Fort Pierce, Florida.
H0	10a	1.6 to +1.1	30 to 35	Greenhouse culture, except in mildest areas of California, Hawaii, Australia and N. New Zealand and similar.

that they define as 'fully frost hardy', which is factually incorrect for the coldest parts of Scotland, let alone most of continental Europe. In reality, the H4 rating means little more than that the plant is hardy at RHS Wisley in southern England. I have therefore adapted the RHS ratings, adding four further hardiness bands, so that my hardiness ratings can be used internationally. These ratings H1–8 correspond to the USDA ratings in the chart below. I'm sure eventually the RHS will be forced to revise, extend and improve their own rating system.

Hardiness is hard to quantify precisely, as it depends on the timing of cold weather as well as the presence or absence of summer heat. Sudden drops in temperature are much more damaging than gradual drops. Many plants that are perfectly hardy in extreme midwinter cold are more vulnerable to damage in early autumn or late spring. Only the 'ironclad' rhododendrons can tolerate the combination of high summer temperatures and very cold winters. The USDA ratings usually contain an upper and lower figure, which applies to cold and heat. Most American gardeners know which USDA band their local area falls into. Maps are available on the internet, if you are not sure.

FLOWERING TIME (*see* Table 2)

In mild and maritime climates the rhododendron and azalea flowering season can cover seven months or more, beginning in midwinter and ending in late summer. In severe climates, the flowering season is compressed into a 2–3 month period, not starting until late April–May. The vagaries of the British climate cause considerable variation in flowering time from year to year, especially with early-flowering varieties.

R. KESANGIAE.

TABLE 2	FLOWERING TIME			
	FLOWERING TIME	*NORTHERN HEMISPHERE MODERATE*	*NORTHERN HEMISPHERE SEVERE*	*SOUTHERN HEMISPHERE*
VE	Very Early	Dec–Feb	April	July
E	Early	March	Early May	Aug–Sept
EM	Early-Mid	April	Mid May	Sept
M	Mid	1–15 May	Late May	Early Oct
ML	Late Mid	15–31 May	Early June	Late Oct
L	Late	June	June	Nov–Dec
VL	Very Late	July–Aug	July–Aug	Dec–Jan

SEAVIEW SUNSET.

FLOWER COLOUR (*see* Table 3)

Describing flower colours in words is a rather complex business. We now have the scientific means to exactly colour match and record any hue, shade or tint that we please. And yet the describing of flower colour in rhododendrons and other plants is a history of confusion and controversy. One dictionary (Kelly & Judd, 1976) describes 7,500 colour names. Many of these names have been applied to rhododendron flowers: we might have some idea what 'primrose yellow' or 'buttercup yellow' might look like, but what about 'Aureolin yellow', or 'empire yellow'? In order to sort out this confusion, in 1949, a chart called ISCC-NBS was created, with colours referred to by number: 'purplish-red 61C', for example. The Royal Horticultural Society produced a colour fan for matching and describing these colour codes. This did not altogether solve the problem, however: few people thought it worth paying the considerable cost of the colour chart and, worse still, many of the colours in the first printing in 1965 did not match the equivalents in the second in 1995! And, unsurprisingly, nurserymen find that 'vernacular' terms such as 'claret' are a much more appealing way to describe plant colour than the more scientific 'dark purplish pink 70C' when selling their new hybrid roses and rhododendrons. In other words, the needs of the nurseryman are at odds with that of scientific recording.

I am indebted to Donald Voss for elucidating for me the minefield of colour descriptions and the complexity of the issues therein. He points out that yellow, blue, green and violet are less problematic colours, as they basically vary only in darkness or lightness. The more complex colours, in the reddish-purple, red-orange and pink spectra, vary in darkness and lightness and in saturation or intensity. I therefore have included his excellent table, reproduced from the *Journal of the American Rhododendron Society* (Vol. 58, No. 1), which gives equivalent names for these colours. The most controversial

TABLE 3 — SELECTED ISCC-NBS COLOUR NAMES IN THE PURPLE-RED-ORANGE HUE RANGE

Within each colour, purple-red for example, colours become darker top to bottom, and more saturated from left to right. Standard ISCC-NBS colours (e.g. *light purplish-pink*) are in italics, with the associated vernacular colour names listed below in roman (e.g. rose pink or lilac rose).

CHROMA (COLOUR SATURATION)			CHROMA (COLOUR SATURATION)		
LIGHTER	MEDIUM	DARKER	LIGHTER	MEDIUM	DARKER
PURPLE			**PINK – RED**		
very light purple	*brilliant purple*	–	*light pink*	*strong pink*	*vivid pink*
light purple	*brilliant purple*	*vivid purple*	(baby pink,	(flamingo pink)	(carmine)
moderate purple	*strong purple*	*vivid purple*	almond blossom)		
REDDISH PURPLE			*moderate pink*	*strong pink*	*vivid pink*
light purplish pink	*brilliant purplish pink*	–	(flesh, arbutus pink)	(flamingo pink)	(carmine)
(rose pink, lilac rose)	(cameo pink, pink carnation)		*dark pink*	*deep pink*	*deep pink*
moderate purplish pink	*strong purplish pink*	–	(old rose)	(eosine pink, geranium pink)	
(orchid pink)	(deep rose pink)		*greyish red*	*moderate red*	*strong red – vivid red*
light reddish purple	*deep purplish pink*	–	(ash rose, carmine rose)	(blood red, cherry red)	(scarlet, flame red, tomato red, pimento)
(orchid, crocus)	(fuchsia pink, phlox pink)		**YELLOWISH PINK – REDDISH ORANGE**		
moderate reddish purple	*strong reddish purple*	*vivid reddish purple*	*light yellowish pink*	*strong yellowish pink*	*vivid yellowish pink*
(mauve, heliotrope)	(magenta)	(mallow purple, true purple)	(flesh pink, shell pink)	(salmon, peach)	(melon pink, red orange)
PURPLISH PINK – PURPLISH RED			*moderate yellowish pink*	*strong yellowish pink*	*vivid yellowish pink*
light purplish pink	*brilliant purplish pink*	–	(coral pink, peach pink)	(salmon, peach)	(melon pink, red-orange)
(rose pink, lilac rose)	(cameo pink, pink carnation)		*dark yellowish pink*	*deep yellowish pink*	*deep yellowish pink*
moderate purplish pink	*strong purplish pink*	–	(dusty coral)	(shrimp pink)	(rich shrimp pink)
(orchid pink)	(deep rose pink)		*greyish reddish orange*	*moderate reddish orange*	*strong reddish orange/vivid reddish orange*
dark purplish pink	*deep purplish pink*	–	(ash rose, carmine rose)	(burnt orange)	(bright coral red, lobster red)
(clover pink, claret)	(fuchsia pink, phlox pink)		**ORANGE – BROWNISH ORANGE**		
moderate purplish red	*strong purplish red*	*vivid purplish red*	*light orange*	*brilliant orange*	*vivid orange*
(dusty rose, dull lilac)	(bright rose, cherry)	(fuchsia, crimson, raspberry)	*moderate orange*	*strong orange*	*vivid orange*
			brownish orange	*deep orange*	*vivid orange*

or complex is the colour known as 'salmon pink' or 'yellowish-pink'. I prefer the former, but apparently the latter is more scientific. Vernacular terms such as 'peach', 'flesh', 'coral', 'shrimp pink' and 'melon' are also used to describe this colour, very common in evergreen azaleas. I have taken the decision to use the descriptive name where possible rather than the colour/number combination, as most of my readers will not have access to the RHS colour chart to interpret the numbers. I realize this may cause inconsistencies of colour nomenclature, but I'm afraid that no one has yet had the time to track down all 25,000 named rhododendron and azalea cultivars, raised over a two-hundred-year period, to check and record the colours properly. And my two young children have helped me resist the challenge to do it myself.

VIREYA PANORAMA: BRIGHTLY, NE PLUS, VALENTINE AND JAZZ BAND.

PROVEN PERFORMERS LISTINGS AND AWARDS

Using my own extensive correspondence with many growers, as well as surveys conducted by the American Rhododendron Society, The Azalea Society of America, The Royal Horticultural Society and Rhododendron Societies in Australia and New Zealand, I have compiled data on best performers in many areas. The abbreviated initials found at the end of many plant entries are often fairly obvious: 'Scand' for Scandinavia, or 'NZ' for New Zealand, for example. Most of the less obvious ones refer to American Rhododendron Society Chapters. All the abbreviations are listed below. It is important to bear in mind that these surveys tend to reflect the tried and tested older varieties and that many species and cultivars have no ratings due to their scarcity or newness. Many such varieties will, in time, come to receive higher ratings.

Awards need to be fairly and expertly given or they don't merit being taken seriously. The FCC (First Class Certificate) and SPA (Superior Plant Award) are two examples: the former was awarded on the basis of cut flowers alone, the latter were so hard to receive that hardly any plants were awarded. About twenty years ago I sat outside and eavesdropped on an RHS Rhododendron award committee meeting at Chelsea (it's a tent – you can hear what they are saying!). The standard of debate was ill-informed and the committee members befuddled by a long and alcoholic lunch. I have been unwilling to take 'FCC's and 'AM's seriously ever since and so I have decided to ignore both these and the old ARS awards. They are in any case, as far as I can ascertain, barely in use these days. As it is voted for by a committee of experts, re-assessed from time to time and includes tried and tested plants, I have included one award, the U.K. 'Award of Garden Merit'(AGM).

PROVEN PERFORMER CODES

(These are found in *italics* at the end of plant entries.)

AA	Ann Arbor, Michigan
AGM	UK Award of Garden Merit
AT	Atlantic Region, E Canada
Aus	Australia
AZ	Azalea, Georgia, Florida
BH	Birmingham, AL
CA	Bay Area, CA
Cal	California
CC	Cape Cod, MA
CD	Cascade, Bellvue WA
CH	Chattahoochee, AL, Georgia
CN	Cowichan Valley, Vancouver Is., BC
CT	Connecticut
Czech	Czech Republic
DA	De Anza, San Jose, CA

DE	Denmark
Den	Denmark
EG	Eugene, OR
EK	Eureka, CA
Fin	Finland
FS	Fraser South, Vancouver BC
FV	Fraser Valley, Vancouver BC
GA	Georgia
Ger	Germany
GH	Grays Harbor
GL	Great Lakes, USA
GP	Greater Philadelphia
HI	Hawaii
Hol	Holland
Jap	Japan
JF	Juan de Fuca, WA
KK	Komo Kulshan, WA
Latv	Latvia
LC	Lewis County, WA
LH	Lehigh Valley, PE
MA	Middle Atlantic, Virginia
MB	Monterey Bay, CA
MD	Mason Dixon, Virginia
ME	Maine
Mel	Melbourne
MS	Massachusetts
MT	Mt Arrowsmith, BC
MW	Midwest
NG	RSC Niagara Region, S. Ontario
NI	North Island, Vancouver, BC
NK	Kitsap, WA
NN	Nanaimo, Vancouver Is., BC
NO	Noyo, Mendcino, CA
NSW	New South Wales
NY	New York, Long Island
NZ	New Zealand
OL	Olympia, WA
OP	Olympic Peninsula, WA
OZ	Ozark, Oklahoma, Missouri, etc.
PA	Peace Arch, BC
PB	Pine Barrens, NJ
PC	Pilchuck, Snohomish Co, WA
PD	Portland, OR
PN	Key Harbour and Key Peninsula, WA

PNW	Pacific Northwest
PR	Princeton, NJ
PT	Piedmont NC, SC
PV	Potomac Valley, Virginia
SC	Southern California
Scand	S. Sweden, Denmark, Norway
Scot	Scotland
SE	S.E. NC and Tennessee
SH	Shelton, WA
SI	Siuslaw, Coastal OR
SL	Seattle, WA
SO	Soutwestern Oregon
ST	Southern Connecticut
SV	Susquehanna Valley, Pennsylvannia
Swe	Sweden
TC	Tacoma, WA
TN	Tennessee Valley
TO	RSC Toronto Region
TV	Tualatin Valley, OR
TZ	Tappan Zee, NJ, NY
U.K.	United Kingdom
U.S.A.	United States of America
VC	Vancouver, BC
VF	Valley Forge, S. Penn, Delaware
VI	Victoria, Vancouver Is., BC
Vic	Victoria, Australia
WB	William Bartram, SC and Georgia
WI	Whidbey Island, WA
WT	Willamette, OR

R. SINOFALCONERI.

A NOTE ABOUT PATENTING, TRADEMARKS AND PLANT BREEDER'S RIGHTS

Some cultivar names are followed by marks which designate rights to the breeder of the plant concerned. Plants with the designation® or ™ show that the name is a trademark. Within a designated national or regional territory (Germany, or the USA, or Europe) the name may not be used without permission. This essentially means that no one may list the variety for sale by its name (a trademark) without licence. For example, our own nursery 'Glendoick™' is a trademark and all rhododendrons containing the word 'Glendoick™' such as 'Glendoick™ Glacier' are protected from commercial propagation in designated territories.

Another level of protection is the patent (USA) or PBR (Plant Breeder's Rights), applied to some rhododendrons and azaleas. These may not be propagated commercially without permission or licence. Examples include many of the Encore azaleas.

Usually these rights are granted in the first instance for a certain period of years. The protection may then be allowed to lapse or can subsequently be renewed. Amateurs may propagate protected varieties but may not offer them for sale.

NOTES ON TAXONOMY AND TERMINOLOGY

The Genus *Rhododendron* is divided into eight subgenera:

Subgenus *Rhododendron*: the scaly-leaved rhododendrons, including subsection Vireya
Subgenus *Hymenanthes*: the larger-leaved rhododendrons
Subgenera *Azaleastrum*, *Candidastrum* and *Mumazalea*: a strange assortment of rarely cultivated species
Subgenus *Pentanthera*: the deciduous azaleas
Subgenus *Tsutsusi*: the evergreen or Japanese azaleas
Subgenus *Therorhodion*.

I have followed the subgenera in the order listed above, incorporating the relevant hybrids. Subgenera are further divided into groupings: sections and subsections of related species.

In line with almost all recent rhododendron literature, I have followed the so-called 'Edinburgh Revision' of *Rhododendron* species, except where our own and other research has proven to be more up to date or accurate. I have included several newly introduced species named by Chinese botanists. In order to save space, I have rendered subspecies with the same name as the species, *R. wardii* ssp. *wardii* for example as *R. wardii*. This book is not a botanical monograph and, as such, I have used words such as flower and truss in place of corolla and inflorescence, to make the text more readable. Unavoidable botanical terms are explained in the glossary.

Some hybrids are listed with the designation 'g': e.g. 'Loderi' g. This 'g' stands for 'grex' and this means that the name was originally applied to all the seedlings from a particular cross. Usually one or more clones, such as 'Loderi King George' and 'Loderi Venus' are selected and these are usually the ones which go on to be made commercially available. But in some cases such as 'Mayday', 'Hummingbird' and 'Polar Bear', many different clones have been distributed, sometimes from crossings made in more than one garden.

EVALUATING SPECIES AND HYBRIDS FOR DIFFERENT CLIMATIC REGIONS

The size of the genus *Rhododendron* and its enormous distribution mean that evaluating what grows well where is a complex and life-long task. My father, Peter Cox, began this process in his books *Dwarf Rhododendrons* and *Rhododendrons, the Larger Species* and we continued with our joint work *The Encyclopaedia of Rhododendron Hybrids*. To write these we corresponded with experts all over the world and sent out evaluative questionnaires. With the internet, this has become easier and I have received hundreds of invaluable e-mails to help me evaluate newer plants for this book. There are too many named hybrids for anyone to grow more than a tiny fraction of what is out there and, therefore, it is with the hybrids that I have tried to be most selective in praise and criticism. You won't agree with everything I have written and you may think some of my assessments are unfair. Please let me know, as I hope there will be a second edition. Best doers for different climates are noted in italics at the end of the plant entries.

RHODODENDRONS

SUBGENUS RHODODENDRON: LEPIDOTE SPECIES AND HYBRIDS

The lepidote or scaly-leaved rhododendron species are characterized by their small leaves, covered in tiny scales, just visible with the naked eye. This section includes many dwarf and alpine species and the many popular hybrids that have been bred from them. Not all the lepidotes are small: subsections Triflora, Heliolepida, Cinnabarina and Maddenia contain larger growing species. Many in subsections Maddenia and Boothia are tender, making popular indoor plants. The Vireyas from Indonesia and Malaysia are the least hardy of all rhododendrons, requiring a more or less frost-free environment.

SECTION POGONANTHUM: SPECIES AND HYBRIDS

30cm–1.5m. Mostly H4. This group of species and their hybrids are grown for their distinctive daphne-like flowers and aromatic foliage. These connoisseur's favourites, irresistible in flower, have particular requirements: good drainage, cool roots in summer, near neutral soil and very little, if any, fertiliser. Taxonomically isolated from the rest of *Rhododendron*, this group has very seldom been successfully crossed with species outside section Pogonanthum.

ANTHOPOGON VAR. HYPENANTHUM 'ANNAPURNA'

■ **ANTHOPOGON** Semi-dwarf–Low H4 EM. Flowers narrowly tubular with spreading lobes, white, pale yellow, cream to deep rose. Dark leaves. Needs good drainage and cool roots. Aromatic foliage burned as incense by Tibetans and Bhutanese. **'BETTY GRAHAM'** bright pink **VAR. HYPENANTHUM 'ANNAPURNA'** pale yellow daphne-like flowers.

■ **ANTHOPOGONOIDES** Low? H4? EM (L in wild). Flowers narrowly tubular funnel-form, with spreading lobes, greenish white, greenish yellow or whitish pink, 10–20 per truss. Plants cultivated under this name pre-2000 are not correctly named. It has recently been introduced, but may turn out to be hard to cultivate.

■ **CEPHALANTHUM** Dwarf H4 EM–M. Flowers narrowly tubular with funnel-shaped lobes, white to deep rose, 5–10 per truss. A tight compact bush with dark aromatic foliage. One of the best of the section. **CREBREFLORUM Group** the smallest growing forms. **NMAIENSE Group** cream to pale yellow. **SSP. PLATYPHYLLUM** wider leaves, white.

CEPHALANTHUM CREBREFLORUM GP.

CEPHALANTHUM NMAIENSE GP.

CEPHALANTHUM SSP. PLATYPHYLLUM

COLLETTIANUM

■ **COLLETTIANUM** Low H3–4 M. Flowers white, narrowly tubular-funnel-shaped, 5–12 per truss. Pale to bright green leaves. From Afghanistan. Rare and hard to grow.

■ **KONGBOENSE** Low H4 EM. Flowers narrowly tubular with spreading lobes, deep strawberry-red (to pink), 6–12 per truss. Tiny dark green, very aromatic leaves. Upright, fastigiate habit. Needs perfect drainage and cool roots. Not easy to please. **FRAGRANS** is a closely related species from further north that has proven to be almost impossible to cultivate. From Mongolia and Siberia.

KONGBOENSE

■ **PRIMULIFLORUM** Semi-dwarf–Low H4 EM–M. Flowers narrowly tubular with spreading lobes, white to pink, 5–10 per truss. **'DOKER LA'** clear pink, perhaps the best form. Tiny aromatic leaves.

PRIMULIFLORUM

PRIMULIFLORUM 'DOKER LA'

Bark often peeling. Very variable, sometimes straggly, and some forms shy flowering. For the garden, it is best to choose selected forms. **LAUDANDUM** white to palest pink flowers. Very slow. Dark leaves. Lavender forms are hybrids.

SARGENTIANUM

■ **SARGENTIANUM** Dwarf H4 ML. Flowers narrowly tubular with spreading lobes, yellow or white, 5–12 per truss. **'WHITEBAIT'** is a creamy white form. Very compact with deep-green leaves. Not always easy to grow, it requires near neutral soil and cool roots. One of the best species in this section.
■ **TRICHOSTOMUM** Semi-dwarf H4 M. Flowers narrowly tubular with spreading lobes, bright pink, pale pink, cream or white, 8–20 per truss. **'RAE BERRY'** pink, **'COLLINGWOOD INGRAM'** pink. Dark green aromatic leaves. Very fine, one of the best of this section. Grows in dry woodland in the wild. *AGM.*

TRICHOSTOMUM

■ **MARICEE** Semi-dwarf H4–5 M. Flowers narrowly tubular with spreading lobes, creamy-white, in clusters. Leaves small, glossy, dark green. Dense, twiggy, compact plant. Very free-flowering and one of the easiest to please of this section. (*sargentianum* ×) Caperci. *CD, KK, SL* **'LIZ ANN'** is a pale pink sister, not as attractive.
■ **SARLED** Semi-dwarf H4 ML. Flowers narrowly tubular with spreading lobes, pale pink, fading to cream, in rounded trusses. Tiny narrow leaves on a dense, compact plant. (*sargentianum* × *trichostomum*) Ingram. *AGM.*

SARLED

SECTION RHODODENDRON: SPECIES AND HYBRIDS

SUBSECTION AFGHANICA

A single species.

■ **AFGHANICUM** Semi-dwarf H2–3 L. Flowers campanulate, white, in trusses of 8–16. Leaves thick, +/– elliptic, on a rather straggly plant with ascending or prostrate branches. Rarely cultivated, I have only ever seen a handful of plants.

SUBSECTION BOOTHIA

To 2m. H2–3. Smaller than the related *Maddenia* species, with charming white or yellow flowers. Usually epiphytes, so requiring good drainage. Most are hardy in a sheltered site at Glendoick. They also make good pot-plants but, as they are not scented, they are not as popular as the *Maddenia*.

■ **BOOTHII** Low H1–2 EM? Flowers campanulate, dull to bright yellow, sometimes with reflexed lobes, sometimes spotted, in trusses of 3–10. Leaves leathery, ovate to elliptic, upper surface usually with bristles on midrib and margins. Bristly branches. Bark reddish, peeling. Almost lost to cultivation but recently reintroduced from Arunachal Pradesh. **MISHMIENSE Group** flowers spotted red. **LEPTOCARPUM** similar but with tiny flowers. A curiosity, but seldom a beauty.
■ **CHRYSODORON** Low H2 E–EM. Flowers campanulate, bright canary-yellow, in trusses of 3–6. Leaves scaly, hairy when young. Attractive smooth bark. The flowers are a fine colour and the plant is fairly tidy, but it grows early in spring and is not very hardy.
■ **DEKATANUM** Low H3–4 E–EM. Flowers broadly campanulate, deep lemon-yellow, in trusses of 2–3. Leaves +/– ovate. Fine peeling bark. This

CHRYSODORON

species was introduced by Ludlow and Sherriff but remained unrecognized till Peter Cox keyed it out a few years ago.

LEUCASPIS

■ **LEUCASPIS** Semi-dwarf H2–3 E–EM. Flowers almost rotate, white, with black anthers, 1–2 per truss. Recent introductions from Arunachal have more tubular-campanulate flowers. Attractive hairy leaves on a mounding plant of good habit. Needs very good drainage and a sheltered site. The flowers are charming.

MEGERATUM 'BODNANT'

■ **MEGERATUM** Dwarf H3 E–EM. Flowers +/– campanulate, deep or pale yellow or cream, 1–3 per truss. Small dark, elliptic to orbicular, hairy shiny leaves. Needs excellent drainage. Best in a raised bed or in a tree stump. **'BODNANT'** is a fine deep yellow selection.
■ **SULFUREUM** Low H2–3 EM–M. Flowers campanulate, greenish yellow to bright yellow, in

trusses of 3–8. Small, dark, shiny leaves. Bark brown, smooth and peeling. Needs sharp drainage. Flowers can be long-lasting.

SULFUREUM

SUBSECTION CAMELLIIFLORA

A single species.

■ **CAMELLIIFLORUM** Low H3–(4) L–VL. Flowers relatively small, camellia-like, white, cream flushed yellow or pink to crimson, 1–3 per truss. Leaves +/– elliptic. Needs good drainage. A curious and striking plant, tolerant of drought and useful for its late-flowering.

CAMELLIIFLORUM

SUBSECTION CAMPYLOGYNA

A single species.

■ **CAMPYLOGYNUM** Semi-dwarf–Low H3–4 EM–ML. Flowers campanulate, on long stalks, red, pink, purple or white. Many selected forms and variations. **MYRTILLOIDES Group**. Very compact with purple flowers. **'LEUCANTHUM'** compact with white flowers. **CELSUM Group**, tallest growing with larger flowers and leaves. Small scaly leaves are shiny and often glaucous below. Enchanting dwarfs

CAMPYLOGYNUM BODNANT RED

CAMPYLOGYNUM MYRTILLOIDES GP.

CAMPYLOGYNUM 'LEUCANTHUM'

CAMPYLOGYNUM SBEC 0509

with thimble-like flowers, which need cool roots and good drainage. **'PATRICIA'** a hybrid, red-purple, prone to rust. *AGM*.

SUBSECTION CAROLINIANA

A single species.

■ **MINUS** Low H5–8 M–L. Flowers funnel-shaped, purplish pink, pink or white, in a compact truss of 4–12. A compact to straggly shrub with pale-green leaves. One of the hardiest lepidote species and much used as a parent. Little grown in milder climates. We find it has rather a small root system, a trait passed to its hybrids. **CAROLINIANUM Group** contains the toughest and generally the best garden plants. **VAR. CHAPMANII** is a low-altitude heat-tolerant form from Florida.

MINUS CAROLINIANUM GP.

MINUS VAR. CHAPMANII

SUBSECTION CINNABARINA

Species and hybrids. 2–3m. H(3)–4–(5). This group contains some of the most attractive of all rhododendrons with pendulous flowers in shades of reddish purple, orange, salmon and yellow. Due to their susceptibility to powdery mildew, these species and hybrids are less popular than they used to be, but they are worth extra trouble.

CINNABARINUM BLANDFORDIIFLORUM GP.

■ **CINNABARINUM** Medium–Tall H4 M–L. Flowers +/– tubular-campanulate, semi-pendent, red, orange or yellow, or a mixture of colours, in a truss of 2–9. Upright growing with small scaly leaves, often glaucous when young. Most forms are rather susceptible to powdery mildew. Very striking and worth the extra trouble required to keep them disease free. **BLANDFORDIIFLORUM Group**, red

CINNABARINUM ROYLEI GP.

and yellow flowers. Mildew prone. **ROYLEI Group**, reddish-purple flowers; not too mildew susceptible. **SSP. TAMAENSE** Medium H4 M–ML. Flowers +/– campanulate, purple. Almost deciduous. Rarely grown, and seldom as showy as its relatives.

CINNABARINUM SSP. TAMAENSE

SSP. XANTHOCODON Low–Tall H4 M. Flowers +/– tubular-campanulate, yellow (to orange or purple), in hanging clusters of 2–9. Leaves broader than those of ssp. *cinnabarinum*. Less susceptible to mildew. Needs good drainage.

CINNABARINUM SSP. XANTHOCODON

CINNABARINUM SSP. XANTHOCODON CONCATENANS GP.

PURPURELLUM Group purple. **CONCATENANS Group**, deep yellow-orange flowers, compact with blue-grey foliage. **'ORANGE BILL'** FCC clone. **'AMBER'** orange flowers.

KEYSII

■ **KEYSII** Tall H3–4 L–VL. Flowers narrow tubular, bicolour red and orange (rarely one-coloured), in clusters, 2–6 per bud. Leaves thinly textured. Upright and fairly strong growing. Subject to powdery mildew infection. Useful for its late flowering.

ALISON JOHNSTONE

■ **ALISON JOHNSTONE** Low–Medium H4 EM–M. Flowers campanulate, peach and amber-pink, in trusses of 9–10. Attractive glaucous yellow-edged foliage. Compact. Moderately susceptible to powdery mildew. (*yunnanense* × *cinnabarinum* ssp. *xanthocodon* Concatenans Gp.). Johnstone **'PEACE'** creamy white flowers in 7–8 flower lax trusses. **'PINK GIN'** flowers light solferino purple shading to peach in the centre, in a truss of 4–5.
■ **BELINDA** Low–Medium H5 M–ML. Flowers tubular funnel-shaped, deep yellow, in a pendulous truss of 7–8. Leaves small, ovate, dark green, glossy above. As hardy as 'Biskra' so worth growing in cold areas. Likely to suffer from mildew in mild gardens. (*ambiguum* × *cinnabarinum* ssp. *xanthocodon* Concatenans Gp.). Hachmann. **'HACHMANN'S EILEEN'** a sister with more tubular flowers. **'MONDSCHEIN'** a Boskoop hybrid from the same cross. Flowers deep yellow.
■ **BERNICE** Medium H3 M. Flowers crimson, blush white on margins, in trusses of 7. Leaves elliptic with brown scales on leaf underside. Very attractive in flower but not very hardy and rather susceptible to mildew. Quite widely grown in its native New Zealand. (*cinnabarinum*

Blanfordiiflorum Gp. × Royal Flush). Jury. Sisters: **'MOON ORCHID'** pale yellow, pink outside, scented. Red stems. **'BARBARA JURY'** yellow with pink tube, **'FELICITY FAIR'** amber-yellow flushed pink and orange, scented.

BERNICE

■ **BISKRA** Medium H4–5 M. Flower reddish-orange shading to light brown, in a lax truss of about 5. A second clone is deep-pink fading to orange. Leaves elliptic, on a plant of erect and slender habit. One of the hardiest *R. cinnabarinum* hybrids worth trying in cold climates. *FS, PA, PC*. (*cinnabarinum* Roylei Gp. × *ambiguum*). Rothschild.

CINNKEYS

■ **CINNKEYS g.** Medium H3 ML. Flowers tubular, clear light-red in the tube with soft yellow lobes, in multi-bud hanging clusters. Leaves shiny, dark green, narrow. Very striking with long-lasting flowers and well worth extra care. Subject to powdery mildew. **'MINTERNE'** has larger, more orange-red flowers. *U.K.* (*cinnabarinum* × *keysii*). Magor.
■ **CINZAN g.** Low–Medium H3–4 M. Flowers pendant, apricot. There may also be a pink clone in commerce. As with all *R. cinnabarinum* hybrids, subject to powdery mildew. (*cinnabarinum* Blandfordiiflorum Gp. × *cinnabarinum* ssp. *xanthocodon*). Stevenson.
■ **COMLEY g.** Medium H3–4 M. Flowers orange deep-yellow, waxy, campanulate, in a pendant truss of 7–9. Leaves elliptic, blue-green, somewhat aromatic. Subject to mildew. (Lady Chamberlain × *cinnabarinum* ssp. *xanthocodon* Concatenans Gp.). Puddle/Aberconway **'GOLDEN ORFE'** orange-yellow, about 7 per truss.
■ **CONROY** Low–Medium H3 M. Flowers waxy, light orange tinged with rose, in loose trusses of about 6. Glaucous leaves. Upright growth habit. Needs spraying for powdery mildew. *FS*.

CONROY

ORANGE DELIGHT

TREWITHEN ORANGE

(*cinnabarinum* Roylei Gp. × *cinnabarinum* ssp. *xanthocodon*). Puddle/Aberconway.

■ **DORTE REICH** Medium H5 M. Flowers salmon-pink campanulate, 4–6 per loose truss. This should be the hardiest *cinnabarinum* hybrid. Tidy habit. Promising. Free-flowering and striking. May require spraying for powdery mildew. (*minus* Carolinianum Gp. × *cinnabarinum* ssp. *xanthocodon* Concatenans Gp.). Reich.

DORTE REICH

■ **GOLDSTRIKE** Low H4 EM. Flower funnel-campanulate, bright yellow with buttercup-yellow upper lobes, in terminal umbels of 8. Leaves glossy, dark green. Stiff, upright habit. Subject to powdery mildew. *PA, PD.* (*oreotrephes* × Royal Flush selfed). Henny. '**FIRST LOVE**' pink flowers with a darker blotch.

■ **LADY CHAMBERLAIN g.** Tall H2 M–ML. Flower tubular-funnel shaped, pendulous. FCC form has flowers apricot suffused with red, in lax truss of 3–6 flowers. Leaves elliptic, waxy-looking, dark green, blue-green coloured when new. Upright and spreading habit. Almost ungrowable as it is so subject to powdery mildew. (*cinnabarinum* Roylei Gp. × Royal Flush). Rothschild. '**BODNANT YELLOW**' yellow-orange.

■ **LADY ROSEBERY g.** Tall H2 M–ML. Flower tubular-funnel shaped, pendulous pink, in a lax truss. Leaves elliptic, dark green, blue-green when new, with reddish petioles. Upright and spreading habit. Almost ungrowable as it is so subject to powdery mildew. (*cinnabarinum* Roylei Gp. × 'Royal Flush'). Rothschild.

■ **ORANGE DELIGHT** Medium H2 M. Flower funnel-shaped, light orange, in lax trusses of 6.

Leaves elliptic, deep green. Foliage has a slightly spicy fragrance when crushed. Upright, well-branched shrub. Subject to powdery mildew. ([Lady Berry × *cinnabarinum* ssp. *xanthocodon*] × Lady Rosebery). Heller.

■ **POLYROY g.** Medium–Tall H3 L. Pendulous bright pink flowers as we grow it. Other clones are reddish or apricot. Leaves dark green on an upright willowy plant. Similar to 'Lady Rosebery' but not as susceptible to powdery mildew. (*maddenii* Polyandrum Gp. × *cinnabarinum* Roylei Gp.). Ramsden. '**MURIEL GIAUQUE**' deep pink, spotted red.

POLYROY

■ **REVLON** Tall H3–4 M–ML. Flowers tubular orange-scarlet, waxy, in a pendulous truss of about 7. A tall-growing plant with shiny foliage. Subject to powdery mildew. (*cinnabarinum* Roylei Gp. × Lady Chamberlain). Rothschild.

■ **ROYAL FLUSH g.** Medium–Tall H2–3 M. Flowers orange-pink or rose-red depending on the clone, in a loose truss of 5–7. Dark glossy foliage on an upright plant. Flowers are very attractive but this hybrid is not very hardy and is subject to powdery mildew. Much used in breeding other similar hybrids. (*cinnabarinum* × *maddenii*). Ramsden '**FULL HOUSE**' deep-pink flowers, '**ROSE MANGLES**' rose-pink flowers. '**LADY HOLLAND**' fragrant apricot-pink. '**HELEN STRYBING**' white scented flowers.

■ **TREWITHEN ORANGE g.** Low–Medium H3–4 M–ML. Clear orange pendent bells in a truss of about 5. Fairly compact habit. Susceptible to rust and mildew. Very striking and one of the best

hybrids of this colour. More than one clone was distributed: the award clone does not seem to be the best one. (Full House × *cinnabarinum* ssp. *xanthocodon* Concatenans Gp.). Johnstone.

WHAT A DANE

■ **WHAT A DANE** Medium H4–5 M. Flowers waxy, yellow and red, in loose trusses. This exotic looking plant is as hardy as 'Biskra' and may be hardy enough for inland continental Europe and coastal E. North America. De. ([*ambiguum* × *cinnabarinum* Concatenans] × *cinnabarinum* 'Nepal'). Birck.

■ **YUNNCINN** Medium H3–4 M. Flowers violet rose, darker on the outside, in a loose, pendant truss. Leaves small and dark on an upright plant. Roots easily. Prone to mildew. (*cinnabarinnum* × *yunnanense*). Rothschild, Aberconway '**YOUTHFUL SIN**' the best selected form with fine purple flowers.

SUBSECTION EDGEWORTHIA

To 2.5m. H2–4. The three species are characterized by the very hairy leaf under-surface and white or yellow flowers. These species are epiphytes and must have perfect drainage in a raised, partly shaded bed, on a very steep bank, or on rocks or mossy logs in wet areas.

■ **EDGEWORTHII** Low H2–3 M. Flowers funnel-campanulate, white flushed pink, sweetly scented, in trusses of 1–3. Most attractive dark rugose foliage with indumentum on the undersurface. A popular scented species that proves reasonably hardy in a raised bed. One of my favourites. *U.K.*

EDGEWORTHII

■ **PENDULUM** Semi-dwarf H3–4 EM–M. Flowers openly funnel-campanulate, white or cream with a pink calyx in trusses of 2–3. Distinctive foliage is small, bullate and hairy. A rare species, like a dwarf version of *R. edgeworthii*. Needs especially sharp drainage.

PENDULUM

SEINGHKUENSE

■ **SEINGHKUENSE** Semi-dwarf–Low H2–3 E–EM. Flowers rotate campanulate, pale or bright yellow, singly or in pairs. Small bullate, indumented leaves. Makes a fine container plant. Very distinctive. Almost lost to cultivation but now re-introduced and becoming quite widely grown.

SUBSECTION GENESTIERIANA

A single species.

■ **GENESTIERIANUM** Medium–Tall H2–3 EM. Flowers tubular-campanulate, reddish purple, covered with glaucous bloom, in trusses of 4–15.

GENESTIERIANUM

Leaves with white under-surface. Fine peeling bark. Flowers are striking, almost weird. For mild gardens or indoors. Comes into growth very early.

SUBSECTION GLAUCA

60cm–1m. H(2)3–4. Bell-shaped flowers, yellow, white, pink and purple. Aromatic foliage. Often attractive in flower, but not all that hardy and not always easy to please.

BRACHYANTHUM VAR. HYPOLEPIDOTUM

■ **BRACHYANTHUM** Semi-dwarf H3–4 L–VL. Flowers campanulate, on long stalks, 1–2cm long, pale or greenish yellow, 3–10 per truss. **VAR. HYPOLEPIDOTUM** is the commoner of the two subspecies. The differences between the two varieties are of no horticultural significance. Mound forming with very aromatic leaves. Useful for its late flowering.

■ **CHARITOPES** Semi-dwarf H4 EM–M. Flowers broadly campanulate, apple-blossom pink, often

CHARITOPES

two-toned, usually spotted crimson, in a truss of 2–6. From Burma and Yunnan. **VAR. TSANGPOENSE** flowers purple-pink. From Tibet. Leaves dark green, aromatic. Can be very fine but rather bud tender, so best in a sheltered site.

GLAUCOPHYLLUM

■ **GLAUCOPHYLLUM** Semi-dwarf H3–4 EM–M. Flowers campanulate, rose-pink, pinking-purple or white, in trusses of 4–10. **VAR. TUBIFORME** flowers tubular. **VAR. ALBUM** flowers white. Leaves small, dark green, aromatic, greyish or white beneath, on a fairly compact bush.

LUTEIFLORUM

■ **LUTEIFLORUM** Low H3 EM. Flowers campanulate, bright yellow, in a truss of 3–6. Leaves dark, underside blue-grey. Bark smooth and flaking. Rather early flowering and bud tender, best in milder gardens.

■ **PRUNIFLORUM** Low H3–4 ML–L. Flowers campanulate, small, dull crimson to plum-purple, in loose trusses of 3–7. Leaves dark green, aromatic.

PRUNIFLORUM

A bushy grower with peeling bark. The flowers are small but rather striking in colour and this is one of the latest-flowering dwarf species.

■ **SHWELIENSE** Semi-dwarf H3–4 ML–L. Flowers campanulate, yellow, flushed pink, in a truss of 2–4. The plants with pink flowers cultivated under this name do not match the type description. This 'species' is probably a natural hybrid of *R. brachyanthum*.

SUBSECTION HELIOLEPIDA

2–3m+. H3–5. Flowers pink, to purple-mauve, to near-white, usually blotched or spotted. Usually aromatic or very aromatic foliage. Not very heat-tolerant. *R. rubiginosum* is very vigorous and useful for windbreaks in moderate climates.

■ **BRACTEATUM** Low H5 L–VL. Flowers openly funnel-shaped, white flushed rose, with a crimson blotch, 4–6 per truss. Leaves very aromatic. Useful for its late flowering. Hard to propagate and remains very rare. Smaller in all parts than *R. heliolepis*. Wilson 4253 may be the only introduction.

BRACTEATUM

■ **HELIOLEPIS** Medium–Tall H4 L–VL. Flowers funnel-shaped, white, rose to cherry-red or violet heavily spotted or blotched, 4–10 per truss. Deep green leaves are pungently aromatic. Valuable for its late flowering. Needs very good drainage, not as easy to please as *R. rubiginosum* and much less vigorous. **VAR. BREVISTYLUM** and **VAR. FUMIDUM** are geographical variants.

HELIOLEPIS VAR. FUMIDUM

■ **RUBIGINOSUM** Tall H3–4 E–EM. Flowers funnel-shaped, pale- to deep-pink or lavender-pink to near white, 4–8 per truss. Leaves dark green on

RUBIGINOSUM

a vigorous, easily grown plant, which is excellent for interior windbreaks and informal hedging. Not a very fashionable colour and flowers are rather early. Very fast growing. *U.K.*

SUBSECTION LAPPONICA & FRAGARIFLORA

Low-carpeting to compact shrubs, most less than 1m. H4–6. Flowers funnel-shaped (except *R. intricatum* and *R. fragariflorum*), mostly in the purple-blue spectrum, though several species have white or yellow flowers. The Lapponica species are found on high-altitude moorland: they have small or tiny leaves, twiggy growth and are usually free-flowering. They are carpeting plants, best grown in clumps in full light, away from the drips of trees. Many are very hardy but few have much heat tolerance. The best put on a spectacular show. Several species and hybrids have frost-hardy flowers, which is a boon in cold gardens and those prone to late-spring frosts. The Phillipsons made a brave but flawed attempt to sort out the taxonomy of this subsection, but there are still too many 'so-called' species and the number should be reduced further.

■ **COMPLEXUM** Dwarf–Semi-dwarf H5 EM–M. Flowers pale lilac to rosy purple, 3–5 per truss. Tiny

COMPLEXUM

CUNEATUM

leaves on a compact plant. Rare. One of the most attractive Lapponica species.

■ **CUNEATUM** Low H4 E–EM. Flowers rose-lavender to deep rose-purple, 3–6 per truss. Leaves to 1.7cm long. The tallest and largest-leaved Lapponica species.

■ **DASYPETALUM** Semi-dwarf H5 EM–M. Flowers bright rose-purple, pubescent outside, in a truss of 1–4. A probable natural hybrid between a member of SS Lapponica and *R. saluenense*.

■ **FASTIGIATUM** Dwarf H5 EM–M. Flowers small, blue-purple (also pinkish or lavender), in trusses of up to 5. Tiny leaves are a lovely glaucous blue in the best selected forms. Probably the best Lapponica species for general planting. **'BLUE STEEL'** is a popular form with good foliage. **'INTRIFAST'** is another fine selection. *AGM.*

FASTIGIATUM

■ **FLAVIDUM** Low H5 EM–M. Flowers pale yellow, in a truss of 1–4. Tiny leaves on a plant of neat, fastigiate habit. The true species is rare in cultivation. The forms with large, white flowers are hybrids.

FLAVIDUM

FRAGARIFLORUM

■ **FRAGARIFLORUM** Dwarf H4 ML–L. Flowers widely funnel-shaped to almost rotate, pale strawberry-pink to pinkish purple, 2–6 per truss. Tiny leaves. Hard to please and rare. Given its own subsection by Cullen but, as it is very closely related to *R. setosum*, I have returned it to SS Lapponica.

■ **HIPPOPHAEOIDES** Low H5 EM. Flowers lavender-blue, bluish purple to lavender-rose, 4–8 per truss. **'HABA SHAN'** fine blue flowers, vigorous. **'GLENDOICK® ICEBERG'** pure white flowers. **VAR. OCCIDENTALE** narrower leaf. Grey-green leaves on an upright bush. April–May. May need spraying for mildew. *S. Fin*. **TSAII** very similar, and probably should be considered a variety of this species. Occurs in N.E. Yunnan and Sichuan. As cultivated this is later-flowering than *R. hippophaeoides*.

HIPPOPHAEOIDES GLENDOICK ICEBERG

HIPPOPHAEOIDES HABA SHAN

IMPEDITUM

■ **IMPEDITUM** Dwarf H5 EM–M. Flowers violet, purple to rose-lavender (purple-blue as cultivated), 1–4 per truss. One of the best and most popular Lapponicas. Tiny leaves on a tight, compact plant. Often confused with *R. fastigiatum* as cultivated. *U.K.* **LYSOLEPIS** considered to be a natural hybrid of *R. impeditum* × *R. flavidum*. Flowers purple or rose-lavender. Seems to have some heat resistance.

■ **INTRICATUM** Dwarf H5 E–EM. Flowers tubular, with spreading lobes, lavender-blue, frost hardy, 2–8 per truss. Small glaucous leaves. Needs perfect drainage and cool summers. The flower shape suggests an affinity with Section Pogonanthum.

■ **LAPPONICUM** Semi-dwarf H5 VE. Flowers magenta-rose, pinkish-purple or purple, 3–6 per truss. A species with a huge circumpolar distribution from Scandinavia to Japan and N. America. Most forms are semi-deciduous and look a bit sad in winter. The flowers can be relatively frost-hardy. Most non-coastal and arctic forms are very hard to cultivate. **PARVIFOLIUM Group**: taller, coastal forms are the easiest to cultivate. **CONFERTISSIMUM Group**: compact forms. A Siberian form is particularly early flowering.

LAPPONICUM CONFERTISSIMUM GP.

LAPPONICUM PARVIFOLIUM GP.

■ **NITIDULUM VAR. OMEIENSE** Dwarf H5 ML–L. Flowers (rosy lilac) to violet-purple-blue, in trusses of 1–2. Later flowering than most Lapponicas. Introduced from Mt. Omei, Sichuan, China by Keith Rushforth. These forms are a good colour. **VAR. NITIDULUM** differs only in scale colour. It appears not to be in cultivation. **CAPITATUM** is similar with a more fastigiate habit and earlier flowering. Usually pale lavender to mid-purple.

NITIDULUM VAR. OMEIENSE

■ **NIVALE** Semi-dwarf H5 M. A variable species with lavender to purple flowers. Very variable from upright to prostrate, but all with small leaves. Needs cool roots and good drainage. **SSP. BOREALE** the easiest to cultivate. **RAMOSISSUM Group**: fine blue flowers. **SSP. AUSTRALE** the southernmost forms. I have never seen a plant cultivated under this name. **BULU** a low-altitude Tibetan variant, which we introduced for the first time in 1995. Proving rather susceptible to dieback.

NIVALE RAMOSISSUM GP.

■ **ORTHOCLADUM VAR. MICROLEUCUM** Dwarf H4 EM–M. Flowers small, pure white. Leaves very small. Slow growing and dwarf. The tiny flowers, effective en masse, are quite frost resistant. **VAR. ORTHOCLADUM** with lavender or purple flowers is seldom grown.

ORTHOCLADUM

POLYCLADUM

RUSSATUM COLLINGWOOD INGRAM

■ **POLYCLADUM** Semi-dwarf H5 EM–M. Flowers blue-purple. **SCINTILLANS Group 'POLICY'.** Freely produced small, pure, intense-blue flowers. This is the only clone commonly available. Arching shoots with tiny leaves. Flowers are a very good colour. *AGM.*

■ **RUPICOLA** Semi-dwarf H5 EM–M. Flowers reddish purple or purple, up to 6 per truss. Small scaly leaves. Fairly compact. Best forms are a striking colour. Hard to propagate, so normally available only from wild collections.

RUPICOLA

RUPICOLA VAR. CHRYSEUM

■ **RUPICOLA VAR. CHRYSEUM** Semi-dwarf H5 EM–M. Flowers pale to bright yellow. **VAR. MULIENSE** virtually identical, this is just botanical hair-splitting. Contrasts well with the purple and blue varieties. Requires good drainage. A parent of several hybrids including 'Chikor' and 'Goldilocks'.

■ **RUSSATUM** Semi-dwarf H5 EM. Flowers blue-purple, purple, reddish purple or lavender, 4–6 per truss. Selected forms have deep-black-purple flowers. Best forms include **'COLLINGWOOD**

INGRAM', **'BLUE BLACK'**, both with very dark purple flowers. Small scaly leaves. Fairly compact, upright or mounding habit. One of the most striking Lapponica species. *AGM* .

■ **SETOSUM** Semi-dwarf H5 EM. Flowers purple to purple-pink, or reddish purple, 1–6 per truss. Small hairy leaves. Hard to cultivate. Closely related to *R. fragariflorum.*

■ **TAPETIFORME** Dwarf H5 EM–M. Flowers purplish blue to violet or rose, 1–4 per truss. Low and compact habit.

■ **TELMATEIUM** Dwarf H5 EM–M. Flowers lavender, pink or purple, 1–2 per truss. Also grown under the names Diacritum Group & Drumonium Group, both very low and compact. Very dwarf. Rarely cultivated.

■ **THYMIFOLIUM** Semi-dwarf H4–5 EM–M. Flowers lavender or purplish, 1–2 per truss. Leaves tiny, usually very narrow, on an erect but low-growing plant. Rare and of limited garden merit.

■ **WEBSTERIANUM** Low+ H4–5 EM–M. Flowers pale lavender-purple, 1–2 per truss. Fastigiate habit and one of the tallest of this subsection, reaching 1.5m or more. Recently introduced and rare.

■ **WONGII** Low–Medium H4 EM–M. Flowers pale yellow, about 4 per truss. A tidy fastigiate habit. A natural hybrid of *R. flavidum* × *R. ambiguum.*

WONGII

■ **YUNGNINGENSE** Dwarf H5 EM–M. Flowers small, pinkish purple, 1–4 per truss. Tiny dull green leaves. Often cultivated under the name Glomerulatum Group.

SUBSECTION LEDA

15cm–2m. H5–7. Clusters of small white flowers. Foliage usually strongly aromatic. The genus *Ledum* has recently been shown through morphological and DNA evidence to be best considered part of the genus *Rhododendron*. (Harmaja, Kron & Judd).

■ **GROENLANDICUM** Low H5 EM–L. Flowers rotate, very small, white, in a balled truss. Hairy leaves with indumentum on lower surface. 'Labrador tea'. One of the best garden plants of this group. Rather straggly. *S. Fin* **NEOGLANDULOSUM** is very similar, often later flowering.

■ **TOMENTOSUM** Low H4–5 ML–L. Flowers rotate, very small, white, with protruding stamens, in many flowered trusses. Leaves narrower than in *R. groenlandicum.* Very aromatic foliage. **'MILKY WAY'**. A fine selected clone. **SSP. SUBARCTICUM** (var. *decumbens*) prostrate or decumbent habit. (Described as a species *R. subarcticum* Harmaja) **HYPOLEUCUM** differs in the white hairs on leaf under-surface. **DIVERSIPILOSUM** from N.E. Asia is not considered distinct by some authorities. **TOLMACHEVII** from E. Russia, probably not in cultivation.

TOMENTOSUM

SUBSECTIONS LEPIDOTA & BAILEYA

30cm–1.5m. H4. Deciduous, semi-deciduous or more or less evergreen. Small purple or yellow flowers.

■ **BAILEYI** Low H4 EM–M. Flowers purple, rotate, in trusses of 4–9. Dark leaves. Sometimes semi-deciduous. Upright sometimes rather sparse habit. Very striking in flower. Given its own subsection, but belongs better with SS Lepidota.

■ **COWANIANUM** Low H4 M. Flowers small, reddish-purple, on bare stems or as foliage develops, 2–5 per truss. Deciduous. A very rare Nepalese species. Some forms are subject to rust fungus. Not very showy, mainly grown by collectors.

COWANIANUM

LEPIDOTUM

■ **LEPIDOTUM** Dwarf to Semi-dwarf H4 L. Flowers small, very variable: yellow, cream, pink or purple, 1–3 per truss. Tiny leaves. Most forms are deciduous or semi-deciduous. Useful for its late flowering. **LOWNDESII** a very rare creeping deciduous species with yellow flowers. Very hard to propagate, so almost unobtainable.

SUBSECTION MADDENIA SPECIES AND HYBRIDS

Ht to 15m, usually much smaller in cultivation, seldom over 3m. H1–3 (occasionally 4). Suitable outdoors for mild climates such as the western seaboard of the U.K. and Ireland, parts of France and Italy, California and Vancouver Island, most of New Zealand and parts of S. Australia. In mild climates they make superb garden plants, producing compact, free-flowering specimens with flowers ranging from lavender and pink though white to yellow. The hardier Maddenia hybrids and species grow well outdoors at Glendoick in a sheltered site. In colder climates they make excellent indoor plants for the greenhouse or conservatory. Many are scented. Most are epiphytic, so they need a coarse growing medium and sharp drainage: they do well in raised beds, old tree-stumps or mossy logs in wet areas. In containers, allow them to become a little pot-bound. They can be hard-pruned after flowering to improve habit. Unless you live in a mild climate, the varieties listed in this section are likely only to be available from specialist nurseries. Many of the Maddenia hybrids have never been officially registered and, therefore, a formal description is hard to come by. Someone in California, in particular, needs to address this issue. This is another subsection which has been poorly served by botanists, who have named far too many species, with inadequate herbarium material and little fieldwork.

CILIATUM

■ **BURMANICUM** Medium H2–3 EM–M. Flowers funnel-campanulate, yellow, greenish yellow or cream, 4–6 per truss. The true species with leaves up to 8cm long is very rare in cultivation. The clone mostly grown under this name with small leaves and small deep yellow flowers is a hybrid. *Cal.*
CRENULATUM a little-known species from Laos with pale yellow flowers and small leaves.
■ **CILIATUM** Semi-dwarf H3–4 E–EM. Flowers +/– campanulate, pale pink-white, 2–5 per truss. Compact with small leaves with hairy margins. One of the hardiest Maddenia species, good outdoors at Glendoick. A parent of many fine dwarf hybrids such as 'Dora Amateis'.
■ **CILIICALYX** Low–Medium H3? EM–ML. Flowers broadly funnel-shaped, white or pale pink, sometimes lightly scented, 2–5 per loose truss. Fairly compact habit. Many plants cultivated under this name are referable to *R. pachypodum* or other related species. This group (*see* under *R. pachypodum*) would better be considered a single variable species. *Mel.*
■ **COXIANUM** Low–Medium H2 EM–M. Flowers tubular funnel-campanulate, strongly scented, 2–4 per truss. Leaves narrow, thick and stiff. Rather leggy habit. A curious species discovered by my parents in Arunachal Pradesh and named after my grandfather.
■ **CUFFEANUM** Low–Medium H1–2 M–ML. Flowers tubular-campanulate, white with a yellow blotch, little or no scent (except as cultivated), about 5 per truss, calyx lobes long. Habit loose and often straggly. The highly scented plants cultivated under this name in California do not match the species description, though some are under number Kingdon Ward 21909. *Cal.*
■ **DALHOUSIAE** Medium H2 ML–L. Flowers large (to 10cm long), tubular-campanulate, greenish yellow, fading to cream, slightly scented, 2–3 per loose truss. Hairy leaves and peeling bark. Very fine. Rather straggly so not one of the best for a pot.
■ **DALHOUSIAE VAR. RHABDOTUM** Low–Medium H2 L–VL. Flowers tubular-campanulate, cream with crimson stripes down the lobes, 2–3 per truss. One of the latest flowering Maddenia. Peeling bark. The flowers are rather a shock the first time you see them: it looks as if someone painted on the stripes. *Cal.*

DALHOUSIAE VAR. RHABDOTUM

■ **DENDRICOLA** Medium H1 M–ML. Flowers funnel-shaped, white, often with a darker flare, sometimes flushed pink, usually fragrant, 2–5 per truss. Similar to *R. pachypodum*. Bark dark-purple to mahogany-red, peeling. **TARONENSE Group**. Plants under this name have fine white flowers with a yellow flare. Good in California.

■ **EXCELLENS** Tall H1–2 ML–L. Flowers large, funnel-campanulate, white, scented, in trusses of 3–5. Large dark green leaves. For indoors except in mildest climates. Plants cultivated under this name do not quite match this species as described.
■ **FLETCHERIANUM** Semi-dwarf H3–4 E–EM. Flowers broadly funnel-shaped, pale yellow, 2–4 per truss. Small leaves with hairy margins. Requires good drainage. One of the hardiest and most dwarf of the Maddenia, best grown outdoors. **'YELLOW BUNTING'** for long the only clone cultivated.

FLETCHERIANUM

■ **FORMOSUM** Low–Medium H2–3 ML–L. Flowers openly funnel-campanulate, white, usually flushed pink, scented or unscented, 2–6 per truss. Leaves fairly small and one of the tidier Maddenia species, very fine in its best forms. **'KHASIA'** a fine large-flowered, scented clone with a yellow blotch.

FORMOSUM KHASIA

FORMOSUM ITEOPHYLLUM

FORMOSUM VAR. INAEQUALE

LEPTOCLADON

LINDLEYI

ITEOPHYLLUM Group The smallest leaved and usually the hardiest forms. *Cal.* **VAR. INAEQUALE** Medium H2 EM–M. Flowers large, white, with a very strong sweet scent, with a yellow blotch, 2–3 per truss. Perhaps the most delicious scent of all rhododendrons. A free-flowering plant for indoors or mildest gardens.

■ **JOHNSTONEANUM** Medium H3 M. Flowers funnel-shaped, creamy yellow, sometimes flushed green or pink, lightly fragrant, 2–5 per truss. Hairy leaves. Upright, rather leggy habit. One of the hardier larger Maddenia species. Can be very spectacular. **LYI** is similar with the corolla covered with scales. Rarely cultivated. **FLEURII** another similar species with white flowers.

JOHNSTONEANUM

KIANGSIENSE

■ **KIANGSIENSE** Low H2? E. Flowers broadly funnel-shaped, white, with a narrow pink stripe, scented, 2 per truss. Leaves small, leathery, oblong-elliptic. Recently introduced for the first time from southern China, so we don't have much idea of its hardiness.

■ **LEPTOCLADON** Medium H2–3 E–EM. Flowers broadly funnel-shaped, pale greenish yellow, frilled, in trusses of about 3. A recently introduced species from Vietnam for greenhouse or mild garden. Proving relatively hardy.

■ **LEVINEI** Low H1–2 EM–M. Flowers broadly funnel-form, small, pure white, scented, 2–4 per truss. Leaves small, oblong to lanceolate, margins hairy. I have only seen one cultivated clone, which is distinctive but not very spectacular.

LEVINEI

■ **LILIIFLORUM** Medium H2–3 L. Flowers narrowly funnel-campanulate, white, scented, 2–3 per truss. Leaves narrowly oblong elliptic (as cultivated), on a plant of upright, rather rangy habit. Useful for its late flowering, one of the latest of the Maddenia, and proving hardier than expected. **CHUNNIENII** a similar species distinguished by having only 5 stamens, rather than the more usual 10–15.

■ **LINDLEYI** Tall H2–3 M–ML. Flowers open funnel-campanulate, white, sometimes flushed or tinged pink, sweetly scented, in a truss of 2–12. Rangy habit. Good drainage required and tends to have a small root system. Spectacular at its best, despite the habit, and some forms are quite hardy in E. Scotland. **GROTHAUSIAE Group** includes the hardier Tibetan forms. **TAGGIANUM** is very similar with wider leaves and a more elongated flower bud.

■ **LUDWIGIANUM** Medium H1–2 EM–M. Flowers funnel-shaped, white, sometimes flushed pink,

with or without a yellow flare, in a truss of 2–4. Not scented. Thick, leathery leaves. A rare Maddenia from northern Thailand.

■ **MADDENII (SSP. MADDENII)** Tall H2 L–VL. Flowers tubular funnel-shaped, scented white, usually flushed pink, orange or purple, with or without yellow flare, in a truss of 2–11. Dark leaves. This comes from further west than ssp. *crassum*, mainly from the Himalaya. The best forms are really spectacular. Useful for its late

MADDENII SSP. CRASSUM

flowering. **POLYANDRUM Group** largest flowered selections. **'PAMELA'** White, with hints of pink and yellow, fragrant, in June–July. *Mel.* **SSP. CRASSUM** Tall H2–3 L–VL. Strongly scented white flowers, often flushed deeper. Usually hardier than var. *maddenii*. Well worth trying in good micro-climates even in gardens as cold as Glendoick. Best in some shade. **'FORT BRAGG CENTENNIAL'** yellowish white, flushed pale greenish yellow. *Mel.*

■ **MEGACALYX** Tall H1–2 M–ML. Flowers white-tinged-pink, nutmeg-scented, tubular-funnel-shaped, with a long lower lobe, in a truss of 2–6. Distinctive bullate leaves. Quite a rangy grower but can be pruned to make a good indoor plant. Spectacular with a good scent, one of the finest Maddenia species.

■ **NUTTALLII** Medium–Tall H1 E–EM. Flowers very large (to 12cm long), funnel-campanulate, white flushed yellow, scented, in trusses of 2–7. A magnificent giant with large rugose leaves. For mildest gardens or indoors, though you'll need a large greenhouse. *NZ.*

MEGACALYX

NUTTALLII

■ **PACHYPODUM** Low–Medium H1–2 ML–L. Flowers funnel-shaped, pale pink-white, usually unscented, 1–4 per truss. Leaves 3–10cm long, not hairy. The lack of scent may account for the relative rarity in cultivation. Many plants grown as *R. ciliicalyx* are better referable to this species. Two so-called species named from cultivated material are: **CARNEUM** pale-pink flowers; **HORLICKIANUM** white flowers, flushed rose. Both should be probably considered synonyms of *R. pachypodum*.

CARNEUM

■ **PARRYAE** Low–Medium H1–2 ML–L. Flowers narrowly funnel-shaped, white, usually fragrant, 2–4 per truss. Leaves obovate, with a sharply pointed tip. One of the latest of the subsection to flower. **ROSEATUM** is considered synonymous by some authorities.

PARRYAE

■ **PSEUDOCILIIPES** Low–Medium? H1–2 EM. Flowers openly funnel-campanulate, white, or white faintly flushed pink, scented, 1–2 per truss. Leaves small. Recently introduced from the wild for the first time and said to be free-flowering.

■ **SCOPULORUM** Low H2 EM–M. Flowers funnel-shaped to funnel-campanulate, white with a yellow blotch, sometimes fragrant, 2–4 per truss. Small +/– elliptic, smooth leaves. A fine Tibetan species that is only suitable outdoors in mildest climates.

SCOPULORUM

■ **VALENTINIANUM** Dwarf H2–3 EM. Flowers small, funnel-campanulate, deep yellow, 1–4 per truss. Dark hairy leaves on a fairly compact spreading plant. Perfect for growing on an old tree stump. We can grow this outdoors in a sheltered site.

VALENTINIANUM VAR. OBLONGILOBATUM

■ **VALENTINIANUM VAR. OBLONGILOBATUM** Low H2–3 M–L. Flowers funnel-campanulate, very deep yellow, 2–4 per truss. Oval hairy leaves. Very different from *valentinianum* and much larger in all parts. Best considered a distinct species. From S.E. Yunnan.

■ **VEITCHIANUM** Medium–Tall H1–2 EM–M. Flowers large, openly funnel-campanulate, frilled, white, often with a yellow blotch, sometimes scented, 2–5 per truss. A fine vigorous species from Thailand and adjacent areas. Bark flaking. One of the most spectacular Maddenia species. Needs very sharp drainage. **CUBITTII Group** white flowers with a strong reddish flare, little scent. **'ASHCOMBE'** a fine selection. **SURASIANUM** also from Thailand and adjacent areas, flowers pale pink.

VEITCHIANUM

VEITCHIANUM CUBITTII GP.

■ **WALONGENSE** Low–Medium H2 EM–M. Flowers funnel-shaped, creamy white with a greenish blotch, scented, in a truss of 3–4. As cultivated from Cox collections in Arunachal Pradesh, India, this has spicy-scented flowers and fine, peeling, mahogany bark. It may be different from further east. *Mel.*

WALONGENSE

MADDENIA AND RELATED HYBRIDS

■ **ACTRESS** Low H3 EM. Flowers white inside, stained red outside, fragrant, about 3 per truss. Bullate foliage. This plant is 75 per cent *R. edgeworthii*. You might as well grow *R. edgeworthii* instead, as it has better foliage. (Lady Alice Fitzwilliam × *edgeworthii*). Harrison.

■ **ALCESTA** Low H3 EM. Flowers pale yellow, 3–4 per truss. Leaves elliptic, on a rounded, well-branched plant. Sun, drought and wind tolerant and outstanding in N. California. Scruffy and poor in Scotland. (*lutescens* × *burmanicum*). Puddle/Aberconway.

■ **ALFRED MARTIN** Medium H4–5 E. Flowers openly funnel-shaped, fragrant, light purplish pink with lighter pink to white edging, brilliant yellow blotch and scattered brown spots, in a ball-shaped truss of 5. Leaves elliptic, flat, wavy margins, bullate, tan indumentum on lower surface. Upright, broad habit. Prefers some shade in California. (*edgeworthii* × Else Frye). Evans.

■ **ALPINE SNOW** Tall H1 EM. Flower with wavy lobes, very fragrant, yellowish white with reddish orange to yellow throat in lax truss of 7–11. Leaves bullate, olive-green with brown scales. Upright rangy habit. ([*lindleyi* × *dalhousiae*] × *taggianum*). Richards **'WHITE WAVES'** creamy-white, scented. Yellowish foliage.

■ **AMBER MOON** Low H2? E–EM. Flowers amber, flushed yellow, in rounded trusses. Habit low and dense, vigorous, best in part shade in California. (complex *burmanicum* hybrid × *moupinense* cross). Scott.

AMBER MOON

■ **ANNE TEESE** Low–medium H2–3? M? Flowers white, flushed solferino purple, striped purple outside, in trusses of 3. Small hairy leaves. Fairly compact. *Mel.* (*ciliicalyx* × *formosum*). Teese.

■ **APRICOT PERFECTION** Low H2? E. Flowers small, apricot-pink in trusses of 2–5. Very compact for a Maddenia hybrid. Best in part-day shade in California. (*burmanicum* × *moupinense*). Scott.

■ **BILL MASSEY (syn. NUTBERGER)** Low–Medium H1–2 EM. Flower tubular funnel-shaped, strongly fragrant, yellowish white with slight pink shading, reverse striped pink in a lax truss of 4–6. Leaves narrowly elliptic, bullate, yellow-green with tan scales. Rounded habit. A cross between the elephant and mouse of this subsection. According to Paul Molinari, the scent is cinnamon and chocolate, which sounds good. *CA.* (*ciliatum* 'Bergie' × *nuttallii*). Vaerlen.

■ **CALIFORNIA GOLD** Semi-dwarf–Low H1 E. Flowers fragrant, greenish yellow with occasional pink markings on reverse, in a lax truss of 5–6. Leaves elliptic, hairy, with indented primary veins, dark green. One of the few yellow scented hybrids. *NO* (Else Frye × El Dorado). Bowman **'MICHAEL'S PRIDE'** unscented creamy yellow flowers.

■ **CANDLELIGHT** Low H2? E. Flowers apricot-pink, flushed with yellow. Mounding and compact habit, with peeling bark. The name will have to be 'Scott's Candlelight' when it is registered. (Else Frye × complex hybrid). Scott.

■ **CAPPUCCINO** Semi-dwarf H2? VE–E. Flower openly funnel-shaped, frilly edges, white with vivid yellow markings in upper lobe, fragrant, in lax trusses of 5. Leaves elliptic, convex, olive-green. Dense, spreading habit. Bud tender, so for mild gardens only. ([Bric-a-Brac × *scopulorum*] × [Bric-a-Brac × *scopulorum*]). Moyles.

■ **CHARISMA** Low–Medium H2 EM. Flowers rose-madder in bud, opening to frilly rose-pink, lined deeper, with a yellow-orange blotch on upper lobe, in trusses of 2–4. Dark-green leaves. Attractive mahogany, peeling bark. Moderately compact. I saw this in New Zealand and thought it very fine. *NZ.* (*ciliicalyx* hybrid (from KW 20280)). NZ Rhod. Assoc.

CHARISMA

■ **CHRYSOMANICUM** Low H2 EM. Flowers primrose-yellow, in a truss of about 8. Leaves dark, shiny, on a compact spreading plant. Rated highly in mild climates but bud tender, so not worth growing in areas with regular spring frosts. *NZ, Aust: Tas, Vict,* (*chrysodoron* × *burmanicum*). Puddle/Aberconway **'CANDLE GLEAM'** flowers primrose yellow, pink edges. **'HEATHER'** creamy yellow with darker spots. **'PIRIANDA HARVEY'** light greenish yellow.

■ **CONCHITA** Medium H2 E. Flowers flat-faced, fragrant, wavy-lobed, phlox pink, spotted crimson, in trusses of 2–3. Leaves small dark green, young growth reddish, with red peeling bark. A good fragrance for a plant with such deep-pink flowers. *CA.* (*ciliicalyx* × *moupinense*). Druecker.

■ **COUNTESS OF HADDINGTON** Medium H2 EM. Flower funnel-shaped, fragrant, white flushed rose, in very lax trusses of 2–6. Leaves large, slightly rugose, bright green with hairy edges.

COUNTESS OF HADDINGTON

Compact, flat-topped shrub. Very bud tender and seldom managed to open a single flower at Glendoick. *AGM.* (*ciliatum* × *dalhousiae*). Parker.

■ **COUNTESS OF SEFTON** Low H2 EM. Pink buds open to white flowers, stained red, fading to pure white, fragrant, in trusses of 2–4. Fairly compact for a Maddenia cross. (*edgeworthii* × Multiflorum). Davies **'SUAVE'** a smaller-flowered hybrid, which is straggly and prone to rust fungus in U.K. but less rust prone in California. I dislike it but Peter Schick thinks it is good.

■ **DENISE** Semi-dwarf H2–3 E. Flowers creamy yellow, tinged apricot-pink that fade to white, with a red blotch, in a truss of 8–9. Fairly compact for a Maddenia hybrid, free flowering and easily rooted. Popular in Australia, especially in Victoria. (Winter Favourite × *chrysomanicum*). Boulter.

■ **DONATELLA** Low–Medium H1–2? E. Flowers large, pale yellow, in trusses of about 3–5. Attractive foliage. Habit rounded and compact. Best with some shade. Showy red buds. (My Lady × [*burmanicum* × *chrysodoron*]). Moyles.

ELSE FRYE

■ **ELSE FRYE** Low H2–3 EM. Flowers fragrant, white flushed pink with a bright yellow throat, in lax trusses to 6. Leaves dark-green with impressed veins. Stems, leaves and buds densely covered with light-brown hairs. Leaf undersides scaly, glaucous light green. Bark reddish-brown fissured grey. More than one clone seems to have been distributed. *CA, NO.* (*ciliicalyx* (so called) × *edgeworthii* (I assume)). Bowman **'ROSE SCOTT'** an 'Else Frye' hybrid with fine pink-flushed flowers. Very prone to rust, so not grown very much.

ROSE SCOTT

FLORAL DANCE

■ FLORAL DANCE Medium H2 EM–M. Flowers frilly, camellia rose with a yellow blotch, funnel-shaped, in trusses of 4. Leaves glossy, ovate with tan indumentum on the underside. The flowers are amongst the frilliest I have seen and it is very striking. Mainly grown in New Zealand. *NZ.* (*nuttallii* × *edgeworthii*). Jury.

■ FORSTERIANUM Medium H2 M. Flower funnel-shaped, frilly lobes, heavily fragrant, white with a yellow flare, in lax trusses of 3–4. Leaves lanceolate, hairy-edged, dark green. Best in semi-shade. Prune to keep from being too straggly. There is also a pinker form. *CA, MB.* (*veitchianum* × *edgeworthii*). Forster.

FORSTERIANUM

■ FRAGRANTISSIMUM Medium H2 EM. Flower funnel-shaped, fragrant, white flushed rose, a bright yellow throat, in lax trusses of about 4. Leaves elliptic, rugose, hairy, olive green. Very leggy growth habit. Suitable outdoors in mild gardens, or potted with long shoots trained around stakes. Subject to mildew and rust. *AGM, CA, EK, MB, SC, Mel.* (*edgeworthii* × *formosum*). Unknown **'SESTERIANUM'** creamy white, with a yellow flare, tinged pink on outside.

FRAGRANTISSIMUM

■ FRAGRANTISSIMUM IMPROVED Semi-dwarf–Low H2 EM. Deep pink in the bud, opening to scented white flowers, blushed pink, resembling the flowers of the pollen parent, in trusses up to 5. Upright, well-branched plant. Habit denser and more compact than 'Fragrantissimum', and worth growing in preference. *CA, EK, MB, SC.* (*edgeworthii* × *formosum* or *ciliicalyx*?). Rollison **'COASTAL SPICE'** a 'Fragrantissimum' hybrid with spicy-scented flowers and hairy leaves.

■ FRAN SUMNER Low H3 E. Flowers open funnel-shaped, deep pink in bud, opening light purplish-pink inside, a deeper shade on the reverse, slightly scented, in a flat truss of 4. Very attractive flowers and should be more widely grown, especially in California. Flowers open over a long period, up to two months. Named after the charming hybridizer whom I was fortunate to meet just before she reached the age of 100. (Seta × *johnstoneanum*). Sumner.

■ HARRY TAGG Low H2–3 EM. Flowers with some fragrance, white, pink tinged, with a pale yellow-green throat, in trusses of 3–4. Leaves oblong-lanceolate, leathery, margins fringed with hairs, dark green, underside pale green, waxy, glaucous, with golden-brown scales. Compact habit. *SC.* (Albescens × *ciliicalyx*). R.B.G Edinburgh.

■ HUMBOLDT SUNRISE Semi-dwarf–Low H2–3? EM. Flower openly funnel-shaped, fragrant, pale yellow with vivid yellow blotch in throat, reverse blushed deep-pink in a lax truss of 5–6. Leaves elliptic to lanceolate, glossy, yellow-green on a plant of upright, broad growth habit. (Else Frye × *johnstoneanum*). Anderson/Braafladt.

■ ILAM PEARL (syn. STEAD'S ASSAMICUM HYBRID) Low H2–3 M. Flowers white, inside yellow, outside tinged red, faintly scented, in a truss of 2–3. Leaves narrowly elliptic, dark green. A fairly tidy Maddenia SS hybrid mainly grown in New Zealand, where it was raised. (*formosum* ×). Stead.

■ JIM RUSSELL Medium–Tall H1–2 E–EM. Flowers large frilly, clear light-pink, scented, in huge, full, rounded trusses. One of the most spectacular Maddenia hybrids we have seen: always creates a sensation. We named this after the great English plantsman who gave it to us. We have no idea who actually made the cross. (*ciliicalyx* × unknown). Unknown/Russell/Cox.

JIM RUSSELL

■ JOHN BULL Low H2–3? EM–M. Flowers pale pink, flushed cream, 4–5 per loose truss. A Scottish hybrid occasionally seen in Argyll gardens but also commercially grown in New Zealand. (*johnstoneanum* × *edgeworthii* (*bullatum*)). Noble.

■ JOHN PAUL EVANS Tall H1–2 EM. Flower campanulate with distinctive recurved petals, pale yellow to white with brilliant orange-yellow throat, in a flat truss of about 5. Leaves bullate, young growth purple, on an upright, well-branched plant. Papery reddish-brown bark. (A selected *R. nuttallii*). Evans **'PARLEZ VOUS'** a similar *R. nuttallii* seedling with large, very fragrant, white flowers.

■ JOY RIDGE Low H2 E–EM. Flowers pale yellow with a deeper-yellow centre, flushed reddish pink. Leaves shiny, on a dense and compact plant. Attractive young growth. Needs shade in California. (Rose Scott × *burmanicum* × *chrysodoron*). Scott.

■ LADY ALICE FITZWILLIAM Low H2 EM. Flower funnel-shaped, with nutmeg fragrance, open pink fading to white with yellow in the throat, in trusses of 2–3. Leaves are deeply veined, with concave edges. Compact plant. Sometimes prone to rust. One of the earliest Maddenia hybrids dating back to before 1880. *AGM.* (*edgeworthii* × *formosum*). Fischer, Son & Sibray.

LADY ALICE FITZWILLIAM

■ LAKE LORRAINE Low–Medium H2 E–EM. Flowers white with brilliant yellow blotch, outside paler yellow, with a faint scent, in flat trusses of 6–8. Fairly compact. Peeling bark. Flower texture rather thin. (*burmanicum* hybrid × *cuffeanum*). Scott.

LAKE LORRAINE

■ LAKE MERRITT Low H2–3 E–EM. Flowers light-pink with deep-red flair, reverse dark red, fragrant. Low and compact. Needs shade in California. One of the few scented Maddenia hybrids that is really pink. (Rose Scott × complex hybrid). Scott.

■ LARTAG Low–medium H2–3? M. Rose-pink in bud, opening to pure white flowers, with a small yellow blotch, funnel-shaped, fragrant, in loose trusses of 4. A spreading plant of loose habit. Free-flowering. (*taggianum* × unknown). Larson/Bowman.

■ **LEMON MIST** Semi-dwarf–Low H2 E–EM. Flower openly funnel-shaped, light yellowish green, in trusses of 2–3. Leaves elliptic, light green on a spreading shrub, almost twice as wide as tall. Needs good drainage. Rather bud tender. *CA*. (*xanthostephanum* × *leucapsis*). Scott. **'PRARIE GOLD'** small yellow flowers. **'HOLLANDAISE'** a Moyles hybrid, pale yellow. Compact mounding habit, lower than 'Lemon Mist'.

■ **LOVELOCK** Low H2 VE. Flowers pale greenish-yellow, darkening toward the base, in a truss of about 5. Leaves dark green, on a plant with mahogany, flaking bark. Opening buds susceptible to frost damage. In mild New Zealand springs, flowers open over a 6–8 week period. (*chrysodoron* × unknown). Dunedin Botanic Garden.

■ **MARTHA WRIGHT** Medium–Tall H2–3 EM. Flowers creamy white, yellow in centre, strongly fragrant, in flat trusses of 4. Small dark leaves on a fairly compact plant. A good choice for strong scent on a reasonably compact plant suitable for pot culture. *Cal.* (*burmanicum* × *fragrantissimum*). Sumner.

MARTHA WRIGHT

■ **MAURICE SKIPWORTH** Low–Medium H2–3 EM. Flowers creamy white to soft yellow with yellow speckling, sweetly scented, 5 per truss. Leaves bullate. Unusually for a pale yellow, this has a strong scent. (*edgeworthii* × *burmanicum*). Skipworth.

■ **MCNABII** Low H2? E–EM. Flowers funnel-shaped, creamy white, strongly scented. Leaves covered with soft hairs. Habit rather straggly, prune after flowering. Said to be one of the best scents of all the Maddenia: Paul Molinari says you can smell it from 100ft away. Register describes flowers as 'crumpled'. Maybe a tree fell on it…. *N. Cal.* (*ciliatum* × *edgeworthii*). Van Houtte **'COWBELL'** same cross, large, pure white flowers. *See also* 'Tinkerbird'.

■ **MEADOWGOLD** Semi-dwarf–Low H1 E. Flower tubular funnel-shaped, light greenish yellow with vivid yellow spots on upper lobe, in trusses of 4–6, from multiple buds. Leaves elliptic, glossy, medium dark green. Compact, dense habit. 'Almost too yellow'. Peter Schick. (*burmanicum* × Lemon Mist). Scott.

■ **MI AMOR** Tall H1 M. Flower very fragrant, large, tubular-funnel-shaped, to 15cm across, white with yellow throat in large flat trusses of 5–7. Leaves dark green above, grey-green below. Open, upright straggly habit. Stunning if you can grow it. *CA, EK*. (*lindleyi* × *nuttallii*). Sumner. From same parentage: **'JANE HARDY'**, **'SOUTHERN CLOUD'**, **'FLORAL FETE'**, **'KALLISTA'**, **'TUPARE'**, **'STEAD'S BEST'**, **'LADY DOROTHY ELLA'** are all very similar.

MI AMOR

■ **MOTH** Semi-dwarf H3 EM. Flowers lemon-yellow, heavily spotted brown, very heavy texture, about 6 in a loose truss. Small dark green leaves on a fairly compact plant. Quite common in New Zealand gardens. A curiosity which makes a good pot plant. (*megeratum* × *boothii* Mishmiense Gp.). Aberconway/Puddle.

■ **MY LADY** Semi-dwarf H1 E. Flower slightly fragrant, white-blushed-pink with a pale yellow throat, in perfect trusses. Leaves bullate, glossy, dark green, on a fairly compact and tidy plant. The flowers are stunning but there is little scent, so it is limited in popularity for growing indoors. CA ([*veitchianum* × *edgeworthii*] × [*veitchianum* × *edgeworthii*]). Sumner.

MY LADY

■ **MYSTERIOUS MADDENII** Low–Medium H2? E–EM. Flowers large, white with hints of pink and gold, very fragrant. Foliage fine. Heat resistant. Spreading and vigorous habit. Very highly rated by Paul Molinari. (? *parryae* × unknown). Kerrigan.

■ **OPAL DAWN** Low–Medium H3 M–ML. Buds of rose-opal flushed cream, opening to camellia rose, fading white with a pink flush, a dorsal flare of greenish-yellow spots, fragrant, in a truss of 4–5. Oblong leaves with brown scales. An interesting cross for mild gardens, quite popular in its native New Zealand. (*davidsonianum* × Countess of Haddington). Gordon.

■ **PARKER SMITH** Low H2 E–M. Flowers light yellowish green with deeper-yellow spots, some flowers double, 4–6 per truss. Yellow-green leaves with hairy margins. Low and compact habit. Flowers over a long period in mild climates, up to five months in N. California. Named after a Californian rhododendron grower. ([*johnstoneanum* × *veitchianum* Cubittii Gp] × *chrysodoron*). Scott.

■ **PATRICIA MARIE** Low H1 E. Flower as grown: very light pink fading to white. According to register there are bold stripes on the flowers. The clone

grown under this name in California does not have the pink stripes. Leaves oblong, recurved margins, with prominent veins, greenish yellow, dark brown scales on underside. Open, upright habit. Similar to 'Mi Amor' but a little pinker. Grows in full sun in N. California. (*nuttallii* × Lind-dal Gp.). Granston.

■ **PAUL MOLINARI** Low–Medium H2 E–EM. Flowers large, pure white with pale yellow eye, with strong fragrance, in a flat truss of 4. Leaves hairy. Habit somewhat rangy, good trailling down a bank. Young growth silvery. Named after the Californian nurseryman and Maddenia expert who supplied lots of good information for this section of the book. (*veitchianum* × Else Frye). Evans.

■ **PINK SKY** Low–Medium H2–3 E–EM. Flowers fragrant, white, tinged pink, 3–5 per truss. Fairly compact. I'm not convinced this is any improvement on the parents. (*edgeworthii* × Else Frye). ?

■ **PRINCESS ALICE** Medium H2 EM. Flower fragrant, white lined pink with a small yellow eye, in a loose truss. Leaves dark green, textured. More compact than 'Fragrantissimum' with better habit and more disease resistance. We have seen several different plants being offered under this name. *CAL.* (*edgeworthii* × *ciliatum*). Veitch.

■ **REINE LONG** Medium H1 EM. Flower very fragrant, rotate, white streaked rose with faint-yellow blotch, in loose trusses of 4–5. Leaves glossy, deeply veined, leathery, with sparse hairs. (*dendricola* Taronense Gp × Else Frye). Bowman.

■ **SABRINA ADLER** Low H1 VE. Flower widely funnel-shaped, frilly edges, lightly fragrant, white with light-red spotting, outside suffused pale pink, aging to white in a lax truss of 2–3. Leaves elliptic, small, dark green on a compact plant, useful for its early flowering. (*ciliicalyx* × *moupinense*). Scott.

■ **SAFFRON PRINCE** Low H2 EM. Flower opens funnel-campanulate, wavy lobes, sulphur-yellow without markings, in flat trusses of 8. Leaves elliptic, on a rounded, well-branched plant. Sun, drought and wind tolerant and outstanding in N. California where it is considered an improvement on its mother 'Saffron Queen'. (Saffron Queen × *burmanicum*). Sumner **'OWEN PIERCE'** light sulphur-yellow. **'SAFFRON MEADOW'** deep yellow. Foliage bronzy.

■ **SAFFRON QUEEN** Dwarf H2 EM. Flower openly funnel-shaped, sulphur-yellow with darker spotting, in lax trusses of 8–9. Leaves glossy green, narrow, on a plant of upright and open growth habit. Prefers some sun. *NO.* (*xanthostephanum* × *burmanicum*). Williams.

SAFFRON QUEEN

■ **SCOTT'S VALENTINE** Low H2 E–EM. Flowers strongly scented, clear pink. Flower buds with multicoloured bud scales. Low and compact, with showy reddish young growth. Best in part-day shade in hot areas. ([*johnstoneanum* × *veitchianum* Cubittii Gp.] × [*moupinense* × Rose Scott]). Scott.

■ **SEPTEMBER SNOW (syn. SPRING SNOW)** Semi-dwarf H1 E. Flower white with brown anthers, in a truss of 4–6. Rounded, rather open habit. Small furry leaves. Needs sharp drainage. I would choose the parents over the hybrid in this case, though it is highly rated in S. New Zealand, which is where it flowers in September. *CA, NZ.* (*leucapsis* × *edgeworthii*). Campbell.

■ **SMILEY** Low H2? E. Flowers white flushed red and pink, fragrant. Low growing and compact, best in some shade. (Else Frye × complex hybrid). Scott.

■ **TAOS** Low H2? E–EM. Flowers tubular funnel-shaped, pale purplish pink, outside flushed light purplish pink, in ball trusses of 4–5. Leaves elliptic, moderate olive-green, reddish-brown scales below. Useful for its very early flowering and flat-topped habit. (*carneum* × Harry Tagg). Moyles.

■ **TAVEUNI** Low H2? E. Flowers creamy-apricot-peach with a red-orange eye. Very low and compact. Best with afternoon shade in hot climates. Named after the Hawaiian island. ([(*burmanicum* × (*johnstoneanum* × *dalhousiae*)] × Alfred Martin). Scott.

■ **THE WINNER** Medium H2? EM–M. Flowers rich yellow with apricot overtones. Deep-green leaves. Upright habit. (Saffron Prince × *dalhousiae*). Moyles.

■ **TYERMANII** Medium H2 M. Flowers, lily-shaped, tinged outside with green and brown, aging to pure white, much yellow in throat, sweetly fragrant, in large lax trusses. Dark, glossy green foliage, bark dark brown, peeling. For very mild gardens only, or indoors. (*nuttallii* × *formosum*). Tyerman '**VICTORIANUM**' large creamy-yellow flowers, 4–5 per loose truss, sweetly scented.

TYERMANII

■ **VIRGINIA STEWART** Medium H1 EM. Flower widely funnel-campanulate, wavy lobes, very fragrant, white with a fading yellow throat, in flat trusses of 3–7. Leaves elliptic, glossy, slightly bullate, scaly. Upright habit. (Countess of Haddington × *nuttallii*). Kerrigan.

■ **VUNA** Low H2? E. Black buds opening flushed rosy red, becoming white with a dark-red eye. Low and compact. This is a startling Maddenia hybrid with more than 10 species in its breeding. (complex Maddenia ×). Scott.

■ **WEDDING GOWN** Low–Medium H1–2 E–EM. Flowers funnel-shaped, yellowish white, with slight flushing of yellow in throat and on dorsal lobe, in trusses of 5–7. A fine Australian hybrid for very mild climates. *Mel.* (*veitchianum* × *burmanicum*). Van de Ven.

■ **WHITE DOVES** Low H1–2 EM. White flowers with a green-yellow throat, fragrant. Compact with dark green foliage. Free-flowering. A New Zealand hybrid, little known elsewhere. (*scopulorum* × *formosum* var. *inaequale*). Jury.

■ **WHITE LILY** Low H1–2 EM–M. Flowers funnel-shaped, very fragrant, white with a yellow throat. Dark-green pointed leaves, on a plant of good habit. Name illegal as there is a Gable hybrid of this name. (unknown)

■ **WHITE WINGS** Semi-dwarf–Low H2–3 M. Large flowers pure white with yellow flare, sweetly fragrant, in neat trusses of 4–5. A compact plant with large foliage, like that of *R. edgeworthii*. (*edgeworthii* × *ciliicalyx*). Scrase-Dickens.

SUBSECTION MICRANTHA

A single species.

■ **MICRANTHUM** Low–Medium H5 L–VL. Flowers very small, white, campanulate, in dense trusses of up to 20. Tiny narrow leaves. Rather sprawling habit. Very hardy but early growth can result in bark-split. The flowers are usually rather insignificant.

MICRANTHUM

SUBSECTION MONANTHA

1–3m. H2–3. This subsection contains the only autumn-flowering non-Vireya species. They have considerable potential as parents of autumn and/or repeat-flowering hybrids. Very good drainage essential. Two are currently in cultivation. Of the others, *R. flavantherum* should be placed in synonymy with *R. kasoense*. The other, *R. conycinnoides*, has purple flowers and has never been in cultivation.

■ **KASOENSE** Medium H2–3 VVL. Flowers tubular funnel-shaped, bright yellow, 1–3 per truss, in September–December. Larger flowers than *R. monanthum* and potentially a better garden plant. First introduced from the wild by the author in 2002. **FLAVANTHERUM** is almost certainly synonymous with *R. kasoense*. **CONCINNOIDES** purple flowers. Not in cultivation at the time of writing.

KASOENSE

MONANTHUM

■ **MONANTHUM** Low H2–3 VVL. Flowers small, tubular, bright yellow, 1–2 per truss, flowering indoors from August to January. Small leaves on a fairly tidy plant.

SUBSECTION MOUPINENSIA

30cm–1m. H4–5. Small-leaved, early flowering, epiphytic species with charming open funnel-campanulate flowers.

■ **DENDROCHARIS** Dwarf H4–5 E–EM. Flowers widely funnel-shaped to almost rotate, pale to deepest pink, 1–2 per truss. Small ovate dark green leaves on a neat, compact bush. Needs good drainage and tends to produce a rather small root system. Probably the finest dwarf species introduced in recent years. Proving to be remarkably hardy. '**GLENDOICK® GEM**' deep pink, fine dark leaves and erect habit. *U.K.*

DENDROCHARIS

MOUPINENSE

■ **MOUPINENSE** (*see* photo previous page) Low H4 VE. Flowers openly funnel-campanulate, pale pink flushed deeper pink or white, usually spotted deeper in trusses of 1–2. One of the earliest species to bloom; flowers are able to withstand a few degrees of frost. Drought resistant. Needs very good drainage and has a small root system.

■ **PETROCHARIS** Semi-dwarf H4 E–EM. Flowers funnel-shaped pure white or pale pink, 1–2 per truss. Compact, with larger leaves than *R. dendrocharis*. Needs very sharp drainage.

PETROCHARIS

SUBSECTION RHODODENDRON

30–60cm. H4–5. Low-growing European native species, which are not always the easiest to please but are useful for their hardiness and late flowering.

■ **FERRUGINEUM** Dwarf–Semi-dwarf H5 L. The 'Alpenrose'. Flowers tubular with spreading lobes, rose-crimson to rose (occasionally white), 6–15 per truss. Dark green scaly leaves. Tough. Best in full sun, away from drips from trees, with sharp drainage. Not always very easy.

FERRUGINEUM

■ **HIRSUTUM** Semi-dwarf H5 L–VL. Flowers tubular, pale to deep pink (occasionally white), 4–12 per truss. Hairy foliage, paler than that of *R.*

HIRSUTUM

ferrugineum. Slow growing. Will tolerate neutral soil and is found in the wild growing on limestone.
FLORE PLENO is a short-lived double-flowered clone.

■ **MYRTIFOLIUM (syn. KOTCHII)** Dwarf H4 ML. Flowers narrowly tubular, rosy to mauve-pink, 3–7 per truss. Very dark green leaves. Handsome when well grown, but rather tricky.

SUBSECTION RHODORASTRA

60cm–2.5m. H5–7/8. Extremely hardy, deciduous and with flowers early in the season on bare branches, these species hardly look like rhododendrons at all. They can be pruned hard after flowering to encourage a bushy habit. Parents of many early-flowered hybrids such as 'Praecox' and 'Weston's Pink Diamond' (*see* page 57).

■ **DAURICUM** Semi-dwarf–Medium H5–8 VE–E. Flowers widely funnel-shaped, purple, rosy purple or white, on bare stems early in the season. Deciduous or semi-deciduous with small leaves. Most forms need good drainage. There are some fine dwarf selections. **'ARCTIC PEARL'** small white flowers. **'HOKKAIDO'** larger white flowers. **'SNOWY MORNING BLUES'** white, E–EM. **'MADISON SNOW'** pure white. **'MIDWINTER'** frost-resistant rose-purple in midwinter on the bare branches. This may be better considered a form of *R. sichotense*.
LEDEBOURII essentially a more evergreen variation of *R. dauricum.*

DAURICUM HOKKAIDO

DAURICUM MIDWINTER

■ **MUCRONULATUM** Tall H5 VE–E. Flowers purple, pink (rarely white). Deciduous, with small thin leaves, on an upright willowy plant. Very tough and good in severe climates. Early growth and flowers often damaged in areas with spring frosts. Prune after flowering to reduce straggliness.
'CORNELL PINK' is the best known pink form.
'MAHOGANY RED' a strange reddish-purple colour. Floppy habit. **'BRIGHT PINK'**, **'STORR'S PINK'** deep pink. **'EASTER BUNNY'** soft lavender. **'PINK PEIGNEUR'** soft pink. AGM, S. Fin. **VAR. TAQUETTII**

MUCRONULATUM CORNELL PINK

(syn. VAR. CHEJUENSE) Semi-dwarf H5 E–EM. Flowers pink or purple, usually singly from multiple buds, on bare stems, before leaves. Low growing and compact, deciduous, often with fine autumn colour. From Cheju Island, Korea. **'CRATER'S EDGE'** reddish-lavender.

■ **SICHOTENSE** Medium–tall H5 VE–E. Flowers purple, larger than those of *R. dauricum* 'Midwinter', otherwise very similar. Semi-deciduous, with remaining leaves turning bronze-purple in winter. Recently introduced.

SUBSECTION SALUENENSIA

Prostrate to 1.5m. H3–5. Flowers purple, pink or reddish. Many forms of these two species make fine garden plants.

CALOSTROTUM GIGHA

CALOSTROTUM SSP. KELETICUM

■ **CALOSTROTUM** Semi-dwarf H4 M. Flowers widely funnel-shaped or rotate, magenta, pink, rose-crimson or purple flat-faced, 1–2 per truss. **'GIGHA'** AGM fine large rosy-red saucer-shaped flowers. Leaves often grey-green or glaucous. Compact and dense habit. **SSP. KELETICUM** Dwarf H4 ML–L. Flowers widely funnel-shaped or rotate, pale to deep purplish crimson. Leaves very small, narrow, dark green on a plant of dense, low-spreading habit. Useful for relatively late flowering. **ROCK 58** is a very fine form with large flowers.

CALOSTROTUM RADICANS

RADICANS Group. Very compact, almost prostrate forms, very slow growing, delightful. *AGM*. **SSP. RIPARIOIDES** Low H4 M. Flowers blue-purple. Mostly grown as **ROCK'S FORM** which often flowers in autumn as well as spring. Attractive glaucous aromatic foliage. Subject to powdery mildew and rust. **SSP. RIPARIUM** Semi-dwarf H4 EM–M. Flowers pinkish purple, 2–5 per truss. **CALCIPHILUM Group**, small pink flowers. **NITENS Group** purple flowers in June–July. Leaves rarely glaucous.

CALOSTROTUM NITENS

■ **SALUENENSE** Semi-dwarf H4 M. Flowers widely funnel-shaped, reddish purple or purple, 1–3 per truss. Leaves dark green or grey-green, often turning bronzy in winter, usually hairy on margins. Compact to open habit. **SSP. CHAMEUNUM** compact habit. **PROSTRATUM Group**, the lowest growing forms, not always very easy to please.

SUBSECTION SCABRIFOLIA

30cm–2m. H3–5. Characterized by clusters of pink-reddish flowers from axillary buds. Straggly plants can be pruned after flowering.

RACEMOSUM

■ **RACEMOSUM** Dwarf–Semi-dwarf H4–5 EM. Flowers widely funnel-shaped, deep to pale pink or white, 1–4 per leaf axil, sometimes from multiple buds. Small leaves, glaucous on leaf lower-surface. Compact or straggly and very variable in flower. Very free-flowering, the best forms are spectacular. **'ROCK ROSE'** fine pink flowers, **'WHITELACE'** pure white flowers. *AGM, Mel.* **HEMITRICHOTUM** downy hairs on the leaves. **MOLLICOMUM** leaves with a pale green underside. Both these so-called species are better considered aberrant forms of *R. racemosum*.

■ **SCABRIFOLIUM VAR. SPICIFERUM** Low H3 EM. Flowers small deep pink, pale pink or white, 2–3 per leaf-axil bud. Small hairy leaves. The best forms have very showy flowers. Borderline hardy at Glendoick. *NZ(s)*. **PUBESCENS** is almost identical but a little hardier. **SCABRIFOLIUM VAR. SCABRIFOLIUM** with rather small white to pink flowers, is rarely grown and is of little garden merit.

SCABRIFOLIUM VAR. SPICIFERUM

■ **SPINULIFERUM** Medium H3 EM–M. Flowers tubular, long-lasting, deep pink to red, with protruding stamens, in upright trusses of 1–4. Bullate leaves with hairy margins on a upright and rather rangy plant, good against a wall. Very distinctive and always attracts comment. A parent of several good hybrids such as 'Razorbill' and 'Ann Carey'.

SPINULIFERUM

SUBSECTION TEPHROPEPLA

0.3–2m. H2–5. Flowers purple, pink, yellow or white/cream. Not all that commonly cultivated.

■ **HANCEANUM** Semi-dwarf H4 ML–L. Flowers funnel-campanulate, white, pale pink or yellow, 5–15 per truss. Dark green leaves, bronzy when young. Compact habit, in the usually cultivated clones,

HANCEANUM 'CANTON CONSUL'

recent introductions are straggly. Requires good drainage and dislikes fertiliser and summer heat. **'CANTON CONSUL'** flowers creamy white, **'NANUM'** lower and slower growing, flowers bright-yellow.

■ **LONGISTYLUM** Low H3 M. Flowers narrowly funnel-shaped, small, white, with a long style (hence the name), 1–3 per truss. Small leaves. Rather loose habit. Dainty but not very spectacular and rarely grown. I have only ever seen one clone.

LONGISTYLUM

■ **TEPHROPEPLUM** Low H3(–4) EM–M. Flowers campanulate to tubular-campanulate, purplish to deep or pale pink, in trusses of 3–9. Leaves usually dark-green, very scaly. Habit compact to sprawling. Bark brown and peeling. A good plant for mild gardens. **DELEIENSE Group** includes forms with the largest leaves and often the largest flowers.

TEPHROPEPLUM VAR. DELEIENSE

AURITUM

XANTHOSTEPHANUM

■ **XANTHOSTEPHANUM** Low H2–3 EM–M. Flowers campanulate, bright to creamy yellow, in a truss of 2–5. Leaves scaly, lower surface glaucous. Bark smooth and reddish brown. A fine yellow for mild gardens. **AURITUM** differs in its cream flowers, sometimes flushed pink.

SUBSECTION TRICHOCLADA

60cm–2m. H3–4. A group of yellow-flowered species, some of which are deciduous and flower on the bare stems. Useful for late-flowering.

■ **CAESIUM** Low H3 ML–L. Flowers funnel-campanulate, small, bright yellow, 2–3 per truss. Leaves semi-evergreen, slightly bristly, glaucous. Flowers tend to hang down in the foliage and this is the least hardy of the subsection.
■ **LEPIDOSTYLUM** Semi-dwarf H4 L. Flowers funnel-campanulate, small, bright yellow, 1–3 per truss. Flowers tend to open under the new growth. One of the finest dwarfs for foliage, most attractive in its hairy, glaucous, blue, young leaves. Habit compact wider than high. Can grow very large in time.

LEPIDOSTYLUM

■ **MEKONGENSE** Semi-dwarf H3 M. Flowers funnel-campanulate, yellow to greenish yellow, spotted or flushed red, 2–5 per truss, usually before or with the new growth. Leaves +/– obovate, deciduous. Virtually identical to R. trichocladum but generally with less-hairy stems and leaves.
■ **TRICHOCLADUM** Low H4 M–L (VL). Flowers funnel-campanulate, yellow to greenish yellow, often spotted or flushed red, 2–5 per truss, usually opening on bare stems before the leaves unfurl. Leaves deciduous, often glaucous, sometime bronze or reddish on young growth, usually hairy.

TRICHOCLADUM

■ **VIRIDESCENS** Low H4 L–VL. Flowers funnel-campanulate, cream to pale yellow, with red spots. Evergreen leaves, young foliage glaucous. Now reinstated as a species. Prone to mildew.
'DOSHONG LA' a good yellow selection.
RUBROLUTEUM Group flowers cream flushed red.

VIRIDESCENS

SUBSECTION TRIFLORA

2–3m+. H3–5. These large-growing, mostly vigorous species are a must for any garden where they can be grown. They are good-natured and many are spectacularly free-flowering. All can be hard-pruned after flowering to keep them in bounds or improve habit. John Bond at Windsor, England practised a chain-saw rejuvenation programme every few years.

AMBIGUUM

■ **AMBIGUUM** Low–Medium H5–6? EM–M. Flowers widely funnel-shaped, greenish yellow to pale yellow, 2–7 per truss. Compact, with shiny dark green leaves, glaucous beneath. One of the hardiest Triflora species. **'GOLDEN SUMMIT'** is a fine dwarf selection. Other selections: **'CROSSWATER'**, **'JANE BANKS'** *U.K, Ger, Scand.*
■ **AUGUSTINII** Medium–Tall H3–4 EM–ML. Flowers widely funnel-shaped, pale to deep purple-blue, or reddish purple (occasionally white), 2–6 per truss, usually very free flowering. Small leaves, usually with some hairs on midrib or margins. New growth often bronze or reddish. This is one of the finest of all species and is a must for moderate climates. Variable in hardiness, paler forms are often hardier. *U.K.* **'ELECTRA'** AGM a fine form, not very hardy, deep purple-blue. **'BARTO BLUE'** popular in Pacific Northwest. **SSP. CHASMANTHUM** Medium–Tall H3–4 M–ML. Flowers blue (or white), with a dark blotch. Leaves sometimes semi-deciduous. Usually later flowering than ssp. *augustinii*. **SSP. RUBRUM** Tall H4 E–EM. Flowers reddish purple, 2–6 per truss. More compact than its relatives and earlier flowering. Not very easy to propagate. The least attractive of the subspecies. A probable natural hybrid. **SSP. HARDYI** Tall H4 M–ML. Flowers white with yellowish green spotting, 2–6 per truss. Stiff leaves. Almost deciduous. Rare but very good at its best.

AUGUSTINII SSP. CHASMANTHUM

AUGUSTINII SSP. HARDYI

■ **CONCINNUM** Medium–Tall H5 EM–M. Flowers purple or reddish purple, 2–5 per truss. Dark-green leaves with dense scales on the lower surface. Compact habit. One of the hardiest species in Triflora. Popular in northern Europe. *U.K.* **PSEUDOYANTHINUM Group** deepest coloured reddish-purple forms. **'CHIEF PAULINA'** royal-purple flowers spotted dark brown. **AMESIAE** is a variant of R. concinnum or a natural hybrid with R. trichanthum.

CONCINNUM

LUTESCENS 'BAGSHOT SANDS'

POLYLEPIS

■ **DAVIDSONIANUM** Medium–Tall H3–4 EM–M. Flowers pink to white, usually with a strong blotch or spotting. A graceful arching bush. Very free-flowering, a real showstopper at its best. Recent research claims this species is resistant to Phytophthora, though I am rather dubious about this. **'FCC'** form clear pink. **'RUTH LYONS'** unmarked deep pink. **'STAR TREK'** pastel lilac-pink. **'CAERHAYS'** blotched pink. *AGM, Mel.*

DAVIDSONIANUM

■ **KEISKEI** Low H(4)5–6 E–EM. Flowers rather thin-textured, pale to mid-yellow, 2–6 per truss. Green leaves often bronze or reddish in young growth. Branchlets tend to be rather brittle. A useful tough species and a parent of many dwarf hybrids. **(VAR. OZAWAE) 'YAKU FAIRY'** Dwarf H5–6 EM–M. Flowers funnel-shaped, clear pale yellow, in trusses of 3–5. Near prostrate habit. One of the most dwarf of all rhododendrons and very slow-growing. Needs a sunny site. *AGM, AT, CT, SO.*

KEISKEI

■ **LATERIFLORUM** Medium–Tall H4 ? Flowers white or yellow. A newly described (by the Chinese) species that appears to be related to *R. triflorum*. Described flowers unseen, which means no one will ever be able to identify it when they find it in flower.

■ **LUTESCENS** Medium–Tall H3–4 E–EM. Flowers pale- to deep-primrose-yellow, usually spotted red. Often attractive reddish-bronzy young growth. Wild collected forms tend to be hardier than named forms but have smaller flowers. *U.K.* **'BAGSHOT SANDS'** bright yellow, not all that hardy. *AGM.*

■ **OREOTREPHES** Medium–Tall H4 EM–ML. Flowers light- or dark-purple, pink or off-white, 1–3(5) per truss. Attractive glaucous foliage and a tidy upright habit. One of the best Triflora species for flowers and foliage. *U.K.* **'BLUE-CALYPTUS'** with very striking glaucous leaves and pink-purple flowers. **'PENTLAND'** two-tone purple flowers.

OREOTREPHES 'BLUE-CALYPTUS'

OREOTREPHES 'PENTLAND'

■ **POLYLEPIS** Medium–Tall H4 EM–M. Flowers pale to deep purple or pinkish purple, 3–5 per truss. Dark, narrow pointed leaves with recurved margins. Seldom grown and not as showy as most of its relatives. **SEARSIAE** differs in the bluish leaf underside.

■ **RIGIDUM** Low–Medium H4 EM–M. Flowers white, lightly scented, 2–6 per truss. Wild forms can also be pink or purple. Small grey-green leaves. A tidy plant with glaucous new growth. One of the most beautiful of the Triflora species. *U.K.*

RIGIDUM

SIDEROPHYLLUM

■ **SIDEROPHYLLUM** Low–Medium H3–(4) M. Flowers white or pale pink, pink, lavender or purple, 3–6 per truss. Usually compact and can be very fine, but not all that hardy. **TATSIENENSE** is similar, white to pink, usually small-flowered, which may be a natural hybrid containing *R. racemosum*.

■ **TRICHANTHUM** (*see* photo overleaf) Medium H4 ML–L. Flowers plum-purple to reddish purple or pale purple-mauve, 3–5 per truss. Dark green leaves, usually with hairy or bristly stems and margins. The best forms are striking, but the poorest forms are a muddy purple. Useful for its late flowering. **'HONEYWOOD'** spectrum violet, outside light.

TRICHANTHUM

■ **TRIFLORUM** Medium–Tall H2–4 ML–L. Flowers yellow, cream, often spotted or flushed red, pink or bronze, 2–4 per truss. Leaves usually glaucous, bark peeling in Himalayan forms. Tibetan forms are hardiest but lack the fine peeling bark. At its best a showy species. **MAHOGANI Group** includes the reddest flowered selections. **VAR. BAUHINII-FLORUM** less hardy with larger flowers.

TRIFLORUM TIBETAN TYPE

■ **YUNNANENSE** Medium–Tall H3–4 M. Flowers pink to white, usually spotted or flared red or deep-pink, 1–6 per truss. Often semi-deciduous. An outstandingly showy plant and the most spectacular Triflora. It is well worth planting a group or clump of several clones. Tolerant of dry and shady conditions. A must for a moderate climate. **'OPENWOOD'** A lavender pink selection. AGM, Mel. **PLEISTANTHUM** should be considered a synonym of R. yunnanense.

YUNNANENSE

■ **ZALEUCUM** Medium–Tall H2–3 E, EM or M. Flowers white, pale pink to purple, the largest flowers in the subsection to 4.8cm long, 3–5 per truss. Dark foliage with grey-blue leaf underside, young growth brown or reddish. Very fine in mild gardens. Early growth requires shelter. **VAR. FLAVIFLORUM** pale yellow, less hardy than the type.

ZALEUCUM

TRIFLORA SS HYBRIDS

■ **CALIFORNIA BLUE** Medium H4–5 EM. Flowers lavender-blue in small compact trusses. Rather leggy, best pruned periodically after flowering for best habit. (? augustinii × unknown). Greer (intro).

■ **CONTINA** Medium–Tall H5 EM–M. Flowers vivid violet-blue, with white stamens, in compact rounded trusses. A good alternative to R. augustinii for cold gardens. (concinnum 'Chief Paulina' × augustinii 'Barto Blue'). Phetteplace.

■ **ELEANORE** Medium–Tall H5 EM–M. Two clones: clear lavender-blue with olive-green spots and amethyst-violet with darker spotting. Leaves small with some colour in the new growth. An upright willowy grower that will take full sun. (rubiginosum × augustinii). Rothschild.

■ **FLORENCE MANN** Medium H4 EM–M. Flowers deep lavender-violet in clusters. Leaves small, on an upright fairly compact plant. Bred for heat tolerance and highly rated in its native Australia as the best of the smaller 'blues' for their conditions. Mel, Tas. (rigidum × Blue Admiral). Bramley **'BLUE ADMIRAL'** violet-blue with prominent stamens. Grown in Australia.

■ **HACHMANN'S MEDLEY** Low–Medium H5 M–ML. Flowers funnel-shaped opening greenish creamy yellow tinged pale yellowish pink, aging pale yellow to pale purplish pink, in multiple bud clusters of 9–20. Leaves ovate, flat, matte green above, scaly, very aromatic. A rather curious and muddy mixture of colours, as to be expected with a yellow crossed with a purple. (ambiguum × concinnum). Hobbie/Hachmann.

■ **STAR SAPPHIRE** Semi-dwarf–Low H4–5 EM. Flower saucer-shaped, vivid purple fading lighter towards the centre with green spotting, outside light purple, in ball-shaped truss of 4–7. Leaves small and scaly, elliptic, dull, olive-green. Upright, dense habit. (augustinii × minus Carolinianum Gp.). Hardgrove.

SUBSECTION UNIFLORA

10–40cm. H3–4. A small group of species for the connoisseur, with charming flowers. All need cool roots, good drainage and a little extra care. R. pemakoense is quite easy.

IMPERATOR

■ **IMPERATOR** Dwarf H3–4 EM–M. Flowers widely funnel-shaped, purplish pink, 1–2 per truss. Tiny narrow pointed leaves. Flowers are large for the leaf size. Semi-deciduous. Best covered with a cloche in winter. Rare and choice. **UNIFLORUM** larger leaves, otherwise similar. Probably a natural hybrid. We were unable to locate it in the wild where it was originally found.

■ **LUDLOWII** Dwarf H4 M. Flowers broadly campanulate (bowl-shaped), yellow, with reddish-brown spots, 1–2 per truss. Tiny deep-green leaves. The flowers are large for the leaf size. Best in a peat bed with good drainage. A choice but rather tricky dwarf. A parent of numerous Glendoick hybrids.

LUDLOWII

■ **PEMAKOENSE** Semi-dwarf H4 EM. Flowers tubular funnel-shaped, pale pinkish purple to near-pink, 1–2 per truss. Small dark green leaves on a very compact, dense plant. Extremely free-flowering, but opening buds and flowers need protection from frost.

PEMAKOENSE

PUMILUM

■ **PUMILUM** Dwarf H4 EM–M. Flowers small, pink, campanulate (bell-shaped), on long stalks, 1–3 per truss. Kingdon Ward's 'Pink Baby'. A charming little plant for the connoisseur with tiny leaves and thimble-like flowers. Grow in a peat bed. Not always easy to please.

SUBSECTION VIRGATA

A single species.

■ **VIRGATUM** Low H2–3 E–M. Flowers funnel to tubular funnel-shaped, pale- to deep-pink, mauve or white, always from axillary buds, 1–(2) per bud. Leaves lanceolate to oblong-oval, on a sprawling and often straggly shrub. Useful for its heat and drought tolerance but rather tender, suitable for mild climates. **SSP. OLEIFOLIUM** is from the eastern end of the distribution, in China. Flowers paler.

VIRGATUM SSP. OLEIFOLIUM

LEPIDOTE HYBRIDS

15cm–2m. H3–8. These are dwarf or low-growing plants that are ideal for the small garden, rock garden or raised bed. Most smother themselves in flower, have small scaly leaves and are dense twiggy growers. The small-leaved alpine varieties are happiest grown in the open, away from the drips of trees, though in areas with hot summers they need some shade.

DAURICUM AND MUCRONULATUM HYBRIDS

1–2m H4–H8. Flowers in clusters, white, pale-yellow, pink, purple to reddish. Small scaly leaves, deciduous or semi-deciduous or evergreen with deep-coloured winter leaves. This group contains a large number of early flowering, generally very hardy hybrids derived from two very hardy species, *R. dauricum* and *R. mucronulatum*. The hardiest are extremely tough and will withstand

temperatures as low as –30°C (–22°F) (USDA 4b). The most widely known are the many forms of 'P.J.M.'. Recently many double-flowered forms have been raised. The downside of these hybrids are the poor winter leaf-retention and the often straggly and floppy habit, especially as young plants. Although very tough, the flowers are not frost hardy and, in mild climates such as the U.K., the early flowers are often spoiled. These are important plants for the landscape in N.E. America. Mostly bred in Massachusetts and Connecticut, they grow best in New England. Few are very heat tolerant, so generally they perform less well as you head south down the U.S. eastern seaboard.

■ **AIRY FAIRY** Low–Medium H6? E. Flower widely funnel-shaped, purplish pink with red spots, in flat trusses of 3. Leaves narrowly elliptic, long, glossy. Semi-deciduous. Upright, stiff-branched growth habit. (*lutescens* × *mucronulatum* 'Cornell Pink'). Maloney **'CORAL GLOW'** is the same cross, flowers pinkish-orange.

AIRY FAIRY

■ **ALICE SWIFT** Low H7 EM. Flower openly funnel-shaped, light reddish purple shading to purplish pink in throat, with vivid purplish-red spots, 12–16 per truss. Leaves elliptic, scaly. Compact, well-branched plant. Flowers have some frost resistance. Later and pinker than 'P.J.M.' with greener winter leaves. Long-lasting flowers. Needs pruning. *GL, MD*. ([*racemosum* × *mucronulatum*] × *minus* Carolinianum Gp.). Yavorsky.
■ **ANGEL POWDER** Low H6 E. Flowers light yellowish-green in bud, opening ruffled white with a strong yellow-green dorsal spot in trusses of 6. Leaves large, semi-deciduous. Good reports as a garden plant on Long Island and New Jersey and this seems be one of the best Delp lepidotes. Buds well in shade. *NY*. (Epoch × *mucronulatum* white). Delp.
■ **APRIL DAWN** Semi-dwarf–Low H8 E–EM. Flower widely funnel-shaped, slightly fragrant, light pink, 3–4 per truss. Leaves elliptic, mahogany in winter. Upright, spreading habit. *CT, MS*. (*minus* Carolinianum Gp. × *dauricum* 'Arctic Pearl'). Mehlquist.

APRIL DAWN

APRIL GEM

■ **APRIL GEM** Semi-dwarf–Low H8 EM. Flower widely funnel-shaped, pure white, double, slightly fragrant, in a lax truss of 2–3. Leaves elliptic, deep olive-green. Broadly, upright plant. The flowers are rather a curious shape and look like those of a Gardenia. The pale leaves rather spoil the effect. ([*minus* Carolinianianum Gp.White × *mucronulatum* 'Cornell Pink'] × [*dauricum* album × *dauricum*] F2). Mehlquist.
■ **APRIL PINK** Semi-dwarf–Low H5 E. Flower funnel-shaped, slightly fragrant, pale purplish pink with heavy red spotting in throat, in a lax truss of 3. Leaves elliptic. Compact growth habit. *MD*. (*minus* var. *chapmanii* × *mucronulatum* 'Cornell Pink'). Kehr.
■ **APRIL REIGN** Semi-dwarf–Low H8 EM. Flower widely funnel-shaped, double, slightly fragrant, pink with a lighter centre. Leaves elliptic, scaly. Upright habit. *MS*. ([*minus* Carolinianum Gp. × *mucronulatum* 'Cornell Pink'] × *dauricum* white form, selfed Mehlquist). Mehlquist. **'APRIL MIST'** double pink.
■ **APRIL ROSE** Semi-dwarf–Low H8 EM. Flower widely funnel-shaped, double, reddish purple. Leaves elliptic. Reddish bronze in autumn. Broadly upright habit. Very good for breeding doubles. Rather prone to root-rot problems. *AT, MS, MW, SH, ST, TO*. ([*dauricum* white × *dauricum*] × [*minus* Carolinianum Gp. × *mucronulatum* 'Cornell Pink'] F2). Mehlquist.

APRIL SONG

■ **APRIL SONG** Medium H7 E–EM. Flower widely funnel-shaped, wavy edged, hose-in-hose, purplish pink, fused stamens form ring of lighter pink, in a ball-shaped truss. Dense and fairly compact. Semi-deciduous. Perhaps my favourite of the double-flowered *R. dauricum* hybrids. *MS*. ([(PJM Group × *mucronulatum*) × *dauricum* album] × [Pioneer × unnamed hybrid form PJM Gp.]). Mezitt **'APRIL LOVE'** is a sister seedling with light purple-pink double-flowers with fused stamens.

APRIL SNOW

THUNDER

■ **APRIL WHITE** Semi-dwarf–Low H8 EM. Flower widely funnel-shaped, semi-double, slightly fragrant, pure white, 3–4 per truss. Leaves dark-green, copper-coloured when new, yellow in autumn. Rounded, dense habit. Semi-deciduous. *CT, MS, ST.* ([(*minus* Carolinianum Gp. × *mucronulatum* Cornell Pink) × (white flowered *dauricum* × *dauricum*)] × [white flowered *dauricum* × *dauricum*]). Mehlquist. There are lots of similar double-white hybrids such as: **'APRIL CLOUD'**, pale yellow-green to white, **'APRIL SNOW'** pure white, **'LILAC CREST'** double-white with a flushing of lilac.

■ **ARCTIC GLOW** Semi-dwarf–Low H6 E. Flower openly funnel-shaped, wavy edges, light purple fading to white in centre, with faint light purple spots on dorsal lobe, 2–3 buds per terminal with 3 flowers per bud. Leaves elliptic, on a dense plant. *ME* (*minus* Carolinianum Gp. × *dauricum* 'Arctic Pearl'). Lewis.

■ **BALTA** Semi-dwarf–Low H7 E. Flower broadly funnel-shaped, pale purple-pink, fading to off-white, in dome-shaped trusses of about 9. Leaves elliptic, semi-glossy, dark green. Upright, dense plant. The muddy off-white colour is not that attractive. *GL.* (*minus* Carolinianum Gp. × PJM). Mezitt.

BALTA

■ **BLACK SATIN** Semi-dwarf–Low H7 EM. Flower light violet-purple with a coral throat, in ball-shaped trusses of about 10. Leaves oblong, age from light green to rusty green and turn dark bronze-purple in winter. Wide, upright habit. *ST.* (*minus* Carolinianum Gp. × *dauricum* Sempervirens Gp.). Mezitt. **'THUNDER'** is very similar with equally dark but more glossy winter foliage. We found both these plants inclined to die off with root problems.

■ **BODEGA CRYSTAL PINK** Low H4–5 VE. Flower openly funnel-shaped, purplish pink with deeper purplish-pink spots, reverse purplish red, in ball-shaped trusses of 3–7. Leaves elliptic, light green, semi-deciduous. Upright habit. A free-flowering very early hybrid let down by its sparse habit in winter. Flowers are vulnerable to frost. Needs sharp drainage. *EK, PC.* (Cilpinense × *mucronulatum* 'Cornell Pink'). Heller.

■ **CARONELLA** Low H7 M. Flower broadly funnel-shaped, light purplish pink, with striped purple-pink markings, in dome-shaped trusses of about 6. Leaves small, elliptic, flat, dark green, semi-deciduous, turning orange-red in autumn. Upright habit. (*minus* Carolinianum Gp., white form × *mucronulatum* 'Cornell Pink'). Mezitt. **'JAY MURRAY'** light purplish pink with brownish orange spotting.

■ **CHAPMANII WONDER** Medium H6 E–EM. Flower openly funnel-shaped, wavy-edged, bright lavender-pink. Leaves elliptic, small and scaly. Bred to be more tolerant than the 'PJM' hybrids of heat and humidity. Needs pruning for compactness. Not worth growing in mild areas. *PT, SE.* (*minus* var. *chapmanii* × *dauricum* album). Wada. **'SENEGAL'** pale yellow-ivory. H7.

■ **CLIFF GARLAND** Semi-dwarf H5 E. Flowers shell-pink with darker spotting, in trusses of 4. Leaves obovate to nearly circular, deep-green, new growth bronzy. Upright habit. Very bud-tender and so of limited merit in spring-frost-prone areas. (Bric-a-Brac × *mucronulatum* pink form). Nearing.

■ **CONEMAUGH** Medium H6 VE–E. Flower star-shaped, lavender-pink, held in small, ball-shaped trusses. Leaves small, glossy, semi-deciduous. Upright, open, twiggy habit. Various forms exist. Flowers rather wishy-washy and habit too straggly to make this a popular plant. (*racemosum* × *mucronulatum*). Gable. **'CONEWAGO'** several clones, pale-pink flowers. H7. Not grown much these days.

■ **EMASCULUM** Low H5 VE–E. Flower funnel-shaped, rosy lilac, with no stamens, in trusses of 2 or 3. Leaves small, fir-green coloured, lightly scaly. An early flowering hybrid that is not as good as 'Praecox' from the same cross, with rather a weak root system, though it may be hardier. (*ciliatum* × *dauricum*). Waterer.

■ **FLODA** Semi-dwarf–Low H8 VE. Flower openly funnel-shaped, purplish-pink edged lighter, fading to white with pink stripes and with a light orange-yellow blotch, in trusses of 3–8. Leaves elliptic, flat, glossy, on a spreading plant. Autumn foliage red. Poor in Scotland with a limp and floppy habit and an inability to decide whether to drop its leaves or not: they hang on making the plant look dead.

(*keiskei* × *mucronulatum* pink form). Waldman. **'CORAL PINK PROLOGUE'** pink and yellow. Foliage rather average.

■ **GLENWOOD ARCTIC DAWN** Medium H6 E. Flower openly funnel-shaped, white tinged with very pale purple, lightly spotted with dark reddish orange, in dome-shaped trusses of up to 15. Leaves elliptic, convex, shiny, dark yellowish green, with brown scales on the under-surface. Leaves retained for 18 months, so of denser appearance than many related hybrids. *PR.* (*minus* Carolinianum Gp. × *dauricum* 'Arctic Pearl'). Lewis.

■ **GLENWOOD SENTINEL** Low H8 EM. Flowers light to pale purple, inside and out, unmarked, in trusses of 3. Leaves yellow-green. Dense and compact habit. Yet another from the PJM cross, this is said to differ in the brighter flower colour. (*minus* Carolinianum Gp. × *dauricum*). Lewis. **'TWISTER'** another 'PJM' type hybrid with twisted leaves. A little earlier than 'P.J.M'. Not exceptional.

■ **GRACE & WILL** Low H5 E. Buds light yellow-green and rose-pink, opening to flowers yellowish-white, paler yellow-green and pink in rounded trusses. Leaves narrowly elliptic, on a plant of rather upright habit. Seems to be quite a good early white with better leaf retention than most. ([*minus* Carolinianum × Mucram] × *lutescens* FCC). Delp.

■ **HELEN SCOTT RICHEY** Semi-dwarf H4–5 VE. Flower widely funnel-shaped, deep purplish pink lightly spotted deep-pink, in terminal clusters of 1–5 buds, with 1–2 flowers per bud. Leaves elliptic, glossy, bullate, dark green, semi-deciduous, new growth bronze, on a plant of upright growth habit. ([*racemosum* × *moupinense*]) × *mucronulatum* 'Cornell Pink'). Scott.

■ **HUDSON BAY** Low H7 EM. Flower openly funnel-shaped, wavy lobes, white, unmarked, in terminal flower clusters, dome-shaped, each three-flowered. Leaves elliptic, long, glossy, on a plant of broad, rounded, well-branched habit. (*minus* Carolinianum Gp. × *dauricum*). Leach. **'YUKON'** white-flowered edged lilac-pink. **'ARCTIC DAWN'** blush-white flowers. Not as widely grown as the Weston and Melquist versions of this cross.

ISOLA BELLA

■ **ISOLA BELLA** Low H5 E–EM. Flowers palest pink, fading to white, with faint green-yellow spotting, in trusses of 3–5. Good foliage. A fine very tough Canadian dwarf hybrid. Like many *dauricum* hybrids the root system and habit are poor when young, though it improves at maturity. (*fletcherianum* × *dauricum* white form). Brueckner.

■ **JUNE PINK** Low H7 ML–L. Flowers openly funnel-shaped, moderate purplish pink, in flat-domed trusses of 8–10. Growing as wide as high. Leaves held one year. The latest to flower of the Weston lepidotes. (Olga Mezzit seedling). Weston.

■ **KICKOFF** Low–Medium H7–8 EM. Buds of violet and strong purple open to light purple flowers, edged strong-purple, dorsal spots greenish yellow in balled trusses of 12. Said to be a good, tough lepidote. Though can be rather leggy, it does remain more or less evergreen. (Achiever × *mucronulatum*). Delp/Anderson.

■ **LANDMARK** Low H8 EM. Flowers deep purplish-red in bud, opening strong purplish red with very faint scarlet spotting, in multi-bud dome-shaped trusses of 25. Leathery leaves, bronze-mahogany in winter, +/– evergreen. A robust, deep-flowered hybrid of the 'P.J.M.' type getting good reviews in E. North America. It really does look almost red, a colour that is rare in hardy lepidotes. Promising. *GP*. (Counterpoint × Carolina Rose). Mezitt. **'RED QUEST'** is not as good.

■ **LAURIE** Semi-dwarf H7 M. Flower openly funnel-shaped, white blushed pink with golden spotting and reddish-purple stripes on reverse in terminal clusters of 28–35 flowers composed of 2–3 inflorescences. Leaves aromatic, narrowly elliptic to elliptic, rounded, long, glossy, dark green. Broad habit with willowy branches. The colour is a rather muddy one between white and pink, but it is tough and adaptable. *ME*. (*minus* white form × P.J.M.). Mezitt.

■ **LAVENDER FROST** Semi-dwarf–Low H7 EM. Flower broadly funnel-shaped, fully double (no normal stamens), very pale purple to almost white with light purple margins, in dome-shaped trusses of about 4. Leaves elliptic, glossy, green, on a fairly compact plant. *MS*. (Laurie × *dauricum* white-flowered). Mezitt. **'MRS J.A. WITHINGTON III'** a sister, double very light purple at margins, shading paler to very pale purple at centre. **'WESTON'S STARBURST'** light lavender with yellowish petaloid stamens.

■ **LEGACY** Low H7 E. Flowers openly funnel-shaped, fully double (no normal stamens), with 15 wavy-edged lobes; strong reddish purple, in ball trusses of 10. Fine mahogany winter foliage. Similar flowers to 'April Rose' like deep purple-pink rosebuds. (April Glory × Princess Susan). Mezitt.

■ **LLENROC** Semi-dwarf–Low H7 M. Flower openly funnel-shaped, wavy edges, pale purplish-pink with yellow blotch, in a dome-shaped truss of about 4. Plant is semi-deciduous with two-thirds of the leaves falling in autumn after colouring up. The plant is sparse and straggly and needs pruning. Best in full sun but not very heat tolerant. (*minus* Carolinianum Gp. × *mucronulatum* 'Cornell Pink'). Mezitt. **'GERTRUDE SAXE'** clear-pink, tetraploid. **'WALLY'** soft-pink, **'WICKATUNK'** bright-pink.

■ **LYNNE ROBBINS STEINMAN** Low H7 E. Flowers ruffled, double pink with yellow throats. Almost deciduous. Not one of the better known early Weston hybrids. Too many have been named. (unnamed hybrid × unknown). Mezitt.

■ **MICROTONES** Medium H7 E. Flowers open funnel-shaped, a blend of light and pale purple and deep purplish pink, 5 per truss. Tall and a bit straggly. Free-flowering and a good doer in the Philadelphia area. The combination of colours is attractive. Needless to say there were five sisters also named, which vary very little. (Achiever × Conemaugh). Delp.

■ **MIDNIGHT RUBY** Low H8 EM. Wavy, reddish-purple blooms with a yellowish eye, 10–15 per balled truss. Leaves small and green in summer, turning dark, rich almost black colour in autumn. (Olga Mezitt × deep-purple seedling from PJM Gp.). Weston.

MILESTONE

■ **MILESTONE** Semi-dwarf–Low H6 EM. Flower frilly, vivid purplish pink, holding colour well, in trusses of 3–10. Leaves small, shiny, turn mahogany-coloured in winter. Foliage retention 10–20 per cent in winter. Dense growth habit. Prefers some sun. (*minus* Carolinianum Gp. × *dauricum*). Mezitt. **'COLT'S NECK ROSE'** a similar hybrid from the same cross. **'ALFREDA WIACZEK'** lavender-pink with paler centres.

■ **MOLLY FORDHAM** Semi-dwarf–Low H7 EM. Flower saucer-shaped, white inside with brilliant greenish-yellow spots, outside white with slight streaking, in flat trusses of 7. Leaves elliptic, flat, semi-glossy, moderate olive-green. A good doer in severe climates. 'Dora Amateis' is less hardy but more attractive. *CT, MD, MS, MW*. (Balta × *minus* Carolinianum Gp.). Mezitt.

■ **NEW PATRIOT** Semi-dwarf–Low H7 EM. Flower openly funnel-shaped, vivid purplish red with white anthers, in ball-shaped trusses of 8. Leaves oblong, glossy, medium green, on an upright, spreading plant. *MS*. ([selected PJM Gp. seedling × pink-flowered *mucronulatum*] × unknown). Mezitt. **'STACCATO'** double deep-silvery-pink flowers. Good autumn colour, leaves bronze in winter. Needs pruning.

■ **NORTHERN STARBURST** Semi-dwarf–Low H8 E. Flower broadly funnel-shaped, frilly edges, heavily textured, purple, fading inside to light-purple centre, in dome-shaped trusses of 4–5. Leaves elliptic, dark greyish reddish brown in late-winter, on a fairly dense plant. Genetically engineered (colchicine) to increase the chromosomes for thicker flowers and leaves. 'PJM on steroids' – Rare Find Nursery. Subject to snow breakage. *OZ*. (PJM Group colchicine treated). Briggs Nursery.

■ **OLGA MEZITT** Low H6 EM. Flower openly to tubular funnel-shaped, light purplish pink with inconspicuous markings in dome-shaped trusses of about 12. Leaves lanceolate, convex, yellow-green, mahogany in winter. A good plant at maturity but we found it straggly and without much rigidity as a young plant. Best with judicious pruning. Very common in E. North America. *AT, AZ, BH, CC, CH, GL, GP, MD, NG, PR, PT, PV, SE, ST, SV, TO*. (*minus* Carolinianum Gp. Compacta × *dauricum* hybrid). 'Olga Mezitt' Sports: **'ROSY MIRACLE'** red stems, **'LITTLE OLGA'** is two-thirds the size of parent.

OLGA MEZITT

■ **OLIVE** Low H6 VE. Flower vivid reddish purple with darker spots, singly or in twos. Leaves small, light green. Upright, rather leggy, sparse habit. Similar to but not as good as 'Praecox'. *FS*. (*moupinense* × *dauricum*). Maxwell.

■ **PIONEER (syn. GABLE'S PIONEER)** Tall H5 VE. Flower rosy mauve-pink, held in multiple trusses of up to 17, from buds in the leaf axils. Leaves elliptic, flat, glossy, olive-green, semi-deciduous. Plant upright, multiple stemmed. Benefits from regular pruning after flowering. *MS, PV*. (*racemosum* × ? *mucronulatum*). Gable.

■ **PJM Group** Medium H8 E. Flower openly funnel-shaped, lilac-purple to light violet. Leaves elliptic, rust-coloured scales, deep mahogany-purple, November to April. Upright, dense growth habit. The number one best-selling E. American hybrid. Poor in S.E. U.S.A.. Rather bud-tender in Scotland. Several selected forms. **'ELITE'** Flowers deep-pink, **'REGAL'** deep purple-pink. **'VICTOR'** strong reddish purple. **'P.J. MEZZIT'** named in England is a poor, shy-flowering clone. *AT, CD, CT, EG, FS, GL, GP, JF, KK, MA, ME, MS, MT, MW, NG, NY, OL, OP, OZ, PA, PC, PR, PT, PV, SC, SE, SI, ST, SV, TC, TO, TZ, WT, S. Fin, Swe, Pol*. (*minus* Carolinianum Gp. × *dauricum* Sempervirens Gp.). Mezitt.

PJM CHECKMATE

PJM ELITE

■ **PRINCESS SUSAN** Semi-dwarf H7 EM. Flower openly funnel-shaped, deep reddish purple, in ball-shaped trusses of 4–5. Leaves oblong, twisted margins, light green, dark mahogany-coloured in winter, on a dense and compact plant. A good looking plant, but not as easy to please as most of its relatives. (Balta × Laurie selfed). Mezitt.

■ **RED QUEST** Low H5–6 EM. Flowers strong purplish red, in trusses of 4. Not as bud-hardy as most of the Weston hybrids of this type and needs shelter and light shade. (Wilsoni × *dauricum* Sempervirens). Weston.

■ **RED SPLASH** Semi-dwarf–Low H7 E. Flower openly funnel-shaped, purplish red in bud, opening reddish purple, in flat dome-shaped trusses of 4. Leaves elliptic, to rounded, aromatic, mahogany-coloured in autumn. Dense habit. (Waltham × P.J.M.). Mezitt.

■ **SIDEKICK** Low H6 E. Flowers broadly funnel-campanulate, strong- and light-purple in bud, opening light-purple, outside strong-purple, anthers moderate-orange, in trusses of 7 (from multiple buds). Compact habit. Later than 'P.J.M.'. There are so many of these hybrids now. (Achiever × P.J.M.). Delp. **'MARGE DANIK'**, **'BOB DANIK'**, **'BOB DANIK JUNIOR'** all reddish purple; surprised the dog did not get one named after it too.

■ **TESSA** Low H4–5 E. Flower lilac-pink with spots in loose trusses. **'TESSA ROZA'** bright-pink. A much finer plant. (AGM). **'TESSA BIANCA'** smaller white flowers. Leaves small, convex edges, emerald-green. Vigorous grower with reddish-bronze bark. (Praecox × moupinense). Stevenson.

TESSA BIANCA

TESSA ROZA

■ **WESTON'S AGLO (syn. AGLO)** Semi-dwarf–Low H8 EM. Flower broadly funnel-shaped, wavy edges, moderate purplish pink with coppery red spotting, in dome-shaped trusses of about 8. Leaves small, scaly, elliptic, glossy, on a plant of open habit. Sun tolerant. Best in full sun and best with a good pruning after flowering to ensure an acceptable habit. A little earlier than sister 'Olga Mezitt'. GL, MS, MW, NG, NY, OZ, PR, ST, TO, TZ, WT. (minus compact form × dauricum hybrid). Mezitt.

■ **WESTON'S CRESCENDO (syn. CRESCENDO)** Low H6 EM. Pale-pink buds opening to flowers deepening in colour as they mature to medium purplish pink, in a balled truss of 15–20. Leaves rounded, larger than on most lepidotes, varying in size, green year-round. (P.J.M. Gp. × unknown). Weston.

WESTON'S PINK DIAMOND

■ **WESTON'S PINK DIAMOND** Low H5 E. Flower flat, saucer-shaped, semi-double, ruffled centre of petaloid stamens, light fuchsia-pink with orange-brown spotting, in ball-shaped trusses of 8–12. Leaves lanceolate, aromatic, glossy, yellow-green, on a vigorous, upright, well-branched, plant. Semi-deciduous with leaves colouring up well in autumn. Flowers are very fine but the lack of winter leaves make it less popular than it would be. CC, GL, MD, MS, NG, PR, TO. (PJM × mucronulatum 'Cornell Pink'). Mezitt.

■ **WHITE SURPRISE** Low H6 EM. Flower widely funnel-shaped, greenish white with greenish-yellow spotting, in ball trusses of 3–5. Leaves elliptic, convex, dull-green, about half turn brilliant yellow in autumn. Upright, open habit. Semi-deciduous and so tends to look rather sparse. Hard prune after flowering. ME, MS. (white-flowered dauricum × white-flowered mucronulatum). Mehlquist.

DWARF LEPIDOTE HYBRIDS

15cm–1.5m. H3–6(7). Low-growing alpine plants that are ideal for the small garden, rock garden or raised bed. Most smother themselves in flower, have small, scaly leaves and are dense, twiggy growers. As with most alpine plants, they must be grown in the open away from the drips of trees, though in warm areas they are best in part-day shade. Few have much heat tolerance. The Glendoick 'bird' hybrids, raised at our nursery, are to be found in this category. Many other fine hybrids have been bred by American Warren Berg.

■ **ALPINE GEM** Dwarf H4 M. Flowers yellow. As cultivated, this has small, deep purplish-pink flowers. The plant that is grown under this name is not 'Alpine Gem' but 'Radmosum'. Tiny leaves on dwarf, compact and spreading plant. The flowers are small and a rather harsh colour. I have never seen the real 'Alpine Gem' (brachyanthum × ferrugineum). Thacker.

■ **ALPINE MEADOW** Semi-dwarf H3 EM. Flowers pure white with brown stamens, 2–5 per truss. Soft attractive fuzzy green leaves. Early flowers need protection. Needs sharp drainage. (leucapsis seedling). Dunedin Rhododendron Gp.

■ **AMBER LANTERN** Semi-dwarf–Low H5 E. Flower funnel-shaped, pale yellow with green spots, marked pink, in flat trusses of 3–7. Leaves elliptic, dull olive-green. Grows wider than tall. Looks very close to straight R. keiskei to my eyes. (keiskei × unknown). Arsen.

■ **AMBROSE LIGHT** Semi-dwarf–Low H5 E. Flower openly funnel-shaped, very pale purple, in ball-shaped trusses of 10. Leaves elliptic with wavy margins, pale green. Upright, spreading, open habit. (Rochester Pink × unknown). Arsen.

■ **ANN CAREY** Low H3–4 E. Flowers tubular, chartreuse, fading to coral-pink. Several clones exist, some with petaloid stamens. New growth bronzy. Vigorous and straggly, best in full light. Can be pruned after flowering. Subject to bark-split in cold gardens. (keiskei × spinuliferum). Lem.

■ **ANNA BALDSIEFEN** Semi-dwarf H5 EM. Flowers brightest clear phlox pink, with deeper-pink margins in terminal racemes, 1–3 flowers per bud. Leaves tiny, on a plant of dense, fastigiate habit. Susceptible to rust. AZ, BH, CH. (Pioneer selfed). Baldsiefen.

■ **AQUAMARINE** Medium H5 M. Flowers brilliant violet, not fading, unspotted, 5–8 per truss. Leaves flat, broadly elliptic-ovate, glossy green, scaly. Fairly late for a dwarf 'blue'. (Lauretta × Crater Lake). Hachmann. Sisters include **'SAPHIRBLAU'** light violet-blue inside and out with blue stamens, **'STATUETTE'** strong violet-blue. Useful taller blues with better foliage than 'Blue Tit' and the like.

SAPHIRBLAU

■ **ARCTIC TERN** Semi-dwarf H4 ML. Flower very small, pure white with slight green in throat, in rounded clusters of 20. Leaves thin and narrow, yellowish green. Needs full sun to keep compact and benefits from a haircut when young. Prone to rust fungus so we stopped growing it commercially at Glendoick. SL. (trichostomum × subsection Leda species). Larson.

■ **AUTUMN VIOLET** Dwarf H7 E. Flowers flat saucer-shaped, frilly edged, violet, unmarked in trusses of 1–3. Leaves oblong, semi-glossy, moderate yellow-green. Tends to flower in autumn on Long Island and similar climates. MS. (impeditum × dauricum hybrid). Mehlquist.

■ **AZURELLA** Semi-dwarf H5 EM–M. Flowers strong-purple, paler in the throat, strong violet outside with red-purple veins, spotted dark purple on lobes, 3–5 per truss. Leaves elliptic to ovate, flat and slightly glossy. Fine bluish-grey leaves. May be subject to mildew in milder climates. (Sacko × calostrotum ssp. riparioides). Hachmann. **'ENRICO'** a sister with dark violet-blue flowers.

■ **AZURIKA** Semi-dwarf H5 M. Aster-violet flowers in tight trusses of 7–8. Tiny dark green leaves on a compact plant. Not one of the better dwarf purple-blues at Glendoick. (russatum × Moerheim). Hachmann. **'HACHMANN'S VIOLETTA'** is a sister with more blue-purple flowers.

■ **BARTO ALPINE** Semi-dwarf–Low H5 EM. Flower funnel-shaped, fuchsia-purple, in rounded truss of 4–5. Leaves elliptic, 2.5cm long, with a nutmeg-like scent, on a bush of upright, dense habit. Not one of the best Lapponica hybrids. JF. (lapponicum hybrid). Barto.

■ **BLANEY'S BLUE** Low H4–5 EM. Flowers funnel-shaped, blue-purple in clusters of 3–5. Leaves green in summer, bronze in winter, on a dense grower. The parentage given is probably wrong, as this plant has small leaves and is low-growing. Highly rated in Pacific Northwest. *CD, EK, KK, MT, OL, PC, PD, VI*. (*augustinii* Towercourt × Blue Diamond). Blaney.

■ **BLAUBART** Semi-dwarf H5 EM–M. Flowers light violet, with dorsal spotting of strong purple, in a truss of 4–6. Small dark green leaves. Compact and spreading. (Azurika × Blue Tit Magor). Hachmann. Sisters: **'BLAUMEISE'** brilliant purplish blue to light violet, **'LUISELLA'** violet-blue.

BLAUBART

LUISELLA

■ **BLUE BARON** Semi-dwarf H5 EM. Flower broadly funnel-shaped, wavy edges, light violet inside, vivid violet outside, in a dome-shaped truss of 20. Leaves oblong, glossy, dark green, bronze in winter, on a compact, mounding plant. Trumpeted as the deepest-coloured dwarf-purple-blue for the east coast of N. America. Not very heat or sun tolerant and needs good drainage, so may be of limited value. (Gletschernacht × Waltham). Mezitt.

■ **BLUE DIAMOND** Semi-dwarf–Low H4–5 EM. Clusters of violet-blue flowers of various shades, depending on the clone, up to 5 per truss. Leaves green in summer, turning bronze in winter. Many clones exist, most suffer leaf spot. *CN, EG, FS, OL, SH, SI, WT*. (Intrifast × *augustinii*). Crosfield **'BLUE POOL'** medium blue-purple flowers. Seems to be a good doer with some heat tolerance. **'OUDIJK'S FAVOURITE'** pale violet-blue.

■ **BLUE EFFECT** Semi-dwarf H5 EM–M. Flowers brilliant violet to vivid purple, outside vivid purple, base of lobes lightly spotted dark red, in a dense balled truss of 2–5(7). Small dark green leaves. Compact. Large flowers for a dwarf 'blue' hybrid. (Sacko × Blaney's Blue). Hachmann.

BLUE DIAMOND

■ **BLUE RIDGE** Low H5 M. Light lavender-blue (campanula-violet), in small trusses of 4–5. Small elliptic scaly leaves. Hardier than *R. augustinii* itself. (Russatunii × *augustinii*). Haag.

BLUE SILVER

■ **BLUE SILVER** Semi-dwarf H5 E–EM. Flowers reddish purple, in small trusses of 5–7. Small grey-blue leaves on an upright but tidy plant. Extremely tough, said to withstand −32°C (−26°F). Its main attribute is its frost-resistant flowers. (*hippophaeoides* × unknown). Hobbie.

■ **BLUE TIT** Low H5 M. Flowers violet-blue, 3–5 per truss. **'MAGOR'** is the best form I have seen. Very tough and relatively late-flowering. Most forms apart from 'Magor' tend to suffer leaf spot and chlorosis. (*impeditum* × *augustinii*). J. Williams & Magor. **'AUGFAST'** has dark lavender-blue flowers and yellowish young growth. **'BLUETTE'** pale blue flowers.

BLUE TIT 'MAGOR'

■ **BLUEBIRD** Semi-dwarf–Low H4 EM. Flowers bright purple-blue in a truss of 7–10 (best clone), others I have seen are washed out mauves, fit for the bonfire. Dense, small foliage on a finely textured plant, wider than high. Leaves inclined to chlorosis and leaf spot. No sign of *R. intricatum* in this cross. (*intricatum*? × *augustinii*). Puddle/Aberconway.

■ **BLUENOSE** Low H6 EM. Flower openly funnel-shaped, light violet, fading to very pale purple, in lax trusses of 3–5. Leaves narrowly elliptic, pale yellow-green, on an upright, open plant. This has large and impressive flowers of a luminous blue-purple. I am impressed so far, though the pale leaves may be a minus point. *AT*. (unnamed *augustinii* hybrid × *dauricum* Sempervirens Gp.). Brueckner.

BLUENOSE

■ **BLUMIRIA** Semi-dwarf H5 M. Flowers vivid purple to light violet, unmarked, in trusses of 4–6. Dark green leaf, margins recurved. Good foliage. (Azurika × Blue Tit Magor). Hachmann.

■ **BOB'S BLUE** Semi-dwarf–Low H4-5 EM. Flower funnel-shaped, open lavender then change to luminescent violet-blue, in trusses of 3–5 flowers. Leaves small, leathery, dark bronze-green in summer turning to maroon in winter. Upright growth habit. *CD, CN, MT, PA, SC, SH, VI*. (Ilam Violet × Blue Diamond). Rhodes.

■ **BO-PEEP** Semi-dwarf–Low H3 E. Flower funnel-shaped, creamy yellow with yellow-green spotting, 2–3 flowers per truss. Leaves small, recurved, glossy, on an upright somewhat rangy plant. Early into flower and growth, so needs shelter, but one of the few very early yellow dwarf hybrids. Suffers bark-split from spring frosts at Glendoick. (*lutescens* × *moupinense*). Rothschild. **'FINE FEATHERS'** white and yellow, blushed pink. Bud tender.

■ **BOSKOOP ASTARA** Low H5 E. Very bright pink flowers on sparsely leaved or near-bare stems. Small pointed leaves. Semi-deciduous. The flowers are a shocking pink colour. Rather straggly as a young plant but better with age. Fine if you like the colour. (*mucronulatum* ×). Boskoop.

■ **BRAMBLING** (*see* photo overleaf) Low H4 EM. Flowers two shades of brightest pink in multiple loose clusters. Fine dark foliage on a vigorous but well-branched plant. One of the best bright pink dwarf hybrids for moderate climates: an outstanding new Glendoick bird dwarf. (Razorbill × *racemosum*). Cox.

BRAMBLING

■ **CAROLINA ROSE** Semi-dwarf H5 M. Masses of pink flowers fading to white from multiple buds. Several clones. Said to be an azaleodendron, which is frankly nonsense: there is no sign of *R. prinophyllum* in it. This is a *minus-racemosum* type hybrid and very good it looks too in the Pennsylvania area. (*minus* Carolinianum Gp. × *racemosum* or *racemosum* hybrid). Knippenberg.

■ **CHARME LA** Semi-dwarf H8 EM–M. Flowers of heavy substance, openly funnel-shaped, wide, violet-purple, in lax trusses of 3–5. Small convex scaly leaves. One of the hardiest dwarf hybrids, said to take –32°C (–26°F). Flowers are large for the foliage. Not all that easy to root. (*minus* Carolinianum Gp. × *pemakoense* Patulum Gp.). Brueckner.

CHIKOR

■ **BRIC-A-BRAC g.** Semi-dwarf–Low H3 VE. Flower small, pure white or pinkish white, brown anthers, in lax trusses of 3. Leaves small, round, hairy, new growth bronze-coloured. Bark at maturity is shiny, papery, peeling. Spreading habit. Needs good drainage. Very early and buds are frost sensitive so only useful for milder areas. Some clones are pinker than others. (*leucaspis × moupinense*). Rothschild. **'PIRIANDA PINK'** a seedling of 'Bric-A-Brac' with flowers light cardinal-red to deep purplish pink, white centre.

■ **BRILLIANT** Dwarf–Semi-dwarf H4 M. Small bright red, campanulate flowers in loose trusses of 3–5. Small thin dark green leaves. New growth bronzy red. Slow growing, creeping habit. Said to be lime and heat tolerant. Rather brittle and prone to breakage. This looks like a rhododendron crossed with an evergreen azalea and not a Ledum × as claimed. (Elizabeth × evergreen azalea). Lem.

■ **BRITTANY** Semi-dwarf–Low H6 M. Widely funnel-shaped flowers, pale yellow, fading to pale and light yellowish-pink, outside moderate pink, 6 per lax truss. Oval, bronzy leaves and red-brown stems. Fairly compact. Bred for extreme hardiness, not worth growing in milder areas. (Bowie × *keiskei* (dwarf form)). Leach.

CHARME LA

■ **CHIFFCHAFF** Semi-dwarf H4 EM. Flower pale chartreuse-yellow, in loose trusses of 5–6. Leaves dark green, turning mahogany-bronze in winter. Compact and dense habit. Paler than most of the yellow Glendoick bird hybrids. Good reports from Vancouver Island. *U.K.* (*hanceanum* Nanum × *fletcherianum*). Cox.

red. Foliage is poor and flowers are pale, so probably not worth growing these days. (*keiskei × trichocladum*). Crown Estate.

■ **CILPINENSE** Semi-dwarf H3 E. Flower funnel-shaped, pale pink shaded darker pink, in trusses of 2–3. Leaves elliptic, shiny, green with a fine covering of light hair. Compact and rounded habit. Avoid dense shade. Very bud tender and rarely flowers well at Glendoick. 'Lucy Lou' is better. *AGM, CD, CN, SI, TC, VI.* (*ciliatum × moupinense*). Puddle/Aberconway. **'GRAHAM'** pale-pink, **'PINK SILK'** pale-pink, deeper than 'Cilpinense', light-purplish. **'BOULTER'S PINK GEM'** pink, shading to pale purplish pink, spotted darker.

CILPINENSE

■ **CRANE** Semi-dwarf H5 EM. Buds pale greenish yellow, opening palest creamy yellow both inside and out, unmarked, in trusses of 3. Small leaves. My own hybrid, a white version of 'Ginny Gee', which is hardy, very free-flowering and easy to

BRITTANY

CHIFFCHAFF

■ **CHIKOR** Semi-dwarf H4 M. Yellow, flat-faced flowers with reddish spots in a truss of 3–6. Leaves tiny and slightly shiny. Compact and rounded. A delightful dwarf that needs cool roots and moist but well-drained soil. Good in Scotland but rather a struggle in the Pacific Northwest. Not very suited to container production. The first Cox bird. *SO, Sco.* (*rupicola* var. *chryseum × ludlowii*). Cox.

■ **CHINK** Low H4 E–EM. Flowers pale chartreuse-yellow, some darker spotting, drooping, campanulate, in lax trusses of 5. Leaves semi-deciduous and often with ugly leaf-spot, new growth

CAROLINA ROSE

CRANE

please. One of the best white dwarf hybrids in Scotland. AGM. (*keiskei* Yaku Fairy × *racemosum* Whitelace). Cox **'JUNE BEE'** and **'FAIRY MARY'** are similar but with a slight pink tinge to the flowers.

■ **CRATER LAKE** Medium H4–5 EM. Flower flat saucer-shaped, brilliant violet, unmarked, in trusses of 3. Leaves elliptic, yellowish. Plant upright, new growth bronze-yellow. One of the best Lapponica hybrids for the Pacific Northwest. Grows to a substantial height in time. EG, NO, OL. (*augustinii* Barto Blue × Bluebird). Phetteplace.

■ **CREAM CREST** Semi-dwarf H4 E. Flower cup-shaped, bright creamy yellow, in trusses of 6–8. Leaves very glossy and deep green. Spreading habit. Attractive and free-flowering, but rather too early into flower for cold gardens, where it is often frosted. SI. (*rupicola* var. *chryseum* × Cilpinense). Wright.

■ **CROSSBILL g.** Medium H3 E. Flowers tubular, pale yellow, with protruding stamens, in clusters. Some clones have red, pink or orange markings or flushing. Leaves small, on an upright, vigorous and straggly plant, best in full light. Can be pruned after flowering. Prone to bark-split. The flowers are fine in the best forms. (*keiskei* × *spinuliferum*). Lem.

■ **CURLEW** Semi-dwarf H4–5 EM–M. Flower openly campanulate, 5cm across, bright mid-yellow, spotted red, in compact trusses of 1–3. Leaves small, shiny, dark green, on a dwarf, compact plant. Needs shade in hotter climates, and good drainage. Avoid fertilizer. Expanding buds need frost protection. The best selling of the many Glendoick bird hybrids. Large flowers for the leaf size. AGM, CN, KK, VI. (*ludlowii* × *fletcherianum*). Cox.

CURLEW

■ **CUTIE** Semi-dwarf–Low H3 M. Flowers lilac-pink in clusters of up to 19. A dwarf bush of grey-green leaves. Prone to rust. The sickly name probably also accounts for its declining fortunes. (*calostrotum* hybrid × unknown). Greig.

■ **DALKEITH** Semi-dwarf H4 EM. Flowers small, lavender-pink, in trusses or clusters of up to 17. Leaves tiny on a compact plant. Very free-flowering. Good reports from the south of South Island, New Zealand where it was bred. (Uniflora SS ×). McLaughlin.

■ **DEMING BROOK** Dwarf H5 M. Flower pale yellowish pink, outside shaded pale purplish pink, in trusses of 6. Leaves narrowly elliptic, flat, yellow-green, on a plant of dense habit. Free-flowering from multiple buds. Similar to 'Ginny Gee'. (*keiskei* Yaku Fairy × unknown). Foster.

■ **DORA AMATEIS** Semi-dwarf–Low H6 EM–M. Flower broadly funnel-shaped, slightly fragrant, white with faint green spotting, in lax trusses of 6–8. Leaves recurved, mid- to pale green. Bronze leaf-colour if grown in full sun. Prefers some shade for best performance in hot climates. Grows twice as wide as tall. One of the finest white dwarf hybrids. Foliage is sometimes yellowish and plant

DORA AMATEIS

can be rather brittle. AGM, AT, AZ, BH, CC, CH, EK, FS, JF, MD, MS, MT, NO, NY, OP, PC, PD, PR, PT, SE, SI, SL, SV, TC, TZ, WT. (*minus* Carolinianum Gp. × *ciliatum*). Amateis.

■ **EGRET** Dwarf H4–5 EM. Flowers tiny, bell-like, white slightly tinged pale green toward the throat, in loose trusses of 2–6. Leaves small, shiny, dark green, on a compact plant (unless in shade). Quite unlike any other hybrid. Can suffer mildew and rust. AGM, SL, SO. (*campylogynum* × *racemosum* White Lace). Cox.

EGRET

■ **EIDER** Semi-dwarf H5 EM. Flowers pure white, with black anthers, long lasting, in compact trusses of 5–8. Flowers relatively frost-resistant. Foliage yellowish green. The plant normally produces a rather inadequate root system but seems to be able to live with this. One of the finest early flowering pure-white hybrids. (*minus* Carolinianum Gp. × *leucapsis*). Cox.

EIDER

■ **ERNIE DEE** Semi-dwarf H4 EM. Flower campanulate, moderate purplish pink with red spots, in a terminal inflorescence composed of 4–8 two-flower trusses. Leaves narrowly elliptic, slightly rugose, dark green, on a well-branched plant that grows twice as wide as tall. PA. (*dauricum* × *racemosum*). Caperci.

■ **EUAN COX** Dwarf H4 ML. Flowers light yellow, spotted brickdust-red, in trusses of 4. Small oval dark glossy green leaves. Tight habit, very slow growing, one of the most dwarf of all hybrids, easier to grow than either parent. The only hybrid made by my grandfather Euan Cox. Dislikes heat, fertilizer and poor drainage. (*ludlowii* × *hanceanum* Nanum Gp.). Cox.

EUAN COX

■ **FAISA** Semi-dwarf–Low H7 M. Flower openly funnel-shaped, reddish purple in bud, opening to a blend of light purple and moderate purplish pink in trusses of 6. Leaves light green, small and scaly. A tough lepidote hybrid that is becoming quite popular in N.E. U.S.A. The flower colour is unusual. Rare Find Nursery catalogue says: 'impossible to kill'. Watch this space. MW, NG, TZ. (Achiever × *polycladum* Scintillans Gp.). Delp. Several sisters named are very similar: **'TICKLEY'**, **'DELP'S MIGHTY MITE'**.

FAISA

■ **FLEURETTE EVANS** Semi-dwarf–Low H3 E. Flower tubular funnel-shaped, pale purplish pink with deeper-pink throat, in lax trusses of 3–4. Leaves lanceolate, glossy, olive-green to yellow-green, of broad, compact habit. CA. (Seta × Seta). Moyles.

■ **FROSTHEXE** Dwarf H5 M. Flowers tubular-funnel-shaped (daphne-like) strong-violet with a deep reddish-purple base, in clusters of 4–6. Leaves narrow, dark green, A striking hybrid, which crosses the normally incompatible boundary between subsection Lapponica and section Pogonanthum. (*anthopogon* × *lapponicum*). Reich.

FROSTHEXE

■ **GINNY GEE** Semi-dwarf H5 EM. Flowers white with pink flushing at edges both inside and on reverse, fading to light pink or white, in terminal clusters of multiple buds of 3–5 flower-trusses. Leaves elliptic, with some red-bronze colouring in cold climates, on a very compact, very dense plant. One of the most popular of all dwarf hybrids and extremely free-flowering: you can't see a leaf. Sun, drought and heat tolerant. AGM, AT, CC, CN, EK, FS, GP, JF, KK, MB, MD, ME, MS, MT, NY, OL, OP, OZ, PA, PC, PD, PR, PT, SE, SH, SI, SL, SO, TC, TZ, VI, WT. (keiskei Yaku Fairy × racemosum). Berg.

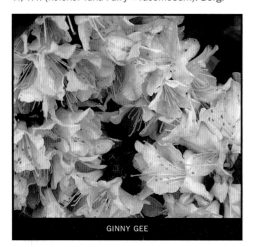

GINNY GEE

■ **GLENWOOD IVORY** Semi-dwarf H6 E–EM. Flowers off-white, tinged purplish pink, with some orange-yellow spotting, in terminal trusses of about 7. Leaves lanceolate, dark on a dense plant. Subtle colour with yellow overtones. ([Carolina Nude × dauricum white] × keiskei (epiphytic)). Lewis.
■ **GLETSCHERNACHT (syn. STARRY NIGHT)** Semi-dwarf–Low H4–5 EM. Flower deep-violet, in a truss of 7–8. Leaves yellowish green. Compact, dense shrub. Launched with fanfare in E. North America a few years back, but not heat tolerant, so of limited use. CC, PC. (russatum × Blue Diamond). Hachmann. **'AZURWOLKE'** very similar. **'HYDON MIST'** pale lavender flowers. **'BLUE CHIP'** purple-violet. **'GRISTEDE'** violet-blue. Dark green leaves. Sometime gets rust.
■ **GOLDEN BEE** Semi-dwarf H4 EM. Flowers openly funnel-shaped, brilliant mimosa-yellow with vivid yellow throat, unmarked, in lax trusses of 5–6. Small leaves are reddish bronze in winter and partly deciduous in cold winters. Compact and slow-growing. Very deep yellow. Surprisingly good in

GOLDEN BEE

Long Island. The plant is brittle and does not transport very well. (keiskei Yaku Fairy × mekongense Melinanthum Gp.). Berg. **'GOLDEN PRINCESS'** is almost identical. Warren Berg, the raiser, says that it has better foliage.
■ **GOLDEN ORIOLE g.** Low H3 EM. Flowers pale yellow, in a lax truss of about 3. Small leaves on a straggly, upright plant with fine peeling bark. Needs a mild garden or protected site for its early flowers and growth. (moupinense × sulfureum). Williams. **'TALAVERA'** yellow. **'BUSACO'** yellow flushed pink.
■ **GOLDILOCKS (PBR U.S.A.)** Semi-dwarf H4 E–EM. Flowers small, deepest yellow, held in multiple trusses. Leaves tiny, dark green on a compact and dense grower. We gave this up due to severe problems with rust fungus and bud tenderness. But it is one of the deepest yellow dwarf hybrids. The name cannot be registered as there is an older hybrid of this name. EK. (xanthostephanum × rupicola var. chryseum). Kerrigan.
■ **GOOSANDER** Semi-dwarf H3 EM. Flower saucer-shaped, pale yellow slightly green flushed, with dark red spots, in trusses of 3–5. Leaves small, dark green, reddish bronze in new growth. Semi-deciduous after cold winters and the flowers hang their heads too much, so not one of the best Cox birds. (ludlowii × lutescens). Cox.
■ **HINDSIGHT** Low H6 EM. Openly funnel-shaped, very pale purple, edged light purple with vivid yellow-green dorsal spots, in trusses of 6. Surprisingly large leaves. I have heard good and bad things about this plant. Some say it is shy flowering. It looks like Carolinianum with larger flowers and leaves. It looked impressive to me when I saw it. (Epoch × [Achiever × pemakoense]). Delp.

HINDSIGHT

■ **HOCKESSIN** Medium H8 EM. Flower apricot fading to an off-white, in racemes. Leaves tiny, hairy, on a rather straggly plant. This is one of Nearings's series known as the Guyencourt hybrids: at least nine F1 and F2 hybrids were named, which are all rather similar. (pubescens × keiskei). Nearing. Sisters: **'BRANDYWINE'**, **'CHESAPEAK, 'DELAWARE', 'LENAPE', 'MONTCHANIN'**. Flowers are muddy white, yellow or apricot, and most are straggly. Not grown much these days.
■ **HONSU'S BABY** Semi-dwarf H3 EM. Flower white with pale purplish-pink margins, giving an appearance of pink, in trusses of 4. Leaves small and pointed. Compact, mounding habit. Branches are rather brittle. PD, WT. (keiskei 'Yaku Fairy' × scabrifolium var. spiciferum). Spady. **'TURACAO'** A Glendoick hybrid from the same cross with slightly pinker flowers. Pinker than 'Ginny Gee' but not as hardy.

HONSU'S BABY

■ **ILAM VIOLET** Semi-dwarf–Low H3 EM–M. Flower dark violet-blue, in compact trusses of about 11. Leaves small, dark green, slightly glossy, reddish when young and bronzy in winter. Leaves aromatic. Best in some shade in New Zealand away from the far south. CN, PA. (augustinii 'Electra' × russatum). Stead.
■ **IMPEANUM** Dwarf H4–5 M. Flowers rotate, cobalt blue-lilac, in a truss of about 5. Small ovate leaves. Suitable for the rock garden with an almost prostrate habit. (impeditum × hanceanum). R.B.G. Kew.
■ **INCREDIBLE** Dwarf H5 E. Flowers open funnel-shaped, light purple inside, light violet outside, in balled trusses of 15. A theoretically impossible cross, hence the name, which miraculously seems to have worked. We have it at Glendoick and it is nothing to write home about. But it shows what you can do if you break or ignore the rules of genetics. (yakushimanum × dauricum). Reich. **'IMPOSSIBLE'** a sister, is very similar.
■ **IVORY COAST** Low H7 VE–E. Flower pale yellowish green fading to white in trusses of 5–7. Small leaves on a semi-deciduous dense plant. A useful low, early flowering hybrid for severe climates. Not worth growing in mild gardens. (keiskei × dauricum 'Arctic Pearl'). Leach.
■ **JERICHO** Semi-dwarf–Low H7 M. Flowers light yellow-green in bud, opening pale yellow-green with pale yellow dorsal spots, 6 per truss. Leaves are small and oval on a plant that can sprawl and flop. Hard prune after flowering for best habit. CC. (keiskei Mt. Kuromi × minus 'Epoch'). Leach.
■ **JOSEFA BLAU** Semi-dwarf H4–5 M. Flowers light violet with brilliant violet margins, to 8 in a loosely balled truss. A new German 'blue', which is later than most and of fine colour. The short pedicle gives it a distinctive look. I'm not convinced that it is the cross it purports to be, as I can't see any R. edgeworthii in it. (russatum × edgeworthii?). Reich.
■ **JOSEPH DUNN** Low H6 EM. Flower open funnel-shaped, wavy edges, pale purplish pink, in ball-shaped trusses of 20–25. Leaves elliptic, dull green with scales below and on stems on a plant of dense, rounded-growth habit. Useful as a late-flowering low lepidote-pink for cold gardens that is very free-flowering. A good doer at Glendoick. PR. (minus Carolinianum Gp. × racemosum). Lewis. **'EASTER ROSE'** is a sister with rosy pink flowers. **'PINK POMPOM'** pink in rounded trusses.

JOSEFA BLAU

JOSEPH DUNN

■ **KARIN SELEGER** Dwarf H8 EM. Flowers frost-hardy, purple in trusses of 5–7. Leaves tiny, scaly, on a dense, low grower. One of the hardiest dwarfs of this type, but not very heat tolerant and we find it rather inclined to die off. (*impeditum* × *dauricum*). Brueckner.

KARIN SELEGER

■ **LACKAMAS BLUE** Low H4–5 EM. Flower saucer-shaped, lavender-blue with a white star-shape in the centre, in trusses of 3–4. Leaves small, medium-green, new growth bronze, on a plant of upright habit. (*augustinii* form or seedling). Kerr.

■ **LAURETTA** Semi-dwarf H5–6 EM–M. Flowers brilliant violet, tinted reddish, unspotted in trusses

of 2–4. Leaves small, dark glossy green, erect compact habit. (Sacko × Gletschernacht). Hachmann. **'ENZIANA'** strong-violet, paler throat.

■ **LAVENDULA** Semi-dwarf–Low H5 M. Flower frilly, deep lavender with darker-coloured spots, in trusses of about 4. Leaves aromatic, dark green, turn bronze-coloured in winter. A compact grower that is a solid performer in Scotland, even if the colour is unfashionable. ([*russatum* × *saluenense*] × *rubiginosum*). Hobbie.

LAVENDULA

■ **LITTLE IMP** Dwarf H4–5 E–EM. Flower moderate bluish purple in small clusters. Leaves grey-green. Dense, twiggy grower. Easier to grow than *R. impeditum* in warm climates. CA. (*impeditum* × Blue Diamond). Barber.

■ **LITTLE LOU** Dwarf H3 E. Yellow buds open to funnel-campanulate flowers, greenish yellow, tinged apricot, 2–4 per truss. Leaves obovate or elliptic, small, hairy, deep green. Slow growing and needing sharp drainage. A good plant for the small garden in mild areas. (Lucy Lou × *valentinianum*). Sumner. Other *R. valentinianum* hybrids: **'PARISIENNE'** sulphur-yellow fading to cream. Popular in New Zealand. **'GOLDFINGER'** primrose-yellow, large calyx.

■ **LUCY LOU** Semi-dwarf–Low H3 E. Flower campanulate, pure-white with black stamens, in lax trusses of 3 to 5. Leaves elliptic, hairy and scaly and dark green. Compact, dense and broadly branching habit. Surprisingly frost-resistant buds. Very similar to 'Snow Lady' but with better habit. (*leucapsis* × [*ciliatum* × *leucapsis*]). Larson.

LUCY LOU

■ **MACOPIN** Semi-dwarf–Low H7 EM. Flower pale-lavender/lilac, held in ball-shaped clusters. Leaves small shiny, dark green. The flower colour deepens as it ages. PR, GP. (*racemosum* × Wyanokie?). Nearing.

■ **MAGGIE** Semi-dwarf H5 EM–M. Flowers dark blue-purple in compact rounded trusses. Small leaves on a dense, twiggy plant. Flowers are a good colour. (St Merryn × Azurika). Hachmann. **'RONNY'** a sister with dark violet-blue flowers.

■ **MALTA** Semi-dwarf–Low H8 E. Flower widely funnel-shaped, pale purplish pink, flushed darker, no stamens, in ball-shaped trusses of 2–6. Leaves elliptic to narrowly elliptic, bronze/mahogany in the winter. Grows wider than high, a bit straggly as a young plant. Good in full sun in Ohio. Not very heat tolerant in S.E. U.S.A. (Gable's Pioneer × Gable's Pioneer). Leach.

MALTA

■ **MANITOU** Semi-dwarf–Low H5 EM. Flower openly funnel-shaped, white rapidly changing to pale purplish pink with a purplish-pink throat and small, red spots, in ball-shaped multi-bud inflorescences of up to 35. Leaves elliptic, flat, rounded, semi-glossy, olive-green, brown scales below. The most highly rated of the many Nearing hybrids of this type. AT, AZ, BH, CH, MS, PT, SE. (Conestoga × unknown). Nearing.

■ **MARY FLEMING** Semi-dwarf H7 EM. Flower campanulate, pale yellow-cream with blotches and streaks of salmon, in a truss of 2–3. Small leaves. Bronze young growth. Sun and heat tolerant and one of the most highly rated dwarfs for N.E. U.S.A. The same cross has been made many times: CC, FS, GP, MD, ME, MS, NY, PR, PT, PV, SE, SV, TZ. ([*racemosum* × *keiskei*] × *keiskei*). Nearing. **'ARSEN'S PINK'** pale pink, **'YELLOW SPRING'** pale yellow and pink.

MARY FLEMING

■ **MAURY SUMNER** Low H3 EM. Flowers tubular, rosy red, in clusters. Low and spreading, best in sun for habit. A striking *R. spinuliferum* hybrid. Not all that easy to root. *NO, DA*. (Seta × *spinuliferum*). Sumner.

■ **MERGANSER** Semi-dwarf H4 M. Flowers funnel-shaped, light greenish yellow, in a truss of 3. Dark green foliage, bluish-grey underneath, on a very compact dense plant. This looks like a yellow *R. campylogynum*. Best in areas with cool summers. Sensitive to fertilizer. Easy to root, free-flowering and very attractive. *AGM*. (*campylogynum* white × *luteiflorum*). Cox.

MERGANSER

■ **MOERHEIM** Dwarf H5 M. Flowers pale (aster) violet, freely produced. Small dark foliage turns maroon in the winter, on a compact plant. I've never understood why such an insipid colour should be so popular. I suspect it is simply because it is easy to produce commercially. It is reliable, but I would not grow it. *AGM*. (*impeditum* hybrid). Moerheim.

■ **MOTHER GREER** Dwarf–Semi-dwarf H5 M. Flowers funnel-shaped, lilac, in clusters. Compact, with small leaves. Rather prone to disease but flowers are good and somewhat frost-resistant. (*hippophaeoides* hybrid). Greer.

■ **MOYLES' LEONARDO (syn. LEONARDO)** Semi-dwarf H3? M? Flowers pure pink in rounded clusters. Dwarf and mounding with a spreading habit. Should be very heat tolerant for a dwarf. Good in sun. Promising for N. California. (*minus* var. *chapmanii* × *tephropeplum*). Moyles.

■ **MULTIFLORUM** Low H2–3 E–EM. Flowers blush pink in trusses of 2–3 from axillary buds. Olive-green obovate leaves. A rather tender dwarf-hybrid suited to mild climates. (*ciliatum* × *virgatum*). Davies.

■ **NIGHT EDITOR** Low H4–5 E. Flower dark purple with light reddish-purple throat, dark violet spots and light reddish-purple lines, in a ball-shaped truss of 6–7. Leaves elliptic, glossy, mostly yellow-green, on an upright, dense grower. *PD*. (*russatum* seedling). unknown/Sheedy.

■ **NIGHT SKY** Semi-dwarf H5 EM–M. Flowers deep violet-blue, paler in throat, in trusses of about 5. Leaves small green, not turning colour in winter. A neat but vigorous, compact bush with good foliage. Later than most similar 'blues'. (Blue Steel × Russautini Gp.). Russell.

NIGHT SKY

■ **OBAN** Dwarf H4–5 M. Flowers funnel-shaped, strong purplish red in bud, opening deep to strong purplish pink throughout, spotted, in loose trusses of 2–4. Small thin pale green leaves on a very dwarf plant best in full sun, as it dislikes damp winter foliage. Not very easy to grow well but quite a number of nurseries still list it. We have stopped growing it. (Grouse × *keiskei* Yaku Fairy). Cox.

■ **OCEANLAKE** Semi-dwarf H4–5 EM. Flower saucer-shaped, deep violet-blue, in trusses of 4–6. Leaves small, medium green, reddish bronze in winter. Compact, dense habit. Can be sheared. *PA, WT*. (Blue Diamond × Sapphire). Wright.

■ **PATTY BEE** Semi-dwarf H5 EM. Flower openly funnel-shaped, light green-yellow with no markings, in lax trusses of 6. Leaves small smooth, narrowly elliptic to elliptic on a dense, spreading grower. One of the finest yellow dwarf-hybrids, not very deep coloured but with large flowers and healthy foliage. Dislikes too much fertilizer. Early flowers may need protection. *AGM, CN, FS, ME, MS, NY, OL, OP, PD, PT, SE, TC, VI, U.K*. (*keiskei* Yaku Fairy × *fletcherianum*). Berg. **'PETER BEE'** named after Peter Cox. Pale-yellow flowers. Fine foliage with narrow leaves.

PATTY BEE

■ **PENHEALE BLUE** Low H4 EM–M. Wisteria-blue, flushed spinel-red (or deep purple-blue) in compact multi-bud trusses of up to 20 flowers. Leaves turn reddish bronze in winter. One of the best hybrids of this type, with good flowers and foliage. *AGM*. (*concinnum* Pseudoyanthinum Gp. × *russatum*). Colville.

PENHEALE BLUE

■ **PIKELAND** Dwarf H4–5 EM. Flowers pale rose, fading to white, spotted deep purplish pink, 6–7 in a balled truss. Leaves small, dark green, scaly below, on a rounded plant growing as wide as tall. Highly rated by Hank Schannen and others in the New Jersey and Philadelphia areas of E. U.S.A. *GP*. (*keiskei* × *campylogynum*). Herbert.

■ **PINK DRIFT** Dwarf H5 EM. Flower funnel-shaped, magenta-pink. Leaves tiny on a slow-growing, dense, tough little plant. The colour is a rather unpleasant mauve and the plant is prone to rust and mildew. It has definitely seen its day. (*calostrotum* × *polycladum*). White.

■ **PINK MAGIC** Low H4–5 EM. Flower tubular funnel-shaped, light purplish pink with speckled brown throat, 15–16 flowers per ball-shaped truss from multiple buds. Leaves narrowly elliptic, flat, rounded, glossy, rugose, open habit, twice as wide as high. A pink version of 'Dora Amateis' but not as good. (*minus chapmanii* × *ciliatum* pink form). Kehr.

■ **PINK SNOWFLAKES** Semi-dwarf–Low H4 E. Flower openly funnel-shaped, white flushed soft pink, darker-pink spotting, in terminal clusters, about 3 flowers per bud. Leaves elliptic, glossy, medium green, with bronze new growth. Upright habit. Rust prone. Very free-flowering. *CD, SI*. (*racemosum* × *moupinense*). Scott.

■ **PINTAIL** Semi-dwarf H4 EM. Flowers brightest pink in multiple trusses from leaves, axils and terminal buds. Small medium-green leaves on a

PINTAIL

fairly compact plant with good foliage. We replaced 'Anna Baldseifen' with this hybrid, which is almost as bright in colour but less susceptible to disease. (*racemosum* × Snipe). Cox.

■ **PIPIT** Dwarf H3–4 ML. Flowers flat-faced, pink with darker markings in trusses of 2–3. Very slow and low growing, semi-deciduous. A natural hybrid from Nepal. Needs extra care. We cover it with a cloche in winter. (*lowndesii* × *lepidotum*). Cox.

PIPIT

■ **PRAECOX** Low H4–5 E–EM. Flower funnel-shaped, rosy lilac, in clusters of 2–3. Leaves thin, dark green, shiny above, pale below. A famous old early flowering hybrid that is spectacular in mild springs. The flowers are not frost hardy. Best with a good haircut after flowering to keep it compact. *AGM*. (*ciliatum* × *dauricum*). Davis.

PRAECOX

■ **PRINCESS ANNE** Semi-dwarf H4–5 EM–M. Flower campanulate, pale yellow with a faint greenish tinge in trusses of 4–10. Leaves small, bright green, bronze when young and often bronze-red in winter. Tight, compact habit. Hardy and easy, though leaves inclined to be yellowish and flowers are not very large. *AGM, NY, SO, TC*. (*hanceanum* Nanum × *keiskei*). Reuthe.

PRINCESS ANNE

■ **PTARMIGAN** Dwarf H4–5 EM. Flower funnel-shaped, pure-white with black stamens, in terminal clusters of 2–3, opening in batches over several weeks. Leaves small, dark green. Spreading and sprawling habit. The 'Snow Grouse' is one of the best early hybrids for the U.K. as it usually manages to open flowers between frosts. A bit straggly when young, filling in with age. *AGM, Nova Scotia*. (*orthocladum* var. *microleucum* × *leucaspis*). Cox.

PTARMIGAN

■ **PUNCTA g.** Low H4–5 L. Flowers small, pink in small rounded trusses. An early Victorian hybrid, useful for its late flowering. Inclined to die-off from fungal diseases. Best in full sun. I saw a whole series of different clones of this at Drumlanrig Castle in Scotland, so there are obviously several forms. (*ferrugineum* × *minus*). unknown.
'MYRTIFOLIUM' Flowers lilac-pink with red spots.
■ **PURPLE GEM** Semi-dwarf–Low H7 EM. Flower bright purplish violet, in ball-shaped trusses. Leaves aromatic, rusty olive-green, new growth greyish blue, turning bronze in winter. Dense, rounded habit. A sister of 'Ramapo' and generally not as good, and slightly less hardy. Some heat resistance. Over-planted in E. U.S.A. *MD, SC, TO, WT*. (*fastigiatum* × *minus* Carolinianum Gp.). Nearing/Hardgrove.
■ **QUAIL** Dwarf H4 EM–M. Bright-red buds open to deep reddish-pink flowers in a loose truss of 2–4. Small dark-green convex leaves on a compact, very free-flowering plant. The flowers last best in part-day shade. Almost a true, red, lepidote dwarf. (*keiskei* Yaku Fairy × *glaucophyllum*). Cox.

QUAIL

■ **QUAVER** Semi-dwarf–Low H3 E. Flower funnel-campanulate, creamy yellow with black stamens, in loose trusses of 4–6. Leaves elliptic, with hairy margins, deep-green. Dense, compact habit. Needs sharp drainage. (*leucaspis* × *sulfureum*). Rothschild.

■ **RACIL** Semi-dwarf–Low H4 EM–M. Flowers pale pink in multi-budded trusses forming large clusters. Leaves, small, dull, often sparse, on a rather open plant. Free-flowering but not all that hardy and prone to bark-split and rust. There are obviously several clones. Doubtful if worth growing these days. (*racemosum* × *ciliatum*). Holland.
■ **RADISTROTUM** Dwarf H5 M–ML. Flat-faced purple flowers. Tiny grey-green leaves on a spreading, very dwarf plant mainly grown in Continental Europe, sometimes wrongly under the name 'Radicans'. (*calostrotum* ssp. *keleticum* Radicans Gp. × *calostrotum*). Arends.
■ **RAMAPO** Semi-dwarf H7 EM. Flower light violet-purple, in clusters. Leaves bluish green, aromatic, on a fairly dense compact plant. A highly rated dwarf hybrid for cold climates. The flower colour is rather insipid, but the foliage is excellent. Heat tolerant and takes sun. Virginia and southwards it struggles. *AT, CN, FS, KK, MD, NG, PT, SE, TC, TO, WT, S. Fin.* (*fastigiatum* × *minus* Carolinianum Gp.). Nearing. **'GRAPE JAM'** same cross by Delp, darker flowers. Lots of similar sisters were named too. I doubt they'll ever touch 'Ramapo' for popularity.

RAMAPO

■ **RAZORBILL** Semi-dwarf–Low H4 EM. Flower tubular-shaped, rose-pink with variable darker-pink overtones, in upright clusters of 6–14. Leaves medium-green, crinkly, hair-fringed, scaly underneath, growing wider than tall. The most compact *R. spinuliferum* hybrid, with most attractive and unusual flowers. Sometimes hard to root. *AGM*. (*spinuliferum* × unknown). Cox.

RAZORBILL

■ **REICH'S SCHNEEWITCHEN** Semi-dwarf H6 M. Flowers creamy pink in bud, opening yellowish white, with yellow spots, in trusses of 6–9. Leaves rather thin and inclined to chlorosis, on a compact, spreading dwarf that should be one of the hardiest dwarf hybrids. Winter leaves reddish in cold climates. Worth trying in E. U.S.A. and Canada. (*minus* Carolinianum Gp. × *keiskei* Yaku Fairy). Reich.

■ **REUTHE'S PURPLE** Dwarf H4 M. Flowers bright purple-violet, rotate-campanulate, in trusses of 1–3. Small dark semi-deciduous leaves. Useful for its late flowering for a dwarf. Somewhat inclined to die-off in parts, so of limited commercial merit. (*lepidotum* × unknown). Reuthe.

REUTHE'S PURPLE

■ **RHEIN'S LUNA** Low H6 EM. Flowers funnel-shaped, light-purple margins, shading very light purple throat in ball trusses of 4–6. Leaves small, semi-glossy moderate olive-green. Rather leggy and open, best pruned every few years for best shape. An alternative to *R. augustinii* for cold areas. (*minus* Carolinianum Gp. × Russautinii Gp.). Rhein.

■ **RIK** Semi-dwarf H5 EM. Flower widely funnel-shaped, yellowish white or white flushed light pink and edged purplish pink, in a truss of 10–18. Leaves elliptic. Winter foliage and stems are red. Dense, mounding habit. (*racemosum* × *keiskei*). Yavorsky **'VINESTAR'** pale canary-yellow, spotted orange. The plant in the U.K. under this name is not correct.

■ **ROBERT SELEGER** Semi-dwarf H5 M. Flowers small, pale rose, spotted deeper, very freely produced. Leaves pale green on a very dense plant that is late flowering for a dwarf, so good for gardens with late frosts. Flowers thin textured. *Ger.* (*calostrotum* hybrid?). Hobbie.

ROBERT SELEGER

■ **ROSE ELF** Semi-dwarf H3 E. Flowers campanulate, open light pink, fading to white flushed pink, in loose clusters. Leaves small, glossy, dark green on a dense, mound-like and spreading plant. Drought resistant. Opening buds and flowers are very sensitive to frosts and it rarely flowers at Glendoick. (*racemosum* × *pemakoense*). Lancaster.

■ **ROUNDHILL** Semi-dwarf H5 E–EM. Flowers pale yellow, unmarked, in rounded clusters. A compact plant, growing wider than high. Very free-flowering. (*keiskei* × *hanceanum*). Moyles.

■ **SACKO** Semi-dwarf H5 M. Flowers deep blue-purple (campanula-violet), in rounded trusses of 4–7. Leaves small, elliptic, glossy dark green. Very tough and quite easy. Healthy foliage and compact habit. Later than most similar hybrids of this colour. (*russatum* × Moerheim). van Vliet.

■ **SAINT BREWARD** Semi-dwarf–Low H3–4 EM–M. Flower shallow-campanulate, sea-lavender-violet, darker at edges, held in tightly packed ball-shaped trusses. Leaves dark green covered with downy hairs. Upright, dense bush, wider than high. Foliage hangs downward in winter and early spring. The flowers are excellent, but it is not very hardy and the foliage can be poor. (*impeditum* × *augustinii*). Magor. **'ST TUDY'** is more or less identical.

■ **SAINT MERRYN** Semi-dwarf H4–5 EM. Flowers broadly funnel-shaped, strong-violet, in a small tight truss of 2–4. Tiny dark, pointed leaves on a dense and mounding dwarf. Flowers are a very fine colour, but plant is inclined to die off, so we have discontinued it. AGM. (Saint Tudy × *impeditum*). Harrison **'BLUE STAR'** a sister with deep purple-blue flowers. Not as good.

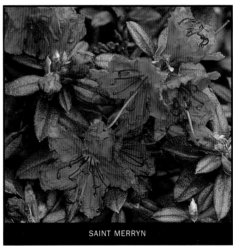
SAINT MERRYN

■ **SAPPHIRE** Semi-dwarf–Low H4–5 EM. Flower light purplish blue, in trusses of about 4. Leaves small. Less compact than most Lapponica hybrids (Blue Tit × *impeditum*). Knap Hill Nursery.

■ **SATIN SHEETS** Low H3? EM–M. Flowers silvery lavender-pink. Plant is low and spreading and needs sharp drainage. One of the few *R. tephropeplum* hybrids. (*tephropeplum* × unknown). Scott.

■ **SCHNEEFLÖCHEN** Semi-dwarf H5 M. Flowers small, white with dark stamens in multiple clusters up the stems. Tiny grey-green leaves on a somewhat straggly plant. Prone to disease and rather poor habit in Scotland. Said to be a hybrid of *R. trichostomum* but I don't believe it. I think it is probably *R. racemosum* × a white Lapponica. *Ger.* (*trichostomum* ×?? Or *racemosum* ×). Brehmer.

■ **SCOTIAN BELLS** Dwarf H5 EM. Flowers campanulate purplish pink. Small, very deep green, glossy leaves on a compact plant. This may be one of the hardiest *R. campylogynum* hybrids. (*campylogynum* Celsum Gp. × *mucronulatum* var. *taquettii* Crater's Edge). Weagle.

■ **SENORA MELDON** Low H4 EM. Flower widely funnel-shaped, pale violet-blue, in trusses of 2–5, in terminal clusters of 3–5 trusses. Leaves small, aromatic, emerald-green, new growth bronze, on a dense, rounded plant. (*augustinii* 'Lackamas Blue' × Blue Diamond). Goheen.

■ **SETA** Medium H3 E. Flower tubular-campanulate, pink with a much paler base, the reverse darker-pink, giving a striking striped effect, in trusses of about 3–5. Leaves dull, dark green. Upright rangy growth habit and subject to mildew, but it is very attractive. *Mel.* (*spinuliferum* × *moupinense*). Puddle/Aberconway.

■ **SHAMROCK** Semi-dwarf H4 E–EM. Flower yellowish green with slight strong yellow-green spotting fading to light yellow in trusses of 8–9. Leaves small elliptic, yellowish green, on a dense and spreading shrub. This is a popular commercial plant, but to my mind the flowers are pale and rather small and I don't rate it highly. It is also very early. SO. (*keiskei* dwarf form × *hanceanum*). Ticknor.

■ **SHORTY** Low H6–7 M. Flowers light purple with moderate reddish-orange spots and strong reddish-purple throat and red stamens, in trusses of 6. Low and compact. A rather shocking colour. (Epoch F2 × Hi Tech). Delp. Sister **'PIPSQUEAK'** is very pale purple.

■ **SNIPE** Semi-dwarf H3–4 M. Flower pale pinkish white shaded pale violet with maroon spots, 3–5 per loose, terminal cluster. Leaves convex, glossy, pale green on a dense, compact plant. Very free-flowering but rather bud-tender and prone to powdery mildew. Supermarkets love to sell liner-sized plants with lots of buds. (*pemakoense* × *davidsonianum*). Cox. **'PHALAROPE'** is a very similar sister seedling with slightly more purple in the flower.

■ **SNOW LADY** Semi-dwarf–Low H4 E. Flower pure white, dark brown anthers, in lax trusses of 2–5. Leaves small +/− ovate, hairy, on an upright fairly dense plant. Not as compact as 'Lucy Lou'. A fine early flowering plant for moderate areas. Gets straggly in shade. Subject to powdery mildew. NI, MT, OP, SH, VI. (*leucapsis* × *ciliatum*?). Exbury/Lancaster.

■ **SONGBIRD** Semi-dwarf–Low H4–5 EM. Flower campanulate, violet-blue, in clusters of 20. Small, glossy foliage on a dense, compact plant. Reliable autumn flowering in the U.K. OL, TC, WT. (*russatum* × Blue Tit). Horlick.

■ **SOUTHLAND** Semi-dwarf H6 M. Flower open-campanulate, light yellowish pink fading to cream flushed pink, with brown speckles in throat,

SOUTHLAND

in ball-shaped trusses of 10. Leaves small, yellow-green, elliptic. Heat and sun tolerant and free-flowering with an unusual colour for such a hardy dwarf. Sometimes suffers die-back. Not worth growing in mild climates. *PR, PT, SE.* (*minus* var. *chapmanii* × *keiskei*, prostrate form). Kehr.

■ **SPICIL** Low H4 VE–E. Flower very pale purple, with lilac on margins, in small terminal clusters. Small, oval leaves are heavy textured, dark green with red stems. Plant habit is upright and compact. If not frosted, flowers can be long-lasting. *SC.* (*scabrifolium* var. *spiciferum* × Cilpinense). Dunedin Bot. Garden.

■ **STRAWBERRY CREAM (syn. FLIP)** Low–Medium H4 M. Flowers yellowish pink, outside striped and faintly blotched deeper pink, in trusses of 5–6. Shiny, dark, oval leaves on an upright, almost fastigiate, bush. Most attractive and unusual. Has been used in further breeding. *U.K.* (*flavidum* hybrid × Lady Rosebery). Brandt. **'BARNABY SUNSET'** flowers pale yellow, pink on the reverse. **'CHARTREUSE'** probably a synonym of 'Barnaby Sunset'.

STRAWBERRY CREAM

BARNABY SUNSET

■ **SWIFT** Semi-dwarf H3–4 M. Flowers greenish yellow, strongly spotted orange-red, in trusses of about 3. Small, dark green leaves on a slow-growing, compact bush. Flowers are slightly smaller than those of 'Curlew' but a bit later flowering and more bud-hardy. (*keiskei* Yaku Fairy × *viridescens*). Cox.

■ **TEAL** Semi-dwarf–Low H4–5 M. Flower widely campanulate, clear light yellow in trusses of 5–8. Leaves narrowly elliptic, pale green on an upright but compact plant with reddish peeling bark. We have discontinued it due to rust. *MT.* (*brachyanthum* ssp. *hypolepidotum* × *fletcherianum*). Cox.

SWIFT

■ **TIFFANY** Semi-dwarf H6 EM. Flower star-shaped, semi-double, reflexed, primarily pink with mixture of apricot and yellow shading, in trusses of 3–7. Leaves lanceolate, small, on a fairly compact plant. Good in New England but less successful to the north and south. *SV.* (Anna Baldsiefen × *keiskei*). Baldsiefen.

■ **TINKERBIRD** Semi-dwarf H3–4 M. Flowers pure-white, flushed pink in bud, in a loose truss of 3–4. A real breakthrough: a compact, scented dwarf, which grows outdoors at Glendoick. Best in a sheltered site. Surprisingly bud hardy. Also good as a pot plant. (*ciliatum* BLM 324 × *edgeworthii* (hardiest form)). Cox. **'COWBELL'** is an earlier version of this cross, which is less hardy and less bud hardy.

TINKERBIRD

■ **TOW HEAD** Dwarf H6 EM. Flower rotate-campanulate, white flushed pale greenish yellow with orange-yellow spots, in trusses of up to 5. Leaves small, elliptic, glossy, scaly. Probably the hardiest hybrid of *R. ludlowii*. Not very heat tolerant. *CT, ST.* (*minus* Carolinianum Gp., white form × *ludlowii*). Leach.

TOW HEAD

■ **TREE CREEPER** Dwarf H4 EM–M. Pink buds opening to flowers pink on outside, cream inside, giving a two-tone effect, in trusses of 2–4. Dense and compact habit. Very free-flowering. Flowers last best in part-day shade. A sister of 'Quail' with a very different flower colour. (*keiskei* 'Yaku Fairy' × *glaucophyllum*). Cox.

TREE CREEPER

■ **VEESPRITE** Semi-dwarf H5 EM. Flowers small, Persian rose, in terminal clusters of 3–5. Small leaves on a twiggy grower. Good on Long Island. (*impeditum* × *racemosum*). Forster.

■ **VIBRANT VIOLET** Semi-dwarf–Low H4 E–EM. Flower widely funnel-shaped, vivid violet with brownish-orange anthers, in terminal clusters composed of 4–5 trusses each with 5–6 flowers. Leaves near elliptic to wider than lanceolate, concave, small, dull, dark yellowish green, on a round, well-branched shrub. *CD, PC, SL.* (*impeditum* × *augustinii*). Fujioka.

■ **WACHTUNG** Semi-dwarf H4–5 EM. Flowers small, lavender-blue. Tiny green leaves on a very compact plant. A witch's broom-type sport of the well known 'Ramapo'. Yavorsky.

■ **WAGTAIL** Semi-dwarf H3–4 M. Flowers small, yellow, strongly spotted red, 1–3 per truss. Small thin-textured leaves. Semi-deciduous and so can look poor in winter. Much easier to grow than *R. lowndesii* but we have ceased growing it, as it is rather susceptible to rust. (*lowndesii* × *keiskei* 'Yaku Fairy'). Cox.

■ **WALTHAM** Semi-dwarf H7 M. Flower small, tubular funnel-shaped, wavy edges, purplish pink, in dome-shaped trusses of 8. Leaves elliptic, dark green, on a compact plant. Prone to leaf spot unless grown in shade. (Laetevirens × *minus* Carolinianum Gp.). Ticknor.

■ **WEE BEE** Dwarf H3 EM. Flower openly funnel-shaped, pale pink inside, deeper pink outside with red rays down each lobe, in lax trusses of 3–5. Very free-flowering. Leaves elliptic, flat, on a very dense, compact plant. This fine dwarf is rightly one

WEE BEE

of the world's best selling dwarf hybrids. *AGM, OP, SH.* (campylogynum Charopoeum Gp. × *keiskei* Yaku Fairy). Berg. **'TOO BEE'** is a sister seedling with smaller darker flowers, not so free flowering.

■ **WESTON'S MAYFLOWER** Low H5–6 M. Flowers deep purplish pink, in domed trusses of about 7. Compact, slow-growing, forming a mound wider than tall. (Laetevirens × *minus* Carolinianum Gp. × *minus* Carolinianum Gp. × Myrtifolium). Mezitt.

WESTON'S MAYFLOWER

■ **WHEATEAR** Semi-dwarf H4 E–EM. Flowers tubular funnel-shaped, light pink striped with pale greenish yellow, fading to white, in trusses of 3–7, in multiple bud-clusters. Small leaves on a spreading, vigorous plant, with bronzy new growth. (keiskei Yaku Fairy × spinuliferum). Cox. **'WAXBILL'** is a sister with pale pink flowers. The flowers of both these hybrids are striking and they are more compact and hardier than most *R. spinuliferum* hybrids.

WHEATEAR AND WAXBILL

■ **WIGEON** Semi-dwarf H5 M. Flowers light purple-pink flushed rose, with red spotting on upper lobes, short red stamens, in trusses of about 5. Leaves greyish green, new growth silvery. One of the hardiest Glendoick dwarfs. Good in coastal New England. Prone to mildew in some climates. (*minus* Carolinianum Gp. × calostrotum 'Gigha'). Cox.

WIGEON

■ **WILSONI (syn. LAETEVIRENS)** Low H6 M. Flowers small, rose-pink, tubular, in small tight trusses of about 12. Small dark green slender leaves on a well-branched, sun-tolerant plant. Rather brittle and inclined to fall off its roots. Useful for its hardiness and sun and wind tolerance but not all that free-flowering. Susceptible to gall fungus. *S. Fin.* (*minus* Carolinianum Gp. × ferrugineum). unknown.

WYANOKIE

■ **WINDBEAM** Medium H8 EM. Flowers pale pink, fading to off-white, spotted red, in small trusses of about 8. Several clones exist with deeper or paler flowers. Leaves pale green, aromatic. Willowy and rather straggly habit. Tough, sun tolerant, heat tolerant and easy. Not worth growing in mild climates. Very widely grown in Eastern North America. *AZ, BH, CC, CH, GP, MD, ME, NG, PT, PV, SE, SV, TO, TZ.* (Conestoga × unknown). Nearing. **'WINDBEAM 2'** is more compact. **'WYANOKIE'** also more compact with paler flowers.

WREN

■ **WREN** Semi-dwarf H4 M. Flowers clear yellow, with red spotting, in small tight trusses of 3–5. Leaves small, dark green, glossy, recurved, turning bronze in winter. Prostrate habit and slow growing. Branchlets are rather brittle. The most successful Cox yellow in E. North America. *SO.* (ludlowii × keiskei 'Yaku Fairy'). Cox.

YAKU FAIRY (KEISKEI)

■ **YAKU FAIRY (KEISKEI)** Semi-dwarf H5 EM. Flowers pale greenish yellow, 2–5 per truss. Very slow-growing and prostrate habit. An excellent parent of dwarf hybrids such as 'Ginny Gee', 'Crane' and 'Wren'. Needs to be grown with winter sun in Scotland or it goes black. Covers itself with flowers. (keiskei var. *ozawae* selection). Starling.

YELLOW DANE

■ **YELLOW DANE** Dwarf H5 EM. Bright yellow flowers in small tight trusses of about 3. Tiny dark green leaves on a compact, twiggy plant. The flowers are a good colour. Susceptible to rust and mildew in mild climates. *Den.* (rupicola var. *muliense* × hanceanum Nanum Gp.). Kristensen.

■ **YELLOW EYES** Semi-dwarf–Low H6 EM. Flower broadly funnel-shaped, pure-white with prominent spotting of greenish yellow, in dome-shaped trusses of 8–9. Leaves elliptic, dull green, densely scaly, turning bronze in winter. *PT, SE.* (Wyanokie × unknown). Fitzburgh.

■ **YELLOW HAMMER** Medium H4–5 E. Flowers small, tubular-campanulate, bright yellow, terminal and in the leaf axils, up and down the branches. Tiny dark green leaves on upright grower. Prune after flowering for best habit. Often flowers in autumn too. Needs good drainage. A good cut-flower. *AGM.* (*sulfureum* × *flavidum*). Williams.

YELLOW HAMMER

SECTION VIREYA: SPECIES AND HYBRIDS

Vireya rhododendrons are found on mountains in Indonesia, Papua New Guinea, Malaysia, the Philippines and other parts of S.E. Asia, with one (or two) species in Northern Australia. Unless you live in an area where frosts are almost unknown, such as favourable parts of North Island, New Zealand, parts of Australia, California or Hawaii, you will have to grow these plants indoors in a more or less frost-free greenhouse or conservatory. For sheer flamboyance with brightest yellows, oranges and reds, not to mention multicoloured flowers, the Vireyas have few equals. In the wild, Vireyas can reach 5m or more, but in cultivation such large plants are seldom seen. Larger growers will reach 2m or more, while some of the smaller growers scarcely reach 30cm. As they come from near the equator, Vireyas tend not to respond to seasons and can, therefore, flower or grow at any time of year. There are several hundred species and many hybrids to choose from. In areas where they can be grown outdoors, you may be able to find Vireyas at your local garden centre. In colder regions, they are only available from specialist nurseries.

The four essential steps to successful Vireya Culture
■ **Keep them frost-free.** Some high-altitude Vireyas can take a degree or two of freezing, but it is safer to keep them frost-free. If you live in a very mild climate you can grow them outdoors year round and they can, therefore, be planted in the garden. For everyone else, they need to be indoors during colder parts of the year and so, usually, they are grown in containers.

■ **Sharp drainage.** Compost with very sharp drainage is essential: more Vireyas fail through soggy roots than probably any other cause. Most Vireya experts have their own pet compost-formula, but you won't go far wrong with a mixture of 15–25 per cent peat, with the rest a mixture of coarse bark and coarse perlite. If the peat is fine, then reduce the quantity and add more of the other two ingredients. We add slow-release fertilizer to the mix but you can equally well liquid-feed. Chelated iron is a good addition if the leaves turn chlorotic. Don't overdo the feeding: it soon burns the leaf tips and can be fatal. Little and often is the safest way. Vireyas live in trees or on steep banks and cliffs and they like to have a restricted root-run. They hate being over-potted and they often die of it, so move up a single pot-size at a time. Don't be afraid to repot a plant with a small root-system back into the same container, perhaps with some new compost. Water your plants and then let them dry out a bit between waterings, but not to wilting stage. Californian water has been detrimental to Vireya culture due to the disinfectant Chloramine. You may need to filter water if this is a problem.

■ **Heat and Light.** Vireyas need plenty of light and a cool, humid atmosphere, so they are not suitable as houseplants in centrally heated houses. Greenhouses and conservatories are best. Indoors, you can grow Vireyas in beds, usually raised beds. The peat house at the Royal Botanic Garden, Edinburgh is a good example. But containers are more common: the advantage being that that they can be moved outdoors in summer, where they require less looking after. A number of species and hybrids are suitable for hanging baskets: examples include *R. lochae, R. christii*, 'Charming Valentino' and 'St Valentine'. In borderline climates where there is some frost, you can use a lathe house for a few degrees of frost protection. The one at Pukeiti, New Zealand is a good example. If you keep your plants indoors all year, don't let the pots heat up in the sun: it encourages root fungal-disease, which can be fatal. Indoors, good ventilation is essential; if you can't keep your greenhouse cool, better to put the plants outside. They also require a humid atmosphere, which discourages leaf-tip burn and other foliage problems. Those of us who grow Vireyas in cold climates, far from the equator, struggle to give them enough light in winter. At the Royal Botanic garden in Edinburgh and at Glendoick we use sodium lights to extend the day length in midwinter. Conversely, in regions nearer the equator, it is shade that is needed. Bill Moynier recommends eastern and northern exposure for southern California, to avoid the heat of midday and afternoon.

■ **Pruning and maintenance.** Many Vireyas are naturally straggly and they benefit from regular pinching and pruning to attain the best habit. Pinching a single growth-bud as it elongates usually results in several side-shoots breaking from below. Where flower buds are formed, the growth buds will automatically break from below. Vireyas can suffer from insect pests, such as aphids and vine weevil, and they have their own strain of mildew. These can be controlled in the same way as I advise for non-Vireya rhododendrons (*see* pages 22–8).

VIREYA SPECIES

This is just a selection of the best and most widely grown of over 300 Vireya species. The sizes that these plants attain in the wild far exceed what is normally seen in cultivation, when a 2m by 2m plant would be considered large. The smaller and compact varieties range from less than 30cm to 1m in height.

■ **ACROPHILUM** Flowers orange-yellow, about 3 per truss. Small leaves on a compact plant. Recently introduced, and likely to become one of the most popular species with great potential as a parent. One of my favourite Vireya species.

■ **AEQUABILE** Flowers campanulate, orange, 2–12 per truss. Leaves elliptic, densely scaly. Young growth brown. Compact and easy but slow-growing.

AEQUABILE

■ **APOANUM** Flowers orange-red, small but freely produced. Leaves small, bluish green, on a fairly compact plant. Recently introduced.

■ **ARMITII** Flowers trumpet-shaped, white tinged pink, well-scented, 3–7 per truss. Leaves green, with brown scales on underside. There are many species with tubular white flowers. Some of these include: **TUBA**, white, hanging flowers, **MAIUS** white, strong scent, **LORANTHIFLORUM** white, lightly scented, **LURALUENSE** small, white, unscented flowers.

■ **AURIGERANUM** Flowers funnel-shaped, bright yellow, sometimes flushed orange in a truss of 8–14. Leaves green, thin. Very spectacular and needs plenty of room. Quite easy.

■ **BLACKII** Flowers tubular funnel-shaped, pendulous, bright red, in trusses of 3–7. Almost round, thick leaves with very short leaf petioles or leaf stalks. Slow to bloom when young.

■ **BROOKEANUM** Flowers funnel-shaped, pale-yellow, orange or red, sometimes bicoloured, in a truss of 3–12. '**MANDARIN**' bicolour: yellow and orange. Leaves medium to large, +/– elliptic. The bicoloured forms are the most popular.

■ **BURTII** Flowers cylindrical with a straight tube, small, red, in pendulous trusses of 1–2. Small leaves and twiggy compact habit. Repeat flowering up to six times a year.

■ **CARRINGTONIAE** Flowers trumpet-shaped, white, fragrant, 3–9 to a truss. Leaves obovate to elliptic. One of the fine, fragrant, white-flowered species, fairly easy to please but takes a number of years to flower.

■ **CHRISTI** (*see* photo overleaf) Flowers cylindrical, bicolour, with yellow tube and red-orange lobes, very striking, in a truss of 1–4. Leaves distinctive: ovate with a long, pointed tip, on a compact and good-natured plant. One of the finest species for flowers and foliage.

CHRISTI

JASMINIFLORUM

LAETUM

■ **CHRISTIANAE** Flowers small, orange lobes and yellow tube, in loose or hanging trusses of 2–7. Fairly compact with smallish leaves. Used in hybridizing.

■ **COMMONAE** Flowers cream, pink or red, tubular-campanulate, 3–8 per truss. Small, thick oval leaves on a small upright-growing plant. One of the hardiest Vireya species, it can take a little frost.

■ **CRUTTWELLII** Flowers trumpet-shaped, white, in erect or semi-erect trusses of 4–9. A vigorous, well-branched plant with obovate leaves. Named after Rev. Norman Cruttwell, a missionary in New Guinea who collected Vireyas.

■ **DIELSIANUM** Flowers tubular, curved, pink, in trusses of 2–4. Leaves +/− elliptic. An easy and free-flowering species. Best-doer list from Hawaii chapter ARS.

■ **GOODENOUGHII** Flowers tubular-flared, white, up to 10 per truss. Leaves large and rounded. Medium-sided to 1–2m. Flowers at first have a distinctive collar of bud scales. What a great name.

■ **GRACILENTUM** Flowers small, cylindrical to narrowly funnel-shaped, hanging, red or deep pink, singly or in pairs. Tiny pointed deep green leaves on a very dwarf, bushy, slow-growing plant.

■ **HELLWIGII** Flowers tubular funnel-shaped, dark red, of thick texture, velvety, 2–5 per truss. Leaves almost round, covered with dark scales when young. Slow to bud-up as a young plant. Can grow quite tall.

■ **HERZOGII** Flowers white, tubular, beautifully scented, 5–15 per truss. Leaves grey-green, aromatic. × **INUNDATUM** is very similar.

■ **HIMANTODES** Small saucer-shaped white flowers covered in dark scales in a truss of 8–10. Very dark, narrow, pointed leaves. The unusual flowers and foliage never fail to attract comment. Not all that easy to grow.

HIMANTODES

■ **JASMINIFLORUM** Flowers tubular, scented, white or palest pink in a truss of 3–20. Leaves elliptic, scaly. One of the best of the white, scented species.

■ **JAVANICUM** Flowers orange in a usually rounded truss of 4–12. Dark-green glossy leaves. Good habit. One of the finest species, free-flowering and of good habit.

JAVANICUM

■ **KONORI** Large white funnel-shaped flowers of heavy substance, fragrant, in a truss of 3–20. Large, dark, scaly leaves, thick branches and tall habit. Takes a few years to start to flower.

KONORI

■ **LAETUM** Flowers deep-yellow in trusses of 5–9. Habit is rather rangy but can be controlled with pinching and pruning. One of the finest yellow species in flower.

■ **LAMRIALIANUM** Flowers tubular, bicolour, yellow and orange. Relatively large leaves for the flower size. Striking.

■ **LEUCOGIGAS** Flowers deep-pink to white, often marked deeper pink, in trusses of 5–8. Leaves +/− elliptic to 30cm. Large and slow-growing, spectacular in flower. Much used as a parent. **'HUNSTAN'S SECRET'** is a fine white clone.

■ **LOCHIAE or VIRIOSUM** Deep red to deep pink, loose to pendulous flowers, 2–7 per truss. Quite slow-growing and compact. The one native Vireya species in Australia has suddenly been split into two. What was considered *R. lochiae* is now *R. viriosum*. And some similar entity is now *R. viriosum*. The two look almost identical and it looks like taxonomic hair-splitting to me.

LOCHIAE

■ **MACGREGORIAE** Flowers pale- to deep-yellow, orange, pink or red, small, but in usually full rounded trusses of 7–15. Small leaves on a compact manageable plant. One of the easiest species to grow. **'SCOTCHBURN WHITE'** is white form or natural hybrid of this species.

MACGREGORIAE

NERVULOSUM

RUGOSUM

STENOPHYLLUM

■ **NERVULOSUM** Flowers small, orange-red, 1–6 per truss. Distinctive dark green, very narrow leaves. This is probably the easiest to cultivate of the narrow-leaved species. Quite easy. It may be a natural hybrid.

■ **ORBICULATUM** Flowers tubular with wide, open, large lobes, pale pink, fragrant, in trusses of 2–6. Leaves light green, broadly obovate to sub-circular, on a spreading plant. **'HIGHLAND ARABESQUE'** is a hybrid of this species with tubular pale-pink, scented flowers and oval leaves. **SUAVEOLENS** is a closely related species, with tubular, scented, white flowers.

■ **PHAEOCHITON** Flowers tubular, cream, pink, red (or rarely yellow), hanging, 2–5 per truss. Leaves and stems covered with red-brown scales, on a fairly compact plant.

■ **POLYANTHEMUM** Flowers narrowly funnel-shaped, bright orange or pinkish orange, 25–30 per truss. Quite a large grower with silvery to brown young growth. Unusually for a deeply coloured flower, this is strongly scented.

■ **PRAETERVISUM** Flowers cylindrical, pink or pinkish violet, hanging down, in loose trusses of 3–7. The longest pendent flowers of any Vireya species make this easily distinguished. Quite easy to grow.

■ **RETIVENIUM** Flowers bright clear-yellow, or yellow flushed orange, usually scented, 4–7 per truss. A rather straggly grower that needs pruning.

■ **RETUSUM** Flowers red, 2–10 per truss. Small dark green leaves to 4cm. Compact and slow-growing, hardly spectacular but attractive.

■ **ROUSIAE** Flowers pure white, 3–4 per truss. Slow-growing and compact. This is one of the finest dwarf species; it is certain to become very popular and should also make a good parent.

■ **RUBINEIFLORUM** Flowers campanulate, red, solitary. Tiny leaves with relatively large flowers, on a spreading grower to 10cm. **SAXAFRAGOIDES** is another tiny cushion-forming species to 20cm with red to pink, usually solitary, flowers.

■ **RUGOSUM** Flowers pink to purplish pink, hanging, in a truss of 8–14. Handsome dark rugose leaves covered with brown scales. Can grow very large in the wild, but usually low and compact in cultivation. Flowers can be rather harsh-coloured.

■ **STENOPHYLLUM** Flowers orange, turning red with age, 1–5 per truss. Very narrow dark green pointed leaves. Fairly easy to cultivate and very striking.

■ **SUPERBUM** Flowers large, strongly scented pink, cream or white in a truss of 3–5. Leaves to 12cm, +/– elliptic, young growth covered with brown scales. Quite tall and vigorous and takes a few years to flower.

■ **TAXIFOLIUM** Flowers open-faced, white, in trusses of about 3. Tiny, very narrow leaves, which look like conifer needles. Very rare, nearly extinct in the wild. Very distinctive and relatively easy to grow.

■ **WOMERSLEYI** Flowers pendulous, red, in trusses of 1–3. Leaves small (to 1cm), on a plant of erect or arching habit that can be rather straggly. Flowers produced all year round.

■ **WRIGHTIANUM** Flowers deep red (almost black-red), hanging, in trusses of 2–3. Leaves small, dark green, on a small, bushy, upright plant.

■ **ZOELLERI** Flowers funnel-shaped, bicolour yellow and orange, in trusses of 4–8. A vigorous, upright plant very popular with hybridizers with its large and spectacular flowers.

ZOELLERI

SUBSECTION PSEUDOVIREYA

Height to 1.5m, compact to spreading, usually epiphytic shrubs. Flowers small, yellow, lilac-pink to white, waxy. These species are hardier than the rest of the Vireyas and most can be grown outdoors in milder parts of Britain. As they are epiphytic, they are best grown outdoors on mossy rocks and logs and in very well-drained planting medium indoors. All are rare in cultivation.

■ **EUONYMIFOLIUM** Dwarf H1–2 EM–ML. Flowers campanulate, small (about 1cm long), 1–2 per truss. Tiny dark green leaves. Flowers are a good colour but are small and often held singly, so it cannot be said to be spectacular. **SORORIUM** is virtually identical and may be synonymous. **ASPERULUM** another similar species with small, single, deep-yellow flowers and spatulate leaves.

■ **KAWAKAMII** Dwarf–Semi-dwarf H2–3 L–VL. Flowers small, clear bright-yellow, in late summer, in trusses of 4–7. Leathery evergreen leaves. Best on mossy rock, tree-stump or raised bed. Hardy outdoors in milder parts of S. and W. Britain and similar climates.

ROUSIAE

TAXIFOLIUM

KAWAKAMII

RUSHFORTHII

ASUTASAN

■ **RUSHFORTHII** Low H2–3 ML–L. Flowers deep-yellow, in trusses of 3–8. Leaves small, grey-blue-green. Said to be hardy to –8°C (18°F), so it should be suitable outdoors in mildest part of U.K. and Pacific Northwest, U.S.A.

■ **SANTAPAUI** Dwarf H1 VL. Flowers campanulate, small, white, 1–4 per truss. Small dark green leaves. Very compact. Discovered by my parents, Peter and Patricia Cox, in 1965, in India. The least hardy of this subsection.

SANTPAUI

■ **VACCINIOIDES** Dwarf H1–2 VL. Flowers campanulate, white tinged pink in trusses of 2–4. Tiny dark green leaves on a fairly compact, spreading plant, not all that easy to cultivate. Very late flowering, but not very floriferous. It does look very like a small vaccineum. A curiosity.

VIREYA HYBRIDS

■ **ALEKSANDR (syn. ALEKSANDR ISIAHAVITCH)** Flowers large, scented, pink with creamy yellow throat. Medium grower to 1.5m.
■ **ALISA NICOLE** Flowers shortly funnel-shaped, deep purplish pink, 2–3 per truss. Compact to 30cm. Usually summer flowering. Snell.
■ **ANATTA GOLD** Flowers deep yellow with brown throat, 7–8 per truss. Good sun tolerance. A fairly compact plant to 1.5m. Schick/Snell.
■ **ARAVIR** Flowers very narrowly tubular funnel-shaped, pure white; strongly scented, 7–10 per rounded truss. Leaves elliptic, flat, scaly on the underside. Repeat flowering. Good for hanging baskets. Sullivan **'FELICITAS'** is very similar.
■ **ARTHUR'S CHOICE** Flowers deep yellowish pink, shading to vivid reddish orange, 6–7 per loose truss. Low and spreading to 1m. Good for hanging baskets. Clancy.

■ **ASUTASAN** Flowers deep-orange/red in a domed truss. Compact, with pointed leaves, to 1.5m. Snell.
■ **BEEJAY BAY** Flowers large, deep-orange with a yellow throat, 8–10 per truss. Vigorous, moderately upright in growth, to 2m. Snell. **'FANTASIA'** Vivid orange-and-yellow bicolour. Both are hybrids of *R. baenitzianum*.
■ **BELLENDEN CORAL** Flowers tubular-campanulate, coral-pink, scented, in trusses of 9–12. Leaves broadly ovate, on a vigorous grower to 1.2m. Cullinane.
■ **BLAZE OF GLORY** Flowers medium sized, flared, brilliant red, with a cream centre, 5–8 per truss. A compact bush to 1.5m. Snell.

BLAZE OF GLORY

■ **BRIGHTLY** Flowers Dutch vermilion (deep orange-red), 6–7 per truss. Foliage is deep-green and glossy. Shade tolerant. Buds-up young and repeat flowering. Moderately compact to about 1m. A striking colour. Blumhardt.

BRIGHTLY

■ **CALAVAR** Flowers deep-pink at tips, throat light yellow, outside light yellow-green, carnation-scented, in a flat or slightly conical truss of 5–7. Open habit. Free-flowering. Lelliott.
■ **CAMEO SPICE** Flowers trumpet-shaped, carrot-red, shading to Spanish-orange, with pink lobes, carnation-scented, in trusses of 4–8. Leaves elliptic, densely scaly, large, on a large vigorous, open shrub to 1.5m. Repeat flowering. Lelliott/Blumhardt.
■ **CAPE COD CRANBERRY** Flowers narrowly tubular funnel-shaped, strong-red throughout; strongly carnation-scented, in a flat truss of 5–8. Habit bushy and robust. Chaikin.
■ **CAPE COD SUNSHINE** Flowers tubular funnel-shaped, brilliant yellow shading to light greenish yellow aging to orange-yellow in a lax-to-domed truss of 8–15. Leaves elliptic to narrowly obovate on a plant of upright, open habit. An impressive yellow with good trusses. Hunnewell/Chaikin. **'YELLOW BALL'** is similar.
■ **CARILLION BELLS** Flowers deep purplish pink with a light yellowish-pink throat, 2–3 per truss. Low and compact to 60cm. Repeat flowering and one of the best dwarf choices. Withers/Snell.
■ **CHARMING VALENTINO** Flowers deep-pink to red, 3–4 per truss. A bushy plant suitable for containers or hanging baskets. Similar to 'St Valentine' with paler flowers but larger flowers and greater vigour than its parent, though not as free flowering as a young plant. Schick/Snell.
■ **CHERRY LIQUOR** Flowers cherry-red with a cream centre, with a fine scent. Upright to 2m, and quite straggly, best with some pruning. Buds up well. Snell.
■ **CORAL FLARE** Flowers tubular funnel-shaped, salmon-pink with deeper rims, in a truss of 3–7. Low spreading habit to 1.2m. Long-flowering in summer. Snell.
■ **CORAL SEAS** Flowers funnel-shaped, tubular; lobes strong-orange suffused pink, inside throat and tube yellow, 6–9 per flat truss. Leaves ovate, on a medium-sized, fast-growing, upright, dense bush. Saperstein.

CORAL SEAS

■ **CRAIG FARAGHER** Flowers tubular, strong-pink, with pale purplish pink, 6–8 per truss. Compact to 60cm. Flowers on and off all year, in some climates it seems to flower continuously. Faragher.
■ **CRISTO REY** Flowers tubular funnel-shaped, vivid-orange, gradually shading to brilliant orange-yellow in throat, 6–8 in a domed truss. Leaves elliptic, dark yellowish green. Blooms twelve months of the year in S. California. Sullivan.

CRAIG FARAGHER

FAIRY DANCER

GWENEVERE

■ **DEEP HEAT** Flowers glowing shades of vermilion, 5–8 per truss. Compact and bushy to 1m or more. Snell.

■ **DONVALE PINK** Flowers tubular funnel-shaped, white fading to pink, opening moderate purplish pink with thin, white stripes on outside, scented, in a truss of 7–11. Leaves lanceolate, margins decurved, glossy green. Ht to 1.5m. Rouse/Shannassay.

■ **DR HERMAN SLEUMER** Flowers tubular, with flaring lobes, red-pink, fading to creamy white to green in the throat, outside creamy white, carnation scented, in trusses of about 6. Leaves large, scaly on a fairly tidy plant to 1m. A natural hybrid named after the pioneer of Vireya taxonomy. Lelliott.

DR HERMAN SLEUMER

■ **DRESDEN DOLL** Flowers large, apricot-pink-cream, 8–10 per truss. Leaves often edged red. Compact upright habit. Best in some shade outdoors. Not always easy to grow. Rouse/Snell.

■ **ELIZABETH ANN SETON** Flowers narrow tubular funnel-shaped, very light pink throat, flushed and rayed deeper, with contrasting red stamens, 12–16 per truss. Leaves elliptic, glossy, dark green above with red buds, veins and midrib, on a compact, bushy plant. Sullivan.

■ **FAIRY DANCER** Flowers small, very widely funnel-shaped, deep yellowish pink in trusses of 3–5. Small leaves on a dwarf and compact plant. Repeat flowering over a long period. A bit tricky, but very fine at Glendoick. Cullinane.

■ **FANCIFUL** Pink and yellow, lightly scented flowers in a domed truss. Habit bushy, to 1.5m. This and those which follow are hybrids of 'Gardenia Odyssey'. Snell: **'GOLD BULLION'** yellow,

with an apricot blush. **'HIGHLAND PEACE'** lemon, edged pink, scented. **'LEMON SPICE'** large lemon-yellow. **'NEESA'** pastel-primrose, scented. **'ZIRCON'** pure yellow.

■ **FELINDA** Flowers pale purplish pink with deep-pink rays, tending to reflex with age, 7–8 per domed truss. Deep-green leaves on a plant to 60cm. Moynier.

■ **FIREPLUM** Flowers deep-red with a paler throat. Leaves shiny, on a fairly compact plant. Free-flowering. Sullivan/Withers/Snell.

■ **FIRST LIGHT** Soft pastel-pink flowers with light fragrance, in a truss of 10–16. Shiny leaves. Repeat flowering at various times of year, with peak early in winter. To 1.5m. Lelliott.

■ **FLAMENCO DANCER** Flowers pale yellow to gold, suffused apricot in fine trusses, usually in winter. Leaves elliptic, dark green, on a vigorous plant that is taller than most hybrids. Lelliott **'BUTTERMAID'** is very similar with deeper-yellow flowers. **'THAI GOLD'** butter-yellow in rounded trusses.

■ **FLAMINGO BAY** Flowers reddish orange, shading to yellowish pink, edged deeper, lightly fragrant, in a domed truss of 4–8. Leaves elliptic, semi-glossy and moderate olive-green. A trailing habit, good for hanging baskets. Ht to 60cm. Jensen.

■ **GEORGE BUDGEN** Flowers tubular funnel-shaped, Indian-yellow shading to marigold-orange, 5–6 per flat truss. Upright and tall growing. Free flowering. A good doer in the Bay area of California. More compact than sister 'Simbu Sunset'. Lelliot/Sullivan.

■ **GILDED SUNRISE** Flowers funnel-shaped, lemon-yellow, suffused apricot, in a truss of 7–8. Leaves elliptic, on an open, vigorous shrub to 2m+. Reliable and sun tolerant. Lelliott/Perrott.

■ **GREAT SCENT-SATION.** Flowers deep-pink, fading to light pink in the throat, scented, 5–8 per truss. Leaves rough. Fairly compact, spreading to 1m by 1m. Withers/Snell.

■ **GWENEVERE** Trumpet-shaped very fragrant flowers, white lobes tinged pink in the tube, with contrasting pink stamens. Large rounded leaves. Summer flowering. Very highly rated. Snell.

■ **HALOED GOLD** Flower greenish when first open, turning yellow, edged with a thin band of orange-red. Vigorous and upright to 2m. Sun tolerant. Blumhardt.

■ **HARRY WU** Flowers broadly funnel-shaped, light orange-yellow tube and strong yellowish-pink lobes, outside yellowish pink and yellow, in a flat truss of 6. Leaves elliptic, margins decurved. Voted one of the best Vireya hybrids, Hawaii. Named after a Chinese dissident. Sullivan.

■ **HIGHLAND WHITE JADE** Flowers creamy white, with a touch of green at the base of the tube, sweetly scented, 5–8+ per loose truss. Compact, and bushy plant to 1.5m. Rouse/Snell.

■ **HOT GOSSIP** Flowers pale red, aging to claret-red, 6–8 per truss. Leaves oblanceolate. Compact with good foliage. Ht to 1m. Jury.

■ **INFERNO** Flowers campanulate, hanging, orange-red fading to yellow throat, 6–8 per truss. Leaves veined. Habit narrowly upright. Free-flowering. Blumhardt.

■ **JAVA LIGHT** Flowers capsicum-red, shading to orange in the throat, about 10 per truss. Vigorous and straggly habit. Often flowers twice a year with one flowering in midwinter. Sun and heat resistant. Stanton. **'JAVA ROSE'** flowers deep orange-red, double. Best Vireya hybrid list from Hawaii. One of the few double Vireyas. **'NIUGINI FIREBIRD'** orange, tinged red.

■ **JENZELLE** Flower large, tubular-funnel shaped, white to blush-pink, scented. Leaves large on an open, spreading bush to 1m by 2m. Snell. **'PEARLY WHITE'** pure-white, strongly scented tubular flowers. Dark foliage.

■ **JOCK'S CAIRN** Flowers narrow tubular-funnel-shaped, strong-red with a vibrant-pink throat in trusses of 10–14. Vigorous to about 1.3m. On the 'best Vireya hybrids list' from Hawaii. A good choice for a container. Sullivan.

■ **JUST PEACHY** Flowers soft apricot-peach, 10–12 per truss. Compact, spreading, almost prostrate habit, good for hanging baskets. In some climates it flowers all year round. There is also a Delp elepidote under this name, so this may have to be re-named.

JUST PEACHY

KIANDRA

MARGARET OF SCOTLAND

NE PLUS ULTRA

■ **KIANDRA** Flowers tubular funnel-shaped, vivid reddish orange, 7–14 per flat truss, in winter. Leaves lanceolate on a vigorous plant to 60cm. Clancy.

■ **KISSES** Flowers light greenish yellow, lobes deep yellowish pink. Bushy upright shrub, free flowering, to 1.2m. Blumhardt. **'LITTLE KISSES'** pink with a cream centre, smaller growing. Needs pruning when young.

KISSES

■ **LAWRENCE** Flowers open-funnel-shaped with a long narrow tube, bright-red, in a lax truss of 5–7. Leaves obovate, tinted red when young, aging to light green. Vigorous, 1.5–2m. One of the hardiest, said to survive several degrees of frost. Sullivan.

■ **LEONORE FRANCIS** Flowers, tubular funnel-shaped, bright cherry-red-pink with a cream throat, 12–14 per domed truss. Leaves elliptic, dull- and mid-green above, paler below, with tiny scales. The contrast between throat and lobes is very striking. Needs pruning. Ht 1m. Repeat flowering. Sullivan.

■ **LIBERTY BAR** Flowers tubular funnel-shaped, deep yellowish pink, 10–15 per truss. Leaves elliptic, shrub to 1.5m. Stanton/Rouse.

■ **LITTLE ONE** Flowers tubular funnel-shaped, strong yellowish pink with a deeper throat, in trusses of 2–3. Small pointed leaves. Very compact, has been used as a low hedge in Australia, sometimes rooting as it spreads. Free-flowering. Clancy.

■ **LITTLEST ANGEL** Flowers tubular-campanulate, vivid-red, 4 per truss. Leaves elliptic on a miniature with good foliage. Voted one the best Vireya hybrids, Hawaii. 40cm. Similar to 'St Valentine'. Snell.

■ **MARGARET OF SCOTLAND** Flowers funnel-shaped, reddish orange, edged deeper, throat paler, flushed reddish purple, in a balled truss of 15–20. Leaves lanceolate, flat, glossy, petioles strong purplish red. Magnificent flowers. Cullinane.

■ **MARSHAL PIERCE MADISON** Flowers tubular funnel-shaped, ruffled, strong-pink, highly scented, 14–16 per domed truss. Leaves narrowly elliptic, moderate olive-green. Very impressive, though the colour is a bit sickly sweet! Sullivan.

■ **MOONWOOD** Flowers yellowish white (ivory), with a pale yellow throat, strongly scented, in a truss of 10–12. Dark scaly leaves on a fairly compact, spreading plant to 0.6m. Repeat blooming in S. California. Moynier **'CRÈME SERENE'** honey-cream, ruffled, fragrant.

MOONWOOD

■ **MOUNT PIRE** Flowers deep orange-red with red stamens, 7–8 per conical/lax truss. Glossy dark green leaves. Rangy habit that needs pruning. Voted one of the best Vireya hybrids Hawaii. Stanton/Moynier.

■ **NARNIA** Flowers inside a yellow-orange bicolour, outside yellow, 6–11 per rounded truss. Best Vireya hybrids listing, Hawaii. Ht to 1.5m. Repeat flowering in mild climates. Moynier.

■ **NE PLUS ULTRA** Low. Flowers funnel-shaped, crimson-scarlet, 8–15 per truss. A very fine Victorian hybrid, still grown today. Best with some pruning. Veitch **'TRIUMPHANS'** is very similar and may be synonymous.

■ **ORANGE CASCADE** Flowers orange and yellow, in small trusses. Compact to 1m. Flowers 2–3 times a year. Snell.

■ **ORANGE FLAMBÉ** Flowers bright orange, 10–15 per truss. Long pointed leaves. Vigorous and rangy to 2m, but can be pruned. Snell.

■ **OUR MARCIA** Flowers long tubular funnel-shaped, tube pale yellow, lobes strong-red, fading to deep purplish pink, in trusses of 10–12. Vigorous and bushy to 1m. Rouse.

OUR MARCIA

■ **PANDASHAY** Flowers large, bicolour orange/red with yellow centres, 7–8 per truss. Tall, vigorous bushy growth, to 1.5m or more. Snell.

■ **PINK DELIGHT** Flowers tubular funnel-shaped, pink, in large trusses. Bushy and can get rather leggy if not pruned. Ht to 1.2m. A fine old nineteenth-century hybrid still popular today. Easy and flowers all year round in mild climates. Veitch.

PINK DELIGHT

■ **PRINCESS ALEXANDRA** Flowers waxy, longer in the tube than in *R. jasminiflorum*, white tinged blush, with pink stamens, fragrant, about 8 per truss. Leaves long and slender. A well-branched low bush. Veitch. **'POPCORN'** smaller flowers creamy white in packed trusses of 10–14.

■ **QUEENSLAND** Flowers large, fragrant, deep rich-pink. A selection from the Super Nova Group.

■ **RASPBERRY CORDIAL** Flowers small, raspberry-red, 6–8 per loose truss. Leaves dark green, linear/narrow, on a compact plant. The plant looks like the hardy *R. roxieanum*. **'CORDIAL ORANGE'** orange and red, narrow leaves.

■ **RED ROVER** Flowers coral-pink deepening to red, 10–12 per truss. Spreading habit. Summer flowering, sometimes again in winter. Jury.

■ **RIO RITA** Flowers funnel-campanulate, pale to deeper pink with a yellowish-white tube, 8–9 per large, loose truss. Leaves ovate, flat, glossy, with rusty brown scales on young growth. Repeat flowering. Blumhardt.

■ **ROB'S FAVOURITE** Flowers tubular funnel-shaped, vermilion, 10–12 per truss. Leaves elliptic, with scattered, light brown scales. Flowers are rather small for the leaf size. Easy to grow and tolerant of sun or shade. Usually summer flowering. Blumhardt.

■ **SAINT CECILIA** Flowers elongated tubular funnel-shaped, white, with purplish-pink markings at sinuses in a domed truss of 4–5. Leaves elliptic, large, margins decurved, glossy and dark yellowish green. Ht to about 1.2m. Sullivan.

■ **SATAN'S GIFT** Flowers large, deep-pink with yellow throat, scented, 8–10 per truss. A tall and leggy grower to 1.8m. A great name! Jury.

■ **SAXON GLOW (PBR)** Flowers light red to pink, held up on long pedicels. A neat and compact plant that repeat-flowers. Patented and becoming available in Europe through Dutch auctions. Blumhardt. Other *R. saxafragoides* hybrids include: **'SAXON BLUSH'** small, salmon with paler throat. **'SAXON BONNIE BELLE'** salmon. **'JIMINY CRICKET'** pink-red, long pedicels.

SAXON GLOW (PBR)

■ **SCARLET ROBE** Deep-red lobes, with a white throat. A strong, open-growing bush to 2m. Flowers are show-stopping. The name will need to be changed as there is an azalea with this name. Perhaps 'Snell's Scarlet Robe' – or does that sound a bit odd? Snell.

■ **SHANTUNG PINK** Flowers strong-pink, throat strong yellowish pink, scented. Leaves oblong. Ht to 2m. Rouse/Snell. **'SHANTUNG ROSE'** a sister, lightly perfumed rose-pink with a yellow centre.

■ **SHAYA** Flowers deep rose-pink, scented, 5–8 per truss. Vigorous but bushy, to 1.5m. Snell.

■ **SILVER THIMBLES** Delicate white flushed pink bells, 3 per truss. Small leaves, compact with red stems. Ht to 0.6m. Long flowering period. Blumhardt **'LITTLE BO PEEP'** is very similar.

SILVER THIMBLES

■ **SIMBU SUNSET** Flowers funnel-shaped, strong reddish orange, shading to brilliant orange-yellow in the throat, 4–6 per truss. Leaves elliptic, with sparse brown scales. Stems deep-red in first year. H. T. Lelliott. **'APASSIONATA'** raspberry-pink lobes, inside throat cream. **'CADMIUM ORANGE'** large bi-coloured orange and yellow. **'ROSIE POSIE'** orange-red with yellow centre, sometimes double.

■ **SOUVENIR DE J.H. MANGLES** Flowers chrome-orange, suffused rose-pink, centre light-rose, tube pale yellow. A Victorian hybrid still grown. Ht to 1.2m. Veitch.

■ **ST VALENTINE** Pendulous red flowers, 3–5 per truss. Compact and easy to please. Ht to 0.7m. A good beginner's plant. Lelliott. **'CAPE COD VALENTINE'** an improved version with larger flowers. **'LITTLE MARIA'** similar but more compact.

ST VALENTINE

■ **STRAWBERRY PARFAIT** Flowers large, wavy-edged, pink fading to creamy-white throat, lightly scented, 8–10 per truss. Bushy habit. Ht to 1.5m. Snell.

■ **SUNNY** Flowers tubular funnel-shaped, vivid-yellow, lobes strong yellowish pink, 8–15 per truss. Bushy and vigorous to 2m. Clancy/Snell. **'SUNNY'S BROTHER'** yellow and orange-red. **'GOLDILOCKS'** small golden-yellow flowers (not to be confused with the Kerrigan hybrid).

■ **SUNSET FANTASY** Flowers long tubular funnel-shaped, brilliant orange-yellow, edged vivid reddish orange, 5–8 per truss. Leaves elliptic. Flower shape and colour are striking. Buds-up young. Snell.

■ **SUNSET GOLD 50** Deep-orange flowers, shading to yellow in the throat in a large truss of 25–30+. Leaves long, narrow and pointed. Strong, upright growth to 2m or more. Best pruned. Snell.

■ **SWEET WENDY** Flowers soft-pink with a creamy-yellow centre, 5–8 per truss, scented. Medium bushy habit, to 1.5m. A 'good doer'. Withers.

■ **TEREBINTHIA** Flowers scented, rippled lobes, bright pink, 12–18 per truss. Fairly compact to 1.2m. Lelliot/Sulivam/Moynier.

■ **TOFF** Flowers large, cream-yellow, edged pale-salmon-pink on lobes, 8–10 per truss. Bushy and vigorous to 1.75m. Snell.

■ **TROPIC GLOW** Flowers golden yellow, shaded orange-red on lobes, 4–6 per truss. Leaves elliptic, on a shrub to 2.5m. Best Vireya hybrids, Hawaii. 'Simbu Sunset' is similar, with larger flowers. Lelliott.

■ **TROPPO** Orange and yellow bicolour, 12–15 per truss. A vigorous tall, open bush to 2m or more. Good habit in sun with pruning. Snell.

■ **ULURU** Flowers deep red, lobes deep orange-red; lower lobe and throat intense yellow; tube short, light yellow, 10–14 in a domed truss. Leaves ovate, dark glossy green with prominent veining. Spectacular, in a fine truss. Saperstein.

■ **VLADIMIR BUKOVSKY** Flowers long tubular funnel-shaped, vivid reddish orange, inside of tube vivid yellow, unmarked, 7–12 per truss. Leaves elliptic to narrowly obovate, glossy and smooth, with red petioles. Best Vireya hybrids, Hawaii. One of the few compact spreading orange hybrids. Lelliot/Sullivan.

■ **WATERMELON DREAM (syn. PEACH DREAM)** Flowers large, scented, watermelon-pink, 10–16 per truss. Leaves large (to 25cm). Ht to 1.75m. Fine foliage. Kenyon.

■ **WATTLE BIRD** Flowers tubular-campanulate, Strong orange-yellow, 7–9 per truss. Leaves ovate. Much used in further breeding. Rouse.

SUBGENUS HYMENANTHES: ELEPIDOTE (NON-SCALY LEAVED) RHODODENDRON SPECIES

The elepidote rhododendrons are most people's idea of the 'typical' rhododendron with relatively large leaves and large, full trusses of flowers. The advantage of growing elepidote species is that they tend to have more interesting foliage than the hybrids. The disadvantage is that, in most cases, you have to wait a few years for flowers. Most of the species require shelter from winds and plentiful organic matter mixed into the soil for best results, though some species, such as those in subsection Fortunea, are pretty tough and easy. The spectacular large-leafed species are found mostly in subsections Falcon-era and Grandia.

SUBSECTION ARBOREA

3–5m, ultimately some can reach 10m or more in time. H3–4. Long-lived trees or large shrubs, magnificent in full flower, with flowers in fine rounded trusses, usually red, pink or deep lilac, E–ML. A great choice for moderate climates.

ARBOREUM

■ **ARBOREUM** Tall H2–4 EM–M. Flowers tubular campanulate, variable in colour: red, pink, pinkish purple, white or two-toned, in a rounded or conical truss of 15–20. Usually handsome leaves, stiff and leathery, to 20cm long, with grey or brown indumentum on leaf underside. This wonderful tree-like species is variable in foliage and hardiness. It regenerates well after cutting, fire or cold damage. **VAR. ROSEUM** pink flowers. **SSP. CINNAMOMEUM** pink, carmine or white, leaves with dark brown indumentum. *Mel, U.K. (west).* **SSP. ALBOTOMENTOSUM** Medium H2–3 EM. Flowers cherry-red. Dark foliage. A dwarf slow-growing form from Mt Victoria, Burma. Should be considered a variety of ssp. *delavayi*. **SSP. DELAVAYI** Medium–Tall H2–3(4) M. Flowers deep-crimson to carmine, 15–20 per truss. Leaves dark and glossy, under-surface with a thin white to fawn indumentum. This subspecies occurs further east than ssp. *arboreum*, into China. *Mel.* **SSP. ZEYLANICUM** Medium–Tall H2 M. Flowers crimson (occasionally pink), 10–20 per rounded truss. Deep-green bullate leaves. Very leggy, tree-like habit. The only rhododendron species from Sri Lanka. Very handsome foliage. **SSP. NILAGIRICUM** H2 deep-crimson/crimson-rose. From South India. Heat, drought and fire tolerant, it regenerates after bush fires in the wild.
■ **LANIGERUM** Low–Medium H3–4 VE–E. Flowers scarlet-crimson or pink, in a full rounded truss of 20–35. Leaves silvery when young, leathery, with a thin layer of whitish to fawn indumentum on the lower surface. One of the finest early flowering species with magnificent trusses. Needs a sheltered site.

LANIGERUM

■ **NIVEUM** Low–Medium H4 EM–M. Flowers deep magenta to deep lilac, in rounded trusses of 15–20. Leaves with white, grey or fawn felted indumentum on lower surface. A wonderful and distinctive species, the colour of which is not to everyone's taste. *AGM.*

NIVEUM

SUBSECTION ARGYROPHYLLA

2m+ (10–15 years), ultimate height to 6m. H4–6. Flowers white to pink or purple in April–July. Leaves with white to fawn indumentum. Most are tough plants of good habit, fairly easy to grow with fine foliage and showy flowers.

■ **ADENOPODUM** Low–Medium H6 EM–M. Flowers funnel-campanulate, pale rose, in a flat-topped truss of 6–8. Dark narrow leaves with white to fawn indumentum on the underside. Hardy and free-flowering but foliage can be chlorotic. *Scand, Ger.*

ADENOPODUM

■ **ARGYROPHYLLUM** Medium–Tall H5 M–ML. Flowers funnel-campanulate, white to deep-rose, with or without spots in a truss of 4–12. Leaves 6–9cm long, shorter than in ssp. *nankingense,* with white indumentum. Hardy and usually of good habit. Quite free-flowering at maturity. **SSP. HYPOGLAUCUM** leaves glaucous below. **SSP. NANKINGENSE** Medium H5 M. Flowers funnel-campanulate, rich-clear-pink to lilac-purple, 4–12 per truss. Shiny dark-green leaves with silvery indumentum on the underside. A tough and quite easy species suitable for cold climates. **'CHINESE SILVER'** AGM is a selected free-flowering form. **SSP. OMEIENSE** usually white flowers, small leaves, generally a poor grower. **PINGIANUM** deep-pink flowers. *Scand, U.K., Ger, MA.*

ARGYROPHYLLUM SSP. NANKINGENSE

■ **COELONEURON** Medium H5 EM–M. Flowers +/– campanulate, pink to purplish, 4–9 per truss. Handsome leaves with pale-rufous indumentum below. Previously incorrectly placed in SS Taliensia. Recently introduced from Sichuan, China.
■ **CORYANUM** Medium H4–5 EM–M. Flowers funnel-campanulate, white, spotted red, 20–30 per dense truss. Stiff narrow leaves with thin indumentum on lower surface. Very rare. Most cultivated plants I have seen as this species, including the AM form, are wrongly named. The large number of flowers in the truss is the key character for this species.

CORYANUM

■ **DENUDATUM** Medium H4–5 EM–M. Flowers campanulate, light-pink, rose or wine-red with nectar pouches, in lax or rounded trusses of 8–10. Attractive shiny rough leaves with grey-brown indumentum. Closely related to *R. floribundum*. Recently introduced from China.

DENUDATUM

FLORIBUNDUM

INSIGNE

ARGIPEPLUM

■ **FLORIBUNDUM** Medium H4–5 EM. Flowers widely campanulate, pink-purplish-lavender with blotch and spots, in a truss of 5–12. Olive-green bullate leaves with a white to greyish woolly indumentum on the lower surface. Handsome when well-grown, with distinctive flowers. Foliage inclined to chlorosis.

■ **FORMOSANUM** Low H3–4 EM–M. Flowers widely funnel-shaped, white-pale-pink, with red spotting, in a loose to rounded truss of 7–20. Narrow leaves with pale buff indumentum on the lower surface. This species requires heat to grow well and it is not easy in Scotland. Said to be very fine in the wild in Taiwan.

FORMOSANUM

■ **HAOFUI** Medium H4 ML–L. Flowers broadly campanulate, small, white, with a large number of stamens, 5–9 per truss. Leaves narrow and smooth with a thin layer of brown indumentum on the lower surface. Rather prone to chlorosis and may need lime. Very late into growth.

■ **HUNNEWELLIANUM** Medium H4–5 E. Flowers widely campanulate, white tinged pink to pale-pink, spotted darker, in a loose truss of 4–8. Distinctive oblanceolate (narrow pointed) leaves with white indumentum on the lower surface.

■ **INSIGNE** Medium H5 ML–L. Flowers widely campanulate, pale- to deep-pink, spotted and lined deeper, in a loose to compact truss of 8–15. Rigid leathery dark green leaves with a plastered indumentum on the lower surface that looks metallic. Compact and dense growing, and useful for its hardiness and late flowering. Perhaps the best species of this subsection. *AGM.*

■ **LONGIPES** Medium H4–5 EM–M. Flowers funnel-campanulate, pink to purple in a loose truss of 8–15. Narrow leaves with pale brown indumentum on lower surface. Leaves inclined to chlorosis. Recently introduced for the first time.

■ **RIRIEI** Medium H4–5 VE–E. Flowers campanulate, lilac-purple to reddish purple, with deep violet nectar pouches, in a truss of 4–10. Leaves grey-green, under-surface with a thin layer of compacted silvery white indumentum. One of the earliest species to flower, lasting well if there is no frost.

■ **SIMIARUM** Low–Medium H2–3 EM–M. Flowers open-campanulate, pink, (white), with a few darker flecks in a lax truss of 4–7. Leaves narrowly elliptic to broadly oblanceolate, lower surface with a thin compacted indumentum. This species has a reputation for very good heat tolerance. It is worthless in cool climates such as Scotland, where it languishes and dies.

■ **THAYERIANUM** Low–Medium H5 L–VL. Flowers funnel-campanulate, small, white or white flushed pink, in a loose to compact truss of 10–20. Stiff pointed leaves on a slow-growing, upright but dense shrub with good foliage retention. The flowers are rather small. The latest flowering of this subsection.

THAYERIANUM

SUBSECTIONS BARBATA AND FULGENSIA

2–5m. Large shrubs to small trees with beautiful peeling bark, H3–4, leaves usually bristly, often very showy when young. Glowing flowers scarlet to crimson in compact trusses in February–April.

■ **ARGIPEPLUM (syn. SMITHII)** Medium–Tall H3–4 E–EM. Flowers scarlet to crimson, in a compact rounded truss of 10–19. Leaves with a thin layer of indumentum on the lower surface. This is essentially an eastern form of *R. barbatum*. Bark reddish to brown, flaking to reveal smooth under-surface.

■ **BARBATUM** Medium–Tall H4 VE–E. Flowers scarlet to crimson-scarlet in compact trusses of 10–20. Leaves +/– elliptic, stems usually with bristles. Beautiful reddish-plum smooth bark. Needs shelter and good drainage. One of the finest red-flowered species. Fairly hardy but needs wind protection. *U.K.*

BARBATUM

■ **EROSUM** Medium H3–4 E–EM. Flowers crimson to deep rose-pink, in compact trusses of 10–15. Obovate to oval hairy leaves with thin layer of indumentum on lower surface. Beautiful reddish-plum smooth bark. A striking plant for sheltered gardens. Flowers not as showy as those of *R. barbatum*.

EROSUM

EXASPERATUM

■ **EXASPERATUM** Medium H3–4 EM. Flowers bright brick-red to reddish pink, in compact trusses of 10–15. Bristly stems and large handsome leaves, a striking beetroot-colour when young. Bark peeling, reddish brown. A first-class foliage plant, one of the finest of all larger species.

FULGENS

■ **FULGENS** Medium H4 VE–E. Flowers deep blood-red to bright scarlet, in a compact and rounded truss of 8–14. Handsome rounded leaves with fawn indumentum on lower surface. Fine peeling bark. A fine slow-growing species with good flowers and foliage. Needs good drainage. Given its own subsection, but fits better here.

SUCCOTHII

■ **SUCCOTHII** Low–Medium H4 E–EM. Flowers crimson-scarlet, in compact, rounded trusses of 10–15. Leaves with very short petioles are held in whorls with the tips pointing upwards. Purplish smooth bark. Somewhat susceptible to powdery mildew. Needs good drainage.

SUBSECTION CAMPANULATA

1–3 or 4m. Compact shrubs to small trees. H3–5. Leaves to 18cm long, elliptic, obovate, lower surface with a dense, fawn-rusty-brown indumentum, or a loose or scattered indumentum or almost glabrous. Flowers white, cream, pink, purplish red, rosy purple, blue-lavender, with +/– spotting. Fine foliage plants with variable flowers. Not very heat tolerant.

CAMPANULATUM AERUGINOSUM YOUNG GROWTH

■ **CAMPANULATUM** Medium–Tall H4–5 E–M. Flowers lavender, white, mauve or purple, in a loose to compact truss of 6–18. Leaves to 18cm long, elliptic, with dense fawn to rusty-brown indumentum on the lower surface. Very variable in quality of foliage and flowers, the best forms are very fine. Needs good drainage. **'WAXEN BELL'** small flowers. **'ROLAND COOPER'**, **'KNAP HILL'** large flowers and large handsome leaves. **SSP. AERUGINOSUM** Low H5 EM–M. Flowers pinkish purple, 6–18 per truss. Glaucous metallic-blue young growth, amongst the most striking in the genus. Leaves remain grey-blue year round in the best forms. Under-surface with thick, pale indumentum. Compact and dense habit. Needs good drainage. Mainly grown for its foliage. **'BLAUSCHIMMER'** a fine Hachmann selection.

CAMPANULATUM

WALLICHII HEFTII

■ **WALLICHII** Medium H4 EM–M. Flowers deep- or pale-mauve, purple or pinkish, 5–10 per loose to compact truss. Dark-green leaves with a thin layer of black to brown indumentum or none, on leaf underside. The foliage is generally not as good as that of *R. campanulatum*. **HEFTII Group** white flowers, leaves glabrous.

SUBSECTION CAMPYLOCARPA

2–4m in 10 to 20 years. H3–5. Leaves glabrous, flowers in loose trusses, usually yellow or pink, occasionally white, April–June. Usually very free-flowering and amongst the finest species. All require good drainage, best mound-planted in heavy soil or wet conditions.

■ **CALLIMORPHUM** Medium H3–4 ML–L. Flowers campanulate, pink to deep-rose, blotched deeper-pink, 4–8 per loose truss. Neat small oval leaves on a fairly slow-growing compact plant, which flowers from a fairly young age. Needs good drainage and shelter from late-spring frosts. **VAR. MYIAGRUM** White flowers.

CALLIMORPHUM

■ **CAMPYLOCARPUM** Medium–Tall H4 EM–M. Flowers pale- to bright-yellow, with or without a faint red basal-blotch, in a loose truss of 3–10. Leaves elliptic to ovate, with no hairs or glands. Usually free-flowering at maturity. One of the finest yellow species. **SSP. CALOXANTHUM** Low–Medium H4 EM–M. Flowers pale yellow, sometimes with red blotch, 3–10 per loose truss. Small orbicular leaves, foliage often glaucous. Smaller in all parts than var. *campylocarpum*. It is worth seeking out selected forms with good foliage.

CAMPYLOCARPUM

CAMPYLOCARPUM SSP. CALOXANTHUM

■ **SOULIEI** Medium H5 M. Flowers openly cup-shaped or saucer-shaped, deep- to pale-pink or white, with or without a crimson blotch, in a truss of 5–14. Leaves oval, glaucous-green when young. One of our real favourites. Best in low-rainfall areas, requiring extra good drainage. Sensitive to fertilizers, sprays and weed killers. Needs shelter owing to early growth.

SOULIEI

■ **WARDII** Medium–Tall H4–5 ML–L. Flowers yellow, saucer-shaped, with or without a crimson blotch, in a rounded to loose truss of 5–14. Leaves orbicular to ovate, smooth and glabrous forming a large shrub or small tree. Very variable in flower, foliage and hardiness. Needs good drainage. **LUDLOW** and **SHERRIFF** forms are late, with flowers with a pronounced red blotch. **VAR. PURALBUM** white flowers.

WARDII LUDLOW AND SHERRIFF

WARDII VAR. PURALBUM

SUBSECTION FALCONERA

2–4m (10m ultimate ht). H2–5. Forming large bushes or small trees with huge handsome leaves with woolly to smooth indumentum. Flowers in big trusses, white, pink, purple, deep cherry-red, yellow, often blotched and spotted, February–May. These large-leaved species make magnificent foliage plants and are a must for every garden in moderate areas, as long as you can provide wind shelter.

■ **ARIZELUM** Medium–Tall H3–4 EM–M. Flowers cream, pale-pink or yellow, flushed or lined pink, apricot or reddish, in compact trusses of 15–25. Leaves to 25cm long, upper surface with silvery covering on new growth, lower surface with woolly cinnamon indumentum. Pink to reddish bark. A medium to large flat-topped tree. One of the finest large-leaved species for foliage. Flowers very variable. **RUBICOSUM Group**, flowers crimson to cerise.

ARIZELUM

■ **BASILICUM** Medium–Tall H3–4 E–M. Flowers white-cream, often flushed or lined pink, usually with a dark blotch, in a packed truss of 15–20. Leaves to 36cm long, dark green on upper surface, lower surface with woolly greyish-cream indumentum, petiole flattened. Forms a flat-topped tree. **GRATUM** is virtually identical.

■ **CORIACEUM** Tall H3 EM–M. Flowers white, sometimes flushed rose, with a red blotch and sometimes spots in a truss of 15–20. Leaves to 25cm long with pale indumentum on lower surface. Fine 'kid-glove-like' young growth. Flowers variable in quality from spectacular to very poor.

CORIACEUM

■ **FALCONERI** Tall H3 EM–M. Flowers off-white, cream or pale-yellow with a purple basal blotch, long-lasting, in a usually dense truss of 12–20. Handsome rugose leaves to 35cm long with rust-coloured indumentum below. One of the most magnificent of all species with very handsome leaves and flowers, but needs shelter. *AGM*. **SSP. EXIMIUM** Tall H3 EM–M. Flowers open rose and fade to cream in a truss of up to 20. Leaves oval or obovate-elliptic, to 25cm long, upper surface with persistent silvery indumentum, lower surface with deep-cinnamon indumentum. One of the best of all species for foliage.

FALCONERI

FALCONERI SSP. EXIMIUM

GALACTINUM

REX SSP. FICTOLACTEUM

■ **GALACTINUM** Medium–Tall H5 EM–M. Flowers white flushed pink to pale-rose with deeper blotch and spots, in rounded trusses of 9–15. Leaves to 35cm long, with pale-cinnamon indumentum on lower surface. One of the hardiest of the subsection. Tough but leaves inclined to be chlorotic. *Scand, Ger.*

■ **HEATHERIAE** Medium H3–4 EM–M. Flowers cream, pale-pink (?), in rounded trusses of 15 or more. Leaves to 25cm long, lower surface with woolly cinnamon indumentum. Similar to *R. arizelum* but differing in the oblanceolate leaves over three times as long as broad. Petiole winged. Probably derived from natural hybrids with *R. fulvum* ssp. *fulvoides.*

■ **HODGSONII** Tall H4 EM–M. Flowers pink to purple to reddish purple, usually fading to cream, with or without a blotch, in a compact truss of 15–25. Leaves to 35cm, dark green on upper surface with silvery to cinnamon indumentum on lower surface. Fine cream to cinnamon peeling bark, showy on mature plants. One of the hardiest big-leaved species. Flowers can be a harsh colour. **HODGSONII AFF** (Rudong La) leaves with handsome reddish-brown indumentum on underside.

HODGSONII

■ **PREPTUM** Medium H4 EM–M. Flowers white with a purple base, 10–20 per truss. Leaves to 12cm long, oblong to ovate-lanceolate, lower surface with thick white to fawn indumentum. This is a natural hybrid, one parent being *R. coriaceum*, the other seems to vary. Lots of strange plants are cultivated under this name.

■ **REX** Tall H4 EM–M. Flowers white flushed pink with a dark reddish-purple blotch and or spotting, in large rounded trusses of 12–30. Leaves dark green, to 35cm, with fawn indumentum on lower surface. Magnificent in flower and foliage and one of the best large-leaved species for cold areas.

SSP. FICTOLACTEUM Tall H4 EM–M. Flowers white or white flushed pink or lilac with a crimson blotch in a compact truss of 12–25. Dark, shiny leaves to 10cm, narrower than those of ssp. *rex*, lower surface with rusty-brown indumentum. One of the hardiest big-leaved species and free-flowering once mature. *AGM.*

■ **ROTHSCHILDII** Tall H4 E–M. Flowers white, creamy yellow or pale pink, sometimes with a basal blotch, in a truss of 12–17. Dark green leaves to 35cm, lower surface with a granular indumentum. One of the hardiest big-leaves.

ROTHSCHILDII YOUNG FOLIAGE

■ **SEMNOIDES** is very similar to the above, with a slightly different indumentum texture. This so-called species is a swarm of natural hybrids of *R. arizelum* and *R. praestans* where they meet on the mountainside.

■ **SINOFALCONERI** (*see also* photo page 37) Tall H3–4 EM–M? Flowers pale- to rich-yellow in a truss of 10–12. Leaves to 25cm, upper surface rugose, lower surface with light-brown indumentum. A recently introduced tree-forming species with fine foliage. Hardy so far at Glendoick.

SINOFALCONERI FOLIAGE

SUBSECTIONS FORTUNEA AND AURICULATA

2–3m, ultimately to 6m, medium to large shrubs or small trees, H(2)–4–5. Flowers white or pink, sometimes blotched, often scented in February–August. Leaves with no indumentum. Some of the finest and most versatile species, easy to grow, every garden should have a selection. This subsection contains the hardiest scented rhododendron species.

■ **ASTEROCHNOUM** Tall H5 EM Flowers funnel-campanulate, white, tinged pink with a blotch, in large rounded trusses of 15–20. Leaves to 20cm, lower surface with a sparse discontinuous whitish indumentum. Closely related to (and may be a hybrid of) *R. calophytum* and should be equally hardy.

■ **AURICULATUM** Tall H5 VL. Flowers funnel-shaped, white (occasionally pink), with a greenish blotch, fragrant, in a loose truss of 6–15. Handsome large leaves to 30cm. Vigorous and can grow very large. The latest to flower of the larger species, into August in the U.K. It tends to grow very late in the season, so soft growth is vulnerable to early frosts. Otherwise very tough.

AURICULATUM

■ **CALOPHYTUM** Tall H5–6 VE–EM. Flowers openly campanulate, white to pale-pink, with a dark-red blotch, 15–30 per truss. Leaves to 30cm, narrow, stiff and pointed, lower surface glabrous or with indumentum on the midrib. A tough, handsome species suitable for cold climates. Best with wind shelter. *AGM.* **VAR. OPENSHAWIANUM** Smaller leaves and 5–10 flowers per truss.

CALOPHYTUM

DAVIDII

FORTUNEI

HEMSLEYANUM

■ **DAVIDII** Tall H4–5 E–EM. Flowers openly campanulate, lilac to rose, spotted purple in truss with a long rachis of 8–10. Handsome stiff leaves, glabrous and dark green. The 'true' species was introduced in the late 1990s. Plants that pre-date this are wrongly named. This is distinctive; flowers young and should be tough.

■ **DECORUM** Tall H4 ML–L. Flowers openly funnel-campanulate, white to pale pink, with or with markings, scented, in fine rounded trusses of 7–14. Oval-elliptic leaves. Very vigorous, tolerant of dry conditions. A versatile and easy species. *AGM.* **SSP. DIAPREPES** later flowering and less hardy, often with larger flowers.

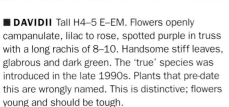

DECORUM

■ **FORTUNEI** Tall H7 ML–L. Flowers open to funnel-campanulate, near-white, pale-pink or lavender-pink-lilac, scented, in a loose sometimes pendulous truss of 5–12. Leaves glabrous, with a purple leaf-stalk. The hardiest scented species, much used in hybridizing. Also useful for its heat tolerance. **SSP. DISCOLOR** Tall H5 L–VL. Flowers usually white, also pale pink-lavender. Usually later flowering than ssp. *fortunei*. Leaves glabrous, often with reddish-brown new growth. Tough and quite easy. **HOULSTONII group**. Usually with narrower leaves and earlier flowering as cultivated. *AGM.* **KWANGFUENSE** appears to be related to Houlstonii Group. Recently introduced from a botanic garden in China.

■ **GLANDULIFERUM** Medium–Tall H4–5? ML–L. Flowers funnel-campanulate, white or pale pink, with a yellow/green flare, scented, in a loose truss of 5–7. Large handsome glabrous leaves to 20cm, new growth bronzy. Outstanding, vigorous, recently introduced species, which should become widely grown.

GLANDULIFERUM

■ **GRIFFITHIANUM** Tall H2–3 M. Flowers widely campanulate, very large (to 15cm across), sometimes fragrant, white or white tinged pink, in a loose truss of 3–6. Glabrous leaves to 30cm long. Fine peeling bark. Magnificent tree-forming species with amongst the largest flowers in the genus. Requires shelter.

GRIFFITHIANUM

■ **HEMSLEYANUM** Tall H4 VL. Flowers widely campanulate, pure white (occasionally tinged pink), fragrant, in a truss of 5–10 or more. Leaves to 30cm, with wavy edges, very distinctive, leaf-base auricled. A giant tree-forming species useful for its fine late flowers with a good scent.

■ **HUIANUM** Medium H4–5 EM–M? Flowers open-campanulate, deep rosy-purple/rose-red, in a truss of 6–12. Leaves glabrous, habit fairly compact. A distinct newly introduced species, should be tough.

■ **MAOERENSE** Tall H5–6? ML–L. Flowers campanulate, white, in trusses of 9–10. Leaves thick, oblanceolate, rarely obovate. Very vigorous and large growing. A recently described species from NE Guangxi, China, which looks close to *R. fortunei*, so should be tough.

■ **ORBICULARE** Medium H5 EM–M. Flowers campanulate, deep pink to purplish pink, unmarked, in a loose truss of 7–10. Glabrous almost round leaves, making a striking foliage plant. Tough and easy to please. Some forms have a rather harsh flower colour, so require careful placing in the garden. *AGM.* **SSP. CARDIOBASIS**, leaves more elongated, larger. All I have seen as ssp. *cardiobasis* look like *R. fortunei* hybrids.

ORBICULARE

■ **OREODOXA** Tall H6 E–EM. **VAR. FARGESII** Flowers campanulate, clear-pink to lilac-pink, 6–12 per truss. (AGM). **VAR. OREODOXA** Flowers generally earlier and paler, white to pale pink, leaves usually narrower. Small glabrous leaves curl up in dry weather. A fine early flowering species, which blooms young and has frost-resistant flowers. Forms a small tree.

OREODOXA VAR. FARGESII

PLATYPODUM

■ **PLATYPODUM** Low–Medium H4–6? EM–M. Flowers open-campanulate, pinkish red in a truss of up to 12. Leaves broadly elliptic, thick, with a very short winged-petiole. A handsome foliage plant that comes into growth very early. Introduced by my father, Peter Cox, its wild habitat in Sichuan is seriously threatened. Extremely rare.

■ **PRAEVERNUM** Medium H6 VE–E. Flowers campanulate, white with a purple blotch, about 10 per truss. Leaves with recurved margins to 18cm long. Very closely related to *R. sutchuenense* but tends to be more compact and the flowers are paler.

■ **SEROTINUM** Tall H3–4 L–VL. Flowers widely funnel-campanulate, white, sometimes flushed rose, fragrant, with or without a red blotch, in a loose truss of 7–8. A recent introduction from the wild with distinctive handsome wavy foliage. Very vigorous: should grow very large. The type specimen was very late flowering but recent introductions flower in June–July.

■ **SUTCHUENENSE** Medium–Tall H5–6 E–EM. Flowers widely campanulate, pale-pink to mauve-pink, spotted red, about 10 per truss. Large handsome leaves to 30cm long. One of the easiest larger-leaved species to grow. Best to shelter from wind and to protect early flowering. *U.K.* **VAR. GIRALDII** has a striking deep-pink blotch.

SUTCHUENENSE

■ **VERNICOSUM** Medium–Tall H4–5 EM–M. Flowers widely funnel-campanulate, pale-pink, bright-pink to lavender-pink, occasionally white, usually spotted crimson, in a rounded truss of 5–12. Glabrous leaves variable in size. A consistently good species that is easy to grow and forms a rounded bush. Requires good drainage.

■ **YUEFENGENSE** Low H5? M–L. Flowers light purple, 5–10 per truss. Leaves oval-ovate. This recently described species looks quite distinctive, as it is more compact and lower growing than most of its relatives.

SUBSECTION FULVA

Shrubs or trees, ultimately to 6m, H4, leaves with indumentum, white to rufous, flowers campanulate to funnel-campanulate, usually pink blotched, March–April. Long-lived and very free flowering once mature.

■ **FULVUM** Medium–Tall H4 EM–M. Flowers lilac-pink, with a deep blotch, in rounded trusses of 8–20. Dark shiny leaves with a fine rusty indumentum below. Often makes a small tree. Best with shelter to protect early flowers. **SSP. FULVOIDES** has larger leaves with thinner indumentum.

FULVUM

■ **UVARIIFOLIUM** Tall H4 E–EM. Flowers rose-pink, blotched deeper in a compact truss of 6–20. Leaves with greyish indumentum on the under-surface, new growth silvery. Forms a small tree. **VAR. GRISEUM** small truss of white or palest-pink flowers. From Tibet.

UVARIIFOLIUM

SUBSECTION GLISCHRA

2–5m, small to large shrubs, H3–4, hairy or bristly, leaves sometimes with indumentum, flowers usually pink, less often white, March–May. Many have striking and interesting foliage and are long-lived.

■ **ADENOSUM** Medium H4 EM–M. Flowers rose-pink or white tinged pink, blotched or spotted red, 6–8 per truss. Dark hairy leaves on a rounded bush. Free-flowering. Rare and should be better known.

■ **CRINIGERUM** Medium H3–4 EM–M. Pink to white flowers with pink flushing and/or red spotting in a truss of 10–20. Fine deep-green leaves with buff indumentum on the lower surface. Showy young growth. Variable in flower quality.

ADENOSUM

CRINIGERUM

■ **GLISCHROIDES** Medium H3–4 E–EM. Flowers white flushed rose or pink to pinkish purple, with a maroon blotch in a loose truss of 6–10. Bristly bullate leaves with a thin indumentum on the lower surface. New growth often showy with red bud-scales. Early new growth best with shelter.

GLISCHROIDES

■ **GLISCHRUM** Medium H3–4 M. Flowers rose-pink to purplish to almost white, prominently blotched and spotted crimson, in a truss of 5–15 flowers. Leaves pale- to dark green, bristly on lower surface and margins also sometimes on upper surface. Stems and leaf stalk bristly. A handsome plant for moderate climates. **SSP. RUDE** flowers pale pink, leaves pale green, hairy on upper surface. **VESICULIFERUM** differs in the white hairs on leaves and stems. I have never seen a cultivated or wild plant of this species.

GLISCHRUM

RECURVOIDES

KESANGIAE

GLISCHRUM SSP. RUDE

■ **HABROTRICHUM** Medium H3–4 M. Flowers rose-pink to purplish, blotched crimson, in a compact truss of about 15. Leaves dark green, with red bristles on margins, buds, stems and leaf stalk. Impressive when well grown but rather fussy and needs very good drainage.

HABROTRICHUM

■ **RECURVOIDES** Semi-dwarf H4 E–EM. Flowers white flushed pink or rose-pink, with crimson spots, in a loose truss of 4–7. Densely hairy with handsome dark-green leaves with indumentum on lower surface. One of the finest dwarf species for foliage.
■ **SPILOTUM** Semi-dwarf–Low H3–4 EM–M. Flowers pink with a bold basal blotch in a loose truss of 5–12. Small pale-green leaves, new growth with small bristles. Fairly tidy and compact. Probably of natural hybrid origin.

SUBSECTION GRANDIA

Forming large bushes or small trees with huge handsome leaves with usually plastered pale-coloured indumentum. Flowers in big trusses of 10–30, white, pink, purple, deep cherry-red, yellow, often blotched and spotted, February– May. Magnificent foliage plants, requiring a sheltered site to protect the enormous leaves. They grow best in mild areas with high rainfall.

■ **BALANGENSE** Low–Medium H4–5 EM–M. Flowers white to cream, lined pink or with reddish spots or blotch, in a fairly loose truss of 13–15. Leaves to 15cm long, pointed, lower surface with whitish indumentum. A recent introduction with handsome foliage. Better placed in SS Taliensia.

BALANGENSE

■ **GRANDE** Medium–Tall H2–3 E–M. Flowers cream or pale yellow with a reddish blotch and sometimes spots in a truss of 15–25. Leathery leaves to 35–45cm with silvery indumentum on lower surface. Needs a sheltered site to protect early growth.

GRANDE

■ **KESANGIAE** Tall H4 EM–M. Flowers purple-pink, rose-pink or white, in a compact truss of 15–20. Deep-green leaves to 30cm long with thin or no indumentum on the underside. A recently named species from Bhutan only just starting to flower in cultivation. Needs shelter from wind to avoid broken leaves.
■ **MACABEANUM** Tall H3–(4) E–EM. Flowers yellow, blotched purple in a large, usually full, rounded truss of up to 30. Deep-green shiny elliptic leaves to 35cm, under-surface with fawn-whitish indumentum. A must if you can grow it. Regenerates well from the base after winter damage. Recent introductions from higher altitudes may be hardier. *AGM.* **WATTII** is a probable natural hybrid of *R. macabeanum*, probably crossed with *R. arboreum*.

MACABEANUM

■ **MONTROSEANUM** Tall H3 VE–E. Flowers pale to deep purplish pink, with crimson veining and spots, in a rounded truss of 15–20. Leaves to 40cm, stiff, dark green and rugose, lower surface with silvery to buff plastered shiny indumentum. Forms an upright or domed small tree. Needs wind shelter and protection from late frosts. Very fine at its best.

MONTROSEANUM

PRAESTANS

■ **PRAESTANS** Medium H4 E–M. Flowers white, creamy pink to magenta-rose, usually with deeper blotch and or spots, in a truss of 10–25. Leaves to 35cm, under-surface with layer of plastered indumentum, petiole flattened and winged. One of the hardiest large-leaved species. Slow-growing and takes many years to flower.

■ **PROTISTUM** Tall H2–3 VE–E. Flowers pale-rose to crimson-purple, often fading, with or without a blotch and spotting, in compact to lax trusses of 20–30. Leaves to 50cm long, lower surface indumentum takes years to appear, often around the edges only. For very mild sheltered gardens. Best on Scottish west-coast islands and in New Zealand. **VAR. GIGANTEUM** 'Pukeiti' purple, fading, a fine form. **MAGNIFICUM** is very similar, with leaves that develop indumentum at a younger age.

PROTISTUM YOUNG GROWTH

■ **PUDOROSUM** Medium H4–5 E–EM. Flowers pink to mauve-pink with or without a blotch, in a rounded truss of 15–25. Leathery stiff leaves to 30cm, dark-green upper surface, lower surface

PUDOROSUM

with silvery-fawn indumentum. Persistent bud-scales hang down between the leaves. Slow growing. One of the hardiest of the big-leaves.

■ **SIDEREUM** Tall H3 ML–L. Flowers cream to clear-yellow with a purple blotch, in a truss of 12–20. Leaves to 25cm, leathery, upper surface matt, lower surface with a thin silvery-white to fawn indumentum. Later flowering than other big-leaved species. Should be better known.

■ **SINOGRANDE** Tall H3 EM–M. Flower creamy white to pale yellow with a large crimson blotch in a large truss of 12–30. Leaves the largest in the genus up to almost 1m in length. A magnificent giant, which can reach over 10m in height. Best in mild, sheltered gardens. Will not start flowering till it reaches a considerable size. A must if you can grow it. *AGM*.

SINOGRANDE

■ **WATSONII** Low–Medium H4–5 EM–M. Flowers white to cream, with or without reddish spots or blotch, in a fairly loose truss of 10–16. Leaves to 20cm, yellow midrib on upper surface, plastered indumentum on lower surface. Not of much merit as a garden plant as flowers tend to be small and growth comes very early.

WATSONII

SUBSECTION IRRORATA

2–3m, ultimately to 6m, medium to large shrubs, H2–4, most with no indumentum, flowers white, pink, red, March–May. While some are a little tender, they are worth protecting under trees as the flowers are usually good and frequently heavily spotted.

ABERCONWAYI HIS LORDSHIP

■ **ABERCONWAYI** Low–Medium H4 ML–L. Flowers saucer-shaped, white spotted crimson, in erect trusses of 6–12. **'HIS LORDSHIP'** is the most popular form. Stiff pointed leaves on a slow-growing, upright plant. Free-flowering and quite easy to please. *Mel.*

■ **ANNAE** Medium H2–4 M–L. Flowers white, cream or pink in a fairly loose truss of 7–12. Shiny glabrous leaves. Variable in hardiness. **SSP. LAXIFLORUM** larger flowers but more tender.

ANNAE

■ **ANTHOSPHAERUM** Medium–Tall H2–3 EM–M. Flowers pink, lavender, magenta, lilac or near-red, with nectar pouches, blotched and spotted deeper, in a truss of 7–15. Leaves thick and usually stiff, lower surface pale. Very variable in flower, sometimes very fine, often poor. Rather early into flower and growth. **LUKIANGENSE** has dark leaves with a waxy sheen. Flowers pink to purple-pink.

ANTHOSPHAERUM

■ **ARAIOPHYLLUM** Medium–Tall H2–3 EM–M. Flowers white or pale pink, with a crimson blotch and spots in a truss of 6–8. Leaves lanceolate, of thin texture, glabrous but midrib sometimes woolly. A pretty plant for mild gardens. Rare.

■ **GONGSHANENSE** Medium–Tall H2–3 VE–E. Flowers tubular-campanulate, light red, with nectar pouches, in packed trusses of 18–21. Bullate, narrow leaves. A recently named species, new to cultivation. Likely to be suitable for mild areas only.

GONGSHANENSE FOLIAGE

■ **IRRORATUM** Tall H3–4 E–EM. Flowers pink or white, often with heavy purple-red spotting, in compact trusses to 15. **'POLKA DOT'** pale-pink, heavily spotted purple, **'SPATTER PAINT'** pink with red spotting, Leaves glabrous, variable in size. The best forms of this species are very showy. Early flowers and growth require shelter. **SSP. POGONOSTYLUM** the most southerly and tender forms. H2–3. *Mel.* **BREVINERVE** flowers purplish or pink, without spots, from N. Guangdong, N. Guangxi, S.W. Hunan, S.E. Guizhou. Chinese botanists have described far too many taxa in SS Irrorata.

IRRORATUM

■ **KENDRICKII** Tall H2–3 EM–M. Flowers crimson, scarlet or pink in a rounded truss of 8–20. Closely related are **RAMSDENIANUM** red, purple-red or pink flowers, leaves wider than the above. **TANASTYLUM** rose-purple, magenta or crimson. Leaves stiff, narrow and sharply pointed. This species can be very fine but it needs a mild climate and shelter to be at its best.

RAMSDENIANUM

■ **WRAYII** Tall H1–2 VE–E. Flowers widely campanulate, white flushed pink, 10–18 per truss. Leaves with thin indumentum on lower surface. The most tender of the subsection. Heat tolerant. Rarely cultivated but should be good in warm climates.

SUBSECTION LANATA

Height 0.3–4m, bushy to erect shrubs or small trees. H4–5. Branchlets and buds *densely tomentose*, leaves lower surface a dense light-brown to rufous indumentum. Flowers yellow, white or pink with spotting. Attractive in both leaf and flower but rather fastidious as to soil conditions. Though hardy, they require some shelter, as they flower and grow early in the season. Very low heat-tolerance.

■ **FLINCKII** Low–Medium H4 EM–M. Flowers cream, creamy yellow or pale pink, usually spotted red, in a truss of 3–8. Orangey brown indumentum on both leaf surfaces eventually wearing off above. Easier to grow than its relative *R. lanatum*. A handsome foliage plant.

FLINCKII

LANATOIDES FOLIAGE

■ **LANATOIDES** Tall H4–5 VE–E. Flowers white with red spotting, in a dense truss of 10–15. A magnificent foliage plant with thick fawn indumentum on the lower surface and light-brown new growth which turns silvery. Mature leaves dark green. One of the rarest and most desirable species. New introductions by the author.

■ **LANATUM** Medium H4–5 EM. Flowers cream to yellow, spotted red, in a truss of 5–10. Thick leaves, with brownish indumentum on leaf lower surface. New growth, buds, stems brown. A challenge to grow, needing sharp drainage and plenty of organic matter.

LANATUM

■ **LUCIFERUM** Medium H4–5 E. Flowers funnel-campanulate, cream spotted red, in a truss of 8–10. Deep-green leaves with splendid yellowish-brown indumentum on the underside and silvery-yellow new growth. Needs perfect drainage. Introduced by the author. **CIRCINNATUM** very similar if not synonymous, said to differ in the leaf shape. Both come from S. Tibet.

LUCIFERUM FOLIAGE

■ **TSARIENSE** Low H4 EM. Flowers pale-pink, cream or white, flushed pink, spotted crimson, 3–5 per truss. **'YUM YUM'** a good selection. Smallish dark-green leaves with rusty indumentum on lower surface and a veil of persistent indumentum on the upper surface. **POLUNINI Group** larger leaves. **TRIMOENSE Group** paler leaves with paler indumentum.

SUBSECTION MACULIFERA

Small to mostly medium shrubs ultimately to 4m, H4–5, leaves with hairs or indumentum, flowers white, pink, red, often blotched, February–May. Several very fine species with first-rate foliage and flowers. All are very hardy.

■ **ANWHEIENSE** Low H6 M. Flowers funnel-shaped, pale pink to white, flushed pink, frost resistant, in rounded trusses of 6–10. Leaves pale green with no hairs or bristles. A tough plant with surprisingly frost-hardy flowers, on a dome-shaped bush. Foliage tends to yellowish. *Scand, Ger, U.K.* **ZIYUANENSE** said to be related to *R. anwheiense*, from Kwangsi, China.

ANWHEIENSE

■ **LONGESQUAMATUM** Tall H5 ML–L. Flowers openly campanulate, rose with a crimson blotch in a truss of 6–10. Deep-green leaves with shaggy hairs on lower surface midrib and stems and persistent bud scales. Useful for its late flowering and unusual appearance.

LONGESQUAMATUM

■ **MACULIFERUM** Medium H5 E–EM. Flowers openly campanulate, white to pale pink, with a bold purple blotch, in a truss of 7–10. Pale-green leaves, lower surface midrib with indumentum, on a fairly compact tough plant. Flowers are quite showy but foliage is not all that interesting. **OLIGOCARPUM** is closely related, with purple flowers.

■ **MORII** Low–Medium H4–5 EM. Flowers widely campanulate, white to white flushed rose with red spotting and/or blotch in a loose to compact truss of 5–15. Leaves mid-green, glabrous, new growth with slight silvery covering that soon rubs off. Best forms are very free flowering at maturity. Some forms are early into growth. Remarkably hardy and worth growing on coastal N.E. America.

OLIGOCARPUM

MORII

■ **OCHRACEUM** Low–Medium H4–5 E–EM. Flowers +/- campanulate, scarlet to crimson-scarlet tight rounded trusses of 6–12. Narrow leaves with light-brown indumentum in lower surface. Slow growing and compact. This is undoubtedly one of the most important new introductions in recent years.

OCHRACEUM

■ **PACHYSANTHUM** Low H6 E–EM. Flowers funnel-campanulate, white to pale-pink with yellow or red spots or blotch, in a rounded truss of 10–20. Outstanding foliage: leaves with indumentum on lower surface and silvery covering on upper surface, which persists all summer. Very compact habit. A great all round plant, one of the finest of all species. *AGM.*

PACHYSANTHUM FOLIAGE

■ **PACHYTRICHUM** Medium H5 E–EM. Flowers campanulate, with nectar pouches, pink or white with a deeper reddish or purple blotch in a loose to rounded truss of 7–17. Leaves with recurved edges, branches with bristles. Very variable in flower quality, the best forms are very fine.

PACHYTRICHUM

■ **PSEUDOCHRYSANTHUM** Semi-dwarf–Medium H4–5 EM–M. Flowers campanulate, pink in bud opening white or pale pink, usually spotted red, in a loose truss of 5–10. Thick and rigid pointed leaves with indumentum on the lower surface midrib. Young growth covered with silvery hairs that persist for several months. Habit neat and compact in most forms. A fine species for flower and foliage. Dislikes fertilizer. *AGM.*

PSEUDOCHRYSANTHUM

SIKANGENSE Medium H5 M–L. Flowers campanulate, white, pink or purple, with or without blotch or spots, in rounded trusses of 5–15. Leaves glabrous. Young growth sometimes silvery. Useful for its fine flowers and hardiness. Rare. **VAR. EXQUISITUM** Flowers white, blotched and spotted deeper. Leaves with some indumentum on lower surface.

SIKANGENSE

STRIGILLOSUM

STRIGILLOSUM Medium H4 E–M. Flowers tubular-campanulate, with nectar pouches, deep-red to crimson-scarlet, in usually flat-topped trusses of 8–12. Distinctive recurved leaves and bristly branches. One of the best early flowering red species, which is quite hardy but needs shelter for its early growth and flowers.

SUBSECTION NERIIFLORA (WITH VENATORA AND GRIERSONIANA)

Prostrate to small to medium-sized to large shrubs, H3–5, many with handsome foliage with indumentum on leaves. Flowers tubular-campanulate, except where noted, in loose trusses, mostly red but also orange, yellow, pink, white or bicolour in March–July. Many make good garden plants with flowers in striking colours and combinations of colours. Some are rather shy-flowering, especially as young plants. Most need good drainage and are best in cool climates.

APERANTUM Dwarf–Semi-dwarf H4 EM–M. Flowers small, waxy, red or pink, in lax trusses of 4–6. Small leaves with a glaucous lower surface. Shaggy persistent bud-scales hang down between the leaves. A neat compact species that needs cool roots and good drainage.

APERANTUM

BEANIANUM Low H3–4 E–EM. Flowers waxy, crimson-scarlet (or pink), in a loose to rounded truss of 6–10. Dark hairy leaves with fine rufous indumentum on lower surface. Branches with bristles. Early flowers, needs a protected site.

BEANIANUM

CATACOSMUM Low–Medium H3–4 E–EM. Flowers scarlet to rose-crimson, tubular campanulate, in loose trusses of 5–9. Oval leaves with fine rufous indumentum on the underside. Hard to propagate so remains rare. Dislikes fertilizer.

CATACOSMUM

CHAMAE-THOMSONII Dwarf–Semi-dwarf H4 E–M. Flowers campanulate, carmine, crimson or pink, waxy, in a loose truss of 1–5. Larger than its close relative *R. forrestii* Repens, forming compact mounds. Most plants under this name are natural hybrids of *R. forrestii* crossed with other species

growing nearby such as *R. sanguineum* and *R. selense*. **VAR. CHAMAEDORON** leaves with some indumentum. **VAR. CHAMAETHAUMA** flowers pale- to deep-pink.

CITRINIFLORUM Semi-dwarf H4 EM. Flowers yellow or cream, often flushed pink, in loose trusses of 2–6. **VAR. HORAEUM** flowers orange-red to carmine-red. Small leaves with grey-brown indumentum on under-surface. The orange forms of var. *horaeum* are very striking.

CITRINIFLORUM

CITRINIFLORUM VAR. HORAEUM

DICHROANTHUM Semi-dwarf H4 ML–L. Flowers salmon to orange in loose trusses of 3–8, very variable. This species and its various forms has some of the best orange flowers in the Elepidote species and this has been much used in breeding. All need cool roots and good drainage. **SSP. APODECTUM** orange-red, small dark leaves. **SSP. SCYPHOCALYX** orange to yellowish, compact. **SSP. SEPTENTRIONALE** flowers yellow, salmon or orange, small narrow leaves to 10cm long with a silvery to fawn indumentum on the underside.

DICHROANTHUM SSP. SCYPHOCALYX

■ **EUDOXUM** Low H4 EM–M. Flowers rose-pink, magenta or bluish crimson in a loose truss of 2–6. Several varieties exist with different flower colours. Small dark-green leaves with little or no indumentum on the underside. A natural hybrid of *R. selense* crossed with *R. sanguineum* or one of its relatives.

■ **FLOCCIGERUM** Low–Medium H3–4 E–EM. Flowers waxy, variable in colour, red, pink, cream or a combination of colours in loose trusses of 4–7. Narrow leaves with patches of indumentum on the lower surface. Very variable. Most forms are showy in flower, though the colour combinations can be a bit shocking. **ALBERTSENIANUM** closely related, with red flowers, rare.

FLOCCIGERUM

■ **FORRESTII** Dwarf H4 E–EM. Flowers waxy, campanulate, brightest scarlet, in a truss of 1–2. Leaves oval, deep-green. Creeping, near prostrate or mounding habit. Needs cool roots and part-day shade but shy flowering if it does not get enough light. **REPENS Group** lowest growing, creeping habit. **TUMESCENS Group** taller-growing with a dome-shaped habit. **SSP. PAPILLATUM** has a glaucous leaf underside.

FORRESTII REPENS

■ **GRIERSONIANUM** Low H3 L. Flowers bright geranium-scarlet, in a flat-topped but open truss of up to 12. Narrow leaves with light-coloured indumentum on lower surface. Useful for its late flowering and much used as a parent of red hybrids. Late growth is vulnerable to early autumn frosts. *U.K. (west) & Ireland.*

■ **HAEMATODES** Semi-dwarf H4 M. Flowers scarlet to crimson, often with a large calyx, in a flat-topped truss to 12. Leaves dark green, lower surface with a thick woolly rufous indumentum. Compact habit. Needs good drainage. One of the finest low red species.

GRIERSONIANUM

HAEMATODES

■ **HAEMATODES SSP. CHAETOMALLUM** Low H4 E. Flowers scarlet to crimson, in a loose truss of 4–12. Leaves larger and rougher than ssp. *haematodes* with some indumentum on upper surface and dense woolly indumentum on lower surface. Rare and quite hard to please. **VAR. CHAMAEPHYTUM** low and more glabrous. Introduced by the author from Arunachal Pradesh.

■ **MALLOTUM** Tall H3–4 VE–E. Flowers fleshy, crimson in a rounded truss of 7–15. Leaves to 15cm long, obovate, thick and bullate with a reddish-brown indumentum on the lower surface. An outstanding foliage plant with impressive flowers. Not always easy to please and requires good drainage.

MALLOTUM

■ **MICROGYNUM** Low H4 EM–M. Flowers campanulate, waxy deep crimson-scarlet in a loose truss of 3–10. Deep-green leathery leaves with a thin buff-to-cinnamon indumentum on the lower surface. Compact habit. One of the easiest of this subsection to grow, with good flowers and foliage.

■ **MINIATUM** Low–Medium? H4–5 EM. Flowers crimson with darker nectar pouches, about 5 per truss. Small leaves with white indumentum on lower surface. Introduced by the author for the first time from Tsari S. Tibet. It is not related to *R. sherriffii* as previously thought and best placed in SS Neriiflora.

MINIATUM

■ **NERIIFLORUM** Low–Tall H3–4 E–EM. Flowers scarlet, crimson, in a compact to loose truss of 5–12. Leaves glabrous, lower surface usually glaucous, bark often smooth with a peeling layer. Very variable in flower quality. **EUCHAITES Group** tall growing, usually with fine flowers. **SSP. PHAEDROPUM** H2–3. Flowers red, rose, yellow or orange, 5–12 per truss.

NERIIFLORUM

■ **PARMULATUM** Semi-dwarf H4 E–EM. Flowers pale-yellow, cream or pink with heavy purple spotting, in a truss of 4–6. Neat dark rugose leaves without indumentum on the lower surface. One of the easier species in this subsection to please, but takes a few years to flower.

PARMULATUM

■ **PIERCEI** Low H3–4 E–EM. Flowers crimson, 6–8 per truss. Dark shiny foliage with indumentum on the lower surface. One of the easiest and most vigorous of this subsection.

■ **POCOPHORUM** Medium H3–4 E–EM. Flowers light- to deep-crimson in a loose to rounded truss of 10–20. Leaves dark green with thick brown indumentum on the lower surface. Taller growing than most of its relatives and can be very showy. **COELICUM** crimson flowers. **VAR. HEMIDARTUM** leaves with discontinuous indumentum on lower surface.

■ **SANGUINEUM** Semi-dwarf H4 EM–M. Flowers red, pink, yellow or white in a loose truss of 6–8. Leaves dark green, lower surface with silvery to grey indumentum. Neat compact habit. Needs cool roots and good drainage. **VAR. HAEMALEUM** flowers black-red, **VAR. DIDYMOIDES** flowers white or yellow, flushed pink or red.

SANGUINEUM VAR. HAEMALEUM

SANGUINEUM SSP. DIDYMUM

SSP. DIDYMUM Semi-dwarf H4 L–VL. Flowers blackish crimson, in loose trusses of 3–6. Dark-green narrow leaves with indumentum on the lower surface. One of the few late-flowering dwarf species. Needs good drainage and near neutral soil. Apply dolomitic lime if foliage is chlorotic or growth weak. Buds-up young.

■ **SPERABILE** Low H3–4 E–M. Flowers scarlet to crimson, 3–5 per truss. Leaves with a dense but loose cinnamon indumentum. **VAR. WEIHSIENSE** bright-red flowers in often good trusses. Indumentum white. Hardier and more showy than var. *sperabile*.

■ **SPERABILOIDES** Low H3–4 EM–M. Flower crimson to deep red, 4–5 per truss. Leaves with speckled indumentum on under-surface. Free-flowering from a young age.

■ **TEMENIUM** Low H4. Flowers white, yellow, pink or red in a loose truss of 2–6. Leaves +/– glabrous on upper and lower surface. A compact and dense low-mounding plant. **VAR. DEALBATUM** flowers rosy pink. **VAR. GILVUM** flowers cream-yellow.

■ **TRILECTORUM** Semi-dwarf H4–5 EM–M. Flowers pale yellow, 2–3 per truss. Small glabrous leaves. Discovered by Ludlow & Sherriff and first introduced by the author from Arunachal Pradesh, India in 2002. Very compact.

■ **VENATOR** Low–Medium H3–4 ML–L. Flowers scarlet, in loose trusses of 4–10. Leaves rugose, oblanceolate, on a fairly compact bush. Easy and useful for its latish flowering. Only recorded from the Tsangpo Gorge, Tibet and Arunachal.

VENATOR

SUBSECTION PARISHIA

Large shrubs, 3m, ultimately to 6m, H2–3, leaves with loose often quickly shedding indumentum. Fine flowers, usually scarlet, May–August. Late growth. Renowned for their magnificent late flowers; wonderful in mild and west-coast gardens. Parents of numerous Exbury hybrids.

■ **ELLIOTTII** Medium–Tall H3 L–VL. Flowers funnel-campanulate, scarlet, in flat-topped or rounded trusses of 10–20. Leaves to 11cm long, glabrous at maturity except for lower surface midrib. New growth covered with silvery or brown hairs. One of the best red species for mild climates.

ELLIOTTII

■ **FACETUM** Tall H2–3 L–VL. Flowers tubular-campanulate, clear bright-red in rounded trusses of 10–20. Excellent in mild gardens, hardy in a sheltered position at Glendoick. Late growth may need protection. Useful for its late flowering.

FACETUM

■ **KYAWII** Tall H2(–3) L–VL. Flowers tubular-campanulate, bright-crimson to scarlet, 10–20 per truss. Long leaves, to 30cm. Young growth covered with silvery hairs. A magnificent but very rare species for mildest gardens.

SUBSECTION PONTICA

Prostrate to medium, occasionally large shrubs, mostly H5 so really tough and able to withstand open situations. Leaves with or without indumentum. Flowers white, pale yellow, to pink or purple. Most species are late-flowering from late-May to June and July.

■ **AUREUM** Dwarf H5 E–EM. Flowers widely campanulate, thin-textured, creamy yellow, usually with some deeper spotting, in a loose truss of 5–8. Leaves usually small, to about 8cm long, glabrous. A neat low-growing, hardy species that does best in cool climates. Grows well as far north as Tromso, Norway. Tends to flower in autumn in moderate climates. Limited use as a parent, due to thin-textured early flowers. *Scand, Ger.* **NIKOMONTANUM** is a natural hybrid of *aureum × brachycarpum*.

■ **BRACHYCARPUM** Semi-dwarf–Medium H5–8 ML–L. Flowers broadly funnel-shaped, pale pink or white, often lined or flush pink, with brown-green spotting/flare, in a rounded truss of 10–20. Flowers often hidden under new growth. Handsome foliage usually with a thin layer of indumentum on lower leaf-surface. Extremely hardy but often very early into growth. An important parent for breeding extreme hardiness. Dwarf forms called var. *roseum* are particularly good. **TIGERSTEDTII Group** (*see* photo overleaf) the hardiest of all species. **SSP. FAURIEI** leaves glabrous, *S. Fin, Baltic reps, Swe.*

BRACHYCARPUM

BRACHYCARPUM TIGERSTEDTII

DEGRONIANUM

MACROPHYLLUM

■ **CATAWBIENSE** Medium H8 ML–L. Flowers funnel-campanulate, lilac-purple, pinkish purple, occasionally white, in rounded trusses of 8–20. Leaves with margins curved downwards, pale- to mid-green, glabrous when mature. New growth with silvery tomentum. One of the hardiest of all species and much used to breed 'ironclad' hybrids. Not very satisfactory in mild climates such as the U.K. **VAR. ALBUM ('CATALGLA' & 'POWELL GLASS')** white with a yellow throat. Much used in breeding. *S. Fin, E. U.S.A., Canada.*

CATAWBIENSE POWELL GLASS

■ **CAUCASICUM** Low H4–5 EM–M. Flowers broadly campanulate, creamy yellow, sometimes flushed pink, spotted green in a rounded truss of 6–15. Leaves with a thin layer of indumentum on underside. Compact habit. Needs sharp drainage and cool roots. Rare and not always very easy to please. **'CUNNINGHAM'S SULPHUR'** pale yellow. Narrow twisted leaves.
■ **DEGRONIANUM** Low H7 M–ML. Flowers pink to rose, occasionally white, in a loose to rounded and compact truss of 6–15. Leaves with recurved margins, deep-green, lower surface with a felted fawn to rufous indumentum. There have been numerous confusing name-changes with this species and older names, such as *R. metternichii*, are still commonly used. A useful hardy species. **SSP. HEPTAMERUM** Larger, with flat leaves and usually five- to seven-lobed flower. **VAR. HONDOENSE** seven-lobed corolla, **VAR. HEPTAMERUM** five to seven-lobed, **VAR. KYOMARUENSE** five-lobed. *Scand, Ger, New Eng.*
■ **DEGRONIANUM SSP. YAKUSHIMANUM** Low H7 ML–L. Apple-blossom-pink buds open to flowers, pale rose to white, spotted red or unmarked, in a

DEGRONIANUM SSP. YAKUSHIMANUM 'KOICHIRO WADA'

rounded truss of 5–10. The 'yak' parent species. Excellent foliage: silver indumentum above and fawn below. Forms a compact mound. Very hardy and tolerates full sun. Will continue to be known as *R. yakushimanum*, whatever the botanists think, and they should have just left things as they were. **'KOICHIRO WADA' FCC** is the most famous clone – usually grafted. *Scand, Ger, U.K., Hol, Fra, U.S.A., Can, NZ, Aust.*
■ **HYPERYTHRUM** Low–Medium H7 M. Flowers funnel-campanulate, white, spotted or unmarked, in a fairly tight truss of 7–12. Leaves with recurved margins, glabrous. New growth brown. Useful for its hardiness and heat resistance. **'OMO'** Award of Merit form, pure-white.

HYPERYTHRUM

■ **MACROPHYLLUM** Medium–Tall H4 ML–L. Flowers broadly campanulate, deep- to pale-pink, occasionally white, often blotched or spotted, in tall trusses of 10–20. Glabrous, thin-textured leaves on a rather straggly upright shrub. Quite shade- and drought-tolerant once established. The only large western U.S.A. species.

■ **MAKINOI** Low H5 ML–L. Flowers funnel-campanulate, rose-pink, pale pink or off-white, sometimes spotted, in a compact truss of 5–8 or more. Narrow recurved leaves, often pale green or yellowish, lower surface with tawny indumentum. New growth usually silvery. A fine foliage plant. Prefers near-alkaline soil and may need lime to avoid chlorotic leaves. Useful for its late flowering. *AGM.*

MAKINOI

■ **MAXIMUM** Low–Medium H7–8 L–VL. Flowers small, campanulate, white, pink-tinged with a yellow blotch in a rounded truss of 12–30. Leaves dark green, with a thin layer of brown indumentum on the lower surface. Very hardy and useful for its tolerance of shady conditions. Leaves go yellow in too much sun. Habit rather sprawling and untidy. *S. Fin, E. N. Amer.*
■ **PONTICUM** Medium H4 L. Flowers campanulate, pale to deep pinkish-purple, usually blotched or spotted deeper, in a compact truss of 6–20. Narrow dark green glossy glabrous leaves. Compact to straggly, adaptable to sun or shade. This species is an out-of-control weed in much of the milder, wetter parts of the British Isles and it ought to be illegal to plant it. Once used as an understock for grafting, the suckers are often all that remain, having overcome whatever was grafted on top. Not good in Eastern U.S.A. *Mel.*

MAXIMUM

UNGERNII

■ **HIRTIPES** Medium H4 E–EM. Flowers near saucer-shaped, pink to white, usually spotted deeper, in trusses of 3–4. Dark-green obovate leaves and bristly stems. Can be very attractive in flower but rather early, so best with some protection. *U.K.*

MARTINIANUM

PONTICUM GROWING WILD IN SCOTLAND

SUBSECTION SELENSIA

Shrubs to small trees, up to 6m, but usually 3–4m. Branchlets often with hairs or bristles. Leaves glabrous, or with a loose or thin indumentum. Flowers funnel-campanulate to campanulate, with no nectar pouches, white, pink or reddish purple, with or without spots. Not as widely grown in gardens as the related members of subsection Campylocarpa.

■ **BAINBRIDGEANUM** Low–Medium H4 EM–M. Flowers pink or cream, 4–8 per lax truss. Leaves with indumentum on the leaf underside. A natural hybrid of *R. selense*. Other natural hybrids of *R. selense* include: **ERYTHROCALYX** (cream flowers) and **ESETULOSUM** (white flushed pink-purple).

■ **MARTINIANUM** Low H5 EM–M. Flowers pink, bell-shaped, in loose trusses of 1–4. Small glabrous leaves. A slow-growing compact plant. **EURYSIPHON** is a natural hybrid with creamy-white flowers flushed rose.

■ **SELENSE** Low–Tall H4 EM–M. Flowers white or pink, usually spotted red, in a truss of 3–8. Leaves small, +/– glabrous, often glaucous. Best in a fairly bright situation. The 'tramp' of the rhododendron world, this species is very promiscuous in the wild, hybridizing with many of its neighbours, seldom with attractive results. **SSP. DASYCLADUM** branchlets bristly. **SSP. JUCUNDUM** pink flowers with small red blotch. **SSP. SETIFERUM** leaves with indumentum on underside.

■ **SMIRNOWII** Medium H7 ML–L. Flowers funnel-campanulate, pink to rose-purple usually spotted deeper, in a loose to compact truss of 6–15. Fine foliage with indumentum on the leaf lower-surface. Useful for its hardiness and relatively late flowering. *S. Fin.*

BAINBRIDGEANUM

SELENSE

SMIRNOWII

HIRTIPES

■ **UNGERNII** Medium H4–5 L–VL. Deep-pink buds open to funnel campanulate white flowers, sometimes flushed pink, spotted green, in compact, upright trusses of 20–30. Large handsome leaves to 25cm long, with woolly white indumentum on under-surface. New growth with light, silvery tomentum. Prefers to be grown in shade: too much sun causes burning and yellowing of the leaves. Useful for its late flowering.

SUBSECTION TALIENSIA

Dwarf to medium-sized, often compact. Most 1–2m in ten years, ultimately 2–4m. A few very dwarf and slow: 30–50cm. Most very hardy, H4–5. The majority have fine foliage with silvery or white to rufous indumentum, very popular with collectors. The white to pink, occasionally yellow, flowers can take some years to appear but many are worth growing for their foliage alone. All require good drainage and are long-lived in good conditions.

ADENOGYNUM

BEESIANUM

BUREAVII ARDRISHAIG

■ **ADENOGYNUM** Low H5 EM–M. Flowers white or pink, spotted deeper in a truss of 4–12. Leaves dark green with thick olive-brown indumentum on the lower surface, on a compact plant. Flowers at a young age. × **DETONSUM** is a natural hybrid of *R. adenogynum* × *R. vernicosum* with pink flowers.

■ **AGANNIPHUM** Low H5 EM–M. Flowers white to rose, often heavily flushed deeper, in compact trusses of 10–20. Leaves glabrous on upper surface, lower surface with a spongy grey-white indumentum. **VAR. FLAVORUFUM** has splitting indumentum on the leaf underside. Two former species now reduced to Groups: **GLAUCOPEPLUM Group** intermediate with *R. phaeochrysum*. **DOSHONGENSE Group,** thin indumentum. **BATHYPHYLLUM** a natural hybrid with *R. proteoides* with fine foliage.

■ **ALUTACEUM** Low H5 EM–M. Flowers white to flushed rose sometimes with a crimson blotch or spotting in rounded trusses of 10–20. *R. alutaceum* is a series of natural hybrids between *R. roxieanum* and other species in SS Taliensia. Fine foliage, leaves with fawn indumentum on lower surface. **TRIPLONAEVIUM Group** narrow leaves with thin indumentum. **VAR. RUSSOTINCTUM** and **VAR. IODES** are distinguished by the texture and colour of their indumentum.

■ **BALFOURIANUM** Low–Medium H5 EM–M. Flowers rose-pink, with a deep-pink calyx, in rounded trusses of 6–12. Leaves with greyish-pink indumentum on the lower surface. One of the finest Taliensia species.

■ **BEESIANUM** Medium H4–5 EM–M. Flowers white to deep rose, often with bold, deep pink-reddish blotch or spotting in rounded trusses of 10–20. Handsome leaves to 30cm long, with a thin layer of indumentum on the under surface. A challenge to grow successfully requiring good drainage and cool roots. Best grafted.

■ **BHUTANENSE** Low H5 EM–M. Flowers deep to pale pink, spotted or blotched deeper, in a rounded truss of 10–15. Dark-green leaves with brown indumentum on the lower surface. New growth brown. Takes many years to flower. Not very easy on its own roots but grafted plants grow much better.

BHUTANENSE

■ **BUREAVII** Medium H6 M. Flowers white to pale pink flushed deeper, in a loose truss of 10–20. A superb foliage plant, one of the finest in the genus. Rich rusty-red indumentum on leaf under-surface and shoots. New growth a lovely brown colour. The most popular species in SS Taliensia. *AGM.* **'ARDRISHAIG'** twisted leaves and larger than normal flowers. **PUBICOSTATUM** is a natural hybrid with *R. sikiangense*.

■ **BUREAVIOIDES** Medium H6 EM–M. Flowers pink to white, with reddish spotting, in a truss of about 15. Usually with larger leaves and a shorter leaf stalk than *R. bureavii*. A fine foliage plant.

■ **CLEMENTINAE** Medium or less H5 EM. Flowers rose, pink or white, flushed pink, with red to pink markings, in a rounded truss of 10–15. Leaves handsome, ovate, greenish, greyish-green or blue with spongy buff indumentum on the underside. Very fine foliage, but rather reluctant to flower even at maturity. **SSP. AUREODORSALE** a distinct taxon from N.E. Sichuan. Jens Nielsen, who introduced it from the wild, thinks it is a distinctive species.

CLEMENTINAE NEW GROWTH

■ **DIGNABILE** Medium H4 EM–M. Flowers pink, cream or white, with or without blotch or spots, in a rounded truss of 8–15. Leaves to 18cm long with a barely visible layer of brown indumentum on the leaf underside. Closely related to *R. beesianum*. A challenge to grow successfully requiring good drainage and cool roots; I recommend grafting it.

BALFOURIANUM

BUREAVII FOLIAGE

ELEGANTULUM

■ **ELEGANTULUM** Semi-dwarf H4–5 E–EM. Flowers pale pinkish purple, with deeper spotting, in a fairly compact truss of 10–20. Handsome dark narrow leaves with rufous-brown indumentum on lower surface. Free-flowering and ideal for the smaller garden. Needs good drainage.

■ **FABERI** Low–Medium H5 EM–M. Flowers white to pale pink, spotted or blotched deeper, in neat trusses of 7–20. Leaves small (to 11cm), pointed, lower surface with a thin brown indumentum. New growth silvery. Tough but not one of the most striking members of SS Taliensia for foliage.

FABERI

■ **LACTEUM** Low–Medium H4 EM–M. Flowers pale- to clear-canary-yellow with or without a bold red blotch or red spotting, in a rounded truss of 15–30. Leaves dark-green obovate, to 17cm long, lower surface with a thin grey-brown indumentum. Best in a very acid, well-drained soil in a cool climate. A magnificent yellow species at its best: it grows best when grafted.

LACTEUM

■ **MIMETES** Low H5 E–EM. Flowers white to rose, spotted, about 6–7 per truss. Leaves with thin layer of indumentum on lower surface. Not very easy to grow and tends to suffer disease. Rare and probably a natural hybrid. **VAR. SIMULANS** leaves with splitting indumentum on lower surface.

■ **NIGROGLANDULOSUM** Medium H5 E–EM. Flowers small, white or pale pink, spotted, in a rounded truss of 8–10. Leaves narrow, to 20cm long, with tawny indumentum on leaf underside. Rare.

PHAEOCHRYSUM

■ **PHAEOCHRYSUM** Low–Medium H5 EM? Flowers white to pink, spotted, in loose to compact and rounded truss of 8–15. Leaves with thin to medium brown indumentum on leaf underside. Variable in foliage and flower quality. Needs very good drainage. **VAR. LEVISTRATUM** leaves with felted indumentum on lower surface. **VAR. AGGLUTINATUM** leaves with plastered indumentum on lower surface. A yellow form, which I introduced from Tsari, Tibet, will probably be described in its own right.

■ **PRATTII** Medium H5 EM–M. Flowers white, spotted red, in neat, flat-topped trusses of 6–14. Leaves to 19cm long, one of the largest-leaved Taliensia, with a thin layer of brown indumentum on underside. Flowers are rather small for the leaf size but it makes a handsome specimen.

■ **PRINCIPIS** Medium–Tall H5 E–EM. White to pink flowers, spotted or unspotted, in rounded truss of 10–30. Dark, pointed leaves with spongy fawn indumentum on leaf underside. One of the most free-flowering species in the subsection but rather early flowering.

PRINCIPIS

■ **PRONUM** Dwarf H5 EM–M. Flowers white, cream or pale pink in a flat topped truss of 6–10. Leaves small (to 7.5cm) green or glaucous blue with white-fawn indumentum on the underside. Very compact and slow-growing and takes many years to flower. A collector's plant, well worth growing for foliage alone.

■ **PROTEOIDES** Dwarf H5 E–EM. Flowers (rarely) pale pink to white, spotted deeper, in a small rounded truss of 5–10. Leaves small, to 4cm long, with thick brown indumentum on the lower surface. Young growth brown. Much sought after by collectors for its tiny leaves and neat dense compact habit. Perfect for the rock garden.

PRONUM FOLIAGE

PROTEOIDES FOLIAGE

■ **PRZEWALSKII** Low–Medium H6 EM–M. Flowers white to pale pink, often small, usually with some spotting, in a truss of 10–15. Leaves with thin indumentum on the under surface or glabrous with no indumentum. Leaves often have white bloom on them. This species is very hardy but not very garden worthy in flowers or foliage. Glabrous forms are known as **VAR. DABANSHANENSE**.

■ **PURDOMII** Low–Medium H6 EM–M. Flowers white to pale pink, with a red blotch, in a truss of 10–12. Leaves glabrous. Most plants cultivated under this name are misidentified.

■ **ROXIEANUM** Semi-dwarf–Medium H5 EM. Flowers white, flushed rose, with red blotch or spotting in rounded trusses. Leaves narrow (except var. *cucullatum*), dark green on upper surface, lower surface with fawn to rufous indumentum. The slow-growing narrow-leaved forms are the most popular garden plants. One of the best species in this subsection. **VAR. OREONASTES** leaves very narrow, **VAR. CUCULLATUM** leaves relatively wide, indumentum thick. **GLOBIGERUM Group** narrow leaves and thick indumentum. **VAR. PARVUM** short leaves.

ROXIEANUM VAR. OREONASTES FOLIAGE

■ **RUFUM** Low–Medium H5 EM. Flowers white to deep pink, sometimes flushed deeper, in a truss of 6–12. Leaves shiny on upper surface, lower surface and stems with thick white-grey indumentum. Flowers tend to be rather small.

■ **SPHAEROBLASTUM** Medium H5 EM–M. Flowers white, sometimes spotted or flushed pink. Leaves dark green with reddish-brown indumentum on the lower surface. Handsome in flower and foliage. **VAR. WUMENGENSE** leaves larger or wider; from N.E. Yunnan.

■ **TALIENSE** Low H5 EM–M. Flowers cream to white flushed pink, often heavily spotted red, in a flat-topped to rounded truss of 10–20. Leaves dark green with tawny-brown indumentum on the lower surface. Compact and dense habit with fine flowers and foliage.

■ **TRAILLIANUM** Low–Tall H5 EM–M. Flowers white, sometimes flushed pink, with or without deeper spots or blotch, in a small compact truss of 6–15. Leaves dark green with thin brown indumentum on the lower surface. Often fine foliage, but flowers can be small. **VAR. DICTYOTUM** appears to be a natural hybrid.

■ **WASONII** Semi-dwarf–Low H5 EM–M. Flowers pale yellow with red spotting, in a flat-topped truss of 8–15. Dark-green leaves with a thin to dense reddish-brown indumentum on the lower surface. A compact and dense growing plant. **VAR. WENCHUANENSE** flowers cream to pale pink. **RHODODACTYLUM Group** pale pink.

WASONII

■ **WIGHTII** Low–Medium H5 E–EM. Flowers cream to pale yellow, usually spotted red, in a truss of 12–20. Leaves with a thin layer of brown indumentum on the lower surface. Slow growing and quite hard to please, best grafted. The plant for many years grown under the name '*wightii*' with a lop-sided truss of cream flowers is a hybrid and looks quite distinct.

WILTONII

■ **WILTONII** Low–Medium H5 EM–M. Flowers white to pale pink, often flushed deeper pink, spotted and blotched pink red, in a lax or flat-topped truss of about 10. Handsome bullate leaves with thick cinnamon indumentum on the lower surface. A handsome plant which looks very distinctive. *AGM.*

Small trees, or bushes ultimate height 2–3m. H3–4. Leaves with little or no indumentum. Flowers red or pink, yellow or cream. Many have very fine peeling or coloured bark. Some are susceptible to mildew.

■ **CERASINUM** Low–Medium H4 ML–L. Flower thick-textured, with deep nectar pouches, in a truss of 3–5. There are two flower-types: '**CHERRY BRANDY**' white to pale pink with a darker band around the corolla; '**COALS OF FIRE**' red flowers. Leaves small (to 10cm), dark green, glabrous. Compact and fairly slow-growing with a long flowering period. Often opens some of its flowers in autumn. Very striking.

CERASINUM CHERRY BRANDY

■ **CYANOCARPUM** Medium H4 E–EM. Flowers pink to white, often flushed deeper and with nectar pouches and a dark basal blotch, in a flat-topped truss of 6–11. Leaves elliptic to orbicular, glabrous, sometimes glaucous. Rather prone to powdery mildew. Rare and sometimes difficult to please.

CYANOCARPUM

■ **ECLECTEUM** Low–Medium H4 E–EM. Flowers tubular-campanulate, usually in shades of pink, also cream, white or yellow, unmarked or spotted or stained deeper, in a loose to compact truss of 6–12. Leaves +/– obovate, +/– glabrous. A variable species which can be very fine. Prone to powdery mildew infection.

ECLECTEUM

■ **FAUCIUM** Medium H3–4 EM or M. Flowers pink, occasionally white tinged pink, spotted to blotched deeper, in a rounded truss of 5–10. Leaves smooth, glabrous, green. Fine, pink, smooth, peeling bark. Bronzy young growth. Very attractive at its best but rather early into flower and growth. **HYLAEUM** is almost identical, less hardy with larger leaves. **SUBANSIRIENSE** fleshy red flowers, early. Fine peeling bark and pink smooth trunks.

FAUCIUM

■ **HOOKERI** Medium H3–4 E–EM. Flowers in shades of red or pink, with nectar pouches, in rounded trusses of 8–18. Leaves with 'hook'-like hairs on underside veins. Fine peeling bark. A fine tree-like species for mild gardens.

HOOKERI

MEDDIANUM

THOMSONII

■ **MEDDIANUM** Low–Medium H3–4 E–EM. Flowers scarlet (occasionally deep rose) with nectar pouches, in trusses of 5–10. Leaves obovate to elliptic, glabrous. Subject to powdery mildew. Very showy red flowers from a fairly young age. Rare and should be better known. **VAR. ATROKERMESINUM** less hardy, and more tree-like in habit.

■ **SHERRIFFII** Semi-dwarf–Low H4 E. Flowers funnel-campanulate, small, waxy, deep red, in a loose truss of 4–6. Leaves oval, small, dark green with a chocolate-coloured indumentum on the lower surface. Needs sharp drainage and not always easy to please. Slow-growing and rather lacking in vigour.

■ **STEWARTIANUM** Low H4 VE–E. Flowers tubular-campanulate, white, cream, yellow, pink or a combination of colours, sometime spotted deeper, in a loose pendulous truss of 3–7. Leaves +/– elliptic, glabrous or with a thin layer of indumentum on the lower surface. Rarely offered and rather subject to powdery mildew.

STEWARTIANUM

■ **THOMSONII** Medium–Tall H4 EM–M. Flowers in shades of red, waxy, with a large calyx and nectar pouches, in a loose truss of 3–12. Leaves +/– ovate, glabrous, often glaucous. A smooth and peeling bark. Most forms are susceptible to powdery mildew. One of the finest red species. Variable in flower colour and quality and hardiness. **SSP. LOPSANGIANUM** Low H4 E–EM. Flowers deep to medium red, waxy, in a loose truss of 3–5. Leaves +/– oval, dark green, glabrous or with a very thin layer of indumentum on the leaf underside. Slow growing, compact to upright. From Tsari, Tibet and Arunachal Pradesh.

■ **VISCIDIFOLIUM** Low H3–4 M. Flowers coppery red to coppery orange, flushed deeper on outside, spotted deeper, with crimson nectar pouches, in a loose truss of 1–3. Oval leaves are sticky on lower surface. Thin stems with smooth bark. Somewhat subject to powdery mildew.

VISCIDIFOLIUM

A single species.

■ **WILLIAMSIANUM** Semi-dwarf H4 EM–M. Flowers pink, campanulate, in loose trusses of 2–3. Leaves small, smooth and orbicular, bronze when young. Not for frost pockets. Parent of many fine hybrids. Forms a perfect dome-shaped mound in a sunny position, with fine flowers and foliage. *AGM*.

WILLIAMSIANUM

LARGER ELEPIDOTE HYBRIDS

This section contains what many people think of as 'typical rhododendrons' with large rounded trusses of often spectacular flowers. Most grow 2m by 2m or more in 10–20 years and the larger ones can attain well over 4m by 4m at maturity. In hardiness they range from H7/8 (known as ironclads), often able to withstand extremes of heat and cold, to tender hybrids (H2), suitable for mild maritime climates only. There are thousands of named hybrids in this category and more are named each year.

■ **A. BEDFORD (syn. ARTHUR BEDFORD)** Tall H4–5 ML. Flower openly funnel-shaped, light mauve, with darker lobes, with a brownish-red blotch, in dome-shaped trusses of 11–16. Leaves thick, glossy, dark green with reddish-purple stems, on a plant of open, upright habit. Sun tolerant. A good flower but a rather ungainly, coarse and upright habit. *AZ, MA, MB, PT, PV, SE.* (unknown × *ponticum*). Lowinsky.

A. BEDFORD (SYN. ARTHUR BEDFORD)

■ **ABE ARNOTT** Medium H4–5 M. Flowers orchid-purple, with a heavy blotch on upper lobe and throat, in trusses of 16. Leaves dark green. Best in sun to keep well-branched. A useful parent of blotched hybrids. (Marchioness of Lansdowne × Lee's Dark Purple). Weber.

■ **ABENDSONNE (syn. VORWERK ABENDSONNE)** Medium H4–5 M. Flowers brilliant-red suffused orange, with an orange calyx, in loose trusses. Rounded olive-green foliage. (John Waterer × *dichroanthum* ssp. *scyphocalyx*). Hobbie.

■ **ABRAHAM LINCOLN** Low–Medium H8 M. Flowers light magenta-crimson, strong-red slowly fading to pink in rounded trusses of about 14. An ironclad hybrid now seldom grown. (*catawbiense* × unknown). Parsons.

■ **ABRAXAS** Low H5 ML. Flowers orange with outside and centres deep pink, with a large calyx, in a loose truss of 5–7. Leaves tend to be rather pale and yellowish. A promising new hybrid that may be the best Hachmann 'orange'. (Olga × Clivia). Hachmann. **'CHIWAWA'** a later flowering orange and red combination on a compact plant. **'ORANGE FLIRT'** pale orange-yellow with a pink rim on a compact plant.

■ **ACCLAIM** Low H4–5 M. Flower openly funnel-shaped, slightly fragrant, purplish red with a small, dark eye deep in throat, in ball-shaped trusses of 16. Leaves elliptic, flat, yellowish green, on a rounded, well-branched plant. Hard to root. *PT, SE.* ([Pygmalion × *haematodes*] × Wellfleet (exact combination unknown)). Dexter. Sisters: **'ACCOMPLISHMENT'** red and white bicolour. **'ARONIMINK'** large deep rose-red with small brown flare. Open habit. **'KELLEY'** reddish purple with some spotting. **'TRIPOLI'** red flowers, rather shy-flowering.

■ **ADELE'S YELLOW** Low H5 L. Buds cream and pink, flowers primrose-yellow, widely funnel-campanulate, in a lax truss of 14. Plant broad and semi-dwarf, branching well. Heat tolerant and may be a good parent for heat-tolerant yellows. Not very free-flowering. A sister called 'Susan Kay' was also named. (*maximum* × *wardii*). Fetterhoff.

■ **ADONIS g.** Medium H3 ML–L. Flowers pale pink in loose trusses. A vigorous spreading plant, suitable for mild climates only. Not one of the better *R. griersonianum* hybrids. (Vanessa × Sunrise). Puddle/Aberconway.

■ **ALADDIN** Tall H4 L–VL. Flower openly funnel-shaped, rose-pink, deeper in throat, outside pink flushed orange, in loose trusses of about 14. Leaves large, long and rather narrow. Hairy stems. One of the best and toughest late-flowering hybrids of this colour with good foliage, better than 'Azor'. Late growth can be frost-vulnerable. Takes a few years to flower. (*griersonianum* × *auriculatum*). Crosfield.

ALADDIN

■ **ALARM** Tall H4? E–EM. Flowers deep crimson, with a white centre and brown spotting, in a conical truss of 14. An old early-flowering hybrid that now appears mainly to be grown in Australia where it is a good performer. There are two hybrids under this name in Europe. (unknown). A. Waterer.

■ **ALBARELLO** Low–Medium H5 ML. Flowers cream, flushed pale lavender, with a yellow-green blotch, in a compact rounded truss. Leaves dark green, recurved. (Holger × Schneebukett). Hachmann.

■ **ALBATROSS g.** Tall H4 L. Flower 12cm across, fragrant, light pink or near-white. 'AM' form has slightly blush pink-white flowers with reverse slightly tinged pink, in lax trusses of 12. Other clones are '**EXBURY**', blush-pink and '**TOWNHILL**', white with pink edging. Leaves 15cm long, retained one year. Sparse growth habit on a tree-like plant. A useful late-flowering hybrid for a sheltered site. (Loderi g. × *fortunei* ssp. *discolor*). Rothschild.

■ **ALBERT** Medium H6 ML–L. Pale lilac-blue with a lighter centre and a yellow-green blotch, in a dense rounded truss of about 16. Matt foliage on a rounded, spreading plant. Buds-up young. Not very easy to root. Ger. (Viola × Everestianum). Seidel. '**BISMARK**' is a sister with purplish-pink flowers fading to white.

■ **ALBERT CLOSE** Low H6 L. Flower bright rose-pink with chocolate-red spotting in throat, in conical trusses of 23. Leaves bluish green, on a straggly, open grower. Tolerates sun and heat. Leaves are insect resistant. One of the first Canadian hybrids. CT, PV. (*maximum* × *macrophyllum* or Mrs Jamie Fraser). Fraser/Gable.

■ **ALBERT SCHWEITZER** Medium H4–5 ML–L. Pink flowers with a deeper flare in trusses of 13–14. A vigorous, tough hybrid of neat habit. AGM, Ger, Fra. (unknown). Van Nes.

■ **ALBUM ELEGANS** Tall H7 ML–L. Flower white flushed mauve, fading to white, with a greenish-yellow blotch and darker spots, in a dome-shaped truss of 12–18. Leaves dark green. Spreading, open habit. MA, E Can. (*catawbiense* hybrid or selection). H. Waterer. '**ALBUM NOVUM**' is very similar.

ALENA

■ **ALENA** Medium H5 M. Flowers lightly scented, pure-white, with lemon-yellow spotting, in rounded trusses of 11–14. Vigorous but bushy and dense. A fine Czech hybrid. Flowers are rather prone to weather marking. A bit slow to bud-up and best in plenty of light to make it flower, though flowers last best with some protection. Becoming popular and proving good in Scotland and E. U.S.A. PB, NY, U.K. (Cunningham's White × *decorum*). Kyndl.

■ **ALEXIS** Low–Medium H6 ML–L. Flowers open funnel-shaped, reflexed, light purple, with a large dark-red flare, in a conical truss of 15–17. Leaves dark green and glossy, on a fairly compact plant. (Hyperion × Herme). Hachmann. Sisters: '**GUNDULA**' paler lavender with a large reddish flare, '**MARSALLA**' white, tinged lilac with a large red flare. Like 'Sappho' and rather leggy. '**DURANTIK**' pale purple with a deeper blotch.

■ **ALFRED** Medium H6 ML–L. Frilled violet flowers with faint yellow-green markings, in a rounded truss. Leaves narrowly ovate. Vigorous. Tough and one of the most attractive of the many Seidel hybrids from the late nineteenth and early twentieth centuries. Somewhat susceptible to bud-blast fungus. (Everestianum selfed). Seidel. '**EFFNER**' bred from 'Alfred' and very similar.

■ **ALICE** Tall H4–5 M. Flower clear deep pink with lighter-pink centre, ages to pale rose-pink and then to near-white, large calyx, in trusses of 14–18. Upright-slender habit. Vigorous grower. Tolerant of sun. AGM, CD, EK. (*griffithianum* × unknown). J. Waterer.

■ **ALICE STREET** Low H4–5 M. Flowers lemon-yellow in a full truss. Glossy foliage, dense habit and good branching. Foliage not very good. Largely superseded but an important parent of yellows for H. Hachmann in Germany. (Diane × *wardii*). Koster.

■ **ALMA MATER** Tall H8–9 ML–L. Flowers light purple with an olive blotch, 15–19 per truss. Leaves glossy on a well-branched plant, best in light shade in Latvia where it was raised. Latv. (*catawbiense* × Mrs P.D. Wiliams). Kondratovičs. '**LITA**' Phlox-purple with olive-green spotting, in rounded trusses. Now available from Hachmann's nursery, Germany.

ALWAYS ADMIRED

■ **ALWAYS ADMIRED** Low H6 M–ML. Peachy-pink flowers flushed yellow in rounded trusses. Compact habit with 'Scintillation'-like foliage. (Scintillation × *haematodes*). Wister.

■ **AMANDA JOAN YOUNG** Low H6 ML–L. Flowers bright rose with a paler purple centre blotched orange-yellow, giving a peachy-apricot effect, in balled trusses of 7–9. Low and compact growth habit. A tough hybrid for this colour. PB. (Vulcan × Dexter seedling). Anderson.

■ **AMARETTO** Low H4 ML. Flower funnel-campanulate, creamy orange tinged blood-red, in flat trusses of 12–16. Leaves ovate, smooth, glossy, dark green. Compact habit. Flowers look rather muddy from a distance. (*dichroanthum* ssp. *scyphocalyx* × Hachmann's Marina). Hachmann. '**KINNOR**' flowers orange inside, deep pink outside and on margins, in a loose truss. '**MASKARILL**' orange with deep-pink margins.

■ **AMBASSADOR** Semi-dwarf–Low H4–5 ML. Flowers of deep pink, upper-petal lighter pink, in trusses of 20. Good habit. Not very much grown these days. (Jan Dekins × Madame de Bruin). Rotterdam.

■ **AMBER TOUCH** Low H4 ML–L. Flowers moderate yellowish-pink edges, fading to light yellow, with strong-red nectaries, outside strong yellowish pink, in a truss of 16. Leaves dark green, dense habit. (Nadia × Sedona). Barlup.

■ **AMERICA** Medium H7 ML. Flower dark red with a slight bluish cast, in a ball-shaped truss. Dull, matte-green leaves. Open, sprawling habit. Best in full sun. An 'ironclad', the hardiest of the old reds. Needs pruning to keep in shape. (Parsons Grandiflorum × dark-red hybrid). Koster.

■ **AMOR** Medium H3–4 L. Flowers small, white tinged pink, with red spotting, in lax trusses of about 10. Leaves with thin indumentum. Poor foliage and feeble flowers. At least it is late. (*griersonianum* × *thayerianum*). Stevenson.

■ **AMPHION (syn. F.I. AMES)** Medium–Tall H6 ML. Flowers rose-pink, with bold-white centre, in loosely rounded trusses of 21. Large broad glossy dark-green leaves, deeply veined. (Sometimes also spelled 'Ampion'.) (*catawbiense* × unknown). A.Waterer.

■ **ANAH KRUSCHKE** Medium H6 ML. Flower widely funnel-shaped, strong reddish purple with a deep purplish-red blotch, in ball-shaped trusses of 10–12. Leaves elliptic, glossy rounded habit. Heat and sun tolerant. 'Has a very strong root system and makes an excellent landscape plant'. G. Woodard, Long Island. AZ, CA, EG, EK, MB, MT, NO, OL, PT, SC, SE, SI, WT. (*ponticum* seedling). Kruschke.

ANAH KRUSCHKE

■ **ANANOURI** Low–Medium H4–5 ML. Flower openly funnel-shaped, frilly, medium-red with an inconspicuous eye in a truss of 12. Leaves elliptic, dull green, on an upright, well branched, vigorous grower. (Britannia × *fortunei* ssp. *discolor*). Phipps.

■ **ANATEVKA** Low H5 ML. Flowers deep purple-lilac with a large darker flare, in a rounded truss. Leaves dark green, edges recurved. One of a large series of new Hachmann dark purples; probably too many have been named, time will tell which are the best. Hachmann. '**KANGARO**' purple fading to paler in centre, with dark flare. '**MUGAMBO**' deep purple, darker flare, fairly compact.

■ **ANDANTINO** Medium H5 EM–M. Flowers large, deep pinkish-red, of heavy texture, in rounded trusses. Leaves thick, dark green. The first successful hybrid of 'Taurus' as far as I know. Should be good. Buds-up younger than 'Taurus'. Ger. (Taurus × Carola). Hachmann. '**ATTRAKTION**' a similar sister seedling.

■ **ANGELO g.** Tall H4–5 L. Flowers blush-pink outside, white with pale green spots within, in a tall truss of 12. Large dark-green leaves. A very large growing plant that takes a few years to flower. Not easy to root. Several clones from different gardens were released, from Exbury and Sheffield Park. (*griffithianum* × *fortunei* ssp. *discolor*). Rothschild.

■ **ANGEL'S DREAM** Low H4–5 ML. Double pink flowers with reddish spots, sweetly scented. Lance-shaped leaves. Fairly well branching but best with vigorous pruning to keep in shape. (Whitney's Orange × *fortunei* ssp. *discolor*). unknown.

■ **ANICA BRICOGNE** Tall H5 ML–L. Flowers pale mauve to orchid-pink, with a green-and-yellow flare, in rounded trusses. Light-green leaves on a dense plant. Some heat and sun tolerance but foliage can yellow in the sun. Free-flowering and easy to root. A very old hybrid from the 1850s. (*catawbiense* ×). Leroy.

■ **ANITA** Medium H3–4 ML. Flowers campanulate, apricot-pink, fading to cream tinged pink. Rather sparse open habit. Little grown. There is also a Seidel hybrid with this name. (*campylocarpum* × *griersonianum*). Puddle/Aberconway.

■ **ANNA** Tall H4–5 M. Flowers deep pink, with a red blotch in the throat, fading to light pink, in trusses of 10–12. This is the P.A. form; there are other clones. Leaves long, narrow, and deeply veined. New growth is bronze-coloured. (Norman Gill × Jean Marie de Montague). Rose/Lem.

■ **ANNA ROSE WHITNEY** Tall H4–5 ML. Flower funnel-shaped, deep rose-pink, spotted brown in throat, in ball-shaped trusses of 10–21. Leaves of heavy texture, matte-green. Vigorous, rapid growing shrub. Needs plenty of room to develop. Heat tolerant and surprisingly hardy. Subject to powdery mildew. I'm sure the seed parent was a hybrid and not pure *R. griersonianum*. AZ, JF, MT, NO, OP, PT, SE, TC. (?*griersonianum* × Countess of Derby). Whitney. Two sisters: '**LUCKY STRIKE**' salmon-pink; '**VAN**' deep pink, heavily spotted.

■ **ANNE GLASS (syn. MRS POWELL GLASS)** Medium H7–8 ML. Flowers pure-white, with a pale-green throat, in a large, rather lax truss. Leaves can be rather poor and it tends to be straggly and of open habit. (Catalgla × *decorum*). Gable. '**STOCKHOLM**' is the same cross.

■ **ANNE'S DELIGHT** Medium H4 EM–M. Primrose-yellow with a small red blotch in the throat, 14 per rounded truss. Glossy slightly twisted leaves. Easy to root and buds-up young. (unknown). Whitney/Sather.

■ **ANNIE DALTON** Medium H6 ML–L. Flowers apricot-pink (fuchsine-pink) in lax trusses. Leaves long and narrow with a slight twist. ([*decorum* × *griffithianum*] × America). Gable. Sister '**MADONNA**' has white flowers with a yellow throat, fading to lavender-pink. Much used as a parent. '**HERBERT'S FIND**' pink, orange and lavender in a rounded truss.

■ **ANNIVERSARY GOLD** Semi-dwarf–Low H4 EM–M. Flower saucer-shaped, light greenish yellow with brilliant greenish-yellow throat, in ball-shaped trusses of 10–12. Leaves narrowly obovate, matte-green. Upright, open habit. Not a good doer in Scotland with unattractive distorted foliage. ([King of Shrubs × Crest] × Golden Star). C. Smith.

■ **ANTIGUA** Medium H4–5 M. Flowers azalea-pink shading to Naples-yellow, base of throat blood-red, dorsal blotch, in lax trusses of 10. Compact, growing as wide as high. (Mary Belle × Dexter's Apricot). Becales/Herbert.

■ **ANTONIO** Tall H4 ML. Flowers rose-pink, frilled, blotched and spotted deeper, fading to pale pink, sweetly scented, in a truss of about 10. Hard to root, slow to bud-up and rather shy-flowering. There is also a red Standish and Noble hybrid with this name. (Gill's Triumph × *fortunei* ssp. *discolor*). Rothschild.

■ **ANTOON VAN WELIE** Tall H4–5 ML. Flower pink with a yellowish centre and red spots, in trusses of 17. Leaves large and thickly textured, waxy, jade-green. Easy to root, vigorous, heat resistant. PNW, CA, AUST, NZ. (Pink Pearl × *catawbiense*). Endtz.

■ **APRICOT FANTASY** Tall H4–5 M. Flower openly funnel-shaped, lightly fragrant, light yellowish pink, with light orange-yellow throat and yellowish-pink edging, vivid-red spotting, in a ball-shaped truss of 16–17. Leaves light green, narrowly obovate, convex, often poor. Upright habit. Sister of the dramatic but ungrowable 'Paprika Spiced'. (Hotei × Brandt's Tropicana). Brockenbrough.

■ **APRICOT GLOW** Semi-dwarf–Low H5 ML. Flower funnel-shaped, pink-edged shading to pale orange-yellow at centre and base of lobes, in flat trusses of 10–14. Leaves obovate, convex, long, glossy, dark yellowish green, retained three years. Thin indumentum on leaf underside. Dense growth habit. (*maximum* × Ostbo's Low Yellow). Hunnewell/Ticknor/Brooks.

■ **APRICOT NECTAR** Semi-dwarf–Low H4–5 M. Flower vivid-red edges fading to orange and a dark-red base, orange veins in centre, in loose to ball-shaped truss of 14. Leaves oval, pointed. Compact habit. Sun tolerant. ([*dichroanthum* × *neriiflorum*] × [*fortunei* ssp. *discolor* × Fabia] × Jalisco). Lyons.

■ **APRICOT ROAD** Medium H4 L. Flowers strong-red on lobes, upper lobes spotted green, throat and back of tube pale yellow, held in trusses of 10. Fine foliage. A popular commercial plant in New Zealand. (unknown). Harris/Henry.

■ **APRICOT SHERBERT** Low–Medium H3 M. Buff apricot-colour flowers, with a large calyx of the same colour, in a compact truss. Long, oval leaves on a mound-shaped plant. (Comstock × Dido). Greer.

■ **APRICOT SUN** Medium H3 M. Flowers tubular-campanulate, inside light yellowish pink with strong-pink lobes, in flat trusses of 10. Matte-green narrow leaves. Rather leggy. Flowers look apricot in colour. (*fortunei* ssp. *discolor* Houlstonii Gp. × Veta). Boulter. '**DESERT SUN**' orange-pink with a yellow centre.

■ **APRITAN** Semi-dwarf H4–5 ML. Flower broadly funnel-shaped, fragrant, purplish pink edged with pale-yellow centre, outside light purplish pink, in dome-shaped trusses of 10–11. Leaves narrowly elliptic, dull, yellowish green. (unknown × unknown). Dexter.

■ **ARCTIC GOLD** Semi-dwarf–Low H7 ML. Flower openly funnel-shaped, wavy lobes, pale yellow with a greenish-yellow blotch, in ball-shaped trusses of 20. Leaves elliptic. Dense growth habit. Very free-flowering. This looks yellow from a distance and is proving to be a good parent of hardy yellows. Excellent, tough and easy to please. MS, PV, PB, NY. (white *catawbiense* hybrid × yellow-centred *catawbiense* hybrid). Mezitt.

■ **ARGENTINA** Low–Medium H8 EM. Vivid purplish-red unfading flowers, of heavy substance in ball-shape trusses of 21–25. Leaves obovate, slightly convex. Good growth habit and dense foliage. ([*catawbiense* white × *yakushimanum*] × Fanfare × Gertrude Schäle or unknown). Leach.

■ **ARGOSY** Tall H4–5 VL. Flower openly funnel-shaped, white with yellow centres and crimson rays, sweetly scented, in trusses of 6–8. Leaves elliptic, matte-green, waxy glabrous, with green petioles stained faintly crimson. Upright grower. Tree-like at maturity. AGM. (*fortunei* ssp. *discolor* × *auriculatum*). Rothschild.

■ **ARKADIUS**® Medium H5–6 ML. Flowers open funnel-shape, strong purplish pink, with a white band along midveins inside, conspicuous blotch of dark greenish yellow, in a conical, rounded truss of 14–16. Leaves elliptic-ovate, glossy dark green. (Scintillation × Furnivall's Daughter). Hachmann.

■ **ARKONA** Medium H5 EM. Flowers pale pink, edged deeper, with a bold-red blotch in a full rounded truss 15–17. Leaves long (25cm) and handsome. Flowers are very striking. Takes a few years to flower and best with some shelter. Foliage can be rather yellow. (Ann Lindsay × *calophytum*). Hachmann. '**MONTEVERDI**' deeper-pink with a smaller blotch.

■ **ARKTIS** Low–Medium H7 ML–L. Flowers light purple, in a rounded truss. One of a race of German *R. insigne* hybrids, this looks one of the poorest. Said to be very hardy, but the colour is not very attractive. (*insigne* × unknown). Vorwerk.

■ **ARNOLD PIPER** Low–Medium H4 M. Flower widely funnel-shaped, purplish-red fading to rose with age, with deep-red spots and blotch, in ball to dome-shaped trusses of 15. Leaves narrowly elliptic to elliptic, yellow-green. New growth is brownish green. Rounded habit. One of the 'Walloper Group'. *CA.* (Anna × Marinus Koster). Lem.

■ **ARTHUR OSBORNE** Semi-dwarf–Low H3 VL. Flowers dark red, trumpet-shaped, in very lax trusses of about 6. Small dark slightly hairy leaves with thin indumentum, on a fairly low plant, one of the latest flowering dwarf hybrids for moderate climates. Late growth is inclined to suffer frost damage. Rather susceptible to mildew. Needs good drainage. (*sanguineum* ssp. *didymum* × *griersonianum*). R.B.G. Kew.

■ **ARTHUR WARREN** Low H4–5 ML–L. Flower funnel-shaped, frilled, soft-orange edged red with deeper spots and markings, in open-topped trusses of 10–12. Leaves elliptic, medium-green, with thin fawn-coloured indumentum. Spreading habit. (Mrs Lindsay Smith × Dido). Slocock.

■ **ASCOT BRILLIANT** Medium H4 EM–M. Flowers blood-red, spotted darker, trumpet-shaped, in trusses of 12–15. Open tree-like habit. An old hybrid that is free-flowering and still worth growing. Fine bark. (*thomsonii* × unknown). Standish.

■ **ATROFLO** Tall H5 M–ML. Flower openly funnel-shaped, bright rose-pink with darker spots, in lax flat trusses of 10–12. 'Atroflo #1' larger flowers and stragglier habit. 'Atroflo #2' is marginally hardier, with tidier habit but smaller flowers. Leaves long, narrow, matte-green with thick fawn indumentum. Useful as a tall hedge. No sign of 'Atrosanguineum' or *R. floccigerum*, which are said to be the parents. Almost certainly a *R. smirnowii* hybrid, perhaps × *griersonianum*. *NY, MA.* Gable. **'GAY PRINCESS'** is a seedling of 'Atroflo', which appears rather similar.

ATROFLO

■ **AUGIE KEHR** Medium H6 M. Flowers fully double, with wavy edges, deep yellow with a green calyx. Dark-green leaves on a free-flowering plant of somewhat upright habit. Needs sharp drainage and foliage can burn in sun. (Queen Annes × Golden Star). Kehr. **'DOUBLE GEM'** is a better double, paler yellow, with a more leggy habit.

■ **AUGUST MOON** Low H4 E. Flowers pale yellow, fading to ivory with light-red spotting, in a compact to loose truss of 16–19. Dense, bushy and compact. Bred to flower early in Australia to avoid the summer heat. Hard to root. Buds-up young. *Aust.* (Nobleanum or Marion × Unique). Boulter.

■ **AUGUSTE VAN GEERTE** Tall H4 ML. Flowers magenta-lavender in large trusses. Very close to pure *R. ponticum*, but more heat tolerant. Sun tolerant. Good in Victoria, Australia. (*ponticum* × unknown). Van Geerte.

■ **AUNT MARTHA** Tall H5 M. Reddish-purple flowers with some yellow markings, in a tight truss. Dense dark-green leathery foliage. Free flowering, heat and sun tolerant, but not much of a colour. Very near *R. ponticum*. (*ponticum* hybrid × unknown). Clark.

■ **AUSTRALIAN CAMEO** Low H3? M. Flowers funnel-shaped, light orange-yellow flushed pink, in trusses of 20–24. Launched with fanfares in Australia, but the foliage is not very good. There are so many Lem's Cameo hybrids to chose from and this is not one of the best. (Apricot Gold × Lem's Cameo). Van de Ven. **'AUSTRALIAN SUNSET'** a sister with flowers strong orangey-yellow inside, moderate reddish-orange outside.

■ **AUTUMN GOLD** Medium H4–5 M. Flowers salmon-orange with pink-and-orange shading and a yellow eye, in lax trusses of about 10. Leaves bright green, on a well-branched, spreading shrub. Heat tolerant but the thin leaves can suffer sunburn. Rather slow to bud-up and subject to powdery mildew. *PNW.* (*fortunei* ssp. *discolor* × Fabia). Van Veen.

■ **AVALANCHE** g. Tall H4 E. Flower fragrant, pure-white with a small, magenta-rose blotch and flushing, in trusses of 12–14. Takes several years to flower. Leaves thick, elliptic-oblong, up to 22cm long, deep green with green petioles. AGM. (Loderi g. × *calophytum*). Rothschild. **'SAUSALITO'** bright pink, blotched deeper. Forms a dome-shaped tree. **'ABIGAIL'** is similar with flowers white, pink tinged, in large, ball-shaped trusses.

■ **AVONDALE** Low H4–5 M. Flower widely funnel-campanulate, strong-red with black spotting on dorsal lobes, in ball-shaped trusses of 14. Leaves narrowly elliptic, glossy, olive-green. Upright, well-branched plant. Best with afternoon shade. ([Pygmalion × *haematodes*] × Wellfleet (exact combination unknown)). Dexter. **'DEXTER'S RED VELVET'** a similar hybrid from the same raiser.

■ **AWARD** Medium H4 ML–L. Flower openly funnel-shaped, fragrant, white with pink edges, greenish-yellow blotch and yellow throat, fading to pure-white with green spots, in a ball-shaped truss of 15. Leaves narrowly oblong. New growth greenish copper. Upright and open habit. Scent has been described as 'root beer'. Subtle colouring fades quickly to white. (Anna × Margaret Dunn). James.

■ **AZONEA** Tall H6 L. Flower tubular funnel-shaped, deep pink to strong purplish pink with sparse brownish-orange spots, in ball-shaped trusses of 12. Leaves elliptic, pale green. Upright habit, moderately well-branched plant. (Azor × Catanea). Nearing.

■ **AZOR** Medium H3 L. Flowers salmon-pink with ruddy-brown flecking toward the base, in loose trusses. There are several clones, some better than others. Most are straggly and have rather poor leaf retention. A useful late pink-hybrid with very bright pink flowers. (*griersonianum* × *fortunei* ssp. *discolor*). Stevenson. **'AZOR'S SISTER'** from a later cross may be the best form. **'AZMA'** very similar but earlier flowering.

■ **AZURRO** Low H5 L. Flower deep purple with dark-red blotch in a rounded truss of 11–14. Almost as deep as 'Purple Splendour' but a better grower. Rather sprawling when young, but tidy with age. Dull convex leaves. Not the hardiest deep purple. *U.K. Ger.* (Danamar × Purple Splendour). Hachmann. **'RASPUTIN'** very similar. **'POLARNACHT'** beetroot-purple with a deeper blotch.

AZURRO

POLARNACHT

■ **BABĪTES BALTAIS** Medium H8–9 ML–L. Rose-purple buds open to white flowers with yellow spotting, in trusses of about 15. A vigorous, upright grower. Best in a woodland site in some shade in its native Latvia. The given parentage cannot be correct for a plant as hardy as this. *Latv.* (Cunningham's White × Elizabeth). Kondratovičs.

BABĪTES BALTAIS

■ **BABĪTES LAVANDA** Medium H8–9 ML–L. Light purple with yellow-green spotting in the throat. Leaves thick, light green on a spreading and bushy plant. Very flowering and easy to root. Good in sun or light shade. *Latv.* (*catawbiense* × unknown). Kondratovičs. Similar hybrids: **'IRINA'** phlox-purple, foliage tends to be chlorotic. **'KĀRLIS'** lilac with brown-green spotting. **'LĪGO'** purple with green spots. Needs part shade. Late flowering. **'SPRĪDĪTIS'** amethyst-violet. **'ULDIS'** violet-purple with green-yellow blotch. Straggly.

■ **BABYLON** Medium H5 EM. Flower very large, satiny white with a red-brown blotch, in a rounded truss. Leaves glossy, medium-green. Dense, rounded, rigid branches. Needs wind shelter and takes a good few years to start flowering. *CT.* (*calophytum* × *praevernum*). Reuthe.

■ **BACHER'S GOLD** Low–Medium H3–4 ML. Flowers broadly funnel-shaped, salmon-pink, shading to yellow centre; cream stamens, brown anthers. Longish light-green leaves that need protection from sun. Flowers are good-sized. (Unknown Warrior × Fabia). Bacher.

■ **BAGSHOT RUBY** Medium H5 M–ML. Ruby-red flowers with a few spots and white anthers, in a conical truss of about 14. Dark, dull-green foliage on a fairly dense grower. Best in some shade in hotter climates. (*thomsonii* ×). J. Waterer.

■ **BALALAIKA** Low H6 M. Flowers orange-pink with lavender on outside, yellow centre, in loose trusses of 6–10. Leaves small, dark green. Dense, rounded shrub. Hardy for a hybrid of this colour and form. (Omega × *dichroanthum* ssp. *scyphocalyx* hybrid). Hachmann.

BALALAIKA

■ **BALI** Low H7 M. Flower light purplish pink with a pale yellowish-green throat, reverse deep purplish pink, in flat trusses of 14–17. Leaves elliptic, pale green. Rounded, spreading habit, 1.5x wider than tall. Likes filtered afternoon sun. (*catawbiense* var. *album* × [*neriiflorum* × *dichroanthum* × *fortunei* ssp. *discolor*]). Leach. **'NUANCE'** is a less popular sister seedling.

BALI

■ **BALLET** Medium H6 M. Flowers purplish pink, with a greenish-yellow blotch, a compact, conical truss. Similar to 'Scintillation'. Sun tolerant. (Dexter hybrid × Catalgla). Pride. **'SATIN DOLL'** a sister with rose-pink flowers with ruffled edges, contrasting white anthers, in large domed trusses. **'PINK SCALLOP'** pink edges, light centres, with a striking blotch on upper lobe.

■ **BAMBINO** Low H4 EM. Flower lightly fragrant, light yellowish pink with red flare on dorsal lobe, in ball-shaped trusses to 12. Leaves elliptic, bronzy in new growth. Broad, well-branched plant. Not a great plant in flower colour, foliage or performance. *PA.* ([Britannia × *yakushimanum*] × Lem's Cameo). Brockenbrough.

■ **BANGKOK** Medium H7–8 M. Flowers open funnel-shaped, of heavy substance, pale to strong coral-pink, centre soft orange-yellow, blotch and spots dark reddish, in a lax truss of 13. Dark-green convex leaves. Easy to root. (white *catawbiense* × [*dichroanthum* × (*griffithianum* × *auriculatum*)]). Leach. Two sisters: **'DUET'** pale-yellow flowers, rimmed in pink, green blotch and spotting in throat, fading to cream; **'MONACO'** pastel orange-pink flowers with yellow throat, fading to off-white.

■ **BARBARA HOUSTON** Medium H3–4 L. Flower openly funnel-shaped, light orange-yellow, pink edges and with large red spots, in dome-shaped trusses of 9. Leaves narrowly elliptic to elliptic, bullate, on a rounded, well-branched plant. (Virginia Scott × Belvedere). Larson.

■ **BARITON** Medium H5 ML. Flower deep reddish-purple, centre light purple, with a dark blackish-red blotch, exterior purple tinged reddish purple, in ball-shaped trusses of 14–16. Leaves elliptic, glossy, dark green. Upright habit. A handsome plant with good flowers and foliage. *PC.* (A. Bedford × Purple Splendour). Hachmann.

BARITON

■ **BARNSTABLE** Medium H4–5 M. Flower very fragrant, pale purplish-pink paling to centre with greenish-yellow spotting and two greenish-yellow rays in throat, in ball-shaped trusses of 10. Leaves elliptic, rounded habit. Good fragrance but not one of the better known Dexter hybrids. (Fortunea SS × [unknown × unknown]). Dexter.

■ **BASS RIVER** Low H4–5 M. Flower openly funnel-shaped, frilly, purplish-pink spotted greenish yellow, with prominent stamens, in ball-shaped trusses of 14. Leaves elliptic, flat to slightly wavy, glossy olive-green. Spreading growth habit. (unknown × unknown). Dexter.

■ **BEA'S GLORY** Semi-dwarf–Low H4 EM. Flower widely funnel-shaped, pale yellow-green shading to light greenish yellow in throat with two small red rays, in a flat truss of about 12. Leaves elliptic, wavy margins on a spreading, dense plant.

([(Naomi × *decorum*) × *orbiculare*] × [(*wardii* × *dichroanthum* × *fortunei*)]). Emmerich.

■ **BEATRICE KEIR** Medium H4 EM–M. Flowers greeny yellow, of thick texture, in full rounded trusses of 18–20. Bushy habit. Hard to root, slow to bud-up and subject to mildew, so now little grown. (Logan Damaris × *lacteum*). Crown Estate. **'JOHN BARR STEVENSON'** lemon-yellow with red spots.

■ **BEAU BRUMMELL** Medium H4–5 L. Flower funnel-shaped, waxy, dark blood-red, speckled black, black anthers, in ball-shaped trusses of 20–30. Leaves dull, grey-green with brown indumentum. Open, sparse and sprawling plant habit. (Essex Scarlet × *facetum*). Rothschild.

■ **BEAUFORT** Medium H7 M. Flowers fragrant, white, tinted mauve, in trusses of 12–14. Compact with large insect-resistant leaves. This should be a good parent for hardy white, scented hybrids. (Boule de Neige × *fortunei*). Gable.

■ **BEAUTIFUL DAY** Low–Medium H4–5 L. Flower openly funnel-shaped, brilliant-yellow, narrowly striped light orange-yellow, in ball-shaped trusses of 12. Leaves with blue-green cast with yellow midribs and red stems. Rounded, well-branched plant. Best in partial shade to avoid sunburned foliage. Buds up as a four- to five-year-old. Prone to powdery mildew. (Hotei × Crest). Whitney. **'ANITA DUNSTAN'** is a sister with yellow flowers tipped orange.

■ **BEAUTY OF LITTLEWORTH** Tall H4–5 M. Flowers large, pure-white with purple-red spots on upper petal at throat in large upright trusses of 16–19, often bent down by their own weight. Leaves medium-green and glossy, on a vigorous plant, which can become leggy. Slow to bloom as young plant. **'LAMELLEN'** is similar, with pale-mauve flowers. *MB.* (*griffithianum* × *campanulatum*?). Mangles.

■ **BEGULA** Low–Medium H5 M–ML. Flowers campanulate, purplish red, +/− unmarked, in a loose truss of 12–13. Leaves ovate, flat, matte-green, on a fairly compact plant. Rather a harsh colour and flowers are loose. (Polarnacht × *orbiculare*). Hachmann. Other German *R. orbiculare* hybrids include: **'MONIKA'** rose-red, **'ROTGLOCKE'** loose trusses of red flowers.

■ **BELKANTO**® Low H6 ML. Pale yellow tinged pale yellowish-pink, greenish-yellow spots, in a ball-shaped truss of 14–17. Leaves dull, medium-green. Compact, broad growth habit. Said to be a good doer and becoming quite widely grown all over Europe. (Mrs J. G. Millais × Golddekor). Hachmann.

■ **BELLE HELLER** Medium H5 M. Flower white with a large golden blotch, in ball-shaped trusses. Leaves large, dark green. Good sun and heat resistance. Rather straggly, open and untidy. Useful for exposed sites. Susceptible to bud-blast fungus in some climates. (Catawbiense Album × white *catawbiense* seedling). Shammarello.

■ **BELLEFONTAINE** (see photo overleaf) Low H6 L. Flower openly funnel-shaped, wavy lobes, fragrant, deep purplish pink with olive-brown flecks on dorsal lobe, in a dome-shaped truss of 10. Leaves narrowly elliptic, glossy, dark green, thin white indumentum on the lower surface. Upright habit. *AT.* (*fortunei* × *smirnowii*). Pike. **'KATHERINE DALTON'** (see photo overleaf) pale lavender-pink, scented. **'FUNDY'** rose, paler centre, scented. There are also other clones under generic name **'SMIRFORT'**.

BELLEFONTAINE

BEN MOSELEY

KATHERINE DALTON

■ **BELLEVUE**® Low–Medium H6 ML–L. Flowers open funnel-shaped, deep purplish pink, slightly shaded vivid purplish red, outside deeper, with dark-red markings on the dorsal lobe, in a truss of 15–18. Leaves elliptic to ovate, slightly recurved, matte-green, on a compact, rounded plant. Buds up well as a young plant. Tough but not all that exciting. (Erich Herrmann × Germania). Hachmann.

■ **BELLRINGER (syn. CONSOLINI'S BELLRINGER)** Medium H5 M. Flower light greenish yellow, funnel shaped, slightly fragrant, with a moderate reddish-brown freckled flare that fades to brilliant yellow-green, in dome-shaped trusses of 17. Leaves elliptic, smooth, on a handsome and tidy plant. This looked a great plant in the New Jersey/Philadelphia areas and came through the harsh 2003–4 winter well. Raised by Dexter's head gardener. *MA, Long Island*. (*fortunei* × *wardii* ?). Consolini/Pilkington.

■ **BELLROSE** Semi-dwarf H6 EM. Flower openly funnel-shaped, purplish pink with purplish-red flare and spotting, outside strong purplish pink, in trusses of 10–12. Leaves elliptic, semi-glossy, olive-green with plastered indumentum on lower surface. (*smirnowii* × Lady Armstrong). Vossberg.

■ **BEN MOSELEY** Medium H7 ML. Flower openly funnel-shaped, light purplish pink with darker edges and deep reddish-purple blotch, in ball-shaped trusses of 12. Leaves elliptic, glossy. Compact, rounded habit. One of the best Dexter hybrids in this shade, highly rated in E. U.S.A. *GP, ME, PR, PT, SE, TZ, PB*. (*fortunei* × unknown). Dexter. **'DOT'S CHERRY JUBILEE'** has larger deeper flowers but otherwise looks very similar.

■ **BERGENSIANA**® Medium H6 ML–L. Light-pink flowers shading deeper towards the edges, flushed pinkish purple with a large blotch of reddish pink in a rounded, dense truss of 13–15. Leaves elliptic-ovate, dark and glossy. Named for City of Bergen, Norway. (Mme Jules Porges × Hachmann's Diadem). Hachmann. **'CASSATA'** palest pink with a small red flare. **'BELAMI'** white with a large red flare.

■ **BERGIE LARSEN** Low–Medium H3 L. Red buds open to flowers of heavy substance, orange-yellow inside, cadmium-orange outside, with light-red spots in trusses of 12. Plant broad and well-branched. In tissue culture in the U.K. Leaves oblong, bullate, dark green. Mounding habit. Give afternoon sun protection. (Jasper × Lady Bessborough). Larson.

■ **BERG'S YELLOW** Low–Medium H4 M. Very bright yellowish-green flowers in full rounded trusses. Leaves yellow-green. Not all that easy to grow in our experience. (Mrs Betty Robertson × Fred Rose). Berg.

■ **BERLINALE** Medium H6 ML–L. Flowers broadly funnel-shaped, pale purplish pink, streaked deep purplish pink, centre paler, outside purplish red, in a domed truss of 13–15. Leaves elliptic, slightly glossy. Compact, slightly wider than high. (Tarantella × Seestadt Bremerhaven). Hachmann. **'MADDALENA'** similar.

■ **BERLINER LIEBE** Medium H5 ML. Flowers rose-pink, centre paler, with brown spotting, fading to a harsh bluish pink, in compact trusses of 14–21. Thick pointed leaves on a compact, dense plant. I'm not keen on the colour of this, but it seems robust. (*insigne* × El Alamein). Bruns. **'MARIANNE VON WEIZSÄCKER'** bright red with darker markings.

■ **BERN** Medium H5 EM. Flower saucer-shaped, pastel-pink with lighter centre and prominent magenta-rose blotch on upper lobes, in dome-shaped trusses. Leaves medium-textured, light green. Dense, spreading habit. (*decorum* × unknown). Bacher.

■ **BERNARD SHAW** Tall H4–5 EM. Large clear-pink flowers with a darker blotch, in large trusses. Large handsome leaves. Takes a while to bud-up and needs shelter. (*calophytum* × Pink Pearl). Reuthe.

■ **BERNSTEIN** Medium H6 ML. Flower saucer-shaped, wavy lobes, soft yellow-orange with conspicuous bright orange-red blotch in trusses of 12–15. Long narrow leaves tend to be chlorotic. I have seldom seen a healthy looking plant of this hybrid, though it seems to be quite popular and it is very hardy for this colour. (Goldsworth Orange × Mrs J.G. Millais). Hachmann. **'HACHMANN'S LIBELLE'** greenish-yellow flowers. Not as hardy. **'FORLANA'** light creamy yellow with red spotting.

■ **BERRY PUNCH** Medium H3–4 M–ML. Flowers strong purplish-red, with deep-magenta spotting, outside deeper, in a domed truss of 12. Leaves with yellowish indumentum on the underside. Sun or part shade. Dense habit. (*yakushimanum* hybrid × [C.I.S. × Jingle Bells]). Kesterson.

■ **BERYL CORONET** Semi-dwarf H5 M. Flower openly funnel-shaped, light purple in centre, darker purple on edge, with dark greenish-yellow spotting on dorsal lobe, in ball-shaped trusses of 11. Leaves oblong, semi-glossy, olive-green. (unknown × unknown). Cowles.

■ **BESSE HOWELLS** Semi-dwarf–Low H8 ML. Flower frilly, deep purplish red or burgundy-red with a deep-red blotch, in ball-shaped truss. Leaves shiny, slightly wrinkled on a free-flowering and easily rooted plant of compact but sprawling habit. Tough and a good all-round performer. The colour is very unusual. *GL, ME, NG*. (red *catawbiense* hybrid × Boule de Neige). Shammarello. **'TONY'** bright cherry-red flowers with darker spotting. **'SPRING PARADE'** light red, no blotch.

BESSE HOWELLS

■ **BETSIE BALCOLM** Medium H4 M–ML. Flowers openly funnel-shaped, currant-red, unmarked, with red stamens, in a conical trusses of 13. Plant dense, rounded, branching well; leaves bullate, new growth tinged red. (Princess Elizabeth × Elizabeth). McGuire.

■ **BETTY ANDERSON** Low H4–5 EM. Buds reddish purple, flowers amethyst-violet, fading to near-white in the centre, reverse darker and striped, in trusses of 10. Leaves +/– elliptic, yellow-green, on an upright, fairly dense grower. (Van Nes Sensation × [Mars × Purple Splendour]). Anderson.

■ **BETTY ARRINGTON** Medium H6 L. Flowers fragrant, rose-madder with a prominent flare, in a fine rounded truss of 17. Medium-green rather thin-textured leaves. Rarely offered as difficult to root. Sometimes shy flowering, and autumn blooming in some climates. (Dexter hybrid). Dexter/Arrington.

■ **BETTY GOHEEN** Low H4–5 E. Flower greenish yellow with pink margins, in dome-shaped trusses of 7–8. Leaves elliptic to narrowly elliptic, glossy, yellow-green, on an upright, spreading shrub. (Fabia × Hawk). Goheen.

■ **BETTY HUME** Medium H5 ML. Flowers open-funnel-shaped, clear-pink, frilled, in loose trusses, sweetly scented and of good substance. Plant grows wider than tall. Compact, spreading habit. One of the tougher Dexter hybrids and flowers are good. (*fortunei* × unknown). Dexter.

■ **BETTY WORMALD** Medium H4–5 M. Flower pink with pale-pink centre and light-purple blotch in large conical trusses of 10–12. Pale-green leaves on a fairly vigorous, upright plant. Similar to 'Pink Pearl'. Heat tolerant and quite good in drier climates. Sometimes has a small root system. (George Hardy × red hybrid). Koster.

■ **BIBIANI g.** Tall H3 E–EM. Flower openly funnel-shaped, waxy, crimson-red with sparse maroon spotting, in ball trusses of about 14. Leaves long, narrow, glossy, dark green with silver-brown indumentum. Vigorous, dense, upright growth habit. A fine early flowering red, good for milder gardens with few spring frosts. *EK, NZ, Mel.* (Moser's Maroon × *arboreum*). Rothschild.

■ **BIG DEAL** Semi-dwarf H6 M–ML. Flower openly funnel-shaped, pale yellow with dark greenish-yellow blotch, in ball-shaped trusses of 18–20. Leaves elliptic, concave, on a spreading, dense-branching plant. Yellow from a distance, this is one of the hardiest plants of this colour. *MS, GP, PB.* (unnamed hybrid cross). Mezitt.

BIG DEAL

■ **BIGGI DIXON** Low–Medium H4 ML. Flowers creamy-yellow flushed orange-pink with a red blotch, with a large calyx, in a rounded truss of up to 13. Leaves elliptic, bullate, glossy. A new hybrid by one of the few contemporary rhododendron breeders in England. (Linsweger Gold × Dido). Dixon. **'GOLD CUP'** deep yellow, thickly textured flowers, 7 per truss.

■ **BIKINI ISLAND (syn. BIKINI)** Low H7 M. Flower openly funnel-shaped, of heavy substance, red, unmarked, in dome-shaped truss of 13. Leaves elliptic, flat, deep green. (Scarlet Blast × [*catawbiense* × *yakushimanum*] × [Fanfare × Gertrude Schäle]). Leach.

BIKINI ISLAND

■ **BILLY BUDD** Medium H3–4 ML. Flowers waxy turkey-red, in a dense, flat-topped truss of 10–12. Leaves with wavy margins, with traces of indumentum on the underside, on a compact, bushy plant. Not all that hardy and not one of the best reds of this size. (*elliottii* × May Day). Hanger. **'KIEV'** another similar hybrid with dark-red flowers with contrasting red anthers.

■ **BLACK MAGIC** Low–Medium H4 ML. Flower very dark red, opening from black-red buds, in a ball-shaped truss. Medium, matte-green leaves on a well-branched plant with an upright growth habit. Best in filtered sunlight in areas with hot summers to avoid yellowing foliage. A little shy-flowering, but an impressive colour. *TC.* (Jean Marie de Montague × Leo). Greer.

BLACK MAGIC

■ **BLACK PRINCE** Medium–Tall H4 M–ML. Flowers very dark purple, spotted deeper. Free-flowering, of rather open habit and hard to root. A very old hybrid, now little grown outside Australia, where it does well. There is also a red Brandt hybrid with the same name. (unknown). Veitch.

■ **BLACK SPORT** Medium H4–5 ML–L. Flower dark reddish-purple with an almost black eye, in a ball-shaped truss of about 17. Leaves small, dark green, twisted, on a plant of upright, open, round habit. Tends to flower in Autumn. (Britannia × Purple Splendour). Nelson/Briggs. **'KATHIE JO'** from the same cross has wine-red flowers. **'BLACK BEAUTY'** is a similar older hybrid with a straggly habit.

■ **BLAZE** Low–Medium H7 M. Flowers strong-red, rims deeper, light-pink blotch, in rounded trusses of 16–18. Foliage medium-sized, petioles dull red, downy. (Mars × *catawbiense* (red form)). Leach.

■ **BLEWBURY** Semi-dwarf H4 M. Flower openly campanulate, white with throat spotted reddish purple, in trusses of 18–20. Several different clones exist. Leaves narrowly elliptic, pointed, with recurved edges, lower surface with pale-brown woolly indumentum. I could never see why anyone would choose this over its parent *R. roxieanum*, but it has proven popular. *AGM, PA.* (*roxieanum* × *anwheiense*). Crown Estate. **'ENBOURNE'** (*anwheiense* × *aberconwayi*). Flowers white, speckled darker. Inferior to its parents.

■ **BLINKLICHT®** Low H4–5 M. Flowers open from dark-red buds, to cherry-red with darker margins, in a truss of 15–21. Leaves elliptic, dark green. Hachmann named too many selections from this cross. (Nova Zembla × Mars). Hachmann. **'HACHMANN'S LAGERFEUR'** strong-red. **'NICOLINE'** deep red. None are as good as 'Feuerschein' (q.v.). (*See* also 'Sammetglut'.)

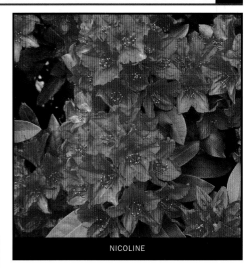

NICOLINE

■ **BLITZ** Semi-dwarf–Low H3 M. Flower funnel-campanulate, dark red, unmarked, in loose trusses of 10–14. Leaves medium-sized, dark green with fawn indumentum on the under surface, on a dense plant growing wider than high. Sometimes flowers in autumn. Quite heat tolerant for a *R. haematodes* hybrid. (*haematodes* × G.A. Sims). Clark.

■ **BLONDIE** Medium H5 ML. Flowers pale yellow with orange-and-yellow blotch in throat. Slow to bud-up and hard to root but used as a parent for other yellows. Compact habit. ([Nereid × *fortunei* ssp. *discolor*] × Russell Harmon). Leach/Pride. Two sisters: **'BLAZEN SUN'** and **'PEACHES AND CREAM'** were also named.

■ **BLUE BOY** Medium H5 L. Flower openly funnel-shaped, strong-purple with a prominent near-black blotch, in tight ball-trusses of 18–20. Leaves narrowly elliptic, dark green. Upright, open habit better than most 'blues'. *FS.* (Blue Ensign × Purple Splendour). Watson. Sister **'BLUE HAWAII'** has larger, light-coloured flowers.

■ **BLUE DANUBE** Tall H4–5 ML. Flower lavender-blue with a greenish blotch, in dome-shaped trusses of 20–25. Leaves dark green. A tall, sprawling plant. Flowers of good texture and free-flowering. (*fortunei* ssp. *discolor* × Purple Splendour). Knap Hill Nursery.

■ **BLUE ENSIGN** Low H6 M. Flower pale lavender-blue with a prominent dark blotch, in ball-shaped trusses of 15–18. Leaves, large, dark matte-green with a tendency to black leaf-spot. Dense, spreading habit. Heat tolerant. *BH, CH, JF.* (unknown × unknown). Slocock. **'BLUE FROST'** frilled lavender flowers with a golden eye. Good foliage.

■ **BLUE JAY** Medium H5 ML–L. Flower small, pale lavender-blue, edged violet, purple blotch, spotted brown on upper lobes, in small trusses of about 15. Leaves dark and glossy, on a compact plant. Heat and sun tolerant. The flowers are rather insignificant and they don't last well in warm or wet weather. *CA.* (*ponticum* seedling or Blue Ensign ×). Larson.

■ **BLUE PACIFIC** Medium H4–5 ML. Flower openly funnel-shaped, light reddish-purple with a dark reddish-purple blotch and spots, in ball-shaped trusses of 10–16. Leaves narrowly elliptic to oblanceolate, glossy, yellow-green. Said to perform best in some shade. We found it had rather dejected hanging foliage and never grew very well. Said to be a favourite of weevils. (Purple Splendour × Susan). Whitney.

BLUE PETER

■ **BLUE PETER** Medium H5 M–ML. Flowers light lavender, with frilled edges, throat near-white, overlaid with a prominent purple flare, 15 per conical truss. Leaves elliptic, concave, glossy, matte dark green. Vigorous and sprawling plant. Heat and sun tolerant. Foliage is often burned in E. U.S.A. winters, perhaps due to thin leaf-texture. Weevils like the leaves too. *AGM.* (unknown). Waterer, Sons and Crisp. **'DERREL KING'** mauve with a deeper flare. A New Zealand hybrid of 'Blue Peter'.
■ **BLUE RHAPSODY** Medium H4–5 ML. Flower openly funnel-shaped, reddish purple, with white stamens, a darker blotch and spots, in ball-shaped trusses of 12. Leaves narrowly elliptic to oblanceolate, yellow-green, on an upright, stiffly branched, rather sparse grower. (A. Bedford × Purple Splendour). Whitney. **'BLUE LAGOON'** a sister with blue-purple flowers with a deeper eye. **'IMPERIAL'** bluish purple with black flare, red stems. Buds-up young.
■ **BLUE RIVER** Medium H4–5 M–ML. Flower pale lavender-violet, in ball-shaped trusses of 17. Leaves elliptic, dark green, thin-textured, on a compact plant. Far from blue, the flowers are rather pale lavender. (Van Nes Sensation × Emperor de Maroc). Lyons.
■ **BLUEBELL (syn. 'BLUE BELL')** Low–Medium H4–5 M–ML. Large, compact trusses of shapely campanulate flowers, wide edges of light-purple tinged blue, centre white, a few yellowish dorsal spots. A vigorous plant. There were two plants

under this name: 'Bluebell' (one word) and 'Blue Bell' (two words); I think they are now used interchangeably for the same plant. Tall and upright. I like the unusual flowers. (Unknown). A. Waterer. **'NICHOLAS'** a Rothschild hybrid of similar colour, which is rather straggly.
■ **BLUESHINE GIRL** Medium H4–5 ML. Flowers open from deep-pink buds to cream, with a yellow centre and red basal-blotch, in loose trusses. Leaves, petioles and flower buds a fine glaucous green. Not all that free-flowering. The summer foliage is quite striking. (Soulkew × *wardii*). Hobbie/Wüstemeyer.
■ **BLUNIQUE (syn. BLUENIQUE)** Low H4–5 EM. Flowers cream with lavender-blue spotting in throat, in ball-shaped trusses. Fairly compact habit. An odd cross which turns out to be better than it sounds. (Blue Peter × Unique). Hall.
■ **BLUTOPIA** Medium H6 L. Flower openly funnel-shaped, deep purple with greenish-yellow spotting on dorsal lobe, in a ball-shaped truss of 12–15. Leaves elliptic, slightly twisted, dark green, on a broad, upright grower. Said to be one of the best hybrids of this shade. It looked a good plant at Hachmann's nursery. (Catawbiense Grandiflorum × Arthur Bedford). Hachmann.
■ **BODDAERTIANUM** Tall H4 EM. Flowers open pale pink, fading quickly to creamy white, spotted maroon-purple, in a tall truss of 18–20. Leaves matte, narrow and bullate with a thin indumentum on the lower surface. Surprisingly hardy for a *R. arboreum* hybrid and seems to be sun tolerant. A very old hybrid, still grown commercially. (*arboreum* × *ponticum*). Van Houtte.
■ **BONITO g. & cls.** Medium H4 L. Flower pale blush-pink, fading to white, sweetly scented, with heavy chocolate-brown spotting on the upper lobes, in large, rounded trusses. (AM clone). Another clone has yellow-green markings in the throat. Leaves medium-green. Dark greyish-green leaves, on an upright, vigorous plant. (*fortunei* × Luscombei). Rothschild.
■ **BONNIE BABE (syn. CECIL'S CHOICE)** Semi-dwarf–Low H3–4 M–ML. Flower openly campanulate, yellow with more intense colour in throat and cardinal-red spots, reverse shaded red, with a large yellow calyx, in dome-shaped trusses of 10–14. Leaves elliptic, dull, yellowish green, on a rounded, well-branched plant. (Inca Gold × unknown orange hybrid). Elliott.
■ **BONNIE DOONE (syn. KIRSTY)** Low H3? M–ML. Yellow flowers with red markings. Very compact. Best with shelter from wind. Free-flowering. A New Zealand hybrid. (?Gold Mohur × Ilam Apricot). Yates.
■ **BORDÜRE** Low–Medium H5 M–ML. Flowers white with a bold deep-pink edging, with a dark red-purple blotch, in a tight compact truss. A striking new Hachmann hybrid with a more compact habit that its parent 'Hachmann's Charmant'. (Hachmann's Charmant × Schneespiegel). Hachmann.
■ **BORNEO** Medium H7 EM. Flower pale yellow with bright-yellow centre in ball-shaped truss of 8–10. Leaves oblong, flat. Dense, spreading habit. Free-flowering. One of the earliest flowering elepidote Leach hybrids. (*catawbiense*, white form × [*dichroanthum* ssp. *apodectum* × Loderi White Diamond]). Leach.
■ **BOULE DE NEIGE** Medium H8 M. Flower openly funnel-shaped, wavy edges, pure-white with a few green-yellow spots, in a truss of about 10. Dull-green, leathery, upward-pointing leaves on a

compact and tight-mounding plant. Not very heat tolerant so best in northerly gardens. Foliage prone to lace-wing damage in full sun in E. North America. A successful parent. Highly rated in many areas: *CT, MS, MT, SV.* (*caucasicum* × *catawbiense* hybrid). Oudieu.
■ **BOULTER'S CREAM** Tall H3–4 EM–M? Flowers large, yellowish white with darker spotting, in a truss of 10–15. Leaves elliptic. A tall, vigorous, tree-forming hybrid that seems only to be grown in its native Australia. (unknown). Boulter.
■ **BOULTER'S ROBYN (syn. ROBYN)** Medium H4 EM. Flowers strong reddish purple along lobe edges, shading to very pale purple in throat, outside strong reddish purple at lobe edges shading to very pale purple near calyx, unspotted, in a truss of 14. Leaves wavy edged, moderate olive-green. (Van Nes Sensation × Marion). Boulter. **'HEATHERDALE'** a lilac-pink sister seedling.
■ **BRANDT RED** Semi-dwarf H4 M. Flowers ruby-red, in flat-topped trusses. Dark-green foliage with indumentum on the leaf underside. (Grosclaude × Britannia). Brandt.
■ **BRAVO!** Tall H8 E. Flower light purplish-pink, lighter in centre, sparse dorsal brown spotting, in truss of 11–12. Handsome foliage on a rather leggy plant. Sun and heat tolerant, easy to grow, free-flowering and resistant to insects. Flowers fade quickly in full sun. Extremely hardy and flowers well after severe winters. (*catawbiense* var. *album* × [*fortunei* × (*arboreum* ssp. *arboreum* × *griffithianum*)]). Leach.
■ **BREMEN** Semi-dwarf–Low H4–5 EM–M. Flowers scarlet in a loose truss of up to 12. Leaves with silvery new growth. Not all that hardy. There is another 'Bremen': a *R. williamsianum* hybrid with loose trusses of pink flowers. (*haematodes* × *catawbiense* ×). Bohlje.
■ **BRIGADOON** Low–Medium H3 M–ML. Flowers cherry-red, with a large calyx, giving a hose-in-hose appearance, in loose trusses of about 8. Yellow-green foliage. Prone to bark-split in Scotland and killed stone-dead. An appalling plant without any merit, released untested in tissue culture in Washington, U.S.A., claimed to be double, which it is not. I don't believe that it is a 'yak' hybrid. (unknown × *yakushimanum*?). Larson/Minch.
■ **BRIGGS RED STAR** Medium H4 EM–M. Flowers in flat truss of 12–14, openly funnel-shaped, heavy-textured, inside strong-red, with strong-red veining, and with dark-red speckles in throat. Leaves thickly textured, pale olive-green, on a sturdy plant. A 'frankenrhododendron', created in a test tube to be tetraploid. (Jean Marie de Montague treated with colchicine). Briggs.

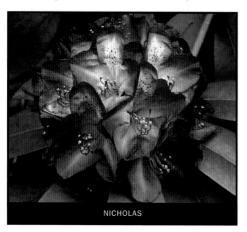

NICHOLAS

BRIGITTE

■ **BRIGITTE** Low H5 ML. Flower medium-vivid-reddish-purple at margins shading toward centre to pale pink-and-white with a yellow-green blotch in a ball-shaped truss of 14–18. Leaves elliptic, glossy, deep green on a compact, dense, plant. Very fine in many gardens and seems to be best grafted. Not always free-flowering when young. (*insigne* × Mrs J.G. Millais). Hachmann.

■ **BRITANNIA** Low H4–5 ML. Flowers campanulate, bright scarlet-red, in ball-shaped trusses of about 15. Leaves large, deeply veined, dull, yellowish green. Sun tolerant but foliage can look an unhealthy yellow. Takes four to five years to flower freely. Hard to root. Why this plant is still grown is largely beyond me. It does flower reliably, I suppose. (Queen Wilhelmina × Stanley Davies). Van Nes.

BROWN EYES

BUD FLANAGAN

BRITANNIA

■ **BRITTENHILL** Medium H5 M. Flowers large, bright red, with black freckling. Vigorous and upright habit. Somewhat similar to 'Markeeta's Prize' but not nearly as well known. (Jean Marie de Montague × Red Loderi). B. Smith.

■ **BRITTENHILL BUGLE** Medium–Tall H4 EM–M. Flower openly funnel-shaped, vivid-red with a star-shaped eye almost black at edges and lighter in centre, reverse with red lines near centre of lobes, in ball-shaped trusses of 9–10. Leaves narrowly, elliptic, yellowish green with brownish young growth. *CA.* (Karkov × [Loderi King George × Earl of Athlone]). B. Smith.

■ **BRONZE WING** Low H4 EM–M. Pink buds open to creamy white with rosy edges in an open-topped truss. Leaves heavy textured on a plant of low, bushy habit. New growth deep bronze-red. *Aus, NZ.* (unknown). Teese.

■ **BROUGHTONII** Tall H4–5 EM. Flower rose-red with dark-red spots, in a large truss of about 20. Leaves narrow, long, with light indumentum on the under-surface. Upright growth habit. One of the earliest hybrids ever made, pre-1835. *Vic.* (*arboreum* × unknown). Broughton.

■ **BROWN EYES** Medium H7 M. Flowers pink with a golden-brown flare in throat, in a rounded truss. Deep-green twisted foliage on a vigorous and tough plant. Heat tolerant. One of the most highly rated Dexters in E. U.S.A., but in the U.K. it tends to have dejectedly hanging, twisted, yellow leaves. (*fortunei* × unknown). Dexter.

■ **BRUCE BRECHTBILL** Low H4–5 EM. Flower openly funnel-shaped, pale pink with light-yellow throat, in ball-shaped trusses of 10–12. Leaves elliptic, glossy, olive-green. Plant has a compact, dense habit. Best in full sun in north to ensure that it flowers well. The pink form of the well-known 'Unique'. Consistently highly rated. *AGM, CA, EK, FS, NO, PA, SI, TC, U.K.* (bud sport of Unique). Brechtbill.

BRUCE BRECHTBILL

■ **BRUN'S GLORIA** Medium H5 L. Flowers creamy yellow with a faint pink tinge, with yellow-green markings on the dorsal lobe, outside creamy yellow with a very faint pink tinge in loose trusses of 10–17. Leaves elliptic, flat, pale green. Pleasant pastel-coloured flowers but not much to get excited about. (Prof F. Bettex × Goldsworth Orange). Bruns. '**CHAMPAGNE COCKTAIL**' a new English hybrid with a blend of pastel-pink flowers in late June.

■ **BRYCE CANYON** Semi-dwarf–Low H4 M. Flower openly funnel-shaped, light orange fading to light yellow with age, red blotch deep in throat, reverse tinged light orange in dome-shaped trusses of 10–14. Leaves oblanceolate, yellowish green, new growth bronze. Upright, well-branched habit. (King of Shrubs × Idealist). Childers.

■ **BUCHANAN SIMPSON** Medium H4–5 EM. Flowers phlox-pink, wide, throat speckled reddish olive, base of corolla yellowish, in trusses of 8–10. Bright green recurved leaves. Compact with sturdy stems. (*oreodoxa* var. *fargesii* × unknown). Greig.

■ **BUD FLANAGAN** Medium–Tall H4–5 ML–L. Flowers small, and thin-textured, mauve, with large flash of deep chestnut, in rounded trusses of 18–20. Dark-green leaves on a tough and sturdy bush. A good parent of blotched hybrids. (*ponticum* × unknown). Rothschild.

■ **BUMBLEBEE** Medium H5 ML. Flowers phlox-purple, with a maroon-and-black eye, in trusses of 25–27. Dark glossy green foliage. Robust. One of the best hybrids of this colour for New Zealand. *Aus.* (Purple Splendour × Blue Peter). King. Sister seedlings include '**RONKONKOMA**' amethyst-violet flowers, darker edges and reverse and '**BLUE CROWN**' spectrum-violet, lighter centre, blotched medium-greyed-purple.

■ **BURGUNDULA** Low–Medium H5 ML–L. Flowers deep reddish-purple, paler on midveins and in throat, outside deep reddish-purple, with an almost black dorsal blotch, in a dense rounded truss of about 18. Leaves elliptic to ovate, dark green, on a fairly compact spreading plant. Holger Hachmann sees this as an improved 'Baritone'. (Azurro × Blue Boy). Hachmann.

■ **BURGUNDY** Medium H6 ML. Flower star-shaped, burgundy-red, with white or red stamens, in dome-shaped trusses of about 15. Good habit and foliage. There appear to be two clones, the best is the one with white stamens. It seems to flower well even in semi-shade. *PNW.* (Britannia × Purple Splendour). Rose.

■ **BURNABY CENTENNIAL** Low H4 M. Flowers funnel-shaped, strong-red with deep yellowish-pink flare in throat and with light spotting of strong-red on all lobes, in compact trusses of 20–25. Leaves with slightly wavy margins, moderate olive-green above. A promising and striking new hybrid. (Leona × Etta Burrows). Trayling/Finley.

■ **BURNING BUSH** Low H4 ML–L. Flowers waxy, campanulate, tangerine-red, in loose trusses of 5–10. Leaves with indumentum on underside. A low spreading bush. Subject to mildew. Grown in New Zealand. I'm not sure why anyone would grow this in place of its more distinctive parents. (*haematodes* × *dichroanthum*). Rothschild.

■ **BUSUKI**® Low H5 ML. Flowers funnel-shaped, strong-red, in a rounded truss of 19. Leaves elliptic. A compact, slow-growing and tough red with fine trusses. (Tarantella × Small Wonder). Hachmann.

BUSUKI

■ **BUTTER BRICKLE** Semi-dwarf–Low H4 M. Flower openly funnel-shaped, frilly, light-yellow edges darkening to brilliant-yellow towards centre, star-shaped cardinal-red blotch in throat and red spotting, in ball-shaped to flat trusses of 12. Leaves elliptic to lanceolate, flat, dark green, new growth bronze. Round and compact growth habit. Not nearly as good as 'Nancy Evans' from the same cross. (Hotei × Lem's Cameo). Lofthouse. **'PALOUSE'** from Barlup, same cross, yellow with red throat and spotting.

■ **BUTTER YELLOW** Medium H4 M. Flowers bright yellow in a rounded truss. A vigorous, fairly tidy plant. (Crest × Golden Yellow). Hill.

■ **BUTTERFLY** Medium H4 M. Flowers pale yellow, spotted red, in rounded trusses of 11–15. Leaves ovate, smallish, on a somewhat open grower. Some heat tolerance. (campylocarpum × Mrs Milner). Slocock.

■ **BUTTERMINT** Semi-dwarf–Low H4 M. Flower campanulate, light yellow with moderate-pink on edges and reverse, in flat-topped trusses of 15. Leaves elliptic, new growth bronzy green. Dense and compact habit. Best grown in some shade in sunny climates to avoid sunburn. Susceptible to lace wing. (Unique × [Fabia × dichroanthum ssp. apodectum]). Mauritsen.

■ **C.I.S.** Medium H3 M–ML. Flower yellow-orange with a bright red-orange throat and large red calyces, in a lax truss of about 9. Leaves matte-green and twisted on an upright and sparsely branched plant. Prone to powdery mildew, leaf spotting and sunburn. The flowers are very attractive but we found it too problematic and threw it out. (Loder's White × Fabia). Henny.

■ **C.O.D.** Low H4–5 M. Flowers fragrant, white and pink, dark throat, deep-yellow blotch, pink flush on reverse, in a rounded truss. Fairly compact habit. The initials are those of the Cape Cod hybridizer Charles Dexter. (fortunei × unknown). Dexter/Everitt.

■ **CADIS** Medium H6 ML. Flower fragrant, frilly, light pink in flat trusses of 9–11. Leaves narrow, to 30cm long. Vigorous and dense, heat tolerant and good in full sun or shade. Takes five to six years to bud-up and the flowers tend to get hidden in the new growth. CT, GP, MA, PV. (Caroline × fortunei ssp. discolor). Gable. **'ROBERT ALISON'** pink with golden throat. **'DISCA'** flowers a few days earlier than 'Cadis'.

■ **CALFORT BOUNTY (syn. BOUNTY)** Tall H4–5 EM–M. Flowers scented, white, with a reddish throat, in large rounded trusses of 12–15. There are other clones. Leaves lanceolate, pale green,

stiffly held on a large mushroom-shaped bush. More robust than 'Loderi' and almost as fine. Needs some wind shelter to protect leaves. Not as hardy as would be expected from the parents. Perhaps the cross should be remade. (calophytum × fortunei). Ingram.

■ **CALSAP** Medium H7–8 ML. Flower tubular-funnel-shaped, white with a dark-red blotch, reverse flushed very pale purple, in a conical truss of 18. Leaves oblong, convex, emerald-green. Plant needs sun for dense habit. Leaves rather thin and yellowish and does not have the best root system, but the flowers are good and it is one of the best very hardy hybrids of this colour. AT, CC, MS, NG, PT, SE, TO, S. Fin. (Catalgla × Sappho). Michener. **'MARIA STENNING'** very light purple with reddish-purple flare on upper lobe, in dome-shaped trusses of 24. More compact than its parent 'Calsap'. **'EASTERN SAPPHO'** another fine pale-lavender-blotched hybrid that looks promising.

CALSAP

■ **CAMPANILE** Medium H5 ML–L. Flowers broadly funnel-shaped, edged reddish pink, centre almost white, with a yellow-green flare which changes to red, in conical trusses of 13–17. Leaves dark green, convex. Striking star-shaped flowers. ([Hachmann's Diadem × Holger] × Ignatius Sargent). Hachmann.

■ **CANADIAN BEAUTY** Tall H4 ML. Flower openly funnel-shaped, pale-pink centre, edge shading darker, 2 yellow rays, in a truss of about 16. Leaves elliptic, thick, with slight twist. A Walloper hybrid, which is not as good as 'Lem's Monarch' or 'Point Defiance'. (Mrs Horace Fogg × Point Defiance). Lofthouse. Three sisters named were: **'SIERRA SUNRISE'** pale pink, **'SIERRA BEAUTY'** a little darker, **'LADY OF SPAIN'** carmine.

■ **CANARY** Low H5 EM. Flowers lemon-yellow, in tight trusses of 7–13. Rugose leaves almost always look chlorotic and insect-damaged. For a long time this was one of the few hardy yellows, but it is an ugly plant and I would not give it garden space these days. (campylocarpum × caucasicum). Koster.

■ **CANARY ISLANDS** Low H6 ML. Flowers light greenish yellow with dorsal lobe slightly darker yellow, a deep-red blotch and spotting, in trusses of 16. Glabrous, elliptic foliage of glossy green. Reported to be very shy-flowering in some climates, but seems to do well in Ohio where it was raised. ([catawbiense var. album × fortunei ssp. discolor] × [Fabia × (Mary Belle × Catalga × Peking)]). Leach.

CAPE WHITE (SYN. WHITE SUPREME)

■ **CAPE WHITE (syn. WHITE SUPREME)** Medium H5? ML. Flowers pure-white, from lavender buds, in full rounded, ruffled trusses of 17. Leaves narrow, dark green, glossy on an upright rather leggy plant. Tough and came through the harsh 2003–4 winter well in E. North America. (decorum/fortunei hybrid). Cowles.

■ **CAPISTRANO** Low–Medium H6 ML–L. Flower funnel-campanulate, frilly edges, pale greenish yellow with no markings, in dome-shaped trusses of 15. Leaves elliptic, flat, dull, deep green. Dense, mounding habit. Reports indicate this plant may be the long sought-after breakthrough of a really hardy yellow. Compact and with better foliage than most Leach yellows, this is definitely the best of them. PB, GP, NY, MS. (Hindustan × [catawbiense × {fortunei ssp. discolor × Fabia} × {Russell Harmon × Goldsworth Orange}] × Golden Gala). Leach.

CAPISTRANO

■ **CAPRICCIO** Low H4 ML. Flowers funnel-shaped, hose-in-hose, at first deep purplish pink inside and out, fading inside to light orange/light yellowish-pink ground, spotted red, in a dense truss of 11–17. Foliage not always very good and not as hardy as its parent 'Hachmann's Brasilia'. I think it looks muddy but it will appeal to some. (Hachmann's Brasilia × Whitney's Orange). Hachmann.

CALFORT BOUNTY

CAPTAIN JACK

CAROLINE

CATAWBIENSE ALBUM

■ **CAPTAIN JACK** Tall H4 ML–L. Flower waxy, dark blood-red with darker spotting, held in rounded trusses of about 15. Leaves long, with rolled edges. Leggy and open habit. Prefers some shade for best performance and leaves can be chlorotic. It is worth putting up with the habit and foliage for the outstanding flowers: one of the best red hybrids of all. (Mars × *facetum*). Henny.

■ **CARACTACUS** Tall H8 L. Flowers rich purplish crimson, in rounded trusses of 14–17. Leaves deeply veined, yellowish in full sun. Compact habit. A harsh, unfashionable colour, but very tough. (*catawbiense* hybrid). A. Waterer.

■ **CARAMBA** Medium H5 EM. Flowers deep pink, fading toward the centre, with a bold purple-red blotch, in rounded trusses of 16–18. Leaves to 24cm long, on a stiff but tidy plant. (Kokardia × *calophytum*). Hachmann. **'DOMINIK'** very similar. **'SARASTRO'** pale pink with a bold dark-red blotch.

■ **CAREX** Medium H4 E. Flower light pink with darker-pink edges, freely spotted maroon, in trusses of about 8. Greyish-green leaves. Pyramidal habit. Prefers some afternoon shade. Not really an improvement on the parents, which I would grow in preference. (*irroratum* × *oreodoxa* var. *fargesii*). Rothschild.

■ **CARITA** g. Low H4–5 M. **'AM'** flowers pale primrose-yellow in loose trusses. **'GOLDEN DREAM'** yellow, fading to cream, **'CHARM'** flowers flushed peach-pink on yellow in loose trusses. **'INCHMERY'** rose and yellow fading to cream. Leaves elliptic, shiny on a tree-like plant. Buds up at six to seven years old. Needs a sheltered site in part shade in hotter climates to avoid sunburn. Not all that commonly available nowadays. (Naomi × *campylocarpum*). Rothschild.

■ **CAROL AMELIA** Tall H4 VL. Flower openly funnel-shaped, wavy lobes, fragrant, white tinged pale yellow with red spots, reverse flushed pink, in open, lax trusses of 8–10. Leaves narrowly elliptic, yellowish green, on an upright, tree-like plant. For late flowering, a good alternative to 'Polar Bear' with yellow-tinged flowers. Takes several years to bud up and requires some shelter. (Polar Bear × Evening Glow). Holden. **'JANE HOLDEN'** salmon-pink, **'ADA AGNES ARCHER'** deep rose-pink, both late.

■ **CAROL JEAN** Tall H5 EM. Flowers carmine with a dark blotch on dorsal lobe, deeper-red in the throat, in trusses of 14. Leaves elliptic, on a compact plant that takes a few years to flower. (Vulcan × Robin Hood). Klupenger.

■ **CAROLINE** Low H6 ML. Flowers lightly scented, orchid-lavender in a large loose truss. Leaves light green, slightly twisted, on an upright-growing but dense, vigorous shrub. Full sun or part shade, but fragrance more pronounced in a sunny location. Very heat tolerant and phytopthora resistant and should be used far more in breeding for heat resistance. Flowers can be rather hidden in the foliage. *AZ, BH, CH, GP, MA, MD, PR, PT, PV, SE, SV, TZ.* (*decorum*? × *brachycarpum*?). Gable.

■ **CAROLYN GRACE** Low H4 EM. Flowers soft-yellow shading to chartreuse in centre, of good texture, in a loose but compact truss of 7–10. Leaves dark green, shiny, elliptic, with a red-brown petiole. Sun tolerant. (*wardii* × unknown). Grace.

■ **CARTE BLANCHE** Low H7–8 ML. Flowers, deep purplish pink in bud, opening light purplish pink and aging to white, with brilliant-yellow spots, in domed trusses of 18–20. Leaves with recurved margins on a fairly compact plant, probably only worth considering in severe climates. (*brachycarpum* × Bonfire). Shapiro.

■ **CARY ANN** Semi-dwarf–Low H4–5 M. Flower openly funnel-shaped, coral-red, in conical trusses of 17. Leaves elliptic on a fairly slow-growing and compact plant that flowers freely. Let down by its rather thin foliage, which tends to be chlorotic and which is often munched by weevils. *MB.* (Corona × Vulcan). Wright. **'RED CLOUD'** similar, slightly deeper flowers, less compact.

■ **CASANOVA** Low H7 M. Flower openly funnel-shaped, opening from reddish-pink buds to pale yellow with an orange-yellow dorsal blotch, reverse flushed medium-shell-pink, in trusses of 12–14. Leaves elliptic, glossy, dark green. A fine and very attractive pale yellow for severe climates, though perhaps not as good as 'Capistrano'. *NG, MA.* (Newburyport Belle × Good Hope). Leach.

■ **CATALINA** Low–Medium H6 ML. Flowers funnel-campanulate, with overlapping, flat-edged lobes, moderate purplish-pink throat with strong purplish-red margins aging to white in throat with pink margins, in dome trusses of 16. Leaves flat, obovate, on a spreading plant. (unknown). Leach.

■ **CATAWBIENSE ALBUM** Tall H8 ML. Buds lilac, open to pure-white flowers, with greenish-yellow spots in balled trusses of 18. Deep-green convex leaves. Very tough and good in exposure. The classic ironclad white-hybrid and much used as a parent. We find it susceptible to root rot in Scotland. *CT, GP, MD, MS, MT, PR, SV, TO, TZ.* (*catawbiense* hybrid). A. Waterer.

■ **CATAWBIENSE BOURSAULT** Medium H7–8 ML. Purple flowers with a few darker markings, in a rounded truss of about 17. Dense and spreading habit. Tough plant that takes heat and sun. Not quite ironclad hardy but tougher than 'Catawbiense Grandiflorum'. Seldom grown in mild areas. *AT, MA, MS, NG, TO.* (*catawbiense* hybrid or selection). Boursault.

CATAWBIENSE BOURSAULT

■ **CATAWBIENSE GRANDIFLORUM** Tall H7 ML. Lilac flowers with a yellow-red blotch in the throat, in a full rounded truss. Leaves smooth, dark green, slightly shiny. Vigorous grower, sun and heat tolerant. Probably less hardy than 'Catawbiense Boursault'. *MB, S. Fin.* (*catawbiense* hybrid or selection). A. Waterer.

■ **CATHARINE VAN TOL** Medium H6 ML. Flower rosy carmine with yellowish-green spots, centre paler, in a rounded trusses of 16–20. Deep-green leaves. Rather open habit. *Ger, Bel, Den.* (*catawbiense* × unknown). Van Tol.

■ **CAUCASICUM PICTUM** Medium H5 EM–M. Flowers pale pink, frilly, with a dark blotch in rounded trusses of 14. Narrow pale-green leaves. A 1850s hybrid, occasionally still grown commercially. Much easier to grow than *R. caucasicum* itself. (*caucasicum* ×). Ord of Manchester, before 1853.

■ **CAVALCADE** Medium H4–5 M. Flowers brilliant-scarlet in a loose truss. Narrow leaves. There are so many red hybrids of this type and this is not one of the best. (Essex Scarlet × *griersonianum*). Waterer, Sons and Crisp. **'C.P. RAFILL'** is similar with orange-red flowers.

■ **CELEBRITY** Medium H4–5 L. Flower pink, with a yellow eye, fragrant, in large rounded trusses. Leaves dark green, heavily veined. Best in some shade. There is also a Delp hybrid under this name, registered as 'Delp's Celebrity' (*fortunei* unknown). Greer intro.

■ **CELESTE** Medium–Tall H5 ML–L. Fuchsia-pink flowers, 8–12 per truss. An upright and vigorous hardy hybrid. (Alice × *fortunei* ssp. *discolor*). Waterer, Sons and Crisp. '**SPÄTLESE**' a similar hybrid with heavily spotted medium-pink flowers.

■ **CETAWAYO** Low–Medium H5 ML. Flowers very dark, almost blackish purple, unmarked, pale, contrasting anthers in trusses of about 12. Leaves glossy, dark green. Not all that vigorous. The flowers are an astonishing deep colour, but they are rather small. *AGM.* (unknown). A. Waterer. '**BLACK ADDER**' another deep reddish-purple from L. Newcomb.

■ **CHAPEAU** Tall H4–5 L. Flowers lavender-pink darkening to purple, with a white centre, with a dark-crimson eye, in a rounded truss. Leaves matte-green, bullate, on a rather open, spreading plant. Not one of the best of this colour. (Britannia hybrid × Purple Splendour). Broxson, Disney.

■ **CHARLES LOOMIS** Low H5 EM. Flowers blush-pink, fading to white, with red spotting, in a compact, rounded truss. Leaves narrow and recurved. Buds-up young and with a dense habit. Bred in Louisiana for extreme heat tolerance using *R. hyperythrum*. *PB.* (English Roseum × *hyperythrum*). Thornton.

■ **CHARLES THOROLD** Low H6 ML–L. Flowers maroon-purple with a yellow flare and white anthers. Dark green foliage. Good habit. Low and compact. An old Waterers hybrid which has been rediscovered. (unknown × unknown). A. Waterer.

■ **CHATHAM** Medium H5 EM. Flowers fragrant, lavender-pink with a paler centre, with red spotting, 11–12 per truss. Leaves medium yellow-green, on a fairly compact, free-flowering plant. (*fortunei* × unknown). Dexter.

■ **CHEER** Medium H5–6 EM. Flowers moderate purple-pink, with red spots and red blotch, in a conical truss of 8–21. Leaves smallish, shiny, jade-green. Dense, compact and mounding habit. Opens a proportion of flower buds in autumn in some climates. Tough; a little early flowering but always seems to put on a good show. *U.K.* (Cunningham's White × red *catawbiense* seedling). Shammarello. '**SPRING GLORY**' larger purplish-pink flowers with a cherry-red flare.

■ **CHERRIES AND CREAM** Semi-dwarf–Low H4 EM. Flowers funnel-shaped, of heavy substance, strong-red in bud, opening outside deep purplish pink, inside pale orange yellow, in flat trusses of 14. Leaves shiny, narrowly elliptic, new growth bronzy, on a fairly compact, well-branched plant. ([Fabia × *bureavii*] × Lem's Cameo). Workman/Imrie.

■ **CHERRY CUSTARD** Low H4 M–ML. Flower buds mandarin-red, open to medium saffron-yellow, with coral-red stripes, also on the reverse, in flat trusses of 10–12. Leaves long and narrow on a spreading plant with decumbent branches. Leaves have a very thin indumentum on underside. (Elsie Straver × Fabia Roman Pottery). Lofthouse.

■ **CHERRY FLOAT** Medium H4–5 M. Flowers strong purplish-red with moderate purplish-pink centre, with solid dorsal blotch of dark red, and spotting, in a compact truss of 15. Leaves dark green and glossy. Said to be sun tolerant but others have found this not to be the case. Not exceptional. (Naomi hybrid). Lofthouse.

■ **CHEVALIER FELIX DE SAUVAGE** Medium H4–5 EM–M. Flower funnel-campanulate, frilly, coral-rose-red with dark-red blotch in upright, ball-shaped trusses of 9–15. Leaves elliptic, recurved, on a mounding, dense plant. Can be prone to leaf spot and not as hardy as some similar *R. caucasicum* hybrids. Buds-up young. *AGM.* (*caucasicum* × unknown hardy hybrid). Sauvage. '**CORRY KOSTER**' frilled light-pink flowers with white margins and a cherry-red flare. Straggly.

■ **CHEYENNE** Medium H4–5 M. Flower funnel-shaped, with some fragrance, yellow with faint orange-brown marking in upper throat in an open-topped truss of 8–9. Leaves oblong, on a compact plant, which needs shade in hot/sunny climates to avoid sunburn. (Jalisco × Loderi). Greer.

■ **CHINA** Medium H4–5 M. Flowers cream with a rosy-carmine throat in a rather untidy truss to 13. Leaves heavily textured, are liable to be chlorotic or suffer leaf spot. Also prone to lace bug and red spider. Forms a rather open tree-like bush. A plant of rightly waning popularity. Clone 'A' has smaller more yellow-cream flowers. (*wightii* (hybrid) × *fortunei*). Slocock.

■ **CHIONOIDES** Low H6 ML. Pink-tinged buds open to small pure-white flowers with a yellow flare in small compact trusses of up to 14. Small dark narrow leaves on a compact, broad, dense plant. Wind and sun tolerant. Not very spectacular but very reliable and appears on good-doer lists from all over the world. *GP, MD, MS, PT, SE.* (*ponticum* hybrid). J. Waterer. '**THE BRIDE**' pure-white, spotted green-and-yellow. Dense growing.

■ **CHITWOOD** Low H3 M. Flowers yellow shading to white in the centre, blotched and flared yellow in a balled truss of 13–16. Leaves oblong, margins flat or down-curved, dull dark green. (Hotei × Van Nes Sensation). Stockman.

■ **CHOREMIA** g. Low–Medium H3 E. Flowers waxy, campanulate, crimson, about 10 per truss. Dark foliage with silvery-grey indumentum. Several clones exist. Rather prone to root rot, slow to bud up and prone to bark-split, so not often grown these days. *AGM.* (*haematodes* × *arboreum*). Puddle/Aberconway. '**CASTLE OF MEY**' Flowers deep red, waxy, campanulate, in flat trusses.

■ **CHORUS LINE** Semi-dwarf H4 EM. Flower openly funnel-shaped, fragrant, pale purplish pink with purplish-red margins, light yellow-orange flare on upper lobe, in dome-shaped trusses of 20. Leaves elliptic, convex, glossy, dark green. Upright and spreading grower. Foliage tends to be yellow and chlorotic. Considered one of the better Lofthouse hybrids. (Lem's Goal × Pink Petticoats). Lofthouse.

■ **CHRISTMAS CHEER** Low H5 VE–EM. Flower pink in bud, opening blush-pink with deeper stripes, fading to very pale pink in small rounded trusses of about 8, opening in batches over a long periods, sometimes up to two months. Small pale-green leaves on a low and mounding, dense grower. Drought tolerant. Needs shade in hotter climates. Very free flowering. This is the outstanding early flowering hybrid for moderate climates *EK, MT, OL.* (*caucasicum* × unknown). Methven.

CHRISTMAS CHEER

■ **CIRCUS** Low H4–5 ML. Flower openly funnel-campanulate, strong yellowish pink aging to pale orange-yellow with yellow spots edged pink, in ball-shaped trusses of 12–14. Leaves narrowly elliptic, glossy, new growth with a brown dusting. This hybrid really is a sick-inducing mixture of colours for my tastes but someone must like it. (Fabia × Purple Splendour). Grace.

■ **CLADIAN VARIEGATED (syn. CLAYDIAN VARIEGATED)** Low–Medium H5 ML–L. Small white flowers with a yellow flare in small tight trusses. Narrow pointed leaves of three colours, green, yellow and white. Rather lacking in vigour and foliage looks pretty scruffy, but the variegation is quite impressive. Sometimes suffers leaf-tip burn and fungal disease in summer. (Madame Masson sport). unknown.

■ **CLARA CURRY** Medium H6 ML. Flowers ruby-red, in rounded trusses of 12–14. Leaves dark green, young growth reddish. Plant upright, with broad habit. Heat tolerant. (Vulcan × America). Hughes.

CHEER

CHIONOIDES

■ **CLARA RAUSTEIN** Low H4–5 M. Flower widely funnel-campanulate, apricot to warm-yellow fading to light greenish yellow, in ball-shaped trusses of 10. Leaves elliptic to narrowly elliptic, glossy, yellow-green, on a sturdy plant. ([*decorum* × *fortunei* ssp. *discolor*] × [*wardii* × (*dichroanthum* × *fortunei*)]). Raustein.

■ **CLAUDINE** Medium H6 ML. Flowers purplish pink with paler margins, spotting on dorsal lobe of yellowish brown, in trusses of 16–19. Leaves with a slight twist. Fairly upright habit. Rather curious pink flowers of the 'Corona' type. (Sammetglut × Daisy). Hachmann. **'PALERMO'** very frilly dark pinkish-purple flowers.

■ **CLEMENTINE LEMAIRE** Medium H6 ML. Flowers bright pink with yellow blotch in tight trusses of 15–23. Foliage deep green. No longer grown very much. (Unknown). Moser & Fils.

■ **COLLEGE PINK** Medium. H3–4 M. Rose bengal buds open to paler-pink flowers, in compact trusses of 15. Fine glabrous elliptic foliage and good habit. Free-flowering and highly rated in its native New Zealand. *NZ.* (Noyo Chief × unknown). Massey College.

■ **COLONEL COEN** Medium–Tall H5 M. Flowers deep purple, with darker spotting, in a dome-shaped truss. Leaves are shiny and wrinkled and tend to be chlorotic. Free-flowering, vigorous and tough. Habit upright. Though the flowers are good, it seldom makes a pretty plant. (*ponticum* × unknown). Ostbo.

COLONEL COEN

■ **COLONEL ROGERS g.** Tall H4 EM. Flowers rose-purple fading to pale purplish pink, in tightly packed rounded trusses of 15–20. There are several clones. Leaves medium-green, rugose, with pale indumentum. This is a 'big-leaved' hybrid, which takes a good few years to bud-up and which needs a sheltered site. It looks like a washed out *R. niveum*, which may not be to everyone's taste. (*falconeri* × *niveum*). Rogers.

■ **COMMAND PERFORMANCE** Medium H4–5 EM–M. Flowers white rimmed pink with a dark blotch, in a tall truss. Exceptionally dark green leaves. Jim Barlup has high hopes for this new and as-yet-unregistered hybrid. (Hachmann's Charmant × Snow Candle). Barlup.

■ **COMMONWEALTH** Medium H7 M. Flower broadly funnel-shaped, deep red, in dome-shaped trusses of 18. Leaves elliptic, wavy and recurved edges, glossy. Open growth habit. Very free-flowering. (Henry's Red, open pollinated). Mezitt.

■ **COMSTOCK** Semi-dwarf–Low H4–5 M. Flower openly funnel-campanulate, orange-yellow with deeper throat and apricot-and-yellow streaks, in flat, lax trusses of 8. Leaves broadly elliptic to obovate, medium-green, on a broad, well-branched plant. Hard to root. (Jalisco × Jasper). James.

■ **CONGO** Medium H7 M. Flowers white, with yellow markings, opening from buds flushed spiraea-red, in spherical trusses of 16. Leaves +/– elliptic. Plant much broader than high. (*catawbiense* white form × Goldfort). Leach. **'LUXOR'** a sister with cream flowers, spotted orange.

■ **CONNECTICUT YANKEE** Low H8 L. Flower openly funnel-shaped, opens vivid purple and ages to light purple, edges slightly darker, light olive flare, in dome-shaped trusses of 16–20. Leaves elliptic, dark green, on a vigorous, but compact plant. *MS.* (unnamed lavender *catawbiense* type × unknown). Mehlquist/Brand.

■ **CONQUISTADOR** Low H4 M. Flowers frilled, strong purplish red at edges, shading to strong-pink towards light yellow-green centre, reverse strong-red and yellow in a truss of 11–17. Leaves dull green, thin. (Firebird × Autumn Gold). Bulgin.

■ **CONSOLINI'S WINDMILL** Tall H4 ML. Flower fragrant, openly funnel-shaped, wavy edges, vivid purplish red with a white band inside along each lobe, with a yellowish-green flare on the upper lobe, in ball-shaped trusses of 13. Leaves elliptic, rather pale green. Upright, spreading habit. A rather 'shocking' flower that some might consider in bad taste. We found it was not very hardy at Glendoick. *OZ, NY.* (unknown × unknown). Consolini. **'XEROX'** white with pink edging and a yellow-green throat.

CONSOLINI'S WINDMILL

■ **COOKIE** Low–Medium H5 EM. Flowers rose with a maroon spot in throat and maroon flushing, fragrant, in large trusses of up to 10. Leaves medium green and glossy. (Queen O' the May × Fawn). James.

■ **CORAL FANTASY** Low H4 M. Flowers coral-pink, to yellowish white, with a red flare in the throat, and a large irregular calyx, in lax trusses of 7–8. Glossy leaves, edges flat or curled. Upright habit. (Fabia (Exbury) × Spring Parade). Elliott.

■ **CORAL MIST** Semi-dwarf–Low H4 EM. Flower openly funnel-shaped, frilly edges, inside pale yellow-pink with a pale-yellow blotch and red spots, outside deep purplish pink, shading to pale purplish pink at base in ball-shaped trusses of 19. Leaves elliptic, semi-glossy, olive-green.

CORAL MIST

Disappointing so far at Glendoick where trusses are small and pale coloured, but this may well be a tissue-culture problem: it is very fine in its raiser's garden. (Nancy Evans × Mrs Furnival). Barlup. **'LIGHT YEARS'** pink margins, pale yellow inside with reddish markings. Good foliage.

■ **CORAL REEF (GLORIANA g.)** Low–Medium H4 L. Flowers salmon-pink, pink margins, slightly flushed in throat, in open, lax trusses of about 12. Fairly compact, spreading. Similar to 'Tortoiseshell'. (Fabia × Goldsworth Orange). Hanger.

■ **CORINNE BOULTER** Medium H4 M–ML. Flowers funnel-shaped, inside light purplish pink, fading with age and with an orange-yellow flare in the throat, in conical trusses of 10–15. Leaves ovate, flat, matte-green. (*fortunei* ssp. *discolor* Houlstonii Gp. × Van Nes Sensation). Boulter.

■ **CORMID** Medium H4 M. Flowers light mauve, spotted deep purple, with a green centre, in trusses of about 14. Well-branched, spreading habit, dark leaves. (Midnight × Coronation Day). Van de Ven. Sisters include: **'MAX MARSHLAND'** light magenta-rose, blotched red, **'PURPLE GOWN'** tyrian-purple, blotched ruby-red, **'YVONNE DAVIES'** white, striped rose.

■ **CORNISH CROSS g.** Tall H3 EM. Flowers, of heavy substance, deep pink to red, fading through pink to nearly white inside, in large loose trusses of about 9. **'EXBURY CORNISH CROSS'** crimson. Large glossy leaves of medium-green. Bark smooth maroon-brown to coppery brown. Forms a large tree. Many forms, raised in several gardens. Susceptible to powdery mildew. (*griffithianum* × *thomsonii*). Smith, Rothschild.

■ **CORNUBIA** Tall H2–3 VE–E. Flower blood-red, held in large conical trusses of about 12. Takes five plus years to bloom. Leaves large, medium-green, rather sparse. Upright, and spreading habit. In mild areas plant grows tree-like. *EK, MB.* (*arboreum* × Shilsonii). Fox. **'ILAM CORNUBIA'** has a better truss and is more compact. **'WYN RAYNOR'** another fine red of this type, slightly more compact.

■ **CORNUBIA VARIEGATED** Low–Medium H3 EM. Flower blood-red, held in large conical trusses of about 12. Leaves about 70–80 per cent variegated, yellow-white, The most spectacular variegated rhododendron I have seen. Commercially available in New Zealand and should be good in mild areas elsewhere. (Cornubia sport). Duncan & Davies.

■ **CORONA** Low H4–5 ML. Flowers rose-pink, paler in the centre, cup-shaped, in neat tall trusses of about 15. Dense habit and moderately slow-growing. Not good on its own roots and better grafted. A striking flower and a good parent. Brittle branches. Some heat resistance but best in light shade in sunny areas. (Unknown). J. Waterer.

CORONA

■ **CORONATION DAY** Tall H4 M. Very large flowers, fragrant, tinged delicate china-rose, crimson basal blotch, in large loose trusses of 11. Habit surprisingly compact. Sensitive to sun and wind. Much used as a parent in Australia. Not good on its own roots and best grafted. (Pink Shell × Loderi). Crosfield. **'AROMA FROM TACOMA'** large fragrant pink flowers. Tacoma is famed for its paper factory smell.

■ **CORTEZ** Tall H4 E. Flower openly funnel-shaped, red with throat fading to pink, a few vivid-red spots on the upper lobe, in dome-shaped trusses of 16–18. Leaves narrowly elliptic, glossy, bullate, dark green with faint coppery-brown hairs below. Upright, spreading habit. The given parentage should have produced thick indumentum, so the *R. basilicum* was probably wrongly named. ([Mars × *yakushimanum* K. Wada] × *basilicum*). Cisney/Goheen.

■ **COSMOPOLITAN** Medium H5 M–ML. Flowers light pink, fading to paler pink with a deep-red flare in a compact truss of 10–18. Leaves rugose, dark green. Tough and easy. Foliage can be rather yellowish and the flowers are somewhat thin-textured. Autumn flowering in some areas. *NI.* (Cunningham's White × Vesuvius). Hagen, Boskoop.

COSMOPOLITAN

■ **COTTON CANDY** Tall H4 M. Flower fragrant, pastel-pink, very large, in conical truss of 12–18. Leaves dark green. Upright and spreading habit. Very vigorous grower. Snow and wind may cause stem damage and this was a problem at Glendoick. Sun tolerant and resistant to root rot. *PNW, NZ.* (Loderi Venus × Marinus Koster). Henny & Wennekamp.

■ **COUGAR** Medium H4 EM. Flowers bright rose, fading to lighter pink, scented, about 15 per truss. Well-branched with attractive foliage. A pink 'Loderi' seedling with deeper-pink flowers than its parent. (Loderi King George × unknown). Drewry/German/Weeks.

■ **COUNTESS OF ATHLONE** Tall H5 ML. Purple buds open to large wavy-edged pale-mauve flowers which fade, marked yellow, in a conical truss of about 15. Leaves glossy on a fairly compact, free-flowering plant, which is fairly sun tolerant. Pest-resistant foliage. (Geoffrey Millais × Catawbiense Grandiflorum). Van Nes.

■ **COUNTESS OF DERBY** Medium H4–5 ML. Flower rose-pink with reddish-brown spots, in conical trusses of about 17. Thick pale green leaves. Vigorous, inherited from its well-known parents. *MT.* (Pink Pearl × Cynthia). White. **'PINK PERFECTION'** a sister with pale pink flowers in conical trusses.

■ **COUNTY OF YORK (syn. CATALODE)** Tall H6 M–ML. Flower lightly scented, white with an olive-green blotch in throat in dome-shaped trusses of 13. Leaves glossy, convex (unusually so) and light green. Sprawling, open growth habit. Used as understock for grafting. Flowers are very impressive but the plant is an untidy thug and needs to be hidden behind better-behaved varieties. *AZ, GP, MA, PT, SE, SV.* (Catawbiense Album × Loderi King George). Gable.

COUNTY OF YORK

■ **COURT JESTER** Low H4 M. Flowers vivid red with light yellow-green centres, with an unusual red-striped calyx, 9–13 per domed truss. Leaves narrow and dark green. (Vulcan × Sun Devil). Bulgin. Four sisters also named: **'PEACH NUGGET'** pastel-peach, **'ELROSE COURT'** coral-pink, deepening, **'SATAN'S FURY'** red with a brown-red throat and dark spotting, **'LIGHT TOUCH'** coral flowers.

■ **CRANBERRY LACE** Low H2 M. Flower widely funnel-shaped, frilly edges, purplish pink with paler throat and purplish-red central star, purplish-red margins in a dome-shaped truss of 15–16. Leaves elliptic, glossy, dark green, Spreading plant with dense habit. Better foliage than sister 'Elsie Watson', buds young with fine flowers. (Anna × Purple Lace). Fujioka.

■ **CRANBERRY SWIRL** Medium H3 M–ML. Flowers purplish pink, darker margins, with a deep-red flare, 10–14 per domed truss. Leaves elliptic, flat. Useless in Scotland, so bud-tender it never opened more than a single flower, even after mild winters. It seems to be more successful in N. California. *N. Cal.* (Lem's Cameo × Coronation Day). Davis.

■ **CREAM GLORY** Medium H4 M. Flowers deep cream, of heavy substance, openly funnel-campanulate, fragrant, in dome-shaped trusses of 8–9. Rounded habit. Attractive foliage. Subject to powdery mildew. (Comstock × Cheyenne). Greer.

■ **CREOLE BELLE** Low H4 ML. Flower widely funnel-shaped, wavy edges, brightest pink with a deep-red flare and spots, in dome-shaped trusses of 16–18. Leaves elliptic, smooth and dark. Upright and dense habit. The colour is decidedly 'hot'. Roots easily, buds young and leaves quite resistant to insects. *KK.* (Vulcan × Harvest Moon). Thompson.

■ **CREST (syn. HAWK CREST)** Tall H3–4 M. Orange buds open to funnel-campanulate flowers, primrose-yellow, somewhat darker in the centre of the upper lobes, in dome-shaped truss of about 12. Leaves glossy, dark green, on an upright grower. Best with some shelter. A famous yellow, still hard to beat. Lots of tissue-culture mutants have been sold under this name. These should be burned. *AGM, JF, TC.* (*wardii* × Lady Bessborough). Rothschild.

CREST

■ **CRETE** Low H7 EM. Flowers light-purple, quickly fading to white, with a few ochre spots, in domed trusses of 12. Leaves elliptic, convex, lower surface with heavy tan indumentum. New growth tan-coloured. Plant broader than tall. A useful very hardy 'yak' for severe climates but the flowers are not as good as those of 'Ken Janeck'. *MS, VI.* (*smirnowii* × *yakushimanum*). Lancaster. **'SILVER LADY'** a similar German hybrid.

■ **CRIMSON CONSTELLATION** Semi-dwarf H5 ML. Flower open funnel-shaped, dark-red edges shading to white star-shaped centres, reverse is deep red, in dome-shaped trusses of 12–14. Leaves elliptic, convex, glossy and olive-green, on an upright grower. This looked very fine when I saw it in the late Dick Brook's garden. He was an expert judge of good hybrids and this is excellent. Good reports from all over N.E. U.S.A. *MS, GP, PB.* (Aviva Ann × Small Wonder). Brooks.

■ **CRYSTAL YELLOW** Low–Medium? H4? M–ML? Flowers pale yellow-green, with a darker yellow-green throat and spotting, in a truss of about 16. Not properly registered, so information about this plant is rather sketchy. (Keystone × Cecil). Delp.

■ **CUNNINGHAM'S BLUSH** Tall H5 M–ML. Flower lilac-pink, marked red, fading to blush-pink, in lax trusses of about 10. Leaves narrow, dark green on a dense and spreading plant. Tough and ideal for windbreak, screening or underplanting of trees. Not very exciting. There are several clones of this in its native Scotland, in various shades of pale pink. *Sco. (caucasicum × ponticum* var. *album*?). Cunningham.

CUNNINGHAM'S BLUSH

■ **CUNNINGHAM'S WHITE g.** Low H6 M–ML. Flowers white with greenish-yellow spotting in upper lobes. Several clones exist. The most common forms have small flowers in a lax truss of 7–8. Leaves dark green on a plant of dense, spreading habit. Tolerant of neutral soil. One of the best selling varieties in Europe and also much used as a rootstock. There are probably hundreds of clones in Scotland. We have over ten at Glendoick. The best clone (**syn. 'CUNNINGHAM'S SNOW WHITE'**) has a full rounded truss with a yellow blotch. *Sco, Ger, Hol.* (*caucasicum × ponticum* var. *album*). Cunningham.

CUNNINGHAM'S WHITE

■ **CUP DAY** Tall H3–4 ML. Flowers of tyrian-rose, heavily spotted on all lobes, in a truss of about 12. Poor foliage and seldom grown commercially. Much used as a parent by Karel Van de Ven in Australia. (Albatross × Fusilier). Van de Ven. **'SUCCESS'** Flowers rose-bengal.

■ **CYNOSURE** Medium H6 ML. Flowers open funnel-shaped, lightly scented, strong purplish pink at margins and shading rather abruptly to a very pale purple centre with a strong orange-speckled flare, in a domed truss of 10. Leaves narrowly elliptic, slightly convex, glossy, on a vigorous,

dense and spreading plant. The best hybrid named from this cross. Flowers well in sun or shade. *PB, NY.* (Essex Scarlet × *fortunei*). Shapiro.

■ **CYNTHIA** Tall H6 M–ML. Flower rose-pink-purple with deeper red-staining on the upper lobe, in conical trusses of up to 24. Leaves medium-green, elliptic, tend to hang down in winter months. Sun and heat tolerant. A hot colour but a very old reliable and tough plant. Somewhat susceptible to mildew, but it seems to grow and flower well despite infected leaves. Highly rated. *AZ, BH, CH, JF, MT, PA, PC, PD, PT, SE, SH, SI, SL, U.K.* (*catawbiense* hybrid). Standish & Noble. **'JANET WARD'** a sport with pink flowers with white edging.

CYNTHIA

■ **CYPRUS** Low H7 M. Flower openly funnel-shaped, white with red dorsal blotch, in domed trusses of about 20. Leaves elliptic to narrowly elliptic, glabrous, light green. Round, compact habit. Free-flowering and vigorous. Not worth growing in mild climates. (Mrs Furnival × *catawbiense* var. *album*). Leach. **'PERSIA'** a little taller with pinker flowers.

DAD'S INDIAN SUMMER

■ **DAD'S INDIAN SUMMER** Low H4 M. Flower openly funnel-shaped, red fading to deep yellowish pink to deep pink at edges, outside red aging to deep pink, in dome-shaped trusses of up to 30.

Leaves oblong, slightly concave, glossy, olive-green, upright habit. This appears to be better than its parents. (Pink Petticoats × Ring of Fire). Thompson. **'DAD'S AT A DISTANCE'** very strange grammar in this name… a sister with yellow with orange margins.

■ **DAIRYMAID** Low H5 M. Cream flowers lined pale pink, with red spots in throat in compact trusses of about 10. Leaves elliptic, glossy on a compact, well-branched plant. (*campylocarpum* × unknown). Slocock. **'DEVONSHIRE CREAM'** creamy yellow with a red blotch, **'SOUVENIER DE W.C. SLOCOCK'** creamy yellow, flushed pink with red spots. **'MRS MARY ASHLEY'** salmon-pink, shaded cream, spotted red.

■ **DAMARIS g.** Low H4 M. **'LOGAN DAMARIS'** is probably the only clone now available. Clear lemon-yellow flowers in loose trusses of 10–12. Leaves glossy, elliptic on a vigorous, upright plant. A fine yellow hybrid, perhaps best grafted. Not all that widely grown nowadays. (Doctor Stocker × *campylocarpum*). Magor.

■ **DAME NELLIE MELBA** Tall H4 EM. Flower bright pink with brownish-red spotting, in a large truss of about 12. Leaves dark green and glossy, on an upright dense grower. Large trusses may cause branches to bend sideways. May need part shade to protect foliage against sunburn. *MB, NO.* (Standishii × *arboreum*). Loder.

■ **DAMOZEL** Tall H4 ML. Flower funnel-shaped, deep rose-pink (AM clone) or bright red, spotted darker red (more commonly seen clone with no clonal name) in dome-shaped trusses of 14–17. Leaves narrow, dark green with thin brown indumentum on the leaf underside. Rather sparse foliage. Grows wider than tall. Some heat tolerance. (A.W. Bright Rose × *griersonianum*). Rothschild. **'FIRE BIRD'** glowing salmon to red flowers. Vigorous and rather rangy.

■ **DANUTA** Low–Medium H5 M–ML. Flowers broadly funnel-shaped, pale purplish-pink with a small dark-red blotch in the throat, in a compact rounded truss of 11–13. Leaves elliptic, slightly glossy, with a thin indumentum on the lower surface. (Bellefontaine × [Lumina × Perlina]). Hachmann. **'ULRIKE JOST'** Flowers white, margins with deep pink, small red blotch in the throat.

■ **DAPHNOIDES (syn. IMBRICATUM)** Low H6 L. Flowers purplish pink, small, in small rounded trusses like pom-poms. Leaves deep green, glossy, oval, pittosporum-like, on a densely foliaged, tight growing, vigorous shrub. A curiosity that is sun tolerant, tough and popular in some parts of the world, but not in the U.K., as the flowers are *R. ponticum*-like. *SC.* (*ponticum* sport). Methven.

■ **DAVID** (*see* photo overleaf) Medium H4 EM. Flowers brilliant blood-red, with white anthers, frilly margins, campanulate, in loosely formed trusses of 16–19. Leaves narrow and pointed on a very upright plant that forms a narrow tree. Good at Glendoick as mature plant, but young plants look too sparse to be appealing and so it is slowly slipping out of commerce. (Hugh Koster × *neriiflorum*??). Swaythling.

■ **DAVID FORSYTHE** Low H7 ML. Flower dark-scarlet, held in ball-shaped trusses of about 8. Leaves dark green on a plant of dense, spreading habit. Flowers similar to those of 'Mars' but the plant is hardier. (*catawbiense* var. *compactum* × Mars). Baldanza.

DAVID

■ **DAVID GABLE** Medium H6 EM–M. Flower deep purplish pink with a deep-red blotch in throat, in trusses of about 8. Leaves matte-green. Plant is sun tolerant, free-flowering, easy to root and a good all-round doer but the branches can be brittle. Leggy if grown in shade. *GP, PT, PV, SE.* (Atrosanguineum × *fortunei*). Gable.

■ **DAWN** Medium H4 M. Flowers white blushed phlox-pink, with a small brown blotch, in flat-topped trusses of 8. Average foliage. Little grown. (*griffithianum* × unknown). Waterer, Sons and Crisp.

■ **DAWN'S DELIGHT** Medium–Tall H3–4 M–ML. Flowers large frilly soft-pink, veined rose-pink and spotted crimson, in a conical truss of about 14. Leaves dark green and glossy on a fairly compact grower. One of the first *R. griffithianum* hybrids raised. Little grown these days but in many old collections. (*griffithianum* × *catawbiense* hybrid). Mangles.

■ **DELP'S STARDUST** Low H4 EM. Flowers pale greenish yellow, with moderate-orange spots, and light greenish-yellow throat. A compact fairly neat grower. (Ronald Otto Delp × Golden Star). Delp.

■ **DELP'S SUNSHEEN** Medium H6 M. Flowers openly funnel-shaped, light yellow and pale greenish yellow with strong reddish-orange freckles, in lax-domed trusses of 12. Pale-green foliage. Good reports from the midwest. The truss is rather loose but the colour is good. (Sweet Lulu × [*vernicosum* × (Nereid × *fortunei* ssp. *discolor*)]). Delp.

■ **DELTA** Medium H5 M–ML. Flowers phlox-purple with a pale green-brown blotch, in trusses of 15. An easy, dense growing plant which buds-up well. Not very exciting but reliable and hardy. (*catawbiense* hybrid × *ponticum* ×). Boot and Co.

■ **DENALI** Tall H4–5 M. Flower openly funnel-shaped, tyrian-rose with reddish-orange spots on dorsal lobe, in ball-shaped trusses of 12–15. Leaves elliptic, flat, on an upright, well-branched plant. Heat resistant but not very sun tolerant. *KK.* (Vanessa Pastel × [Anna × Marinus Koster]). Elliott.

■ **DERRELL KING** Medium–Tall H4–5 ML. Flowers mauve, with a deep-purple centre, held in dense trusses. Dark-green leaves on a vigorous plant. Quite widely grown in New Zealand. (Peter Koster × Blue Peter). King.

■ **DEXTER'S AMYTHEST (syn. AMETHYST)** Medium H5 ML. Flower funnel-shaped, light purple at margin shading to very pale purple at base, with a tan to yellowish-green flare, in ball-shaped trusses of 12. Leaves elliptic, on a plant of rather open habit. Easy to root. *PV.* (unknown). Dexter.

■ **DEXTER'S APPLEBLOSSOM (syn. APPLEBLOSSOM)** Medium H5 ML. Flower fragrant, white with edging deep purplish pink, blotched yellow-green with darker spots in a flat truss of 12–15. Leaves glossy on a broad, rounded, well-branched plant. Free flowering. One of the best pink-and-white Dexter hybrids. (unknown). Dexter.

■ **DEXTER'S APRICOT** Medium H4 ML. Flower openly funnel-shaped, fragrant, light purplish-pink with dark-pink edge and yellow-green blotch, in flat trusses of 12–15. Leaves oblong, glossy. Broad, rounded habit. One of the less hardy Dexter hybrids. (unknown). Dexter. Probable sisters: **'DEXTER'S BRICK RED'** pink-red, **'DEXTER'S CREAM'** fragrant, cream, **'DEXTER'S SPRINGTIME'** cream, edged pink, **'DEXTERS' VANILLA'** fragrant, cream and salmon.

■ **DEXTER'S CHAMPAGNE** Medium H6 EM. Flower broadly funnel-shaped, off-white, pale yellowish pink at margins with pale-yellow centres and a yellow-green flare, in dome-shaped trusses of 14. Leaves elliptic, flat, thick-textured, semi-glossy. A rather lanky and weak plant, which is shy flowering unless planted in plenty of light. The impressive flower is often a show winner. *GP.* (unknown). Dexter.

DEXTER'S CHAMPAGNE

■ **DEXTER'S GIANT RED** Low H4–5 L. Flower openly funnel-shaped, slightly frilly, reddish pink with dark-red blotch, with light-red spotting, in conical trusses of 12–15. Leaves elliptic, glossy olive-green. Very vigorous and sprawling but matures into a reasonably shapely specimen. Spectacular, but only reliably hardy in mildest parts of coastal E. North America, though recent milder winters have increased its popularity. *AZ.* (unknown). Dexter.

■ **DEXTER'S GLOW** Tall H4–5 ML–L. Flower openly funnel-shaped, frilly, fragrant, strong purplish red with lighter throat, darker around corolla edges, in a flat to lax truss of 8–10. Leaves oblong, glossy, olive-green, on a well-branched plant. Not one of the hardiest Dexters, so limited availability. (unknown). Dexter.

■ **DEXTER'S HARLEQUIN** Medium H4–5 M. Flower widely funnel-shaped, frilly, deep purplish pink at edges, fading to near-white at centre, in ball-shaped trusses of 10–15. Leaves elliptic to narrowly elliptic, flat with slightly undulate edges, slightly glossy, olive-green, on an upright grower. Free-flowering and striking in flower, though not to everyone's taste. ([Pygmalion × *haematodes*] × Wellfleet). Dexter.

■ **DEXTER'S HONEYDEW** Low H4–5 ML. Flower openly funnel-shaped, wavy edges, very pale purple at margins, fading to greenish-white centre and a light-yellow throat, in a ball-shaped truss of 6–7. Leaves narrowly oblong, wavy margins, on a plant of spreading habit, wider than tall. 'Great flower, terrible plant,' Hank Schannen. Can't argue with that. (unknown). Dexter. **'MARJIE KAY HINERMAN'** fragrant, very pale purple, white interior, yellow blotch.

■ **DEXTER'S ORANGE** Low H4 ML. Flower openly funnel-shaped, deep-pink, shaded orangey, with brownish-orange blotch, in a flat to lax truss of 8. Leaves elliptic, small, glossy, olive-green. Dense habit with branches that can touch the ground. Not really orange at all, unless you have a fertile imagination, but the two flower colours combine to make it look orange from a distance. (unknown). Dexter.

■ **DEXTER'S PEPPERMINT** Low H4 ML. Flower openly funnel-shaped, very fragrant of peppermint, light purplish pink with light yellowish-green blotch. Leaves oblong, glossy, olive-green, on a plant of upright, open habit. (unknown). Dexter.

■ **DEXTER'S PINK** Medium H4–5 ML. Flowers pink, spotted brown, with a tiny deep-reddish blotch in the throat, in full rounded trusses. Leaves narrowly elliptic to elliptic, glossy, olive-green. Broad, rounded, well-branched habit. Free-flowering. Very similar to and may be the same as 'Sandwich Appleblossom'. (unknown). Dexter.

DEXTER'S PINK

■ **DEXTER'S PINK GLORY** Medium H4 ML–L. Flower open funnel-shaped, frilly, fragrant, deep purplish pink with yellow-green and deep-red spotting on dorsal lobe, in flat trusses of 6–8. Leaves narrowly elliptic to elliptic, glossy, olive-green. Plant of broad, rounded well-branched habit. Not as hardy as previously thought, so a plant for coastal parts of E. North America. (unknown). Dexter.

■ **DEXTER'S PURPLE** Low H6 M. Flower broadly funnel-shaped, inside light-purple at edge, shading lighter in centre with a vivid-red flare in throat, outside light purple tinged with reddish purple at base, in a ball-shaped truss of 16. Leaves elliptic, flat, dull to semi-glossy, yellow-green, on a plant of broad, somewhat open habit. One of the hardiest Dexter hybrids with good foliage and habit. *AZ, BH, CH.* (unknown). Dexter.

■ **DEXTER'S SPICE** Tall H4–5 ML. Flower openly funnel-shaped, frilly, very fragrant, large: up to 13cm across, white with pale yellow-green spots in throat of dorsal lobes, in lax trusses of 5–7. Leaves elliptic, glossy, olive-green. Upright, broad habit that can be rather sparse. Magnificent in flower with a very impressive scent, which rivals 'Loderi'. Hard to root, it is best grafted. Needs filtered light in most climates. (unknown). Dexter.

■ **DEXTER'S VICTORIA** Tall H5 ML. Flower openly funnel-shaped, frilly lavender with a greenish-brown blotch, in conical-shaped trusses of 12–15. Leaves elliptic, glossy, olive-green on a plant of upright, rounded habit. Not always very free-flowering but quite attractive and with good foliage. (unknown). Dexter.

■ **DIDO g.** Medium H4 M–ML. Flowers orange-pink, yellow centre, in lax trusses. Several clones exist. A sturdy, compact plant with stiff and rounded light-green leaves. An important parent, in the background of many fine hybrids, such as 'Lem's Cameo'. (*dichroanthum* × *decorum*). Wilding.

■ **DIVA g.** Medium H4 ML. Flowers deep-pink with brown spotting in an open to rounded truss. Other clones have reddish or orange-pink flowers. Long narrow leaves on an open, rather leggy, spreading plant. Free-flowering but rather prone to mildew. Not grown much these days. (Ladybird × *griersonianum*). Rothschild. **'EARL OF DONOUGHMORE'** another similar hybrid with bright-red, orange-tinged flowers.

■ **DOCTOR ARNOLD W. ENDTZ** Medium–Tall H4–5 M–ML. Flowers carmine-pink, frilled, tinted lilac, with a yellowish centre in a compact truss of 12–14. Leaves slightly twisted on a compact, free-flowering plant. Sun tolerant. (Pink Pearl × *catawbiense* ×). Endtz. **'DR A. BLOK'** very similar. **'VIRGO'** Fringed flowers light-pink on opening, fading to white, with a large reddish brown, spotted blotch, in tall trusses of 17–18.

■ **DOCTOR H.C. DRESSELHUYS** Tall H4–5 ML. Flower aniline-red (or raspberry-red) fading to lighter in the centre, in a tall truss of about 21. Leaves dark-green on an upright, rather sparse grower. *NY, MA, Ger. Nor.* (unknown). den Ouden.

■ **DOCTOR STOCKER** Medium H4 M. Flowers creamy white, lightly spotted and streaked brown-and-crimson, in very loose trusses of 6–8. Leaves dark, glossy and insect-resistant, on a plant growing wider than high. Not grown much these days, but a useful parent. (*caucasicum* × *griffithianum*). North.

■ **DOCTOR V. H. RUTGERS** Medium H6 ML. Flowers aniline/crimson-red with frilled edges and brown markings, in compact trusses of about 16. Leaves dark and recurved on a spreading, dense grower. *MA, PV, NC, Ger.* (Charles Dickens × Lord Roberts). den Ouden. **'VAN WEERDEN POELMAN'** a sister with crimson flowers marked brown.

■ **DOLCEMENTE** Low H5 M–ML. Flowers broadly funnel-shaped, outside and edges deep purplish-pink, centre and throat vivid brilliant-yellow, in rounded trusses of 10–12. Leaves dark green, ovate. Less hardy than most Hachmann hybrids of this colour such as 'Hachmann's Brasilia' but much more attractive in flowers and foliage. (August × Fred Wynniatt). Hachmann.

■ **DOLLY MADISON** Medium H7 M. Flower openly campanulate, white with reddish-brown dorsal blotch in a full truss of about 12. Leaves oblanceolate, semi-glossy, dark green with yellowish-green petioles. Plant grows 2 times wider than tall. Flowers are large and plant is very vigorous. Probably not worth growing in mild areas. (*catawbiense* var. *album* × [*fortunei* × (*arboreum* × *griffithianum*)]). Leach.

■ **DOMINIK** Medium H5 EM. Flowers campanulate, pale purplish pink inside with large dark-red dorsal blotch and spots, edged light purplish pink inside and out, in rounded trusses of 16–18. Leaves elliptic-lanceolate, large (up to 19.7cm long), matte-medium-green, yellowish-green edges above. A tough but early-flowering hybrid that needs some shelter. Takes a few years to bud-up. (*calophytum* × Kokardia). Hachmann. **'CARAMBA'** is a similar sister.

■ **DON KELLAM (syn. KELLAM'S ORANGE)** Medium–Tall H4 M–ML. Flowers broadly funnel-shaped, pale-yellow in throat, shading through pale orange-yellow to pale yellowish pink at outer edge, spotted and blotched maroon with rays of pink on outside, in trusses of 8–10. A vigorous but not very hardy plant, which seems to be an F2 Dexter hybrid. (Dexter's Giant Red? × Dexter's Orange). Cowles.

■ **DONATOR** Medium H5 ML–L. Flowers deep purplish red, shaded strong-purplish-red on veins both inside and out, paler in throat; conspicuously blotched dark red, in trusses of 11–12. Leaf undersurface with fawn-coloured hairs, especially on veins and on petioles. (Lee's Best Purple × Purple Splendour). Hachmann. **'LIBRETTO'** a sister seedling, flowers deep reddish purple shading inwards to greenish yellow. **'TONIKA'** deep reddish purple, green throat.

■ **DONCASTER** Semi-dwarf–Low H4–5 M–ML. Flower dark crimson-red with black spots, in trusses of about 15. Leaves concave, wavy edged, stiff, shiny, dark green. Compact, spreading habit, sometimes rather sparse and open. Free-flowering and with some heat tolerance. Not one of my favourites and now superseded. A much used parent. Susceptible to bud blast. (*arboreum* × unknown). A. Waterer.

■ **DONNA HARDGROVE** Semi-dwarf H4–5 M. Flower widely funnel-campanulate, open apricot-pink and age to light orange-yellow, edged strong orange-yellow in a lax truss of 8. Leaves elliptic to lanceolate, medium-green. Plant rounded and well-branched but rather sparse, as leaves are only held one year. Only hardy in milder and coastal parts of seaboard of E. North America. (*fortunei* × [*wardii* × *dichroanthum*]). Hardgrove.

■ **DONVALE RUBY** Low H3? E–EM. Flower tubular-campanulate, vivid scarlet-red, in trusses of 14–16. Leaves elliptic, pale green. Heat tolerant. Parentage sometimes given as (*arboreum* × Britannia). *Mel.* (Lamplighter × *arboreum*). O Shannassy.

■ **DORINTHIA** Low H3–4 EM. Flowers clear-shiny-red with wavy lobes, in a loose truss of 6–9. Leaves dark green with fawn indumentum on the lower surface. There may be more than one clone around. *NZ, Vic.* (Hiraethlyn × [*haematodes* × *griffithianum*]). Puddle/Aberconway.

■ **DOROTHY AMATEIS** Medium H6 ML. Flowers deep rosy purple of good substance with a deeper-purple flare, in a tall, rounded truss. Leaves glossy on a sprawling plant that is rather prone to root problems in hot climates. One of the hardier deep-purple hybrids, though there are some good new ones coming onto the market that have a better habit. (America × Purple Splendour). Amateis.

■ **DOROTHY RUSSELL** Medium H4–5 EM. Flower large, openly funnel-shaped, wavy edges, deep rose-red with dark-red spots in ball-shaped trusses of 21. Leaves elliptic, flat, olive-green, on an upright spreading shrub. Flowers do not last long in warm areas and foliage can burn in sun, but this is one of the reddest Dexter hybrids and it is fine at its best. Best with some pruning as a young plant. (Pygmalion × [haematodes × Dexter No 8] (exact combination unknown)). Dexter.

■ **DOUBLE DATE** Medium H4 M. Flowers rose-pink, double, with mostly petalloid stamens, about 10 per conical truss. Matte leaves on a rather sparse and straggly plant. Rather slow to bud-up. Not bad, but not one of the best double-hybrids and not very widely available. (Unknown). Whitney/Sather.

■ **DOUBLE EAGLE** Medium H4 M. Flowers yellow with a maroon-red flare in the throat. Good foliage. Grown in California and New Zealand. The name is illegal, as there is already an azalea with this name; it will probably become 'Korth's Double Eagle'. (Bump's Orange × Skipper). Korth.

■ **DOUBLE FACED** Semi-dwarf–Low H7 ML. Flower widely funnel-campanulate, hose-in-hose, purplish red with dark-red dorsal spots, reverse reddish purple and purplish pink in a truss of 15. Leaves ovate on a fairly compact plant. (America × Ann Rutledge). Delp.

■ **DOUGLAS McEWAN** Medium H4–5 M. Flowers rosy scarlet with a few black spots, in a truss of about 12. Leaves large, medium-green, curving upwards at the tip on a rather rangy grower. (*griffithianum* × Monsieur Theirs). Van Nes.

■ **DOUGLAS R. STEPHENS** Low H5 EM. Flower openly funnel-shaped, spinel-red with dark-red blotch in throat and spots, fading to pink, in conical trusses of 14. Leaves elliptic, glossy, thick, dark green. Upright rather open habit. I'm not sure that this is any great advance over its popular parent 'Jean Marie'. (The Hon. Jean Marie de Montague × unnamed hybrid). Stephens. **'FREEMAN STEVENS'** is a sister, which differs in a less pronounced blotch.

■ **DRAGONFLY** Tall H3–4 VL. Flowers large, carmine-red fading to fluorescent-pink, lightly fragrant, in loose trusses. Leaves hairy, narrow and long. An enormous vigorous tree, which takes a while to start flowering and which needs shelter for its late growth. Best in part-day shade to allow the late flowers some protection. (*auriculatum* × *facetum*). Rothschild.

■ **DREAM OF KINGS** Low H4 ML. Flower openly funnel-shaped, wavy lobes, light reddish pink with darker dorsal-blotch, in a conical truss of 16–20. Leaves narrowly elliptic to elliptic, glossy. Upright, moderate branching habit. A great name. (A. Bedford × Purple Splendour). Frederick, Jr.

■ **DUKE OF YORK** Medium H5 ML. Flower rosy pink, fading to near-white in the centre, brown spots, held in loose trusses of about 12. Leaves large, medium-green. Open growth habit. *Ger.* (*fortunei* × Scipio). Paul. **'DUCHESS OF YORK'** is a sister with fragrant salmon-pink flowers with a brownish blotch.

■ **DURANGO** Medium H3 EM–M. Flower funnel-campanulate, purplish pink with red blotch and red nectaries in dome-shaped trusses of 18. Leaves elliptic, with recurved margins, dark green, underside with tan indumentum that ages to brownish orange, on a plant of dense habit. (Ruby Bowman × *elliottii* 'War Paint'). Goheen.

DUKE OF YORK

■ **EBONY PEARL** Tall H4 M. Flowers a rather harsh pinkish purple, in conical trusses of 12–18. Dark bronze-purple foliage, young growth red. This should be a great plant with impressive coloured foliage, but it appears to have such a weak root system that we can't make a decent plant of it on its own roots and I think it should be grafted. (Pink Pearl sport).

■ **EDELTRAUD** Medium H5 ML. Flowers deep to moderate purplish pink, conspicuous blotch of very dark purplish red, in dense trusses of 13–16. Leaves convex, mid-green. Flowers are striking. (Hachmann's Ornament × Furnivall's Daughter). Hachmann. **'KALAMAIKA'** a hybrid of 'Edeltraud' with pink flowers, blotched red. **'MODERATOR'** pale-pink fading to white, with a large red-purple blotch.

■ **EDITH BOSLEY** Medium H6 ML. Flower openly funnel-shaped, deep reddish purple at margins shading through purple to reddish purple in centre, with dark-red spotting, in a flat truss of 12–15. Leaves elliptic, flat, glabrous, olive-green on a spreading, open plant. Very hardy for a dark-purple, with a smallish truss of fine colour, a little later than most similar hybrids. Habit a bit leggy. (Dexter Bosley 1035 × Lee's Dark Purple). Bosley.

EDITH BOSLEY

■ **EDITH BOULTER** Low H4? EM–M. Flowers frilled lavender-pink, with darker margins, in ball-shaped trusses of 15–18. Leaves elliptic on a compact and dense plant. Bred for Australia, so heat and sun tolerant. *Aus.* (Marion (Cheal's) × Unique). Boulter. **'MUNDAI'** a sister with magenta flowers. **'KATE BOULTER'** salmon-pink.

■ **EDITH MACKWORTH PRAED (syn. EDITH PRAED)** Medium H4–5 EM–M. Flower bright crimson-red, paler towards the throat with dark crimson markings, in conical truss of about 13. Foliage reasonable but unremarkable on a plant of upright habit. *MB.* (Doncaster × *griffithianum* hybrid). Koster.

■ **EDITH PRIDE** Semi-dwarf–Low H8 L. Flower small, funnel-shaped, pink with pale-yellow spotting and small white blotch, in ball-shaped trusses of 22. Leaves narrowly elliptic, on a plant of rounded, well-branched habit. A really tough hybrid suitable for under trees and exposed sites. Heat tolerant and with better foliage than 'Boule de Neige'. *Nova Sc, IN.* (English Roseum × *maximum*). Pride.

■ **EDMOND AMATEIS** Medium H7 EM–M. Flower rotate funnel-shaped, white with a prominent two-rayed, dark-red blotch, in a ball-shaped truss of 13. Leaves glossy, medium-green, on a plant of upright habit. Easy to root. (*catawbiense* var. *album* × Dexter seedling). Amateis.

■ **EDUARDS SMILĢIS** Medium H8–9 ML–L. Flowers frilly, pansy-violet with an almost-black flare, in a dense truss of about 18. Leaves matte green. Loose and upright habit, best pruned. Best in part shade in its native Latvia. *Latv.* (*catawbiense* × Purple Splendour). Kondratovičs. **'JĀNIS'** dark red-purple with a black blotch in trusses of up to 17.

EDUARD SMILĢIS

■ **EDWARD DUNN** Low H4–5 L. Flowers apricot and pink, in dome-shaped trusses of 10. Moss-green leaves, spreading habit. ([*neriiflorum* × *dichroanthum*] × *fortunei* ssp. *discolor*). Ostbo. **'PHYLLIS BALLARD'** from the same cross has orange/coral-red flowers.

■ **EDWIN O. WEBER** Tall H4–5 ML. Flower flat saucer-shaped, purple, with large vivid yellowish-green blotch on dorsal lobe and green spots, in flat trusses of 28. Leaves narrowly elliptic, dark green, on a plant of upright growth habit. (Purpureum Elegans × Madame Albert Moser). Weber.

■ **EHRENGOLD** Medium H5 M. Flowers pale yellow fading to ivory, with slight pink tinges at margins, in rounded trusses of 10–15. Leaves convex, broadly ovate, pale greenish yellow. Needs good drainage. A tough German hybrid. Probably not worth growing in mild gardens. (*wardii* Astrocalyx seedling). Hobbie. Other similar German hybrids are **'STADT WESTERSTEDE'** and **'KARL SAUERBORN'**, both pinkish fading to yellow-cream. **'ANNA ALBERTZARD'** creamy yellow with light spotting.

EHRENGOLD

■ **EL CAMINO** Tall H4–5 M. Flower openly funnel-shaped, wavy lobes, pinkish red with red blotch and spotting on dorsal lobe in a rounded truss of about 13. Leaves elliptic, long, thick, light green, slightly wavy, on an upright and spreading plant. *JF.* (Anna? × Marinus Koster?). Lem or Whitney.

EL CAMINO

■ **ELBY** Semi-dwarf H4–5 EM. Flower deep-pink, centre light yellowish pink, red throat and spotting, outside red with rays down centre of each lobe, in flat trusses of 6–9. Leaves elliptic to narrowly elliptic, convex, olive-green, underside with brownish-orange indumentum. Upright, rounded, well-branched plant. ([Fabia × *bureavii*] × [King of Shrubs × *smirnowii*]). Lem/Newcomb.

■ **ELEGANS** Tall H5 M. Flowers deep-rose, of a rather coarse colour, with red spotting in a small rounded truss. A strong vigorous bush. An old hardy classic no longer grown much in Europe but which still turns up in nurseries in America, Australia and New Zealand. I suspect that the plant grown 'down under' may in fact be the *R. arboreum* hybrid raised by J. Booth, with the same name. Heat resistant. *Aus.* (Altaclarense × *catawbiense*).

■ **ELISKA** Semi-dwarf–Low H4–5 ML–L. Flowers yellow, star-shaped with long narrow lobes, in rounded trusses. Leaves oval on a slow-growing, compact plant. The flowers are a curious and unusual shape. (Rotgold × Mareike). Hachmann.

■ **ELIZABETH DE ROTHSCHILD** Tall H4–5 M–ML. Flower openly funnel-shaped, very pale yellow with maroon spotting in throat, in a ball-shaped, well-packed truss of about 18. Leaves elliptic, dark green. Upright habit. Hard to root, slow to bud up and rather mildew-susceptible, but the flowers are very fine. Best in a sheltered site. *MT.* (Lionel's Triumph × Naomi seedling). Rothschild.

■ **ELIZABETH OF GLAMIS** Medium H4 M. Flowers light greenish yellow deepening to brilliant greenish yellow, with a very small vivid reddish-orange eye in throat, in rounded trusses of 12. Handsome foliage on a tidy grower. Hard to root so usually grafted. Chosen to be named after her, by Elizabeth, the Queen Mother, a keen rhododendron collector, on a visit to Glendoick. ([Tidbit × *caucasicum*] × [*wardii* × (*yakushimanum* × Crest)]). Cox.

ELIZABETH OF GLAMIS

■ **ELIZABETH TITCOMB** Medium–Tall H4–5 M. Pink buds open to white flowers, of heavy substance, in tall conical trusses of about 15. Leaves dark green, on a vigorous grower. (Marinus Koster × Snow Queen). Larson. **'DIANE TITCOMB'** and **'JULIE TITCOMB'**, two sisters, are both white flushed or edged pink.

■ **ELLA** Medium H6 ML–L. Flowers a rather harsh crimson-pink in rounded trusses. A tough old German hybrid seen in old collections there. There are at least three other hybrids with this name; a Rothschild white and a sister of Henny's 'Tidbit' may still be around. (*smirnowii* × Mrs Milner). Seidel. Several sister seedlings: **'DARIUS'** purplish pink, **'DIETRICH'** carmine-rose, **'ERNA'** carmine and the similar **'DONAR'** light-crimson with white edges and dark markings.

DONAR

■ **ELLIE SATHER** Low H3–4 EM. Flowers funnel-shaped, strong purplish-red throughout, in flat-balled trusses of 10. Oval leaves with thick indumentum on the underside. Needs sharp drainage and not very heat tolerant. (*haematodes* × *mallotum*). Elliott/Heuston.

■ **ELSA CRISP** Medium–Tall H4 L. Flowers rose, paling towards centre with deeper margins and crimson speckling, in a conical truss of 14–20. A vigorous, upright plant with rather brittle branches. (Mrs E.C. Stirling × unknown). Waterer, Sons and Crisp.

■ **ELSIE STRAVER** Medium H4–5 EM. Flowers greenish yellow, tinged apricot with a red blotch in the centre, in rounded trusses of 12–16. Pale-green leaves tend to turn yellow. Popular in the 1970s and 1980s, but it is such an ugly, leggy plant and there are so many good yellows, that it really is time to let this die out. (*campylocarpum* × unknown). Straver.

■ **ELSIE WATSON** Low H4 EM–M. Flower frilled, pale purplish pink with a dark-purple star in the throat, purple-red edges, outside purplish red, in trusses of 22. Leaves leathery and dark green, spreading habit. This is a tough and easy plant with striking flowers. There have been badly produced tissue-culture plants distributed, which gives this hybrid a bad name. *CA.* (Anna × Purple Lace). Fujioka.

ELSIE WATSON

■ **ENCHANTED EVENING** Low H4 ML. Flowers soft salmon-yellow with stripes of peach-orange, spotted dark-green, 10–12 per lax truss. Long elongated, pointed dark-green leaves. Good in sun, exposure. Similar to 'King of Shrubs' but hardier. (Unknown). Whitney/Sather.

■ **ENGLISH ROSEUM** Medium–Tall H8 ML. Flower soft rose-pink, in dome-shaped trusses. Leaves smooth, glossy, medium-green. Good dense habit. Plants can get very large. An 'ironclad', tolerant of humidity, sun and cold. A standby for severest climates, doubtful if worth growing in mild gardens. *AZ, GP, MA, MD, PT, SE, S. Fin.* (*catawbiense* × unknown). A. Waterer.

■ **ENTICEMENT** Low H4 M. Flower pale purplish pink with deep pink, with rays of orange-brown spotting in throat, in a lax truss of 9–12. Leaves narrowly elliptic to elliptic, glossy, dark green. New growth is red. Upright habit. Buds-up young. Insects like the foliage. (Sunup-Sundown × Lem's Cameo). Lofthouse. **'PINK PORCELAIN'** rose-pink with

salmon-yellow centre. **'SIERRA STARS'** soft-pink flowers with red edging and deep-pink throat. **'SIERRA SUNSET'** carmine-red flowers, edged shell-pink, perhaps the best flower.

■ **ERATO®** Medium H6 ML. Flower funnel-shaped, deep-red with darker spots in a compact truss of 14–17. Leaves elliptic, dull, medium-green. For flowers, this the best of the Hachmann reds in our opinion, though foliage tends to be rather yellow and the root system is not the strongest. (Oratorium × Feuerschein). Hachmann. **'TROCADERO'** bright red.

ERATO®

■ **ERCHLESS** Medium H5 ML. Flower funnel-shaped, frilly, pale purplish pink with a dark-red flare in compact truss of 9–10. Leaves elliptic, glossy, medium-green. Vigorous grower, open, spreading habit. (C.O.D. × Mrs Furnival). Phipps.

■ **ERUPTION®** Low–Medium H5 ML. Flowers funnel-shaped, white centre and throat, margins inside and out of strong-red, in rounded trusses of 14–16. Leaves elliptic, edges flat to slightly recurved, matte dark-green, on a dense, compact plant. Very spectacular flowers. (Tarantella × Seestadt Bremerhaven). Hachmann.

ERUPTION®

■ **ETTA BURROWS** (*see* photo overleaf) Medium H4 E–EM. Flower campanulate, bright blood-red, in a ball-shaped truss of 30. Leaves fir-green, with hairs on the under-surface midrib and hairy stems. Foliage resembles that of parent *R. strigillosum*. One of the best of the many Larsen *R. strigillosum*

ETTA BURROWS

hybrids. *CA, NI, TC, VI.* (Fusilier × *strigillosum*). Larson. **'DOUBLE WINNER'** and **'CROSSROADS'** have red flowers and similar foliage.

■ **EUROPA** Tall H3–4 VL. Flowers bright rosy lilac in a loose truss. Very attractive, large dark-green leaves, forming a tidy, mushroom-shaped bush. One of the best of the late-flowering hybrids. Needs shelter. (*ungernii* × *kyawii*). Rothschild.

EUROPA

■ **EVENING GLOW** Medium H4–5 L. Flower bright-yellow with a prominent calyx, in lax trusses of about 6. Leaves narrow, matte, light green, on an upright plant. Useful for its late flowering but foliage is thin and inclined to yellow and it takes a few years to flower freely. It appears to be surprisingly heat-resistant. (*fortunei* ssp. *discolor* × Fabia). Van Veen. Several sisters were named: **'MARYKE'** soft-pink, yellow, fading to white. (*See* also 'Autumn Gold'.)

EVERESTIANUM

■ **EVERESTIANUM** Tall H5 ML–L. Frilled trusses of rosy lilac with deeper spotting, 15–20 per rounded truss. Vigorous and free flowering in sun or shade. A pre-1850 hardy hybrid. (*catawbiense* × unknown). A. Waterer.

■ **EXBURY CALSTOCKER** Tall H4–5 E. Flower campanulate, creamy white with maroon blotch on upper lobes, in huge trusses of up to 23. Leaves are large and thick. A giant woodland hybrid, which needs wind shelter. (*calophytum* × Dr Stocker). Rothschild.

■ **EXCALIBER** Medium H4 M. Flowers two-toned, deep-rose margins with a light-pink to white centre with a basal red blotch, in huge trusses of 28–32. Leaves pale green, new growth bronze. Upright habit with stiff branches. Very spectacular in flower, but the influence of the dreadful 'Pink Petticoats' means that the habit is poor and the foliage chlorotic, unless you pour extra fertilizer on it. Jim Barlup hybrids of this type are better. (Lem's Cameo × Pink Petticoats). Lofthouse.

■ **EXOTIC** Medium H3 M. Flowers fragrant, reddish, blended yellow and pink, in trusses of 10–12. Leaves large, matte green, tending to be chlorotic, on an upright, rather open plant. Hard to grow well and hard to root. Sensitive to fertilizer. Fine when well-grown. (Loderi King George × Ostbo Y3). Bovee. **'STANLEY ANGELL'** scented rose-pink with a small reddish flare.

■ **EXTRAORDINAIRE** Medium H4 M. Flowers with pink margins and a creamy throat with a prominent red flare, over a yellow ground, fading to creamy pink. Dark-green leaves on a rounded plant. The combination of white with the yellow and red is very attractive. (Gold Medal × Olin O' Dobbs). Greer.

■ **EYE PLEASER** Medium H5–6? M–ML. Flowers cream with a well-defined reddish-bronze blotch. Leaves glossy, deep-green, on a dense and tidy plant. A little-known Delp hybrid, which looked good when I saw it at Rare Find, NJ. (Harvest Moon × Ice Cube). Delp.

■ **FABIA** Medium H3–4 ML–L. **'FABIA AM'** Flowers salmon-orange-salmon, in loose trusses of 7–10. **'FABIA TANGERINE'** pale salmon-orange in trusses of 7–10. **'FABIA ROMAN POTTERY'** pale orange. Leaves smooth, matte-green with reddish-brown indumentum. Mounding growth habit. Most attractive and one of the best of the orange varieties. Best with some shelter. The AM clone is by far the best one. (*dichroanthum* × *griersonianum*). Puddle/Aberconway. **'LEDA'** vermilion to orange-scarlet flowers.

FABIA

■ **FAGGETTER'S FAVORITE** Tall H4–5 EM–M. Flower lightly fragrant, cream-white flushed deep purplish-pink fading to white, bronze speckles on dorsal lobe, in trusses of 11–13. Leaves glossy, medium-green, may hang downwards. Best in light shade to avoid leaf burn. Compact habit. Rather hard to root and takes a few years to bud up. *AGM, EG.* (*fortunei* × unknown). Slocock.

FAGGETTER'S FAVORITE

■ **FAIRWEATHER** Semi-dwarf–Low H4–5 M. Flower openly campanulate, strong yellowish-pink fading to pale yellow, in ball-shaped trusses of about 15. Leaves mostly oblanceolate, slightly bullate, underside with tan indumentum, new growth with a light dusting of white tomentum, on a rounded, compact shrub. ([Fabia × *yakushimanum*] × Hello Dolly). Brockenbrough.

■ **FAIRY LIGHT (syn. FAIRYLIGHT)** Low–Medium H3 L. Flowers bright pink or soft salmon-pink (two different forms), in loose trusses. Narrow leaves on a spreading plant. A little known hybrid similar to 'Vanessa'. (Lady Mar × *griersonianum*). Rothschild.

■ **FASTUOSUM FLORE PLENO** Tall H6 ML. Flower double to semi-double with petalloid stamens, lavender-blue with darker spotting and small green-brown flair, in an open trusses of 15–17. Leaves dull-green and convex on a bush of upright, broadly rounded habit. The best double-flowered large hybrid and an outstanding versatile plant, tough, sun and wind tolerant with long-lasting flowers. Free-flowering and easy. *AGM, EK, MB, TC.* (*catawbiense* × *ponticum*). Francoisi.

FASTUOSUM FLORE PLENO

■ **FATIMA** Low–Medium H5 M–ML. Yellow with large reddish-brown blotch. A new Hachmann yellow, not yet registered or in commerce at the time of writing, but for which the raiser has very high hopes. (Surtaki × Goldstück). Hachmann. **'SARISKA'** a sister.

■ **FEUERSCHEIN®** (syn. **HACHMANN'S FEURSCHEIN, FIRELIGHT**) Medium H5 M. Flowers scarlet, with brown spots, white-tipped anthers, in trusses of 14. Leaves dark green, tending to be a bit yellowish, on an upright but fairly compact plant. Considered to be the best of the many named from this cross. PBR granted for Holland. (Nova Zembla × Mars). Hachmann.

■ **FIDELIUS** Medium H5 ML–L. Flowers star-shaped, deep purplish-pink paling to almost-white in the centre, outside purplish pink, with a strong greenish-yellow flare, in a rounded upright truss of 17. Leaves ovate, convex, somewhat twisted, with some indumentum on the lower-surface midrib. (Judy Spillane × Erato). Hachmann.

■ **FIJI** Low–Medium H7 L. Dark-red buds open to flowers of deep-pink (claret-rose) with pale-yellow rays and brown spotting in the throat, in trusses of 13. Growing wider than high, the plant habit is low and sprawling. Fine flowers are let down by the habit. David Leach tried to withdraw the plant but it is still in commerce. (Russell Harmon × Goldsworth Orange). Leach.

■ **FINLANDIA** Low H6 EM. Flowers pure white, of heavy substance, open from pink buds, in spherical trusses of 12. Leaves small, convex, down-turned, on a rounded, well-branched plant. The foliage is very distinctive. (Catalgia × [Adrian Koster × *williamsianum*]). Leach. Sister seedling: **'APPLAUSE'** flowers white, faint ivory shading, openly campanulate, in trusses of 11. Flower perhaps better than 'Finlandia'.

■ **FIRE RIM** Semi-dwarf–Low H3 M–ML. Flower openly funnel-shaped, frilly edges, light yellow with purplish-red edge, deep-red nectaries, red filaments and style in ball-shaped trusses of about 20. Leaves elliptic, concave with wavy edges, dull, rather pale olive-green, on a dense grower. Buds-up young and with striking flowers but, as with every 'Pink Petticoats' hybrid, the foliage can look a bit pale and sickly. (Nancy Evans × Pink Petticoats). Barlup. **'SWEET DREAMS'** two-toned pink. **'DREAMWEAVER'** white with red blotch.

FIRE RIM

■ **FIRE WINE** Medium H4 ML. Flower openly funnel-shaped, frilly, bright purplish red with darker spotting, in flat trusses of about 16. Leaves narrowly elliptic, medium-green, on a moderately well-branched plant growing wider than high. Heat resistant and free-flowering but this colour meets with a fair amount of resistance from some gardeners. (Purple Splendour × Fire Bird). Greer.

■ **FIREGLOW** Medium H3 ML. Turkey-red flowers, in a loose truss of about 10, said to be faintly fragrant, which is doubtful. Leaves wavy, twisted, with some indumentum on the lower surface, on a large-growing shrub. ([Roseum Superbum × H.M. Arderne] × *griersonianum*). Crosfield.

■ **FIREMAN JEFF** Semi-dwarf H5 EM–M. Flower widely funnel-campanulate, red with brown spots on 3 dorsal lobes, in a ball-shaped truss of about 10. Leaves lanceolate, dark green with orange indumentum. Grows wider than tall. (The Hon. Jean Marie de Montague × Grosclaude). Brandt.

■ **FIRESTORM** Semi-dwarf–Low H8 L. Flower openly funnel-shaped, bright deep-red, unmarked, in dome-shaped trusses of 15–16. Leaves elliptic, dark green with lighter midribs, young growth lime-coloured. Spreading habit. Very hardy for a red, but not worth growing in mild climates. *MS, ST.* (Vulcan × Chocolate Soldier). Mehlquist.

■ **FLAMING SNOW** Tall H6 M. Flower slightly fragrant, openly funnel-shaped, open light pink and quickly fade to almost white with deep pink to purplish red spots, in ball-shaped trusses of 10–12. Leaves oblanceolate to narrowly obovate, glossy, yellowish green, on a plant of upright, dense habit. One of the hardier Dexters and the colour is unusual. Best with a little shelter or light shade. (unknown × unknown). Dexter.

FLAMING SNOW

■ **FLAMING STAR** Medium H4 M–ML. Flowers with red-orange edges fading to yellow centres, in a rounded truss. Leaves glossy, dark green, new growth bronzy. (Ring of Fire × Lem's Cameo). Thompson. **'FLAMING COMET'** a sister with frilly yellow flowers with red edges. **'RED GOLD'** orange-red margins, yellow centre, in balled trusses.

■ **FLAMINGO** Medium H5 M–ML. Pale pink, cream centre with a small red blotch, in a loose truss. A Hobbie hybrid. There is also a *R. griersonianum* hybrid with this name. (Kate Waterer × *wardii* L&S). Hobbie.

■ **FLAUTANDO** Low H6 L. Flowers small, narrowly funnel-shaped, rather pendent, wavy lobes, light yellow with pink rims, spotted reddish, outside empire-rose, in a truss of 10–14. Small dark-green leaves on a compact plant. Not spectacular but quite a useful tough late-flowering hybrid. Not really free-flowering enough. (*brachycarpum* ssp. *fauriei* × Goldsworth Orange). Hachmann. **'MARIMBA'** pink flowers marked yellow-green. **'HACHMANN'S BANANAFLIP'** flowers pale greenish yellow.

■ **FLORA MARKEETA** Low H4–5 M. Coral-pink buds open to ivory-white flowers, blushed coral, deeper on markings and reverse, in a rounded truss of about 10. Leaves glossy dark green on a plant of fine compact habit. It takes several years before it starts to flower freely. (*thomsonii* × [Unique × Luscombei]). Markeeta.

■ **FLORENCE ARCHER** Semi-dwarf–Low H2 L. Flower campanulate, brilliant-yellow, with yellowish-green spots, in dome-shaped trusses of about 8. Leaves broadly elliptic, yellow-green, on a somewhat open plant, growing as wide as high. Foliage is insect resistant. Flowers are supposed to be edged red, but they were not on the plants we grew. (*wardii* × Marcia). Larson.

■ **FLORIADE** Medium H4–5 ML. Flowers deep-pink, with a heavy sienna-brown flare in the throat, in a full rounded truss of 14–20. Leaves pale green, inclined to chlorosis, on a rather untidy plant. There are so many hybrids of this type and this is not one of the best. (unknown). Van Nes.

■ **FLUIDUM** Medium H5 M–ML. Flowers pale purplish-pink fading to whitish in the centre, with an orange-yellow flare. Compact and spreading habit. Foliage rather yellowish. (Orangina × Belkanto). Hachmann.

■ **FOREVER YOURS** Low H4–5 EM. Flower openly funnel-shaped, wavy edges, vivid-red at the edge, shading to white centre with a red spotted throat, in a ball-shaped truss of 16–18. Leaves elliptic, concave, glossy, on a plant of spreading, open habit. Red stems. Like its parent 'Creamy Chiffon' rather hard to please. (Creamy Chiffon × Vulcan). McCulloch.

■ **FORT BRAGG GLOW** Medium H1 EM. Flower openly funnel-shaped, strong purplish red with dark-red throat and slight dark-red spotting on all lobes, in a ball-shaped (somewhat lax) truss of 11–14. Leaves elliptic, olive-green, on a rounded plant. (Ruby Bowman × *elliottii*). Druecker.

■ **FORTUNE g.** Tall H3 EM–M. Flowers cream-primrose-yellow with a large crimson blotch, in a huge truss of 25–30. Massive bullate leaves, with indumentum on the lower surface, up to 40cm long, on a giant tree-forming plant that requires plenty of shelter. You have to have plenty of patience waiting for this to flower: it can take ten to twenty years. Needs to be grafted. (*falconeri* × *sinogrande*). Rothschild.

■ **FRAGRANT RED** Medium H3 EM. Flowers funnel-shaped, strong purplish red in bud, opening vivid purplish red with two deep-red flares on upper dorsal-lobe, strongly scented, in ball trusses of 14. Leaves glossy, moderate olive-green, narrowly elliptic. One of the deepest-coloured larger hybrids with fragrance and should be used in further breeding. (Loderi Venus × Jean Marie de Montague). Watson.

■ **FRANCESCA** Tall H5 ML. Flower tubular-campanulate, crimson, opening from black-red buds, in full rounded trusses of 19–25. Leaves ovate, with slightly recurved margins, on a plant of broad, rounded, rangy open habit. A very fine colour with an impressive truss for a hybrid so hardy. Flowers can suffer sun scorch. This plant was patented but it may have lapsed. *AT, BH, CH, MS.* (Britannia × Dexter #202). Consolini.

■ **FRANK BAUM** Low–Medium H4 L. Flowers carmine, shading to a yellow centre, in tight trusses. The watermelon-like flowers are let down by the chlorotic and thin leaves. (Mars × Jasper). Seabrook.

FRANCESCA

■ **FRANK GALSWORTHY** Semi-dwarf–Low H6 L. Flower maroon-purple with a distinctive yellow-and-white blotch, in ball-shaped trusses of 15–20. Leaves, narrow, slightly twisted, dull, deep-green. Round, rather sparse habit. Nothing else looks quite like this and it always attracts comment, it's a pity it is not very good doer. *AGM, CA.* (*ponticum* × unknown). A. Waterer.

FRANK GALSWORTHY

■ **FRECKLE PINK** Medium H4 EM. Flowers campanulate, ruffled, solferino-purple, speckled deeper, in truss of 12. Used extensively as a parent for further breeding by its raiser. (Marion × Midnight). Van de Ven.

■ **FRED CUMMINS** Medium H4 E–EM. Flowers glowing-scarlet, in full rounded trusses. Habit is tree-like and dense, with good foliage. Very good in N. California where it is best with some shade. (*arboreum* × [Elizabeth × *arboreum*]). Scott.

■ **FRED HAMILTON (syn. GLEN'S ORANGE)** Semi-dwarf–Low H4–5 ML. Flower widely funnel-campanulate, vivid-yellow with yellowish-pink edges and stripes on inside and outside, spotted yellow-green, in flat trusses of 9–12. Leaves elliptic to narrowly elliptic, matte, long, dark green, on a broad, well-branched plant. This should be a good parent for raising orange hybrids with its gene pool. ([*neriiflorum* × *griersonianum*] × *dichroanthum*). Lem.

■ **FRED WYNNIATT g.** Tall H4–5 ML–L. Flowers pale yellow with rose flushing, with large calyx, in flat-topped trusses of about 10. A tree-forming plant. Five further clones were named but not all are commercially distributed. Named after a head gardener at Exbury, where it was raised. (*fortunei* × Jalisco). Rothschild. **'BACH CHOIR'** purplish pink and light yellow. **'STANWAY'** dark-yellow striped pink. Handsome foliage. **'TRIANON'** rose-pink with a yellow throat.

■ **FRENTANO® (syn. FLENSBURG)** Medium H7 ML. Flowers of heavy texture, pale purple-pink with deeper spotting, in a rounded truss. Dark-green leaves. Tough but flowers are not all that attractive. (Scintillation × Germania). Hachmann.

■ **FRESCO** Low–Medium H4–5 EM. Flowers saucer-shaped, purplish pink, paler in centre, with a few dark spots, in trusses of 7–10. Leaves stiff, with narrow pointed tips, on an upright, well-branched plant. (*aberconwayi* × Ruby Bowman). Goheen/Bulgin.

■ **FRONTIER** Medium H3 ML. Flower openly funnel-shaped, strong yellowish-pink with pronounced light greenish-yellow markings, fading to cream, in a ball-shaped truss of 14. Leaves oblong, new growth pinkish brown. Upright, rounded growth habit. Strong grower when established. A rather muddy flower colour, but the foliage is quite handsome. Prone to mildew. (Letty Edwards × Crest). Elliott.

■ **FULL MOON** Low–Medium H4–5 M. Flowers canary-yellow in a fairly full truss of about 11. Leaves glossy, veined, slightly rolled on a rounded or flat-topped bush. Foliage poor in sun, and rather attractive to munching insects. We found it rather prone to mildew and I don't think it really makes the grade these days. (Hawk × Harvest Moon). Henny.

■ **FURNIVALL'S DAUGHTER** Medium H4–5 M. Flower fuchsine-pink with a deep-red blotch in the upper lobe, in trusses of about 15. Egg-shaped leaves large and rugose and can be rather yellow. Upright fairly dense habit but sometimes has a rather small root system. Good at its best, but it often looks a bit sickly and dejected. A good parent for Hans Hachmann. *AGM.* (Mrs Furnival seedling). Knap Hill Nursery.

■ **GANDY DANCER** Low–Medium H4–5 EM. Golden yellow, in large trusses. Dark-green roundish glossy foliage on an upright plant. Not properly registered. ([Crest × Lionel's Triumph] × Diane). Larson.

■ **GARNET** Tall H3 M–ML. Flowers deep salmon-rose, flushed red, in large upright trusses. A giant tree-forming hybrid now little grown. (*griffithianum* × Broughtonii). P.D. Williams.

■ **GENERAL EISENHOWER** Medium H5 M. Flowers ruffled, large, rose-red, in tall trusses of up to 18. Leaves of heavy substance on a vigorous, sturdy plant. The flowers are a rather harsh colour between red and pink, but it is a showy and robust plant. (*griffithianum* hybrid). Kluis.

■ **GENGHIS KHAN** Low–Medium H4 M. Flowers scarlet-red with a large calyx, in a truss of 15. Leaves thin, with a thin indumentum on the lower surface, on a dense and bushy plant. This plant was so shy-flowering at Glendoick we threw it out, bored with waiting for something to happen. It must flower better in the Pacific Northwest. (Britannia × Felis). Brandt.

■ **GENOVEVA** Medium H7 ML. Flowers white, tinged pale-lilac with a yellow-green blotch, in a rounded truss. Leaves recurved on a compact and dense, very tough plant. One of the most attractive of the Seidel hybrids. *Ger.* (catawbiense × unknown). Seidel. Similar ones include: **'HERME'** pale-rose to white, edged rose, **'HERO'** white with green throat, **'HYMEN'** pale lilac.

■ **GEORGE CUNNINGHAM** Medium H4 M. Flowers white with purple spotting over a wide area, in a loose truss of up to 14. Leaves thick and dark green, heavily veined, with thin layer of indumentum. In lots of old U.K. collections, but rarely grown commercially. (*arboreum* × *campanulatum*). Cunningham.

■ **GEORGE GRACE (syn. GRACE)** Medium–Tall H3 M. Flowers rhodamine-pink, with the lobes slightly recurved, in trusses of 15. Leaves oblong to oblong-elliptic. Grown in Australia. (Loderi × Borde Hill). Henny.

■ **GEORGE SWEESY** Low–Medium H3 M. Flowers open funnel-shaped, wavy margins, deep purplish-pink, spotted orange, outside strong-red, in trusses of 12. Leaves medium-sized, dark green. Growth habit rounded and upright, wider than tall. Best in light shade. (Vera Elliot × Dr A Blok). Elliott.

■ **GEORGE'S DELIGHT** Semi-dwarf–Low H4 M. Flower widely funnel-shaped, pale creamy yellow with pale-red picotee edges, in dome-shaped trusses of 13. Leaves elliptic, light green, usually chlorotic and spotty in Scotland, on a broad, well-branched plant. Much better in the Pacific Northwest than I have seen it in the U.K. Rather superseded by 'Lem's Cameo' hybrids such as 'Naselle'. *CN, JF, MT.* (Whitney yellow hybrid selection #6002 × Crest). Whitney.

GEORGE'S DELIGHT

■ **GERMANIA** Semi-dwarf–Low H6 ML. Flowers luminous-rose, paler at centre with deeper-rose edges, faint orange-red blotch, in a truss of 12–19. Compact plant, growing wider than tall, with glossy, medium dark-green leaves. *Ger.* ([Antoon Van Welie × *williamsianum*] × Catherine Van Tol). Hobbie.

■ **GIBRALTAR** Medium–Tall H2–3 EM–M. Large, deep-red flowers, spotted black, held in large rounded trusses. Leaves bright chestnut-colour when young. A tall plant with a rather loose and sparse habit, only hardy enough for mild, sheltered gardens. (Bibiani × *elliottii*). Rothschild.

■ **GI-GI** Medium H5 ML. Flower openly funnel-shaped, vivid purplish red (rose-bengal) with deep-red spotting, in a ball-shaped truss of 15–18. Leaves narrowly elliptic to elliptic, rather pale green, on a plant of broad, dense habit. Not a particularly attractive colour, but free-flowering, drought and heat tolerant and pretty tough. Needs shade in southern Eastern U.S.A. *GP, MA, NY, PR, PT, PV, SE, TZ.* (unknown × unknown). Dexter.

GI-GI

■ **GILL'S CRIMSON** Tall H3–4 E. Bright blood-red, long-lasting flowers, in rounded trusses. An upright, sturdy plant, useful for its early flowering in hot climates. Takes a good few years before it starts flowering. *CA, Aust, NZ.* (*griffithianum* ×). Gill.

■ **GILL'S TRIUMPH** Tall H2–3 EM. Flowers open from blood-red buds and quickly fade to pink, in large rounded trusses. Large leaves on a giant tree-forming plant that needs shelter and a mild garden. (*griffithianum* × *arboreum*). Gill. Others made the same cross. **'BEAUTY OF TREMOUGH'** pink, **'GLORY OF PENJERRICK'** red, fading to pink and **'GLORY OF LEONARDSLEE'** red, fading to off-white.

■ **GLAMOUR** Low–Medium H3 M. Flowers deep cherry-red, with orange flushing, in trusses of 10. Leaves elliptic. Habit low and spreading. Used as a parent by Hydon nurseries. (*Margaret* × *griersonianum*). Rothschild.

■ **GLENDA FARRELL** Low H4–5 M. Flower openly funnel-shaped, wavy to frilly lobes, bright orange-red with dark specks and a red blotch, fading to reddish pink, in a ball-shaped truss of 13. Leaves long on a fairly compact plant. Plant well-branched, broader than tall. Probably the most impressive of the Dexter 'reds' and highly rated, but not worth growing in mild areas where red hybrids are really red. Sometimes flowers in autumn. (unknown × unknown). Dexter.

■ **GLENDOICK® BUTTERSCOTCH** Medium H4 M. Flowers shades of peach, and apricot which looks like butterscotch from a distance, in fine rounded trusses of about 12. Attractive shiny foliage, reddish bronzy when young, on a slow-growing, compact plant. Best with some shelter. For foliage and flower this is one of the best 'Lem's Cameo' hybrids for Scotland. (Lem's Cameo × Whitney's Best yellow). Cox.

■ **GLENDOICK® FROLIC** Semi-dwarf–Low H4–5? EM–M. Flowers white strongly flushed red-purple, fading toward the centre, upper lobe with a bold red-purple blotch and spotting, in a compact slightly loose truss of 12–13. Leaves narrowly oblong, with a thin layer of indumentum on the underside. A dramatic slow-growing hybrid with narrow leaves, which will appeal to species enthusiasts. Hard to root, usually grafted. (*roxieanum* Oreonastes Gp. × *spilotum*). Cox.

GLENDOICK® BUTTERSCOTCH

■ **GLENDOICK® HONEYDEW** Tall H4 ML. Peach buds open to flowers of pale yellow suffused with peach/melon, in loose trusses. Compact and bushy with pale-green leaves. Flowers last best with some shade. (Percy Wiseman × September Song). Cox. Glendoick® is a registered trademark.

■ **GLENDOICK® ICECREAM** Low–Medium H4–5? M–ML. Flowers pale cream-yellow with a small red blotch and some red spotting, in a rounded truss of about 17. Leaves mid-green, on a very dense, compact plant, which is very free-flowering from a young age. A promising hybrid raised by the author. Needs sharp drainage. (Nancy Evans × Cunningham's White). Cox.

■ **GLENDOICK® MYSTIQUE** Tall H4 ML. Flowers glowing salmon-peach in fine rounded trusses of 10–15. Dark green, large leaves on a compact, dense grower. The colour is very fine and the plant is handsome, and we think this is one of the best larger Glendoick hybrids. (Percy Wiseman × September Song). Cox.

GLENDOICK® MYSTIQUE

■ **GLENDOICK® PETTICOATS** Low–Medium H4–5? M–ML. Flowers frilled, apricot fading to creamy yellow, with a red throat and light spotting, with a frilled calyx, in a rounded truss of 17. Leaves ovate lanceolate, on a compact plant very free-flowering from a young age. The flowers are much better than would be expected from the cross and change colour as they fade. (Nancy Evans × Cunningham's White). Cox.

■ **GLENDOICK® VELVET** Medium H5 M–L. Dark-purple flowers with a deeper blotch, in a compact rounded truss of about 11. Dark-green leaves with reddish stems on an upright but tidy grower. For Scotland this has the best foliage and habit of the many dark-purple hybrids with a 'Purple Splendour' ancestry. (Azurro × Rasputin). Cox.

GLENDOICK® VELVET

■ **GLENFIDDICK** Medium H4 M. Flowers nasturtium-red fading to yellow with a green ring in the tube, in a truss of about 10. Leaves obovate. Vigorous and rather open-growing. Raised in New Zealand. Rather a curious spelling: not the same as the whisky. (Pacific Queen × *wardii*). Grant.

■ **GLENNA** Low H4 EM–M. Flowers pink, frilly, flushed deeper-pink, with a creamy-yellow throat and orange eye, in a large rounded truss of about 19. Leaves with wavy margins, semi-glossy, dark green. Rounded habit. Needs good drainage. (Hotei × One Thousand Butterflies). Barlup.

■ **GLOXINEUM (syn. DEXTER'S GLOXINEUM)** Medium H6 ML. Flowers large, luminous pink with a golden flare, spotted darker, with a light scent, in large rounded trusses. One of the hardiest Dexter hybrids. Leggy and vigorous. Best in light shade. (*fortunei* × unknown). Dexter/de Wilde.

■ **GOLD MOHUR** Tall H3–4 ML. Flowers funnel-shaped, golden yellow, with pink markings on the margins, in a loose truss of 10–12. Leaves with recurved edges, rather thin, brittle and easily burned. Late flowering. Much used as a parent. A scruffy plant that failed to do well in the U.K. (Daydream × Margaret Dunn). Brandt. Sisters: **'GOLDEN PHEASANT'** yellow-orange, **'SHAH JEHAN'** yellow, spotted orange.

■ **GOLDBUCKETT (syn. GOLDEN BOUQUET)** Medium H6 M. Flowers creamy yellow with prominent red-brown to ruby spotting, in a rounded truss of 10–14. Leaves ribbed, dark and shiny. Like all yellows, this needs good drainage. Not a very deep yellow, but a tough plant and good in Northern Europe. A poor performer in N.E. U.S.A., where the summer heat causes root and foliage problems. *Ger, Scand.* (Scintillation × *wardii*). Hachmann.

■ **GOLDBUG** Semi-dwarf–Low H3 M. Flowers open red and fade out via orange to yellow, strongly spotted red over the whole corolla, in a loose truss of up to 9. Leaves twisted on a compact plant. Some love this, others think it in appalling taste. It is certainly very spotty. Needs shade to protect foliage. (*wardii* × Fabia). Henny. **'DEL'** Rose-coloured flower with blotch of greenish yellow, in trusses of about 12.

■ **GOLDEN COACH** Medium H4 M–ML. Flowers large, open-campanulate, outside deep-yellow, inside greenish yellow, with red spotting, in full rounded trusses of 8–9. Leaves pale bluish green, elliptic, on a fairly compact plant, rather subject to powdery mildew. (Elizabeth de Rothschild × Jalisco Elect). Drayson.

■ **GOLDEN FLEECE** Medium H4 ML. Flowers golden yellow with wavy-edged lobes. Good foliage. Rather open habit. Not easy to root. Showy flowers. (Goldsworth Orange × Yvonne). Slocock.

■ **GOLDEN GALA** Semi-dwarf–Low H7 ML. Flower widely funnel-shaped, wavy lobes, pale yellowish green (looking cream) with light yellowish-green spots on dorsal lobe, in ball-shaped trusses of 14. Leaves elliptic, glossy, olive-green, on a compact plant, broader than tall. Reasonable foliage and habit, but as Dick Brooks points out, there is nothing 'golden' about it: it is cream. Not worth growing in mild areas. *AT.* (Great Lakes × Good Hope). Leach.

■ **GOLDEN GATE** Semi-dwarf–Low H4 ML. Flower star-shaped, reddish pink with salmon-orange edge and a golden-yellow throat, in an open truss of 5–6. Leaves are deep-green and glossy. Dense, compact plant. Not as hardy as the very similar 'Sonata' but perhaps more free-flowering as a young plant. *TC.* (*dichroanthum* ssp. *scyphocalyx* × unknown). unknown.

■ **GOLDEN GENIE** Medium H3–4 M. Flower openly funnel-shaped, wavy edges, light greenish yellow, in a tall, dome-shaped truss of 8–10. Leaves elliptic, convex, shiny, on a dense, upright grower. Buds young. Sometimes chlorotic. Leaves insect resistant. *VI.* (Lem's Cameo × Crest). Brady.

■ **GOLDEN HARBINGER** Medium H5 M–ML. Flowers soft-yellow in a rounded truss. Leaves glossy. Heat tolerant. Recently released and not yet properly registered at time of writing. (Frilled Cream × Mary Garrison). Ring. A sister with the glorious name of **'CARNAL'** has flesh- or peach-coloured flowers with a touch of lavender.

■ **GOLDEN HORN** Low H2–3 ML. Flowers orange and deep-salmon, tubular trumpet-shaped, with a large calyx, in a loose, flat-topped truss of 9–11. Dark green leaves with brown indumentum on the underside. Compact. Needs good drainage. (*dichroanthum* × *elliottii*). Rothschild. **'PERSIMMON'** Flowers waxy orange-red, with dark speckling, no large calyx.

■ **GOLDEN RUBY** Low H4 M. Flowers moderate-red in bud, opening brilliant- to light-yellow, edged deep-pink, finally turning to golden yellow, 9–10 per truss. Compact and dense habit. Not very free-flowering, and not of much merit at Glendoick. (Jalisco hybrid × Sonata). Lofthouse.

■ **GOLDEN SCEPTER (syn. SCEPTER)** Low–Medium H6 M–ML. Flowers funnel-shaped, light greenish yellow with a slightly darker blotch, in ball trusses of 14. Leaves elliptic with decurved margins. Very tough for a yellow, but not all that attractive. (yellow hybrid × Goldsworth Yellow). Mezitt.

■ **GOLDEN STAR** Medium H4 ML. Flower openly funnel-shaped, wavy lobes, light yellow, without spots, in ball-shaped trusses of 7. Leaves elliptic, smooth and handsome. Long a standard and favourite yellow for coastal parts of Eastern U.S.A., such as Long Island and Massachusetts. We can't grow it due to powdery mildew. *MA, Long Island.* (*fortunei* × *wardii*). Hardgrove. **'AMAZEMENT'** very similar to 'Golden Star' and may be a synonym.

■ **GOLDEN WIT** Low H4 M. Flowers small, pale primrose-yellow, quite heavily spotted red, in compact trusses of 7–9. Leaves dark-green, small, on a slow-growing compact plant. Needs sharp drainage. Not very spectacular, but reliable and tidy. (*dichroanthum* × [Moonstone × Adrastia]). Witt/Michaud.

■ **GOLDFEE** Low H5 M. Coppery orange-yellow buds, flowers pale greenish yellow tinged light orient-pink, fading later, dorsal spots oxblood-red, in a compact truss of about 15. Leaves elliptic, glossy, dark green. Compact habit. ([*wardii* × Alice Street] × [Omega × *wardii*]). Hachmann.

■ **GOLDFLIMMER** Low–Medium H6 ML–L. Flowers lavender-pink, small, in a compact rounded truss of 9–14. Attractive variegated foliage (yellow and green). Mounding, compact habit. A tough, easy and reliable plant mainly grown for its leaves. Very commonly offered in Europe. Damaged in 2003–4 winter in New Jersey/Philadelphia. (*See also* 'Molten Gold'.) *SL, PB, GP, GER, U.K.* (unknown sport). Hobbie.

■ **GOLDFORT** Medium H5 M. Pink buds open to pale-yellow flowers with pink margins and a greenish-yellow centre. Leaves light green, on a plant of open and straggly habit. Heat resistant. Rather slow to bud up. Probably had its day but, of its time, one of the few hardy yellow-hybrids. (Goldsworth Yellow × *fortunei*). Slocock.

■ **GOLDIKA** Medium H4–5 ML. Flowers reflexed, deep-yellow with a small basal blotch. Leaves ovate on a rather sparse plant. This is almost 100 per cent *R. wardii* and it looks like one of the hardy Ludlow & Sherriff forms from Tibet. (*wardii* seedling). Hobbie. **'PRIMULA'** is a similar sister seedling. **'TROMPENBURG'** pale yellow with a deep-red blotch.

■ **GOLDINETTA®** Low–Medium H5 M–ML. Flowers pure light-yellow-green, unmarked, in a rather lax truss of 12–14. Leaves deep-green. Very fine yellow flowers are unmarked with no trace of spotting. (Marina × New Comet). Hachmann. **'SIMSON'** flowers pale pure yellow, unmarked. Vigorous.

■ **GOLDKOLLIER (syn. GOLD NECKLACE)** Low–Medium H4–5 ML. Flowers bright yellow, reverse and opening buds flushed orange, spotted reddish brown. Leaves to 10cm long. Not yet in commerce at the time of writing, but the Hachmanns think it will be a good commercial plant. (Kupferberg × Goldstück). Hachmann.

GOLDKOLLIER

GOLDKRONE®

■ **GOLDKRONE®** (syn. GOLD CROWN) Semi-dwarf–Low H4–5 M. Flower openly campanulate, golden yellow with sparse dark-red spotting on dorsal lobe, in compact trusses of about 12. Leaves rounded, slightly curled, dark green. Compact, mounding habit. Needs good drainage. Very free flowering. An outstanding yellow for northern climates with cool summers. *AGM, Ger, Den, Swe, U.K.* ([*wardii* × Alice Street] × Hachmann's Marina). Hachmann.

■ **GOLDSCHATZ (syn. GOLDPRINZ)** Tall H4–5 M. Flowers funnel-campanulate opening from reddish buds to light greenish-yellow inside and out, with dorsal spotting and basal blotch of strong-red, in rounded compact truss of 15–17. Leaves small, sometimes rather yellowish on a compact grower. Not all that vigorous and a little floppy as a small plant, better with age. Suffers sunburn in Switzerland. (Festivo × Alice Street). Hachmann. **'SEPTEMBER-FLAIR'** similar, often flowering in September, less hardy. **'GOLDZWERG'** yellow with a small red flare.

GOLDSCHATZ

■ **GOLDSWORTH CRIMSON** Medium–Tall H4 M. Flowers bright red, fading to paler in the centre, spotted black, reverse darker, in a compact domed truss of 12–16. Dark, glossy leaves on a fairly compact spreading plant, which can become very large in time. Flowers are striking and rather unusual. Heat and sun tolerant and popular in the southern hemisphere. *Aus, NZ, S. Cal.* (*griffithianum* × Doncaster). Slocock.

■ **GOLDSWORTH ORANGE** Medium H4–5 M. Flowers salmon-pink with orange tones fade to creamy pink, spotted brown, in a loose truss of about 10. An upright but dense and compact grower, leaves with red petioles. Heat-tolerant but flowers last best in some shade. Much used for breeding orange hybrids, but the epithet 'orange' is a bit far fetched. Rather prone to mildew. (*dichroanthum* × *fortunei* ssp. *discolor*). Slocock. **'GOLDGLANZ'** a hybrid which is three-quarters 'Goldsworth Orange', light-yellow flushed orange in flat trusses.

GOLDSWORTH ORANGE

■ **GOLDSWORTH YELLOW** Low H5 ML. Apricot buds open to buff-yellow flowers of thin texture, with olive-green markings, in broad, domed trusses of about 15. Dense plant with yellowish-green leaves, medium size. Sprawling habit. This is one of the first hardy yellow hybrids raised, but it is not really worthy of much attention these days with so many hardy yellows on the market. (*caucasicum* × *campylocarpum*). Slocock.

■ **GOMER WATERER** Medium H6 ML–L. Flower white flushed mauve-pink at the edges with yellow-brown flare in the upper lobe, in trusses of up to 24. Leaves broadly elliptic, thick and leathery, recurved, matte, dark. Dense and compact. Heat resistant and sun tolerant. A consistently highly rated hybrid, one of the best late hybrids for general planting. Leaves sometimes yellowish. *AGM, CA, FS, Ger, MB, NI, OZ, PT, SC, SE, WT, U.K.* (*catawbiense* × unknown). J. Waterer.

GOMER WATERER

■ **GOOD NEWS** Low H4–5 ML–L. Flower with wavy lobes, crimson-scarlet, in lax trusses of 12–15. Leaves with slight tan indumentum on the underside, new growth pale-green with fawn tomentum. Compact shrub, grows wider than tall. Shy flowering in Scotland. (Britannia × Romany Chal). Henny.

■ **GORDIAN** Low H5 M. Flowers pale greenish-yellow shaded deeper, with small red blotch in the centre, with yellow stamens and style, in a rounded truss of about 11. Leaves often twisted, on a fairly compact plant. The flowers are said to be very attractive. (Belladonna × Fred Wynniatt). Hachmann. **'MAIFEUER'** pure-yellow, unmarked flowers. **'MIRABELLA'** cream shaded yellow with a rim of salmon-pink. **'SANTORINA'** perhaps the best of this cross: pale yellow with orange-red tone and red blotch, thick textured.

■ **GORDON VALLEY SUPREME (syn. PERSIAN LADY)** Medium H4 M–ML. Flowers rhodamine-pink in bud, opening lighter, paling in centre to blush-white, frilled, with a light scent, and a red flare, in trusses of 9–10. Fairly compact but vigorous. Popular in New Zealand where it was raised. (Queen Souriya ×). Harris/Henry.

■ **GOSH DARN!** Low H6 ML. Flowers openly funnel-shaped, light yellowish-pink, pale orange-yellow and strong yellowish-pink with strong yellowish-pink dorsal spots and throat, in trusses of 18. Vigorous and tough, good in Philadelphia area. Much used as a parent by W. Delp and should be good for breeding tough, heat-tolerant offspring. (Catalgla × Caroline). Delp.

■ **GRACE SEABROOK** Medium H4–5 EM. Flower currant-red at margins shading at centre to blood-red, in tight trusses of about 12. Leaves large, pointed, very thick and dark green on a sturdy, tidy plant. It buds up at four to five years of age and reliably after. A little early flowering, but an outstanding colour, one of the finest of all reds. 'Taurus' is very similar. *AZ, CC, EG, EK, MT, PA, PT, SE.* (The Hon. Jean Marie de Montague × *strigillosum*?). Seabrook.

GRACE SEABROOK

■ **GRAF LENNART** Low–Medium H4–5 EM. Flowers pale yellow, campanulate, with red spotting and light-pink flushing, in a loose truss of 9–12. Leaves small and ovate-elliptic. A neat upright grower that is very free-flowering. Flowers are pale but attractive and rather earlier than its many sister seedlings such as 'Goldkrone' (q.v.). *U.K.* ([*wardii* × Alice Street] × Hachmann's Marina). Hachmann. **'GOLDRAUSCH'** orange buds, yellow flowers.

GRAF LENNART

■ **GRAF ZEPPELIN** Medium H6 ML. Flower bright clear-pink with darker edges, in ball-shaped trusses of up to 10. Leaves dark green, shiny, slightly twisted. Upright and spreading growth habit. Tough and easy but not very exciting. (Pink Pearl × Mrs C. S. Sargent). Van Nes.

■ **GRAFFITO®** Medium H6 ML–L. Flowers light pink, shading deeper towards the edges, with a large blotch of deep-red, in a rounded dense truss of 17–19. Narrowish, dark-green pointed leaves on a densely clothed plant, one of the best of this colour. (Mme Jules Porges × Hachmann's Diadem). Hachmann.

GRAFFITO®

■ **GRAHAM HOLMES** Low H3–4 ML. Flowers neyron-rose with a small red mark in the throat, in a truss of 15. Compact with good foliage. Mainly grown in New Zealand where it was raised from American seed. (unknown). Holmes.

■ **GRAND SLAM** Medium–Tall H4–5 ML. Flowers deep-pink, with wavy edges, lobes with darker spotting in the throat, in a cone-shaped truss up to 30cm tall. Large glossy green leaves, and sturdy stems on a somewhat irregular, coarse plant. Great if you like giant pink confections but a bit too 'Barbara Cartland' for my taste: she overdid pink to perfection. (Trude Webster × Lydia). Greer.

■ **GRANDMA'S HAT** Medium H4 ML. Flower greenish white with deep purplish-red edges and dark-red blotch and spots, reverse deep purplish red, in a ball-shaped truss of 18–20. Leaves oblanceolate to lanceolate, flat, dull, dark yellowish-green, on an upright, well-branched but rather leggy plant. (unknown × unknown). Lem?

GRAZIELA

HACHMANN'S BRASILIA

■ **GROSCLAUDE** Low H3 M. Flowers bright, blood-red, specked brown, in loose trusses of 6–12. Dark green recurved leaves with dark rusty-orange indumentum on the under-surface. Flowers small and not very well presented but the foliage is good. Rather prone to bark-split at Glendoick. (*haematodes* × *facetum*). Rothschild. **'W.F.H.'** Lax truss of brilliant-scarlet. Leaves with indumentum.

■ **GWEN BELL** Medium H4–5 ML. Flower saucer-shaped, slightly wavy edges, deep purplish pink with a small blotch of dark-red spots. Leaves elliptic, semi-glossy, dark yellowish green, on a plant of open, irregular habit. One of the Walloper group. (Anna × Marinus Koster). Lem.

■ **GWILLT-KING** Medium H3 M–ML. Flowers turkey-red, with spotting on upper lobe, in a semicircular truss. Leaves bullate, with woolly indumentum on the underside. Handsome, but only suitable for mild coastal gardens. Not hardy at Glendoick. (*arboreum* ssp. *zeylanicum* × *griersonianum*). Haig. **'RUDDIGORE'** deep-red flowers.

■ **GWYNETH MASTERS** Tall H4? ML–L. Cardinal-red flowers, spotted on upper lobes, with 5 dark nectaries in throat, in trusses of 20–21. Attractive glossy deep-green foliage, bushy habit. Becoming commercially available in New Zealand. (unknown). Masters.

■ **HAAGA** Low H7 L. Flower openly funnel-shaped, wavy edged, inside fuchsine-pink, outside with brownish-red spots, in dome-shaped truss of 15–20. Leaves elliptic, glossy, dark green. New growth yellowish. Upright growth habit. An excellent plant for very harsh climates. Foliage resistant to sun/frost winter weather. Flowers are small and thinly textured, so not worth growing in mild areas. *S. Fin., Swe, Pol.* (*brachycarpum* Tigerstedtii Gp. × Doctor H.C. Dresselhuys). Uosukainen/Arb. Mustila.

HAAGA

■ **HAAG'S CHOICE** Low H5 M–ML. Flower pinkish lavender, in conical trusses. Leaves elliptic, dark green. Dense growth habit. Leaves best in filtered sun. *PT, SE.* (*fortunei* or *fortunei* hybrid × Charles Dickens). Nearing/Gable.

■ **HACHMANN'S ANASTASIA®** (syn. **ANASTASIA**) Low–Medium H5 ML–L. Flowers pale pink flushed deeper-pink, of good texture, frilly, in a full rounded truss of 11–13. Large ovate dark-green leaves on a fairly compact plant growing wider than high. (August × Lem's Monarch). Hachmann. **'CARUSO'** deep-pink, fading towards the centre. **'ROMILDA'** pink, fading towards the centre. **'VALKÜRE'®** deep-pink paling to off-white in the centre. **'CHARIS'** pink paling in the centre. **'HAITHABU'** pink with darker spotting.

■ **GRAZIELA** syn. **GRAZIELLA** Medium H4–5 M. Flowers small pinkish purple, with small red spots, in a rounded truss of 8–15. Very distinctive narrow pointed leaves, on an easily grown, outstanding foliage plant extremely free-flowering and one of the best semi-dwarf hybrids. (*ponticum*? sport?). Eschrich/George/Hilliers/Hachmann. **'HAMPSHIRE BELLE'** looks identical to me, perhaps someone took cuttings to Germany?

■ **GREAT EASTERN** Low H4–5 ML. Flower fragrant, deep purplish pink paling to light purplish pink with blotch of greenish-yellow rays, in ball-shaped truss of 16. Leaves elliptic, flat, margins slightly undulate, mucronate, new leaves glossy, yellow-green, retained one to two years. Plant is broader than tall. (unknown × unknown). Dexter.

■ **GREAT SCOTT** Tall H4 ML–L. Flowers pure-white with reflexed lobes, strongly blotched maroon, in a tight rounded truss of 14. Smooth, deep-green leaves on a rather leggy, sprawling plant. (Mrs J.G. Millais × Cheyenne). Greer. A sister **'RAZZLE DAZZLE'** has pink flowers with deeper margins and a deep-maroon blotch.

■ **GREAT SMOKEY** Medium–Tall H6 M. Large conical trusses of light mauve-pink flowers with a prominent reddish-purple blotch. A fast-growing, vigorous plant. Parent 'Hardy Giant' is a hybrid of *R. rex* ssp. *fictolacteum*. (*vernicosum* × Hardy Giant). Haag.

■ **GREER'S CREAM DELIGHT** Medium H5 ML. Large tight trusses of creamy flowers, with darker throat markings. Good foliage on a compact, very floriferous, heat-tolerant plant. (Barto Ivory × Barto Lavender). Greer.

■ **GRENADIER** Tall H3 L. Flower waxy, blood-red with a deep-black throat, in ball-shaped trusses of about 12. Leaves large, dark green, with loose indumentum on the lower surface, on a straggly plant that produces late, frost-vulnerable growth. Needs protection from sun in hot climates. (Moser's Maroon × *elliottii*). Rothschild.

■ **GRETCHEN** Medium H6 ML. Flower pink with a red throat, in dome-shaped trusses. Upright, dense habit. There were several clones distributed. #1 is the best. ([*decorum* × *griffithianum*] × Kettledrum). Nearing/Gable.

■ **GRIERSPLENDOR** Low H4–5 M. Flowers red-purple, blotched darker, in a loose truss. Leaves narrow on a vigorous spreading plant. Not a very fashionable colour. Almost unknown in its native U.K., I have never seen a plant there. Grown in North America and New Zealand. (*griersonianum* × Purple Splendour). Loder.

■ **HACHMANN'S BRASILIA (syn. BRASILIA)** Medium H5 M. Flower light brownish-pink-yellow, the colour looking orangey rose with yellow, slight spotting of brownish yellow in a small, ball-shaped truss of about 17. Leaves elliptic, lightly twisted, light green, on a compact grower. Muddy, small flowers, of poor texture. W. U.S.A. tissue-culture plants of this were quite appalling. Ask for a refund. The real thing is better. *Ger, Scand.* (Hachmann's Marina × [*wardii* var. *wardii* × Alice Street]). Hachmann.

■ **HACHMANN'S CHARMANT®** Low H6 ML. Flower white, with a marginal band of purplish-red to deep purplish-pink inside, with a conspicuous blood-red blotch on dorsal lobes, in conical trusses of 17–19. Leaves glossy, dark green, on a compact spreading plant. One of Hachmann's finest hybrids for flower, but a little lacking in vigour as a young plant. Definitely recommended. Not good in N.E. U.S.A. *OZ, U.K.* (Hachmann's Diadem × Holger). Hachmann. **'RICARDA'** a sister with pink flowers, blotched green-gold.

HACHMANN'S CHARMANT

■ **HACHMANN'S CONSTANZE** Tall H5 ML–L. Flowers magenta-rose with blotch of ruby-red, calyx reddish green, in a truss of 18–20. Leaves convex, dull dark green on a fairly dense plant. We grew this for a while, but it did not impress; it is popular in colder part of Europe. (Humboldt × Kluis Sensation). Hachmann.

■ **HACHMANN'S DIADEM** Medium H5 ML–L. Light purplish-pink flower with a large, conspicuous blotch of cherry-red, in a rounded truss of 10–13. Handsome dark-green glossy leaves. Tough and tolerant of exposure. One of the best hybrids of this type. Not very easy to root. We have reports of sunburned leaves in Switzerland. *Ger, U.K.* (Hachmann's Ornament × Furnivall's Daughter). Hachmann. **'HERBSTFREUDE'** pink with deeper blotch, tends to bloom in autumn in Germany.

HACHMANN'S DIADEM

■ **HACHMANN'S ESKIMO** Medium H5 ML. Flowers yellowish white, outside just touched with very pale purple along veins, conspicuously marked deep yellowish green, in rounded, conical trusses of 14–16. Leaves with some pale-brown indumentum on underside. (Gloriosum × Herme). Hachmann.

■ **HACHMANN'S FELICITAS** Low H5 ML. Flowers pale yellow, wide edging of medium- to pale-pink, spotted red fading to yellowish green, in a truss of 13–17. Leaves ovate-broadly elliptic, mid-green. Flowers are a subtle blend of cream and pale pink, best in part-day shade to preserve the colour. (Goldkrone × Perlina). Hachmann.

■ **HACHMANN'S GOLDSPRENKEL** Low–Medium H5 M–ML. Flowers pale yellow, strongly spotted red all over upper lobe, in a rounded truss. A striking new hybrid, though the yellow/red combination won't be to everyone's taste. The name 'Goldsprenkel' is already used for a German cultivar with variegated leaves, so I have assumed that this will have 'Hachmann's' appended to it when registered. (Suella × Goldstück). Hachmann. **'PEGGY'** flowers cream, with deep-red flare and spotting.

■ **HACHMANN'S JUNIFEUER** Low–Medium H5 L. Flowers strong-red, darker towards edges, with yellow spotting, in trusses of 14–17. A useful late-flowering hybrid, a bit let down by its foliage and leggy habit. (Mary Waterer × Moser's Maroon). Hachmann. **'JUNIPERLE'** a sister seedling with flowers strong purplish red, shading inwards lighter, marked greenish yellow. **'LAUSITZ'** another similar hybrid, a little earlier flowering.

■ **HACHMANN'S KABARETT**® Low H5 ML–L. Flowers frilled, light purple, with a large dark-red to purple blotch on 3 lobes, in a dense balled truss of about 12. Dark-green glossy leaves, on a compact plant. (Hyperion × Hachmann's Diadem). Hachmann. **'PFAUENAUGE'** light pinkish purple, paling towards the centre with a large reddish-purple flare.

PFAUENAUGE

■ **HACHMANN'S MARIANNE (syn. MARIANNE)** Low–Medium H5 M. Flowers open funnel-shaped, light yellow-green to pale greenish yellow, with deep-red markings on 3 dorsal lobes, 13–15 per truss. Leaves mid-green, slightly glossy. ([*wardii* × Alice Street] × Mareika). Hachmann.

■ **HACHMANN'S MARYLOU** Low H4–5 ML. Flowers cream flushed pink-and-yellow with orange spotting, in a rounded truss. Compact and spreading. An attempt to improve on 'Paprika Spiced'. The Hachmanns think this is very promising. (Paprika Spiced × Hachmann's Corinna). Hachmann.

■ **HACHMANN'S MERCATOR** Tall H5 EM. Flowers light purple paling to near-white in the centre, overlaid with a bold dark-purple blotch, outside deeper-purple, in large rounded trusses of about 11. Leaves to 14cm long, elliptic. Takes a few years to flower and best with some shelter. The flower is striking. (Polarnacht × *praevernum*). Hachmann. **'OSTERSCHNEE'** another *R. praevernum* hybrid with pure-white flowers with a bold red blotch. Early. Very striking.

■ **HACHMANN'S MIKADO** Medium H5 ML. Pale salmon-pink buds open to salmon flowers immediately fading to pale yellowish, with a red flare in compact, rounded trusses of 15–17. Leaves elliptic, with decurved margins, with a dense fawn indumentum on the under-surface. A vigorous and attractive hybrid. ([Lumina × Perlina] × Lachsgold). Hachmann.

■ **HACHMANN'S PARSIFAL (syn. PARSIFAL)** Medium H5 EM–M. Flowers vivid purplish red tinged strong purplish red, in a fairly compact truss of 15–20. Leaves elliptic, light green. A rather hot colour. (Mars × Direcktör E. Hjelm). Hachmann.

■ **HACHMANN'S PICOBELLO**® **[PBR] (syn. PICOBELLO)** Medium H5 ML–L. Flowers pure

HACHMANN'S PICOBELLO® [PBR]

white with a blackberry-coloured blotch, in rounded trusses. Dark green glossy, handsome foliage. This is one of the first named Holger Hachmann crosses (son of Hans). It looks very fine with deep foliage and striking flowers. One of the best of this colour. (Pfauenauge × Schneespiegel). Hachmann. **'PINGUIN'** lavender with a bold deep-red-purple flare.

■ **HACHMANN'S RIMINI (syn. RIMINI)** Low H5 M. Flowers broadly funnel-shaped, from deep-pink buds light-yellowish-green/pale-greenish-yellow, tinged pale purplish-pink at edges with brilliant greenish-yellow blotch, in trusses of 8–10. There is already a Rothschild hybrid called 'Rimini', so I have assumed it would be registered with the Hachmann epithet. Named after the Italian seaside town. (Goldbuckett × Nippon). Hachmann.

■ **HACHMANN'S ROSABELLA** Low H5 ML. Flower funnel-shaped, wavy-edged, purplish red paling to almost-white in throat with yellowish-green markings, in tight spherical trusses of 15–18. Leaves elliptic, shiny, olive-green, on a broad, compact plant. (Donar × Furnivall's Daughter). Hachmann.

■ **HACHMANN'S ROSARKA** Low–Medium H5 M–ML. Flowers light carmine-red, wavy-edged, with faint dark-red markings, in trusses of 11–14. Leaves dark green, stiff, with impressed veins, on a compact bush. Flowers are long-lasting. The flower colour is rather harsh but the plant is handsome. *Ger.* (*insigne* × Spitfire). Hachmann. **'EUROPA '93'** red with dark-red spotting, in a rounded truss.

HACHMANN'S ROSARKA

■ **HACHMANN'S ROSITA (syn. ROSITA)** Low H5 ML. Flowers roseine-purple, paling towards the centre, with yellow-dyed dorsal spotting, in a truss of 8–9. Dark green recurved leaves. A fairly compact plant. We found the leaves tended to be yellowish and it was not a very attractive flower colour. It seems to do well in Germany and Scandinavia. (Kokardia × [Mars × *yakushimanum*]). Hachmann. **'LUMINA'** a sister seedling: flowers mallow-purple, in trusses of 13. **'MANUELA'** frilly, lavender-pink.

■ **HACHMANN'S SAYONARA (syn. SAYONARA)** Medium H5–6? ML? Reddish purple with a deeper blotch in a rounded truss. A promising and striking new Hachmann introduction likely to be introduced around 2008. (Soubrette × Sarasate). Hachmann. **'SARASATE'** reddish purple with a deeper blotch. Being discontinued but much used as a Hachmann parent.

■ **HAIDA GOLD** Medium H4 M. Flowers light greenish-yellow with a yellow-green throat, in trusses of 10. Foliage is smooth, bluish green and quite handsome but the plant came into growth so early in Scotland, it was always frosted. (*wardii* × Goldfort). Bovee & Mayo/Rhodes.

■ **HAITHABÜ**® Medium H5–6 ML. Medium pinkish-purple paling towards the centre, with red spotting, in a rounded truss of 16–18. Thick, deep-green leaves. A hardy variation on the 'Walloper' theme. (Walküre × Germania). Hachmann.

■ **HALFDAN LEM** Medium H4–5 M. Flower openly funnel-shaped, red, fading to slightly lighter in the centre, and fading to pinkish red, with darker spotting on dorsal lobe, in conical trusses of about 13. Leaves narrowly elliptic, glossy, dark green, on an upright grower. Best in plenty of light to avoid a rangy habit. Good, but not the best colour of the large Pacific Northwest reds; 'Markeeta's Prize' is better. *CD, EK, MT, WT*. (The Hon. Jean Marie de Montague × Red Loderi). Lem.

HALFDAN LEM

■ **HALLELUJAH** Low H6 EM. Flower widely funnel-campanulate, vivid purplish red, in ball-shaped trusses of 10–13. Leaves thick and rigid, narrowly obovate, ends twisted downward, dark green, on a stiff, upright grower. May need shade to avoid sunburn. Not very good in Scotland but highly regarded elsewhere. *CD, EK, NI, PA, SH*. (The Hon. Jean Marie de Montague × Kimberly). Greer.

■ **HANSEL** Low H4–5 M. Flower pinkish orange, heavily speckled with red dots, in a lax truss. Leaves dark green, with felted orange indumentum on underside. Upright, dense habit. A good foliage plant with quite attractive flowers. (*bureavii* × Fabia). Lem. '**GRETZEL**' salmon-pink flowers shaded orange. '**FABUR**' from the same cross, flowers trumpet-shaped, pastel-coral-pink.

■ **HARDGROVE'S ROYAL STAR (syn. ROYAL STAR)** Tall H6 L. Flower openly funnel-shaped, wavy edges, purplish red with dark purple blotch in dome-shaped truss of 16. Leaves elliptic, slightly recurved, semi-glossy, dark yellowish green, plant upright, well branched, with a somewhat open habit. (Moser's Maroon × unknown). Hardgrove.

■ **HARDY SPLENDOUR** Semi-dwarf H4 M. Flower openly funnel-shaped, frilly edges, deep reddish purple shading to purplish red in throat with dark-purple spotting, in dome-shaped trusses of 12–15. Leaves elliptic, flat, dull green, on a plant of spreading habit growing twice as wide as tall. (Purple Splendour × Purpureum Grandiflorum). Shapiro.

■ **HAROLD AMATEIS** Low–Medium H5 M. Flowers campanulate, cardinal-red with dark-maroon throat and darker spots, in trusses of about 20. Leaves rugose, depressed midrib, underside with slight fawn indumentum. A fine truss but slow to bud up and rather shy-flowering. Some suggest grafting it. Should probably be used for further breeding. Surprisingly red for a red × white cross. (*maximum* × *strigillosum*). Amateis.

■ **HAROLD STOCKMAN** Low H4? M. Flowers broadly funnel-campanulate, strong-red in bud, opening the same colour throughout, with sparse dark-red dorsal spotting, in domed trusses of 5–9. Leaves oblong, dull dark green, new growth reddish. (Kubla Khan × Spanish Lady). Stockman.

■ **HARRISVILLE** Semi-dwarf–Low H8 ML. Flower openly funnel-shaped, reddish purple shading to light purple with a white dorsal-flare and brilliant greenish-yellow dorsal spots, in a conical truss of 16. There are lots of sisters and further selfings of this cross, all of which are very hardy. *NG*. (Newport F4). Delp.

■ **HARVEST MOON** Medium H4–5 EM. Flowers pale creamy yellow with red spotting in the throat, in dome-shaped trusses of 10–13. Glossy pale-green rugose leaves. Not as good as its hybrid 'Maharani'. (Mrs Lindsay Smith × *campylocarpum* hybrid). Koster. Sister seedlings are '**DIANE**', '**JERSEY CREAM**', '**ADRIAAN KOSTER**', '**ZUIDERZEE**' all creamy white with red spotting.

■ **HAWK g.** Tall H3–4 M. Flowers yellow with a blotch in compact trusses. Many clones were named. The best (apart from 'Crest') is 'Jervis Bay' with frilled yellow flowers with a red blotch. Leaves elliptic. These are the sisters of the well known and superior 'Crest' (q.v.). 'Hawk A.M', 'Buzzard', 'Falcon', 'Kestrel' are all little-grown. (*wardii* × Lady Bessborough). Rothschild.

■ **HAZEL** Medium H4–5 EM. Flower widely funnel-campanulate, pale purplish pink with deeper-pink edges, both inside and outside and with slight brown spotting, in ball-shaped truss of 12–15. Leaves narrowly oblong to narrowly elliptic, glossy, dark green, underside with a woolly tan-to-brown indumentum, on an upright, moderately branched plant. (*bureavii* × unknown). Unknown/Greer.

■ **HAZEL FISHER** Low–Medium H4–5 M–ML. Flowers with shades of yellow, flushed lavender and apricot with a maroon eye. Leaves dark green and twisted. (Mrs Lammot Copeland × Mary Drennen). Larson. Numerous sisters from this cross were also named: '**BUTTERED POPCORN**' yellow, '**DINY DEE**' orange buds open yellow, '**SPUN GOLD**' amber-yellow. '**PACIFIC GOLD**' brilliant-yellow, '**HJALMAR H. LARSEN**' pale yellow, edged red.

■ **HEART'S DELIGHT** Tall H5 M. Flower openly funnel-shaped, frilled, china-rose shading to rose-red, with a cardinal-red blotch in throat becoming spots on dorsal lobe, in ball-shaped trusses of 14. Leaves elliptic, dull, green, on an upright grower. (Mrs A.T. de la Mare × Britannia). Manenica. '**ERMINE**', said to be the reverse cross, has pure white flowers: I think things must have been mixed up…

■ **HEAVENLY SCENT** Low H4 M. Flowers large, medium-pink, scented, in a high but lax truss. A large stately grower, with medium-green shiny leaves. Mainly grown for its scent. (*fortunei* × unknown). Whitney/Sather. '**PERFUME**' probably a sister, pink with red spotting and a spicy scent.

■ **HEIDI'S LOVE** Low H4 EM. Flowers openly funnel-shaped, strong-red in bud, opening pale yellow with light purplish-pink margins, entire flower and calyx fade to yellowish white with slight flush of light purplish pink, in a truss of 15. Deep-green leaves on a plant growing wider than tall. (Nadia × [*yakushimanum* × Pink Petticoats]). Barlup.

■ **HELEN DEEHR** Semi-dwarf–Low H4 E. Flower openly campanulate, wavy to frilly edges, vivid-red with no markings, in ball-shaped trusses of about 15. Leaves elliptic, convex, glabrous, dull yellow-green, underside with tan indumentum, on a vigorous grower, growing wider than high. (Unknown Warrior × Noyo Brave). Moynier.

■ **HELEN DRUECKER** Medium H3 M. Flower funnel-shaped, recurved lobes, rose-red at margins shading to china-rose at centre, in a truss of 14–16. Leaves leathery, deep-green, on a fairly dense plant suitable for mild gardens. *CA*. (*elliottii* × Betty Wormald). Druecker. '**JIM DREWRY**' crimson, spotted oxblood-red. Probably a sister seedling.

■ **HELEN EVERITT** Medium H6 ML–L. Flower fragrant, openly funnel-shaped, pure-white with partly formed stamens, in ball-shaped truss of 5–7. Leaves elliptic, glossy, medium-green, on a rounded, well-branched plant. Parentage given is my own observation. Flowers are fine but the plant is rather hard to root. *ST*. (*fortunei* × *decorum*?). Everitt.

■ **HELEN MARTIN** Medium H5 M–ML. Buds purple-red, and open light purple-red with a lighter centre and a dark purple-red blotch. Leaves dark green, on a very dense plant. Heat resistant. A promising new Dutch hybrid, which should become available soon. (Cunningham's White × Cosmopolitan). Huisman.

■ **HELENE SCHIFFNER** Low H4–5 M. Pale lilac buds open to flowers of pure-white with very faint yellowish to brown markings, in domed trusses of 12–14. Leaves greyish green with red petioles. The foliage needs some sun protection in hotter climates. The flowers are a very pure white and the plant is slow-growing, suitable for the smaller garden. Habit is rather upright and irregular. *AGM, FS, VI*. (unknown × unknown). Seidel.

HELENE SCHIFFNER

■ **HELLIKKI** Low–Medium H8+ L. Flower wavy-edged, unmarked purple, in dome-shaped trusses of 8–12. Leaves with light tomentum on new growth and slight indumentum on the underside as the leaf matures. Not worth growing in mild climates; perhaps the poorest of the Helsinki University group of hybrids and looks particularly sad in a pot. *S. Fin*. (*smirnowii* hybrid × unknown). Uosukainen/Arb. Mustila.

■ **HELLO DOLLY** Low H5 M. Flower openly funnel-shaped, deep-pink blending to light yellow in throat, a few light-green spots in throat, fading to light yellow with age, in a lax truss of 6. Leaves narrowly elliptic, underside with light-beige indumentum, on a rounded, well-branched, dense plant. Prefers some afternoon shade in N.E. U.S.A. Some problems with floppy habit and breaking off at the roots. Hardy for a plant with such tender genes. (Fabia × *smirnowii*). Lem. **'ODESSA'** a German version of the cross with salmon-rose hose-in-hose flowers.

■ **HELSINKI UNIVERSITY (syn. HELSINGIN YLIOPISTO)** Medium H8+ ML. Flower openly funnel-shaped, wavy-edges, waxy appearance, strong purplish-pink inside with a few dark-red spots in dorsal sector in dome-shaped trusses of 12–18. Leaves red when new, turning green as they age. Upright habit. Rated as hardy to −34.5 to −37.2°C (−30.1 to −35°F) USDA 3b. Foliage is deep-green, glossy and handsome. Not worth growing in mild areas but invaluable for severe climates. *S. Fin.* (*brachycarpum* Tigerstedtii Gp. × unknown). Uosukainen/Arb. Mustila.

HELSINKI UNIVERSITY

■ **HENRY'S RED** Low H8 M. Flower openly funnel-shaped, deep crimson-red with darker throat, in ball-shaped trusses of 12–15. Leaves oblong, flat to convex, dark green, slightly twisted, on an upright, rather open plant. One of the hardiest reds with flowers of this quality and it was impressive at Weston nursery. *CT, MS, S. Fin.* (red *catawbiense* seedling × unknown). Mezitt.

HENRY'S RED

■ **HERBSTGRUß** Low H5? M/VL. Flowers pale purple to white with a large red flare, 10–11 per compact truss. In N. Germany, where it was raised, 60–70 per cent of flowers open in autumn in warm summers. It may not flower in autumn in other climates. (Kalamaika × Perlina). Hachmann.

■ **HERMANN BACKHUS** Medium H5 ML–L. Pure-white with a small dark-red blotch. Dark green leaves. Commercially available in Germany. (unknown). Backhus.

■ **HERNANDO** Medium H4–5 EM. Flower openly funnel-campanulate, opening light greenish yellow with a slight pink tinge, fading to pale yellow, in lax trusses of 16–18. Leaves elliptic, flat, dull, dark yellowish green. Spreading, open habit. Needs good conditions and never likely to become a commercial plant with this parentage. (*lacteum* × [yellow-flowered Loderi Gp. selection × Golden Dream]). Goheen.

■ **HIGH GOLD** Medium H4–5 M. Flowers deep, bright, true lemon-yellow with wavy edges, in large, rounded trusses. Dark green leaves roundish at ends on a vigorous plant with excellent branching habit. This was mixed up commercially with 'Top Hat' for some time, so there are many plants around wrongly named. (Damaris × Crest). Eichelser. **'LEMONADE'** is a sister of 'High Gold' with similar flowers, perhaps less free-flowering. **'TOP HAT'** very similar but lower growing with less shiny leaves.

■ **HILLE** Low–Medium H4 E–EM. Flowers pale yellow, tinged pink in bud, opening cream, all lobes speckled dark red, in compact, rounded trusses of 9–13. Buds-up young and has handsome foliage. Flowers are impressive if you like heavy spotting. Rather early flowering, so the opening buds are vulnerable to frost. (*irroratum* 'Polka Dot' × Graf Lennart). Wieting/Genzel. **'OSTERGOLD'** a similar sister.

HILLE

■ **HILLSDALE** Medium H8 M. Flowers neyron-rose, of good substance, with a yellow-brown flare in the throat, in a conical truss of about 18. Deep-green glossy foliage. Bred to withstand the extremes of temperature, both heat and cold, in its native Indiana. Disease and insect resistant. Promising. *IND.* (Chesterland × *fortunei*). Schroeder.

■ **HINDUSTAN** Tall H7 M–ML. Flower openly funnel-shaped, wavy lobes, yellow-orange flushed reddish pink with orange spots, in a dome-shaped truss of about 17. Leaves elliptic, dull, dark green, on a plant of poor habit which sprawls untidily. The flowers, which take a few years to appear, are impressive, but the habit lets it down. ([*maximum* × Goldsworth Orange] × [America × Gertrude Schäle]). Leach. **'ORANGE PRIDE'** orangey pink with yellow tones.

■ **HOLDEN** Low H6 EM. Flower bright rose-red, slightly tinged blue, fading to pale pink, with small red spots, in ball-shaped trusses. Leaves leathery, shiny, partly twisted, dark green. Compact plant, wider than tall. Heat tolerant. One of the most highly rated Shammarello hybrids from Nova Scotia south to Virginia. Buds-up young. Later flowering than sisters 'Cheer' and 'Spring Glory'. *TO.* ([*catawbiense* × unknown] × Cunningham's White). Shammarello.

■ **HOLLANDIA** Tall H4–5 M–ML. Flowers carmine-pink shading to a paler centre, spotted dark red, in a conical truss of 14–18. Leaves and habit similar to 'Cynthia' on a plant no longer much grown outside Holland. (Pink Pearl × Charles Dickens). Endtz.

■ **HOLY MOSES** Low–Medium H4–5 ML–L. Flowers flat-faced, pale yellow with salmon-pink stripes on the lobes in a flat truss. Leaves like those of *R. smirnowii*, with indumentum on lower surface. Hardier and more sun-tolerant than most hybrids of this colour. (Souvenir of Anthony Waterer or *smirnowii* × King of Shrubs). Lem.

■ **HONEY BUTTER** Low–Medium H4 M. Flower funnel-campanulate, inside light yellowish pink edged with pink; outside deep-pink, in domed trusses of 14. Leaves elliptic, rounded, moderate olive-green, Buds young. One of the many fine 'Lem's Cameo' hybrids from Jim Barlup. The colour may not be to everyone's taste. (Nancy Evans × [China × Lem's Cameo]). Barlup. **'HORIZON WILDFIRE'** pink edges, yellow centre, red flare.

■ **HONG KONG** Medium H7 M. Flower widely funnel-campanulate, pale yellowish green with bright greenish-yellow blotch deep in throat, in flat trusses of 13. Leaves elliptic, shiny, yellowish green. Susceptible to leaf spot, root rot and die-back in hotter areas. For us, this was one of the worst hybrids we ever tried, with poor foliage and habit, shy-flowering and susceptible to mildew. 'Capistrano' is much better. (*catawbiense* var. *album* × Crest). Leach.

HONG KONG

■ **HORIZON DAWN** Low H3 EM. Flower openly campanulate, of heavy substance, wavy edges, pale yellow with brilliant-yellow throat, in ball-shaped trusses of 12–14. Leaves elliptic to narrowly elliptic, convex, on a compact, dense plant. *CD.* ([Hotei × Tropicana] × [*yakushimanum* × (Alice Franklin × Virginia Scott)]). Brockenbrough.

■ **HORIZON GARNET** Medium H4 M–ML. Flowers strong-red with blackish-red spotting on all lobes, in a conical truss of 25. Leaves elliptic with down-curved margins, on a vigorous upright grower, best in some shade. (Anna × Kilimanjaro). Brockenbrough.

HORIZON LAKESIDE

■ **HORIZON LAKESIDE** Medium H3–4 M. Fine yellow flowers with a red flare in the throat, in a full rounded truss of about 15. Free-flowering and compact. Needs a sheltered site. The flowers are striking and distinctive. The rather twisted foliage is inclined to yellow in less than ideal conditions. ([Nancy Evans × Lem's Cameo] × Skipper). Brockenbrough.

■ **HORIZON MONARCH** Tall H3 M. Flower openly funnel-shaped, greenish yellow with a small, vivid-red flare in large ball-shaped trusses of up to 20. Thick textured handsome leaves and stems on a dense and compact plant. A very impressive hybrid, which rivals the Rothschild *R. lacteum* yellows in flower, but is much easier to please. Like most yellows, can suffer from mildew. *AGM, CA, EK, MB, SO, TC, VI.* (Nancy Evans × Point Defiance). Brockenbrough.

HORIZON MONARCH

■ **HOTEI** Low–Medium H4 M. Flower funnel-shaped, light yellow shaded brilliant canary-yellow with a darker throat, in a ball-shaped truss of 12. Leaves narrowly elliptic, dark green on a compact and tight growing plant. Needs light shade in most climates. Once the deepest yellow, but now superseded by others. It needs perfect drainage and takes a while to bud up. A parent of many good hybrids. *JF, MT, NI.* (Goldsworth Orange × [*souliei* × *wardii* var. *wardii*]). Sifferman.

HOTEI

■ **HUGH KOSTER (syn. HUGO KOSTER)** Tall H4 M–ML. Flowers bright-crimson with pale stamens, black spots and lighter centres, up to 16 per truss. Leaves shiny with wavy margins on a sturdy bush. Foliage needs to be protected from hot sun. Prone to leaf spot. *Mel.* (George Hardy × [Doncaster × unknown]). Koster. Sister **'PETER KOSTER'** is very similar with red stamens.

HUGH KOSTER

■ **HUMBOLDT** Medium H6 ML. Flower light rose-purple with dark-purple blotch, in ball-shaped trusses of 16–20. Leaves ovate, matte-green, on an upright, well-branched plant. Good in cold parts of E. North America. *CN, Ger, NY, PB.* (*catawbiense* × unknown). Seidel. **'HOLSTEIN'** bred from 'Humboldt' is equally hardy with similar flowers. **'MARINA DOMSCHKE'** a 'Humboldt' hybrid with lavender flowers blotched red.

HUMBOLDT

■ **HURRICANE** Medium H4 M. Flowers strong purplish pink with darker-pink edges, blotched and spotted dark red, in ball-shaped trusses of about 15. A plant of broad, rather irregular habit. A good plant in the Pacific Northwest but the tissue-cultured plants that most of us grew were terrible, so it got a bad name. Flower larger than that of 'Mrs Furnival' with a smaller blotch. (Mrs Furnival × Anna Rose Whitney). Whitney/Sather. **'HELEN JOHNSON'** carmine-rose with a darker flare.

■ **HUSSAR (syn. HUZZAR)** Low–Medium H3 M. Blood-red flowers with brown speckling on long pedicels, in a loose truss. A compact, free-flowering plant, not very commonly grown. ([*facetum* × Fabia] × May Day). J. Waterer.

■ **HYPERION** Medium H4–5 ML. White flowers, flushed mauve, with a chocolate blotch, 9–19 per rounded truss. Dark green leaves on a fairly rangy plant. Similar to 'Sappho' but in a flatter truss. (unknown). G. Waterer.

■ **HYPERMAX** Low H6 M. Flowers white to pale lavender, edges deeper, with purple-red spotting, in trusses of 14. Leaves very dark green with a thin layer of indumentum on the lower surface. A fairly low, vigorous plant, which should be extremely heat tolerant and would make a good parent for this attribute. Handsome foliage. (*hyperythrum* × *maximum*). Delp.

■ **ICE CREAM** Medium H4 L. Flowers of camellia-rose, white throat, pale-olive spots on upper petal, funnel-shaped, in dome-shaped trusses of 12–14. Vigorous and spreading. This should be scented, but does not appear to be. (Dido × *fortunei*). Slocock. **'VANILLA'** A clone with paler flowers. **'HANSUNANNA'** creamy-light-yellow, reverse pink-red.

■ **ICE CUBE** Medium H6 ML. Flowers ivory-white with a blotch of lemon-yellow, funnel-shaped, in conical trusses. Dark leaves, new growth with light silvery tomentum. Habit vigorous and rather open. Did not grow well in Scotland: leggy with yellowish foliage. Some heat tolerance and popular on U.S. East Coast. (*catawbiense* white × Belle Heller). Shammarello.

■ **ICE MUSIC** Low–Medium H4 ML. Flowers broadly funnel-shaped, frilled white with circular red eye and yellow flare on upper lobe, outside white with light-pink midribs, in a rounded truss of about 16. Leaves dark green on a compact plant. The flowers are striking. (Nancy Evans × Pirouette). Barlup.

■ **IDEALIST** Medium H4–5 M. Flowers pale greenish yellow, dark-red throat, widely campanulate, in trusses of 10–12. Glossy rounded leaves with a purple petiole. Vigorous and upright but dense. Requires a sheltered site. Not a very strong colour. (*wardii* × Naomi). Rothschild. **'QUEEN ELIZABETH II'** pale greenish yellow, no great improvement on its parent 'Idealist'.

■ **IGHTHAM YELLOW** Medium H4 M–ML. Apricot buds open to flowers of pale yellow with a tiny red blotch. Flowers have a faint scent. Leaves elliptic, inclined to chlorosis. Comes into growth early. 'Lemon Lodge' from the same cross seems to be a better plant. *Vic.* (*wardii* × *decorum*). Reuthe. **'JESSICA DE ROTHSCHILD'** pale yellow marked pink.

■ **IGNATIUS SARGENT** Medium H8 ML. Frilled flowers deep-rose-red with deeper blotch in a truss of 13–23. Leaves heavily textured and dark green. Rather open growing when young. (*catawbiense* hybrid). A. Waterer. Similar hybrids from the same stable include **'CHARLES DICKENS'** purplish crimson, spotted black, and **'H.W. SARGENT'** magenta-rose, near-red.

■ **ILAM ALARM** Tall H2–3 EM–M. Flowers red with a paler centre and pale stamens, in a full rounded truss. Leaves dark and rugose on a tree-like very leggy plant. Needs a few years to start flowering. Mostly grown in New Zealand, where it was raised. (*arboreum* ssp. *zeylanicum* × *griffithianum*). Stead.

■ **ILAM CANARY (syn. CANARY)** Medium H4 M. Flowers large, pale yellow, with a red blotch, long-lasting, in rounded trusses. Good foliage on a rather open plant, best in plenty of light. ([*campylocarpum* × *fortunei* ssp. *discolor*] × Loderi seedling). Stead.

■ **ILAM CERISE** Medium H3 M–ML. Flowers vivid-red (cerise) with a white throat and a small red eye, in tall trusses of 14–15. Leaves dark on a vigorous, upright plant. The best form has unfading flowers. A second clone has fading flowers. (Lady de Rothschild × *arboreum*). Stead.

■ **ILAM CREAM (syn. ILAM CREAM LODERI)** Tall H3 M. Flowers, pink in bud, opening pale greenish white, suffused pink around lobes, in loose trusses of 10. Vigorous, open habit. One of New Zealand's best hybrids. NZ. Award of Distinction. (Loderi g. ×). Stead. **'TOWNTALK'** deep-cream flushed pink. **'MARSHMALLOW'** orchid-pink with darker flare in the throat, scented.

■ **ILAM ORANGE** Medium H3? EM. Flowers deep orange-pink, fading to yellow, with a red basal-blotch, in a lax truss of 5–8. Leaves glossy, with red petioles, on a fairly compact spreading plant that grows wider than high. Needs very sharp drainage and protection from hot sun. Mainly grown in Australia and New Zealand. ([*arboreum* ssp. *zeylanicum* × Pink Pearl?] × *dichroanthum*). Stead.

ILAM ORANGE

■ **IMPI** Medium H3 ML–L. Flowers small, funnel-shaped, slightly frilly, very dark red appearing to be almost black, in sparse and loose trusses of 10–12. Leaves dark green with light white tomentum, bright-red stems. Upright, compact grower. The flowers are small and so dark you hardly notice them. A curiosity, useful for its late flowering. (*sanguineum* var. *didymum* × Moser's Maroon). Rothschild.

■ **INAMORATA g.** Medium–Tall H5 L. Flowers creamy yellow with a red blotch and or spotting in a loose truss of 8–12. Leaves in most forms have purple pedicels. Useful for late flowering. Both Rothschild and Hobbie/Robenek made the cross. The German version, sometimes sold as 'Robenek's Inamorata' is hardier. (*wardii* × *fortunei* ssp. *discolor*). Hobbie, Rothschild.

■ **INCA GOLD** Low–Medium H4–5 EM–M. Flower light yellow with maroon rays, in trusses of 10–12. Leaves oval elliptic, bluish green. Rounded habit. (× *chlorops* hybrid). Lancaster.

■ **INDEPENDENCE DAY** Low–Medium H4–5 L–VL. Flowers rosy red with pale-pink centre and a dark eye, 13–19 per compact truss. Usually flowers around 4 July, hence the name. Leaves smooth, light green, on a rounded, mounding plant. Foliage inclined to be yellow and the plant does not have much rigidity, inclined to sprawl. If the foliage and habit were as good as the flowers, this would be first rate. (unknown). A. Waterer.

INDEPENDENCE DAY

■ **INDIANA g.** Low H2–3 L. Flowers orange-red, speckled red, in lax trusses. Leaves recurved. Spreading habit. Very little grown. Useful for late flowering but rather tender. (*kyawii* × *dichroanthum* ssp. *scyphocalyx*). Rothschild.

■ **INHERITANCE** Tall H4–5 M. Flower broadly funnel-shaped, wavy edges, deep purplish pink with sparse purplish-red dorsal spots, in dome-shaped trusses of 16. Leaves elliptic, dull, dark yellowish green, lower surface with sparse indumentum. A good heat-tolerant plant for N. California where it is popular. (Jock × Antoon van Welie). Farwell.

■ **INVITATION** Semi-dwarf–Low H4 EM. Flower openly funnel-shaped, purplish pink with lighter centre, spotted greenish yellow with red areas at base extending upwards, reverse with pink lines in ball-shaped trusses of 20. Leaves narrowly elliptic, dull, olive-green, on a rounded, dense plant. One of the highest rated Barlup crosses. Jim thinks it is one of his best yellows. (Anita Dunstan × Lem's Cameo). Barlup. **'CALICO DANCER'** a sister with pale creamy-yellow flowers, darker with the upper lobes flushed pink.

■ **IRENE STEAD (syn. I.M.S.)** Tall H3–4 M. Flowers soft-pink, lightly scented, in huge blousy trusses. Upright tree-like habit, leaves with deep red-purple petioles. Best in filtered shade. Only lightly scented compared to its parent 'Loderi', but the truss is more sturdy. (Loderi hybrid). Stead. **'MRS PERCY McLAREN'** shell-pink to peachy-pink flowers, with a light fragrance. Needs wind shelter. **'THE DREAM'** phlox-pink, in trusses of 10. **'WAXEYE'** white with yellow-green eye.

■ **ISABEL PIERCE** Tall H3 M. Flower openly funnel-shaped, deep purplish pink fading to paler in centre, prominent reddish-brown blotch, striped deep-pink from base to edges, in ball-shaped trusses of 9–10. Leaves narrowly elliptic, dark green, on a plant of broad, upright growth habit. We find the foliage and habit rather unattractive though the flowers are good. TC. (Anna × Lem's Goal). Lem.

■ **ISABELLA g.** Tall H2–3 L–VL. Flowers pale pink to white, scented, in large loose trusses. **'EXBURY ISABELLA'** white, **'ISABELLA NEVADA'** pale pink. Large leaves on a giant tree-forming hybrid, which is not as hardy as 'Polar Bear' and so is much less grown. (*auriculatum* × *griffithianum*). Rothschild + others. **'BLANCMANGE'** is very similar.

■ **IVAN D. WOOD** Medium H4 ML. Flowers pale neyron-rose, centre orange-buff, fading to Naples-yellow, and then to cream. Light-coloured leaves on a rather open plant. Hard to root. Needs some shade to hold the flower colour. NZ. ([King of Shrubs × Fawn] × Dido). Coker. **'CORAL QUEEN'** is a deep coral-pink sister seedling. **'PACIFIC PRINCESS'** pink with orange-buff centre.

■ **IVANHOE g.** Medium H3 M. Flowers brilliant-scarlet, mottled darker, in loose trusses. Leaves long and narrow on a rather straggly plant. Not very hardy and mainly grown in New Zealand. Not one of the better hybrids of this type. (Chanticleer × *griersonianum*). Rothschild.

■ **IVERY'S SCARLET** Tall H2 VE–EM. Flower deep-red with darker spots on dorsal lobe, in a dome-shaped truss of 12–14. Narrow light-green leaves, on a rather leggy, sparse, upright grower. This hybrid is popular in Australia and New Zealand. In parts of California it flowers on and off all winter. Heat, sun, drought and wind tolerant, so ideal in hot climates. Mel. (unknown × unknown). Unknown. **'RED DAZZLE'** a New Zealand hybrid of R. *arboreum* × 'Ivery's Scarlet' with early, frilled, brilliant-scarlet flowers.

■ **JACKSONII** Low H6 E–EM. Flowers bright-pink, with deeper red-pink edges and red spotting in the throat, in a truss of 12–14. Leaves thin with a light brown indumentum on the underside. Habit is spreading with decumbent branches that can layer themselves. Flowers are early but are somewhat frost resistant. There are several different plants being grown under this name. (*caucasicum* × *arboreum* or Nobleanum). Jackson?

■ **JADE** Low H3 EM. Flowers pinkish orange fading to greenish yellow in tight trusses. A fairly compact, spreading plant. Free-flowering. Mainly grown in the Pacific Northwest where it was raised. (Fabia × Corona). Henny.

■ **JALIPEÑO** Semi-dwarf–Low H3 EM. Flower widely funnel-shaped, frilly lobes, strong-red with a few dark-brown spots and brown nectaries at base, in a conical truss of 16–18. Leaves lanceolate, bullate, dark green. Rounded, dense habit. Free-flowering and buds-up young. ([(Fabia × *haematodes*) × Earl of Athlone] × Jean Marie de Montague). Goheen.

■ **JALISCO g.** Low H3 ML. Yellow flowers, some dark red spotting, in loose trusses of 8–10. **'ECLIPSE'** primrose-yellow, **'ELECT'** primrose-yellow, paler lobes, **'EMBLEM'** pale yellow. **'JUBILANT'** buttercup-yellow. Several more were named. Leaves smooth and usually dark green. Take a few years to bud up and rather tender. Flowers hang down a bit, so the truss is not the best. An important and often used parent. (Lady Bessborough × Dido). Rothschild.

■ **JAMES BURCHETT** Tall H5 L–VL. Flowers white, slightly tinged mauve, with a yellow-green throat, in a dense truss of 15–18. Fairly dark foliage on a dense, free-flowering plant. Unfortunately it is hard to root, which means that it is not as popular as it should be. One of the toughest and best behaved of the late-flowering hybrids. AGM. (*fortunei* ssp. *discolor* hybrid). Slocock. **'WILHELM SCHACHT'** large white flowers on a tall and leggy plant. Named after the German alpine expert.

■ **JAMES DEANS** Medium H2–3 M–ML. Flowers strong purplish pink fading to moderate purplish pink to apricot-pink, in trusses of 14. Leaves large and handsome, lower surface with indumentum. New growth silvery. (*griersonianum* × *grande*). Jury/Deans. **'GRIERGRANDE'** There are several clones of this cross under this name in New Zealand collections. A handsome plant which would be widely grown if it were a little hardier. **'LES JURY'** pink.

■ **JAN DEKENS** Medium–Tall H4–5 ML. Flowers large bright-pink, deeper on edges paling in the centre to pale pink, in compact conical trusses. A strong, vigorous plant with large, boldly curled leaves. Like a more compact and deeper pink 'Pink Pearl'. (Unknown). Endtz/Blaauw. **'AMBASSADEUR'** deep-pink in large rounded trusses.

■ **JANET BLAIR (syn. JOHN WISTER)** Tall H6 M. Flower lightly scented, frilly, light pink with golden-bronze rays on the upper lobe, in a ball-shaped truss of 9 or more. Large glossy, deep-green leaves have a slight wave in them, on a dense, well-branched plant which grows wider than tall. Tough and heat tolerant. One of the finest Eastern American hybrids, a good performer everywhere. Much used as a parent. AT, AZ, BH, CC, CH, GP, MA, MD, ME, MS, NY, OL, OZ, PR, PT, PV, SE, SO, ST, TO, TZ. (unknown × unknown). Dexter.

JANET BLAIR

■ **JANET'S FLAIR** Tall H4–5 M. Flower slightly fragrant, purplish pink in bud, opening pale yellow with greenish-yellow spotting in throat and flare on dorsal lobe in ball-shaped truss of 20. Leaves oblong, glossy, moderate olive-green on a plant of open upright and spreading growth habit. An interesting cross that points the way to other hardy yellows for E. North America. (Janet Blair × Autumn Gold). Brack. **'JANET'S FANTASY'** apricot-cream with orange spots. **'BROOKHAVEN'** pale yellow with a deeper flair in a full rounded truss.

■ **JEAN MARIE DE MONTAGUE (Syn. THE HONOURABLE JEAN MARIE DE MONTAGUE)** Medium H4–5 M. Flower somewhat waxy textured with frilly edges, bright crimson-red with darker spotting in the throat, in round trusses of up to 14. Leaves heavy textured, dark matte-green. Dense habit. Thrives in heat and sun. Highly rated in Pacific Northwest, but to me the colour is rather pale and I think the plant is over-praised. And the full name is excessive: most people call her 'Jean Marie'. AGM, CA, CN, EG, JF, KK, MB, Mel, MT, NI, NN, NY, OL, OP, PD, PT, SC, SE, SH, SI, SO, TC, WT, U.K. (*griffithianum* × unknown). Van Nes.

JEAN MARIE DE MONTAGUE

■ **JEAN RHODES** Medium H4–5 M. Flowers neyron-rose, throat dark chrysanthemum-crimson, in trusses of 14. Leaves large, deep-green, on a tall and vigorous plant. Leaves insect resistant. Takes five to six years or longer to bud up. More than one clone has been distributed under this name. (Naomi × Mrs Horace Fogg). Rhodes.

■ **JEANETTE CLARK** Low–Medium H3–4 E–EM. Flowers funnel-shaped, pale purplish pink, in a truss of 12. Leaves elliptic. Sun tolerant. (unknown). Boulter. **'LAUREL CLARK'** Flowers deep purplish pink both inside and out, with deeper spotting on the dorsal lobe.

■ **JEANNE CHURCH** Low–Medium H3 E–EM. Pink buds open pink with a red flare, fading to creamy yellow in truss of up to 21. Roughly textured thick leaves resembling *R. macabeanum*, though shorter and rounder. From New Zealand where it, and its sisters which follow, are popular commercial plants: (*macabeanum* × Unique). NZ Rhod. Assoc. **'SPICED HONEY'** Flowers apricot and cream with a red blotch, in large trusses of 16–18. **'BEAUTY OF BEN MOI'** creamy white with maroon blotch.

■ **JEDA** Semi-dwarf H4 EM. Flower widely funnel-campanulate, pale orange-yellow with heavy spotting of vivid reddish orange on all lobes, outside deep yellowish pink, in flat trusses of 7. Leaves elliptic, flat, glossy, dark green. (Butter Brickle × [Sunup-Sundown × unnamed hybrid]). Lofthouse.

■ **JENNIE DOSSER** Tall H4–5 L. Flower funnel-shaped, slightly ruffled, light purple with a deep purplish-red blotch, in a tall truss of about 14. Leaves deeply veined, medium-dark-green. Upright habit. Another plant under this name is described as dark red, which is more likely from the cross. (Britannia × Trilby). Dosser.

■ **JENS JÖRGEN SÖRENSEN** Low H6–7 ML–L. Flowers pale pink, in a small rounded truss. Compact with rounded growth habit. This looks like a selection of *R. makinoi* to me, rather than a hybrid. S. Fin. (*makinoi* ×). Knorr.

■ **JESSIE'S SONG** Low H4 M–ML. Flowers pink with a yellow centre and red blotch, in rounded trusses. Leaves semi-glossy, moderate olive-green. (Nancy Evans × Golden Anniversary). Barlup. **'WINGS OF GOLD'** similar. **'RISING SUN'** another hybrid of 'Golden Anniversary' with creamy-yellow flowers with a large red flare. **'TWEEDY BIRD'** a sister with deeper-yellow flowers and a small red flare.

■ **JINGLE BELLS** Semi-dwarf–Low H3 M. Flower tubular funnel-shaped, orange fading to creamy-yellow, with a vivid-red throat, black anthers and stigma, in a lax truss of 8–10. Leaves elliptic, medium-green, on a compact, dense, rounded shrub. New growth bronze-tinged. This is one of the finest of the multi-coloured exotic-looking hybrids for moderate climates and it always attracts attention in flower. *Aust, NZ, SO, U.K.* (Fabia × Ole Olson). Lem.

JINGLE BELLS

■ **JOAN LESLIE HAMMOND** Low–Medium H4–5 ML. Flowers open funnel-shaped, very light purple at margins shading to very pale purple at centre, with a prominent, solid, dark-purple flare in throat, in domed trusses of 16–18. Leaves dark-olive-green. A striking flower. Commercially available in Europe through Hachmann's nursery. ([Holy Moses × Albatross] × Abe Arnott). Newcomb.

■ **JOE PATERNO** Medium H7 ML. Flowers white with a strong greenish-yellow dorsal blotch, in a rounded truss of about 20. Leaves elliptic to obovate, flat to convex, deep-green. A reliable budder. A good tough white. (Catawbiense Album × Swansdown). Pride.

JOE PATERNO

■ **JOHN COUTTS g.** Low H4 L. Flower glowing-salmon-pink, deeper in throat, very smooth texture, large open trusses. Dense somewhat sprawling habit. Useful late-flowering hybrid, but inclined to make frost-vulnerable late-growth. ([Grand Arab × *griffithianum*] × *griersonianum*). R.B.G. Kew. **'FLAMINGO'** H3 bright-rose in a rounded truss. Mainly grown in New Zealand these days.

■ **JOHN PAUL II** Semi-dwarf H7 M. Flower openly funnel-shaped, frilly edges, deep-red with pale yellow-green streaks on dorsal lobe, in ball-shaped trusses of 15–18. Leaves elliptic, glossy, dark green. Plant habit upright, and spreading, somewhat open. Some people rate the Pope's rhododendron very highly in E. U.S.A., though the red colour is somewhat harsh. I have reduced the exaggerated hardiness rating it was given. (Mars × [The Hon. Jean Marie de Montague × Cheer]). Minahan.

■ **JOHN WALTER** Medium H5 ML–L. Flowers slightly frilled, crimson-red with a bluish tinge, in trusses of about 20. Leaves slightly rough in texture, dull olive-green, with traces of indumentum on the leaf under-surface. (*catawbiense* × *arboreum*). J. Waterer.

■ **JOHN WATERER** Medium H4–5 L. Flowers crimson with brown speckling, in a truss of about 17. Leaves lanceolate with a thin layer of indumentum on the lower surface. A fairly vigorous, compact plant, now little grown. (*catawbiense* × *arboreum*). R. Waterer.

■ **JOHNNY BENDER** Medium H3–4 M. Flower currant-red with darker spotting, in ball-shaped trusses of 5–8. Leaves narrowly concave, dull, dark green, slight light-tan indumentum easily rubbed off. Upright grower. Bud-tender in Scotland and never flowered properly. 'Markeeta's Prize' is a much better alternative. The name raises eyebrows in the U.K. (The Hon. Jean Marie de Montague × Indiana). Seabrook.

■ **JONATHAN SHAW** Low H5 L. Flower vivid violet-purple shading to purplish red in the centre, with a prominent black flare, in ball-shaped trusses of 19. Leaves dark green, twisted, with wavy margins. Dense, spreading growth habit, compact for a dark-purple hybrid. The foliage tends to yellow in Scotland, though this may be due to poor tissue-cultured plants. *CC*. (Melanie Shaw × Brenda Lee). Leonard. **'MELANIE SHAW'** frilled flowers of deep-purple, a black blotch, centre reddish, 14–18 per truss.

JONATHAN SHAW

■ **JOSEPH WHITWORTH** Tall H4–5? ML–L. Flowers deep-maroon, well-textured, in a full rounded truss of 12–16. Leaves dark, tinged grey, on a tall but bushy grower. Good habit, foliage and easy to root. An old English hybrid now mainly grown in Australia where it does well. (*ponticum* × ?). J. Waterer.

■ **JOSEPHINE EVERITT** Medium H5 ML. Flower fragrant, clear-pink in a blend of two different shades, in a well-shaped truss. Leaves yellow-green, always looking sickly with us in Scotland, though it seems to do better elsewhere. Tough and the flower is good. *PT, SE*. (unknown × unknown). Dexter/Everitt.

■ **JOY BELLS** Tall H3 M. Flower large, cream-coloured suffused green with a crimson blotch, in large trusses. Leaves large and best with wind shelter. Silvery-brown new growth. Takes years to flower. I'd grow *R. macabeanum* or one of the other parent species in preference. (*macabeanum* × Fortune). Joyce/Hayes.

■ **JUAN DE FUCA** Medium H4–5 L. Purple buds open to aster-violet with a dark purple-blue flare in the throat, in a ball-shaped, 12-flower truss. Dark glossy leaves on a plant of dense upright habit. Easy to root and free-flowering. (Blue Ensign × *ponticum*). Larson.

■ **JUDY SPILLANE** Medium–Tall H4–5 L. Flower openly funnel-shaped, lightly fragrant, light purplish pink, fading quickly to white, with a prominent greenish-yellow blotch, in ball-shaped trusses of 14. Leaves elliptic, flat, olive-green. Rounded, dense habit. Like a paler, later version of its parent, the well-known 'Janet Blair'. A bit slow to bud up as a young plant. *GP*. (*maximum* × Janet Blair). Wister.

■ **JUNGFRAU** Medium–Tall H4 ML. Flowers creamy white in throat shading to pale-rose, in huge conical trusses of 24–32. Leaves dark, on a strong vigorous grower with an upright habit, best with some shelter. (Marie Antoinette × unknown). Rothschild.

■ **JUNIFREUDE** Low H6 L. Flowers strong purplish red, shading strong purplish-pink throat, dorsal markings moderate olive-green to yellow-green, 13–16 per truss. Leaves ovate-elliptic, dark, green, glossy. (Omega selfed). Hachmann.

■ **JURASSIC FANTASY** Low–Medium H5–6 M. Flowers cream, flushed pink with large bold blotch, in a rounded truss. Handsome deep-green leaves with very thin layer of brown indumentum on the underside. A great name for a plant that looked promising when I saw it at Rare Find nursery. A great name. (*yakushimanum* × *rex* ssp. *fictolacteum* hybrid). Schannen.

■ **KALIMNA** Medium H3–4 EM–M. Flowers medium neyron-rose shading to paler-rose in the centre, light yellowish brown on upper lobe, in a truss of about 20. Leaves twisted, on a fairly dense compact plant. Bred to flower early avoiding the heat of the late spring in its native Australia. Hard to root. Heat tolerant. *Aust*. (Edith Boulter × Unknown Warrior). Boulter.

■ **KAPONGA** Tall H3 EM. Flowers scarlet-red, in tight balled trusses. An upright bush of dark-green leaves with silver reverse. One of New Zealand's best hybrids with an impressive truss. *NZ distinction*. (*arboreum* × Ivery's Scarlet). Holland.

KAPONGA

■ **KAREN TRIPLETT** Low H3 M. Flower medium-yellow with a darker throat and large calyx, in trusses of 10–12. Leaves dark green and slightly twisted, on a plant of dense, compact habit. Copper young growth. The flowers are impressive at Glendoick. (Seattle Gold × unknown). Larson.

■ **KARIBIA**® Low H5 ML. Orange-yellow buds open pale yellow in loose trusses of up to 9. Leaves light green on a compact plant. (Brinny × Marinella). Hachmann.

■ **KATE WATERER** Medium H5 ML. Flowers rose-pink with a white, green and yellow centre in a truss of up to 17. Plant upright but fairly compact. Not as hardy as most of the Waterer *R. catawbiense* hybrids, so only of use in moderate climates. *AGM*. (*catawbiense* × unknown). J. Waterer.

■ **KATHRYNA** Tall H6 M. Flower purplish red with dark-red blotch on dorsal lobe, reverse lighter, in a ball-shaped truss of 23. Leaves elliptic, flat, held distinctively at right angle to stem. Upright, broad habit. (unknown × unknown). W. Smith.

■ **KATHY VAN VEEN** Low H4 EM–M. Flower outside vivid-red, inside variable: some flowers are mottled or striped, some have a lighter throat, with red spotting, in a domed truss of 15. Upright, dense plant. Foliage and habit is as in 'Jean Marie de Montague'. (Jean Marie de Montague sport). Rhein/Van Veen.

■ **KERUBIN** Semi-dwarf–Low H4 M. Flower pale yellow inside, outside pale-yellow/light-yellowish-pink with orange-yellow spots, in ball-shaped trusses of 8–13. Small leaves on a very dense, compact plant. (Golden Gate × New Comet). Colombel.

■ **KETTLEDRUM** Low H7 ML. Flowers purplish crimson, with darker marking, in a compact truss of about 16. Leaves ovate-obovate, dark glossy-green. (*catawbiense* × unknown). A. Waterer.

■ **KILIMANJARO** Medium H4 ML–L. Flower large, funnel-shaped, wavy-edged, luminous currant-red, spotted dark-red inside, in ball-shaped trusses of 18. Leaves narrowly elliptic, dark green. Upright habit. Poor branching and tending to straggle. The flowers are very fine and it is hardier than most of the Rothschild late-reds. *CA* (*elliottii* × Dusky Maid). Rothschild. **'BEEFEATER'** huge red trusses. Tender. Foliage easily sunburned. **'EDMUND DE ROTHSCHILD'** finest deep-red flowers. Needs shelter. **'JUTLAND'** deep-scarlet.

KILIMANJARO

■ **KING OF SHRUBS** Medium H4 ML–L. Flowers of good substance, apricot from a distance, yellow stripes from the throat flare, merge with orange at edges, margin banded rose, in lax trusses of 9–10. Leaves dull, pale green, inclined to be a bit chlorotic, on a rather open, leggy plant. (Fabia × *fortunei* ssp. *discolor*). Ostbo.

■ **KING TUT** Medium H7 M–ML. Flower rose-pink, deeper on the reverse, tinted yellow, with brown spots in centre, in a ball-shaped truss. Leaves convex, medium-green, with yellow stems. Needs pruning to maintain shape. The flowers are too *ponticum*-like for the U.K. but it is tough. Heat tolerant. There is said to be another clone under this name in Germany with darker flowers. *Ger, Scand.* ([*smirnowii* × America ?] × red *catawbiense* seedling). Shammarello.

■ **KING'S BUFF** Medium–Tall H3 M. Flowers buff, with dark-red speckles in throat. Leaves glossy, mid-green, glabrous. (Earl of Athlone × Lady Primrose). King.

■ **KING'S MILKMAID** Low–Medium H4 ML. Flowers soft-cream with a mustard-yellow flare, in dense, rounded trusses. Leaves glabrous, oblong-elliptic, light green. A New Zealand hybrid, which is quite highly rated there. (J.G. Millais × Gladys). King.

■ **KINGSTON** Medium H3 M. Flowers carrot-red fading to orange-buff, edges rhodonite-red, in lax trusses of 8–10. Plant upright, rounded, as wide as high, glossy, dark-green foliage, new leaves terracotta-brown. The flowers are a good colour but the truss is poor and the plant is tender and suffers foliage burn in Scotland. (Lem's Cameo × Polynesian Sunset). Holmeide & Poot Smith.

■ **KIWI MAGIC** Low H3–4 M. Flowers deep-pink in bud, open light-pink, centre yellow, overall effect at a distance yellowish pink, in trusses of 13–14. Leaves pale green on a fairly low spreading plant. Grows well in filtered light. This looked good in New Zealand but proved to be very poor, tender and sickly in Scotland. Horses for courses. ([*yakushimanum* × Dido] × Lem's Cameo). Jeff Elliott.

KIWI MAGIC

■ **KLUIS SENSATION** Medium H4–5 ML. Flower funnel-shaped, slightly frilled, bright-scarlet, spotted crimson, in tight trusses of 17–18. Leaves heavy-textured, concave, mid- to yellow-green with curled edges. Compact and slow-growing and a little lacking in vigour. Heat and sun tolerant. Susceptible to bud blast. A popular commercial hybrid especially in Europe. *AGM.* (Britannia × unnamed *griffithianum* hybrid). Kluis.

■ **KLUIS TRIUMPH** Medium H4–5 ML. Flower deep-red, reflexed, of good substance, in a fine truss of 12–16. Leaves dark, dull-green on a fairly tidy plant. Hard to root and usually weak on its own roots, evidently best grafted. A successful parent. (unnamed *griffithianum* hybrid). Kluis.

KOKARDIA®

■ **KOKARDIA**® Medium H5 ML. Flowers rosy-mauve-pink, flecked ruby-red, with a prominent dark-brown blotch in small ball-shaped trusses of 12–16. Leaves pointed, dark green, on an upright but fairly dense shrub. The flowers are striking but rather small for the leaf size. Hard to root, best grafted. *Ger, Scand.* (Humboldt × Direktoer E. Hjelm). Hachmann. **'HACHMANN'S ORNAMENT'** is a sister seedling with earlier flowers, mallow-purple with a deeper flare.

■ **KONSONANZ** Medium H5 ML–L. Flowers open funnel-shaped, purplish pink, shading to very pale purple in throat, edges strong purplish pink, with a conspicuous dark-red blotch, in fairly compact trusses of 14–15. Leaves broadly ovate, matte and dark green above. Flowers are striking and unusual. Tough. (Scintillation × Perlina). Hachmann.

■ **KRISTEN MARIE** Semi-dwarf H5 ML. Flower with deeply cut lobes (star-shaped), white with a yellow flare and purple-red edge, 15–16 to a truss. Leaves elliptic, convex. Grows wider than high. From New Jersey and a good tough plant for E. North America. The pink-rimmed flowers are striking. (Chionoides × Graf Zeppelin). Shapiro.

■ **KUBLA KHAN** Medium H4–5 M. Flower mandarin-red at edges fading to paler in the centre, with a very large currant-red blotch and rays of spots of same colour, in ball-shaped trusses of about 11. Leaves yellowish green, tending to chlorosis. Give plant light-shade for best looking foliage. The foliage (inherited from Britannia) lets it down: I've seldom seen a plant that was not sickly. (Britannia × Goldsworth Orange). Brandt.

KUPFERBERG

■ **KUPFERBERG** Low H5 M–ML. Flowers campanulate, pale orange-yellow with very dark yellowish-brown dorsal spots, in rounded trusses of 10–12. Leaves small and dark green on a slow-growing upright plant. The flowers are quite a good orange-brown and it is one of the toughest plants of this colour. It has potential as a parent. Hard to root, so usually grafted. (unknown, containing *R. dichroanthum*). Wieting.

■ **LABAR'S RED** Medium–Tall H5 M. Purplish pink (definitely not red) in rounded trusses. Leaves and habit acceptable. Easy to root and free-flowering. Its main attraction is extreme heat-tolerance and it obviously has further breeding potential. It is redder than most *R. catawbiense* hybrids. *IND.* (*catawbiense* hybrid). La Bar's Nursery.

■ **LACKAMAS CREAM** Low–Medium H4 M. Cream flowers with flushes of pink in loose trusses of 10–12. Leaves bluish green, elliptic, on a well-branched plant. (form of × *chlorops*). Lancaster.

■ **LADY BESSBOROUGH g.** Medium–Tall H4 ML. Apricot buds open to creamy-white flowers with maroon in the throat in loose trusses of about 10. (FCC clone). Leaves dark and shiny, on a vigorous, upright plant. A parent of 'Crest'. (*fortunei* ssp. *discolor* × *campylocarpum*). Rothschild. **'ROBERTE'** salmon-pink flowers fading to yellow-cream. Lem's **'OLE' OLSON'** is the same cross. Flowers pale yellow. Much used as a parent by Lem and others. **'QUEEN SOURIYA'** pale yellow, edged pink, scented.

■ **LADY BLIGH** Medium H4–5 ML. Dark-pink buds open to large pale-pink flowers with darker-pink edges, fading to paler, in tall trusses. Leaves dark green, on a fairly compact plant. Mainly grown in the Pacific Northwest. Newly open and fading flowers give a nice contrast. (*griffithianum* hybrid). Van Nes.

■ **LADY CLEMENTINE MITFORD** Low H4–5 ML. Flower soft-pink with darker edge and a white centre, in ball-shaped trusses of 16–18. Medium-sized, recurved foliage, new growth silvery, on a dense and spreading plant. Heat and sun tolerant. Over 130 years old and still worth growing. (*maximum* × unknown). A. Waterer.

LADY CLEMENTINE MITFORD

■ **LADY DECIES** Tall H4 ML–L. Flowers blush-lilac or light mauve, with a yellow eye in a dense truss of about 20. A vigorous, leggy grower. An old English hybrid now mainly grown in the southern hemisphere. *Vic.* (*griffithianum* × unknown). J. Waterer.

■ **LADY ELEANOR CATHCART** Medium H4 EM. Flowers clear-pale-pink with a narrow, dark-maroon flare, in a small rounded truss of 12–15. Leaves dark grey-green, under-surface with rusty indumentum, new growth silvery. Long-lived with an upright, rigid habit. Heat resistant. Dates back to the 1850s. (*arboreum* × *maximum*). A. Waterer. **'LADY ANNETTE DE TRAFFORD'** is similar, differing in the paler flowers and wider leaves.
■ **LADY OF JUNE** Medium–Tall H4–5 L. Flowers purplish pink, centre paler, with a yellow-red blotch, in a domed truss of about 16. Glossy olive-green leaves on a vigorous, upright and spreading plant. New growth silvery, turning brown. Takes a few years to start flowering. (Lady Eleanor Cathcart × *decorum*). Dexter/Wister.
■ **LADY PRIMROSE** Low–Medium H4 EM–M. Flowers pale primrose-yellow, spotted red, in a loose truss of 10–12. Leaves small, elliptic, light green, under-surface with a very thin indumentum, on a fairly slow-growing plant best in some shade. The flowers and pale foliage are not a good combination. Barely worth growing these days. (*campylocarpum* hybrid). Slocock.
■ **LADYBIRD** Tall H4–5 L. Flower ruffled, deep coral-pink with a deeper eye, spotted yellow, in dome-shaped trusses. Leaves glossy, dark green. Vigorous grower with open habit. Rather slow to bud up. A useful and fairly tough late-flowering hybrid, which would be more popular if it were easier to root. *Nl.* (*fortunei* ssp. *discolor* × Corona). Rothschild.
■ **LALIQUE** Tall H4 M. Flowers white, tinged delicate-pink and lilac, with wavy-edged lobes, sweetly scented, in conical trusses of 14–15. Leaves dark green on a vigorous, open, upright plant. Best in some shade. *NZ Distinction.* (Loderi or *griffithianum* seedling). Holmes.
■ **LAMPLIGHTER** Medium H4 M. Flower bright light-red with a salmon-pink glow, in tall conical trusses of 10–12. Leaves rounded, medium-green. Compact and open habit. Not one of my favourites. *Mel.* (Britannia × Madame F.J. Chauvin). Koster.
■ **LANGWORTH** Medium H5 M. Flowers large, funnel-shaped, white, with throat streaked greenish brown, in wide, conical, rather lax trusses of 16. Dark, dull-green handsome leaves on a vigorous plant. The flowers are impressive and as it is now in tissue culture, it is suddenly seeing its popularity grow, 40 years after it was named. Should be a good parent. (*fortunei* × Sappho). Slocock.
■ **LANZETTE** Low H6 ML. Flowers broadly funnel-shaped, light-pink tinged lilac, brownish-red dorsal markings, light-pink outside, in flat, lax trusses of 10–12. Narrow lanceolate leaves, margins recurved, with loose white indumentum above when young, under-surface with thick tawny indumentum. (*makinoi* × *degronianum*). Hachmann. **'THE PORCUPINE'** is a Canadian hybrid from the same cross.
■ **LAST HURRAH (syn. ATHENS)** Semi-dwarf H6 V–VL. Flower near-white, tinged and spotted yellow green, in ball-shaped trusses of 13. Leaves dark olive-green, of heavy texture. A spreading grower, much wider than high. Named for its consistent fall/autumn flowering in September in some climates. (Belle Heller × *aureum*). Leach.
■ **LAVENDER GIRL** Medium H5 M–ML. Flower lightly fragrant, pale lavender edged rosy mauve, fading at centre, with golden-brown marking in throat, in dome-shaped trusses of 16–20. Leaves glossy, on a vigorous but dense grower. Tough, sun and wind tolerant; a good choice if you like the subtle flower colour. *AGM.* (*fortunei* × Lady Grey Egerton). Slocock.

LAVENDER GIRL

LAVENDER PRINCESS

■ **LAVENDER PRINCESS** Low H7 M–ML. Flower lavender-mauve with pink-and-lilac blush, in a rounded truss. Leaves dark-green on a compact plant. A reliable and free-flowering hybrid that is one of the toughest of all the many Dexter introductions. (*fortunei*? × unknown). Dexter/Bosley.
■ **LAVENDER QUEEN** Medium H5 M–ML. Flower frilly, bluish lavender with a faint brown blotch, in ball-shaped truss. Leaves glossy, smooth, medium-green. Dense, growing wider than high. Buds young, free-flowering and quite heat tolerant. Some think its flowers are ugly. (*catawbiense*, red form × Boule de Neige). Shammarello.
■ **LEE'S BEST PURPLE** Tall H6 L. Violet flowers with yellow, green and red markings, in loose to rounded trusses of 13–23. Smooth, dark glossy foliage. Sun and heat tolerant. Later flowering than 'Lee's Dark Purple'. (*catawbiense* × unknown). Lee.
■ **LEE'S DARK PURPLE** Tall H6 ML. Flower royal-purple with a greenish-brown flare, in dense rounded trusses. Leaves deep-green and glossy with wavy edges. A rugged purple plant, now improved on by Hachmann and others breeding dark-purples for severe climates. Bred in the 1850s. *MD, PT, SE.* (*catawbiense* × unknown). Lee.
■ **LEE'S SCARLET** Low H4–5 VE. Flower dark rosy crimson fading to deep-pink with bright-red spots and blotch, in trusses of 10–17. Leaves with indumentum on underside. Closely related to 'Nobleanum'. Flowers can come out well before Christmas in mild northern hemisphere gardens. Heat tolerant. *VI.* (*caucasicum* × unknown). Lee.

■ **LEGEND** Medium H4 ML. Flowers white with a pink rim, in huge trusses (up to 25cm tall) of up to 15. A polyploid with thick foliage on a sturdy plant. Similar to the parents, but budding younger and with more pronounced pink edging to the flower. (Point Defiance × Lem's Monarch). Barlup.
■ **LEMON LODGE** Medium H4–5 M. Flowers flat-faced, pale primrose-yellow with tiny spots in the throat in rounded trusses. Leaves smooth and greyish green, on a reasonably compact plant. Very popular in New Zealand: every garden I saw seemed to have one. Hard to root, so perhaps most are grafted? Grows OK at Glendoick, but nothing special. *NZ Distinction.* (*wardii* × *decorum*). Pukeiti. **'GOLDEN JUBILEE'** a similar hybrid with scented creamy-yellow flowers, flushed pink. **'DUCHESS OF ROTHSAY'** pale yellow, shaded deeper.

LEMON LODGE

■ **LEM'S CAMEO** Low H4 M. Flower with wavy lobes, strong purplish pink at edges shading to light yellowish pink at throat with a strong-red dorsal blotch, reverse shaded red, in dome-shaped trusses of 17–20. Leaves elliptic, dark green, new growth mahogany. An astonishing and dramatic plant that has proven to be one of the best of all parents. Needs fertilizer and shelter and tends to grow rather sparsely. Tricky to root, so not as widely grown as it might be. *AGM, CA, CD, CN, EK, JF, KK, NN, OL, PA, PD, TC, VI.* (Dido × Anna). Lem.

LEM'S CAMEO

■ **LEM'S MONARCH** (*see* photo overleaf) all H4–5 M. Flower openly funnel-shaped, pale pink to white with pink margins and two narrow rays of red spots in upper lobe, in giant dome-shaped trusses of 16. Leaves ovate, thick, with slightly wavy margins, dull, olive-green, on a fairly tidy plant, which can grow very large. The giant two-toned trusses cause jaws to drop and it is surely one of the finest American hybrids for moderate climates. *AGM, EG, MB, OL, OP, PA, SI.* (Anna × Marinus Koster). Lem.

LEM'S MONARCH

LEM'S STORMCLOUD

■ **LEM'S STORMCLOUD** Medium H5 ML. Flowers openly campanulate, glossy deep-red, paling at centre, with white stamens, with a light dorsal blotch. Leaves are twisted and not very attractive, on a rather sparse, upright grower. The striking flowers are let down by the foliage and habit. (Burgundy × Mars). Lem.

■ **LEM'S TANGERINE** Low H4–5 ML. Flower openly funnel-shaped, yellowish pink with deeper edges, red throat, reverse reddish orange, in trusses of 10–14. Leaves lanceolate, glossy, olive-green. Upright, open habit. Not very fine as a plant, but proving to be an good parent for orange-red hybrids. (Margaret Dunn × [Anna × King of Shrubs]). Lem.

■ **LEO** Medium H4–5 ML. Flower of heavy substance, campanulate, bright crimson-scarlet with pink filaments and brown anthers, in ball-shaped trusses of 20–25. Leaves elliptic, medium-green, underside with traces of indumentum. A tall, upright, sturdy grower, which is one of the hardier of the Rothschild reds. Leaves can be yellowish. Similar to 'Captain Jack'. (Britannia × *elliottii*). Rothschild.

■ **LEONA** Low H4 ML. Flowers rich-pink, white in centre, with rose flare, in trusses of up to 15. Upright, rather open habit. East to root, sun tolerant and buds-up young. (Corona × Dondis). Henny.

■ **LEONARDSLEE GILES** Medium H4 EM–M. Flowers large, pale pink fading to white, in domed trusses of up to 12. Large thickly textured leaves on a tall tree-forming plant that is best with some shelter. Named after the garden in S. England where it was raised. (Standishii × *griffithianum*). Loder.

■ **LETTY EDWARDS g.** Medium H4 M. Pink buds open to pale sulphur-yellow flowers that fade to cream, lightly spotted darker, in rounded trusses of 10–12. Leaves medium-green with red petioles, on a fairly compact plant, best with some shade for best foliage. Several poor clones have been distributed. The AM clone seems to be the best. (*campylocarpum* × *fortunei*). Clarke. **'SAKI'** pale pink-cream in a tight truss.

■ **LIGHTHOUSE** Medium–Tall H3 E–EM. Flowers campanulate, strong-red throughout, one dark spot at base of throat, in conical trusses of 17–24. Leaves elliptic, margins decurved, glossy dark-green. (*arboreum* × Sir John Waterer). Van de Ven.

■ **LILA PEDIGO** Low–Medium H4 M–ML. Flowers chartreuse-yellow with light-red spotting, ruffled edges, in a large rounded truss. Leaves elliptic, on a compact, free-flowering plant. Very prone to powdery mildew, so we had to give it up, which is a pity as the flowers and foliage are good. (Odee Wright × Crest). Pedigo. **'SUNSET BAY'** another 'Odee Wright' hybrid with pale yellow, pink-tinged flowers.

■ **LILOFEE** Medium H5 ML. Flowers funnel-shaped, strong reddish purple, blotched dark purple on a dark-red to deep purplish red ground, with conspicuous white stamens, in rounded trusses of 14–16. Leaves dark green, on an upright but fairly compact plant. ([Nova Zembla × Purple Splendour] × Purple Splendour). Hachmann.

LILOFEE

■ **LIONEL'S TRIUMPH** Medium H4 M. Rose-pink in bud, opening to rich creamy-yellow flowers, with pink margins and crimson spotting, fading later, in large rounded trusses to 16. Large stiff leaves. Magnificent flowers but not easy to please, requiring good drainage and spraying for mildew. Takes a few years to bud up. (*lacteum* × Kewense). Rothschild. **'FRED ROSE'** lemon-yellow with red spotting. A second US-raised clone has unblotched flowers.

■ **LISETTA**® Low H5 M–ML. Flowers waxy, strong-red, with a white throat, in rounded trusses of 16–20. Dark-green glossy leaves on a dense compact plant. Colour holds well and does not fade. I tried to use 'Ovation' as a parent but got nowhere: Hachmann has succeeded and it seems a good variety to use further. (Ovation × Erato). Hachmann. Several similar sisters: **'ALLEGRETO'** loose trusses, **'BRISANZ'** paler-red, **'SARDANA'** hose-in-hose red.

■ **LITTLE GEM** Semi-dwarf H3–4 EM. Flower widely funnel-campanulate, moderate- to deep-red, unmarked, in lax truss of 7–8. Leaves oblanceolate to narrowly obovate, glossy, yellow-green, underside with light greyish-brown indumentum, growing wider than tall. (Carmen × *elliottii* K.W. 7725). Whitney.

■ **LOCH AWE** Tall H4 EM. Peach buds open pale yellow fading to cream suffused with peach/melon, spotted red, in a rounded truss of 15. Large handsome leaves with a thin greyish indumentum on the underside. Forms a large dense rounded bush. Very fine. Needs wind shelter and a little protection for its early flowers. (Percy Wiseman × *macabeanum*). Cox.

LOCH AWE

■ **LOCH LEVEN** Medium H3–4 ML. Flowers reflexed, medium-yellow, with a small red basal-blotch and red spotting, in full rounded trusses. Leaves dark green, bronzy on the young growth, on a rigid, slow-growing and tidy plant. One of the latest flowering 'Lem's Cameo' hybrids, so avoiding the bark-split and frosted buds that afflict some of them in Scotland. (Lem's Cameo × Whitney's Best Yellow). Somers/Cox.

LOCH LEVEN

■ **LOCH LOMOND** Medium H4 M. Apricot-peach buds open to flowers of rich deep-yellow, with some apricot flushing, in a full rounded truss. Leaves small, pointed and dark green on a very slow-growing, compact bush with bronze new growth. Buds-up young and very free-flowering. Recently named, we think this is very fine. (complex *wardii* & *yakushimanum* F2). Cox.

LOCH LOMOND

LODERI KING GEORGE

■ **LOCH TAY** Tall H4 M. Flowers open light yellow, fading to cream, with extensive red spotting, about 13 per truss. Narrow dark-green leaves on a compact and dense plant of narrowly upright habit. Needs good drainage and takes a few years to flower freely. Part-day shade is best in hot climates. Best grafted, as its Hotei parentage makes it susceptible to root problems. (Hotei × *caucasicum*). Cox.

■ **LOCH TUMMEL** Low H4–5 EM. Flowers white with a reddish-purple blotch in full trusses of 15–18. Leaves lanceolate, like those of its parent *R. pachysanthum*, but with a thinner layer of indumentum. The flowers are impressive. A natural hybrid from Taiwanese seed. (*pachysanthum* × *morii*). Cox.

LOCH TUMMEL

■ **LODAURIC ICEBERG** Tall H4 L. Flower funnel-shaped, frilly edged, very fragrant, white with a red blotch in the throat, in flat-topped trusses of about 15. Leaves elliptic, glabrous, medium-green. Can grow to tree size. We found that this flowered earlier than is claimed, so it is not as desirable as 'Polar Bear'. The flowers are said to stand more sun than most clones of 'Polar Bear'. *AGM*. (Loderi g. × *auriculatum*). Slocock. **LODAURIC g**. cross originally made by Crosfield/Ramsden.

■ **LODERI KING GEORGE** Tall H4 M. Huge palest-pink flowers fade to white with faint green markings, very fragrant, in loose trusses of 9–12. There are dozens of near identical clones. The best white clones are **'PATIENCE'**, **'SIR EDMUND'**, **'SUPERLATIVE'** and **'WHITE DIAMOND'**. Long pale-green smooth leaves on a tall upright tree-forming plant. One of the finest hybrids ever raised and with a very strong scent. The leaves are subject to leaf spot and yellowing, and needs wind shelter. *AGM, CA, CN, EK, JF, MT, NI, NN, PD, VI*. (*griffithianum* × *fortunei*). Loder.

■ **LODERI VENUS** Tall H4 M. Flower fragrant, pink, fading to light pink, faint green markings, in loose trusses of 9–12. Other pink clones include: **'PINK DIAMOND'** the pinkest clone, good foliage, **'SIR JOSEPH HOOKER'** pink with veining, **'GAME CHICK'** palest pink. Leaves and habit as 'Loderi King George'. Hard to root, so now in tissue culture. At least 12 more clones were named but I doubt if there was any point in naming more than about four or five. It has just led to confusion, as they are often mixed up in the trade. *EG, EK, NO, PD*. (*griffithianum* × *fortunei*). Loder.

LODERI PINK DIAMOND

■ **LODER'S WHITE** Medium–Tall H3–4 M. Mauve-pink buds open to white flowers with pink edges fading with age to white, and with small red spots in throat, in conical trusses of about 12. Leaves pale- to medium-green, slightly recurved, on a plant

LODER'S WHITE

of dome-shaped, compact habit. Fairly heat resistant and good in sun or shade. Free flowering and very fine from about five years of age. Given parentage would not yield such a hardy plant. *AGM, CA, MB, MT, OL, Mel*. (*arboreum* ssp. *cinnamomium* × *griffithianum*?). Mangles.

■ **LODESTAR** Low H7 ML. Flower widely funnel-shaped, pale lilac fading to white, blotch greenish yellow, in trusses of 15. Leaves elliptic, convex, on a rather open-growing plant growing wider than tall. *WT*. (*catawbiense* var. *album* × Belle Heller). Leach. **'SWANSDOWN'** is the reverse cross: white flowers tinged pink, blotched yellow, in a tall truss.

■ **LOFTHOUSE LEGACY** Medium H4 M. Flowers openly funnel-shaped, light orange-yellow at centre, darkening to light-orange at edges, outside light-orange, in ball-shaped trusses of up to 30. Leaves elliptic, glossy. Free-flowering. (Butter Brickle × Viennese Waltz). Lofthouse.

■ **LOON'S CALL** Low–Medium H4 M–ML. Flowers creamy yellow with a deeper centre, with a red flare at the base, with a winged calyx, in a rounded truss of about 12. Leaves elliptic with flat margins. Compact habit. (Mindy's Love × Satin Gold). Barlup.

■ **LORD ROBERTS** Low–Medium H6 L. Flowers small, deep-red with a black blotch, in small rounded trusses of 12–22. Leaves small, dark green, rugose, on a fairly compact plant. Tough and late flowering; the flowers are small but of good colour. Best in some shade in hotter climates. Easy to root and buds-up young. *AGM, MB, NI*. (*catawbiense* × unknown). Mason. **'MAX SYE'** small red flowers spotted black, in May.

LORD ROBERTS

■ **LOUIS PASTEUR** Medium H4 ML. Flowers two-toned, brilliant light-crimson margins shading to white centres, deep-pink exterior, in large, dense, rounded trusses of about 24. Spreading, straggly habit. Hard to root. Nice flower, shame about the habit. (Mrs Tritton × Viscountess Powerscourt). Endtz.

■ **LUCIDIUM** Medium H4 ML. Flowers rosy-purplish-lilac with an almost white centre and red spotting in the throat, in a compact truss of 15–21. Glossy foliage on a dense, loose, spreading bush, free-flowering and easy to root. A old English hybrid still commercially available in Australia. *Vic*. (*ponticum* × ?). A. Waterer.

■ **LUNAR QUEEN** Tall H2–3 M–ML. Flowers large, cream, in trusses of 9. Similar to the better known 'Roza Stevenson'. A vigorous tree that needs wind shelter. (*griffithianum* × Hawk). Harrison.

■ **LUSCOMBEI g.** Tall H4 M. Flowers large, deep rose-pink with a ray of crimson, trumpet-shaped, in loose trusses of 10–12. Leaves elliptic, dark and shiny, with a plum-coloured petiole, on a tall, broadly dome-shaped bush with attractive foliage. Common in older U.K. gardens but seldom offered commercially as it buds up slowly. (*fortunei* × *thomsonii*). Luscombe. **'PRIDE OF LEONARDSLEE'** deep-pink, a good selection from the same parentage.

LUSCOMBEI

■ **LUSH** Medium H7 ML. Flowers frilled, white and very pale purple with deep-red flare, in a rounded truss of 14. An absurd number of untested clones were named from this cross: I have managed to count nine of them: they don't seem to differ much. Instead of waiting to assess which were the best, they were named at five years old, far too soon to ascertain if they are any good. There ought to be a law against it. (Abe Arnott × White Peter). Delp.

■ **LYDIA** Tall H4 ML–L. Flower rotate funnel-shaped, rose-red with upper lobe marked cardinal-red, in tight trusses of 12–14. Leaves elliptic, dark green on a fairly compact plant. The flowers are of a very strident colour. We find it hard to propagate. (Antoon Van Welie × Day Dream). Greer.

■ **MACARENA** Low–Medium H5 ML. Flowers creamy yellow with a pink border, orange from a distance, in a rounded truss. One of the new Hachmann orange-hybrids. (Belladonna × Fred Wynniatt). Hachmann.

■ **MADAME CARVALHO** Medium H6 ML–L. Flowers white, flushed mauve, with green spots, in ball-shaped trusses of about 16. Leaves dark green on a dense handsome plant. Susceptible to Rhododendron Fly. Looks like a relative of 'Gomer Waterer'. (*catawbiense* × unknown). J. Waterer.

■ **MADAME COCHET (syn. MME CACHET)** Medium H4–5 ML. Flowers deep-lilac with a white centre and yellow blotch, in a truss of 10–22. Rather open-growing. Easy to root. Free-flowering. (*ponticum* or *catawbiense* ×). Bertin.

■ **MADAME DE BRUIN** Medium H5 ML. Flower cerise (bluish red), with dark-brown spots, in trusses of 18–20. Light-green leaves with a yellow midrib. Upright and rapid growing with rather brittle branches. Poor heat and sun tolerance in warmer climates. A poor truss and a horrible colour, I should avoid it at all costs. (Prometheus × Doncaster). Koster.

■ **MADAME FR. J. CHAUVIN** Medium H5 EM. Flowers rosy pink, paling to near-white in the centre, with a small red blotch, 10–12 per lax truss. Leaves long and narrow, light green, on an upright plant. Heat tolerant. *Cal.* (*fortunei* × Unknown). Koster.

MADAME DE BRUIN

MADAME MASSON

■ **MADAME MASSON** Medium H6 M. Flower star-shaped, white with a golden-yellow blotch, in conical trusses. Glossy, smooth green foliage on a dense, spreading plant. A good doer in moderately severe parts of the North American east coast. (*catawbiense* × *ponticum*). Bertin.

■ **MADLEEN** Medium–Tall H5 EM–M. Flowers in shades of light- and mid-purplish-pink, with greenish-yellow spotting in the throat, in rounded trusses of 9–11. Leaves dark green, ovate with slightly recurved margins. Grows slightly wider than high. (Astor × Oldenberg). Hachmann.

■ **MADRAS** Medium H7 ML. Flower cardinal-red, dorsal blotch of maroon, widely funnel-shaped, in a rounded truss of 19–21. Rather sprawling habit. Leaves +/– elliptic. David Leach tried to withdraw this plant but it is still commercially available. (Mars × Fanfare). Leach. **'BURMA'** a sister with cardinal-red flowers spotted black. Better habit.

■ **MADRID (syn. SEVILLE)** Medium H7 ML. Flowers moderate purplish pink (roseine-purple) with a bold ruby-red blotch, fading to pale purplish pink in trusses of 12–14. Leaves dark green, on a plant broader than tall. Not very widely grown. (Dexter #1 × America). Leach.

■ **MAGIC MOOD** Low H4 M–ML. Flowers light greenish yellow and pale yellow inside, strong red freckling on all lobes and throat, deep yellowish-pink outside, in trusses of 9. Leaves oblong-lanceolate. (Dechaem × Dexter's Honeydew). Delp.

■ **MAHARANI** Tall H5 M. Flowers creamy white, tinged and spotted pink, with a red throat overlaying a yellowish ground, in rounded trusses of 12–16. Handsome bullate foliage and thick stems on a

MAHARANI

SIMONA

dense spreading plant. Leaves sometimes rather yellowish. At its best this is a spectacular plant. *Ger, Nor, U.K.* (Harvest Moon × Letty Edwards). Hachmann. **'SIMONA'** a sister seeding with more pink in the flower when first open.

■ **MALAHAT** Medium H3 L. Flowers scarlet-red with darker throat and dark-red spots, in trusses of 14. Leaves long, pointed, underside with sparse coppery-brown indumentum, mainly on the midrib. One of Larsen's many *R. strigillosum* hybrids. Not as widely grown as 'Etta Burrows'. *CN.* (Gill's Triumph × *strigillosum*). Larson.

■ **MALETTA** Medium H4 L. Flower pale purplish pink with a yellow-green flare, in a conical truss of 13–15. Leaves elliptic and slightly obovate. Compact habit. ([*auriculatum* × *fortunei* ssp. *discolor*] × [*ungernii* × unknown]). Yates.

MANDA SUE

■ **MANDA SUE** Low H4 M. Flower openly funnel-shaped, creamy white with pink edges, aging to white, in trusses of 12–14. Leaves elliptic, light green, on an upright, rounded plant. The flowers are a subtle pastel colour, and last best with part-day shade. Buds-up young and free-flowering. *EK.* (Vulcan × Elspeth). Baker.

■ **MANDARIN DAY** Low H3 EM. Flower broadly funnel-campanulate, heavy textured, wavy edges, vivid reddish orange with reddish-orange nectaries and spots in throat, in a flat domed truss of 10–12. Leaves elliptic, flat or down-curved margins, broadly, dull, olive-green. ([*chlorops* × *decorum* ssp. *diaprepes*] × *venator*). Goheen.

■ **MANDERLEY** Low H4–5 ML. Flower campanulate, bright-red with darker-red spots in domed but lax trusses of 12–13. Deep glossy-green leaves are heavily textured. Mounding habit. (Scandinavia × Fabia). Slootjes. '**MANDALAY**' is another, more tender, hybrid with loose deep-red flowers. The spellings of these two sometimes get mixed up.

■ **MARBLE ARCH** Low H5 M. Flower funnel-shaped, ruffled, lightly scented, pale purplish pink fading to white, dark-purple blotch in throat, in ball-shaped trusses of 13. Leaves oblong, glossy, dark yellowish-green leaves. ([*smirnowii* × Avalanche Gp.] × Spellbinder). Miller/Gustafson.

■ **MARCHIONESS OF LANSDOWNE** Medium H6 L. Flower violet-rose with a distinctive maroon-black blotch, in dome-shaped trusses of about 14. Deep-green leaves on a vigorous plant. Habit poor and sprawling and, even with judicious pruning, it never makes a particularly handsome specimen, but the flowers are striking. (*maximum* × unknown). A. Waterer.

■ **MARGARET DUNN** Low H4 ML. Flowers apricot-pink, flushed shell-pink, openly funnel-shaped, in loose trusses of 8–9. Leaves narrow, slightly elliptic. Free-flowering once established. (*fortunei* ssp. *discolor* × Fabia). Swaything. '**GOLDEN BELLE**' large flowers of orange-and-yellow tones, with deep-pink edges. *See also* 'King of Shrubs'.

■ **MARGARET K. HINERMAN** Low H5–6? M–ML. Flowers pink. Leaves dark green and glossy. Compact habit. Bred in the midwest. (Nassau Red × Dexter's Honeydew). Hinerman.

■ **MARGARET MACK** Medium H4 EM. Flowers widely campanulate, frilled, soft lilac-pink, paler in centre, upper lobe spotted deep-rose, about 15 per conical truss. Leaves rich-green, twisted and wavy, on a plant of sprawling habit, best in sunny location. *MB.* (Marion × Annie E. Endtz). Boulter. '**YOU BEAUT**' orchid-pink flowers. '**GINA LOLLOBRIGIDA**' orchid-purple.

■ **MARIANKA**® Low–Medium H5 ML–L. Flowers white, with a touch of deep-pink with a deeper blotch, in a rounded truss. Several of this cross have been named. The Hachmann family told me they thought this was the best selection from this cross. (Soubrette × Sarasate). Hachmann.

■ **MARIA'S CHOICE** Low H3 M. Flowers hose-in-hose, funnel-shaped, light-yellow, lobes moderate yellowish-pink, in trusses of 15–18. An Australian 'Lem's Cameo' hybrid. *Vic.* (Apricot Gold × Lem's Cameo). Van de Ven. '**TILLY ASTON**' stripes of strong yellowish pink and moderate reddish orange, shading to deep yellowish pink on lobe edges, throat vivid reddish orange, outside strong reddish orange.

■ **MARIE FORTIE (syn. MADAME MARIE FORTIE)** Medium H5 ML–L. Dark wine-red with a darker blotch, in a compact truss of 14–23. An old hybrid that is still produced commercially in Belgium, where it was raised. (unknown). Fortie.

■ **MARIE STARKS** Low H5 EM. Flower openly funnel-shaped, light greenish yellow, deeper on lobes, with dark-red blotch and red spotting in a ball-shaped, somewhat lax truss of 14–18. Leaves elliptic, flat, glossy, yellow-green, on a rounded plant. *MT, PC.* ([*yakushimanum* × Fabia] × Odee Wright). Murray/Starks.

■ **MARILOO g.** Medium–Tall H4 EM. Flowers cream to pale yellow, with darker spotting, in fine rounded trusses of 15–20. There are several clones: '**A**', '**B**', '**FCC**', (all pale lemon), '**EUGENIE**' (cream) and '**GILBURY**' (pale-pink). Leaves yellowish green, twisted in some clones, on a sturdy fairly compact plant. Fine at its best, but it is temperamental, shy flowering when young, with yellowish foliage which is sensitive to spring frosts. Not good in heat and needs to be grafted. (Dr Stocker × *lacteum*). Rothschild. '**REPOSE**' creamy white, flushed green. Another Rothschild *R. lacteum* hybrid, as is the earlier-flowering cream '**GALACTIC**'. Both rather hard to please.

MARILOO

■ **MARINUS KOSTER** Medium H4 M. Flowers rose-pink, with a lighter centre, spotted brown-purple, in tall conical trusses of 10–12. Thick foliage on a vigorous, sun-tolerant, pest-resistant bush, which is easy to root and free-flowering. Koster.

MARINUS KOSTER

■ **MARION** Medium E–EM. Flowers Tyrian-rose, margins frilled and upper-petal spotted orange, reverse Tyrian-rose. Much used as a parent by Boulters nursery in Australia to breed early hybrids. (unknown). Cheal & Son.

MARKEETA'S PRIZE

■ **MARKEETA'S PRIZE** Medium H4–5 M. Flower heavy-textured bright scarlet-red with a few dark-red spots, in trusses of 12. Leaves thick, heavy and dark green. Thick stems on a stiff, upright but dense and well-behaved plant. I think this is the best of the May-flowering, large, western American reds. *AGM, CA, MB.* (Loderi Venus × Anna). Markeeta. '**MARKEETA'S FLAME**' very similar but with pinkish-red flowers.

■ **MARLEY HEDGES** Medium H5 M. Flower openly funnel-shaped, frilly, white edged reddish purple, purple-red dorsal blotch, reverse reddish purple, in a ball-shaped truss of about 24. Leaves dark green, elliptic, on an upright, well-branched shrub. *OL.* (Anna × Purple Splendour). Watson. '**KATRINA**' a sister with strong purplish-red flower with a large black blotch and black spots.

MARLEY HEDGES

■ **MARQUIS OF LOTHIAN** Tall H4 EM. Flower reddish-pink outside, paler within, in loose rather floppy truss of 7–10. A tall vigorous tree-like plant with beautiful cinnamon bark. Needs wind shelter. New Zealand's oldest hybrid, pre-1880. (*thomsonii* × *griffithianum*). Martin.

■ **MARS** (*see* photo overleaf) Low–Medium H5 ML. Flower campanulate, waxy, deep-red, with white stamens, in ball-shaped trusses of 12–14. Leaves narrow, dark green, ribbed, slightly twisted. Plant rather slow-growing and compact. This has a magnificent flower and has been the most successful parent of hardy red hybrids. The foliage tends to be pale green or yellowish. *Ger, U.K.* (*griffithianum*? × unknown). Waterer, Sons and Crisp.

MARS

MAY DAY

■ **MARTHA PHIPPS** Tall H5 ML. Flower openly funnel-shaped, pale-yellow flushed pink, reddish-orange inside, greenish-yellow in throat, in a compact truss of 7–10. Leaves narrowly elliptic, glossy, on an upright, moderately branched plant. (unknown × unknown). Phipps.

■ **MARY BELLE** Low H6 M. Flower widely funnel-shaped, frilly, salmon-peach with cardinal-red blotch and spotting, in a flat-topped, ball truss. Leaves elliptic, crinkled, light green, tending to yellowish. Plant best with filtered light. One of the hardier hybrids of this colour but let down by its rather sickly foliage, which does not set the flowers off well. Not worth growing in mild climates. *CC, GP.* (Atrier × Dechaem). Gable.

■ **MARY BRIGGS** Dwarf H4 EM–M. Flower funnel-campanulate, blood-red, in compact trusses of 8–10. Leaves lanceolate to elliptic, dark green. Low growing and open habit. (*haematodes* × Elizabeth). Wyatt.

■ **MARY DRENNEN** Medium H4–5 L. Flowers light aureolin-yellow, in trusses of 11–12. Leaves large, olive-green, on a well-branched plant. (Angelo × *wardii*). Larson.

■ **MARY GUTHLEIN** Semi-dwarf–Low H4 M. Flower broadly funnel-shaped, lightly scented, pale orange-yellow, unmarked, in flat trusses of 7–9. Leaves elliptic to oblong, dull, moderate yellowish green. Shrub has upright, freely branching, vigorous habit. ([Scintillation × Inamorata] × [(*fortunei* × *wardii*) × *dichroanthum*]). Murcott.

■ **MARY TASKER** Medium H3–4 L. Flowers buff-pink with yellow edges and red throat, in loose trusses of 9–11. Fine healthy leaves on a plant of good habit. Free-flowering. Very popular in New Zealand. *NZ.* (Jalisco × Fawn). Tasker.

■ **MASPALOMA** Low H6 ML. Deep pinkish red with a large almost black blotch and a mass of spotting over almost the whole flower, 12–15 per rounded truss. Leaves glossy, dark green. (Soubrette × Sarasate). Hachmann. **'CHARLESTON'** is a similar sister seedling.

■ **MAVIS DAVIS** Semi-dwarf–Low H4 M. Flower openly funnel-shaped, heavy substance, pale yellow with reddish-orange margins, in trusses of 10–12. Leaves elliptic or obovate, flat, dull-green. Vigorous grower. Best grown in filtered light. The flower is striking but we found it a poor grower, though this may be due to tissue-culture problems. (Orange Marmalade × Lem's Cameo). Davis.

■ **MAXECAT** Tall H4–5 M. Flower broadly funnel-shaped, light pink with yellow blotch and dark-pink spots, in a conical truss of 15–20. Leaves lanceolate, semi-glossy, dark green, new stems red, on a plant of dense habit. Heat tolerant and root-rot resistant. More than one clone exists. Apparently, tissue-cultured plants under this name

may in fact be 'Maximum Roseum'. *MA, PT, SE.* (*maximum* × *catawbiense*). Gable.

■ **MAY DAY g.** Semi-dwarf–Low H3 EM. Flower bright signal-red (or orange-red) with a large calyx, in a loose truss of about 8. Leaves dark green with thick tan-coloured indumentum. Grows wider than tall. Several clones exist, some more tender than others. *EK, SL.* (*haematodes* × *griersonianum*). Williams. **'IBEX'** bright crimson.

■ **MAY MOONLIGHT** Medium H4–5? M–ML. Flowers pale yellowish pink with a greenish throat, unmarked, in a truss of 8–9. Leaves narrowly elliptic–elliptic, flat, moderate yellow-green. (unknown). Dexter/Wister.

■ **MEADOWBROOK** Tall H6 ML–L. Flower frilly, pink with a white blotch and green spots, in a conical truss of about 22. Leaves elliptic, moderate olive-green. Habit as broad as tall. (Mrs C.S. Sargent × Everestianum). Vossberg.

■ **MEDUSA g.** Low H3–4 M. Flowers Spanish-orange shading on lobes to mandarin-red, heavily speckled with light brown, in very loose pendulous trusses of 7–10. Leaves dark green, underside with thin brown indumentum. Plant dense, compact. This is close to true orange, but the flowers hang down, making it hard to see the colour. We find it rather tender in E. Scotland. Heat tolerant and easy to root. (*dichroanthum* ssp. *scyphocalyx* × *griersonianum*). Puddle/Aberconway.

■ **MEL ALLEN** Medium H4 EM–ML. Light orchid-pink with pale-yellow flair, in a rounded truss. Fairly dense habit, good used as a screen. This is probably a selection of *R. ponticum*. (*ponticum* × unknown). Allen. **'CLEO'** light lavender-blue, flowering over several months in California. Bushy.

■ **MELIDIOSO** Low H4–5 ML. Flowers medium purplish pink shading through orange-yellow to pale greenish yellow in the centre, in trusses of 15. Medium glossy-green leaves on a slow-growing and compact plant. (Herme × *dichroanthum* ssp. *scyphocalyx* hybrid). Hachmann.

■ **MENDOSINA®** Medium H6 ML–M. Flowers rosy mauve with a prominent dark black-purple blotch, in a truss of about 17. Leaves dark green, convex. (Kokardia × Ignatius Sargent). Hachmann.

■ **MERLEY CREAM** Medium H7 M–ML. Flower openly funnel-shaped, greenish-white tinged pink, with a yellow flare in the upper lobes, in a dome-shaped truss of about 12. Leaves elliptic, flat, yellow-green, on a dense, upright plant. One of the hardiest Dexter hybrids. Leaves are rather pale and can look a bit sickly. *PB.* (unknown × unknown). Dexter.

■ **MICHAEL WATERER** Medium H6 L. Flowers small, crimson-magenta, with a black flare, in a compact truss of about 15. Leaves narrow on a fairly compact, sun and exposure-tolerant plant.

Easy to root. Much used as a parent. (*arboreum* × *ponticum*). J. Waterer. **'PROMETHEUS'** scarlet-crimson with white stamens and black markings.

■ **MIDNIGHT** Medium H4–5 M. Flower frilly, reddish purple with large deep-red blotch, in trusses of about 16. Shiny, glossy-green leaves on an open-growing and vigorous plant. One of the most popular Australian hybrids, also commercially available in Europe and North America. *Aust, CA, NZ.* (Cup Day × Purple Splendour). Van de Ven. **'NIGHTWATCH'** a sister with dark pink flowers with a maroon blotch. Very leggy.

■ **MIDNIGHT BEAUTY** Low–Medium H5 ML. Flowers with reflexed lobes, deep reddish purple with a large deep-purple flare, in a rounded truss. Dark green leaves, compact habit. Holger Hachmann has very high hopes for this new hybrid of a striking and unusual colour. Unlikely to be on the market till 2007–8. (Frank Gallsworthy × Jonathan Shaw). Hachmann. **'MIDNIGHT LADY'** a similar sister.

MIDNIGHT BEAUTY

■ **MIDNIGHT MYSTIQUE** Medium H4 EM. Flower openly funnel-shaped, very pale purple with wide margin of dark purplish red and with yellow-bronze spots, in dome-shaped trusses to 30. Leaves oblong, dark green, stiff, on a rather irregularly shaped, straggly plant. The extraordinary flowers are let down by the untidy and rather sparse habit. Not all that easy to root. Fujioka and Barlup have used this as a parent. (Midnight × One Thousand Butterflies). Fujioka.

MIDNIGHT MYSTIQUE

■ **MIDSUMMER** Medium H5 L–VL. Flower rose-pink with a golden flare on upper lobe, in compact trusses of about 13. Open, spreading habit on a sun and heat tolerant plant that tends to have yellowish foliage. It is a pity the leaves and habit are poor, as the flowers are good and it is useful for its lateness. (*maximum* × unknown). Waterer, Sons and Crisp.

■ **MIKKELI (syn. SAINT MICHEL)** Low H8 ML. Flower white with pink markings and green spots, in dome-shaped trusses of 10–18. Leaves dark green, slightly hairy. New growth covered with white tomentum. Dense habit. An excellent choice for severest climates, rated to withstand –34.5 to –37.2°C (–30.1 to –35°F), which is USDA zone 3b! Not worth growing in mild areas. *S. Fin.* (*brachycarpum* Tigerstedtii Gp. × *smirnowii*). Uosukainen/Arb. Mustila.

■ **MINDY'S LOVE** Low–Medium H4 M. Flowers strong-pink in bud, opening pale greenish yellow with throat and 3 upper lobes pale orange-yellow, with two faint strong-red streaks, in domed trusses of 21. Leaves dark green, on a fairly compact plant that needs good drainage. Flowers are very fine pure-yellow, almost unmarked, but the *R. lacteum* blood may make it a bit fussy. Lots of good reports. Flowers said to be long-lasting. (Nancy Evans × Lionel Triumph). Barlup.

■ **MINNA'S PURPLE** Low H7 ML. Flowers openly funnel-shaped, deep purplish red with darker margins and darker-red dorsal flare, in domed trusses of 12. Glossy leaves. Tough, but not very exciting. (*catawbiense* hybrid). Mezitt.

■ **MINNETONKA** Semi-dwarf–Low H8 M. Flower widely funnel-shaped, light-purple with lighter centre and vivid yellow-green spots on upper lobe, in dome-shaped trusses of 15. Leaves elliptic, glossy, medium-green, on a dense and spreading shrub. (*ponticum* × unknown). Motzkau.

■ **MOLLIE COKER** Medium H4 EM. Flowers scented, roseine-pink, with a purplish-red blotch in full rounded trusses. Leaves long and dark on an open, tree-forming plant. Buds up at four to six years of age. There are two clones in New Zealand. #30 has a yellow-brown blotch. #106 has a red-purple blotch and is more compact. (Irene Stead O.P.). Coker. **'THE DREAM'** is similar.

■ **MOLTEN GOLD** Medium H5 L. Flowers pinkish purple in small rounded trusses of 10–15. Leaves with bold yellow flashes on them. Hardy but the variegated growth is sometimes frosted or sunburnt. I think it can also be damaged by fertilizer and fungicides. Perhaps the best variegated rhododendron so far. *U.K.* (Sport of Goldflimmer). Morleys. **'BLATTGOLD'** from Germany is to all purposes identical: we cannot see any difference between them. The English version is likely to win the popularity contest due to the name.

MOLTEN GOLD FOLIAGE

■ **MONSIEUR MARCEL MÉYNARD (MARCEL MÉYNARD)** Medium H5 ML–L. Flowers small, very deep violet-purple with green speckling in throat, 9–15 in a rather loose truss. Leaves small, recurved, dark green. Flowers are very dark purple but rather small. Becoming quite popular in the U.K. as it is now in tissue culture. (unknown). Croux & fils.

■ **MOONSHINE g.** Medium H4 M. Various clones: **'AM'** primrose-yellow, **'BRIGHT'** pale lemon-yellow, **'CRESCENT'** clear-yellow, **'SUPREME'** primrose-yellow, stained deeper, in trusses of 14–16. Dark-green leaves on an upright but fairly dense plant. Quite good in flower, but somehow these hybrids are not amongst the best and they never really became widely grown. (Adriaan Koster × *wardii*). Wisley.

■ **MOONWAX** Tall H4 M. Flowers lightly fragrant, Naples-yellow centre, light-mauve edges, unmarked, in dome-shaped trusses of 12. Light-green glossy foliage on an upright, stiffly branched plant that grows into a large mushroom-shaped bush. The subtle-coloured flowers need some shade to hold their colour. (Holy Moses × Albatross). Newcomb.

■ **MOSER'S MAROON** Tall H5 L. Flowers small, dark-red with black spots, in compact, rounded trusses of 15–16. Leaves bullate, with striking coppery-red new growth, which remains red-tinged all summer. Rather upright and leggy in habit. Hard to root and rather slow to bud up. More of a curiosity than a beauty. (*maximum* ×). Moser.

MOSER'S MAROON FOLIAGE

■ **MOTHER OF PEARL** Tall H4 ML–L. Rich-pink buds open delicate-pink, fading to pure-white, faint brownish spots, in a truss of about 11–17. Leaves yellowish green on an upright plant that forms a tree-like bush. Not as popular as 'Pink Pearl'. (Sport of Pink Pearl). J. Waterer.

■ **MOUNT CLEARVIEW** Medium H4 M. Flower openly purple with purplish-red throat and dark-red dorsal spotting, reverse strong reddish purple, in dome-shaped trusses of 14. Leaves narrowly elliptic to elliptic, dull, yellowish green, on a plant of rounded habit. (Van Nes Sensation × Purple Splendour). Newcomb.

■ **MOUNT EVEREST** Medium H4–5 EM. Flower campanulate, faintly fragrant, pure-white with brown speckles on upper lobe and throat, in trusses of 10–12. Leaves dull green. Dense, vigorous grower. *Aust, CA, NZ.* (*campanulatum*? × *griffithianum*). Slocock.

■ **MOUNT MAZAMA** Medium H4 M. Flower funnel-shaped, fuchsia-red, spotted brighter-red, with dark-red nectar pouches, and stripes on reverse, in a balled truss of 15. Leaves elliptic, rather pale green. Grows wider than tall. (Britannia × Loderi). Grace.

■ **MOUNT SIGA** Medium H4–5 EM–M. Flowers openly funnel-shaped, slightly fragrant, peach-pink in trusses of 7–10. Leaves light green. A natural hybrid from Rock 18139, which many people grow as *R. vernicosum* in E. North America. A good performer in moderately harsh climates with heat- and some drought-tolerance. Colour varies a little from year to year. (from seed of *R. vernicosum* Rock 18139 × unknown). Gable. **'KULU'** is another selection from this number with pinker flowers. **'DOCTOR JOSEPH ROCK'** flowers peach-pink, shading to deeper in the throat. **'JAMES ALLISON'** pale ivory.

■ **MOUNTAIN AURA** Semi-dwarf–Low H6 ML. Flower white with blue/lavender edge, in ball-shaped truss of 10. Leaves dark forest-green, on a spreading plant which grows three times wider than high. (Dorothea × unknown red hybrid). Nearing.

■ **MRS A.T. DE LA MARE** Medium H6 M. Buds blush-pink, open to slightly fragrant, large white flowers with green spots in throat, in dome-shaped trusses of 12–14. Leaves glossy, dark green. Occasionally throws fused and misshapen leaves. Upright, spreading habit. A fine tough scented-hybrid. Flowers are easily weather-marked. *AGM, CD.* (*fortunei* × Halopeanum). Van Nes. **'ADMIRAL PIET HEIN'** a sister seedling with fragrant pastel-rose flowers in tight trusses.

MRS A.T. DE LA MARE

■ **MRS BERNICE BAKER** Medium–Tall H4 M. Red buds open two-tone rose-pink, lighter centre, in large conical trusses. Rather open habit. Foliage inclined to hang in winter. (Dawn's Delight × *fortunei*). Larson.

■ **MRS BETTY ROBERTSON** Medium H4–5 M. Flower pale yellow with pink flush, aging to cream, with a red blotch on dorsal lobe, in dome-shaped trusses of 6–8. Leaves rough-textured, twisted, deep-green, on a plant of compact habit. Sister of 'Harvest Moon' and quite a successful parent of yellow hybrids. Easy to root and free-flowering. *TC.* (Mrs Lindsay Smith × *campylocarpum* × unknown). Koster.

■ **MRS C.B. VAN NES** Medium–Tall H4 M. Rose-red buds opening almost red, fading to a pretty, soft-pink in a rounded truss of about 12. Leaves medium-green, glossy, on a plant of rather open habit, which does not respond well to pruning. Free-flowering once mature but takes a few years to bud up. Flowers are attractive and quite long-lasting. Some heat resistance. *Vic.* (Princess Juliana × Florence Sarah Smith). Van Nes.

■ **MRS CHARLES E. PEARSON** Tall H4–5 M. Flower widely funnel-shaped, pale pinkish mauve, fading paler, with heavy chestnut-brown spotting, in tall conical truss of 10–12. Leaves matte, deep-green, on a plant of upright habit. A tough, dense plant that takes a few years to bud up. Sun and heat tolerant. Not a very popular colour in the U.K. *AGM, EK.* (Coombe Royal × Catawbiense Grandiflorum). Koster.

■ **MRS CHARLES SARGENT** Medium–Tall H8 ML. Flowers rosy pink to dark carmine-rose with a small yellow blotch, in rounded tight trusses of about 20. A very tough ironclad, whose only drawback is the rather open and sometime floppy habit. It grows well all over E. North America and into the midwest. Also good in colder parts of Europe. (*catawbiense* hybrid). A. Waterer. **'QUEEN MARY'** rose-pink flowers, H5–6.

■ **MRS DAVIES EVANS** Low H5 L. Flowers frilled, strong reddish purple (imperial-purple), with a white blotch and yellow spots, in compact globular trusses of about 19. Vigorous plant of compact habit. Free-flowering. *AGM.* (unknown). A. Waterer.

■ **MRS E.C. STIRLING** Tall H4–5 M. Flower ruffled, blush-pink, fading to white, shaded in upper lobe with mauve, with upward pointing protruding stamens, in a conical truss of about 17. Growth habit upright and leggy when young, later spreading and open. Heat tolerant, though foliage can yellow in sun. *EK, NI, Mel, NZ.* (*griffithianum* × unknown). J. Waterer.

■ **MRS FURNIVAL** Low H6 M. Flower widely funnel-shaped, rose-pink, paler at centre, conspicuous reddish-brown blotch and vivid-red markings, in trusses of 12–14. Medium-green leaves on a compact, rather slow-growing plant. Sun and heat tolerant and highly rated in many areas. Somewhat hard to root. *AGM, CC, EG, FS, OP, PC, PD, SH.* (*griffithianum* hybrid × *caucasicum* hybrid). A. Waterer. **'SPRINGTIME'** (syn. **'WILLIAMS'**) similar but a little later flowering.

MRS FURNIVAL

■ **MRS G.W. LEAK** Tall H4 EM. Flower light pink with brownish-purple blotch, in conical trusses of about 12. Leaves dull, olive-green on an upright grower. Leaves may suffer from harmless black spotting. Easy to root. Susceptible to lacebug and red spider in Australia. A popular garden plant in moderate areas. Buds-up at about four to five years old. *CA, EK, MB, Sl.* (Coombe Royal × Chevalier Felix de Sauvage). Koster.

MRS G.W. LEAK

■ **MRS GEORGE HUTHNANCE** Medium–Tall H3 EM. Flowers open funnel-campanulate, primrose-yellow with red flecking, in a truss of 15–16. Leaves dull green, to 15cm long, with silvery indumentum on the underside. Vigorous but fairly tidy. Popular in New Zealand. (*macabeanum* × unknown). Huthnance. Other similar crosses include: **'PINK FRILLS'** cream flushed pink with a red blotch, **'INA HAIR'** cream with rose spotting, **'GRAND MYSTERY'** pale rose, with a ruby blotch, **'GOLDEN DAWN'** primrose-yellow with red spotting, said to be scented, **'EYESTOPPER'** pale yellow, fading to white.

■ **MRS HELEN KOSTER** Medium H4–5 ML. Flowers star-shaped, pale-lilac to white, with a large red-purple blotch. Leaves dark green, on a compact plant. Another hybrid with lilac flowers and a yellow flare is incorrectly sold under this name in North America. (Mrs J.J. Crosfield × Catawbiense Grandiflorum). Koster.

■ **MRS HOWARD PHIPPS** Medium H5 M. Flower funnel-shaped, medium orchid-pink, in large compact trusses of 13. Leaves elliptic, matte-green, on a plant of compact, well-branched habit. (unnamed hybrid × Naomi). Phipps.

■ **MRS J.G. MILLAIS** Medium H4 ML. Flowers flat-faced, white, tinged pink, with a large yellow flare, flushed red, in large trusses of about 14. A very vigorous, sprawling plant, hard to make into a tidy plant. Easy to root, buds-up young and the flowers are very striking. (unknown). A. Waterer.

■ **MRS JOHN WATERER** Tall H4–5 L. Flowers rosy crimson with dark-crimson spotting, in a truss of about 18. Leaves stiff, slightly convex, leathery, on a vigorous, tall but dense grower. One of the first named late-flowering hardy hybrids, pre-1850. (*maximum* hybrid). J. Waterer.

■ **MRS LAMMOT COPELAND** Low H4–5 L. Flowers clear greenish yellow, in trusses of 12–15. Leaves large shiny dark-green. Fertilizer-sensitive. The deep flower-colour has attracted hybridizers in the Pacific Northwest to breed from it. (*wardii* × Virginia Scott). Larson.

■ **MRS LIONEL DE ROTHSCHILD** (syn. **LADY DE ROTHSCHILD**) Medium H4 M. Flowers white, flushed/edged pink with a crimson blotch and spotting in a rounded truss of about 16. Leaves shiny on a dense and sprawling plant, which has a tendency to fall off its roots so is better grafted. The flowers are impressive. Grown under the name 'Lady de Rothschild' in North America. *AGM, TC.* (*griffithianum* × Sappho?). A. Waterer.

■ **MRS P. DEN OUDEN** Medium H6 M. Flowers deep-crimson, with a ray of olive-green spots in the throat, in a rounded truss of up to 20. Slow-growing, compact and spreading. Highly rated in Europe and North America. *Ger, Hol.* (Atrosanguineum × Doncaster). den Ouden. **'VAN DER HOOP'** pale crimson to deep-pink flowers with dark-brown spots. **'PROFESSOR F. BETTEX'** bright-red, tinged purple in a full truss.

■ **MRS R.S. HOLFORD** Medium H6 ML–L. Flowers rosy salmon, flushed strawberry, lightly spotted crimson, widely funnel-shaped, frilly edged, in large tight trusses of 10–20. Leaves medium-green, oblong-ovate, on an upright, rounded plant. *AGM.* (*catawbiense* hybrid). A. Waterer.

■ **MRS TOM AGNEW** (syn. **MRS T. AGNEW**) Tall H4 L. Mauve-pink buds open to white flowers with a conspicuous yellow-brown flare, which changes to reddish, in a truss of about 16. New growth sometimes obscures the flowers. An old English hybrid still available from a few specialist nurseries. (unknown). J. Waterer.

■ **MRS TOM H. LOWINSKY** (syn. **MRS T.H. LOWINSKY**) Medium H6 L. Flower pale lavender fading to white with a bold brownish-orange blotch, in trusses of up to 14. Dark shiny, textured leaves on a vigorous grower of fairly tidy habit. One of the best late-flowering hardy hybrids with striking flowers. Heat tolerant. Highly rated in many parts of the world. Grown equally as 'Mrs Tom Lowinsky.' & 'Mrs T.H. Lowinsky'. *AGM, AZ, MT, NI, Bel Ger, Scand.* (unknown × unknown). A. Waterer.

MRS TOM H. LOWINSKY

■ **MRS W.R. COE** Tall H4–5 ML. Flower deep-pink with a crimson-red throat, in a dome-shaped truss. Leaves large, deeply veined, on a vigorous, fairly compact plant. Heat tolerant, easy to root and usually free-flowering. (*fortunei* × unknown). Dexter/Coe.

■ **MULTIMACULATUM** Medium H8 ML. Flowers small, white with a red flare, in a compact domed truss of 7–16. Leaves slender, dark green. A very tough 1860s hybrid similar to 'Cunningham's White', which was a favourite of Gertrude Jekell. The flowers resemble small butterflies. (*ponticum* × *brachycarpum*). A. Waterer.

■ **MUNCASTER MIST** Low H4–5 EM. Flower campanulate, blue with darker-blue markings, in conical trusses. Leaves large, grey-green on a compact plant that takes a good few years to flower. It was distributed in tissue culture for some reason, though it is only of specialist interest. *PA.* (*campanulatum* × *floribundum*). Pennington-Ramsden.

■ **MY JANE** Low H5 M–ML. Flowers light-yellow with rays of red spots in the throat, in domed trusses of about 16. Dark-green leaves. A new E. American hybrid now being tissue-cultured, so it will shortly be quite widely available. (Arctic Gold × [Hardgrove's Deepest Yellow × Phipps Yellow]). Anderson/Jasionowski.

■ **MYSTIQUE** Medium H3–4 M–ML. Flowers Naples-yellow, edged with porcelain-rose with a red throat, in a truss of up to 16. Good foliage on a fairly compact plant. Raised in New Zealand. (Mai Tai × Nancy Evans). Sligh.

■ **NANCY EVANS** Semi-dwarf–Low H3 M. Flower openly funnel-shaped, yellow with some early orange shading on lobes and reverse, with a large calyx, in perfect ball-shaped trusses of 19. Leaves narrowly elliptic to elliptic, shiny, medium-green, bronze-coloured when new. A free-flowering, compact plant with bronzy new growth. Needs sharp drainage. One of the best hybrids of this colour. *AGM, EK, FS, MB, MT, NN, OL, PA, SL, SO, TC, VI.* (Hotei × Lem's Cameo). Brockenbrough.

NANCY EVANS

■ **NANTUCKET** Low–Medium H7 ML–L. Flowers broadly funnel-shaped, strong purplish red, with a coppery-coloured, spotted, dorsal flare, in domed trusses of 15. Leaves glossy, elliptic, margins decurved. (*catawbiense* hybrid). Mezitt.

■ **NAOMI g.** Medium H4–5 M. Flowers, with pink and yellow blends, in frilly trusses, lightly scented. Finest is '**NAOMI EXBURY**': pale pink shading to yellow-white centre, about 14 to the truss. Other clones include: '**A.M.**' pale pink, '**NAUTILUS**' rose flushed orange, '**STELLA MARIS**' lilac-pink, tallest growing, '**MOLLIE BUCKLEY**' pink-purple, speckles orange. Hard to root, take a few years to bud up and are subject to powdery mildew. At least seven further clones were named. (Aurora × *fortunei*). Rothschild.

NASELLE

■ **NASELLE** Low–Medium H4–5 M. Flower openly funnel-shaped, wavy edges, china-rose shading to maize-yellow at base of three upper lobes and burnt-orange spotting, in trusses of up to 15. Leaves elliptic, pale green, very pale maroon when new, on a plant of rounded habit. One of the most striking Cameo hybrids. *EK, KK, NO, VI.* ([CIS × unnamed hybrid] × Lem's Cameo). Elliott. '**GALA**' a sister with flowers with rose edges to pale centre, scented, spotted red in a truss of 15.

■ **NATHAN HALE** Low H4–5 ML. Flower openly funnel-shaped, fragrant, purplish red with purplish-pink centre and a red blotch, in a ball-shaped truss. Leaves elliptic, rounded, yellowish green, sometimes prone to spotting, on a compact and rounded plant. (unknown × unknown). Dexter/Schlaikjer.

■ **NELDA PEACH** Semi-dwarf H4 M. Flower openly funnel-shaped, light yellowish pink with bright-yellow throat, in ball-shaped trusses of 12–15. Leaves elliptic, flat. A good flower, but not always easy to please. (unnamed peach-coloured hybrid × Lem's Cameo). Robertson/Davies.

■ **NEPAL** Tall H8 ML. Rose-pink buds opening to large white flowers tinged pink, said to be lightly fragrant, in rounded trusses. Leaves glossy, long, medium-green. Vigorous and can attain a considerable size. Impressive flowers. *NI.* (*catawbiense* var. *album* × [*wightii* × *fortunei*]). Leach.

■ **NEW CENTURY** Low H7 M. Flowers pale yellowish green to ivory-white, with darker-yellow margins and a blotch of darker-yellow, in balled trusses of 15–18. This is really white rather than yellow. Compact and slow-growing and useful for the small garden. (*catawbiense* hybrid × [pale yellow × Bristol Cream]). Mezitt.

■ **NEW COMET** Medium H4 M. Flowers mimosa-yellow, flushed pale-pink and green, in thick textured trusses of about 12. Leaves elliptic, glossy. Slow to bud up and hard to root. Rarely offered these days. (Idealist × Naomi Exbury). Wisley. '**EMERALD ISLE**' flowers chartreuse-green/pale-yellow, stained deeper in the throat, in a loose truss of about 9.

■ **NEWCOMB'S SWEETHEART** Low H4 M–ML. Flower openly funnel-shaped, fragrant, pale purplish-pink darkening with age and edged light purplish pink, with a red blotch, in a ball-shaped truss of 11. Leaves narrowly elliptic, flat, dull, yellow-green, on a plant growing wider than tall. Good foliage and fine flowers. (Pink Walloper × *decorum*). Newcomb. '**NORRIE KING**' a similar New Zealand hybrid with pink flowers with a deeper flare.

■ **NIMBUS** Medium H4 ML. Flowers cream flushed pink, fading to white, in a compact rounded truss of about 8. Leaves large, on a large tree-like plant that needs a sheltered site. (Snow Queen × Cornish Cross or Loderi). Wisley.

■ **NIMROD g.** Tall H4 EM. Flowers pale pink, heavily spotted purplish red, in large, well-filled trusses of about 22. Long broad leaves on a plant early to flower and into growth and which takes many years to flower freely. Needs shelter and plenty of room. (*irroratum* Polka Dot × *calophytum*). Rothschild.

■ **NOBLEANUM** Medium H4 VE–E. Small trusses of pinkish red in mild periods in December–February. '**COCCINEUM**' and '**HANDSWORTH SCARLET**' are two red clones. '**VENUSTUM**' is pink. '**ALBUM**' white, flushed pink. Narrow leaves with a thin layer of indumentum. One of the earliest hybrids to flower, sometimes starting

NOBLEANUM ALBUM

before Christmas. Slow-growing and compact. Some of the pink-and-white clones flower later, in February to March. A wonderful winter-flowering shrub. *U.K.* (*caucasicum* × *arboreum*). Waterer/Smith, and others.

■ **NORFOLK CANDY** Low–Medium H5 M–ML. Flowers cream, flushed orange, with a bold-orange flare, in a truss of up to 16. Dense growing with good foliage. (Milkmaid × Marmora). Russell.

NORFOLK CANDY

■ **NORRIE KING** Medium H4 M. Flowers fuchsine-pink with large maroon flare and white stamens, in broad trusses of 12–15. Leaves ovate-elliptic, glabrous. A vigorous, upright plant that is widely admired and popular in New Zealand. (Mrs G.W. Leak × *decorum*). King. '**HOLMESLEE FLARE**' orchid-pink with a red flare.

■ **NORTHERN STAR** Medium H4–5 L. Flowers lightly fragrant, white, in large trusses of about 15. Leaves large, dark green. We grew this for a while but it was not as late-flowering as it should be from the cross and was nothing out of the ordinary. (*fortunei* ssp. *discolor* × Lodauric Iceberg). Hydon Nursery.

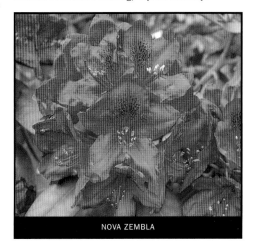
NOVA ZEMBLA

■ **NOVA ZEMBLA** (*see* photo previous page) all H7–8 ML–L. Flower dark bluish red with darker red spots, in ball-shaped trusses. The most popular red for severe climates, but the flowers are rather harsh. Good in full exposure. Fairly heat and sun tolerant but will suffer from phytopthora in S.E. U.S.A. if not given perfect drainage and some shade. A very important commercial plant. *Scand, Ger, Holland, N.E. U.S.A.* (Parson's Grandiflorum × unknown). Koster.

■ **NOYO CHIEF** Medium H3 EM. Flower broadly campanulate, clear rose-red, in ball-shaped truss of 16. Leaves elliptic, glossy, with deep prominent ribs, dark green, underside with sparse fawn indumentum, New growth is bronzy. Vigorous grower with good foliage recommended for mild climates. Its hybrid 'Rubicon' is more compact with darker flowers. *CA, EK, NO, OP.* (*arboreum* ssp. *nilagiricum*? × unknown). Reuthe/Bowman.

■ **NYMPHENBURG** Tall H4–5 L. Flowers large, fragrant creamy white, in lax trusses of about 9. A vigorous, late-flowering white from Germany. Best with some shelter. (*fortunei* ssp. *discolor* × *decorum*). Hobbie.

■ **OBERBURGERMEISTER JANSSEN (syn. MAYOR JOHNSON)** Low–Medium H4 ML. Flowers trumpet-shaped, scarlet, with a dark-brown blotch, in full trusses. Matte-green leaves on a plant of spreading habit. Buds-up young, free-flowering and fairly insect resistant. Not reliably hardy in its native Germany. Translated to 'Mayor Johnson' in the U.K., as the German name is not easy to pronounce! Prone to mildew. (May Day? × Goldsworth Orange?). Bruns.

■ **ODEE WRIGHT** Low H4–5 M. Flower widely funnel-shaped, greenish yellow with carmine-red spotting in throat, in trusses of 12–15. Leaves waxy, glossy, on a compact, dense grower. Best with some shade. Thousands of very poor tissue-cultured plants of this have been distributed. They should be destroyed. The real thing is a fine plant, though rather lacking in vigour. *CD, CN, FS, PD, TC.* (Idealist × Mrs Betty Robertson). Wright.

■ **OFF-SHOOT** Medium H6 EM–M. Flowers funnel-shaped, strong-red in bud, opening pale orange below with strong-pink highlights inside all lobes and moderate-red spotting on dorsal lobe, in a balled truss of 17–19. Mid-green leaves on a fairly tidy plant. A fine flower and quite tough. I saw it in the Philadelphia area where it was impressive. (Holden × Mary Garrison). Rhein.

OFF-SHOOT

■ **OH! KITTY (syn. MISS KITTY)** Low H4 M. Flowers funnel-shaped, large, pastel-pink, with dark-maroon throat, fragrant, in very large conical trusses of 17. Leaves elliptic, convex, dark green on a vigorous plant. A useful addition to the giant Pacific Northwest pinks, of which there are legion, as it has scented flowers. (Cotton Candy hybrid?). Minch.

■ **OKLAHOMA** Tall H3 VL. Flower waxy, currant-red, lightly spotted darker-red, with black anthers and stigma, in large trusses of about 22. Leaves narrowly elliptic with a loose indumentum on the underside. Limited availability. *NZ.* (Bellerophon × Tally Ho). Rothschild.

■ **OLD COPPER** Medium H4–5 L. Flower campanulate, coppery orange fading to orange-yellow with red spotting, in loose trusses of about 5. Leaves elliptic-lanceolate, on a plant of upright habit. Heat tolerant and useful for its late flowering. (Vulcan × Fabia). Van Veen.

■ **OLD PORT** Medium H5 M. Flowers dark wine-red or plum (vinous-crimson), blackish-crimson markings, in a truss of about 15. Leaves very glossy, elliptic, convex. Vigorous and sturdy and of striking colour. I have also seen another plant under this name with deep red-purple flowers, without a blotch, with glossy smooth *R. ponticum*-like foliage. *AGM.* (*ponticum/catawbiense* ×). A. Waterer.

■ **OLGA** Semi-dwarf–Low H5 ML. Flower light yellow, flushed pink, flecked orange-red, fading to salmon, in trusses of about 12. Spreading habit. Free-flowering. The multi-coloured flowers look a bit muddy from afar. *AGM.* (Mrs Lindsay Smith × Dido). Slocock. **'GREENSLEEVES'** pale yellow, tinged pink, heavily spotted.

OLGA

■ **OLIN O. DOBBS** Medium H6 ML. Flowers of good substance, deep reddish purple with a deep red-purple flare, in a truss of 12–15. Like most of the purples, the leaves can be a bit yellow, on a sun-tolerant and quite insect-resistant plant. Free flowering and easy to grow. *MT.* (Mars × Purple Splendour). Dobbs/Greer. Sister **'IRRESISTABLE IMPULSE'** deep red-purple.

■ **OLINDA RUBY** Medium H4 E. Flowers bright red, in full rounded trusses of 15–20. A clever cross looking for an early flowering red with better red flowers than 'Nobleanum'. Popular in Australia. (Nobleanum × Cornubia). Boulter.

■ **OLYMPIC SUN** Low H4 EM. Flower openly funnel-shaped, frilly, greenish yellow, with traces of pink on outside, fading to cream, in domed trusses of 12. Leaves narrowly oblong, flat, dull, dark-olive-green, on a plant of fairly compact habit. (Brandt's Best Yellow × Marcia). Minch.

■ **ONE THOUSAND BUTTERFLIES** Medium H4 ML. Flower widely funnel-shaped, strong purplish pink at edges, shading paler within, with a cardinal-red flare, in ball-shaped trusses of 20–30. Leaves narrowly elliptic to elliptic, glossy, dark yellowish green, on a fairly, well-branched plant. One of Lofthouse's best hybrids and a good parent. *CA, NN, U.K.* (Lem's Cameo × Pink Petticoats). Lofthouse.

ONE THOUSAND BUTTERFLIES

■ **OOH GINA** Semi-dwarf–Low H3 ML. Flower openly funnel-shaped, faintly fragrant, red, with rose edges and star-shaped cardinal-red blotch, in ball-shaped truss of 15. Leaves narrowly elliptic to elliptic, emerald-green, bronze young growth on a plant of rounded habit, with stiff, upright branches, growing broader than tall. (Golden Belle × Lem's Cameo). Burlingame.

■ **ORCHARD ROAD** Tall H4 ML. Flowers funnel-shaped, edges solferino-purple, merging to pastel-mauve, in trusses of 9. Leaves elliptic. Open growing, of vigorous habit. Popular and highly rated in its native New Zealand. (Pacific Queen × *wardii*). Grant. **'KAPUNATIKI'** yellow with red-and-green throat. **'OLWEN'S DREAM'** carmine-scarlet.

■ **ORCHID CORSAGE** Low H5 M. Flower openly funnel-shaped, frilly edges, light-purple margins shading to lighter in centre with a dark-purple blotch and markings on dorsal lobe, in ball-shaped trusses of 15. Leaves oblong, flat, glossy dark green, on a plant of moderately dense habit. (unknown × unknown). Hardgrove/Kordus?

■ **ORIGINAL VAGABOND** Semi-dwarf–Low H5 M. Flower openly funnel-shaped, pale yellow to pale orange-yellow with light orange-yellow flare on dorsal petal, in ball-shaped truss of 12. Leaves elliptic, flat, pale greenish blue on a fairly compact plant. (Janet Blair × Apritan). Gustafson.

■ **OSTBO'S LOW YELLOW** Low H4 M. Flower apricot-pink in bud, open to creamy yellow with apricot-orange centre, in loose trusses. Leaves deeply veined. Dense, compact habit. (unknown × unknown). Ostbo.

■ **OSTERSCHNEE** Low–Medium H5 EM. Palest-pink flowers quickly fade to white, with a bold-red blotch, in a flat truss of 12–14. Dark-green elliptic to ovate leaves. (Mardi Gras × *praevernum*). Hachmann.

■ **OUR GEM** Tall H3 VE. Flowers funnel-shaped, strong purplish red, shading to deep purplish pink in the throat, spotted on dorsal lobe, in domed trusses of 14. A very early 'Nobleanum'-type hybrid grown in Australia. (*arboreum* ×). Olinda Nurseries.

■ **OVATION** Low H6 M–ML. Flowers waxy dark red with a split calyx in a flat-topped truss. Dark foliage, a little inclined to chlorosis. Fine unfading flowers. Much used as a parent by Hachmann. I tried to breed with it too, without success. (Mars × *haematodes*). Nagel. **'MARENGO'** a hybrid of 'Ovation', with fine red flowers.

OVATION

■ **OVERTURE** Low H4 EM. Flower purplish pink, darker-pink on reverse, in ball-shaped trusses of 12. Leaves of heavy substance, narrow, glossy, dark yellowish-green above, underside with a patchy, felted tan indumentum on midrib. Compact, dense growth habit. (Vulcan × *pseudochrysanthum*). Nicolella/Gustafson.

■ **OZ** Low H5–6 ML. Flowers carmine-rose at edges, shading through lemon-yellow to Naples-yellow in throat, spotted orange on dorsal lobe, in dome-shaped trusses of 11–15. Well-branched spreading habit. Surprisingly winter hardy and may be a good parent for breeding hardy oranges. (Catawbiense Album × Fabia). Lem. Sister **'WIZZARD'** apricot and buff with edges of old-rose, yellow streaks flaring from throat, large calyx of apricot.

■ **P.M.A TIGERSTEDT (syn. PETER TIGERSTEDT)** Low–Medium H7 ML–L. Flowers open funnel-shaped, pure white inside and out, with blood-red, triangular spots on dorsal-half of corolla, in domed trusses of 14–18. Leaves convex. Tough, but perhaps less hardy than the other Finnish hybrids. Withstands the combination of frozen soil and winter sun well. Habit is lanky and very slow to fill out, and branches rather brittle. *S. Fin.* (*brachycarpum* Tigerstedii Gp. × Catawbiense Album). Uosukainen/Arb. Mustila.

P.M.A TIGERSTEDT

■ **PACIFIC GLOW** Medium H2 E. Flower openly funnel-shaped, wavy lobes, pink with red throat, unmarked, in ball-shaped trusses of 15–17. Leaves +/– elliptic, dull, medium-green, brown indumentum along sides of midrib and on veins. Compact, rounded, dense habit. Handsome but takes a few years to bud up. Sometimes suffers from the typical 'Loderi' foliage problems and mildew. Hard to root. (Loderi Venus × *strigillosum*). Larson.

■ **PACIFIC QUEEN** Medium H3–4 ML. Red buds open to flowers of azalea-pink with a yellow centre. Best in a sheltered, partly shaded site. May be a sister of 'Ivan D Wood', which it resembles. Popular in New Zealand. ([King of Shrubs × Fawn]? × Dido?). Coker.

■ **PACIFIC SUNSET** Low H2 M. Flower openly funnel-shaped, carmine-red shading to yellow-ochre in throat with red spots on dorsal lobe, in lax truss of 11. Leaves narrowly oblong, dark green, on a plant of broad, rounded habit. (Peach Lady × Malemute). Elliott.

■ **PANA** Low H7 ML. Flower widely funnel-campanulate, purple-red with some white in the throat and deep greenish-yellow spots, stigma dark red, in trusses of 20. Leaves dark green, with woolly, brown indumentum on the underside. Quite widely distributed and hardier than it looks. *NG.* ([*smirnowii* × *yakushimanum*] × [Mars × America]). Delp.

■ **PANAMA** Medium H6 ML. Flower openly funnel-shaped, cardinal-red with deeper-red spots, in dome-shaped trusses of 10–12. Leaves elliptic, rounded, slightly convex, margins slightly wavy, dull, yellowish green, growing twice as broad as tall. (Fanfare × unnamed hybrid). Leach.

■ **PANIA** Low H3–4 M. Salmon-pink with a yellow centre in lax trusses. A popular free-flowering plant in New Zealand. (*dichroanthum* × unknown).

■ **PAPRIKA SPICED** Semi-dwarf–Low H3 EM. Flower widely funnel-shaped, cream, flushed peachy, heavily peppered with paprika-red spots, calyx also speckled, in a truss of 10–12. Leaves small, narrowly elliptic, flat, yellow-green. Rounded habit. Launched with much fanfare and the flowers are spectacular, but it is fussy, needing perfect drainage and I've rarely seen a happy plant. *MT, SO.* (Hotei × Brandt's Topicana). Brockenbrough. **'PAPAYA PUNCH'** yellow-pink, edged orange-yellow.

PAPRIKA SPICED

■ **PARKER'S PINK** Medium H6 ML. Flower openly funnel-shaped, fragrant, purplish red fading to white in throat with red spotting, in a truss of about 12. Leaves elliptic, yellow-green, growing as broad as tall. One of the best and most highly rated Dexter hybrids and one of the toughest. Free flowering and east to root, but needs some shade to avoid foliage yellowing. *AZ, MA, PR, TZ.* (unknown × unknown). Dexter.

PARTY PINK

■ **PARTY PINK** Medium H7 M. Flowers openly funnel-shaped, purplish pink shading lighter in the centre, with a bronze dorsal-flare, in a ball-shaped truss of 18. Leaves widely elliptic. Plant broad, branching well. This was one of the first winners of the Superior Plant Award in N. America, but it is not a great plant, inclined to straggliness and not too good in a container. The flower is fine. *SPA.* (Mrs Furnival × *catawbiense*). Leach.

■ **PAUL LINKE** Low H3 E. Flowers campanulate, currant-red, in tight, upstanding trusses. Leaves recurved, like those of *R. strigillosum* but wider. Hard to root. If not frosted, flowers are long-lasting. Flowers not as deep red as some of the similar Larsen hybrids. (Glamor × *strigillosum*). Seabrook.

■ **PAUL R. BOSLEY** Low H4–5 M. Flowers pink, with red spotting, in rounded trusses of about 15. Long, very dark green foliage on a fairly compact but sometimes somewhat untidy plant. *GL.* (Dexter #1035 × unknown). Bosley.

■ **PAUL VOSSBERG** Low H5 L. Flower openly funnel-shaped, strong-red with dark-garnet blotch, in ball-shaped trusses of 13–15. Leaves narrowly elliptic to elliptic, flat, dark green, on a rounded, well-branched shrub. (*maximum* × *thomsonii*). Vossberg/Knippenberg.

■ **PAULINE BRALIT** Low–Medium H5 M. Flower openly funnel-shaped, yellowish white shading to pale purplish pink, with brownish-orange rays in throat, in ball-shaped trusses of 9–12. Leaves elliptic, dull green, of heavy texture, on an upright grower. A fine flower. (*fortunei* × Nor'easter). Mezitt.

PAULINE BRALIT

■ **PAWHUSHKA** Medium H4 M–ML. Flowers broadly funnel-shaped, white with narrow green flares on dorsal lobe, in rounded trusses of about 13. Foliage dark green, glossy. Name means 'white wind from the north'. (Palmer × [Loderi King George × Madam Masson]). Bowhan. **'SUGAR & SPICE'** a sister seedling with creamy white, star-shaped flowers with a golden-brown blotch.

■ **PEACH CHARM** Tall H4 EM. Flower broadly funnel-shaped, inside edged pink, shading to light orange-yellow on lobes with two red flares on dorsal lobe, outside deep pink, in a ball-shaped truss of 17. Leaves elliptic, semi-glossy, olive-green. (Nancy Evans × [Whopper × Lem's Cameo]). Brockenbrough.

■ **PEARCE'S AMERICAN BEAUTY** Tall H6–7 ML–L. Flower openly funnel-shaped, frilly, strong purplish red with yellowish-green spots, in ball-shaped trusses of 18. Leaves elliptic, flat, yellow-green; plant broad, with decumbent branches. This plant was raised in the 1930s, rediscovered and named fifty years later. Very tough and a good commercial plant with excellent leaf-retention. Much hardier than officially rated. (Mrs Charles S. Sargent? × Dr H.C. Dresselhuys?). Pearce.

■ **PEEPING TOM** Low H4 EM. Flower flat-faced, white with a deep plum-purple eye, in compact trusses of 10–12. Leaves ovate, dark green on a fairly dense, spreading plant. The flower is striking, but the plant seems a bit lacking in vigour, though this may be due to tissue culture. Hard to root. Foliage seems to be insect resistant. Not bud hardy in Germany. NI. (wardii × Mrs Furnival). Wright.

PEEPING TOM

■ **PEKING** Medium H6 M. Flower openly funnel-shaped, pale greenish yellow, with dark-red blotch and sparse dark-red spotting, in ball-shaped trusses of about 15. Leaves elliptic, slightly concave, dark green, on an upright, well-branched plant. Not all that free-flowering and foliage not very attractive. ([catawbiense var. album × Hawk] × [catawbiense var. album × Crest]). Leach.

■ **PEKKA** Medium–Tall H8–9 ML–L. Flowers pink, spotted brown in a rounded truss. Leaves are glabrous, dark green on a vigorous plant. Extremely hardy but doubtful if worth growing in milder areas. Much less well-known than the other Mustila hybrids. S. Fin. (brachycarpum Tigerstedtii Gp. × smirnowii hybrid). Uosukainen/Arb. Mustila.

■ **PELOPIDAS** Medium H6 ML. Frilled flowers of rosy crimson with brown spotting, in trusses of 24. Leaves elliptic, deep green, with a thin indumentum on the underside. A very early Waterer hybrid from the 1860s. (unknown). J. Waterer.

■ **PENJERRICK g.** Tall H3–(4) EM–M. Flowers campanulate white, creamy yellow, or pink. Several forms exist, some forms fragrant, in lax trusses of about 7. Smooth coppery bark. Plant habit upright, forming a small tree. Considered by some to be the most beautiful hybrid of all. Needs a sheltered site. (campylocarpum × griffithianum). S. Smith.

■ **PEPPERMINT TWIST** Low H5–6 EM. Flower funnel-shaped, pink with a white throat and red spotting, aging to white with pale-pink margins, in trusses of 12. Leaves oblong, decurved margins, glossy-green, on a rounded, dense plant. Bred near Tulsa for heat and humidity tolerance. Probably not worth growing in areas where heat tolerance is not a necessity. Flowers are good but foliage rather thin and ugly. (hyperythrum × Scintillation or other hybrid). Thornton. **'OPAL THORNTON'** another R. hyperythrum cross, with pink flowers with a yellow flare.

PEPPERMINT TWIST

■ **PEPPERPOT** Semi-dwarf–Low H4 EM. Flowers pale yellow, heavily spotted red on dorsal lobes, and light spotting elsewhere, in lax trusses of 8–10. Shiny circular leaves, semi-dwarf. Flowers might be considered to be the worst possible taste! (Goldbug × Unknown Lem hybrid). Elliott.

■ **PESTE'S FIRE LIGHT** Low H4 M. Flowers open from strong-red buds to light yellowish pink with strong-red spotting, with reflexed lobes, in lax trusses of 13. Leaves pale, yellow-green, on a stiffly upright plant. Flowers are unusual and striking. Subject to powdery mildew. (C.I.S. × Fabia). Peste.

PESTE'S FIRE LIGHT

■ **PETER ALAN** Low–Medium H4 M. Deep purplish-blue flowers with a black-purple eye, in full rounded trusses. Foliage deep green, glossy, heavy textured. Plant broad, upright. Good habit and very fine flowers, but plant not a great doer for us in Scotland, and probably not one of the best of the many newer dark purples. ([Blue Peter × Purple Splendour] × Blue Perfecta). Girard.

■ **PETER FAULK** Semi-dwarf–Low H3 E–EM. Flower funnel-shaped, cherry-red with scattered darker spots, in ball-shaped trusses of 16. Leaves narrowly elliptic, somewhat bullate, dark green with patchy tawny indumentum on underside midrib. Hairy stems. Plant broad, rounded, well-branched. An impressive early red, similar to R. strigillosum. EK. (strigillosum × unknown). Faulk.

■ **PETTICOAT LANE** Medium–Tall H3 EM–M. Pale yellow with light-pink edging and red spotting, in a tight truss of up to 21. Handsome, dark green, heavily veined foliage. Young stems red. (Butter Brickle × Noyo Chief). Sligh.

■ **PHIPPS YELLOW (syn. PHIPPS 32)** Low H4–5 M. Flowers light yellow, unmarked, in a domed truss of about 10. Leaves elliptic, semi-glossy, light green, on a well-branched plant. A good shade of yellow for E. America. Used on Long Island for hybridizing. (Golden Star × unknown). Phipps/Woodard/Brack.

PHIPP'S YELLOW

■ **PHYLLIS KORN** Medium H6 M. Flower openly funnel-shaped, creamy white with red dorsal-blotch which fades to light greenish yellow, in trusses of 12. Leaves elliptic to near ovate, glossy, dark green, on an upright, sturdy, well-branched shrub. PT, SE, Ger, Scand. (Diane × Gomer Waterer). Korn. Sister **'ROBERT KORN'** has creamy flowers with less spotting. **'IVORY QUEEN'** creamy white with a bright red flare.

PHYLLIS KORN

■ **PIERRE MOSER** Tall H4–5 E. Star-shaped pink flowers with a lighter centre in a rounded truss. A vigorous, lanky plant that needs pruning to keep in bounds. Seems mainly to be grown in Australia and New Zealand. (*caucasicum* hybrid) Moser & Fils.

■ **PILGRIM g.** Medium H4 M. Large trumpet-shaped flowers of rich clear-pink, sparsely marked darker, in rounded trusses of 8–12. Long, narrow, dark-green leaves, on a sturdy and vigorous open plant. (*fortunei* × Gill's Triumph). Johnstone.

■ **PINEAPPLE DELIGHT** Semi-dwarf–Low H4 EM. Flower widely funnel-shaped, amber-yellow, shading lighter at rims, throat lemon-yellow, in ball trusses of 12–14. Leaves elliptic, somewhat bullate, dark green, plant with a rounded habit. Sister of 'Paprika Spiced'. (Hotei × Brandt's Topicana). Brockenbrough.

■ **PINK CAMEO** Medium H7 ML. Flowers clear-pink, with a pinkish-yellow blotch, in compact conical trusses. Leathery dark-green leaves on a bushy, compact plant. (Boule de Neige × *catawbiense*, red form (possibly hybrid)). Shammarello. **'PRIZE'** clear shrimp-pink flowers, with a yellowish-brown blotch. **'SHAM'S JULIET'** pale pink with a brown blotch. Compact. **'SHAM'S PINK'** rose-pink flowers, darker at edges, light-red blotch.

■ **PINK DELIGHT** Tall H3? M? Clear deep pink or white flowers, edged deep rose-pink. Leaves narrowly elliptic, glossy. There are also eight other 'Pink Delight' rhododendrons and azaleas, just to confuse the issue. *Mel.* (*arboreum* ×). Gill.

■ **PINK FLOURISH** Medium H8 ML. Flowers pale pink, edged and reverse medium-pink with a small yellow-brown blotch, in a large truss of about 15. A vigorous and leggy plant unless planted in full sun. Possibly the hardiest of the Leach hybrids, reported to have flowered after temperatures of –36°C (–32.8°F). (*catawbiense* white × [(*decorum* × *griffithianum*) × red *catawbiense* hybrid]). Leach.

■ **PINK FONDANT** Low–Medium H5 ML. Flowers strong purplish red shading to pale purplish pink in centre, unmarked, outside strong purplish red at margins and midribs, shading lighter at base, in conical trusses of 12. Leaves semi-glossy, dark yellowish green. A good New England plant. (Mars × [Catalgla × *wardii*]). Gable/Pride.

■ **PINK JEANS** Low H4–5 M. Flowers strong purplish red at rims, shading to yellowish white at centre, strong-red spotting and a rose-red star in throat, in domed trusses of 8–10. Leaves dark green, pointed. A sport of the well-known 'Jean Marie de Montague' and looks very similar. (sport of Jean Marie de Montague). Briggs.

■ **PINK LEOPARD** Low–Medium H4 ML. Flowers tubular-campanulate, buds of strong-red, opening strong purplish red to strong pink with dark-red spotting, in a truss of about 10. Narrow, thin-textured leaves. The spotty flowers might appeal to some, but not to me. (Fred Wynniatt × Kilimanjaro). Drayson.

■ **PINK PEARL** Tall H4–5 M. Flower opens pink, fading to blush, paler at edges with a ray of reddish-brown spots, in large conical trusses of about 18. Leaves, thick and pale green. In shade rather sparse and straggly. The 'classic' pink hardy-hybrid, once planted in thousands and still widely grown. A reliable, sun and heat tolerant plant. Grows very tall in time. *MB, NI.* (George Hardy × Broughtonii). J. Waterer. **'TOPSVOORT PEARL'** paler-pink with reddish edging.

PINK PEARL

■ **PINK PETTICOATS** Medium H4–5 M. Flower china-rose at margins, lighter at centre, frilled picotee edges, in large trusses of up to 32. Upright, dense plant, slightly wider than tall. One of the ugliest foliage plants I have ever seen, with leaves hanging sadly, thin and always yellow. It should never have been named. Much used in hybridizing, but most hybrids have inherited the poor foliage. (Jan Dekens × Britannia). Lofthouse.

■ **PINK PRELUDE** Tall H2 E. Flower oblique-campanulate, very pale purple, faintly tinged pink with age, throat circled by light-purple blotch, in trusses of up to 21. Leaves narrowly elliptic, flat, glossy, with tomentum on new leaves and thin indumentum on the lower leaf. Broad, rounded, open habit. Impressive flowers but a bit pointless: I'd grow the parents instead. ([Sarita Loder × *calophytum*] × *macabeanum*). Watson.

■ **PINK TWINS** Low H5 M. Flower widely funnel-campanulate, hose-in-hose, ruffle edged, light-pink-coloured, in ball-shaped trusses of about 15. Leaves ovate to elliptic, rounded, medium-green with yellow petioles. Compact and relatively slow-growing. Slow to bud up as a young plant. Insect-resistant foliage. Good in moderate parts of New England. (red-flowered *catawbiense* × *haematodes* hybrid). Gable.

■ **PLATINUM PEARL** Tall H5 ML. Flower ruffled-edged, pearl-pink aging to white with a dark-red blotch and spots at the base. Leaves light yellow-green. Vigorous grower, upright habit. Some heat resistance. Best in light shade. *AZ, CD.* (Trude Webster × *fortunei* ssp. *discolor*). Greer.

■ **PLUM BEAUTY** Medium H5–6 M–ML. Buds ruby-red opening to flowers of ruby-red and deep- to moderate-red with ruby-red dorsal spots. Leaves deep green. Quite a good colour and now becoming available in Europe. (Vivacious × Old Port). Smith/Delp.

■ **PLÜSCH** Medium H7 ML. Flowers ruby-red with a paler background, faintly spotted brown. Very hardy. An old German hybrid suitable for cold climates. (Mrs Milner × *catawbiense*). Seidel. Sisters and similar hybrids include: **'ERICH'** purple-red, **'GOETHE'** light rose-pink, **'BIBBER'** carmine-red, **'EMMA'** bright carmine-rose.

■ **POHJOLA'S DAUGHTER** Semi-dwarf–Low H8+ M. Lavender buds open to white flowers with some spotting in the throat. Foliage dark green, new growth with greyish indumentum. Needs protection from hot sun. Bred for extreme hardiness. Not worth growing in mild areas. Rated as hardy to –34.5°C (–30°F) but suffers some damage in S. Finland, so ratings are a bit suspect. *S. Fin.* (unknown). Uosukainen/Arb. Mustila.

POHJOLA'S DAUGHTER

■ **POINT DEFIANCE** Tall H4–5 M. Flower of heavy substance, white in centre, edged pink, fading to nearly pure white, in compact trusses of 15–17. Leaves elliptic, leathery, dull, dark green. Upright grower. Stunning in flower, similar to 'Lem's Monarch'. Buds-up as a four-to-five-year-old. *CA, CN, JF, NI, NN, OP, TC, VI.* (Anna × Marinus Koster). Lem. **'REVEREND PAUL'** white with a red blotch. **'GENTLE GIANT'** magenta-pink.

POINT DEFIANCE

■ **POLAR BEAR g.** Tall H4–5 VL. Flower very fragrant, pure white with a narrow green throat, in large, flat trusses of 8–10. Leaves very large, pale green, heavily veined. Many clones were raised from this cross, some hardier than others. One of the finest late-flowering hybrids. Best in woodland conditions to shelter flowers and late growth. *AGM, CN, VI.* (*decorum* ssp. *diaprepes* × *auriculatum*). Stevenson. **'ROYSTON RADIANCE'** huge, late, white.

POLAR BEAR

■ **PONTICUM ROSEUM (syn. MAXIMUM ROSEUM)** Tall H8 L. Flowers pinkish lilac with a deeper blotch, in rounded trusses. Narrow shaped, long, green leaves. Very hardy, heat and sun tolerant. Looks like *R. ponticum* but much tougher. A good rootstock to impart heat tolerance, which does not sucker much. There are said to be at least three clones around in the trade. *ME, PR*. (*ponticum* × *maximum*). unknown/Pride.

■ **PONTICUM VARIEGATUM (syn. SILVER EDGE)** Medium H4 ML–L. Flowers small, lavender-pink, in rounded trusses. Leaves narrow, with white edging, on an upright dense tidy grower. One of the best variegated rhododendrons. Not invasive, unlike pure *R. ponticum*. Occasional reverting shoots should be removed. (*ponticum* sport). unknown.

PONTICUM VARIEGATUM (SYN. SILVER EDGE)

■ **POTLATCH** Medium H4 M–ML. Flowers waxy scarlet, fading to deep pink, long lasting, in loose trusses. Leaves with indumentum on the underside. Compact and handsome. Flowers are distinctive. The name is a Native American word for a large gift. (Thor × unknown). R. Clark.

POTLATCH

■ **PRAIRIE FIRE** Medium H3–4 E. Flowers bright scarlet-red, in rounded trusses. Needs some shade in its native California, but reported to be quite heat tolerant. A fine early red. (Cornubia × Red Olympia). Korth.

■ **PRELUDE g.** Medium H4–5 M. Shrimp-pink or coral buds open to openly cup-shaped, creamy-white flowers, shading to primrose, in flattened globular trusses of 10. The AM clone has pale yellow-cream flowers. Leaves like *R. wardii*, leathery, glossy deep green, on a vigorous but tidy plant. (*wardii* × *fortunei*). Rothschild.

■ **PRESIDENT LINCOLN** Tall H8 ML. Flower lavender-pink with a brownish-gold blotch, in ball trusses of up to 26. Leaves deep green, yellow-green in sun. Very tough and heat-tolerant. Not worth growing in mild areas. *SV*. (*catawbiense* × unknown). Parsons.

■ **PRESIDENT ROOSEVELT** Low H4 EM. Flower bright red fading to white in the centre, in conical trusses of 15–30. Leaves thick, shiny, variegated green-and-yellow. Branches weak and break easily and leaves tend to revert. Sprawling habit. Foliage will burn in hot sun. Probably the best variegated hybrid for flowers, let down by foliage and habit. *MB, NN, SH*. (Limbatum sport ?). Mesman.

PRESIDENT ROOSEVELT

■ **PRETTY WOMAN** Low H4 ML. Flower frilled edges, purplish pink, outside purple, in conical trusses of 20–22. Leaves elliptic, glossy, on a plant of upright, spreading habit. What was distributed in tissue culture under this name does not match the description. (Orange Marmalade × Pink Petticoats). Davis.

■ **PRIDENJOY** Low H4 EM–M. Flower widely funnel-shaped, lightly fragrant, pale yellow flushed light shell-pink, changing to pale greenish yellow, spotted red, throat light yellow, in ball-shaped trusses of 23–28. Leaves narrowly obovate, olive-green, new growth olive-brown. Upright habit. Somewhat mildew susceptible. (Lem's Cameo × Kubla Khan). Newcomb. **'EARL MURRAY'** salmon-orange, paler inside.

PRIDENJOY

■ **PRIMARY PINK** Semi-dwarf H3 EM. Flower with deeply incised lobes, light purplish pink shading to pale purplish pink near throat, in dome-shaped trusses of 24. Leaves elliptic, glossy, dark green. Dense and mounding habit. ([Yaku Sunrise × (C.I.S. × Jingle Bells)] × Lem's Cameo). Fujioka.

■ **PRINCE ABKHAZI** Tall H3 VE. Flower very pale purple with pinkish-red spots, in a ball-shaped truss of 15–18. Leaves narrowly elliptic, glossy medium-green. Upright habit. *VI*. (*irroratum* × unknown). Vaartnou.

■ **PRINCE CAMILLE DE ROHAN** Medium H5 EM. Flower pink to mauve, ruffled and frilly edged, with a distinctive dark-brown blotch, in a dense truss of about 20. Leaves slightly twisted, under-surface with thin indumentum. Dense and mounding habit. Needs well-drained soil. A very early hybrid from the 1850s, still commercially available. (*caucasicum* × *arboreum* or *maximum*?). Van Geersdaele. **PROGRÈS (syn. LE PROGRÈS)** very similar with slightly deeper flowers.

■ **PRINZ KARNEVAL (syn. KARNEVAL)** Low H5 ML. Flowers open funnel-shaped, strikingly bi-coloured, margin light-red, throat white with yellow and yellowish-brown markings; outside light-red, in trusses of 13–18. An indigestible mixture of colours, which is certainly striking. (Louis Pasteur × Goldsworth Orange). Robenek. **'LUDGERSTAL'** dark rose, late.

■ **PROFESSOR HUGO DE VRIES** Medium H4–5 L. Flower funnel-shaped, lilac-rose with red markings, in a conical-shaped truss of about 16. Upright, open and leggy shrub. Free flowering, easy to root and heat tolerant. Has proven to be resistant to Phytophthora and should therefore be used in further breeding. *AGM*. (Pink Pearl × Doncaster). Endtz.

■ **PUCCINI** Medium H6 L. Flowers broadly funnel-shaped, light-purple with darker veins, with a conspicuous blotch of orange-yellow with red marks, in a truss of 12–15. Broadly upright habit. Dull-green convex foliage. ([Furnival's Daughter × Simona] × King Tut). Hachmann.

■ **PUGET SOUND** Tall H4 M. Flowers large, fragrant, reflexed, pink tinged lilac, in a tall truss. Thick glossy leaves on a vigorous, stiffly branched, upright plant. Some heat tolerance. Buds-up as a four-to-five-year-old. (Loderi King George × Van Nes Sensation). R. Clark.

■ **PUKEITI ANNIVERSARY** Medium H4 M. Buds pinkish opening to light-yellow flowers with a deep red throat, in rounded trusses of up to 20. Leaves lanceolate, light green on a tidy compact plant. Named after the famous New Zealand garden. *N.Z.* (Mai Tai × Nancy Evans). Sligh.

■ **PURPLE LACE** Medium H4–5 ML. Flower very frilly, deep red, purple or maroon, paling in the centre. Leaves glossy, on a compact, dense, spreading bush. Some heat resistance. *MB, SL*. (Britannia? × Purple Splendour?). Boskoop.

■ **PURPLE PASSION (PP)** Medium H5? ML. Flowers broadly funnel-shaped, vivid reddish purple with a white blotch and superimposed purple spots, edges strong purplish red, outside vivid-purple, in balled trusses of 12–16. Very hardy for a purple of this shade. Pest- and disease-resistant foliage. Not a good performer in N.E. America, maybe due to tissue culture. There is also a hardier but paler Delp hybrid of this name, which will probably be renamed 'Delp's Purple Passion'. (Purple Splendour × Catalgla). Blough.

■ **PURPLE SPLENDOUR** Low–Medium H4–5 ML. Flowers very dark purple, frilly, with black blotch, in conical trusses of up to 15. Dark-green leaves on a slow-growing plant of upright habit. For a long time in a class of its own, but now superseded by numerous better dark purples. Extremely susceptible to mildew. Has an AGM but it should be rescinded. (*ponticum* hybrid). A. Waterer. **'PURPLE OPAL'** an Australian seedling of 'Purple Splendour' with flowers of rich purple-violet.

■ **PURPUREUM ELEGANS** Medium H8 M. Flower amethyst-violet, marked brown and green, in ball-shaped trusses of about 16. Leaves glossy, medium-green. A robust, upright, well-branched shrub. Easy to root, sun tolerant, free-flowering with a reasonable habit. Not worth growing in mild areas. (*catawbiense* × unknown). H. Waterer. **'PURPUREUM GRANDIFLORUM'** is paler, equally hardy.

■ **QUEEN ANNE'S** Medium H4 EM. Flowers double, very pale violet when first open, quickly fading to white, unmarked, in a balled truss of 10–13. Leaves elliptic, glossy, olive-green on a plant of rather sparse upright habit. Hard to root. Said to be very hardy but it suffered foliage damage at Glendoick. The grammar bothers me. I always wonder: Queen Anne's what? A good parent of doubles. ([*brachycarpum* × *catawbiense*] × unknown white *fortunei* hybrid). Skinner. **'LONG ISLAND'** double fragrant white. Not as well-known.

QUEEN ANNE'S

■ **QUEEN NEFERTITI** Medium H1 M. Flower openly funnel-shaped, light purplish pink with deeper margins and reverse, purplish-red spotting on dorsal lobe, in ball-shaped trusses of about 12. Leaves narrowly oblong to elliptic, dark green, on an upright and vigorous grower. *MB*. (Anna × Loderi Venus). Beck/Korth.

■ **QUEEN OF HEARTS** Tall H4–5 EM–M. Flower campanulate, dark crimson with white stamens, red calyces and small black spots on the upper lobes, in tight, domed trusses of 16. Leaves

QUEEN OF HEARTS

elliptic, on a plant of upright, rather rangy habit. Red stems. The flowers are spectacular but the plant tends to have chlorotic foliage and the flowers can bend the straggly stems over till they hang upside down. (*meddianum* × Moser's Maroon). Rothschild.

■ **RABATZ**® Medium–Tall H4 ML. Clear bright red with yellow stamens and black spotting, in compact trusses of up to 11. Dark-green leaves on an upright plant. This was very free-flowering and a good colour, at the Hachmann nursery. (Double Date × Erato). Hachmann. A sister: **'TARAGONA'** bright red with black spotting in the throat.

TARAGONA

■ **RAINBOW** Tall H4 M. Flower deep pink paling to almost-white in the centre, giving a two-tone effect, in loose trusses. Leaves glossy, slightly rough texture, hang downwards, on an upright plant, as wide as tall. Heat resistant. This English hybrid is mainly grown in the Pacific Northwest. The flowers are striking. (A. Waterer hardy hybrid × *griffithianum*). Slocock.

RAINBOW

■ **RECITAL** Low H4 M–ML. Buds coral-pink, flowers open to soft-yellow with deeper-yellow on upper lobes, short red flares on all lobes, in balled trusses of 20. Dark-green leaves on a compact plant. Buds-up young. Used in further breeding by Barlup: its hybrids also bud-up young. (Mindy's Love × Jessie's Song). Barlup.

■ **RED ADMIRAL g.** Tall H3 E. Flowers blood-red in a full truss, opening gradually over a long period. A tree-forming early red-hybrid. An English hybrid now mainly grown in Australia. (*arboreum* × *thomsonii*). Williams. The same hybrid occurs in the wild as *R.* × *sikkimense*.

RECITAL

■ **RED BRAVE** Low H7 M. Flower dark red with white stamens, in dome-shaped trusses. Leaves medium size, sage-green. A tough red-hybrid with good rating from N.E. U.S.A. (America × Mars). Baldanza/Pride. **'PRIDE'S EARLY RED'** is probably a sister seedling with a very compact habit. The earliest of the hardy red-hybrids.

■ **RED DELICIOUS** Medium H4 ML. Flowers waxy, deep red, in rounded trusses. Leaves thick, dark green, on a dense upright grower. Flowers tend to bleach at the edges in sun, so best with part-day shade. (Jean Marie de Montague × Leo). Greer. **'HEATWAVE'** is a sister with large deep blood-red flowers.

RED DELICIOUS

■ **RED EYE** Medium H5 ML. Flower purplish red with a greenish-gold eye that slowly turns red, in full trusses. Leaves glossy, medium-green. Dense, rounded habit. This just looks like a good form of *R. ponticum* to me, but I suppose if it does not grow wild in your local woods it might be exciting. *BH, CH, PT, SE*. (Anah Kruschke × Purple Splendour). Swenson. **'BLACK EYE'** is a sister seedling with a dark, near-black flare in the throat. **'THE REBEL'** flowers of deep reddish purple, showy white anthers.

■ **RED IMPULSE** Medium H5? ML? Deep-red buds, cardinal-red flowers, dorsal spotting of darker-red. This should be good as the genes are a cocktail of the best hardy red hybrids. ([Vivacious × Nova Zembla] × [Mars × America]). Smith/Delp.

■ **RED JACK** Medium H5? M–ML. Clear-red flowers with black nectaries in compact, rounded trusses of 15–18. Habit rather rangy. This resembles 'Taurus' with fine large flowers and handsome foliage as I saw it at Hachmanns. But this cannot possibly be from the parentage given, it is far too big, so evidently the bees beat the hybridizer. ([Wilgen's Ruby × May Day] × said to be × *forrestii*). Boskoop.

■ **RED OLYMPIA** Tall H3 M. Flower cup-shaped, red lobes heavily spotted black, reverse has darker red lines down centre of lobes, in dome-shaped trusses of 13–16. Leaves narrowly elliptic, dark green, on an upright grower. Flowers don't last very well and hang on rather than falling when over. Some insect resistance. (Anna × Fusilier). Lem. **'MURIEL PEARCE'** is a sister, rose-madder, much red spotting on upper lobes.

■ **RED RIVER** Medium H7 L. Flowers bright red, shading pink toward almost-white centre, yellow dorsal flare lightly spotted in yellow-green, in pyramidal trusses of 16–19. Large rugose leaves, undulate margins. Leggy habit, best with a bit of pinching and pruning. Should be used to breed more hardy late red-hybrids. Suffered in harsh 2004 winter in N.E. U.S.A. (*maximum* × [Mars × Fanfare]). Leach.

■ **RED TOP** Low H4 M. Flowers vivid-red with, darker-red dorsal spotting, with a pronounced calyx, in a truss of 13–14. Leaves elliptic, mid-green. (Lord Roberts × Skipper Hal). Stockman.

■ **RED WALLOPER** Tall H4–5 M. Flowers cherry-red, which fade through shades of rose to pastel-pink, in a large rounded truss. Leaves large, dark green. Open habit, vigorous grower. Several different clones are sold with this name. Lem himself unofficially named a seedling of Anna × Burgundy with this name, but this may no longer be around. *CA, JF, MB, NI*. (Anna × Marinus Koster). Lem.

RED WOOD

■ **RED WOOD** Medium H5 M–ML. Flowers pale rosy lilac, fading to off-white, in rounded trusses. Leaves dark green, bronzy when young, on a tough, stiffly upright plant with red stems. The flowers are not the most spectacular but the foliage, stems and habit are excellent. The parentage has recently been unearthed. (*fortunei* × *insigne*). Hobbie.

■ **REDDER YET** Medium H8 ML. Flowers strong purplish red, with faint-brown spotting, in rounded trusses of about 18. Leaves elliptic, matte green. Very hardy but a rather harsh colour. (America × unknown). Leach/Pride.

■ **REDWAX** Semi-dwarf H3 M. Flower funnel-campanulate, waxy, bright red, unspotted, in lax trusses of up to 15. Leaves dark green, underside with thick tan indumentum, slight tomentum on new growth, on a dense, spreading plant. Seventy-five per cent *R. haematodes* and looks like this species. (*haematodes* × May Day). Henny. **'CHARMAINE'** blood-red waxy flowers, 5–6 per truss. Fine foliage. A little shy-flowering but quite attractive.

■ **RICHARD BOSLEY** Low H5 M. Flower widely funnel-campanulate, deep purplish pink shading to very pale purple inside, with a yellow speckled flare, in dome-shaped trusses of 16. Leaves oblong/obovate, oblique at base, flat, dull, olive-green, upright and spreading habit. (*catawbiense* × unknown). Dexter/Bosley.

■ **RING OF FIRE** Medium H3 EM. Flower light-yellow, edged red-pink, outside mostly red with some light yellow near the base, in dome-shaped truss of 10–12. Leaves elliptic, dark yellowish green. Upright, dense growth habit. Not of much merit in Scotland, with muddy flowers and poor foliage. (Darigold × Idealist). Thompson. **'DESERT SUN'** golden-yellow flowers with a small red blotch. **'GEORGE'S RING'** yellow, rimmed magenta.

RING OF FIRE

■ **RING'S EARLY SPLENDOUR (syn. EARLY SPLENDOUR)** Medium H7 M. Flowers frilled, white with red-purple spotting, in a ball-shaped truss of about 20. Leaves lanceolate, smooth and convex. Should be very heat tolerant and hardy. (*hyperythrum* × Catalgla). Ring.

■ **RIO** Semi-dwarf–Low H7 M. Flower openly funnel-shaped, pale purplish pink with pale-yellow spots, in ball-shaped trusses of up to 16. Leaves elliptic to narrowly elliptic, concave, semi-glossy, light green, on a plant of rounded habit. May be hardier than rated, but not always easy to grow well. (Newburyport Beauty × Newburyport Belle). Leach. **'NORMANDY'** a sister with bright rose-pink flowers, deeper on edges, spotted orange.

■ **RIPE CORN** Medium H4–5 M–ML. Flowers yellow, suffused with orange and pink in rounded/flat-topped trusses. Pale leaves with red petioles. Quite widely grown by U.K. specialist nurseries. (Goldsworth Orange × Naomi Exbury). Slocock.

■ **RITCHIE** Medium H6 ML. Flowers pale purple, edged vivid- and strong-purple, with a beetroot-purple flare and dorsal spots, in trusses of 14. Upright habit. Leaves recurved. The flower is striking. (Calsap selfed). Delp. **'MIKEY'** is similar.

■ **ROBERT BALCH** Medium H2–3 ML–L. Flowers campanulate, rich-red, spotted darker in the throat, in perfectly shaped trusses of 10–16. Leaves glossy, dark green and bullate. Best in part shade. Foliage and flowers said to be wind tolerant. A fine red for mild climates; as yet, little known outside its native New Zealand. (*arboreum* ssp. *zeylanicum* × *elliottii*). Balch/Dunedin B.G.

■ **ROBERT SCHILL** Low–Medium H4 M–ML. Openly funnel-shaped flowers moderate- to light-yellowish-pink with centre of each lobe lightly speckled red, with no calyx, in ball-shaped trusses of 20. Leaves oblong, flat. (Whitney's Orange × Golden Star). Rosenthal.

■ **ROCHELLE** Medium H5 M–ML. Flower slightly fragrant, rose-coloured with a strawberry-red blotch, velvet textured, in ball-shaped trusses of 7. Leaves lanceolate to oblanceolate, medium-green colour. Compact growth habit. *PV*. (Dorothea × Kettledrum). Nearing.

ROCKET

■ **ROCKET** Low H6 M. Flower, heavily frilled, bright-pink blotched red with prominent protruding stamens, in a small conical truss. Leaves, thick, glossy, dark green and heavily veined, coppery bronze when new, on a dense and compact plant. Flowers are small and ugly and I see no merit in this whatsoever. Even worse from tissue culture: flowers seem to have shrunk. *SC*. (Cunningham's White × red *catawbiense* hybrid). Shammarello.

■ **ROCKHILL PARKAY** Low H4 M. Flowers creamy white shading to sulphur-yellow in throat and striped down lobes, with red eye, in a truss of 15–17. Leaves shiny, on a broad, branching plant. (Yellow Rolls Royce × Skipper). Brotherton. **'ROCKHILL SUNDAY SUNRISE'** a sister with primrose-yellow flowers, red in throat.

■ **ROCKY POINT** Low H3 EM–M. Flowers openly funnel-shaped, inside pale yellowish pink with a greyish-red blotch in throat and moderate-red spotting on all lobes, outside with darker streaks of pale yellow, in domed trusses of 15. Leaves dull, moderate olive-green. (Glenna × Claire). Barlup.

■ **ROCKY WHITE** Low H5 M. Flowers with recurved edges, light-lavender on first opening, fading to white, unmarked, with some scent, in a loose truss of 12–14. Leaves elliptic, on a well-branched plant. New growth bronze. (Catalgla × *fortunei*). Herbert.

■ **ROLAND** Medium H6 ML. Flowers moderate purplish red with dark-red spotting, in trusses of 18–21. Leaves elliptic to ovate, slightly undulate, glossy dark-green. Quite a striking colour. (Nova Zembla × Purple Splendour). Hachmann.

■ **ROMY** Medium H4 L. Flowers pale yellowish green, flushed deeper yellow, with strong-red speckling, 13 per truss. Compact plant, spreading broader than tall. Free-flowering. Named after Romy Millais, from Millais nursery where it was raised. (Inamorata × Mrs J.G. Millais). Millais. **'HIGH SUMMER'** light yellow, shading to citrus-yellow in centre, in truss of 8–10. **'GOLDEN SPLENDOUR'** lax trusses of light-yellow with a reddish flare. Another useful late-flowering Millais hybrid.

■ **RONA PINK** Medium H6 M. Flowers fragrant, purplish-pink shading lighter on midribs, with sparse yellow-green spotting on dorsal lobe, in dome-shaped trusses of 12–14. Leaves elliptic, flat, dull, moderate olive-green above, yellow-green below, with a dense, spreading habit. A fine but little known Dexter hybrid with good flowers and foliage. *PR, PB.* (unknown × unknown). Dexter/Koenig.

■ **RONALD OTTO DELP (syn. R.O. DELP)** Flowers openly funnel-shaped, pale- and strong-purplish-pink with pale-yellow flare and throat, deep purplish-red dorsal spots, in trusses of 16. (Lodestar × Mary Belle). Hinerman.

■ **ROSA PERLA** Low–Medium H6 ML. Flowers bright pink in small, slightly loose, trusses of 9–18. Leaves narrow, with thin indumentum on the under-surface, on a compact plant. The flowers are a harsh colour and fade out to pinkish. Leaves tend to be yellowish. (Kluis Triumph × *makinoi*). Bruns. **'BRUNS DIAMANT'** a similar hybrid with bright-red flowers. **'DÜSSELFEUER'** pink flowers, very narrow leaves.

■ **ROSA STEVENSON** Tall H4 M. Flowers pale yellow, in loose rounded trusses of about 10. Dark, rather pale foliage on an upright, fairly open plant. Flowers are very fine. Growth is early. (Loderi Sir Edmund × *wardii*). Stevenson.

■ **ROSAMUNDI** Low H4–5 VE. Flower pale blush-pink with near-white throat and darker-pink tube, in tight ball trusses. Leaves elliptic, bright green. Plant is upright, compact, densely foliaged. This hybrid and the similar 'Christmas Cheer' seem to be mixed up in commerce in some areas. 'Rosamundi' is pinker and later flowering. *VI.* (*caucasicum* × unknown). Standish & Noble.

■ **ROSEUM ELEGANS** Medium H8 ML. Flowers rosy lilac with faint brown markings, in rounded trusses of about 20. Olive-green foliage on a dense and spreading plant of great vigour. Tolerant of cold, sun and heat. A highly recommended ironclad for severest climates. Good for windbreaks. *AT, AZ, GP, MA, MS, NG, PR, PT, SE, SV, S. Fin.* (*catawbiense* hybrid). A. Waterer.

■ **ROSEUM SUPERBUM** Medium H8 ML. Flowers purplish rose, in a rounded truss. Free-flowering and roots easily. Not as good or as widely grown as 'Roseum Elegans'. (*catawbiense* hybrid). A. Waterer.

■ **ROSLYN** Medium H5 ML. Flower widely funnel-shaped, frilled, light purple shading to a lighter centre, unmarked, in ball-shaped trusses of 12. Leaves elliptic, yellow-green, on a vigorous but fairly tidy well-branched plant. Free-flowering, easy to root and considered one of the best tough hybrids of this shade. The flowers look blue from a distance. *E. Canada.* (Purpureum Elegans × Everestianum). Vossberg.

■ **ROSS MAUD** Medium H4–5 M. Flowers deep purplish pink with a vivid-red centre, 16 per balled-truss. Dark-green leaves on a very compact and dense, free-flowering plant. Buds-up young. *Aus.* (Fusilier × Unique). Bramley.

■ **ROSSELLINI** Medium H6 ML. Flowers strong fuchsia-purple, shading roseine to white in throat, dorsal markings green, in compact trusses of 13–16. Leaves recurved, almost ovate. One of the hardier Hachmann hybrids. ([Omega × Roseum Elegans] × Furnivall's Daughter). Hachmann.

■ **ROYAL PURPLE** Low H5 ML–L. Flowers small, deep purple with a bright-yellow eye, in a rounded truss of about 12. Leaves shiny, deep green, on a well-shaped plant. The flowers are not very large but it can look good as a mature plant. Foliage not always good and sometimes susceptible to die-back. (unknown). White or Standish & Noble.

■ **ROYSTON REVERIE** Tall H4 L. Light-yellow flowers with margins of pink, in loose trusses of about 8. Leaves pale green, similar to those of *R. auriculatum*. Late flowering, best in a sheltered site. Hard to root. (*auriculatum* × Fabia). Grieg. **'ROYSTON ROSE'** pale pink. **'ROYSTON SUMMERTIME'** white edged pink, spotted red. **'ROYSTON FESTIVAL'** pink.

■ **RUBICON** Medium H3 EM. Flower bright cardinal-red with black spots, in slightly flat-topped trusses of 17–18. Leaves handsome: very shiny, medium-sized and bullate, on a compact plant. Buds-up young. One of the finest reds for mild gardens; good in sheltered woodland at Glendoick. *CA, PA.* (Kilimanjaro × Noyo Chief). Gordon.

■ **RUBY F. BOWMAN** Medium H4–5 M. Flower rose-pink with a blood-red throat, in dome-shaped trusses of 13–15. Leaves slightly glossy, yellowish green with red petioles, on a vigorous, fairly open, upright plant, which is free-flowering and easily rooted. Sun-, heat- and insect-resistant. *BH, CH.* (*fortunei* × Lady Bligh). Bowman.

■ **RUBY HART** Semi-dwarf–Low H3–4 EM. Flower widely funnel-campanulate, very deep red, in flat to lax trusses of 7. Leaves elliptic, glossy, deep green, underside with brown indumentum, on a dense and mounding plant. The flowers are very striking. *VI.* ([Carmen × Elizabeth] × *elliottii*). Whitney. **'ANITA OWEN'** small dark-red flowers in a lax truss.

RUBY HART

■ **RUSSELL HARMON** Medium H8 L. Flowers magenta-pink with darker spotting, in a large truss of up to 25. Dark-green leaves. A little open but good plant habit. Heat tolerant. This may be a natural hybrid between two tough North American species. Used as a parent by David Leach. (*maximum* × *catawbiense*). Harmon/La Bar's Nursery.

■ **RUTH A. WEBER** Low H4–5 ML. Flower openly funnel-shaped, moderate reddish purple with dark purplish-red spotting on dorsal lobe, in ball-shaped trusses of 17. Leaves narrowly elliptic, dark green, on an upright vigorous grower. (Marchioness of Lansdowne × Old Port). Weber.

■ **SAGAMORE BAYSIDE** Low H4 M. Flowers light purplish pink, wavy edges, yellow-green stripe down centre, outside moderate purplish pink, in trusses of 9. Dull olive-green foliage on a well-branched plant. Free-flowering. (*fortunei* unknown). Dexter/Wister. **'SAGAMORE BRIDGE'** purplish pink, flushed yellow in a truss of 14.

■ **SALTARELLO** Low H6 ML. Flowers funnel-campanulate, strong purplish pink, tinged light purplish pink, dorsal lobe brilliant-light-yellow with dark-red spotting, in slightly loose trusses of 13–15. A compact plant. This is an exotic colour for a plant so hardy. Probably not very heat-tolerant. (King Tut × *dichroanthum* ssp. *scyphocalyx* hybrid). Hachmann.

■ **SAMMAMISH** Semi-dwarf H3 ML. Flower campanulate, wavy to frilly edges, pale purplish-pink, outside strong- and pale purplish-pink in a striped effect, in dome-shaped trusses of about 24. Leaves narrowly elliptic, dull green with sparse cinnamon hairs on underside and at margins, yellow petioles. Open plant habit. *CD.* (unknown × unknown). R. George.

■ **SAMMETGLUT (syn. CRIMSON CLASSIC)** Tall H6 ML. Flower clear-red with white stamens, in a ball-shaped truss of 13–15. Leaves elliptic, slightly glossy, dark green. Upright, open growth habit. Prefers some shade. We found the colour good but the leggy habit was not acceptable and other Hachmann reds are a better choice. (Mars × Nova Zembla). Hachmann.

ROSEUM ELEGANS

RUBY F. BOWMAN

■ **SAMTKRONE**® Medium H4–5 ML–L. Flowers deep red without any bluish tone, in a tall truss (to 25cm). As you would expect from the parents, this is a really fine red in a huge truss. But it may not be as hardy as most of the Hachmann reds. (Tarantella × Kilimanjaro). Hachmann.

■ **SANDWICH APPLEBLOSSOM** Tall H5 ML. Flower openly funnel-shaped, frilly, lightly fragrant, deep purplish pink at margins fading to pale purple in the throat, with greenish-yellow spots, in a ball-shaped truss of 14. Leaves elliptic, flat or concave. Upright, dense habit. Very similar to and maybe the same as 'Dexter's Pink'. (unknown × unknown). Dexter.

■ **SANTA FE** Tall H6 ML. Flowers openly funnel-shaped, strong purplish red with cream-coloured stripes extending down lobes to throat and with moderate-red blotch at base of throat on dorsal lobe, in domed trusses of 14. Leaves smooth, elliptic, dark green. Good habit. Foliage inclined to be poor in Ohio. ([Limelight × (King of Shrubs × smirnowii)] × Limelight). Leach.

■ **SAPPHO** Tall H6 M. Mauve buds open to white flowers with a prominent purple-black blotch, in dome-shaped trusses of about 15. Leaves narrow, olive-green, on an open and unmanageably leggy plant: prune it and it sends up a single shoot in revenge. Subject to rust in some climates. The most famous of the old, blotched, hardy hybrids, irresistible in flower. U.K. (unknown × unknown). A. Waterer. **'MRS J.C. WILLIAMS'** has a less-pronounced blotch but a better habit.

■ **SAPPORO**® Semi-dwarf–Low H5 ML. Flower broadly funnel-shaped, pale purple-pink, quickly fading to white, with a deep purplish-red blotch, in round trusses of 11–14. Leaves elliptic, slightly glossy green above with brown hairs. Compact, moderately open habit. This does not appear to grow well on its own roots and the habit is rather sprawling: the branchlets are too thin to hold the plant up. Best grafted. (Hachmann's Diadem × Hyperion). Hachmann.

■ **SARITA LODER** Low H3 ML. Dark-crimson buds, opening to deep rose or salmon flowers in loose trusses. Long, pointed leaves on an open, upright plant. Best in a sheltered position in some shade. (griersonianum × Loderi). Loder.

■ **SATIN MEMORIES** Low–Medium H4 M. Flowers broadly funnel-shaped, pink to red with two, short, red flares on upper lobe, reverse light-lavender-pink with deeper streaking on midribs, in balled trusses of 16. Dark-green leaves on a compact plant. (Mrs Furnival × Lem's Cameo hybrid). Barlup.

SATSOP SUNRISE

■ **SATSOP SUNRISE** Medium H3–4 ML–L. Flowers pink at edge, fading to pale-yellow centre, with a brownish-orange dorsal blotch, said to be lightly scented, in domed trusses of 13. Leaves yellow-green, on a fairly compact plant, useful for its late flowering. Flowers are a rather curious muddy salmon-pink; quite unusual, but I'm not sure I like them much. (Mrs J.G. Millais × Whitney's Late Orange). Deppiesse.

■ **SCANDINAVIA** Low H4 ML. Flower funnel-shaped, crimson-red, shaded bronze, with a black blotch and spots, white anthers, in a dome-shaped truss of about 14–18. Open, spreading habit. Reddish leaves and stems. Free-flowering and easily rooted. (Betty Wormald × Hugh Koster). Koster.

■ **SCARLET KING** Medium H3 ML. Flower rich- or cardinal-red with deeper dorsal spotting in trusses of 16–18. Several clones: **'KAKA'** very fine colour, **'MAGNOLIA'** more compact, **'HOMESTEAD'** cardinal red, **'ORCHARD'** scarlet. Dark-green foliage with white indumentum. Does well in warm climates. Very fine flowers, but the habit is not very good. Seldom grown outside New Zealand. N.Z. (Ilam Alarm × griersonianum). Stead.

HOMESTEAD

■ **SCARLET ROMANCE** Tall H6 ML. Flower openly funnel-shaped, purplish red, in conical trusses of 18–20. Leaves elliptic, flat, glossy, dark green, on an upright grower. Free-flowering. A pretty harsh colour but a tough red-hybrid. CT, MS. (Vulcan × Sefton × H.W. Sargent). Mehlquist.

■ **SCHNEEAUGE** Medium–Tall H6 M–ML. Flowers pale pink in bud, opening to pure white with a conspicuous blotch of moderate purple-red, in dense trusses of 11–14. Leaves ovate-elliptic, dark green, slightly wavy. Flowers are showy. (Holstein × Progres). Hachmann.

■ **SCHNEEBUKETT (syn. SNOW BOUQUET)** Medium H6 ML. Flowers clear-white with a reddish-brown blotch, in ball-shaped truss of 14–18. Leaves elliptic, bright green. Rounded, open growth habit. Flowers are spectacular but the plant is rather leggy. MS. (Mrs J.G. Millais × Bismarck). Hachmann.

■ **SCHNEESPIEGEL** Tall H5 ML. Flowers white, with a large basal blotch in the throat of moderate purplish red to deep pink, in trusses of 8–13. Dark-green oval leaves on a slow-growing compact and tidy plant that, unfortunately, is hard to root. (Babette × [Hachmann's Ornament × Furnivall's Daughter]). Hachmann. **'BLANKA'** a sister with flowers white, tinged moderate-purplish-red to dark-purplish-pink, with red spotting.

SCHNEEBUKETT

■ **SCHUBERT** Medium H4–5 M. Flower pale orchid (cattleya-lilac – as if we know what that is!), fringed, with a light blotch. A bushy, vigorous plant. (griffithianum). Koster.

■ **SCINTILLATION** Medium H6 M. Flower strong purplish pink shaded lighter towards centre, greenish yellow in throat, in ball-shaped trusses of 11–15. Leaves oblong, glossy, deep green, waxy texture, on a broad, well-branched plant. Heat and cold tolerant, though light shade may be needed for foliage. Free-flowering. This plant receives more accolades in E. North America than any other. Can suffer sunburn. Some people are convinced that there is more than one clone. **'GARDEN GEM'** is said to be larger and deeper-flowered and hardier than the original selection. AT, AZ, BH, CC, CH, CN, CT, GL, GP, MA, ME, MS, MT, NG, NI, NY, PR, PT, PV, SE, SI, ST, SV, TO, TZ, WT. (unknown). Dexter.

SCINTILLATION

■ **SEATTLE GOLD** Tall H4 M. Flowers warm light-yellow, brown markings, in compact trusses. Leaves long and slender, on a plant of fairly compact habit, straggly in shade. Fairly insect-resistant foliage. (Diva × Lady Bessborough). Lem.

■ **SEAVIEW SUNSET** Semi-dwarf–Low H2 E. Flower openly campanulate, inside light-yellow edged with broad band of red-orange, outside deep yellowish pink, in dome-shaped trusses of 16. Leaves elliptic, flat, down-curved edges, semi-glossy, dark green. A handsome plant with impressive flowers. (Nancy Evans × Canadian Sunset). Fujioka.

■ **SECOND HONEYMOON** Medium H3 M. Flowers yellow with deep-red spotting, in a rounded truss. Glossy-green roundish leaves. This just looked like a rather average *R. wardii* to me. (*wardii* cross). Whitney. **'HONEYMOON'** is earlier flowering with chartreuse-green buds open to pale chartreuse-yellow with dull-orange blotch, about 14 per domed truss.

■ **SEPTEMBER SONG** Low H4 M. Flower funnel-campanulate, orange-yellow in centre with deep-pink margins and slight spotting of vivid reddish orange, in a dome-shaped truss of 11, giving an effect of orange from a distance. Leaves slight obovate, semi-glossy, medium-green, on a plant of fairly compact habit. One of the best 'orange' hybrids for moderate climates. I find this a good parent and it has also been used in the U.S.A. *U.K.* (Dido × Fawn). Phetteplace. **'WARM SPRING'** sister with yellow flowers flushed pink. **'AMBERGRIS'** pink, lemon and apricot.

SEPTEMBER SONG

■ **SHAKER SUNRISE** Low H5 ML–L. Flower broadly funnel-shaped, light-purplish and yellowish-pink with brilliant-yellow throat, in domed trusses of 8. Leaves oblong, long, olive-green. Slightly open habit, somewhat wider than tall. (unknown × unknown). Cowles.

■ **SHALIMAR** Medium H4–5 ML. Flower widely funnel-shaped, slightly fragrant, pale lavender, in ball-shaped trusses of 12. Leaves elliptic, yellowish green, on a spreading plant. (Dexter hybrid seedling). Schlaikjer.

■ **SHALOM** Semi-dwarf H4–5 M. Flower openly funnel-shaped, white, shaded purplish pink with purplish-red spotting, in flatted ball trusses of 16. Leaves narrowly elliptic, moderate olive-green. I can't quite see how such a compact plant could come from these parents. (Anna × Antoon Van Welie). Lem/Hess.

■ **SHAM'S CANDY** Low H7 M. Flowers pink, frilly, with bronze blotch on yellow-green background, in conical trusses of 12 flowers. Leaves yellow-green on an upright but tidy plant. The yellow new growth is a feature, though not necessarily a good one. (Pinnacle × Pink Cameo). Shammarello. **'PINNACLE'** a parent of 'Sham's Candy' with vibrant-pink flowers. Very tough but not considered a great plant.

■ **SHANGHAI** Tall H6 ML. Flower widely funnel-shaped, pale purplish pink with lobes flushed deeper-pink and orange-yellow flare, in a dome-shaped truss of about 13. Leaves medium-green, elliptic, on a plant wider than tall, branching moderately. Not especially good. ([Mrs Furnival × *catawbiense* var. *album*] × unnamed, gold-blotched, mauve seedling). Leach.

■ **SHAWME LAKE** Medium H6 EM. Flowers moderate purplish pink with a moderate purplish-red basal blotch. Leaves elliptic, dull dark-green, on an upright grower. (unknown). Dexter.

■ **SHILSONII g.** Medium H4 E. Flowers waxy, blood-red, spotted dark brown, in a usually rounded truss of 12–15. Foliage dark green, elliptic on a tree-forming plant with fine bark. A famous early red-hybrid common in U.K. old collections. Subject to mildew. (*thomsonii* × *barbatum*). Gill. **'EARLY DAYS'** a similar Australian cross with cardinal-red bell-shaped flowers.

SHILSONII

■ **SIERRA DEL ORO** Semi-dwarf–Low H4 EM. Flower openly campanulate, wavy, reflexed lobes, light greenish yellow, with a small red flare, in trusses of 15. Leaves broadly elliptic to elliptic, slightly glossy. Poor leaf-retention and a sickly constitution added to a susceptibility to mildew make this a plant to avoid. (Crest × *lacteum*). Lofthouse.

■ **SIGNORINA** Medium–Tall H5 M–ML. Flowers white, tinged light purplish pink when first open, from pale-pink buds, with a bold dark-red flare, in rounded trusses of 15–17. Leaves ovate, dark glossy green, underside with indumentum on the midrib. (Kalamaika × Perlina). Hachmann.

■ **SILBERREIF** Medium H5 M–ML. Flowers lilac-pink-purple in a rounded truss. Leaves with irregular silver-to-white variegation. Sun tolerant. I don't think this has much merit for mild gardens as the variegation is in thin bands and barely visible from afar. It is very hardy. (Catawbiense Grandiflorum sport). Renken. **'CAROLINA SPRING'** flowers mauve-purple. Leaves with irregular and somewhat unstable white variegation.

■ **SILK RIBBON** Low–Medium H4 M. Fuchsia-pink flowers shading to cream in the centre, with red speckling and a large calyx, in rounded trusses of about 24. Leaves elliptic, glossy and moderate-green. Fairly compact. A fine bicolour flower in an impressive truss. (Anita Dunstan × One Thousand Butterflies). Barlup.

■ **SILVER JUBILEE** Low H4 M–ML. Flowers chartreuse-green fading to pale greenish white, with a crimson blotch in the upper throat, in rounded trusses of 14. Leaves pale green, convex, on a compact and slow-growing plant. Flowers are impressive. (Mrs W.C. Slocock × Coronation Day). George.

■ **SIR CHARLES LEMON** Medium H4 EM. Flower campanulate, ivory-white, faintly speckled red, in rounded, tight trusses. Leaves bullate, underside with bright cinnamon-brown indumentum, new

SIR CHARLES LEMON

growth white. Give sun protection. One of the finest hybrids for foliage: a 'must' for the woodland garden in moderate areas. *AGM, NN, PA, TC, VI.* (*arboreum* ssp. *cinnamomeum* var. *album* × *campanulatum*). Hooker seed/Carclew.

■ **SIR FREDERICK MOORE** Medium H4–5 ML–L. Flower frilly-edged, slightly fragrant, clear-pink with crimson spots in the throat, in flat trusses of about 15. Long, large, deep-green foliage on a vigorous upright plant. Tolerant of heat and, in Australia, resistant to lace bug and red spider. Takes a few years to produce flowers. (*fortunei* × St. Keverne). Rothschild. **'CHARLOTTE DE ROTHSCHILD'** clear-pink.

■ **SIR ROBERT PEEL** Tall H4 VE–E. Flower bluish crimson with dark spots in compact trusses of 18–20. Leaves narrow, mid-green, with this indumentum on the underside, on a very vigorous grower that can get enormous in mild gardens. *Mel, NZ* (*arboreum* × *ponticum*). J. Waterer. This cross was made many times. Some named forms include: **'CORNISH RED'**, **'ALTACLARENSE' g.** The largest cultivated rhododendrons in U.K. are of this cross.

■ **SIREN** Medium H3–4 ML. Flowers campanulate, waxy brilliant-red with darker spotting, in lax trusses. Dark shiny foliage with light indumentum. Hardier than would be expected from the parentage. (Choremia × *griersonianum*). Puddle/Aberconway.

■ **SKERRYVORE MONARCH** Semi-dwarf–Low H4–5 M. Flower openly funnel-shaped, deep purplish pink with slight greenish-yellow spotting on near-white background, in ball-shaped truss of 12. Leaves elliptic, olive-green, growing wider than tall. Not very bud hardy, so in N.E. U.S.A., really only suitable for mildest parts of New England and Long Island. (unknown × unknown). Dexter.

■ **SKYGLOW** Medium H4–5 M–ML. Flower openly funnel-shaped, fragrant, peach with a pale purplish-pink edge and a greenish-yellow blotch, in a flat to lax truss of 10–12. Leaves elliptic, glossy, yellow-green, on an upright, rounded, well-branched plant. Very fragrant and the flowers are fine, but the foliage tends to be yellowish and it needs a sheltered site. (unknown × unknown). Veitch/Baldsiefen. **'ASHES OF ROSES'** probably the same plant.

■ **SMOKED SALMON** Low–Medium H3–4 M–ML. Light-yellow throat shading to pale yellowish pink and to strong-pink at edges, scented of melon, in trusses of 10–12 flowers. Typical 'Lem's Cameo' hybrid foliage: new growth cinnamon. (Lem's Cameo × Coker's Pink). Sligh. Several sister seedlings were named: **'PRETTY JESSICA'**, yellow and pink, with red blotch, **'TAUNTON SUNRISE'** pink with a red blotch.

■ **SMOKEY (syn. SMOKEY #9)** Tall H4–5 ML. Flower broadly funnel-shaped, vivid-purple with black blotch and spotting, in a ball-shaped truss of 15. Leaves elliptic, recurved margins, bullate, semi-glossy, dark bluish green to dark green, copper-brown new growth. Very vigorous, best pinched or pruned when young to achieve an acceptable habit. The flower colour is striking. (Burgundy × Moser's Maroon). Lem.

■ **SNOW CANDLE** Low–Medium H4–5 EM. Flowers funnel-campanulate, light purplish pink in bud, opening yellowish-white inside and out with a moderate-red blotch in dorsal throat, in domed trusses of 23. Thick, glossy leaves. Dense habit with good leaf-retention. Takes a few years to bud up. Jim Barlup finds this a good parent of hardy blotched-hybrids. ([Fancy × *yakushimanum*] × Exbury Calstocker). Barlup.

■ **SNOW PEAK** Medium H4 M–ML. Flowers short funnel-shaped, white with a strong purplish-red blotch, in trusses of 16. Leaves elliptic, hairless. An Australian hybrid, popular in Victoria. (Morio × Mrs E.C. Stirling). Van de Ven.

■ **SNOW QUEEN** Medium H3 M. Deep-pink buds opening to large, funnel-shaped, pure-white flowers, with a tiny red basal blotch in large, dome-shaped trusses of 9–15. Vigorous plant of open habit with large handsome leaves to 20cm long. Needs filtered sun and protection from wind. (Halopeanum × Loderi). Loder. **'WHITE LADY'** a sister with pure-white flowers.

■ **SOLDIER SAM** Low H4 M. Flowers yellow-orange tinged red on outside, in trusses of 12. Small leaves on a compact plant. Needs good drainage. Said to be free-flowering. (Dido × *dichroanthum*). Reuthe.

■ **SONARE** Medium H5 ML. Flowers, vivid purplish red, shading to strong purplish red at edges, with a whitish throat overlaid with strong greenish-yellow markings, in fairly compact trusses of 13–17. Leaves broadly elliptic to ovate, slightly glossy and dark green. (Furnivall's Daughter × Simona). Hachmann.

■ **SONATA** Medium H4–5 L. Flowers small, orange-red, edged with crimson, looking orange from a distance, in small flat trusses of 11–13. Leaves small, dark green, on a dense compact plant. One of the hardier varieties in this shade with a good habit. Needs good drainage. Hardier than the very similar 'Golden Gate'. (Purple Splendour × *dichroanthum*). Reuthe.

SONATA

■ **SOUVENIR DE DR S ENDTZ** Tall H5 M. Flowers widely funnel-shaped, rich-pink with a crimson ray in throat, in domed trusses of 15–17. Plant vigorous, broader than tall, with a dark-green leaf. One of the reliable big pinks from Holland. *AGM*. (Pink Pearl × John Walter). Endtz.

■ **SOUVENIR OF ANTONY WATERER** Tall H5 ML–L. Flowers rosy red with a yellow eye, in domed trusses. Dark foliage on a very vigorous, straggly plant that needs pruning. The colour combination is striking. *AGM*. (unknown). A. Waterer.

■ **SPANISH LADY** Low H4–5 ML. Flowers reddish orange, overlaying yellow, in lax trusses of 8. Leaves narrow and long, on a bushy, vigorous plant. (Evening Glow × Lamplighter). Stockman.

■ **SPELLBINDER** Tall H6 E. Flower widely funnel-campanulate, light purplish pink, spotted deep purplish red, reverse deep purplish pink, in ball-shaped trusses of 16. Leaves large (to 24cm) narrowly elliptic, glossy, bullate, medium-green, on a well-branched, rounded, dense plant. You might have to wait a long time for flowers, but the foliage is handsome. Needs to be grown in shade. *TO*. (Russell Harmon × Robin Hood). Leach.

■ **SPITFIRE** Low H4–5 ML. Flowers deep chrysanthemum-crimson with a dark-brown blotch. Large handsome leaves on a tall but dense plant. (*griffithianum* × Mrs R.S. Holford?). Kluis.

■ **SPRING DAWN** Medium H7 EM. Flowers strong rosy pink with a golden-yellow blotch, in globular trusses. One of the toughest of the Shammarello hybrids. Vigorous but bushy. Heat tolerant. *Mid West*. (pink *catawbiense* hybrid × Mrs C.S. Sargent). Shammarello.

■ **SPRING SPIRIT** Medium H3–4 EM. Flowers large, lemon-yellow with deep purple-red markings at the base, in full rounded trusses of about 17. Large handsome bullate dark-green foliage on a fairly compact and dense plant. This should be a good parent of yellows with large handsome leaves. Early flowers and growth need protection. (Nancy Evans × *macabeanum*). Barlup.

STARBRIGHT CHAMPAGNE

■ **STARBRIGHT CHAMPAGNE** Low H4 EM. Flower broadly funnel-campanulate, with deeply cut lobes with rather pointed tips, pale yellow with a deep-red throat and prominent red spotting, in a dome-shaped rather sparse truss of 15. Leaves oblong, flat, dull green, on a slow-growing dense plant. New growth reddish bronze. A fine 'Lem's Cameo' hybrid with very distinctive and unusual flowers. *Scot*. ([Yaku Sunrise × Hansel] × Lem's Cameo). Fujioka.

■ **STOKES BRONZE WINGS (syn. BRONZE WINGS)** Tall H8 L. Flower a blend of light and very light purple with a greenish-yellow flare and yellow-green spots, in trusses of up to 30. Leaves elliptic. Many people have made the max-cat cross between the two hardy Eastern North American species. (*maximum* × *catawbiense*). Stokes.

■ **STRAWBERRY SWIRL** Low H5 E–EM. Flower frilled, pale pink with darker-pink stripes. Leaves pale green, underside with sparse tan indumentum, heavier on the midrib. Flowers rather thinly textured and do not last very long. Very early flowering, one of the earliest elepidotes for E. North America. (Jacksonii No. 1 × Jacksonii No. 1). Gable.

■ **STRAWBERRY WINE** Low H4 M. Flowers strong purplish pink at edges, shading to light purplish pink in centre, with a flare of moderate-red spots, outside streaked deep purplish pink along midribs, in a balled truss of 15. Leaves dull, moderate olive-green. Buds-up young. Grows wider than tall. Not everyone's colour. (Mrs Furnival × Peggy Roberts). Barlup.

STRAWBERRY WINE

■ **SUGAR PINK** Tall H4–5 M–ML. Flowers light purplish pink, deeper in the throat, spotted very light brown, in a tall truss (up to 30cm high) of up to 12. Very thick-textured stems and leaves on a medium compact, upright, vigorous bush. (Trude Webster × [Fawn × Queen of the May]). Greer.

■ **SUMATRA** Semi-dwarf–Low H6 M. Flower openly funnel-campanulate, waxy, deep-red shading to strong-red in centre, in trusses of 8–10. Leaves elliptic, variable from lightly textured to smooth, leaves darker in sun. Grows twice as wide as tall. Not very heat-tolerant. Does not match up to the Hobbie reds in U.K. and Europe. (America × Gertrude Schäle). Leach.

SUMATRA

■ **SUMMER GLOW** Tall H6–7 VL. Flower rose shading to pale purplish pink at centre, spotted orange-yellow, exterior bright purple; pedicels dark red, in a truss of 13. Leaves elliptic, to 16cm long, medium-green. A useful late-flowering plant for cold areas. Large handsome leaves. *ST*. (Summer Snow × Scarlet Blast). Leach.

■ **SUMMER PEACH** Medium H4 L. Flowers saucer-shaped, pale yellow with upper lobes flushed light yellow and with flares of discrete dark-red spots, outside pale yellow with strong-pink midribs, in balled trusses of 15. Leaves moderate olive-green, on a plant growing wider than high. (Whitney's Late Peach × Phyllis Korn). Barlup.

■ **SUMMER ROSE** Medium H5 VL. Flower widely funnel-shaped, strong purplish red with considerable dark reddish-purple spots on dorsal lobe, in ball trusses of 8–12. Leaves narrowly elliptic, yellowish green, underside with thin tan-to-golden indumentum, Silvery-grey tomentum when new. New stems are red. Upright, rounded habit. Heat resistant but needs shade to avoid sunburn. (*maximum* × Romany Chai). Ticknor/Weston.

■ **SUMMER SNOW** Medium H6 L–VL. Flower funnel-campanulate, white with small, rayed greenish-yellow blotch on dorsal lobe, slightly fragrant, in a dome-shaped truss of 11. Leaves elliptic, to 24cm long, on a vigorous grower that forms a large tree in time. A late-flowering hybrid of the 'Polar Bear' type for severe climates. Needs wind shelter and takes many years to start flowering. Best in dappled- or part-shade. *ME*. (*maximum* × [*ungernii* × *auriculatum* F2]). Leach.

■ **SUMMER SUMMIT** Medium H7 VL. Phlox-pink buds, opening to white flowers flushed orchid-pink at base and exterior, aging to white, with dark olive-yellow dorsal spotting. Leaves elliptic, dark green, on a dense grower. (*maximum* × unnamed hybrid). Leach.

■ **SUNNY DAY** Low H4 EM. Flowers light greenish-yellow, with red spotting, in a truss of 12. Leaves elliptic to narrowly elliptic, dark green, shiny. (Unknown). Whitney. **'SUNDANCE'** pale lemon-yellow in rounded trusses. Glaucous foliage.

■ **SUNSTRUCK** Low H5 M–ML. Flowers strong-red to vivid reddish-orange in bud, opening pale yellow, overcast strong-yellowish-pink at edges, in balled trusses of 12. Pale foliage on a compact spreading plant. We thought the flowers rather muddy and it was prone to mildew. It does grow well in parts of coastal New England where it was raised. (Golden Star × Mary Belle). Leonard.

SUNSTRUCK

■ **SUPER GOLD** Low H3 EM. Flowers deep yellow with orange shading, in a rounded but flat-topped truss of about 15. Leaves dark, convex, on a well-branched plant. Not a very 'super gold' in my opinion, susceptible to root diseases and mildew. The flowers are very deep if you can keep it alive. (Hotei × Joanita). Lofthouse.

■ **SUPERNOVA** Medium H5–6 ML–L. Flowers openly funnel-shaped, heavy textured, inside vivid purplish red, margins shading to mottled vivid-purplish-red centre, dark-red speckles on dorsal lobe, in flat trusses of 10–12. Hank Schannen calls this a Franken-Rhododendron as it has had its chromosomes increased in a test tube and then been cultured. Extra-thick flowers and stems. Not very hardy. (tetraploid Nova Zembla). Briggs.

SUPERNOVA

■ **SUSAN** Medium H4–5 M. Flower bluish mauve, paler towards centre, with darker margins and purple spots, in ball trusses of about 12. Leaves flat, glossy, dark green, with traces of indumentum and purple petioles. Hard to root. The colour is unusual, but it is not all that easy to please and is somewhat mildew-prone. *AGM, NI*. (*campanulatum* × *fortunei*). Williams.

SUSAN

■ **SWAMP BEAUTY** Medium H4 ML. Flower open funnel-shaped, wavy lobes, purple shading to white in throat with heavy maroon spots, in ball trusses of 18. Leaves narrowly elliptic, rather thin on an upright plant rather prone to mildew and poor foliage. A useful late-flowering hybrid with showy flowers. (Purple Splendour × Loderi Superlative). Elliott. **'LADY LUCK'** a sister with orchid-pink flowers with sweet fragrance.

SWAMP BEAUTY

■ **SWEET LULU** Low H6 M–ML. Flowers tubular funnel-shaped, moderate yellowish pink, with a pale-yellow throat and strong-orange dorsal spots, about 12 per truss. Good foliage and habit. This is an exotic looking pale salmon-pink, which seems to be pretty tough. A parent of many further Delp hybrids. (Gosh Darn × Dead Ringer). Delp.

SWEET LULU

■ **SWEET SIMPLICITY** Low H4–5 ML. Flowers ruffled, white with a pink edging, lightly spotted, in ball-shaped trusses of about 12. Leaves dark, glossy, fairly large, on a bushy, compact plant. Lots of incorrectly named plants were distributed in tissue culture under this name in the U.K. (*ponticum* hybrid). Waterer, Sons and Crisp.

■ **SWEET SIXTEEN** Tall H4–5 M. Flower widely funnel-shaped, wavy to frilly lobes, light pink with darker edges and an almost-white centre, in ball-shaped truss of 12. Leaves +/– elliptic, light green, twisted, on a vigorous, stiff rather irregular plant best in part shade. (unknown × unknown). Whitney.

■ **TAHITIAN DAWN** Medium H3 M. Flowers a mixture of bright-yellow, peach and tangerine, in a rounded truss. Leaves large, dark green. Upright habit, poorly branching and rather sparse. (Lem's Cameo × Skipper). Korth.

■ **TALLY HO** Medium–Tall H2–3 L. Flower bright orange-scarlet with darker spots deep in the throat, in loose trusses of 9–14. Medium-dull-green, twisted leaves. Upright, rather straggly growth habit. Needs protection from sun. Late growth is vulnerable to frost damage. Not hardy at Glendoick. Lots of clones exist. (*griersonianum* × *facetum*). Crosfield & Loder.

■ **TAMARINDOS** Low H4–5 M. Flowers openly funnel-shaped, deep reddish purple, shading to very pale purple, with a conspicuous blotch of greenish yellow, in trusses of 9–13. Dark-green leaves on a compact spreading plant. The flowers are quite eye-catchingly two-toned. (Blue Bell × Purple Splendour). Hachmann.

■ **TAPESTRY** Low H7 ML. Flower broadly funnel-shaped, wavy edges, vivid-purple with a dark-purple blotch, in dome-shaped trusses of 18. Leaves elliptic, down-curved margins, dull, dark green, on a compact, dense grower. Tough, sun and wind-tolerant. (Purpureum Splendens × *catawbiense* hybrid). Mezitt.

TAPESTRY

■ **TARANTELLA**® Medium H7 ML. Flowers funnel-shaped, deep-red shading to strong-red, dorsal lobe richly marked dark red on light background, with white stamens, in trusses of 12–14. Dark-green ribbed leaves. A promising new German hybrid with flowers of a rich-red. (Oratorium × Feuerschein). Hachmann. **'NEGRITO'** a sister with strong-red flowers with yellow anthers.

TAURUS

■ **TAURUS** Tall H5 E. Flower campanulate, bright clear-red with darker throat and black spots on dorsal lobe, in ball-shaped trusses of 16. Leaves elliptic, rounded, dark green, with attractive red buds. One of the best red-hybrids ever raised. Best in part shade in hot climates. Hardier than 'Grace Seabrook'. Much tougher than thought: good in Germany, Scandinavia and N.E. U.S.A. *AGM, AZ, BH, CA, CD, CH, CN, EG, FS, KK, MB, NI, NO, NY, OL, OP, PC, PD, PT, SC, SE, SH, SI, SL, VI, WT.* (The Hon. Jean Marie de Montague × *strigillosum*). Mossman.

■ **TED'S ORCHID SUNSET** Medium H4 M. Flowers lilac-pink with a yellow-and-brown flare, in full rounded trusses. Bronze-green leaves, on reddish petioles, on an upright, spreading plant. Foliage is not always very good and it probably needs a little shade. (Purple Splendour × Mrs Donald Graham). Fawcett.

■ **TEMPEST** Medium H4–5 L. Flowers of fine bright red, in loose trusses of 8–10. Upright habit. This would be a good parent for orange-red hybrids. (Mars × Fabia). Wright. **'TEMPEST'S SISTER'** is also available.

■ **TEMPLE MEADS** Semi-dwarf H5 M. Flower openly funnel-shaped, frilled, light yellow with brilliant-yellow spotted blotch on dorsal lobe, in dome-shaped trusses of 12. Leaves elliptic, flat, rounded, dull, yellow-green. (Janet Blair × Hindustan). Gustafson.

■ **TENNESSEE** Low H7 EM. Buds of strong purplish pink open to light purplish pink flowers fading to pale yellowish-pink, with a bold-red dorsal blotch, in a truss of about 16. Leaves elliptic, smooth. (La Bar's White × [Ole Olson × Fabia]). Leach.

■ **TENSING** Low H4 L. Narrowly campanulate flowers of camellia-rose, shading to a tinge of orange in the throat, in loose, flat-topped trusses of about 13. A rather rangy grower. Named after the 1953 Everest-conquering Sherpa. (Fabia × Romany Chai). Hanger.

■ **TERRACOTTA** Low H4 M–ML. Flowers salmon-pink with a cream centre, spotted brown. Fairly compact. A little-known English hybrid. (Mrs Lindsay Smith × Dido). Slocock.

■ **THE DON** Low H3 M. Flowers strawberry-red fading to pink, in large trusses. Leaves fir-green, glossy +/– elliptic. (Doncaster × Griffithianum). Lowinsky.

■ **THE GENERAL** Medium H7 ML. Flowers crimson-rose with a darker-red blotch, in a conical truss. Leaves dark green on a rather leggy plant that needs pinching. Some heat tolerance. Not all that free-flowering. (red *catawbiense* hybrid × unknown). Shammarello. **'ROMEO'** blood-red with deeper blotch. **'SCARLET GLOW'** brick-red, less hardy.

■ **THE MASTER** Tall H3–4 M–ML. Flowers pale pink, flushed rose, spotted deeper, in a large truss of 12. Leaves deep green and healthy. A tall, vigorous grower, inclined to straggliness. Hard to root. It did not produced good trusses in Scotland, so we threw it out. *AGM.* (China × Letty Edwards). Slocock. **'MOTHER THERESA'** creamy-white fragrant flowers.

■ **THE MORNING AFTER** Medium H5 ML. Flowers cream with a red blotch, in a rounded truss. Recently named from the Heritage Plantation. I'm trying to work out what exactly the name refers to… (unknown). Dexter/Cowles.

■ **THOR** Semi-dwarf–Low H3 M. Flower bright scarlet with large calyx held in a lax truss of about 7. Leaves

THOR

dark green, underside with thick indumentum, on a compact, widely branched plant. Similar to 'Mayday' but hardier. (*haematodes* × Felis). Brandt.

■ **THUNDERSTORM** Medium H5 M–ML. Flowers dark red with darker spotting and white stamens, in a compact, dome-shaped truss of about 18. Leaves dark and glossy but rather thin and hanging, on a rather loose, sprawling plant. (Doncaster hybrid). Slocock.

THUNDERSTORM

■ **TIDBIT** Low–Medium H3–4 M. Bright-red buds open to small pale-yellow flowers with a red throat, in lax trusses of 6–7. Leaves dark green, glossy, small, on a dense and compact grower. Flowers are attractive in a subtle way and the foliage is fine. Needs good drainage and in hot climates foliage needs some shade. Good at Glendoick. *AGM.* (*dichroanthum* × *wardii*). Henny.

TIDBIT

■ **TIDDLYWINKS** Low–Medium H4 M. Flowers deep lemon-yellow with a large calyx, giving a hose-in-hose effect. Foliage glossy. A curious looking hybrid, probably not to everyone's taste. (Tidbit × Idealist). Thompson.

■ **TODMORDEN** Tall H5 EM. Flower widely funnel-shaped, deep purplish-pink edges shading to light purplish pink, aging to nearly white, with sparse light yellow-green spots, in ball-shaped trusses of 8–15. Leaves elliptic to nearly oblong, flat to concave, dull, yellowish green. Upright, rounded habit. Quite heat tolerant and easy to root. Bicoloured flowers are impressive. *AZ, GP, ST.* ([Pygmalion × *haematodes*] × Wellfleet). Dexter.

TODMORDEN

TORTOISESHELL ORANGE

TRUDE WEBSTER

TRUE TREASURE

TRAIL BLAZER

■ **TOFINO** Medium H4 ML. Flower openly funnel-shaped, pale greenish-yellow edged purplish-pink, in domed to flat trusses of 15–16. Leaves elliptic, margins undulate, glossy, light green, on a plant of upright habit. *MT.* (Lem's Cameo × [Jalisco × (Crest × King of Shrubs)]). Lofthouse. **'O CANADA'** oh too many Lem's Cameo hybrids! Yellow. **'RUTH MOTTLEY'** a Davis Cameo × with pink flowers with a yellow throat.

■ **TOM EVERETT** Low H4–5 M. Flower lightly fragrant, deep purplish pink paling to near-white in throat, with vivid greenish-yellow faint spotting, in a dome-shaped truss of about 11. Leaves pale green, elliptic, flat with slight wave. Rounded growth habit, slow growing when young. Some heat resistance. One of the most highly rated Dexter hybrids. *PT, PV, SE, SV.* (fortunei × unknown). Dexter.

■ **TOONEYBIRD** Low–Medium H5 ML. Flowers funnel-shaped, yellow at tips of lobes, shading lighter to chartreuse in the throat, with greenish spotting on dorsal lobes, outside golden-yellow, in domed trusses of 12. Leaves semi-glossy, elliptic, dark green. (Joe Gable × Goldsworth Orange). Seeds.

■ **TOP BANANA** Semi-dwarf–Low H3 EM. Flowers clear deep yellow, unmarked, in ball-shaped trusses of about 17. Leaves flat to convex, glossy, bright green. Upright habit, taller than broad. We had to give this up due to very early young growth. The flowers are a good deep yellow. *CN.* (unknown × unknown). Whitney.

■ **TORERO**® Medium H5 ML–L. Flowers deep crimson, not fading, in rounded trusses of 14–17. Leaves dark green, on an upright but fairly tidy plant. We found it was reluctant to make a good root system, but this might be a tissue-culture problem. Grafted in Germany. The colour is a bluer red than 'Erato'. (Oratorium × Feuerschein). Hachmann.

■ **TORNADO** Low–Medium H4 M–ML. Flowers currant-red, with fused or absent stamens, with a faint brown blotch, in loose trusses of 9–14. Compact. Leaves with thin indumentum. Not reliably hardy in Holland where it was raised. ([Wilgen's Ruby × Mayday] × Billy Budd). Boskoop.

■ **TORTOISESHELL g.** Low H3–4 ML. Flower funnel-shaped, in loose trusses. **'WONDER'** pale salmon-pink flushed with orange, **'ORANGE'** salmon-orange, **'CHAMPAGNE'** pale creamy-apricot. Leaves, long, dark green with a red petiole; on an upright but tidy plant. Best in a sheltered site and, in hot climates, part-shade. Easy to root and buds-up young. *AGM.* (Goldsworth Orange × griersonianum). Slocock.

■ **TRAIL BLAZER** Medium H5 M. Flower openly funnel-shaped, pink with a deep-red blotch, in ball-shaped trusses of 19. Leaves lanceolate, shiny, dark green, on a compact grower, growing twice as wide as tall. We found it rather inclined to fall off its roots. Some insect resistance. (Mrs Furnival × Sappho). Wright.

■ **TRAVIS L.** Low H3 M. Flowers fragrant, pure white with a faint greenish-white blotch, in globular trusses. Leaves wavy, light green, on an upright bush. Very early into growth, the new leaves partly hiding the flowers. Not a great plant. (unknown × Albatross). Cannon.

■ **TRILBY** Medium H5 ML. Flower small, deep crimson with a small black blotch, in a conical small truss. Leaves matte, greyish green on a stiff upright plant with red stems. Sun tolerant. Flowers are a good colour and the foliage is better than its sisters such as 'Britannia'. *MB, TC.* (Queen Wilhelmina × Stanley Davies). Van Nes.

■ **TRINIDAD** Semi-dwarf–Low H7 ML. Flower openly funnel-shaped, cream, spotted yellow, with pink-red edges, reverse deep purplish pink, in ball-shaped trusses of 14. Leaves elliptic, flat to convex, dull, dark green. Not always very free-flowering but the flower is a dramatic and exotic mixture for such a hardy plant. Tissue-cultured plants under this name in 1980s were wrongly named. (Calcutta × Tahiti). Leach.

■ **TRIPSDRILL** Low–Medium H5 M–ML. Flowers strong purplish red, inside-centre pale purplish pink, in a compact rounded truss of 12–14. Leaves elliptic,

slightly glossy, mid-green. This is a hardier version of the Walloper-type hybrids, suited for N. Germany. (Tarantella × Elizabeth de Rothschild). Hachmann.

■ **TROJAN WARRIER** Low–Medium H6–7 ML. Flowers strong purplish red, in domed trusses of 14. Leaves elliptic with recurved margins, glossy, twisted, dark green. *MS.* (catawbiense hybrid × unknown). Mezitt.

■ **TRUDE WEBSTER** Medium H4–5 M. Flower openly funnel-shaped, clear deep pink, upper lobe spotted, fading to pale pink, in large upright trusses of 14. Leaves elliptic, glossy, slightly twisted, pale medium-green. Sun tolerant and free-flowering with a better habit than the Dutch pinks. One of the first hybrids to be given the Superior Plant Award in the U.S.A. *AZ, MB, VI, PA.* (Countess of Derby selfed). Greer.

■ **TRUE TREASURE** Medium H4 M–ML. Flowers rose-pink, frilled, with a maroon blotch. Less hardy than many Dexters, so little grown on the East Coast of N. America. Flowers are impressive and it does well in Philadelphia area. (unknown). Dexter.

■ **TURKISH DELIGHT** Medium H5 ML–L. Flowers deep purplish pink, spotted, in large trusses of over 20. Hardy, vigorous and easy. Foliage can be poor, with late growth tending to be yellow. No one seems to know what this plant's origins are. (unknown). unknown.

■ **TWILIGHT PINK** Low H4–5 M. Flower glowing-pink and apricot with a large calyx, in a well-filled, rounded truss. Dense, apple-green, insect-resistant foliage. Compact, rounded shrub. Tissue-cultured plants under this name turned out to be something else. ([fortunei × Alice] selfed × Comstock). Greer.

■ **TWILIGHT SUN** Medium H4 EM–M. Flowers light orange-yellow, tinged randomly with deep yellowish pink, with deep-red nectaries, in a balled truss of up to 17. Leaves semi-glossy, moderate olive-green. (Nancy Evans × unnamed hybrid). Barlup.

■ **TYGO** Medium H3 M. Flower broadly funnel-campanulate, vivid-red, upper half of corolla heavily spotted deep red, in flat dome-shaped trusses of 18–20. Leaves elliptic, long, with down-curved margins, dull olive-green above with sparse tan hairs below, along midrib. (Ruby Bowman × elliottii 'War Paint'). Goheen.

■ **UNA MARY** Low H4 EM. Flower widely funnel-shaped, with deeply cut lobes, light-purple with large part of dorsal lobe densely spotted dark red to almost-black, in ball-shaped trusses of 15. Leaves narrowly elliptic, convex, long, glossy, dark green. Upright, dense growth habit. Flowers are star-shaped, giving quite a striking effect. (Purple Splendour × Van Nes Sensation). Stockman.

■ **UNIQUE** Low H4–5 EM. Pink buds open to a light creamy colour that fades to almost white, with a pink flush and yellow throat, in balled trusses of about 14. Leaves ovate, thick, shiny, deep green. Dense and compact habit. Tolerates full sun but does best in filtered light. AGM, CA, MB, MT, PA, PD, SI, SO, ST, TC, WT, Mel. (campylocarpum × unknown). Slocock.

UNIQUE

■ **UNIQUE MARMALADE** Semi-dwarf–Low H4–5 EM. Flower openly funnel-shaped, frilly, deep pink at outer edge shading to light orange in the centre with darker spots, in ball-shaped trusses of 12. Leaves elliptic, flat, glossy, very deep green, Compact and dense habit. Likes filtered afternoon shade and plenty of morning sun. SH. (Orange Marmalade × Unique). Davis.

■ **UNKNOWN WARRIOR** Medium H3 E. Flower deep rose-red with brown markings, in dome-shaped trusses of 12–18. Leaves pointed, matte green, on an upright, straggly grower. (Queen Wilhelmina × Stanley Davies). Van Nes. **'C.B. VAN NES'** a sister with glowing-scarlet flowers. Foliage poor. **'EARL OF ATHLONE'** blood-red flowers on a straggly upright plant. **'LANGLEY PARK'** deep-red flowers that fade.

■ **URSINE** Medium H5 L. Flowers broadly funnel-shaped, vivid purplish red (bright pink), in a compact truss of 10–12. Leaves ovate, dark green. A useful mid-summer-flowering bright pink, which is one-quarter R. auriculatum. (Silentium × Junifreude). Hachmann.

■ **VALLEY FORGE** Medium–Tall H4–5 ML. Flowers medium spinel-red, spotted in cardinal-red, heavily on dorsal lobe, in trusses of 15–18. Plant upright, rounded, well-branched, with glossy leaves. Not as hardy as might be expected from the cross, so not all that widely grown. Named after a Pennsylvanian town. (Atrosanguineum × [fortunei × williamsianum]). Herbert.

■ **VAN DEC** Tall H4 M. Flowers pale pink with a small yellow blotch in the throat, fragrant. Vigorous and upright habit. Mainly grown in New Zealand, where it is quite highly rated. (Van Nes Sensation × decorum). unknown.

■ **VAN NES SENSATION** Medium H4–5 M. Flower widely funnel-shaped, slightly fragrant, pale orchid-pink with paler centres and red spots in throat, fading to off-white, in dome-shaped trusses. Mid-green, glossy leaves on an upright but dense plant. Some heat tolerance and foliage is fairly insect-resistant. AZ, SI, Mel. (fortunei × White Pearl). Van Nes.

VANESSA PASTEL

■ **VANESSA PASTEL** Medium H3–4 ML. Buds open brick-red, flowers apricot to deep cream with darker bronze-yellow in throat, exterior of orange-buff suffused pink-and-peach, in a truss of about 8. There are two clones, one pinker than the other. Compact habit with narrowish, thin, pale-green leaves. Not all that hardy and can suffer bark-split, but the flowers are amongst the finest of all the many R. griersonianum hybrids. **'VANESSA FCC'** is deeper-pink with poor foliage and straggly habit. AGM. (Soulbut × griersonianum). Puddle/Aberconway. **'AMAURA'** from Bodnant is similar.

■ **VERNUS** Medium H7–8 E–EM. Flowers light pink, star-shaped, in large rounded trusses. Apparently the name should be 'Vernum' to make it agree (Latin), but no one pays any attention to this... Leaves, dull, deep green, on an upright, rather open plant. The earliest flowering of the Shammarello hybrids. Autumn flowering in some climates. Easy to root, sun and heat tolerant and free flowering. (Cunningham's White × red catawbiense hybrid). Shammarello.

■ **VERY BERRY** Tall H4–5 M–ML. Flowers rose-red, in tall (up to 30cm), cone-shaped trusses. Large thick leaves to 25cm long, on a vigorous bush. Some heat tolerance. Great if you like your trusses large and gaudy. (Trude Webster × Jean Marie de Montague). Greer. **'BRIDAL DREAM'** ruffled flowers of medium-pink with darker spotting.

■ **VICKI REINE** Medium H4–5 M. Flower bicolour, deep rose-red at edge fading to white in throat, rose exterior, in trusses of about 12. Leaves deeply veined, dark green on a plant growing as wide as high. Flowers are striking. (unknown). Clark.

■ **VICTOR FREDRICK** Tall H3 M. Flower openly funnel-shaped, vivid reddish orange with a red blotch, reverse with red stripe down centre of each lobe, in conical trusses of 17. Leaves elliptic or lanceolate, dark green, on a spreading, somewhat decumbent plant. (unknown). Lem/Sinclair.

■ **VICTORIA'S CONSORT** Low H7 ML. Flower openly funnel-shaped, yellowish white with a light greenish-yellow eye, in a truss of 11–14. Leaves oblong, yellowish green, on an upright, open-growing plant. Used to be called 'Mauve and Gold', which is perhaps a better name. (unnamed hybrid × unnamed hybrid). Mezitt.

■ **VIENNA WOODS** Medium H4–5 ML. Flower widely funnel-shaped, moderately fragrant, very pale purplish pink, in flat trusses of 10–12. Leaves oblong to obovate, flat, on a plant of upright, dense habit. (Robert Allison × fortunei). Walbrecht/Brooks.

■ **VIENNESE WALTZ** Medium H4 M. Flower funnel-shaped, lightly fragrant, light red at edges shading darker in throat with orange-brown spots, reverse salmon, fading to cream, in densely packed conical trusses of up to 34. Leaves elliptic, mid-green, on a plant of upright, open habit. The packed trusses of flowers are impressive but the foliage is thin and inclined to be yellowish with poor leaf-retention and chlorosis, inherited from 'Pink Petticoats'. PC. (Lem's Cameo × Pink Petticoats). Lofthouse.

■ **VILÉM HECKEL** Medium H7 M–ML. Flowers chrysanthemum-crimson, with a pansy-purple blotch, in a globular truss of 10–16. Leaves elongate-elliptic, slightly glossy. A tough Czech hybrid. (Don Juan × Dr. V.H.C. Dresselhuys). Dvořák.

■ **VINCENT VAN GOGH** Low H5 M. Flowers bright cerise-red on margins, striped white towards the centre, in a small compact truss. Leaves dark, matte green, on a straggly, open-growing plant. Blooms at four to six years of age. The flowers are very striking but the plant is pretty unshapely. (unknown). Koster. **'PRINCESS MARY OF CAMBRIDGE'** similar with smaller, tighter trusses.

■ **VINECREST** Low–Medium H6 M. Flower openly funnel-shaped, wavy lobes, fragrant, light greenish yellow with small reddish-brown rays, in trusses of 12. Leaves narrowly elliptic, convex, olive-green. Upright habit. 'Almost as good as Capistrano,' (Dennis MacMullan). Colour a bit paler. Looked impressive to me in flower. CC. ([(catawbiense La Bar's White × fortunei) × wardii] × wardii Litiense Gp.). Begg.

VINECREST

■ **VINEMOUNT** Low H6 ML. Open funnel-shaped flowers, vivid reddish purple, with a pale-yellow dorsal blotch in trusses of 14. Medium-green foliage. (unnamed hybrid × Labar's White). Forster.

■ **VIRGINIA RICHARDS** Low H4 M. Flower long lasting, openly funnel-shaped, open salmon-pink aging to apricot and then creamy yellow, with pinkish-red spotting, in ball-shaped trusses of 10–12. Leaves deep green, on a rounded, well-branched plant. This was a wonderful plant, the best of its type but, with the onset of powdery mildew, this plant is almost ungrowable in moderate climates unless you are prepared to spray it. *NI.* ([*wardii* × F.C. Puddle] × Mrs Betty Robertson). Whitney. A sister **'LEVERETT RICHARDS'** was also named.

■ **VISCY** Medium H5 ML. Flowers of thick texture, cream, flushed and marked orange-and-yellow, with dark-red spots, in trusses of 4–8. Leaves are large, glossy dark green and insect-resistant. The colour is most unusual, some love it; others don't! Somewhat prone to powdery mildew. (Diane × *viscidifolium*). Hobbie. Two further *R. viscidifolium* hybrids: **'SILJA'** pink flowers in a loose truss, **'GOLDEN YELLOW'** pink outside, yellow inside, flare of orange.

VISCY

■ **VIVACIOUS** Semi-dwarf–Low H4–5 ML. Flower openly funnel-shaped, strong-red, with no markings, in ball-shaped trusses of 10 or more. Leaves narrowly elliptic, medium-green, on a rounded plant, broader than tall. The flowers are rather a harsh colour and we found they bleached in the sun. Highly rated in severe climates. *AZ, BH, CH, MA, PT, SE.* (America × Dr Ross). Forster.

■ **VOLCANO** Medium H3–4? EM. Flowers small, dark red. Fairly compact. Easy to root. Grown in Australia. (unknown). Taylor & Sangster.

■ **VOLUPTUOUS** Medium H4–5 ML. Flower slightly scented, openly funnel-shaped, purplish-red edges, yellow star-shaped centre and cardinal-red throat, deep-crimson spots on dorsal lobe, in trusses of 18. Leaves oblong, glossy, on a plant of upright, dense habit. The overall flower colour is deep pink. (Scintillation × Mary Belle). Brack. **'ERIC'S TRIUMPH'** another 'Scintillation' hybrid with cream flowers flushed yellow and spotted deeper.

■ **VULCAN** Medium H6 ML. Flower blood-red, unmarked, in dome-shaped trusses of about 10. Several different clones are sold under this name, some more compact than others. Leaves long and narrow, dark green, with red stems on a plant of mounding habit, which needs a little shade in hotter climates. A reliable and tough hybrid.

VULCAN

AGM, CH, BH, CN, FS, NI, PT, SE, TC. (Mars × *griersonianum*). Waterer, Sons and Crisp. **'VULCAN TETRAPLOID'** has thicker leaves and flower texture. **'BONFIRE'** is very similar but less hardy and more straggly with rather average foliage.

■ **VULCAN'S FLAME** Medium H6 ML. Flower openly funnel-shaped, bright cardinal-red, in trusses of up to 15. Leaves elliptic, pointed, dark green. Very similar to 'Vulcan' but said to be slightly hardier. *SV.* (*griersonianum* × Mars). Lancaster.

■ **WALLOPER g.** Tall H4–5 M. Flowers pink or pink-and-white, in large trusses. Dark-green leaves, slightly twisted. Halfdan Lem applied the name 'Walloper' to a large group of seedlings, many of which were named: 'Lem's Monarch' and 'Point Defiance' are two. There is no clone under the name 'Walloper' registered. (Anna × Marinus Koster). Lem.

■ **WALTER SCHMALSHEIDT** Low H5 EM. Tubular funnel-shaped flowers of clear, rich-yellow, with a small basal blotch, in trusses of 6–12. Broad, upright, compact bush with glossy, dark-green foliage. Named after one of Germany's foremost rhododendron experts and authors. (*wardii* × Linsweger Gold). Robenek.

■ **WAR DANCE** Low H5 M. Flowers, bright currant-red, with black dorsal blotch and spotting, in trusses of 17–21. Leaves dark green, on a spreading, well-branched plant growing wider than high. Badly handled in tissue-culture giving ungrowable plants. (Mars × Pygmalion). Hall.

■ **WARCHANT** Medium H4–5 M. Flowers orange tones with dark throat, in loose trusses. Leaves dark green, on a spreading and well-branched plant. (Old Copper selfed). Bulgin.

■ **WARLOCK** Medium H4 L. Flower openly funnel-shaped, dark reddish purple with black blotch and spots, in flat trusses of 14. Leaves elliptic, some oblong, dark green, with dark red petioles, new growth maroon, on a broad, well-branched plant. *CA.* (Romany Chal × Purple Splendour). Bledsoe.

■ **WARM GLOW** Semi-dwarf–Low H4 ML. Flower, orange with a darker throat, with slight dark-red spotting, outside reddish orange, in lax trusses of 10–12. Leaves narrowly elliptic, on a rounded, well-branched shrub. ([*dichroanthum* × unknown] × Vida). Greer.

■ **WARWICK** Medium H7 EM. Flower fragrant, pale mauve-pink, in a full, rounded truss. Vigorous grower with a wide, open habit. Young growth tends to partially conceal the flowers. Good reports from New England, though sometimes shy-flowering. (unknown). Dexter.

■ **WAY AHEAD** Low H4–5 EM. Flower widely funnel-shaped, china-rose at edges shading to a white centre, in conical trusses of 14. Leaves lanceolate, rounded, deep green, on a plant of compact and dense, rounded habit. (Cary Ann × Mars). Wright.

■ **WEBER'S PRIDE** Medium H4–5 M. Flower flat saucer-shaped, vivid purplish red with moderate reddish-orange blotch, reverse vivid reddish purple, in conical trusses of 17. Leaves oblanceolate, on an upright, well-branched plant. (Lady Clementine Mitford × Kate Waterer). Weber.

■ **WESTBURY** Semi-dwarf–Low H4–5 M. Flower openly funnel-shaped, purplish pink fading to near-white with brilliant greenish-yellow spotting, in ball-shaped trusses of 12. Leaves elliptic, flat, olive-green, on a plant of compact, rounded growth habit, growing wider than tall. Free-flowering and easy to root. Best in light shade. (unknown × unknown). Dexter/Phipps.

■ **WHEATLEY** Low H5 ML. Flower openly funnel-shaped, frilly lobes, very fragrant, pale purplish pink shaded darker towards edge, with yellowish-green rays in throat, in ball-shaped trusses of 16. Leaves elliptic, medium-green, on a broad, well-branched plant best in filtered light. *AZ, GP, MA, PT, SE.* (Westbury × Meadowbrook). Phipps. **'BROOKVILLE'** a sister with delicate-pink frilled flowers, shaded white, deeper flare and gold throat.

■ **WHIDBY ISLAND** Tall H4 M. Flowers ventricose-campanulate, purplish-red buds open very light purple with narrow edging of vivid-violet, spotted/blotched dark purple, in a rounded truss of 22–24. Leaves to 20cm, dark green, underside with felt-like indumentum, slightly recurved, new growth white. Flowers small, not very free-flowering but the foliage is handsome. *PNW.* (*niveum* × *rex*). Meerkerk.

■ **WHIPPED CREAM** Low H3–4 M–ML. Semi-double pale yellow-green, in rounded trusses. Compact. Free-flowering. (unknown). Coker.

■ **WHITE DIMPLES** Low H7 ML. Flower openly funnel-shaped, yellowish white, in ball-shaped trusses of 20. Leaves elliptic, convex, on a dense grower, best in half-shade. Handsome foliage. Has been a good parent in E. U.S.A. (Noreaster × white hybrid). Mezitt.

■ **WHITE GOLD** Tall H4 M. Flowers pure white, reflexed, with a large dorsal flare, brilliant-yellow, in dome-shaped trusses of 12. Leaves elliptic on a fairly tidy plant. The impressive flowers last best with some shelter. (Mrs J.G. Millias × Cheyenne). Greer.

WHITE GOLD

■ **WHITE LINEN** Medium H4 M. Flowers, from purplish-pink buds, opening white inside and out, unspotted, lightly scented, in full truss of 14. Leaves ovate/elliptic, on a dense compact grower. *N.Z.* (Unique × Lemon Lodge). Sligh.

■ **WHITE PEARL (syn. HALOPEANUM)** Tall H3 M. Flowers pastel-pink, fading to pure white, in tall conical trusses of 9–12. Leaves deep green, glossy, on a vigorous grower. A parent of several hybrids. Heat tolerant, easy to root and sometimes used as a rootstock. *Mel.* (*griffithianum* × *maximum*). Halope. **'GEOFFREY MILLAIS'** white flowers flushed pink, fragrant and frilled, in conical trusses.

■ **WHITE PETER** Semi-dwarf–Low H8 ML. Flower openly funnel-shaped, yellowish white with dark-red flare, outside tinged light-pink along veins, in rounded trusses, often from multiple buds. Leaves elliptic, flat, rounded, glossy, dark green, on a spreading and dense plant. A poor plant in Scotland with yellow foliage. Good in severe climates. *MS.* (Blue Peter × Blue Peter). Mehlquist.

WHITE PETER

■ **WHITE SWAN** Tall H4–5 M–ML. Flowers pale pink, fading to white, with a green basal blotch, in trusses of 16–19. Leaves greyish green on an upright plant that becomes open with age. Heat tolerant. Best with some shade in California. *CA, MB, NO.* (*decorum* × Pink Pearl). Waterer, Sons and Crisp.

■ **WHITESTONE** Semi-dwarf–Low H4 M. Flower fragrant, double, petaloid stamens, white with raspberry-bronze markings in the throat, in a ball-shaped truss of 9–16. Leaves elliptic to oblong, flat, semi-glossy, on an upright, sometimes rather sparse and straggly plant, though some find it compact. Flowers are impressive. Used as a parent for raising double hybrids. (unknown × unknown). Vossberg.

WHITESTONE

■ **WHITNEY'S LATE ORANGE (syn. WHITNEY LATE ORANGE)** Medium H4 ML–L. Flowers salmon-pink/orange, in a loose truss. Leaves thin, pointed and recurved, on fairly compact grower. Best in part shade to avoid yellow foliage. Late growth vulnerable to frost. Not of much merit, with small flowers and poor foliage. (unknown). Whitney.

■ **WHITNEY'S ORANGE** Low H4 M. Flower widely funnel-campanulate, yellowish pink with a vivid reddish-orange blotch and spots and edged in red, in ball-shaped trusses of about 15. Another form is deeper-orange and unmarked. Leaves narrowly elliptic to oblanceolate, convex, dull, medium-green, new growth is yellowish green. A rather sprawling, open-growing plant with decumbent, willowy branches that needs pruning. Flowers are good, foliage and habit poor. (*dichroanthum* × Diana). Whitney.

■ **WHITNEY'S TIGER LILY** Low H3 EM. Flowers mid-pink, fading to pale pink, with red spotting and a large split-calyx. Leaves hairy on a spreading plant which buds-up at three to four years of age. (unknown). Whitney/Sather.

■ **WILD AFFAIR** Medium H4–5 ML. Flowers bright red, with a white centre and light-yellow blotch, in a rounded truss. Leaves dark green, thick, on a rather open and sprawling plant, needing pruning. Flowers are unusual. (Jean Marie de Montague × Moser's Maroon). Greer.

■ **WILGEN'S RUBY (syn. VAN WILGEN'S RUBY)** Low H6 ML. Flowers rose-red, with dark-brown blotch and spotting, outside deeper rose-red, in rounded trusses. Leaves smooth, dark green, on a compact and tidy plant. Easy to root, free-flowering and widely available in Europe. Foliage tends to be yellowish. The red is not a very impressive shade. *Hol, Ger, Fra.* (Britannia × John Walter). Van Wilgen.

WILGEN'S RUBY

■ **WILLARD** Medium H4–5 M. Flower tubular funnel-shaped, mildly fragrant, purplish red with paler throat and faint purplish pink spotting, in a ball-shaped truss of about 12. Leaves elliptic, yellowish green, on a broad, well-branching shrub. Free-flowering. (unknown). Dexter.

■ **WILLIAM ROGERS COE** Medium H5 M. Flowers pale pink-white, with a deep-yellow blotch, in a rounded truss. Leaves elliptic. Tough. Confusingly there is another related hybrid called 'William R. Coe', which has similar flowers with a small crimson blotch and flowers about a week earlier. (unknown). Dexter.

■ **WIND RIVER** Low–Medium H4 M. Flowers broadly funnel-shaped, strong-red in bud; opening pale greenish yellow deepening to light yellow in throat and light purplish-pink edges fading with age, with strong-red ring at base, in balled trusses of 20. Habit upright but fairly dense. A long flowering period. Considered one of the best Barlup hybrids. Buds-up very young. (Mindy's Love × complex cross). Barlup.

WIND RIVER

■ **WINDLESHAM SCARLET** Low–Medium H4–5 ML. Flowers cardinal-red with black spots, in compact, domed trusses of 12–16. Vigorous, compact, with dull, dark leaves. Free flowering. *Fra, U.K.* (Britannia × Doncaster). Frowmow.

WINDLESHAM SCARLET

■ **WINDSONG** Low–Medium H4 M. Flowers open funnel-shaped, light greenish-yellow throughout, with a dark-red nectar pouch, in a ball truss of 17. Leaves glossy, moderate olive-green. Compact habit. (Nancy Evans × [Mrs Betty Robertson × Fred Rose]). Barlup.

■ **WINDSOR LAD** Medium H5 ML. Flowers bluish lilac, with a bold golden eye, in compact trusses of 16. Narrow foliage of medium length, on a well-shaped plant that can become sparse with age. Free flowering and easy to root. (*ponticum* hybrid). Knap Hill Nursery. **'MAHMOUD'** lavender-pink with a large yellow blotch.

■ **WINE FUCHSIA** Medium H4–5 ML. Flowers burgundy-red with a prominent dark-bluish eye, in ball-shaped trusses. Spreading growth habit with olive-green foliage. Flowers are impressive but the parentage suggests a lack of hardiness for much of its native New York state. (Mars × Princess Elizabeth). Stephens.

■ **WINNECONNET** Tall H5 M. Flowers fragrant, pale purplish pink with deeper edges and faint yellow markings in the throat, about 10 per truss. Leaves dark green. (unknown). Dexter.

■ **WISSAHICKON** Medium H5 M. Flower broadly funnel-shaped, purplish red with pink throat and faint brownish-green spots, in a ball-shaped truss of 16. Leaves elliptic, flat, semi-glossy, yellowish green, on a plant of open, leggy, sprawling habit. Sun tolerant. (unknown). Dexter.

■ **WITCH DOCTOR** Low H4 ML. Flowers cardinal-red, heavily spotted over the entire flower, with large calyx, in a loose truss of 6. Fairly compact with deep-green leaves. The flowers hang down and we did not think this was a great plant, though the colour is bright. ([Doncaster × Nereid] × Vulcan). Lem.

■ **WITCHERY** Tall H4 L. Flowers bright red in tall rounded trusses. Leaves covered with a persistent silvery tomentum, which remains all summer. A compact grower with good foliage, useful for its late flowering. Some susceptibility to mildew. *U.K.* (Mars × *facetum*). Henny.

WITCHERY

■ **WOJNAR'S PURPLE** Low H7 ML. Flower openly funnel-shaped, reddish purple with a dark-purple flare, in dome-shaped truss of 15–20. Leaves elliptic, flat, deep green, on a compact plant. The colour is on the reddish side of purple, and I thought it was rather average. It is tough and it buds-up young. *MS.* (unknown × unknown). Wojnar.

WOJNAR'S PURPLE

■ **WYANDANCH PINK** Tall H8 M. Flower openly funnel-shaped, purplish pink with deep-pink spotting on upper lobe, fading to paler, in domed trusses of 10–14. Leaves elliptic, convex, on an upright plant of vigorous, spreading, dense habit. A large-growing tough plant, which is rather slow to bud-up as a young plant. Sun tolerant. *PT, SE, SV, PB.* (unknown × unknown). Dexter.

■ **WYNTERSET WHITE (syn. SNOW, LEACH'S WHITE, KORDUS WHITE)** Medium H7 EM. Flower openly funnel-shaped, at first very pale purple with sparse bronze specks, fading to greenish white, in dome-shaped trusses of 20. Leaves elliptic, flat, dull green, on a dense, spreading plant. One of the best early season whites for severe climates, it has a chequered history as regards its name. *GP, PB.* (unknown). unknown.

WYNTERSET WHITE

■ **YEARS OF PEACE** Medium H6 M. Flowers strong purplish-pink with darker spotting, in a domed truss of 6–10. Leaves elliptic, dark green and glossy. (Mrs C.S. Sargent selfed) Mezitt.

■ **YELLOW PAGES** Semi-dwarf–Low H3 EM–M. Flower openly funnel-shaped, wavy edges, greenish yellow fading to light greenish-yellow, in dome-shaped trusses of 13–15. Leaves elliptic, cordate, flat, dull green. Spreading, dense growth habit. Appears to be a *R. lacteum* hybrid. *NI.* (unknown). Whitney/Briggs.

■ **YELLOW PETTICOATS** Medium H4 M. Flowers frilled, yellow, deeper at edges, in a ball-shaped truss of about 15. Leaves smallish, on a compact plant, not very free-flowering and subject to mildew. Chlorotic foliage. I don't think it is any improvement on 'Hotei'. (Hotei × [Pink Petticoats × *wardii*]). Lofthouse. **'FRILLED PETTICOATS'** a sister with pale green-yellow flowers. Over-hyped and not worth much attention.

■ **YELLOW ROLLS ROYCE** Low H3 ML. Flowers openly funnel-shaped, of heavy substance, brilliant greenish yellow on upper lobes, shading to pale greenish yellow on lower lobes, in ball-shaped trusses. Leaves dark green, glossy, on an upright plant. (Crest × Odee Wright). Clarke.

■ **YELLOW SAUCER** Low H4 M. Flower flat-faced, light-yellow at edges fading to brilliant-yellow in throat, with red spots, in ball-shaped trusses of up to 8. Leaves narrowly elliptic to elliptic, glossy, heavy textured. Plant habit upright and rather sparse. Not very attractive at Glendoick. (*aberconwayi* × [*yakushimanum* 'K Wada' × Fabia] F2). C. Smith.

■ **YVONNE g.** Tall H3 EM. Flowers large, widely funnel-shaped, white blushed pink, with a translucent quality, in flat trusses. **'OPALINE'** a clone with pale-rose flowers, deeper on outside. **'DAWN'** the latest to flower and considered the best of the grex. Large leaves on a vigorous, tree-forming plant. An early Rothschild cross, rather subject to mildew, and needing wind shelter. Takes a few years to start flowering. Normally grafted. (Aurora × *griffithianum*). Rothschild.

■ **ZELIA PLUMECOCQ** Low–Medium H3 M. Large, open, saucer-like flowers of yellow with a pink blush, in tall, handsome trusses. Medium-green leaves, new growth light-bronze. What a great name she has and she's the last hybrid in this section. (Rosy Morn × Crest). Rothschild. There is one called 'Zyxya'…

SMALLER-GROWING ELEPIDOTE HYBRIDS

The elepidote Rhododendrons are most people's idea of the 'typical' rhododendron, with relatively large leaves and large full trusses of flowers. This section contains three groups of small and slow-growing 'typical' large-flowered rhododendrons: Forrestii/Repens hybrids, Williamsianum hybrids, and 'Yak' hybrids. As well as being ideal garden plants, these are perhaps the best choice for growing in containers outdoors, as they are dense, compact, free-flowering and mostly easy to please.

FORRESTII/REPENS HYBRIDS

Semi-dwarf–Low H4–7. *Repens* hybrids are bred from the dwarf forms of red *R. forrestii* and have fine waxy red flowers. They make perfect plants for the smaller garden and are good subjects for containers, being very free-flowering, compact and tough. Very few are heat tolerant, so they are not generally successful in E. U.S.A.

■ **BADEN BADEN** Semi-dwarf H6 M. Flower campanulate, bright red, waxy-looking, in a truss of 3–6. Many clones were named from this cross, most of which are hard to tell apart. Leaves smooth, shiny, twisted and pointed. Habit is dense, compact, wider than tall. Some like the twisted leaves, others don't. CC. (Essex Scarlet × *forrestii* Repens Gp.). Hobbie. **'BAD EILSEN'** has flatter non-twisted leaves. **'MANNHEIM'** taller growing. **'ABENDROT'** a good clone, **'FRÜHLINGSZAUBER'** (syn. **'Spring Magic'**) low growing.

ABENDROT

BENGAL

■ **BENGAL** (*see* photo previous page) Semi-dwarf–Low H5 EM. Flowers scarlet-red in a loose truss. A low, compact spreading plant, popular with wholesaler growers and widely available in Pacific Northwest and Europe. (Essex Scarlet × *forrestii* Repens Gp.). Hobbie.

■ **BETTER HALF** Semi-dwarf–Low H4–5 EM. Waxy pale-red flowers in lax trusses. Dense habit with small pale-green leaves. Consistent autumn bloomer in some climates. Good in W. Norway. Not very exciting. (probably Elizabeth hybrid). Whitney/Sather.

BETTER HALF

■ **BUKETTA** Tall H5 M. Dark ruby-red flowers, faintly marked deeper, in trusses of 10–12. Small dark-green leaves on a compact plant. Not all that free-flowering but the colour is striking. (Spitfire × Frülingszauber). Hachmann.

BUKETTA

■ **BURLETTA (syn. BENJAMEN)** Semi-dwarf H4 E–EM. Flowers funnel-campanulate, unspotted strong-red, with a red calyx, in a loose truss of 5–7. Small leaves with a red underside. An improvement on 'Rosevallon', but not all that vigorous. (Buketta × Rosevallon). Hachmann. **'HACHMANN'S BINGO'**

BURLETTA

paler and a little lower growing. **'WHID BEE'** is not very hardy but has a fine impressive red truss and red leaf-underside.

■ **CARMEN** g. Dwarf H4 EM. Flower campanulate, waxy, dark red in loose trusses of 2–5. Several clones exist. Leaves small, elliptic, deep green, shiny with a rugose surface. Tight, slow-growing. Best in sun in the north but needs cool roots so may need shade in hotter areas. Not heat tolerant. One of the best dwarf red-hybrids for cooler climates. *GB.* (*sanguineum* ssp. *didymum* × *forrestii* Repens Gp.). Rothschild.

CARMEN

■ **CREEPING JENNY** Semi-dwarf H4 EM–M. Flowers bright red, fleshy, in loose trusses of 5–6. Leaves pale green on a plant of irregular habit, but usually with a mixture of prostrate and upright or arching branches. A sister of the well known 'Elizabeth' but more resistant to powdery mildew. *U.K.* (*forrestii* Repens Gp. × *griersonianum*). Puddle/Aberconway.

CREEPING JENNY

■ **DEBBIE** Semi-dwarf H4 EM. Flowers campanulate, blood-red in loose trusses. Dark green leaves on a rather untidy plant, not as compact as 'Carmen' but more heat tolerant. Very free-flowering. (May Day × Carmen). Henny.

■ **DJANGO** Semi-dwarf H6 M–ML. Flowers funnel-campanulate, frilly, strong-red, spotted darker, holding colour well, in a lax truss of 11–13. Leaves elliptic, matte with a few hairs on underside. Compact. Early growth. (Abendglut × *brachycarpum* Tigerstedtii Gp.). Hachmann.

■ **DOCTOR ERNST SCHÄLE** Semi-dwarf H5 EM. Flowers light-scarlet, campanulate, in loose trusses of about 6. Leaves small and flat on a low-growing compact plant. One of the hardiest and showiest Hobbie *R. forrestii* Repens hybrids. (Prometheus × *forrestii* Repens Gp.). Hobbie. Sister **'GERTRUDE SCHÄLE'** is almost identical.

DOCTOR ERNST SCHÄLE

■ **ELISABETH HOBBIE** Semi-dwarf–Low H4–5 EM. Flower frilly, scarlet-red with light dark-red spotting in lax trusses of 6–10. Dozens from this cross were named. They don't differ much. Leaves rounded, shiny, dark green. Dense, compact habit but may become leggy with age. One of the best lower-growing hybrids. A tough compact dome-shaped bush. Takes exposure. *AGM.* (Essex Scarlet × *forrestii* Repens Gp.). Hobbie. **'AKSEL OLSEN'** is less compact and rather untidy.

ELISABETH HOBBIE

ELIZABETH

■ **ELIZABETH** Semi-dwarf–Low H4 EM–M. Flower campanulate, bright red, 6–9 flowers per truss. Often flowers in autumn too in some climates. Leaves medium-green, slightly rugose. Forms a compact shrub, growing wider than high. This once very common and popular plant is so susceptible to mildew that it is years since I have seen a clean plant that was not sprayed. A shame, as it is very fine. *OL.* (*forrestii* Repens Gp. × *griersonianum*). Puddle/Aberconway.

■ **ELIZABETH RED FOLIAGE (syn. OSTBO'S RED ELIZABETH)** Semi-dwarf–Low H4 EM–M. Flower funnel-campanulate, vivid-red throughout, with strong-red speckles on all lobes, in lax trusses of 15. Leaves elliptic, pale green. Mainly grown for the showy reddish-brown new growth, which lasts most of the summer. The foliage can be a magnet for munching insects. A great foliage plant for moderate gardens. (unknown). Ostbo.

ELIZABETH RED FOLIAGE

■ **ELVIRA (syn. ELVIIRA)** Semi-dwarf H8 EM. Flowers cherry-red inside and out, a few darker-red spots, in domed trusses of 6–10. Leaves small and dark on a compact plant. Good for very severe climates, though foliage burns in strong sun. Worthless in mild climates, with thin flowers and poor habit: but this is probably the hardiest Repens cross. Not always easy to please. *S. Fin, Swe.* (*brachycarpum* Tigerstedtii Gp. × *forrestii*). Uosukainen/Arb. Mustila.

■ **FIREDANCE** Low H4 EM. Flowers scarlet-red in loose trusses. Compact with red buds. We grew this at Glendoick, but it was not exceptional and was rather slow to bud. Grown in Pacific Northwest and Australia. (unknown). Whitney/Greer.

■ **FLAMING GOLD** Low H4 EM–M. Flower campanulate, bright red, 6–9 per truss. A sport of the well known 'Elizabeth' with bold, golden variegation on the leaf margins. More compact and reported to be less susceptible to mildew than 'Elizabeth'. Variegation is most noticeable in winter and is almost invisible on the new growth. (sport of Elizabeth). unknown.

FLAMING GOLD

■ **FLORA'S BOY** Low H3–4 EM–M. Bright waxy red flowers on long pedicels, in rounded trusses of 4–5. Compact with attractive glossy leaves. This hybrid holds its flowers up better than most Forrestii hybrids. Its main drawback is that it comes into growth early, which is a problem where there are frosty springs. (*forrestii* Repens Gp. × Jean Marie de Montague). Markeeta.

■ **FRED ROBBINS** Semi-dwarf H3–4 M. Flower crimson-red, calyx red, in trusses of 7. Small leaves, underside with silvery indumentum. Compact, mounding growth habit. (Carmen × Choremia). Brandt.

GLENDOICK®™ RUBY

■ **GLENDOICK®™ RUBY** Semi-dwarf H4–5 EM–M. Flowers waxy deep red with a large calyx and no stamens, in a flat-topped truss of about 5. Dark-green leaves with indumentum on underside. Dark-red buds. Slow-growing with fine foliage. Ideal to grow with the bird hybrids. Needs cool roots and good drainage. (Lampion × Charmaine). Cox.

■ **GLUTKISSEN** Semi-dwarf H4–5 EM. Flowers waxy red, with a large calyx, 3–5 per truss. Leaves flat and glossy. Slow-growing and compact. Looks a bit like 'Scarlet Wonder'. (Ovation × *forrestii* Repens Gp.). Hachmann.

■ **HACHMANN'S CORINNA** Semi-dwarf H5 M. Flowers broadly funnel-shaped, vivid-red inside and out with a large dorsal blotch of dark red and red stamens, in lax ball-trusses of 9–10. One of the most striking Forrestii hybrids I have seen, but not one of the toughest or easiest to grow. Habit semi-prostrate. (Lampion × [Ruth Otte × Feuerschein]). Hachmann.

HACHMANN'S CORINNA

■ **HACHMANN'S ROSINA (syn. ROSINA)** Semi-dwarf H5 EM–M. Flowers tubular-campanulate, strong purplish red, centre a bit paler, in a lax-flat truss of 4–7. Very compact and slow-growing, with a creeping habit. New growth and petioles rose. The flowers open and fade out rather unattractively. Tough. (Roseum Elegans × *forrestii* Repens Gp.). Hachmann. **'FLORTEPPICH'** bright carmine-rose. Very hardy for a *R. forrestii* hybrid.

■ **HACHMANN'S TOPSI (syn. TOPSI)** Dwarf H4–5 EM. Flowers funnel-campanulate, deep purplish pink fading to pale pink, in a loose truss of 2–3(6). Small leaves on a very slow-growing, compact plant, taking ten to fifteen years to reach 15cm in height. The fading flowers are not very attractive. It might be a useful parent of hardy low reds. (*yakushimanum* K. Wada × *forrestii* Repens Gp.). Hachmann.

■ **LIONEL'S RED SHIELD** Semi-dwarf H6 EM–M. Flowers currant-red, in lax trusses of 2–6. Buds almost black-red. Leaves long, dull green on a spreading, floriferous plant. One of the hardiest *forrestii* hybrids and seems to be good in Nova Scotia where it was raised. In Scotland the foliage tends to be rather yellow and plant lacks vigour. (America × Carmen). Brueckner.

LIONEL'S RED SHIELD

■ **LITTLE GLENDOE** Semi-dwarf H3 VE–E. Flowers waxy, cardinal-red, in trusses of 7–9. A rounded, compact plant. Comes into flower in midwinter in its native New Zealand, the earliest of this type of hybrid. *NZ.* (*forrestii* Repens Gp. × *arboreum* ssp. *delavayi*). Jury/Johnstone.

■ **LORI EICHELSER** Dwarf H4–5 EM. Flower campanulate, cherry-red, in loose trusses of 3–4. Leaves broadly elliptic, shiny, rounded, jade-green. Very compact, low-growing habit, four times as wide as tall. Shy flowering in Scotland. (*forrestii* Repens Gp. × Bow Bells). Brandt. **'REVE ROSE'** Flowers deep purplish pink in loose trusses of 3–5.

■ **MOLLY ANN** Semi-dwarf–Low H5 EM. Flower funnel-shaped, wavy lobes, pinkish red with small spots on dorsal lobe, in a lax truss of 7. Leaves broadly elliptic, rounded, glossy, dark green, on a very compact and dense grower. Afternoon-sun protection may be needed in warm climates. Prone to powdery mildew. A fine foliage plant. (Elizabeth × unknown). Freimann.

MOLLY ANN

■ **OSTFRIESLAND** Semi-dwarf H4–5 M. Flower tubular-campanulate, scarlet-red in loose trusses of 6–8. Small leaves and dwarf compact habit. Not as hardy as most Hobbie *R. forrestii* hybrids. (Mme de Bruin × *forrestii* Repens Gp.). Hobbie.

PUMUCKL

■ **PUMUCKL** Semi-dwarf H4–5 EM. Flowers broadly funnel-shaped, strong-red inside and out, margins deep-red unspotted, in lax, rounded trusses of 6–9. Leaves ovate, wavy edge, glossy and dark green above. Slow-growing and compact. (Ruth Otte × Feuerschein). Hachmann. **'ROTKÄPPCHEN'** is a sister, vivid-red inside and out, unmarked. Very low-growing. Ht no more than 30cm.

■ **RANGOON** Semi-dwarf–Low H6 EM. Flower widely funnel-campanulate, moderate to dark red, unmarked, in dome-shaped truss of 7–8. Leaves elliptic, dark green, growing twice as wide as high. Not always very free-flowering, though it budded-up well at Glendoick. (Fanfare × Gertrude Schäle). Leach.

■ **RIPLET** Semi-dwarf H4–5 EM. Flowers open crimson and gradually fade to translucent cream, in lax trusses of 5–7. Leaves small on a stiff, compact, rounded plant. Stunning in flower with the contrast between the older and newer flowers. Unfortunately rather prone to mildew and the early flowers are often frosted. (*forrestii* Repens Gp. × Letty Edwards). Lem. **'ANNA'S RIPLET'** is a sister with non-fading pink flowers. We could not see any merit in it.

■ **ROBINETTE** Low H4 EM. Rose-coloured flowers with a large coloured-calyx, in a loose truss. Leaves small, dark and glossy, on a compact plant. (unknown). Aasland.

■ **ROSEVALLON** Low H3–4 E. Flowers small, bright red, waxy, in a loose truss of up to 5. Small leaves with a persistent purplish-red underside. Compact. Hard to root and rather too early flowering, but certainly a fine curiosity. Said to be derived from *R. neriiflorum* but I don't believe it. Crown Estate.

■ **ROYSTON RED** Semi-dwarf H4 E. Flowers waxy and red, in loose trusses. Oval leaves. Fairly compact. Takes a while to bud up. (*forrestii* Repens Gp. × *thomsonii*). Grieg.

■ **SCARLET WONDER** Semi-dwarf H6 M. Flower campanulate, wavy edged, waxy, bright cardinal-red,

SCARLET WONDER

in lax truss of 5–7. Leaves, ribbed, small, bright green. Compact habit, growing twice as wide as tall. Europe's most popular dwarf red-hybrid and one of the best dwarf reds ever raised. Insects seem to love to eat its leaves and it can be chlorotic. *AGM, MT, VI, Hol, Ger.* (Essex Scarlet × *forrestii* Repens Gp.). Hobbie. **'ANTJE'** very similar with good dark foliage.

■ **SMALL WONDER** Semi-dwarf H6 EM. Flower openly campanulate, waxy-looking, dark red with light centre and five basal nectaries, in ball-shaped trusses of 7. Leaves narrowly elliptic, medium-green with yellow-green stems. Very dense and slow growing. Good in New England, but not very heat-tolerant, so not very good further south. (Fanfare × Gertrude Schäle). Leach.

■ **STEPHANIE** Semi-dwarf–Low H4 M. Flowers funnel-campanulate, strong-red in a flat-to-lax truss of 9. Small light-green bullate elliptic leaves on a compact plant, which seems mainly to be grown in New Zealand. *NZ.* (*forrestii* Repens Gp. × unknown). Whitney/Sather.

■ **URSULA SIEMS** Semi-dwarf H4 E–EM. Flowers intense translucent-scarlet, of good substance, in a loose truss of 8–10. Leaves dark green, +/– oval. A good early dwarf in New Zealand. Too tender for Germany where it was raised. (Earl of Athlone × *forrestii* Repens Gp.). Hobbie. **'MOERHEIM'S SCARLET'** is a similar sister.

■ **WINE & ROSES [PBR]** Semi-dwarf H4 EM–M. Bright-pink flowers in rounded trusses. Leaves with red underside. Compact. Very free-flowering. New growth bronze. This is the best of the dwarf hybrids with red leaf-undersides and the only one so far with pink flowers. Likely to become an extremely popular commercial plant. Cox.

WINE & ROSES [PBR]

WILLIAMSIANUM HYBRIDS

Semi-dwarf–Low H3–6. These hybrids are bred from the species *R. williamsianum* (*see* page 99) which is characterized by its bell-shaped pink flowers and oval leaves, which are bronzy when young. Both these characters can be seen clearly in the hybrids. Most make fine plants for the smaller garden and are good in containers, being free-flowering, compact with fine foliage, and fairly tough. Few are hardy in E. North America.

■ **ADRASTIA** Semi-dwarf–Low H4 EM. Flowers bell-shaped deep pink in trusses of 1–4. Semi-dwarf, very bushy plant habit. Little grown. (*williamsianum × neriiflorum*). Aberconway/Puddle.

■ **ANNEGRET HANNSMAN** Low H5 EM–M. Flowers flat saucer-shaped, rosy-red in bud, opening inside light purplish pink, shading to nearly-white centre; outside bright purplish pink with brownish-green marking in a truss of 7–15. Oval leaves on a compact plant. Tough. Leaves can be a bit

distorted or yellowish. One of the best new *R. williamsianum* hybrids we have seen. (Hachmann's Polaris × Wega g.). Genzel.

ANNEGRET HANNSMAN

■ **APRIL GLOW** Semi-dwarf H5 EM. Flower campanulate, rose-pink with reddish markings and spots, in flat-topped trusses of 7–10. Leaves dark green, ovate, with reddish-brown new growth. A more upright, less dense habit than most *R. williamsianum* hybrids. (*williamsianum* × Wilgen's Ruby). Van Wilgen.

■ **ARTHUR J. IVENS** Semi-dwarf–Low H4–5 ML. Flowers campanulate, rosy pink in a lax truss of 5. Leaves ovate, matte green with red stems, new growth copper-coloured. Shy-flowering and doubtful if worth growing nowadays. (*williamsianum × fortunei* ssp. *discolor* Houlstonii Gp.). Ivens. **'OLDENBURG'** rose, bell-shaped flowers, fading to cream, two weeks later than most other *R. williamsianum* hybrids. Very good in Bremen, Germany.

OLDENBURG

■ **AUGUST LAMKEN** Semi-dwarf–Low H4–5 EM. Flowers deep rose-pink, frilly, campanulate, in a loose truss. Leaves heart-shaped, slightly twisted and dark green. Quite open-growing. Flowers and foliage have a heavy texture and it is one of the hardier *R. williamsianum* hybrids. *Den, Ger.* (Dr. V. H. Rutgers × *williamsianum*). Hobbie.

AUGUST LAMKEN

■ **BOW BELLS** Semi-dwarf–Low H4–5 M. Flower campanulate, deep pink, deeper on reverse, aging to pale pink, in lax trusses of 4–7. Leaves elliptic, glossy and stiff, new growth bronze-coloured. A compact, mounding and fairly dense plant. Not very sun-tolerant but tends to be leggy in shade. Not really one of the best *R. williamsianum* hybrids these days. *AGM, CD, MT.* (Corona × *williamsianum*). Rothschild.

BOW BELLS

■ **BRICKDUST** Semi-dwarf–Low H4–5 M. Flowers rose, ruffled, shaded reddish, 6–8 per loose truss. Leaves oval, on a vigorous but compact plant with bronze young growth. (*williamsianum* × Dido). Henny.

■ **BROCADE** Semi-dwarf–Low H4–5 EM–M. Flowers vivid-carmine in bud, open to frilly peach-pink bells, about 6 per lax truss. Leaves deep green, oval, on stiff branches. One of the showiest *R. williamsianum* hybrids in flower but rather slow to bud up as a young plant, so not often grown commercially. (*williamsianum* hybrid). Rothschild.

■ **CARLENE** Semi-dwarf–Low H3 M. Flowers creamy with pink centres, reverse striped with pink, in a loose truss of 6–8. Leaves elliptic, new growth bronze, yellow petiole, on a compact plant. Too early into growth for cold climates, but the flower is attractive. (Lem's Goal × *williamsianum*). Lem.

■ **CLAUDIUS** Semi-dwarf–Low H5 M–ML. Flowers open funnel-shaped, inside moderate purplish pink, edges strong purplish pink, outside deep purplish pink, with a reddish flare, in trusses of 10–11. Leaves ovate, matte, mid-green. (Scintillation × Karin). Hachmann. **'RODRIGO'** Frilly pinkish-purple flowers with darker reddish-purple spotting in rounded trusses.

■ **COWSLIP g.** Semi-dwarf–Low H4 M. Flowers pale primrose-yellow, campanulate, with pink markings, in a loose truss of about 5. Leaves rounded on a mounding plant. Rather early into growth. Not all that free-flowering as a young plant. There appear to be several clones around. (*williamsianum* × *wardii*). Puddle/Aberconway. **'OXSLIP'** from the same cross is pale pink fading to white.

■ **CREAMY CHIFFON** Semi-dwarf–Low H4 EM. Flower semi-double light-yellow, fading to cream with some brownish orange spots in throat and some pinkish shading, in rather open trusses of 7. Leaves elliptic, glossy on a busy, dense upright grower. Requires sharp drainage. The flowers last for a long time and are attractive, but the plant has a bit of a death wish and is inclined to die off for no apparent reason. (unknown × unknown). Whitney.

■ **DORMOUSE g.** Semi-dwarf–Low H4 EM. Flower campanulate, delicate-pink, deeper edges, held in loose clusters. Leaves oval, copper-coloured when new. A neat, compact, dome-shaped bush. Relatively late into growth, so good for frosty gardens. Its only drawback is that it takes a few years to bud up. (Dawn's Delight × *williamsianum*). Rothschild.

CREAMY CHIFFON

■ **ELIZABETH LOCKHART** Semi-dwarf H4 EM. Flowers deep reddish purple in loose trusses of 3–5. Leaves are a deep reddish-purple colour but they revert readily unless planted in deep shade. Most reports from hot and sunny regions indicate that it is impossible to stop it turning green. Our original shaded plant at Glendoick is still red. (sport of Hummingbird). Lockhart.

ELIZABETH LOCKHART

■ **EVER RED [PBR]** Semi-dwarf H4 EM–M. Dark red-purple flowers in lax trusses of 3 (seldom produced). Leaves dark reddish purple on both upper and lower surface, the colour of *Cotinus* 'Royal Purple'. Very slow-growing with dense compact habit. Likely to become widely grown. (EU plant variety rights applied for; propagation for sale without a licence is illegal.) Cox.

EVER RED [PBR]

■ **GARTENDIREKTOR GLOCKER** Low H5 M. Flowers deep reddish-rose, edges darker, campanulate, in a loose truss of 8–12. Foliage dense, stiff, dark and glossy, ends of the leaves curve downwards, on a fairly compact bush. Not the best leaf-retention of this group of hybrids and takes a while to flower freely. Foliage is sun tolerant. (Doncaster × *williamsianum*). Hobbie. **'DR SCHLAPPER'** dark rose, lighter inside.

GARTENDIREKTOR GLOCKER

■ **GARTENDIREKTOR RIEGER** Semi-dwarf–Low H5 M. Flower saucer-shaped, cream tinged pink with red dorsal spotting, in open-topped trusses of 4–9. Leaves rounded, slightly recurved, with yellow-green petioles. Upright habit. Likes a fair amount of sun for good blooming but optimal foliage requires filtered sun. Being sold as 'Dr Rieger' in the U.K. by some nurseries who can't pronounce the name. *AGM, VI.* (Adriaan Koster × *williamsianum*). Hobbie. **'GRUGAPERLE'** pale pink-white. **'GUSTAV LÜTTGE'** white tinged pale pinkish lilac.

GARTENDIREKTOR RIEGER

■ **HACHMANN'S ANDREA (syn. ANDREA)** Semi-dwarf H5 EM–M. Flowers campanulate, pale-pink inside, deeper-pink outside, in loose trusses. Leaves ovate, dark green on a compact plant. (*williamsianum* × Fantastica). Hachmann.

■ **HACHMANN'S GRISELDA (syn. GRISELDA)** Semi-dwarf–Low H5 EM–M. Flowers funnel-campanulate, pale purplish pink, with some red spotting, in a loose truss of 8–10. Leaves dark green, convex, orbicular to ovate. Like a smaller version of 'Gartendirektor Rieger' (Memoir × *williamsianum*). Hachmann.

■ **HACHMANN'S KONTIKI (syn. KONTIKI)** Semi-dwarf–Low H5 EM–M. Flowers star-shaped, pale-pink overlaid with deep-pink/purplish-pink on veins, in lax trusses of 7–8. Deep-green ovate leaves, convex. This is a real curiosity with the long narrow strap-like petals. It may have breeding potential for more hybrids of this type. (Ovation × *williamsianum*). Hachmann.

■ **HUMMING BIRD g.** Semi-dwarf–Low H4 EM–M. Flowers rose-red of good substance, in campanulate, lax trusses of 4–5. There are lots of clones, some with better flowers than others. Plant compact, dense; leaves round, dark green, leathery. Slow-growing. Foliage can burn in hot sun. The Exbury-raised plants seem to be the best. (*haematodes* × *williamsianum*). Rothschild, Aberconway.

HUMMING BIRD g.

■ **IRMELIES** Semi-dwarf–Low H6 M. Roseine-purple buds, open deep purplish pink, funnel-campanulate flowers, spotted strong purplish red on dorsal lobe, in trusses of 10–11. Dark, elliptic-ovate foliage, creamy-white hairs on underside. Very floriferous. One of the hardiest Hachmann *williamsianum* hybrids. (Oudijk's Sensation × Marinus Koster). Hachmann.

■ **JACKWILL** Semi-dwarf–Low H5 EM. Flowers rose-pink fading to paler, with faint-red markings, in loose trusses. Leaves oval/heart-shaped. An early flowering low-growing hybrid. (Jacksonii × *williamsianum*). Hobbie.

■ **JOCK g.** Low H4–5 EM. Flowers bright rose-pink in a small loose truss. Leaves dark on a dense plant in sun, but leggy in shade. In many old collections in the U.K. Heat and sun tolerant. Prone to mildew. (*williamsianum* × *griersonianum*). Maxwell.

KARIN

■ **KARIN** Semi-dwarf–Low H6 EM–M. Flower ruffled, bright pink, in trusses of 8–9. Leaves oval-shaped, pale green. Compact. Flowers are showy but it suffers from a black leaf-spot, which is harmless but unsightly. Sister 'Linda' is a better bet. (Britannia × *williamsianum*). Boskoop Exp. Station. **'WILLBRIT'** rather harsh deep-pink flowers in lax trusses. **'CANBERRA'** taller and hardier. **'ERICH BEEKEN'** white flushed lilac-rose. **'KARL FOERSTER'** pale rose, darker outside.

■ **KIMBERLY** Semi-dwarf–Low H5 EM. Flower slightly fragrant, light Persian-rose fading to white, in a loose truss. Leaves oval, with purple petioles. Compact habit. Grows rather early, so young leaves are prone to frost damage in some climates. *SO*. (*williamsianum* × *fortunei*). Greer. **'PSYCHE'** is the same cross. **'HELEN CHILD'** pink with red spotting in lax truss.

■ **KIMBETH** Semi-dwarf–Low H4–5 EM. Flower funnel-shaped, brightest deep-pink, unmarked, in flat trusses of 3–5. Leaves elliptic to oblong, pale green, new growth bronze. Plant dense, rounded, broader than tall. The flowers are really bright, but the foliage can be yellowish and it suffers from leaf-tip burn. At its best this is excellent. Purple buds in winter. (Kimberly × Elizabeth). Greer.

KIMBETH

LINDA

■ **LINDA** Low H6 M. Flower openly campanulate, frilly edged, rose-pink, in open, upright truss of 7–8. Leaves ovate, slightly cordate, greenish yellow. Dense, rounded habit. One of the best *R. williamsianum* hybrids for hardiness and reliability. Light-green egg-shaped leaves on a dense compact plant. *U.K.* (Britannia × *williamsianum*). Boskoop Exp. Station.

■ **LISSABON** Semi-dwarf–Low H5 M. Flower moderate-red with vivid-red margins, in lax trusses of 8. Leaves bronze-coloured when new. Compact habit. (Nova Zembla × *williamsianum*). Von Martin/Bruns.

■ **MAUREEN** Semi-dwarf–Low H4 E. Buds strong purplish red, opening to campanulate flowers of pale purplish pink with a yellow cast at the base, in a loose truss. Leaves oval. (*williamsianum* × Lem's Goal). Lem.

MINAS GRAND PRÉ

■ **MINAS GRAND PRÉ (syn. GRAND PRÉ)** Semi-dwarf H5–6 ML. Flower campanulate, pale purplish pink, unmarked, in lax trusses of 10. Leaves small, elliptic, new growth copper-coloured, on a very dense, compact grower. One of the toughest *R. williamsianum* hybrids. Probably not worth growing where *R. williamsianum* itself is hardy. *AT, PB.* (Catawbiense Compactum × *williamsianum*). Swain. **'VATER BÖHLJE'** same cross, rosy pink. Less hardy.

VATER BÖHLJE

■ **MISTY MOONLIGHT** Low H4–5 EM. Flowers pale orchid-pink, campanulate, fragrant, in loose trusses. Foliage glossy-green with reddish-purple petioles, deeply coloured stems and buds, on a vigorous plant, compact with age. (Kimberly selfed). Greer.

■ **MOERHEIM'S PINK** Low H5 M. Flowers very pale pink, deeper near edges, widely funnel-shaped, in trusses of 8. Leaves dull, dark green. Plant compact, vigorous, broader than tall. Habit not as good as the similar 'Osmar'. (*williamsianum* × Genoveva). Hobbie. **'GLOCKENSPIEL'** pale-pink flowers flushed and lined deeper-pink.

■ **MOONSTONE g.** Semi-dwarf–Low H4–5 EM. Flower campanulate, pink, creamy yellow or cream flushed pink, in loose trusses of 3–5. Leaves ovate, smooth, flat, medium-green. Compact habit. Rather early into growth and not very free-flowering as a young plant. *Vl.* (*campylocarpum* × *williamsianum*). Williams. **'IVORY BELLS'** creamy ivory in loose trusses.

■ **NOSUTCHIANUM** Semi-dwarf–Low H4–5 M. Small Kalmia-like light-pink rounded flowers in small trusses. Small twisty leaves. An extremely ugly curiosity. Don't bother growing it though, it's a real dog. It needs to be grafted. We also have Kalmia × *R. maximum*, not much better. (Said to be *R. williamsianum* × *Kalmia latifolia*). Lem.

■ **OLYMPIC LADY g.** Low H4–5 EM. Flower campanulate, opening pale pink, fading to white, in lax trusses of 4–8. Leaves rounded, with red petioles on plant growing wider than tall, of mounding habit. A mature plant is very fine but we found it shy flowering when young and too early into growth. *EK.* (Loderi King George × *williamsianum*). Ostbo/Clark. **'LOLLIPOP LACE'** rich-pink with stripes on the outside lobes paler, frilled, in trusses of 3. From New Zealand.

■ **OSMAR** Semi-dwarf–Low H5 M. Flowers campanulate, light lilac-pink, in loose trusses of 4–8. Small oval leaves, bronze when young on a compact plant. Very free-flowering, tough, late into growth and one of the best *williamsianum* hybrids for Scotland. *AGM, Hol, Sco.* (*williamsianum* × unknown). Van Gelderen.

OSMAR

■ **OUDIJK'S SENSATION** Low H5 EM–M. Flower bright-rose with darker-pink margins and crimson spots, in loose trusses of 5–7. Leaves dark green, cordate, sharply pointed with dark-red petioles. Rather a harsh colour, but tough and easy. *Ger, Hol, Sco.* (Essex Scarlet × *williamsianum*). Hobbie.

PINK PEBBLE

■ **PINK PEBBLE** Semi-dwarf–Low H4 EM. Flowers rosy pink, in loose trusses of 4–5. A dense, compact grower, which buds-up young and comes into growth late. *AGM.* (*callimorphum* × *williamsianum*). Harrison.

■ **ROSE POINT** Semi-dwarf–Low H4 EM. Flower openly funnel-shaped, neyron-rose with red spots, deeper at edges and in stripes, in lax trusses of about 7. Leaves broadly elliptic, slightly convex near edges, light green, with reddish-purple petioles, on a mounding plant which grows wider than tall. (Dido × *williamsianum*). Lem/Fisher & Pierce.

■ **ROTHENBURG** Low H6 EM. Flowers funnel-shaped, light creamy yellow with red spotting, in a loose truss of 5–9. Leaves oval, larger than most *williamsianum* hybrids on a vigorous, upright plant. Rather easily frosted, with a poor root system and prone to mildew. 'Gartendirektor Reiger' is a better alternative. (Diane × *williamsianum*). Bruns. **'RASTEDER SCHLOßPERLE'** cream with red spotting.

■ **ROYAL PINK** Semi-dwarf–Low H6 M. Flowers openly funnel-shaped, pale fuchsine-pink inside, exterior darker-rose, in rounded trusses of 5–6. Leaves broadly elliptic, on a rounded, vigorous, compact plant. The truss holds itself up better than most *R. williamsianum* hybrids. (Homer × *williamsianum*). Hobbie, LeFeber.

■ **SEA-TAC** Low H3 M. Flowers cardinal-red, in ball trusses of 7. Leaves oval, on a rounded compact plant. Named after Seattle airport. (Moser's Maroon × *williamsianum*). Larson.

■ **SNOW CAP** Low–Medium H4 M. Shell-pink buds opening to pure-white flowers without markings, in trusses of 7. Compact and dense. Free flowering. The seed parent was probably not pure *R. souliei*. (*souliei* × Olympic Lady). Whitney.

■ **STADT ESSEN** Low H5 M. Flowers clear-pink, paling towards the centre, in full flat-topped truss of 5–8. Oval leaves, bronzy when young. Very fine flowers in a perfectly formed truss, one of the best of the many *R. williamsianum* hybrids. It would be far more popular were it better on its own roots, but it tends to break off at ground level if not grafted. (*williamsianum* × Louis Pasteur). Hobbie.

STADT ESSEN

■ **TEMPLE BELLE g** Low H4–5 EM. Flowers campanulate, rose-pink, in small loose trusses of 3–5. Oval-rounded leaves. Plant neat, rounded, compact. Takes a few years to start flowering. There does not appear to be a selected award clone of this hybrid, so there may well be several clones in commerce. (*orbiculare* × *williamsianum*). R.B.G. Kew. American versions are: **'MISSION BELLS'** pink, scented and **'JAMES BARTO'** harsh purple-pink. Both have elongated leaves, which indicates that the *R. orbiculare* used was a hybrid.

■ **TIBET** Semi-dwarf–Low H4–5 M. Flowers small, palest pink, fade quickly to white, in a lax truss of 6–8. Leaves elliptic, deep-green, with red petioles, on a compact free-flowering plant. One of the least hardy Hobbie *R. williamsianum* hybrids. *AGM* (Bismark × *williamsianum*). Hobbie.

TIBET

■ **TROMBA** Semi-dwarf–Low H5 M. Flowers open funnel-campanulate, strong-red with deep-red edges, outside strong-red, in domed trusses of 6–8. Leaves ovate, bronzed when young. One of the reddest *R. williamsianum* hybrids but suffered from leaf spot and a lack of vigour at Glendoick. (Gartendirektor Glocker × Buketta). Hachmann.

TROMBA

■ **VERYAN BAY** Low H4 EM–M. Pale-pink campanulate flowers in a loose truss of about 4. Compact habit. Shy flowering and devoid of any merit I can see. Grow the wonderful parents and burn this plant. (*pseudochrysanthum × williamsianum*). Williams.

■ **VINEWOOD** Semi-dwarf–Low H6 M. Flowers purplish pink, reverse deep purplish-pink, in loose trusses of 6. Leaves small, ovate, on a fairly compact plant. (Sham's Ruby × *williamsianum*). Forster.

■ **VULCAN'S BELLS** Semi-dwarf–Low H4–5 M. Flowers rose-red, campanulate, in loose trusses of 6–8. Leaves oval, with pointed tips, new growth pinkish bronze, on a plant growing wider than tall. (Vulcan's Flame × *williamsianum*). Lancaster.

■ **WHISPERINGROSE** Semi-dwarf–Low H4 EM. Flower campanulate, dark-red in bud, opening cherry-red/deep pink, in loose trusses of 6. Leaves oblong-orbicular, slightly down-curved edges, semi-glossy, dark yellowish green, new growth copper-coloured, petioles dark red. Not very free-flowering in Scotland. (*williamsianum × Elizabeth*). Greer.

WHISPERINGROSE

■ **WHITE PIPPEN (syn. WHITE MOONSTONE)** Semi-dwarf H4 M. Flowers light greenish white, campanulate, in loose trusses of 7. Leaves rounded-elliptic. Early into growth and not very free-flowering when young. (*williamsianum × Olympic Lady*). Larson.

WINSOME

■ **WINSOME** Low H4 EM. Flower deep purplish pink, in a loose pendent truss of 4–6. Said to be a grex, but I've only ever seen a single clone. Small, pointed dark-green leaves, bronzy when young, and red stems, on a dense, compact plant. A good tidy plant for mild gardens. Somewhat prone to mildew. Easy to root and buds-up young. Needs light shade in Pacific Northwest. *AGM*. (Humming Bird × *griersonianum*). Puddle/Aberconway.

■ **WINTER SNOW** Low H4–5 M. Flowers white with red spotting, in a tight, upright truss. Small deep-green oval leaves. (Kimberly × *aberconwayi*). Greer.

■ **WISP** Low H3–4 E. Flower openly campanulate, purplish pink, lighter towards centre with purplish-red spots on all lobes, in flat trusses of 5–7. Leaves ovate, deep-green, on a rounded, well-branched plant. Early into growth, so not for cold gardens. (*williamsianum × irroratum* 'Spatter Paint'). Landregan.

'YAK' HYBRIDS

Ht 1–2m in ten to fifteen years H4–7/8. Raised from the compact white-flowered Japanese species *R. yakushimanum* (syn. *R. degronianum* ssp. *yakushimanum*), the 'yak' hybrids in many different colours are now very popular. 'Yak' hybrids have rounded, usually full trusses, usually very freely produced. Most have fading flowers, though some F2 hybrids hold their colour better. They form neat dome-shaped, slow-growing plants, ideal for the smaller garden or container, reaching 1–1.2m or so in ten years. Many have fine foliage with indumentum on the leaves, especially on the young growth. Most flower in May and early June, so avoiding spring frosts. Most are hardy to at least H4–5 and some are very tough. Everyone and his dog has made a 'yak' hybrid or two, me included: there are far too many of them and it should be made illegal to name any more with pink, fading flowers, though I'm bound to be ignored on this one...

■ **AGATEEN** Semi-dwarf–Low H6 M–ML. Flowers deep-pink with greenish-yellow blotch, reverse vivid purplish red, fading to paler, in ball-to-dome-shaped trusses of 15. Leaves yellow-green with plastered brown indumentum on lower surface. Rounded, well-branched plant. (*yakushimanum* × Henriette Sargent). Arsen.

■ **ALEC G. HOLMES** Medium H4–5 EM. Flowers light-lavender flushed pink, with red blotch, in a truss of 15. Free-flowering and compact. Leaves with thin layer of orange indumentum. New growth silver. (*yakushimanum × elliottii*). Holmes. **'LADY IN RED'** Flowers bright red, fading to pink, with black speckles.

■ **ALLEN'S SURPRISE** Low H4 M–ML. Flowers pale phlox-pink with a deeper throat, spotted brown. Dark leaves, underside with felted indumentum, on a compact, rounded plant. Popular in New Zealand. (*yakushimanum* × unknown). Harris.

■ **ALOHA** Semi-dwarf–Low H5 EM. Flower deep-pink fading to pale purplish-pink, in dome-shaped truss of about 19. Leaves elliptic, bullate, olive-green with brown indumentum on under surface. New growth with white indumentum. Dense, rounded habit. Not particularly good. *MT, SC*. (Vulcan × *yakushimanum* Exbury). Phetteplace/Briggs.

■ **AMITY** Semi-dwarf–Low H4–5 M. Flower rose-pink fading to darker-pink with red spotting, with a prominent calyx, in trusses to 15. Leaves dark green with heavy indumentum and silver tomentum when new. Dense, compact habit. ([Grosclaude × Britannia] × *yakushimanum* K. Wada). Elliott.

■ **ANITA GEHNRICH** Semi-dwarf H6 M. Flowers deep-pink fading to pale purplish-pink in throat with red dorsal spotting in a dome-shaped truss of 14. Leaves elliptic, flat, very dark green, glossy with slight brown indumentum on mature leaves, on a plant of spreading, dense growth habit. Differs from the similar 'Solidarity' in the smaller leaves, lower growth-habit, darker flower-colour. *PB, NY*. (The Hon. Jean Marie de Montague × *yakushimanum*). Waldman.

■ **ANN LINDSAY** Low H5 ML. Flowers strong red fading to pink with centres and throat white, unmarked, in trusses of 14–17. Foliage dark green, on an upright plant. Petioles reddish brown. Foliage tends to be yellowish. Flowers are very striking. (Blinklight × [Mars × *yakushimanum*]). Hachmann. **'MANUELA'** a sister with flowers strong mallow-purple, paling in throat, with vivid magenta midveins.

■ **ANNA H. HALL** Semi-dwarf–Low H8 M. Flower pure white, opening from pink buds, in a truss of about 15. Leaves thin, convex, deep-green with thin brown indumentum. Dense, compact growth habit. Heat and sun tolerant. Poor in Scotland and probably not worth growing in mild climates. *N.E. U.S.A., S. Fin.* (*catawbiense* var. *album* × *yakushimanum* K. Wada). Leach. **'GREAT LAKES'** and **'SPRING FROLIC'** are similar sister seedlings.

ANNA H. HALL

■ **ANNIKA** Low H5 M–ML. Flowers purplish pink, with a dark-red blotch, fading to off-white, in rounded trusses of 12–14. Leaves elliptic to ovate, glossy, dark green, with thin indumentum on lower surface. (Sapporo × *yakushimanum* K. Wada). Hachmann.

■ **ANUSCHKA** Semi-dwarf–Low H5 ML. Flower deep reddish-pink fading to lighter-pink in centre, fading to pinkish white, in trusses of 12–16. Leaves pointed, recurved, dark green, Grows wider than tall. Good in sun or shade. *PB, NY, Ger.* (Sammetglut × *yakushimanum* K. Wada). Hachmann. Sister seedling **'ANILIN'** deep purplish pink shaded vivid purplish red inside and out, with white throat. Recurved leaves.

■ **APOLLONIA** Low H5 M–ML. Flowers broadly open funnel-shaped, white, tinged rose at first, with a large deep purplish-red blotch, in a compact, rounded truss of 13–16. Dark green leaves with a dense pale-brown, woolly indumentum on the under-surface. Tall and vigorous for a 'yak' hybrid. (Edelweiß × Perlina). Hachmann. **'SEIDENGLANZ'** white flowers. Very fine foliage.

■ **ARABELLA** Low H5 M–ML. Flowers frilly, pink, with a darker centre and dark-pink fringe, fading to off-white, in a rounded truss. Compact grower, leaves with beige indumentum on the underside. Probably the best of a ridiculously large number of sister seedlings named from this cross. (*yakushimanum* × Kluis Sensation). Sagemuller/Schmalsheidt.

■ **ASTRID [PBR]** Low H6 ML. Flowers strong-red, centre of lobes and throat shading to light red and fading to near-white, with deep-red markings on a lighter ground, in trusses of 19–21. Leaves elliptic, dark green, on a dense plant. Flowers are long-lasting and weather resistant. Buds-up young. Flowers hold colour well. (Fantastica × Hachmann's Feuerschein). Hachmann.

■ **AVIVA ANN** Semi-dwarf–Low H6 ML. Flowers pale purplish-pink shading to strong purplish-pink at margins, reverse strong purplish-pink, in a ball-shaped truss of 15–19. Leaves elliptic, dark green above, with thin indumentum on lower surface. Spreading, dense habit. (*yakushimanum* × Mars). unknown/Brooks.

■ **BAD ZWISCHENAHN** Medium H5 M. Rose-pink frilled flowers with red markings, in a rounded truss of 8–18. Glossy-green leaves. Nothing particular to recommend it as far as I could see. ([Doncaster × *yakushimanum*] × Catherine van Tol). Bruns.

■ **BAMBI** Semi-dwarf–Low H3 M. Red buds open to pastel-coral-pink flowers fading out to cream, 7–9 per truss. Compact, leaves with indumentum on underside, silvery all summer on upper surface. For some reason this was demolished by deer at Glendoick… cannibals. (*yakushimanum* × Fabia Tangerine). Waterer, Sons and Crisp. Sisters **'SHRIMP GIRL'**, **'MOLLY MILLER'**, **'DUSTY MILLER'** all-pink fading to off-white in open trusses. All are muddy in flower and to my taste, horrible.

■ **BARBARELLA** Low H5 M. Flowers light-yellow to cream, strongly edged reddish pink, in loose trusses of 6–8. Small, glossy, dark, narrow leaves on a compact, slow-growing plant. Foliage could be better but flowers are excellent. A bit too slow-growing to make a good commercial plant. (Lampion × [*viscidifolium* × *wardii*]). Hachmann.

■ **BARMSTEDT** Semi-dwarf–Low H5 ML. Flower deep purplish-pink, fading paler, light centres, in conical trusses of 15–18. Leaves recurved, dark green, with silvery young growth. Compact and spreading habit. The best of Hachmann's hybrids from this cross. Good in N.E. U.S.A. *PB, PV, NY.* (Sammetglut × *yakushimanum* K. Wada). Hachmann.

BARBARELLA

■ **BASHFUL** Semi-dwarf–Low H4–5 M. Flower deep rose-pink with a reddish-brown dorsal blotch, ages to off-white, in a truss of about 10. Narrowish leaves on a fairly upright grower. New growth silvery. Heavy blooming when planted in full sun. *AGM.* (*yakushimanum* × Doncaster). Waterer, Sons and Crisp. **'PINK CHERUB'** is a similar sister seedling with paler flowers. **'HELIGOLAND'** rose-pink with yellow markings.

■ **BELVA'S JOY** Semi-dwarf–Low H4 EM. Flower campanulate, red, non-fading, in flat trusses of 15–20. Leaves oblanceolate, glossy, dark-green with white, aging to tan, felt-like indumentum. Upright but dense habit. Surprisingly hardy for the parentage and may rate H5. Good flowers and foliage, and flowers hold their colour well for a red 'yak'. (Noyo Brave × Elizabeth). C. Smith/Sanders. **'FAITH HENTY'** loose trusses of rich red.

■ **BERG'S QUEEN BEE (syn. QUEEN BEE)** Low H4 EM. Flowers palest pink, fading to white, in ball-shaped trusses of 9–12. Leaves with thick cinnamon indumentum on the leaf underside. New growth silvery, persisting all summer. Hard to root. Needs cool roots and good drainage. Best in shade in North America. (*yakushimanum* × *tsariense*). Berg.

■ **BETTY SEARS** Low H5 M–ML. Flowers frilled, pink, spotted red, with some petalloid stamens, in rounded trusses. Compact. Several sisters are also being grown in the Pacific Northwest. (*yakushimanum* × Corona). Whitney/Sather.

■ **BLANKANESE** Low H6 M–ML. Flowers rose in bud, opening to soft rose-pink, fading to pure-white throughout with strong yellow-green spotting, in trusses of 14–17. Leaves ovate, dark matte-green above with brownish indumentum below. This should be a good performer in severe climates, given the parentage. (Scintillation × *yakushimanum* K. Wada). Hachmann.

■ **BLURETTIA** Low H6 M–ML. Flowers with rich-purple wavy margins and pale centres in a balled truss of 11–14. Light-green leaves with a thin layer of indumentum on the lower surface. One of the deepest of the purple 'yak' hybrids but not a very attractive colour and I can't really understand why it is so widely grown, as it looks like *R. ponticum.* (Blue Peter × *yakushimanum* K. Wada). Hachmann. **'BOHLKEN'S LUPINENBERG'** violet-purple with a white and green-yellow flare. One of the best 'yaks' of this colour, from what I've seen. **'YAKU BLUE'** is another impressive German, purple 'yak'.

■ **BOB BOVEE** Semi-dwarf H4–5 EM. Flowers light greenish-yellow with light-red in the throat, in ball-shaped trusses of 10–12. Leaves narrowly obovate

to elliptic, glossy, dark green, with red petioles. Rounded, well-branched plant. This looked very good in Pennsylvania and at Hachmann's nursery in N. Germany. Mildew prone in U.K. (*yakushimanum* K. Wada × *wardii*). Bovee. **'WISHMOOR'** pale pink fading to pale yellow.

■ **BRETONNE** Low H6 M. Flower pinkish red in bud, opening light lavender-pink, in ball-shaped trusses of 18–20. Leaves lanceolate, glossy, deep bluish green. Compact and dense with a mounding habit. Similar to 'Caroline Allbrook'. Sun or part-shade. (*yakushimanum* × Purple Lace). Colombel.

■ **BRIDAL BOQUET** Semi-dwarf–Low H4 M. Flowers some hose-in-hose and some with petaloid stamens, pink in bud, opening inside pale yellow, outside light greenish-yellow, in a ball truss of 6–10. Leaves without indumentum on a compact plant. (unknown *yakushimanum* hybrid). Whitney/Sather.

■ **BRUNS LEUCHTFEUER (syn. LEUCHTFEUER)** Low H5 M. Flowers open funnel-shaped, dark red in bud, opening bright red, with very faint brownish markings in dorsal lobe, in compact rounded trusses of 10–15. Leaves with decurved margins. Winter flower buds a striking red-brown. Shrub compact. (*Frülingszauber* × [*yakushimanum* × Doncaster]). Bruns.

■ **CANADIAN SUNSET** Semi-dwarf–Low H4–5 M. Red buds opening to salmon flowers, fading to creamy-yellow centres, in a rounded truss. Narrow recurved leaves. Red winter buds. Fairly compact. Very average when we grew it. *CN.* (*yakushimanum* × Gipsy King). Henny/Linington.

■ **CAROLINE ALLBROOK** Semi-dwarf–Low H5 M–ML. Flower frilly edged, lavender with paler centre, aging to very pale lavender, in trusses of 16–20. Leaves, elliptic, recurved edges, dark-green with no indumentum. Compact habit. Better than 'Hoppy' and 'Sleepy' with a more compact habit. *AGM.* (*yakushimanum* × Purple Splendour). Hydon Nursery. A sister **'ERNEST INMAN'** with slightly darker flowers was also named. **'WHITE FLARE'** white flowers blotched yellow.

CAROLINE ALLBROOK

■ **CASSIE** Low H4 EM. Magenta buds open to yellowish white with two or three moderate-red flares in the dorsal throat and a slight tinge of light purplish-pink outside, in balled trusses of 17. Leaves dark olive-green with a felted light-greyish/light-yellow indumentum. Rather early flowering for a 'yak' and a handsome plant. (*yakushimanum* × [(Lionel's Triumph × Loderi King George) × *macabeanum*]). Barlup.

■ **CENTENNIAL CELEBRATION** Semi-dwarf H4 EM–M. Flower very light purple with sparse spotting, reverse flushed deeper, fading to palest lavender, in trusses of 20. Leaves narrowly elliptic, dark yellowish-green, Compact, well-branched plant. A poor performer at Glendoick but this may have been due to poor tissue-culture in U.S.A. *PA*. (Purple Lace × *yakushimanum*). Peste.

■ **CHELSEA SEVENTY** Low H4 M–ML. Flowers salmon-pink, blending to rose-pink, fading to creamy pink, in a compact, rounded truss. Compact, leaves with some indumentum, buds purple. (*yakushimanum* × [Jalisco × Fusilier]). Waterer, Sons and Crisp. '**VINTAGE ROSÉ**' flowers large for a 'yak' hybrid, rose-pink with a deeper centre fading to near-white, inclined to burn in sun. Very good foliage, new growth silvery.

■ **CINNAMON BEAR** Semi-dwarf H4 EM. Flower openly campanulate, white with strong purplish-red spotting, in dome-shaped trusses of about 20. Leaves narrowly elliptic, lower surface with heavy cinnamon-brown indumentum, new growth is whitish coloured. Rounded, well-branched habit. Needs some shade in most areas. *TC*. (*yakushimanum* K. Wada × *bureavii*). C. Smith/ Leopold. '**BEAR CLAW**' same cross, fine furry foliage with a slight twist. Flowers pale pink. '**APRILMORGEN**' white with lilac tones.

■ **CINQUERO** Low H4 E. Flower campanulate, deep-pink fading to light-pink with red basal-nectaries, in flattened dome-shaped truss of 12–14. Leaves elliptic, convex, bullate, glossy, with tan indumentum on under-surface, on an upright, dense grower. Early flowering for a 'yak'. (*yakushimanum* K. Wada × *strigillosum*). Goheen.

■ **CITY OF DUNEDIN** Low H4–5 ML. Flowers deep purplish-pink, fading to light purplish-pink, lightly speckled red, in a balled truss of about 11. Dwarf and compact. Yet another pink-fading 'yak' hybrid. Named for one of New Zealand's best rhododendron growing towns. (*yakushimanum* × Red Cloud). Hughes.

■ **CLIVIA** Low H5 M. Flowers star-shaped, two-toned, inside pink, outside deeper-pink, with red spotting, in a compact truss. Leaves deep-green, veined. Compact. (Manderlay × *yakushimanum*). Stockman.

■ **COCONUT ICE** Low H4 M. Flowers white with rose edges and red spotting in rounded trusses of 20–21. Compact with dark-green stiff leaves. A New Zealand-bred 'yak' cross. '**FROSTED ICE**' is a sister with pure-white flowers. (*yakushimanum* K. Wada × *aberconwayi*). Pukeiti. '**MAGIC MOMENTS**' from Lofthouse is white with a large red blotch in trusses of 16–22. '**JEFFERSON CENTENNIAL**' is a Warren Berg hybrid of the same cross.

■ **COLIBRI** Low H5 M–ML. Flowers funnel-shaped, strong rosy-red in bud, opening inside light-pink, outside strong-pink, a few small red spots, in rounded, slightly loose trusses of 10–17. Leaves dark green, underside with thin layer of grey indumentum aging to brownish. (*yakushimanum* × Louis Pasteur). Bruns.

■ **CORAL VELVET** Semi-dwarf–Low H5 EM. Flower yellowish-pink fading to creamy, with a few deeper-pink spots, in flattish trusses of 5. Leaves lanceolate to narrowly elliptic, convex, glossy, deep-green with heavy tan indumentum on underside. Buds and new growth with white indumentum. Upright, rounded habit. (*yakushimanum* hybrid). Wild seed, Greer intro.

CRIMSON PIPPIN

■ **CRIMSON PIPPIN** Semi-dwarf H5 M. Flower of heavy substance, waxy-looking, currant-red, in loose or open trusses of 11. Small elliptic dark-green leaves with a thin tan-white indumentum on the under-surface. Not very sun or heat tolerant. The flowers are dark red for an F1 'yak' but they are rather small and not all that freely produced. *NI*. (*yakushimanum* × *sanguineum* var. *haemaleum*). Larson.

■ **CUPCAKE** Semi-dwarf–Low H4 EM–M. Flowers open deep-pink and fade to light yellowish-pink, with sparse red spotting, in lax trusses of 9. Leaves dark green above, underside with brown indumentum. Dense, spreading habit. Very free-flowering. Much better than the 'yak' Fabia Waterer hybrids such as 'Grumpy' and we have found it a useful parent. Sensitive to fertilizer. *CD, EK*. (*yakushimanum* × Medusa). Thompson.

CUPCAKE

■ **DANIELA** Semi-dwarf–Low H5 ML. Flowers deep purplish-pink, shading inwards pale purplish-pink to white, in rounded trusses of 11–18. Leaves elliptic, dark green, lower surface with sparse tan indumentum. Grows wider than tall. *TC*. ([Nova Zembla × Mars] × [Mars × *yakushimanum* K. Wada]). Hachmann.

■ **DAVE GOHEEN** Low H4 E. Flowers open pale purplish-pink aging to white with yellowish-white edges and a cardinal-red dorsal blotch, with rays of pale pink, in dome-shaped trusses of 14–16. Leaves narrowly elliptic to oblanceolate, dull, yellowish green, with thin indumentum on the underside. Takes a few years to bud up. (*yakushimanum* × *calophytum*). Goheen.

■ **DELP'S DREAM** Semi-dwarf–Low H4–5 H5–6. Flowers brilliant greenish-yellow to light yellow-green in bud, opening pale greenish-yellow with sparse vivid yellow-green dorsal spots, in trusses of 8. Matte, oval leaves, indumentum on the lower surface, on a compact plant. Seems to be tough and heat resistant. Buds up very young. (SiSi × Serendipity). Delp. Far too many from this cross were named: '**JACK LOOYE**', '**SILVERY MOON**', **SOFTVIEW**', '**CISA**' are all sisters, all shades of pale yellow.

■ **DIANA PEARSON** Low H4–5 ML. Flowers pale pink fading to off-white, in trusses of 13. Leaves dull dark green. Vigorous but compact plant. Free-flowering. Never became very popular. (*yakushimanum* × Glamour). George.

■ **DOC** Semi-dwarf–Low H6 M. Flower frilled, light pink with darker-pink edges fading to cream, spots on upper lobe, in a ball-shaped truss of 9. Leaves, dull, medium green on a fairly compact plant. Leaves are prone to sunburn and the flowers are rather average. There are hundreds of better 'yak' hybrids and I would not give space to this one. (*yakushimanum* × Corona). Waterer, Sons and Crisp.

■ **DOCTOR LUTTON** Low H6 ML–L. Flowers white, opening from pink buds, with reddish spotting in the throat, in a rounded truss. A vigorous 'yak' with good foliage and neat habit. Leaves with a little indumentum. *PB*. (Mrs J. G. Millais × *yakushimanum*). Pride.

■ **DONVALE PEARL** Low H4 EM. Flowers bright spinel-red, fading to pink, tubular campanulate, in tight trusses of up to 28. An early flowering 'yak' hybrid, bred to avoid the heat of the late spring in S.E. Australia. *Mel*. (*yakushimanum* × *arboreum* hybrid). O. Shannassy.

■ **DONVALE RUFFLES** Low H4 E–EM. Flowers light purplish-pink on lobe edges, shading to pale purplish-pink in the throat and fading with age to pale purplish-pink, in trusses of 17–22. Leaves elliptic with slightly wavy margins, indumentum on underside. Compact habit. Bred in Australia for early flowering. *Mel*. (Marion × [*yakushimanum* × *arboreum*]). O. Shannassy.

■ **DOPEY** Semi-dwarf–Low H4 M. Flower campanulate, strong-red, paling toward margins with dark-brown spots on upper lobe, in spherical trusses of about 16. Leaves dull green, with silvery new growth. Compact and upright grower. Provide shelter from wind and sun. Flowers hold colour better than almost any other red 'yak' hybrid. Subject to powdery mildew. *AGM*. ([*facetum* hybrid × Fabia] × [*yakushimanum* × Fabia Tangerine]). Waterer, Sons and Crisp.

DOPEY

■ **DOROTHY SWIFT** Semi-dwarf–Low H7 ML. Flower opens pale purplish-pink and fades to white, in a ball-shaped truss of 12–17. Leaves obovate, convex, glossy, dark green above with cream, fading-to-brown, indumentum on the underside. Dense, spreading shrub. *MS.* (*smirnowii* × *yakushimanum*). Mehlquist. **'TODAY AND TOMORROW'** is a sister that looks more or less identical.

DOROTHY SWIFT

■ **DREAMLAND** Semi-dwarf–Low H5 M. Flower pale pink with deeper-pink margins, in ball-shaped, slightly open trusses of about 22. Leaves lanceolate, flat, thick, with a compact, dense growth habit. It buds-up young, is easy to root and is quite popular commercially: don't be tempted though, the flowers are insipid and I have always failed to see any attraction in it. *CA, MB, TC.* (complex '*yakushimanum*' hybrid). Waterer, Sons and Crisp. **'TIMOTHY JAMES'** rose fading to paler. Poor.

DREAMLAND

■ **EDELWEISS** Low H5 M–ML. Pale-pink buds open to white flowers in rounded trusses of 15–17. Dark-green leaves with silvery indumentum on both surfaces. An outstanding foliage plant but not as free-flowering as most forms of 'yak' in Scotland and a little slow to bud-up when young. (*yakushimanum* seedling). Wustermeyer/Wieting.
■ **ELEANOR BEE** Semi-dwarf–Low H4 M. Flowers funnel-shaped, purplish-red fading to white in the centre, fading to pale pink, in a flat truss of about 14. Leaves dark green with indumentum on the lower surface. One of several named hybrids from this cross. Not a Berg hybrid, though it sounds like it is; perhaps there is a copyright infringment… (Vulcan × *yakushimanum*). Bulgin.

■ **ELYA** Semi-dwarf–Low H4–5 E. Flower deep purplish-pink in a loose truss of 7–8. Leaves upper surface dusted with brown indumentum, lower surface with brown indumentum, on a compact plant of good habit. Needs filtered light in Pacific Northwest. ([Fabia × *bureavii*] × *yakushimanum*). Larson.
■ **EMANUELLA** Semi-dwarf–Low H5 ML. Flowers white with strong neyron-rose rims and exterior, with orange spotting. Flowers are said to be weather-proof. Dark-green leaves on a compact plant. An inferior sister of 'Fantastica'. (Mars × *yakushimanum*). Hachmann. Sisters **'MARLIS'**, **' KANTILINE'**, **'SONATINE'**, are all fading two-toned pink 'yak' hybrids, none of which is as good as 'Fantastica'.

FANTASTICA

■ **FANTASTICA** Semi-dwarf–Low H5 M–ML. Flowers open deep-pink, shading to paler-pink in throat, gradually fading to pale pink with a white centre, spotted greenish yellow, in trusses of about 20. Leaves elliptic, dark green with thin tan-coloured indumentum on the underside. Dense somewhat upright habit, sometimes leggy. My favourite pink 'yak' hybrid with very fine two-toned flowers. Outstanding. *See* under 'Emanuela' for several sister seedlings. *AGM, CN, MS, MT, OP, OZ, VI.* (Mars × *yakushimanum* K. Wada). Hachmann. **'NINOTSCHKA'** very similar, with a larger truss.
■ **FESTIVO** Semi-dwarf–Low H4–5 EM. Creamy-orange buds open to cream flowers with red speckles, in loose trusses of 12–14. Leaves dark green with no indumentum. Dense and compact. Not heat tolerant, so poor in N.E. U.S.A. (Hachmann's Polaris × *wardii*). Hachmann. **'MARIETTA'** frilled very pale yellow flowers with red spotting. Dark-green foliage. **'LUCINDA'** a new German 'yak' with medium-yellow flowers with red spotting. **'MAIFREUDE'** pale yellow.

MAIFREUDE

FLAVA BABETTE

■ **FLAVA g. & cls** Semi-dwarf–Low H5–6 M–ML. Flower light yellow with a red blotch in open trusses of about 11. Leaves shiny, medium-green. A compact grower that needs sun to make it flower. Subject to powdery mildew and takes a number of years to flower freely. Rather susceptible to lace-wing damage. One of the hardiest low-yellows but not very heat tolerant. There are many clones: **'BABETTE'** a relatively upright habit, **'LACHBLATT'** best foliage, **'VOLKER'** late-flowering. (*yakushimanum* × *wardii*). Hobbie.
■ **FLIRT** Semi-dwarf–Low H5 M. Flower rose-red with a white throat, outside with rose-red stripes on lobes, in lax trusses of 9–12. Leaves flat, glossy, underside with yellow-brown indumentum. Rounded and dense shrub. Everyone and his uncle seem to have made this cross. (Britannia × *yakushimanum* K. Wada). Elliott. **'FIESTA'**, **'CRICKET'** and **'ANDRÉ'** were also named. They don't differ much. **'SASSY'** frilled pink flowers.
■ **FLORKISSEN** Semi-dwarf H4–5 M. Flowers ruby-red inside shading to purplish-rose-red, fading to moderate-pink, in loose-domed trusses of 8–9. Leaves elliptic on a slow-growing, compact plant. Flowers fade/bleach in the sun. (Lampion × Julischka). Hachmann.

FRED PESTE

■ **FRED PESTE** Semi-dwarf H4 M. Flower cardinal-red, darker in throat and deep-red spots, in a floppy truss of 14. Leaves narrowly elliptic, convex, leathery, dark olive-green, under-surface with fine indumentum. Upright, stiff-branched plant. This would be a good plant if the flowers did not hang down dejectedly. Needs good drainage. ([*yakushimanum* × Corona] × *haematodes*). Peste. **'MARLENE PESTE'** paler flowers.

■ **FROSTED PLUM** Semi-dwarf–Low H5 ML. Flowers open reddish purple with a picotee edge, fading to light purple, with a large flare of light olive, in a balled truss of about 19. Leaves dark green with decurved margins, new growth with a light-brown dusting of indumentum. (*yakushimanum* × Frank Galsworthy). Barlup. **'ORCHID MIST'** lavender flowers with deeper margins and a green flare.

■ **FRÜLINSANFANG** Low H5 M–ML. Flowers intense-pink, paler in the centre, with red spotting, in compact, rounded trusses of 9–14. Deep-green leaves. Compact. (Albert Schweitzer × *yakushimanum* K. Wada). Bruns.

■ **GEN SCHMIDT (syn. GENEVIEVE SCHMIDT)** Low H6 M–ML. Flowers neyron-rose, strong- and spiraea-reds, with cardinal-red dorsal spotting, in a truss of 12. Compact. As usual, Delp named lots of sisters. All are much the same. (America × *yakushimanum*). Delp.

■ **GENERAL ERIC HARRISON** Semi-dwarf–Low H4 EM–M. Flowers bright red with dark-red spotting fading to pink, in rounded trusses. Leaves matte-green on a well-branched plant. One of the earliest flowering 'yak' hybrids. (*yakushimanum* × Shilsonii). Hydon Nursery. Sister 'Georgette' is slightly later with flowers pink fading to white. **'CRIMSON GLOW'** an Australian hybrid of the same cross with red flowers with a lighter centre.

■ **GEORGETTE** Low H4 EM. Flowers pink, fading, 12 per globular truss. Compact plant, glossy foliage, medium dark-green. (*yakushimanum* × Cornish Cross). George.

■ **GHOST** Low H6 L. White flowers with a faint yellow blotch in a conical truss of about 16. Leaves with indumentum on the underside. Heat tolerant and looks like a compact *R. maximum* with little or no blotch. 'Delp's Best' (Paul James). ([*yakushimanum* × *maximum*] × *maximum*). Delp.

■ **GLANZBLATT** Low H5 ML. Flowers rose-pink inside with whitish throat, white midveins, outside deep pink, edges darker, in a dense trusses of 14. Broadly elliptic leaves, very convex, recurved margins, glossy above, thin fawn indumentum on underside. (Tarantella × *yakushimanum* Dekora). Hachmann.

GLENDOICK® VANILLA

■ **GLENDOICK® VANILLA** Low H4–5 L. Flowers pure-white, distinctly vanilla-scented, in a rounded truss of 9–12. Leaves dark green, elliptic, with a thin layer of brown indumentum on the underside, on a dense fairly compact and handsome plant, which is one of the latest 'yak' hybrids to flower. (*yakushimanum* × *hemsleyanum*). Cox. **'GEORGE ARBLASTER'** same cross, white with pink tinges.

GLENDOICK® GOLD

■ **GLENDOICK® GOLD** Low H4 M. Flowers of deepest bright-yellow in small rounded trusses of 9–10. Leaves small, dark green with no indumentum, on a plant of very neat compact habit. Needs good drainage and unlikely to have much heat tolerance. Easily the deepest yellow 'yak' hybrid I have seen. (Cupcake × Goldkrone). Cox.

■ **GOLDEN MELODIE** Low H5 ML. Flowers pale yellow with a green throat, in a truss of 9–14. Low growing with good foliage. The Hachmanns have used this to breed hybrids with handsome leaves. (*yakushimanum* × [Manderlay × Albatross]). Stöckmann.

■ **GOLDEN TORCH** Semi-dwarf–Low H4 ML. Flower pale-yellow fading to cream, faintly spotted deeper yellow, in ball-shaped trusses of 13–15. Leaves medium-sized, matte green on a fairly compact plant. It has always been a mystery to me why this became so popular: the flowers are not golden but cream, the foliage is not very attractive and it tends to get mildew. *AGM, CA.* (F2 *yakushimanum* hybrid. Given parentage is nonsense). Waterer, Sons and Crisp.

■ **GOLDEN WEDDING** Low H4 M. Brick-red buds open to chrome-yellow flowers, in trusses of 10–14. Dark green glossy foliage on a spreading plant. The plants in the U.K. under this name are not 'yak' hybrids at all. Perhaps a mix up? Or maybe the parentage given is wrong. Not a bad plant with deep-yellow flowers. (*yakushimanum*?? × Mrs Lammot Copeland). Larson.

■ **GOLDSTURM** Low H4–5 M–ML. Yellow flowers with a very small blotch, in a compact, rounded truss. Compact habit. Not yet in commerce but the Hachmanns think this may be their best yellow 'yak' hybrid. ([Edelweiss × Olga] × Goldstück). Hachmann.

■ **GOLFER** Semi-dwarf H6 EM. Flower pale purplish-pink with slight brown spotting, reverse striped darker, in dome-shaped trusses of 13.

GOLFER FOLIAGE

Leaves narrowly elliptic, with silver tomentum on new growth that persists all summer, on a very tight-domed bush, which can be an outstanding foliage plant. Foliage needs shade in hotter climates and leaves are sensitive to too much fertilizer. Surprisingly hardy. *MS, OP, PB.* (*yakushimanum* × *pseudochrysanthum*). Berg.

■ **GORDON JONES** Semi-dwarf–Low H4–5 EM. Flower very pale purple aging to white with prominent dark-red spotting, in dome-shaped trusses of 16. Leaves oblong, convex, glossy, dark green. Spreading, dense shrub. Poor in Scotland with leaf spot and poor leaf-retention, but good on Long Island and becoming popular in other parts of America. *NY.* (Sappho × *yakushimanum* Exbury). Murcott.

■ **GRADITO** Low H8 ML. Flowers yellowish white tinged purplish pink with darker edges and margins, upper lobe spotted yellow-brown. Leaves dark green, oblong-elliptic, recurved, with indumentum on the underside. Compact and very hardy. (Blurettia × *smirnowii*). Hachmann.

GREAT DANE

■ **GREAT DANE** Low H5–6 M. Flowers white, tinged with pink, the upper lobe heavily spotted with bright pink, outside pale pink, in a rounded truss. Fine dark foliage with indumentum on the lower surface. New growth silvery. A fine mini-version of a large-leaved species. Hard to root, so usually grafted. (*yakushimanum* × *rex*). Birck. **'REXIMA'** is another selection from the same parents.

GRUMPY

■ **GRUMPY** Semi-dwarf–Low H4–5 M. Orange-coloured buds open to creamy flowers, tinged pink, in a ball-shaped truss of about 11. Leaves deep-green, glossy with orangey indumentum on the lower surface, on a mounding plant. Needs shade in hot climates. Not all that free-flowering and flowers are rather insipid. (*yakushimanum* × unknown). Waterer, Sons and Crisp.

■ **GUSTAV MEHLQUIST** Semi-dwarf H7 ML. Flower dark pink in bud, opening pink and fading to clear-white, in ball-shaped trusses of 15. Leaves elliptic, matte green above with a very thin brownish indumentum on the underside, which later rubs off. Spreading, dense habit. A very tough and reliable plant, but the flower is not all that impressive. *MS*. (C.S. Sargent × *yakushimanum*). Mehlquist/McGuire.

■ **HACHMANN'S BELONA** Semi-dwarf–Low H5 ML. Flower deep purplish-pink spotted dark-red, shade to a brighter-pink centre, in ball-shaped trusses of 12–13. Leaves matte, dark green with dark-brown indumentum. Dense growth habit. Grows twice as wide as tall. *PB, PV, NY*. (Britannia × *yakushimanum* K. Wada). Hachmann.

■ **HACHMANN'S KERSTINE** Semi-dwarf H5 M. Flowers rose, centre of lobes and throat light pink, fading to pale pink, outside rose-pink, in lax trusses of 8. Leaves small, dark green, convex. (Manuela × Alpenglut). Hachmann.

■ **HACHMANN'S MAZURKA** Low H5 ML. Flowers pale purplish-pink with deeper purplish-pink edging, with yellow-green markings in the throat, outside deeper, especially on midveins, 14–19 in a dense, balled truss. Dark-green convex leaves. An impressive truss with attractive two-tone flowers. (Hachmann's Polaris × Florence Sarah Smith). Hachmann.

■ **HACHMANN'S MINKIN** Low H5 ML. Flowers pale yellow-cream in the centre with a bold frilly edging of red fading to pink, in rounded trusses of 15–17. Leaves glossy, dark green, underside with a thin indumentum. A rather muddy and wishy-washy colour, which does not do much for me. ([Hachmann's Lagerfeuer × (Spitfire × Frühlingszauber)] × *yakushimanum* K. Wada). Hachmann.

HACHMANN'S MINKIN

HACHMANN'S POLARIS

■ **HACHMANN'S POLARIS** Low H6 ML. Flower openly funnel-shaped, slightly frilly, light-purple with darker edges, sparse olive spots, in a ball-shaped truss of 15–18. Leaves elliptic. Compact mound with dense foliage. Good in both full-sun and shade, very free-flowering from a very young age. Flower is not a great colour, but it is very tough, versatile and reliable. 'Best Hachmann "yak" in E. North America.' George Woodard. *AGM, ME*. (*yakushimanum* K. Wada × Omega). Hachmann.

■ **HACHMANN'S PORZELLAN (syn. PORZELLAN)** Semi-dwarf–Low H5 M. Flowers pure-white, conspicuously blotched yellow-green, in trusses of 15–17. Leaves with dark reddish-brown indumentum on the underside. Only holds one year's leaves, so tends to look rather sparse. The flowers are impressive. Good in Philadelphia and New Jersey areas. (Mrs J.G. Millais × *yakushimanum*). Hachmann. **'SCHNEEWOLKE'** White flowers, flushed pink, in trusses of 12–17. **'SCHWANENSEE'** white with yellow flare.

■ **HACHMANN'S PRISCILLA (syn. PRISCILLA)** Low H5 EM–M. Flowers strong-red, with pale-pink, fading to almost white midveins, outside strong-red, with strong yellow-green marking on the upper lobes, in a loose, rounded truss of 8–9. Leaves dark green, with prominent ribbing, lower surface with a thin indumentum, on a compact plant. (Rotkäppchen × Schlaraffia). Hachmann.

■ **HAPPY ANNIVERSARY** Low H4 M–ML. Flowers soft-pink fading to almost white, in a rounded truss. A compact bush. Name illegal, as there is already an azalea with this name. (*yakushimanum* × IMS). Van der Ven.

■ **HARKWOOD PREMIERE**® Tall H5 ML. Lilac buds open to pale-lilac flowers that quickly fade to white, with a pronounced reddish-purple blotch, in rounded trusses of 18–20. Vigorous but tidy. One of the best white blotched 'yaks'. Patented, though it may have lapsed. (*yakushimanum* × Bud Flanagan). Harkwood. **'FLANAGAN'S DAUGHTER'** is the same cross and looks very similar. **'BOHLKEN'S SNOWFIRE'**® a promising new German hybrid, with fine white flowers with a bold red-purple flare.

HARKWOOD PREMIERE®

■ **HAWAII** Low H8 M. Flower openly funnel-shaped, frilly edges, vivid purplish-red, with a pale yellow-green dorsal blotch, spotted light greenish-yellow, in dome-shaped trusses of 15. Leaves elliptic, flat, matte green, on a plant of rounded habit. (unknown or *yakushimanum* × unknown). Leach.

■ **HEAD HONCHO** Semi-dwarf–Low H6 EM. Flowers white with twin rays of deep orange-yellow spotting on dorsal lobe, in dome-shaped truss of 16. Leaves elliptic, glossy, dark green, underside with thin layer of brown indumentum, on a dense, spreading plant. Heat tolerant. (Siouxon × Mrs J.G. Millais). C. Smith/Traumann.

■ **HEINJE'S ZAUBERFLÖTE** Low H6 ML. Frilly pale-pink flowers, spotted red, in a rounded truss. Heinje's nursery went way overboard, naming dozens of sister seedlings that, frankly, all look much of a muchness… the usual pink fading to white. (*yakushimanum* × Kluis Sensation). Heinje.

■ **HELGOLAND** Low H6 ML. Flowers frilled, pink with a lighter centre, marked green in a rounded truss of 11–20. Leaves elliptic, deep-green, convex. (Scandinavia × *yakushimanum*). Robenek.

■ **HOOPLA** Low H8 M. Flowers moderate purplish-pink, fading to pale purplish-pink and light yellowish-pink inside and out with prominent blotch of light yellowish-pink fading to pale yellow, in a truss of 10–12. Compact. Semi-glossy leaves with indumentum when young. One of the 'Raise the Roof' series of hybrids named after University of Connecticut basketball team-related themes. (Catalgla F3 × [*haematodes* × *yakushimanum*]). Melquist/Brand.

■ **HOPPY** Semi-dwarf–Low H5 M–ML. Flower frilly, open pale lilac-pink, spotted ochre, fading to white with age, in ball-shaped trusses of 18. Leaves long, thin, dull, dark green. There seem to be several different plants in commerce under this name. Rather prone to disease and the colour is very pale. 'Caroline Allbrook' is better. *PA*. (*yakushimanum* × Doncaster?). Waterer, Sons and Crisp.

■ **HORIZON SNOWBIRD** Semi-dwarf–Low H4 EM. Flower widely funnel-campanulate, yellowish white with pink filaments, brown anthers and yellow stigma, in a ball-shaped truss of 18. Leaves narrowly elliptic, dull green, on a rounded, well-branched shrub. I'm not sure how a white came out of the cross. The flower is quite impressive but the foliage let it down when we grew it at Glendoick. ([Britannia × *yakushimanum*] × [Mrs Lindsay Smith × *yakushimanum*]). Brockenbrough.

■ **HYDON BEN** Low H4 M–ML. Flowers red, fading to pink, in a domed truss of up to 12. Leaves with indumentum on the underside. A handsome foliage plant. (*yakushimanum* × Billy Budd). George.

■ **HYDON DAWN** Semi-dwarf–Low H3 ML. Flower openly funnel-shaped, frilly, light purplish-pink fading paler at edges with a deeper markings and spotting, in compact trusses of up to 16. Leaves glossy, dark green with thin indumentum on the underside, new growth silvery, on a plant of compact growth habit. Not all that easy to root and often grows weakly at Glendoick. *AGM, CD, TC*. (*yakushimanum* × Springbok). Hydon Nursery.

HYDON DAWN

■ **HYDON HUNTER** Low H3 ML. Flower frilled, deep pink which fades paler pink and to white in the centre, with some yellow spotting, in dome-shaped trusses of about 14. Leaves, elliptic, recurved, dark green, on a plant of upright habit. One of the least compact 'yak' hybrids, which is upright and can become leggy. Old plants have reached 3m or more. *AGM.* (*yakushimanum* × Springbok). Hydon Nursery.

■ **HYDON PEARL** Low H4 M–ML. Flowers light purplish-pink with darker markings, 14–16 per truss. Leaves narrowly elliptic on a compact plant. Little grown. (*yakushimanum* × The Master). George.

■ **INGRID MEHLQUIST** Semi-dwarf H7 ML. Flowers small, broadly funnel-shaped, pale pink, maturing to pure white, with burgundy blotch, in ball-shaped trusses of 20–22. Leaves elliptic to slightly obovate, flat, glossy, dark green above, lower surface with pale tan aging to brown indumentum, on a dense, spreading plant. Tough, phytophthora resistant and buds up as a young plant. This may be Melquist's best 'yak'. *PB, CT.* (Besse Howells × *yakushimanum*). Mehlquist.

INGRID MEHLQUIST

■ **IRENE BAIN** Semi-dwarf–Low H4–5 EM. Flower pale-pink when first open, fading to cream, with darker-pink edges, in a tight, rounded truss. Leaves thick, medium-green, with indumentum. Uniform and dense habit. New growth silver. (*yakushimanum* × May Day). Yates/Bain.

■ **ISADORA** Low H5 M–ML. Flowers rosy-pink with paler-pink stripes, with red spotting, in rounded trusses. Dark-green recurved leaves on a compact bush. (*yakushimanum* × Cynthia). Heinje. **'SERAPHINE'** rosy pink with a paler throat and darker spotting. **'GUNBORG'** purplish pink.

■ **JODIE KING** Low H4–5 M. Flowers deep-pink, shading to paler pink, fading, in a rounded truss. Leaves dark and glossy on a compact plant. From New Zealand. (*yakushimanum* × unknown). King.

■ **JUNIFEE**® Low H5 L. Purplish red at edges, shading paler towards the centre to almost white, with yellow spotting, in a dense rounded truss of 16–18. Leaves elliptic to ovate, matte green, on a compact plant that buds up very well as a young plant. (Hachmann's Charmant × Anilin). Hachmann.

■ **KALINKA** Semi-dwarf–Low H6 ML. Flower frilly, deep purplish-pink, pale pink at centre, edges darker, marked yellow-green, in conical truss of 14–17. Leaves elliptic, glossy, dark green, under-surface with thin brown indumentum. Dense habit. Nurseries love it as it sets lots of flower buds, but the flowers are a disappointment in colour and texture and I would not have it in my garden. *CT, PB, VF.* (Morgenrot × [Mars × *yakushimanum*]). Hachmann.

■ **KARMINKISSEN**® Semi-dwarf–Low H5 M. Flowers deep pinkish-red, in loose trusses. Small dark-green leaves. A new Hachmann 'yak' with very bright pink-red flowers when first open. (*yakushimanum* K. Wada × Ruby Hart). Hachmann.

KEN JANECK

■ **KEN JANECK** Semi-dwarf–Low H6 M. Flower openly funnel-shaped, fuchsine-pink, fading to white, upper lobe spotted green, in a compact trusses of 13–17. Leaves oblanceolate, recurved, dark green with thick indumentum on lower surface, young growth silvery. A compact, mounding plant, growing twice as wide as high. The best 'yak' × *smirnowii* hybrid we have seen, this is an excellent and highly rated plant. *CC, GP, JF, MS, MT, MW, NG, NI, NY, PT, SE, SH, TC, TO, TZ, S. Fin.* (*yakushimanum* × *smirnowii*). Janeck. **'DECORA'** looks almost identical.

■ **KEVIN** Semi-dwarf–Low H4 ML. Flowers open ruffled strong-pink and fade to light yellowish-pink, edged darker, in a fairly full balled truss of 12–14. Leaves large for a 'yak', underside with golden-brown indumentum, on a compact, rounded plant. (*yakushimanum* K. Wada × Jade). Bovees.

■ **KING'S RIDE** Low H5 ML. Flowers white, flushed phlox-pink, speckled brown. Dark-green glossy stiff leaves with silvery indumentum on underside. Foliage is quite handsome. (*yakushimanum* × insigne). Windsor. **'OBERSCHLESIEN'** is the same cross. Both are rather shy-flowering, especially when young.

■ **KOKETTE** Semi-dwarf–Low H5 M. Flowers deep-pink outside, inside pale pink to white with a deep-pink rim, in a rounded truss. Leaves deep-green, on a compact plant. Like a deeper, more colour-fast version of 'Fantastica', this is a promising new 'yak'. (Ovation × Schlaraffia). Hachmann.

■ **KRISTIN** Low H4 M. Purple-pink buds open pale-pink flowers with stripes, red spotting, 13–14 per balled truss. Dark-green oval leaves, underside with thin indumentum, young growth tinged reddish. A fine foliage plant with a very dense habit. Easy to root and buds-up young. (*yakushimanum* K. Wada × Bow Bells). Sorenson, Watson.

■ **KULLERVO** Low L. Pink flowers fading to white, upper lobes spotted green, in a rounded truss. Leaves upper surface glabrous with age, dark-green, lower surface with indumentum, young growth densely tomentose. One of the hardiest 'yak' hybrids. *S. Fin.* (*brachycarpum* Tigerstedtii Gp. × *yakushimanum*). Uosukainen/Arb. Mustila.

■ **LADY BOWES LYON** Low H4–5 ML. Flowers, white, tinged rose-pink, darkening to phlox-pink, in large globe-shaped trusses of 20. Relatively tall for a 'yak' hybrid. Little grown. (Pilgrim g. × *yakushimanum*). Hanger.

LAMPION

■ **LAMPION** Semi-dwarf H5 M. Bright rose-red long-lasting campanulate flowers on long pedicles gradually fade to cream-pink, in loose trusses of 5–7. Leaves dark green, ovate-elliptic, under-surface with thin brown indumentum. Prone to stem die-back, especially under trees, so best in the open. A fine, slow-growing plant in Scotland, but it is not heat-tolerant and is borderline hardy in N. Germany. (Bad Eilsen × *yakushimanum*). Hachmann.

■ **LANNY PRIDE** Low H5 ML–L. Flowers openly funnel-shaped, strong- to vivid-red in bud, opening vivid-red, in trusses of 14. Compact. Good reports from parts of the American Midwest. Named after the successful East Coast hybridizer. (Princess Elizabeth × [*yakushimanum* × *smirnowii*]). Moyers/Delp. **'WENDY LYN'** a sister with white star-shaped flower, heavily edged and frilled vivid-red.

■ **LEMON DREAM** Low H5 M–ML. Flowers light greenish-yellow, some flowers double, in a domed truss of 13. Leaves elliptic with upcurved margins with indumentum on underside. New growth silvery. The registered parentage (Nancy Evans × unnamed Whitney seedling) is probably an error and I believe that *yakushimanum* × Creamy Chiffon is correct. McCulloch.

■ **LILLIAN PESTE** Semi-dwarf H4 EM. Flower light yellowish-pink edges shading to light vivid-pink in throat, reverse shaded pink, in ball-shaped trusses of 25–30. Leaves narrowly elliptic, convex, green, underside with heavy brown indumentum. Compact, growing wider than high. *MB.* (*yakushimanum* K. Wada × unknown). Peste.

■ **LOCH EARN** Low H4 M–ML. Flowers pale-yellow deeper in the centre, from orange-yellow buds, in flat-topped trusses of 9–11. Leaves small and pale green on a slow-growing and compact plant. Needs very good drainage. One of the finest yellow 'yak' hybrids with good habit and a mass of flowers that do not fade out. Not very heat tolerant. (Hotei × Cupcake). Cox.

LOCH EARN

■ **LOCH RANNOCH** Low H4 M–ML. Flowers yellow with a small red blotch in the throat, in lax trusses of 11–16. Compact and free-flowering with good foliage. Needs good drainage. (['Tidbit' × *caucasicum*] × [Crest × ('yak' × *wardii*)]). Cox. **'LOCH OF THE LOWES'** is later-flowering without the red spotting. Rather fussy and needs good drainage and cool roots.

■ **LOOKING GLASS** Low H4–5 M. Flowers vivid-red in bud, opening with strong purplish-red centre and margins, mottled deep-purplish-pink and with red spotting in throat, fading to pink, in flattened domed trusses of 16. Dark-green leaves with thin indumentum on the underside. Compact. Nothing particular to recommend it. (*yakushimanum* × China). Gordner/Briggs.

■ **LOVE POEM** Low H4 EM. Flowers pale purplish-pink and aging to pale yellowish-green, with deep purplish-red spotting, in balled trusses of 24. Leaves semi-glossy, moderate olive-green. (Silk Ribbon × *yakushimanum*). Barlup.

■ **MALWINE** Semi-dwarf–Low H4 M–ML. Flowers cream, edged and flushed pale pink, 7–11 per rather loose truss. Leaves relatively large, with a thin indumentum on the underside, on a compact and dense plant. (Hachmann's Marlis × Brinny). Hachmann.

■ **MARABU** Low–Medium H5 L. Flowers white inside, outside strong purplish-red, spotted orange, in a dense truss of 15. Leaves dark green, slightly twisted, on a dense, fairly compact plant. (Tarantella × ['yak' × *smirnowii*]). Hachmann.

■ **MARDI GRAS** Semi-dwarf–Low H5–6? M. Flower pale purplish-pink fading to white, edges and reverse strong purplish-pink, in ball-shaped trusses of 11–12. Leaves oblanceolate, deep-green, underside with reddish-brown indumentum. Plant broader than tall, well-branched. Hard to root. Probably not the cross given, as it is remarkably hardy and a good plant in E. North America. *BH, CH, PD, TC, WT.* (*yakushimanum* K. Wada × Vanessa). Bovee. **'TANYOSHO'** a similar sister.

■ **MASADA** Low H4 ML. Flower of heavy substance, white, lower part of upper lobe heavily spotted vivid reddish-orange, in dome-shaped trusses of 12–14. Leaves narrowly elliptic, matte green, lower surface with light white indumentum, becoming sparse when mature, on a plant of very dense and mounding habit. (*yakushimanum* K. Wada × Vistoso). Goheen.

■ **MELODY** Low H4 M–ML. Flowers rosy-red fading to pink, in a rounded truss. Broad, spreading habit. There is also an older Rothschild hybrid of this name, so this name will have to be changed to 'Whitney Melody' or somesuch. (*yakushimanum* × Leo). Whitney. **'VALERIE KAY'** bright carmine-pink, fading to lighter, frilled, in trusses of 20.

■ **MIKE DAVIS** Low H4 M–ML. Flowers openly funnel-shaped, light purplish-pink shading lighter towards centre with small specks of vivid reddish-orange on dorsal lobe, in trusses of 10–12. Low and compact with large, delicately coloured flowers. New growth bronzy. Grown in California and New Zealand. (*yakushimanum* hybrid × Lem's Cameo). Davis.

■ **MINAS SNOW** Low H6 M. Flower openly funnel-shaped, pure-white with cream anthers and light-yellow stigma, in ball-shaped trusses of 14. Leaves narrowly elliptic, olive-green, lower surface with sparse tan indumentum. Good reports from New Jersey area. A little slow to bud up. Roots easily. *Nova Scotia.* (Cunningham's White × *yakushimanum*). Craig.

■ **MIST MAIDEN** Semi-dwarf–Low H7 M. Flower pale purplish-pink aging to white with moderate-yellow dorsal spotting and deep purple-pink stripe, in ball-shaped trusses of 14–17. Leaves oblanceolate, yellow-green, underside with thick indumentum, on a very dense plant. New growth with greyish-tan indumentum. Heat tolerant. Grows broader than tall. *AT, GP, MD, MS, MW, OL, S. Fin.* (*yakushimanum* seedling). Leach. A similar hybrid is **'JANE GRANT'**, pale-pink fading to white.

■ **MORNING CLOUD** Semi-dwarf–Low H4–5 M. Flower frilly, white flushed pale-lavender-pink, in ball-shaped trusses of 16–18. Leaves dark green, lower surface with creamy-buff indumentum. Compact habit. Rather uninteresting pale flowers, I can't get excited about it, but it is hardy and reliable. *MB.* (*yakushimanum* × Springbok). Hydon Nursery. Sister **'MORNING MAGIC'** has flowers white flushed deep purplish-pink with orange-yellow spots.

■ **MOUNTAIN MARRIAGE** Semi-dwarf–Low H7 ML. Flower funnel-shaped, light yellowish-pink, in ball-shaped trusses of about 20. Leaves elliptic, flat, glossy above, lower surface with tan indumentum. One of the toughest 'yaks', with potential for breeding compact, heat-tolerant hybrids. *PT, SE.* (*maximum* × *yakushimanum*). Kehr.

■ **NEAT-O** Semi-dwarf–Low H4 EM. Flower light purplish-pink margins shading lighter to almost-white in throat with deep purplish-pink spotting, in a ball-shaped truss of 20–25. Leaves elliptic to narrowly elliptic, flat, yellowish green, lower surface with heavy grey-orange indumentum, new growth with silvery-white tomentum, on an upright, rounded plant. A good foliage plant. *PA.* (*campanulatum* × *yakushimanum* K. Wada). Goheen.

■ **NESTUCCA** Semi-dwarf–Low H5 M. Flowers white with greenish spotting in throat, in a dome-shaped truss of 12–15. Leaves elliptic, glossy, dark green. Compact, spreading habit. Tolerates heat and sun. Produces a certain percentage of ugly distorted foliage. Flowers are very fine. *AZ, GP, PT, SE.* (*fortunei* × *yakushimanum*). C. Smith. **'LITTLE WHITE DOVE'** pure-white unmarked flowers.

NESTUCCA

MIST MAIDEN

■ **MOLLY SMITH** Low H4 EM–M. Flower creamy white with prominent orange blotch, in conical trusses of up to 12. Leaves oblanceolate, of heavy texture, green, lower surface with grey-brown indumentum, on a rounded, well-branched plant. (*yakushimanum* K. Wada × Mrs Furnival). C. Smith.

■ **MORGENROT (syn. MORNING RED, RED DAWN)** Low H4–5 M. Flowers open red fading quickly to a pale pink in throat with a dark-red blotch on the dorsal lobe, in conical trusses of 11–13. Foliage is elliptic, dark green with light indumentum on the underside, on a compact, rounded plant. The almost-red flowers are deep for an F1 'yak' hybrid. Foliage rather vulnerable to frost/sun burn, so best in some shade in hot climates. *MS.* (*yakushimanum* K. Wada × Spitfire). Hachmann.

■ **NEW HOPE** Semi-dwarf–Low H4–5 EM. Flower deep purplish-pink at edges fading lighter at centre, purplish-pink spotting on upper lobe, in ball-shaped trusses of 10. Leaves oblanceolate, yellow-green, underside with fawn felt-like indumentum, new growth with silvery tomentum. (*yakushimanum* × Kiev). Bovee.

■ **NICOLETTA** Semi-dwarf–Low H6 ML. Flower opens deep purplish-pink, with a dark-red blotch, fading to off-white, in trusses of 16–19. Leaves dark green, light brown hairs on veins below. Dense habit. Quite a popular Hachmann 'yak', though I'm not all that keen on the slightly dirty colour. (Fantastica × Perlina). Hachmann. **'LUGANO'** is a sister seedling with similar flowers, a little deeper pink.

■ **MARION STREET** Low H4 M–ML. Deep-pink buds open to lighter-pink flowers, white in throat, green spotted, in trusses of 14–16. Pale leaves with felted brown indumentum on the underside. Compact. Nothing exceptional. *AGM.* (Stanley Davies × *yakushimanum*). Street.

MARDI GRAS

NOBLE MOUNTAIN

MARISSA

PERCY WISEMAN

■ **NOBLE MOUNTAIN** Semi-dwarf H4 M. Flower purplish pink with heavy dark-red spotting, in a domed truss of 15. Flowers bleach in the sun. Leaves narrowly elliptic, dull, olive-green on an upright, well-branched plant. I don't think this is one of the better blotched 'yak' hybrids. (*yakushimanum* × Rodeo). Peste.

■ **NORMAN BEHRING** Dwarf H8 L. Flower light purplish-pink with darker edges and yellowish-green spots, in dome-shaped trusses of 18. Leaves narrowly elliptic, flat, glabrous, dull, yellow-green with dark-orange indumentum. Grows wider than tall. (Nova Zembla × *yakushimanum* Pink Parasol). Behring. '**PETER BEHRING**' vivid purplish-red. '**GENESIS I**' pink fading to blush-white. '**MINAS MAID**' moderate purplish-pink.

■ **NOYO BRAVE** Semi-dwarf–Low H4 EM. Flower openly campanulate, wavy lobes, vivid reddish-orange, fading to hot-pink, with a small red blotch, in a ball-shaped truss of up to 22. Leaves elliptic to narrowly obovate, recurved, ribbed, glossy, deep-green, under-surface with thin brown indumentum. New growth with white tomentum. The foliage is good, but I don't care for the flower. *CA, CD, EK, MB, PA, TC.* (Noyo Chief × *yakushimanum*). C. Smith. '**FRANGO**' pink flowers. '**NOYO MAIDEN**' white flowers.

■ **NOYO DREAM** Semi-dwarf–Low H4 E–EM. Flower openly campanulate, frilly edges, deep purplish-pink, in ball-shaped trusses of 19. Leaves obovate, flat, with dark greyish-yellow felted indumentum below. Early flowering for a 'yak' and good in N. California. *CA, EK.* (*yakushimanum* × *arboreum* (exact combination unknown)). Moyles.

■ **NOYO SNOW** Semi-dwarf–Low H3–4 M. Flower yellowish white at centre, edged pinkish, with a light yellow-green dorsal blotch, in a ball-shaped truss of 10–17. Leaves oblong, with down-curved edges, olive-green, on a plant of dense habit. *CA.* (*yakushimanum* × *arboreum*). Moyles. '**ESTACADA**' rose-pink flowers with deeper spotting.

■ **ORANGE MARMALADE** Semi-dwarf–Low H4 M. Flower campanulate, amber-yellow, flushed salmon-pink, in lax trusses of 10–12. Leaves elliptic, flat, on a rounded, well-branched shrub. (*yakushimanum* × Mrs Lammot Copeland). Larson. '**YELLOW PIPPIN**' Flowers open carmine-red, fading to light aureolin-yellow, centre sulphur-yellow, spotted chartreuse-green in trusses of 12.

■ **PEGGIE ROBERTS** Semi-dwarf–Low H4 EM. Flower purplish-pink at edges fading to very pale purple with dark-red spotted streaks radiating from base, in ball-shaped trusses of 14. Leaves elliptic, concave, glossy, olive-green, with dense habit. ([Fancy × *yakushimanum*] × Coronation Day).

Barlup. '**MARISSA**' is a sister with striking white flowers, flushed light pink, with a red flare.

■ **PERCY WISEMAN** Semi-dwarf–Low H4–5 M–ML. Flower cream flushed pale purplish-pink and spotted moderate-orange on the dorsal lobe, fading to creamy white with a yellow throat in a truss of 13–15. Leaves elliptic, glossy, pale green, on a fairly compact and well-branched shrub. An outstanding hybrid, hardier than it looks. Needs good drainage. Very free-flowering from a young age. Somewhat prone to mildew, but easy to control. *AGM, FS, GP, MB, MD, ME, MS, PT, SE, VI.* (Complex F2 'yak' hybrid. Given parentage is wrong). Waterer, Sons and Crisp.

■ **PETER SCHICK** Low–Medium H4 EM. Cherry-pink to white flushed pale-pink, in full trusses. Fine foliage on a dense and compact plant. A good plant for N. California. (['yak' × *arboreum*] × [*arboreum* Pink Delight × *arboreum*]). Moyles.

■ **PIN OAK** Low H5–6 M. Flowers white with a pale-yellow throat in rounded trusses. Convex leaves. Spreading habit. Compact with convex leaves. There are so many similar hybrids, I'm not sure how much we need another new one. (*yakushimanum* × Catalode). Schannen.

■ **PINK PARASOL** Semi-dwarf–Low H7 EM. Flower campanulate, pale mauve-pink, aging through clear-pink to white, in a truss of about 13. Leaves flat, bluish green, underside with tan indumentum, growing twice as wide as tall. A sister of 'Mist Maiden' with pinker flowers. *MW.* (*yakushimanum* × *smirnowii*?). Leach. '**SILVER SOVEREIGN**' another

'yak'-*smirnowii*, which is the most vigorous and tallest of them all.

■ **PINK SHERBET (syn. PINK ICE)** Semi-dwarf–Low H4 EM. Flower light purplish-pink with slightly lighter throat and darker margins, fading to white with age, in a ball-shaped truss of 8–12. Leaves +/- elliptic convex, glossy, underside with yellow-ochre indumentum, new growth with silvery tomentum. Rounded habit. (*yakushimanum* Exbury form × unknown). Larson.

■ **PIRIANDA CHESTNUT FLARE** Low H4 M–ML. Flowers strong-pink with moderate-orange flare on dorsal lobes, in trusses of 18–20. Leaves elliptic. Compact. (Jalisco × *yakushimanum*). Ansell.

■ **PIROUETTE** Low H4–5 M–ML. Flower white with pink edges, fading to white, in trusses of up to 28. A compact grower with rather yellowish-green leaves. It is proving to be a good parent but is nothing exceptional in itself. As usual, too many sisters were named. (*yakushimanum* K. Wada × Pink Petticoats). Lofthouse. '**BARRY RODGERS**' the worst foliage we have seen on a 'yak' hybrid. '**OOH LA LA**' pink fading to white. '**SPRING JOY**' pink fading to white, what a surprise!

■ **PLUM HIGH** Semi-dwarf H4 ML. Flower purple at edges shading to very pale purple in throat with red spotted blotch, outside with purplish-red veins along midribs, in ball-shaped trusses of 18. Leaves elliptic, flat, rounded, dull, olive-green, on a dense grower. A good low-growing purple. *CD.* ([Fancy × *yakushimanum*] × Frank Galsworthy). Barlup. '**DEEP CLOVER**' a sister with reddish-purple flowers, edged darker, with soft-pink flare on upper lobe and green spotting over pink flare.

■ **PONTIYAK** Low H4–5 ML. Large pink-lavender flowers in a tight conical truss. Recurved, medium-green foliage. Mounding habit. Why anyone would even make this cross is a mystery to me. (I admit to making it myself once, and soon threw out the results.) Seems to be quite popular in New Jersey and Pennsylvania. *PA.* (*ponticum* × *yakushimanum*). Kellygreen Nursery.

■ **PORCELAIN PROMISE** Low H4 M–ML. Flowers cream with a light-yellow dorsal flare, in balled trusses of 23. Leaves elliptic, semi-glossy, moderately olive-green, margins up-curved, on a compact plant. Long-lasting and impressive flowers. (Peach Charm × Pirouette). Barlup.

■ **POSY** Low H4 M. Rose-pink fading to rose-madder, in a compact truss of about 22. Handsome, glossy, deep-green leaves. Compact. (*yakushimanum* × College Pink). Gordon.

■ **POWDER SNOW** Low–Medium H4 EM. Buds soft-pink, opening to white flowers with three red flares at base of upper lobe and with light-red spotting on upper lobe, reverse white, in dome-shaped trusses of 20. Fine large foliage with silvery new growth. It's a pity that this is not pale-yellow, as might be expected. This is a good parent to use for breeding heat-tolerant yellow hybrids with good foliage. The lowest growing selection of this cross. (*yakushimanum* × *macabeanum*). Barlup. '**LARAMIE**' pale yellow-green with a red blotch. Good foliage and should be a good parent for heat-tolerant yellows.

■ **PRETTY BABY** Low H4 EM–M. Flowers medium-pink, fading, in rounded trusses. Foliage fine on a dense and compact plant. Some autumn flowering in California. Best with some shade in hot climates. (Hydon Dawn × [Cornubia × Red Olympia]). Korth.

■ **QUEEN ALICE** Low H4 M–ML. Cherry-red buds open to bright-pink flowers, which fade to off-white, in domed trusses of 18–22. Leaves +/– elliptic, medium-green, new growth silvery. Rather boring, but popular with nurseries, so I dare say it is easy to produce. (*yakushimanum* × Alice). Clark.

■ **RENDEVOUS** Low H5 ML. Flowers bright-red fading to almost-white in centre, with bright-red spotting, 17–24 per truss. Leaves deep-green, with silvery tomentum on upper surface. A good foliage plant. Flowers similar to so many 'yak' hybrids. *AGM*. (Marinus Koster × *yakushimanum* K. Wada). Hachmann.

■ **RENOIR** Semi-dwarf–Low H5 M–ML. Flowers rose-pink with a white throat and crimson spots, in rounded trusses of 11. Dark-green leaves, with light indumentum. Free-flowering. I'm not a great fan of this plant: the flowers are rather coarse and the colour bleaches out. *AGM*. (Pauline × *yakushimanum*). Hanger/R.H.S. '**TELSTAR**' rose paling to almost-white inside, red throat.

■ **ROSALIE HALL** Semi-dwarf H3 EM. Flower purplish red fading to deep purplish-pink in the throat, with red markings, reverse deep purplish-pink, in ball-shaped trusses of 19. Leaves obovate, with heavy brownish-orange felt-like indumentum. New growth is greyish-yellow-green. Rounded habit. *PC*. (*yakushimanum* × Double Winner). Newcomb.

■ **ROSE LANCASTER** Low H3 ML. Flower brilliant purplish-pink, unmarked, in ball-shaped trusses of 18–30. Leaves oblanceolate, dark green, underside with thick tan indumentum, new growth with tawny tomentum, on a plant of compact habit. (Tally Ho × *yakushimanum*). Lancaster/Austin.

■ **ROSY DREAM** Semi-dwarf H4 M. Flower deep-pink with lighter throat and slight red spotting, fading to pale pink, in ball- to dome-shaped trusses of 12–16. Leaves narrowly elliptic to elliptic, dull green, young growth with silver tomentum. (*yakushimanum* × Britannia). Larson.

■ **RUTH DAVIS** Semi-dwarf–Low H5 EM. Flower yellowish white with yellowish-green blotch, reverse pink until fully open, in ball-shaped trusses of 17. Leaves oblanceolate, somewhat convex, glossy, lower surface with orange-white felt-like indumentum, slight tomentum on new growth. A rather pointless cross but the plant grows well in E. North America. *GP*. (*yakushimanum* × *degronianum*). Gable.

■ **SAMOA** Low H7 EM-M. Flowers vivid Turkey red, with faint dorsal spotting, 15 per truss. Leaves elliptic, rough upper surface, tiny white hairs on lower surface. Not very widely grown, but seemingly tough and reliable. ([*catawbiense* var. *album* × *yakushimanum*] × [Fanfare × Gertrude Schäle]). Leach.

■ **SCHNEEKRONE** Low H5 ML. Flowers open palest rose fading quickly to clear-white with soft-pink tinge, ruby-red spotting in a rounded trusses of 12–17. Leaves elliptic, convex, pale green on a fairly compact plant that buds-up young. One of the best white 'yaks'. Excellent in severe climates. (Humboldt × *yakushimanum* K. Wada). Hachmann.
'**LAMENTOSA**' white tinged lilac with a red throat. Straggly. '**SILBERGLANZ**' white with deeper spotting.

■ **SENATOR HENRY JACKSON (syn. CHINA DOLL)** Low H4–5 ML. Flowers unmarked pure-white in ball-shaped trusses. Leaves pointed, convex, underside with sparse white indumentum. The best white 'yak' I have seen for flowers but the foliage is poor and the plant is hard to root and not easy to please. Could be improved with hybridizing. *CA, CD*. (*yakushimanum* × Mrs Horace Fogg). Larson.

SCHNEEKRONE

■ **SEVEN STARS** Low H4 M. Flower campanulate, opening pale pink and aging to white with red spotting, lightly fragrant, in a rounded truss of 12–15. Leaves medium-green, recurved, on a dense, upright plant which has reached 4m or more. Subject to powdery mildew and sunburned foliage. One of the tallest 'yaks'. We tried using this as a parent with poor results. (Loderi Sir Joseph Hooker × *yakushimanum*). Crown Estate.

SEVEN STARS

■ **SHOGUN** Low H4 M. Flower lightly fragrant, white with a red throat, in a dome-shaped truss of 10–11. Leaves oblong to narrowly obovate, yellow-green, underside with thin indumentum. Open habit. This has a very impressive flower for a 'yak' and good foliage. Recommended. (*yakushimanum* × Coronation Day). Korth.

■ **SHOWBOAT** Low H4–5 M. Flowers white, frilly with a yellow eye, in a ball-shaped truss of 10–14. Leaves dark green and recurved, underside with light-tan indumentum, on a compact plant. (*yakushimanum* Exbury × Tumalo). Phetteplace.

■ **SILBERVELOURS** Low H5 EM–M. Rounded trusses of pale pink, fading to cream, with deeper spotting, in a truss of 14–16. Leaves with thick indumentum on the under-surface. Compact, dense and slow-growing. Indumentum persisting all summer, especially in full sun. Excellent habit. (*yakushimanum* × *pachysanthum*). Hachmann.
'**VIKING SILVER**' a Sven Hansen selection from the same cross, named at Glendoick: pale pink. Very persistent silvery foliage. '**GLENDOICK® SILVER**' white flowers.

VIKING SILVER

■ **SILBERWOLKE (syn. SILVER CLOUD)** Low H6 M–ML. Flowers of very light purple, spotted yellow-green, reverse shaded darker, in trusses of 12–16. Leaves dark green, on a compact, spreading plant. Healthy and easy but not a very appealing colour. Prone to budblast. (*yakushimanum* × Album Novum). Hachmann.

■ **SILVER SIXPENCE** ML–L. White flowers, blushed empire-rose, spotted yellow, in a loose truss of 8–10. Leaves narrow, yellow-green on a rather sparse upright plant. The flowers are fine, but I have seldom seen a healthy plant of this: it is usually chlorotic, straggly and lousy with disease. Avoid. (unnamed hybrid × unnamed hybrid). Waterer, Sons and Crisp.

■ **SILVER SKIES** Semi-dwarf H4–5 EM. Flowers pale pink with deep purplish-pink edges, in flat trusses of 15–16. Leaves oblanceolate, glossy, dark bluish-green, underside with fawn indumentum, new growth silvery. (*yakushimanum* K. Wada × Medusa). Fujioka.

■ **SKOOKUM** Low H4 M. Flower funnel-shaped, vivid-red with an almost-white throat, in conical trusses of 20. Leaves narrowly elliptic, flat, dull, yellowish green, plant with dense growth habit. The bicolour flowers are quite striking. ([*yakushimanum* × Mars] × America). Larson/Minch. '**SKOOKUMCHUCK**' same cross very similar. The two sisters were evidently mixed up in tissue culture.

SKOOKUM

■ **SLEEPY** Semi-dwarf–Low H5 M. Flower opens lavender with a brown blotch, fades to off-white, in a rounded truss. Long dark-green leaves with purple petioles. An upright and not very dense plant, subject to mildew. The poorest of the seven dwarfs. ([*yakushimanum* × Doncaster] × [*yakushimanum* × Doncaster]). Waterer, Sons and Crisp.

SNEEZY

■ **SNEEZY** Semi-dwarf–Low H6 M–ML. Reddish buds open pink with darker edges, fading to pale pink, with a deep-red blotch, about 16 per compact, domed truss. Thick, deep-green leaves. A vigorous 'yak' hybrid with silvery new growth. Proven to be hardy in Germany and Holland. *U.K., Hol, Ger.* (*yakushimanum* × Doncaster). Waterer, Sons and Crisp.

■ **SOLIDARITY** Low H6 M. Flower light red with a paler throat, fading to pink, with red spots on dorsal lobe, in dome-shaped trusses of 12–13. Leaves, elliptic, flat, leathery, dull-green with sparse light-tan indumentum, on a dense, well-shaped plant that looks like a mini 'Jean Marie de Montague'. One of the most highly rated US 'yak' hybrids, raised by one of the most flamboyant rhododendron experts, the larger-than-life Hank Schannen. Can grow open with age. *GP, MB, OZ, PA, PR, PT, SE, ST.* (Jean Marie de Montague × *yakushimanum*). Schannen. **'PINK FLAME'** red fading to pink.

SOLIDARITY

■ **SUNUP-SUNDOWN** Low H4 EM–M. Flower empire-rose fading to shell-pink, in rather loose trusses of 8–10. Oh dear! Flowers are so sensitive to weather damage, at Glendoick they went brown long before the buds even opened. It does better in New Zealand and California, but the flowers are insipid and I would not give it garden space. The foliage and habit are OK. ([*yakushimanum* × Fabia] × [(Fabia × *bureavii*) × Crest]). Lofthouse.

■ **SURREY HEATH** Semi-dwarf–Low H4–5 M–ML. Flower rose-pink with orange spots and with a light-yellow centre, in a ball-shaped truss of 12–16. Leaves narrow and pointed with silver new growth. Very dense almost congested growth habit. Once very popular in the U.K., but seems to be becoming less grown. I used to like it, but the appeal has waned. ([*facetum* × Fabia] × [*yakushimanum* × Britannia]). Waterer, Sons and Crisp.

SURREY HEATH

■ **SWEET SUE** Low H4 ML–L. Flowers pale pink, with lighter margins, spotted rose-pink. Upright for a 'yak' hybrid. The flowers are not very attractive, especially as they bleach as they fade. Quite late for a 'yak'. ([*facetum* × Fabia] × [*yakushimanum* × Fabia Tangerine]). Waterer, Sons and Crisp.

■ **TAKU** Low H4–5 ML. Flower deep-pink outside, moderate-pink inside with red spots, in dome-shaped trusses of 12. Leaves narrowly elliptic, convex, bullate, dull, olive-green, underside with tan felt-like indumentum that ages to dark-tan. Open, upright growth habit. (Tally Ho × *yakushimanum*). Clarke.

■ **TATJANA** Low H5 ML. Flowers strong purplish-red, paling from edges to centres, in trusses of 14–16. Dark green leaves with woolly indumentum on the underside. *AGM.* (Nachtglut × [Mars × *yakushimanum* K. Wada]). Hachmann. **'PAPAGENO'** soft-rose with white centre.

■ **TEDDY BEAR** Semi-dwarf–Low H5 EM. Flower opens light purplish-pink and fades to white with yellow-brown spots in throat, in dome-shaped trusses of 8–10. Leaves elliptic to narrowly elliptic, glossy and bullate above, orange indumentum on under-surface, with a yellow-green petiole. Spreading, dense growth habit. The seed parent 'Lem's *bureavii*' is a hybrid. *CN, MT, NN, PA, SL, TC, VI.* (Lem's *bureavii* hybrid × *yakushimanum*). unknown.

TEDDY BEAR

■ **TEQUILA SUNRISE** Low H3–4 M. Strong purplish pink, flushed very pale pink at base, bases of dorsal lobes flushed and spotted bright-red, trusses of about 13. A compact 'yak' hybrid. (*yakushimanum* × Borde Hill). Hanger. There is another hybrid under this name from the U.S.A., a 'Lem's Cameo' cross with flowers deep-yellow with orange tones.

■ **TIANA** Medium H4–5 M. Flower frilly, white with a prominent dark red-purple blotch, in trusses of 16. Leaves oblong, convex, dark green, on an upright open and rather sparse plant, which is prone to leaf diseases in Scotland. Flowers are good. *NY.* (Sappho × *yakushimanum* Exbury). Murcott/Brack.

■ **TINA HEINJE** Low H6 M–ML. Red buds open to dark-pink flowers with a dark-red eye, in a rounded truss of 14–16. Large trusses on a compact plant with long curving foliage. For some reason, dozens of very similar sister seedlings were named by Heinje nursery. (*yakushimanum* × Kluis Sensation). Heinje.

■ **TITIAN BEAUTY** Semi-dwarf–Low H4–5 M. Flower wavy edged, waxy, turkey-red in long pedicels, in an open but rounded truss. Leaves textured, deep-green with thin brown-coloured indumentum. Upright, dense growth habit. Rather prone to mildew. One of the best red 'yak' hybrids for moderate climates. ([*facetum* × Fabia Tangerine] × [*yakushimanum* × Fabia Tangerine]). Waterer, Sons and Crisp.

TITIAN BEAUTY

■ **TITIAN BOUQUET** Low H4 M. Flowers purplish pink with darker spotting, 10 per ball-shaped truss. Dark green leaves, good habit. Buds-up very young. (Bridal Bouquet × Titian Beauty). Ward.

■ **TOLKEIN** Low H4 ML. Flowers red, small for the leaf size, in rounded trusses. Leaves stiff, dark green, on a compact plant. Not as good as 'Dopey', which is probably a sister. (Waterer 'yak' hybrids mostly have the wrong parentage given.) ([*facetum* × Fabia] × [*yakushimanum* × Britannia]). Waterer, Sons and Crisp/Mayers. Other sisters include: **'SPARKLER'** bright-red, fading to pink, **'BORDERER'** pink, **'PHEASANT TAIL'** rose-pink flowers, lighter centre.

■ **TRINITY** Semi-dwarf H8 ML. Flower white with faint green spotting, shaded pale purplish-pink on lobe edges and reverse when newly opened, in ball-shaped trusses of 14. Leaves yellowish green, underside with thin indumentum. New growth silver-brown. Rounded growth habit. The best of the hybrids from this cross. *MS, CT, ST.* (catawbiense Powell Glass, selfed × *yakushimanum* K. Wada). Pride. **'FALLING SNOW'** pure white with small yellow markings. Good in S. Finland. **'DOUBLE DIP'** white marked green.

TRINITY

FALLING SNOW

■ **VANILLA SPICE** Low H4 M–ML. Pale yellowish-pink with a large dark-red blotch, in balled trusses of 16. Leaves elliptic, semi-glossy, with no indumentum. A good name. (Silk Ribbon × White Cinnamon). Barlup.

■ **VENETIAN CHIMES** Semi-dwarf H4 M. Flower campanulate, carmine-rose with dark spots, in ball-shaped trusses of 11. Leaves dull green, thinly textured, with no indumentum, on a plant growing wider than tall. As with most Waterers 'yaks' the parentage is wrong: hybridizer Percy Wiseman left a stud book and someone made ignorant guesses… ([*facetum* × Fabia] × [*yakushimanum* × Britannia]). Waterer, Sons and Crisp.

■ **VINEBELLE** Low H6 M. Pink buds open to white flowers with olive-green spotting, in a rounded truss of 12–14. Leaves narrowly elliptic, with a thin tan indumentum on the underside. (Robert Allison × *yakushimanum*). Forster.

■ **WALLY MILLER** Low H6 M. Flowers pink, fading to pale pink in a compact truss. Leaves dark green, on a compact plant. Named after a head gardener at Richmond Park, London, where it was raised. (*yakushimanum* × Glamour). Miller/Mullins.

■ **WANNA BEE** Semi-dwarf H4 EM. Flower with large frilled calyx, pale purplish-pink with vivid reddish-orange flare, outside darker, in dome-shaped trusses of 10–12. Leaves elliptic, slightly convex, glossy, dark yellowish-green in colour and with heavy, buff-coloured indumentum, on a plant of upright, dense growth habit. *PC.* (*yakushimanum* × Jiminy Cricket). Berg/Newcombe.

■ **WELDY** Low H4 ML–L. Flowers frilled pink, fading to ivory, with white filaments, in trusses of 24. Leaves with white woolly indumentum on the underside. ([Pygmalion × *haematodes*] × *yakushimanum*). Kehr/Delp.

■ **WINTER MORN** Low H4–5 M–ML. Flowers yellowish white with some green speckling in the throat, in a rounded truss of about 15. Leaves with indumentum on the underside, new growth silvery white. (Mrs J.C. Williams × *yakushimanum*). Barlup.

YAKU ANGEL

■ **YAKU ANGEL** Semi-dwarf H6 M. Flower white with faint brown dorsal spotting, in ball-shaped trusses of 13–17. Leaves narrowly lanceolate, deep-green, underside with tan indumentum, new growth white tomentose, growing wider than tall. It looks to me that this is crossed with *R. makinoi*. *GP, MW.* (*yakushimanum* seedling). Allen/Greer.

■ **YAKU INCENSE** Semi-dwarf–Low H4–5 M. Flower with spicy scent, deep-pink in bud, quickly turning yellowish white, with some yellow-green spotting in throat, in dome-shaped truss of 14. Leaves oblong, flat, semi-glossy, olive-green, underside with sparse yellow indumentum that ages to orange-yellow. *VI.* (Lackamas Spice × *yakushimanum*). Lancaster.

■ **YAKU PICOTEE** Low H5 ML–L. Flowers openly campanulate, rose-madder, edges and the reverse darker, in compact trusses of 10. Good foliage with thin indumentum on the leaf under-surface. Later than most 'yak' hybrids. Hard to root. (*yakushimanum* × Moser's Maroon). Lancaster.

YAKU PRINCE

■ **YAKU PRINCE** Semi-dwarf H5 M. Flower tubular funnel-shaped, opening purplish pink and aging to a lighter pink, pale purplish-pink blotch and dark reddish-orange spotting, in a ball-shaped truss of 14. Leaves narrowly elliptic to elliptic, olive-green, with moderately heavy dark-orange-yellow indumentum, Upright, rounded, well-branched plant. Probably the best and most widely grown of this cross. *MB, MS.* (King Tut × *yakushimanum* K. Wada). Shammerello. '**WHITE BIRD**' white with faint green spots.

■ **YAKU PRINCESS** Semi-dwarf–Low H6 M. Flower tubular funnel-shaped, open strong purplish-pink with pale purplish-pink blotch and red spots, fading to pale pink, in ball-shaped truss of 15. Leaves elliptic, underside with dark orange-yellow indumentum, new growth silver, on a plant of dense, rounded habit. *ME.* (King Tut × *yakushimanum* K. Wada). Shammarello. Very similar sisters: '**YAKU DUKE**', tallest, '**YAKU DUCHESS**', deepest-pink, '**YAKU KING**' lowest growing.

■ **YAKU SUNRISE** Semi-dwarf H5 M. Flower broadly campanulate, rose-pink, edges and reverse darker, in ball-shaped trusses of 10. Several different clones in commerce. Leaves slightly recurved, dark green with light cinnamon tomentum, underside with thick white indumentum. Afternoon-sun protection is best. *NI.* (Vulcan's Flame × *yakushimanum* K. Wada). Lancaster. Others from same cross are '**YAKU SENSATION**', '**YAKU FANTASIA**' and several others.

■ **YAKUSHIMANUM (syn. DEGRONIANUM SSP. YAKUSHIMANUM)** Low H5 ML–L. The 'yak' parent species. Apple-blossom-pink buds open to full trusses of white. Good flowers and foliage. Excellent foliage: silver indumentum above and fawn below. Forms a compact mound. Very hardy and tolerates full sun. '**KOICHIRO WADA**' FCC. The most famous form. Usually grafted. *AGM, PNW, NZ (s), U.K., Scand, and so on.*

YAKUSHIMANUM

■ **YOURS TRULY** Low H4 M–ML. Buds purplish red, opening to frilled flowers of pale purplish-pink, with strong greenish-yellow dorsal spots, in compact trusses. Foliage with indumentum on underside. (Lady Bessborough × Ken Janeck). Smith/Delp.

SUBGENUS AZALEASTRUM

SECTION AZALEASTRUM

Evergreen shrubs or trees. Height 0.6–8m, generally small shrubs in cultivation, though they may grow large in favourable climates. H2–4. Leaves evergreen, glabrous, young leaves often highly coloured. Flowers rotate to tubular-campanulate with spreading lobes, white, pink, rose, pale to magenta-purple, crimson, with or without spots. The species of section Azaleastrum have rather dainty foliage and pretty and sometimes showy flowers, but can be rather shy-flowering in cultivation. All the species are best suited to warm climates, such as Australia and California. None are widely cultivated.

■ **HONGKONGENSE** Flowers rotate, white, spotted violet, single-flowered from multiple buds. Small elliptic leaves, young leaves often purplish, on a fairly compact and dense grower. Very pretty.

■ **LEPTOTHRIUM** Flowers rotate with short tube and spreading lobes, pale-rose to rich-purple-rose, one per bud, in clusters. Young foliage glossy, bronzy or reddish. Can be spectacular in the wild. Best in mild western gardens in the U.K. Good in New Zealand.

LEPTOTHRIUM

■ **OVATUM** Flowers rotate with short tube, white, pink, or pale purple, single-flowered from leaf axils. Leaves +/– ovate, young growth often red or pink. Needs a hot sunny site to flower. **BACHII Group**. Intermediate with *R. leptothrium*.

OVATUM

■ **VIALII** Flowers tubular-campanulate, deep-red to crimson, single, from multiple buds in the leaf axils. Leaves obovate or obovate-lanceolate. A very striking and distinctive species, recently introduced and proving hardier than expected.

VIALII

SUBGENUS CANDIDASTRUM

A single species.

■ **ALBIFLORUM** Flowers rotate, white, 1–2 per bud, in leaf axils, very late. Small leaves on ascending branches. Hard to cultivate successfully, so seldom seen as a garden plant. Very pretty in the wild. 1–2m.

SECTION CHONIASTRUM

Height to 15m, bushy to erect shrubs to small trees. H1–3. Bark often smooth or peeling, red to brown. Leaves evergreen, usually glossy, young leaves often tinged red. Flowers white, rose to purple, narrowly funnel-shaped with narrow tube, often fragrant. In gardens, this is a neglected group of species with great potential for warm climates, such as S.E. Australia and the milder parts of New Zealand and California.

■ **CHAMPIONAE** Flowers broadly funnel-shaped from pink buds opening to white with yellow spots, slightly fragrant, about 5 per truss. Leaves roughish and bristly. A spreading shrub. Flowers can be very attractive.

■ **HANCOCKII** Flowers widely funnel-shaped, white with a yellow flare, fragrant, in a truss of 1–2. Leaves glabrous. Similar to *R. moulmainense*. 1–4.5m.

LATOUCHEAE

■ **LATOUCHEAE** Flowers pink-purple, funnel-shaped, single. Leaves broadly elliptic to elliptic-lanceolate, stiff and shiny, on an upright to spreading shrub to 4–7m.

■ **MOULMAINENSE** Flowers white, pink or magenta, with a yellow blotch in trusses of 3–5, scented. Widespread over large parts of S.E. Asia, including S. China, Vietnam and Cambodia.

■ **STAMINEUM** Flowers tubular funnel-shaped, white with a yellow blotch, long stamens, in a truss of 3–5. Quite hardy at Glendoick but requires more sun than we have to flower well. Can be spectacular.

SUBGENUS MUMAZALEA

SECTION MUMAZALEA

A single species.

■ **SEMIBARBATUM** Flowers rotate-funnel-shaped, small white, sometimes flushed yellow or pink, one per lateral bud. A rare, taxonomically very distinct, deciduous species, with unusual, bronze-tinted foliage that turns a fine red in autumn. The small flowers get lost in or under the foliage.

SEMIBARBATUM AUTUMN COLOUR

HANCOCKII

AZALEAS

SUBGENUS PENTANTHERA: THE DECIDUOUS AZALEAS

DECIDUOUS AZALEA SPECIES AND HYBRIDS

Height 1–10m, spreading to upright, deciduous shrubs or small trees. H3–8. Flowers white, yellow, pink, purple, orange, scarlet or crimson. This subgenus contains the species referred to as deciduous azaleas. The Mollis and Exbury hybrids are well-known, but the species themselves are becoming more and more popular with their subtle, often scented, flowers. Many are late-flowering, so extending the season. Most deciduous azaleas are very tough and many are heat tolerant. Some species and hybrids can suffer from azalea mildew (*see* page 25).

SECTION PENTANTHERA

Ht 1.5–5m, occasionally to 10m. All are decidu-ous. Corolla narrowly funnel-shaped, sometimes blotched but not spotted. These species are North American except *R. luteum* and are useful for their hardiness and heat tolerance (most of them) and, in many cases, their scent.

■ **ALABAMENSE** Low–Medium H3–4 M–ML. Flowers funnel-form, white with a yellow blotch, fragrant (lemon-scented), in a truss of 6–12. Flowering in April–May in native S.E. U.S.A., later further north. **'TERRY GREER'** (syn. **'FROSTY'**) fragrant white with yellow blotch, good foliage: a very glaucous leaf underside. **'FOUNTAIN'** pale pink. A favourite of lace bugs. **'NANCY CALLOWAY'** yellow/white. *AZ, CH.*

ALABAMENSE

■ **ARBORESCENS (Sweet azalea)** Medium H6–7 L–VL. Flowers tubular, heliotrope-scented, white or pale pink, sometimes with a yellow flare with contrasting purplish-red style, 3–7 per truss. Neat compact habit and useful for late flowering, fine scent and attractive flowers. The best of the white scented-species for Scotland and cool climates. **'HOT GINGER & DYNAMITE'**, **'WHITE LIGHTNING'** both very fragrant, **'SUMMER PARASOL'** low-growing. *Scot, AZ, CH, SE.*

ARBORESCENS

■ **ATLANTICUM (Coastal azalea)** Low H5 M–L. Flowers tubular funnel-shaped, white to white-flushed pink, tube usually deeper, with a musky scent, in a truss of 3–13. An attractive and tough azalea with good foliage, which forms large, relatively low, spreading clumps. It enjoys a moister soil than most of its relatives. It lacks rigidity as a young plant with an untidy habit. **'MILENBERG JOYS'** blush-pink shaded apricot, **'THE PEARLS'** creamy white, tinged pink, with yellow flare. *MA, AZ, CH, SE, MW.*

ATLANTICUM

AUSTRINUM YELLOW

AUSTRINUM

■ **AUSTRINUM (Florida azalea)** Medium H4 M–ML. Flowers yellow to orange-yellow, fragrant, in a truss of 10–24. Leaves covered with downy soft hairs. Closely related to and merges with *R. canescens*. Heat-tolerant and good in hot climates but not suitable for growing in areas with cool summers. Mildew resistant. **'ESCATAWPA'** brilliant-yellow. **'MOONBEAM'** early orange-yellow. **'HARRISON'S RED'** coral-red. There is also a white form (alba). *MA, CH, SE, OZ, AZ, NC, GA, WB, Mel.*

■ **CALENDULACEUM (Flame azalea)** Medium–Tall H5–6 L–VL. Flowers funnel-shaped, orange, sometimes red or yellow, in trusses of 5–9. Upright habit, can eventually reach up to 4m. Tough and good in Scotland. A parent of many of the best orange hybrids. **'TANGELO'** large-flowered orange, flushed pink. *TZ, MA, AZ, CH, MW, S. Fin.*

CALENDULACEUM

■ **CANESCENS (Piedmont azalea)** (*see* photo overleaf) Medium H3–5 M–ML. Flowers funnel-shaped, sweetly scented, pink or white, 6–19 per truss, appearing before or with the leaves. Leaves sometimes greyish white or glaucous. Needs heat to ripen wood, so not suited to Scotland. **'VARNADOES PHLOX PINK'** large bright-pink scented flowers. **'CRANE'S CREEK'** deep-pink. **CANDIDUM Group** with a white-glaucous leaf underside. *MA, AZ, CH, SE, OZ.*

CANESCENS VERNADO'S PHLOX PINK

FLAMMEUM

■ **CUMBERLANDENSE (syn. BAKERI)** Low H5–6
L–VL. Flowers tubular-funnel-shaped, orange or red,
with long stamens. More compact than the closely
related *R. calendulaceum* and a little later to
flower. Often has good autumn-colour. **'SUNLIGHT'**
a pale clone with salmon-yellow flowers. **'CAMP'S
RED'** very fine red flowers, but hard to root.
'CHALIF' salmon-pink-reddish-orange. **'SIZZLER'**
orange-red. *SE.*

CUMBERLANDENSE

■ **EASTMANII** Low–Medium H3 M–ML. Flowers
white, very fragrant, emerge after the new growth.
Some forms have pink-and-yellow markings. A recently
described 'new' species from South Carolina. It is
closely related to *R. viscosum* and is probably derived
from hybrids with one or more of the other native
species. It grows along damp stream-banks.
■ **FLAMMEUM (Oconee azalea)** Low–Medium
H3–4 M–ML. Flowers orange to scarlet, long
stamens and style, in a rounded truss of 6–11,
seldom scented. From Georgia and South Carolina.
Earlier than the related *R. prunifolium* and *R.
cumberlandense*. Heat and sun tolerant but not
suitable for areas such as Scotland with cool
summers. **'RED INFERNO'** a deep selection. **'WOOD
NYMPH'** large bright-orange. *AZ, CH, OZ, SE.*
■ **LUTEUM (syn. AZALEA PONTICA)** Low–Medium
H5–6 M–ML. Flowers funnel-shaped, yellow,
sweetly fragrant, in a truss of 7–17. Spreading and
vigorous. Usually fine autumn-colour. Easily grown
and good for naturalizing in the U.K. Subject to
mildew and not very heat tolerant. Formerly used
as an understock for grafting azalea cultivars.
Found wild in the Caucasus north into Poland.
'GOLDEN COMET' large, long-lasting flowers and
good autumn-colour. *AGM, PNW, AT, S. Fin, Mel.*

LUTEUM AUTUMN COLOUR

LUTEUM

OCCIDENTALE

■ **OCCIDENTALE (Western azalea)** Medium H4
L–VL. Flowers scented, white, flushed pink with
orange-yellow flare, 5–25 or more per truss.
Foliage holds on till midwinter and seldom colours
well. Somewhat prone to mildew and rust fungus in
some climates. The largest flowered, scented,
white azalea species, much used in breeding. Many
selected forms. **'CRESCENT CITY DOUBLE'** fine
double flowers, but rust-susceptible.
'STAGECOACH FRILLS' frilled and ruffled flowers.
AGM, PNW, Mel.
■ **PERICLYMENOIDES (syn. NUDIFLORUM,
Pinxterbloom)** Low–Medium H6–8 M–ML. Flowers
funnel-shaped, pubescent outside, deep-pink,
occasionally white to rose-pink, light but sweet
fragrance, per truss of 6–15, before or with the
leaves. Often stoloniferous and usually quite low-
growing. From a wide area of E. U.S.A. from New
England south to Georgia and Alabama and west to
Tennessee. **'FLAT CREEK FUCHSIA'** pinkish purple
with red tube. *AZ, CH, CT.*

PERICLYMENOIDES

PRINOPHYLLUM

■ **PRINOPHYLLUM (syn. ROSEUM Roseshell
azalea)** Low–Medium H6–8 M–ML. Flowers tubular-
funnel-shaped, clove-scented, in a truss of 4–13,
appearing before or with the leaves. This can reach
5m in the wild, usually much smaller as cultivated.
A very hardy plant from open hillsides and stream
banks in Eastern U.S.A., which often crosses with
neighbouring species. Not very successful in S.E.
U.S.A. **'MARIE HOFFMAN'** large flowers, probably
a hybrid. *S. Fin.*

■ **PRUNIFOLIUM (Plumleaf azalea)** Medium H3–5 VL. Deep-orange-red flowers late in the season. Grows best in some shade. Originates from Georgia and Alabama and the lack of heat means it is not good in Scotland and similar climates. Takes a few years to bud up. Can flower as late as September. **'REBEL YELL'** a fine compact bright red. **'LITTLE RED RIDINGHOOD'** pure-red, not dwarf! **'SEPTEMBER'** a late clone. *PNW, CT, TZ, MA, OZ, MW, CH, AZ.*

PRUNIFOLIUM

■ **VISCOSUM (Swamp azalea)** Medium H5–6 VL. Flowers sweetly-scented, small white tubular, 3–14 per truss, usually after the leaves. Best to seek out selected forms, as some have poor flowers. One of the latest species to flower. Tough. Some forms have glaucous foliage. **'WHITE FOAM'** a fine selection. **'BETTY CUMMINS'** fine pink, reflexed. **'DELAWARE BLUE'** white, bluish-green foliage. *AGM, TZ, MA, MW, S. Fin.* **Var. AEMULANS** slow growing and early flowering form from Georgia and Alabama. **OBLONGIFOLIUM Group**. H3–4. Scented white flowers in May. The Texan form from the western end of the range. Not as hardy as more northern *R. viscosum*. Tolerates deep shade and very heat tolerant, but the flowers are small and it cannot really compete with other azaleas flowering at the same time. **'KATIE FERGUSSON'** a pink form. **SERRULATUM Group**. H3. The Hammocksweet Azalea. Small white, clove-scented flowers in late July–August. Occurring from Texas to Florida and can flower as late as November. Now considered a regional form of *R. viscosum*. **'WHITE PEARL'** fragrant white, dark foliage.

VISCOSUM

SUBSECTION SINENSIA

Flowers funnel-shaped, red, orange to yellow only, upper lobe spotted. Distribution China and Japan only.

■ **MOLLE** Low–Medium H4–5? M–ML. Flowers funnel-shaped, yellow with darker spots, in trusses of 3–10+? Little known, this was recently re-introduced from China, previous introductions seeming to have died out, or mixed into Mollis hybrids. It should have good heat-tolerance. **SSP. JAPONICUM (Syn. *Azalea mollis*)** Low–Medium H6–7 M–ML. Flowers funnel-shaped, red, orange, salmon-pink or yellow, in trusses of 3–13. Very hardy, easy and compact. This species from Japan is the parent of the Mollis azaleas. Indeed most of them are simply selected forms of the species. (*See* under Mollis in the hybrid section, page 183.) *SE, UK, Ger, Hol, AT, S. Fin.*

MOLLE SSP. JAPONICUM

SECTION RHODORA

Corolla +/– rotate-campanulate, two-lipped, white to pink or rose-purple. This section contains two species which share a two-lipped corolla but are otherwise not all that closely related.

■ **CANADENSE (Rhodora)** Semi-dwarf–Low H7–8 EM–M. Flowers rotate-campanulate, two-lipped, upper lip with two short lobes, lower part divided into two distinct lobes, rose-magenta-purple in compact trusses. Small, often blue-green leaves on a compact, slow-growing plant. Very hardy. Best in areas with cool summers. Inspired an Emerson poem. Poor in S.E. U.S.A. **'ALBUM'** white flowers. *AT, S. Fin.*

CANADENSE

VASEYI DEEP PINK AND WHITE FIND

■ **VASEYI (Pinkshell azalea)** Low–Medium H5–6 EM–M. Flowers with very short tube with five wing-like lobes, pale to deep-pink or white, with greenish throat with reddish-orange spots at the base, 5–8 per truss. A very distinctive species with pointed leaves and scarlet autumn-colour. Adaptable and tough. **'TIMBERLINE'** a fine deep-pink. **'PINKERBELL'** pink selection. **'WHITE FIND'** pure-white. *AGM, CT, TZ, AZ, CH, AT.*

SECTION SCIADORHODION

Ht 1–3m (5m in wild). H3–6. Leaves +/– obovate. Flowers white, pale- to deep-pink or purplish pink. Variable in hardiness and ease of cultivation.

■ **ALBRECHTII** Low–Medium H5–6 EM–M. Flowers rotate-campanulate, 3–4cm, rose to deep-rose-purple, 2–5 per truss, with or before the young leaves. Very hardy but early growth needs protection from frost. One of the finest azalea species. Rather prone to rabbit and deer damage. *PNW, CT.*

ALBRECHTII

■ **PENTAPHYLLUM** (*see* photo overleaf) Low (cultivated) Tall (wild) H4–5 E–EM. Flowers rotate-campanulate, pale to deep pink, rarely white, 1–2-flowered before the leaves. Leaves deciduous, elliptic to obovate, often tinged red, bark shiny. A magnificent plant in its native Japan reaching 5m or more, like a small-flowered Magnolia. Smaller in cultivation, and best in areas with hot summers. *PT.*

PENTAPHYLLUM

■ **QUINQUEFOLIUM (Cork azalea)** Low H4–5 EM–M. Flowers small, white, in trusses of 1–3, open before or with the leaves. Leaves small, often with red-brown markings. Slow-growing and hard to establish, though tough and quite easy as it gets older. Very attractive. *PT.*

QUINQUEFOLIUM

■ **SCHLIPPENBACHII (Royal azalea)** Low–Medium H4–5 M–ML. Flowers broadly rotate-funnel-shaped, pale to rose-pink, occasionally white, spotted red-brown, sometimes lightly fragrant, 3–6 per truss. Leaves obovate. Very hardy but early growth needs protection, best in some shade. Considered by many to be the finest azalea species. Seems to be a favourite of rabbits. **'SID'S ROYAL PINK'** is a good form available in N. America. *PNW, CT, TZ, AT, S. Fin.*

SCHLIPPENBACHII

SECTION VISCIDULA

A single species.

■ **NIPPONICUM** Low H4–5 L–VL. Flowers small, white and tubular, 6–15 per truss, hang below the foliage. Bullate oval leaves and peeling bark. Good autumn-colour. The *Menziesia*-like flowers are very distinctive but tend to be rather hidden as they hang down below the attractive leaves.

NIPPONICUM

DECIDUOUS AZALEA HYBRIDS

Hybridized during the last 200 years, these now come in a huge variety of colours. Some flower on the bare branches while others start to grow as the flowers open. Most are very tough, and some, such as the Northern Lights series, are amongst the toughest plants in the genus. Often used for mass planting, in woodland or in borders, the hybrids have amongst the brightest flowers of all rhododendrons. Many varieties are scented and some have fine autumn-colour. As most are relatively late-flowering, they seldom lose their flowers to spring frosts. Useful for windy sites, as the leaves blow off when autumn gales start.

The following are the most commonly grown named-varieties in the various hybrid groups, arranged in roughly chronological order, in terms of their development. In the early days, groups such as Mollis and Exbury were more commonly sold as seedlings to colour, rather than as named varieties.

GHENT

Medium–Tall (reaching 3m in time) H6–8 (USDA 4b–5b) M–L. Flowers mostly purplish-red to pink, pale yellow or white, often flushed yellow or pink. The Ghents are the oldest of the hybrid groups, the earliest selections were raised shortly after 1800. Plants in this group are tough and usually small-flowered (3–5cm).

■ **AAMURUSKO** Orange-red, with yellow upper lobes An old Ghent azalea, which has been named in Finland for its extreme hardiness (to –24°C/–11°F). *S. Fin.*
■ **BOUQUET DE FLORE (syn. FLORA)** Red, blotched yellow, frilly. Good autumn-colour. One of the best late Ghents. **'MARIE VERSCHAFFELT'** is probably a synonym. *AGM, S. Fin.* Verschaffelt.
■ **COCCINEUM SPECIOSUM (syn. COCCINEA SPECIOSA)** Small flowers, brilliant orange-red, with a strong-orange blotch. Slow-growing as a young plant. One of the best known Ghent varieties. More than one clone. *AGM, AT.* Seneclause.

COCCINEUM SPECIOSUM

■ **DAVIESII** Pink buds opening white with yellow blotch. Low growing. There appear to be two clones with this name. One has white flowers with a yellow blotch and no scent. The other has small tubular flowers, white flushed pink, with some scent. (*viscosum × molle*). *AGM.* Davies.

DAVIESII

■ **DIRECTEUR CHARLES BAUMANN (syn. ANN LOUISE)** Deep blood-red, with yellow blotch. Baumann. *S. Fin.*
■ **GRANDEUR TRIUMPHANTE** Single, deep-amaranth, shaded orange. van Houtte.
■ **KULLANNUPPU** Yellow flowers with dark-yellow upper lobes. An old Ghent seedling named in Finland as it shows extreme hardiness. *S. Fin.*
■ **NANCY WATERER** Single large vivid-yellow, spotted orange, scented. *AGM.*
■ **PALLAS** Orange-red or vermilion, with orange-yellow flare. There may be two clones, one orange and one more magenta-pink. *S. Fin.* Baumann.
■ **PRINCE HENRI DE PAYS BAS** There seem to be two plants under this name: with strong-orange or vivid-red flowers. Upright, tall. Verschaffelt.
■ **PUCELLA (syn. FANNY)** Small rose-magenta flowers with an orange flare. Good autumn-colour. Common in older collections but seldom commercially offered now. *AGM, PNW.* Mortier.

PUCELLA

SANG DE GENTBRUGGE

FREYA

NORMA

■ **SANG DE GENTBRUGGE** Small, rich tangerine-scarlet with a deep-orange flare, tube yellow-and-pink. van Houtte.

■ **SPEK'S ORANGE** Vivid-red and orange with an orange blotch. A good compact plant. Register claims it is scented: I don't believe it! *AGM.* Spek.

■ **UNIQUE** Yellowish orange in dense, ball-like, multiple-bud clusters of up to 50 flowers. Upright, tall, rather leggy as a young plant. Verschaffelt.

■ **VISCOSEPALA** Pale yellow to ivory-white, fragrant. Very floriferous. Good autumn-colour. (*molle* × *viscosum*). There were many seedlings released under this name. Waterer.

GHENT RUSTICA OR RUSTICA FLORE PLENO

A series of small, double- (or hose-in-hose) flowered varieties, mostly raised in the late nineteenth century. The subtle and pastel colourings are fashionable again, and these have seen a recent resurgence in popularity. I have included a few modern hybrids derived from the Rusticas, in this section.

■ **AIDA** Double, pale-rose, edged deeper, with a yellow blotch, in a ball-shaped truss. Good autumn-colour. **'RIBERA'** deep-pink. de Smet/Vuylstyke.

■ **BYRON** White, tinged deep-pink, double. **'VELASQUEZ'** palest yellow-white, flushed pink, double. Vuylstyke.

■ **CORNEILLE** Pale-pink, double, with dark pink-red tube. An attractive two-toned combination. *PNW.* de Smet/Vuylstyke.

CORNEILLE

■ **DOUBLE DELIGHT** Double, bright-yellow, fragrant flowers. Good autumn-colour. Free-flowering. A modern hybrid bred from 'Narcissiflora'. Bunnell.

■ **FREYA** Light yellowish-pink, with deeper tips, double. Leaves light green, slight bronze tinging on young growth. de Smet/Vuylstyke.

■ **JACK BUNNELL** Double small-flowered medium-pink, with some scent. Quite widely distributed in tissue-culture. Not as good as 'Homebush'. Good red autumn-colour.

JACK BUNNELL

■ **MILTON** White with orange-yellow blotch, double. de Smet/Vuylstyke.

■ **MURILLO** Pale-rose and deeper-pink, double. de Smet/Vuylstyke.

■ **NARCISSIFLORUM (syn. NARCISSIFLORA) g?** Pale yellow, double, with darker centre and on the outside, in a small, balled truss. Not scented in the clones I have seen, though the register claims that it is. Good autumn-colour. Resistant to mildew. Very popular and one of the best sellers in the U.K. Not always easy to please and can be rather lacking in vigour. *AGM, TZ, PV, S. Fin.* van Houtte.

NARCISSIFLORUM

■ **NORMA** Double rosy red with salmon glow in a ball-shaped truss. There may be two clones under this name, one more orange than the other. Good autumn-colour. Flowers are long-lasting. **'IL TASSO'** reddish orange with paler edges, earlier than 'Norma'. *AGM, S. Fin.* de Smet/Vuylstyke.

■ **PHÉBÉ (syn. PHOEBE)** Double, sulphur-yellow, shaded pink on outside. **'PHIDIAS'** pale yellow. Vuylstyke.

■ **VINECOURT DUKE** Double, deep-pink in multiple-bud trusses of up to 50, moderately scented. *NG.* Smith.

■ **VINECOURT TROUBADOUR** Double reddish-pink, lightly fragrant, often in large multi-bud trusses. Free-flowering with a rather upright habit. A modern hybrid of the 'Rustica' type. Smith.

VINECOURT TROUBADOUR

MOLLIS

Low–Medium (to 2.5m) H5–6 (USDA 5b–6a) M–ML. Flowers to 6cm, red, through orange, salmon, pink to yellow-and-white, in trusses or clusters of 7–13. Flowering a week or two earlier than the Knaphill hybrids, most of the Mollis azaleas are not hybrids at all, but simply selections of the Japanese species *R. molle* ssp. *japonicum*. More compact and spreading than the other hybrid groups. Sometimes sold as seedlings by colour, for example 'Mollis Red'. Selected from 1860s onwards. Most are not as hardy as the Ghent hybrids, but the flowers are larger and they tend to be more heat-tolerant. A few are fragrant. Very few of them are widely commercially available these days, having been eclipsed by their more flamboyant Knaphill cousins.

■ **APPLE BLOSSOM** Light salmon-pink with yellow markings. Resistant to mildew. There is also a white *R. canescens* selection with this name. *Mel.* Wezelenburg.

■ **CHRISTOPHER WREN (syn. GOLDBALL)** Brilliant-yellow with a strong-orange blotch. Vigorous. A good Mollis selection. Endtz.

CHRISTOPHER WREN

■ **DR M. OOSTHOEK** Bright orange-red with a darker flare. Leaves with a silvery underside. A very bright colour, one of the best Mollis of this shade. *Mel.* Oosthoek.

DR M. OOSTHOEK

■ **HORTULANUS H. WITTE** Moderate orange-yellow, strong-orange blotch. A good grower. Koster.

HORTULANUS H. WITTE

KOSTER'S BRILLIANT RED

■ **KOSTER'S BRILLIANT RED** Bright orange-red. This was not a clone, but a strain of good red-seedlings from Holland. Koster.

■ **LEMONORA (syn. LEMONARA)** Apricot-salmon, fading to yellowish, mid. Wezelenburg.

LEMONORA

■ **LIESMA** Bright poppy-red, spotted yellow. *Latv.* Kondratovičs.

■ **POLLY CLAESSENS** Orange, tube reddish-orange. Koster.

POLLY CLAESSENS

■ **QUEEN EMMA (syn. KONINGIN EMMA)** Light-orange flowers, suffused salmon, blotched strong-orange. Wezelenburg.

■ **RADIANT** Strong-red with an orange blotch. Kromhout.

■ **SATURNUS** Orange-red. Boskoop.

■ **SNOWDRIFT** Palest yellow-white with yellow-green markings. Free-flowering but as it is not scented, it is of rather limited popularity. White.

SNOWDRIFT

■ **TEIKA** Camellia-rose with a yellow flare. *Latv.* Kondratovičs.

KNAPHILL (EXBURY)

Medium–Tall (2–3m × 2m) H6–7 (USDA 5a–5b) ML–L. The most flamboyant of the hybrid groups and containing the largest number of cultivars, in many colours: red, orange, salmon, pink, yellow and white, some varieties are scented. Development of these hybrids began at Knaphill nursery and continued at Exbury (both in England). Subsequent work has continued in several parts of the world, including Ilam in New Zealand and, some of the best work of all, at the Arneson and Girard nurseries in the U.S.A. Later Exbury selections were made as the Solent group, but I can't say that they seem any improvement on the earlier selections. The over-naming of hybrids in this group has become absurd: there are hundreds of virtually identical cultivars: frankly, once you have twenty of these, you have all the colour variations you need. In the northern hemisphere Knaphill/Exbury hybrids flower from late-May to mid-June. Those marked as 'early' or 'late' are at the beginning or end of this period.

■ **ANNABELLA** Strong orange-yellow, flushed orange-pink, mid-season. A second clone 'A' has paler flowers. Exbury.

■ **ARCTIC REGENT** White with yellow throat and pink edges, early. One of the 'Solent' series. Exbury.

■ **ARISTA** Hose-in-hose, deep-pink, flushed light-pink, flushed orange-yellow, ruffled, early. Dense habit. A huge truss with up to 28 flowers. Girard.

■ **ARNESON GEM** Large orange-yellow, in full rounded trusses. A fairly compact plant with good foliage. The most spectacular of this colour that I have seen. Destined to become one of the classics. *PNW.* Arneson.

ARNESON GEM

■ **ARNESON LITTLE GEM** Orange-yellow. A new miniature version of 'Arneson Gem' which grows to 45–60cm. I have not seen it, but it sounds interesting. Arneson.

■ **ARNESON PINK** Semi-double, ruffled deep-pink. Arneson.

■ **ARNESON RUBY** Large-flowered, strong-red. Upright but spreading habit. Large trusses for a red azalea. Arneson.

■ **BABĪTES ANITA** Scarlet, blotched orange. *Latv.* Kondratovičs.

■ **BABĪTES INDRA** Large brick-red with a yellow flare. *Latv.* Kondratovičs.

■ **BABĪTES INGA** Vermillion, blotched bright-yellow. *Latv.* Kondratovičs.

■ **BABĪTES LAURA** Nasturtium-red with an orange blotch. *Latv.* Kondratovičs.

■ **BAKKARAT** Orange with a yellow blotch, late. Low growing. Hachmann.

■ **BALZAC** Star-shaped, nasturtium-red, deeper tube, with orange/yellow flash. *PNW.* Exbury.

BALZAC

■ **BARBECUE** Semi-double, light orange-yellow, flushed salmon-pink, with an orange flare. One of the Solent Group. Exbury.

■ **BERRYROSE** Rose-salmon pink, with yellow blotch, with some scent. Foliage is pale, hairy, with young growth coppery brown. Autumn colour. *AGM.* Exbury.

BERRYROSE

■ **BRAZIL** Tangerine-orange, small, frilly lobes, late. Mildew resistant. Exbury.

■ **BRIGHT FORECAST** Light yellowish orange with deeper blotch, fragrant. *PNW, Cal.* Exbury.

BRAZIL

■ **BUTTONS & BOWS** Vivid yellow, blotched orange-red, edged pink, frilled, fragrant. Leaves narrow, with a little bronze colouring. Red autumn-colour. Mildew resistant. *PNW.* Bailey.

BUTTONS & BOWS

■ **BUZZARD** Pale straw-yellow, edged and tinted pink, with a deep-yellow flare, some fragrance. *SE U.S.A., NG.* Knaphill.

BUZZARD

■ **CANNON'S DOUBLE** Pale yellowish-pink with a light-orange flare, fading to cream, double. Outstanding reddish young growth and good autumn-colour. Flower colour is a little insipid. *PNW, MW, AT.* Cannon.

■ **CECILE** Salmon-pink with a yellow flare, 6–7cm across. Not very vigorous. 'Strawberry Ice' is better. Mildew resistant. *AGM, PNW, PV.* Exbury.

CANNONS DOUBLE

■ **CHEERFUL GIANT** Double, ruffled, large, marigold-yellow. Reddish autumn-colour. *PNW.* Sorenson.

■ **CHETCO** Large bright-yellow, with an orange blotch, tube orange-red. Fairly compact. *PV, NG.* Slonecker.

■ **CHOCOLATE ICE** Small, double, cream-white flowers. Compact. Leaves tinged bronze. Flowers are rather small and with little or no scent. Waterer.

CHOCOLATE ICE

■ **CORRINGE** Semi-double, reddish orange, with an orange-yellow blotch, late. Exbury.

■ **CRIMSON TIDE (syn. GIRARD CRIMSON TIDE)** Strong-red, double, with compact petaloid centre in tight trusses. Vigorous grower. Mildew resistant. One of the hardiest Girard hybrids, H7–8. Yellow-orange autumn-colour. *MD, MW.* Girard.

■ **CRINOLINE** White flushed pink, frilled. Exbury.

■ **CROSSWATER RED** Deep-red. Good autumn-colour. Best in light shade. This is mostly *R. cumberlandense.* Millais.

CROSSWATER RED

CSÁRDÁS

FIREBALL

GIBRALTAR

■ **CSÁRDÁS** Orange buds open to semi-double (fused stamens) deep-yellow flushed orange. Young growth bronzy. Hachmann.

■ **DOLOROSO** Deep-red with white anthers. Leaves tinged reddish-brown in young growth. Hachmann.

■ **DON QUIXOTE** Strong-orange, flushed reddish-orange, with a yellow-orange throat. Solent Group.

■ **DOROTHY CORSTON** Deep orange-red. Leaves bronze tinged. Similar to 'Fireball'. Knaphill.

■ **DOUBLE DAMASK** White flushed gold and peach, fragrant, early–mid. Knaphill.

■ **DRACULA** Dark-red buds open to deep, rather bluish red. A great name and a good colour, but scarce, as it is hard to root. Hilliers.

■ **DRURY LANE** Semi-double light-orange-yellow tipped yellowish pink. Exbury.

■ **ELSIE PRATT** Clear carmine-pink with small orange dorsal blotch. Pale-green leaves. Upright and spreading habit, hardy. (Knaphill × Mollis). Pratt.

ELSIE PRATT

■ **EVENING GLOW** Pale pink, tinged yellow, throat yellow. There is also a red Mollis under this name. Ht to about 1m. *SE U.S.A.* Knaphill.

■ **EXBURY WHITE** Large white, blotched orange-yellow, tube pink-tinged. This is a named clone, though seedlings are sold to colour under the same name. Exbury.

■ **FANAL** Vivid orange-red, unmarked. An impressive large-flowered selection. Hachmann.

■ **FEUERWERK** Deep reddish-orange, blotch vivid-orange, fringed, late. Upright habit. Hachmann.

■ **FIREBALL** Deep-red fading to deep-orange, with yellow stamens. Fine reddish young growth and good autumn-colour. One of the best of the deep-orange-reds with fine foliage. *U.K.* Exbury.

■ **FLUFFY** Creamy-yellow partly petaloid double, with a small flare, fading to white, mid. *PNW.* Arneson.

■ **FRIDTJOF NANSEN** Vivid reddish-orange, late. Upright habit. Fleischmann.

■ **FRIEDRICH WÖHLER** Bright orange with yellow flare. Fleischmann.

■ **FRILLY LEMON** Double, lemon-yellow with a deeper blotch, in a balled truss of 14–17. Upright and dense. Arneson.

■ **GALLIPOLI RED** Reddish orange. There is also a paler azalea **'GALLIPOLI'** with pale tangerine, pink-flushed flowers. Resistant to mildew. Exbury.

■ **GENA MAE (syn. GINA MAE)** Double (hose-in-hose) light greenish-yellow with orange tips and centre, 20–25 per ball-shaped truss. The flower substance is very good, so the flowers are long lasting. Clement/Kowalsky.

GENA MAE (SYN. GINA MAE)

■ **GEORGE REYNOLDS** Large deep-yellow, shaded green with yellow blotch on the upper lobe. An attractive Knaphill with a vigorous upright growth-habit. One of the original parents of the Exbury strain. *PNW.* Exbury.

■ **GIBRALTAR** Vivid-orange, flushed reddish orange, with a yellow flare, frilled. Extremely free-flowering from young age. The world's most popular deciduous azalea. Mildew resistant. *AGM, PNW, MA, PV, CH, AZ, NG, AT, GL, SE U.S.A., Mel.* Exbury.

■ **GINGER** Strong-orange, flushed pink, with golden flare, early. Resistant to mildew. *PNW.* Exbury.

■ **GIRARD PINK DELIGHT** Double, yellowish pink, very fragrant, in rounded truss. One of the few full double large-flowered azaleas with scent. Girard.

■ **GIRARD RED POM POM** Double, red, in a rounded truss. Mildew resistant. Claims to be fragrant, but I don't believe it. *MD.* Girard.

■ **GIRARD SALMON DELIGHT** Semi-double, ruffled, strong-pink flushed yellowish-pink. Upright habit, yellow-and-orange autumn-colour. Mildew resistant. Girard.

■ **GIRARD YELLOW POM POM** Hose-in-hose (double), vivid-yellow, with occasional orange flushing, fragrant, in a rounded truss. Somewhat mildew resistant. *MD, GL.* Girard.

GIRARD YELLOW POM POM

■ **GLOWING EMBERS** Vivid reddish-orange, with orange blotch. Late. Exbury.

■ **GOG** Orange-red with yellow flash, flushed dark-red on outside, said to have some scent, early. Vigorous with good autumn-colour. Slocock.

■ **GOLD CREST** Brilliant-yellow with an orange-yellow blotch. Leaves tinged red. *MA.* Knaphill.

■ **GOLDEN DREAM** Strong orange-yellow. *Cal.* Exbury.

■ **GOLDEN EAGLE** Strong reddish-orange with orange-yellow midrib and a prominent vivid-orange blotch. Compact habit. Exbury.

■ **GOLDEN FLARE** Vivid-yellow with reddish-orange blotch. *PNW.* Metselaar.

■ **GOLDEN HORN** Yellow with deeper flare, tinged rose on outside, fading to cream, mid–late. Leaves greyish, new growth bronze. Exbury.

■ **GOLDEN ORIOLE** Golden yellow, deep-orange blotch, mid–late. Tall and vigorous. Exbury.

■ **GOLDEN SUNSET** Light yellow, tinged red, with an orange blotch. Leaves slightly tinged bronze. Exbury.

■ **GOLDFLAMME** Brilliant-orange suffused reddish orange, reverse orange tinged deep-pink, late. Some stamens petaloid. Hachmann.

GOLDEN ORIOLE

HACHMANN'S SATOMI

HOTSPUR (RED)

■ **GOLDPRACHT** Yellow-orange blotched deep-orange. Hachmann.

■ **GOLDTOPAS** Orange-yellow, strongly blotched orange. Dark-green foliage is reddish brown on the young growth, probably the best of any Exbury hybrid. One of the most impressive yellow-hybrids, but we don't find it all that easy to propagate. Hachmann.

GOLDTOPAS

■ **HACHMANN'S FABIOLA** Double, deep rich-pink, flushed reddish, in a balled truss. Hachmann.

■ **HACHMANN'S FLAMENCO (syn. FLAMENCO)** Large-flowered orange-red. Hachmann.

■ **HACHMANN'S JOANITA** Double, carmine-pink, blotch vivid-orange to orange-yellow. Upright habit. Hachmann.

HACHMANN'S JOANITA

■ **HACHMANN'S SATOMI (syn. SATOMI)** Pink buds open white flushed pink with a golden-yellow flare, early. Hachmann.

■ **HACHMANN'S STEFANIE** Light purplish-pink with a large vivid-orange-yellow blotch, mid. Hachmann.

■ **HACHMANN'S SUNNY BOY** Reddish orange with a strong-orange blotch, 8–14 per rather lax truss, stamens sometimes petaloid. Young leaves purple-bronze. Hachmann.

■ **HARVEST MOON** Yellow, openly tubular, with a barely visible yellow flare and frilled edges. Good habit, but not very vigorous. An outstanding almost unblotched yellow. Slocock.

■ **HARWELL** Deep-pink, in a fine large truss. Knaphill.

■ **HOMEBUSH** Semi-double, deep carmine-pink, in a ball-shaped, pompom-like truss. Autumn colour. Mildew resistant. A successful parent of double azaleas, especially from Girard nurseries. *PNW, MD, MA, PV, NG, AT, SE U.S.A., Mel.* Knaphill.

HOMEBUSH

■ **HONEYSUCKLE** Pale pink with an orange blotch. Street says there are two forms, one paler than the other. Exbury.

■ **HOTSPUR (RED)** Orange-red with orange flare, mid. This is sold under the names 'Hotspur', 'Hotspur Orange' and 'Hotspur Red'. There may be more than one clone, but all I have seen have been deep-orange from red buds. *AGM.* Exbury.

■ **ILAM CREAM** Pink in bud, opening pale yellow-green, fading to white, with pink flushing on the margins. Seedlings were also sold under this name. Ilam.

■ **ILAM GOLD** Bright orange-yellow. **'ILAM DEEP GOLD'** is very similar with deeper orange-yellow flowers. Ilam.

■ **ILAM LOUIE WILLIAMS (syn. LOUIE WILLIAMS)** Soft-pink and white with a gold flare. Leaves with a glaucous underside. Ilam.

■ **ILAM MELFORD FLAME (syn. MELFORD FLAME)** Vivid orange-red, frilled to 7.5cm, mid-season. Ilam.

■ **ILAM MELFORD LEMON (syn. MELFORD LEMON)** Strong orange-yellow with apricot flare, long lasting. Reddish young foliage, good red autumn-colour. Ilam.

■ **ILAM MING (syn. MING)** Large, vivid-orange with yellow flare. Ilam.

■ **ILAM RED GEM** Red, orange flare, yellow stamens. Ilam.

■ **ILZE** Nasturtium-red, blotched yellow. *Latv.* Kondratovičs.

■ **J. JENNINGS (syn. J.J. JENNINGS)** Red. Compact habit. Mildew resistant. Exbury.

■ **JACK A. SAND** White flushed pink and yellow, tube pink, some petaloid stamens. Foliage sometimes bronzy, autumn-colour purple. *PNW.* Wood/Sand/Eichelser.

JACK A SAND

■ **JOHN EICHELSER** Deep-pink semi-double with a golden flare in the throat, lightly fragrant. *PNW.* Eichelser/Gangsei.

■ **KENTUCKY MINSTRAL** Strong-orange-yellow and orange. *PNW.* Knaphill.

■ **KILIAN** Double, orange buds opening to light purplish pink, flushed deeper, in a balled truss of 11–13. Hachmann.

■ **KING'S RED** (*see* photo overleaf) Vivid-red in a balled truss. Slow-growing, not very vigorous. Leaves seem to be pale and rather spotted. Habit not very good. *ME.* King.

KING'S RED

KLONDYKE Red-orange in bud, opening bright golden-yellow, early for an Exbury. Coppery-red new growth and good autumn-colour. Resistant to mildew. Can get rust where Hemlock is grown. *AGM, PNW, SE U.S.A., NG.* Exbury.

KLONDYKE

KNAPHILL RED Deep-red, small flowers, mid. Good autumn-colour. Knaphill.

LADY ROSEBERY Deep yellowish-pink with touches of red. This lucky lady had a rhododendron and an azalea named after her. Exbury.

LAPWING Pale-yellow tinged orange-and-pink, with greenish blotch, sweetly scented, early. Knaphill.

LIMETTA® Yellow with a deep-yellow flare in the throat. Loose erect habit. Hachmann.

MARION MERRIMAN Brilliant-yellow, flushed and blotched orange-yellow. Leaves light green, glossy. *Cal, AZ.* H. Waterer.

MARY POPPINS Bright orange-red with an orange dorsal blotch, wavy margins, 12–16 per rounded truss. Leaves bronzy when young. Unknown.

MARY POPPINS

MIDAS TOUCH Deep golden-yellow, in large trusses. Hughes/Ilam.

MOLALLA RED Strong-red, wavy-edged and funnel-shaped, in a ball-shaped truss. *AGM, PNW.* Arneson.

MÖWE Small, frilled, pale pink fading to white with a yellow flare. Hobbie/Wieting.

MOUNT RAINIER Light yellow in bud, opening to white with a yellow blotch, lightly scented. Upright habit. *PNW.* Arneson.

MOUNT RAINIER

MT SAINT HELENS

MT SAINT HELENS (syn. GIRARD'S MT ST HELEN) Yellowish pink with an orange blotch, lightly fragrant, in a truss of 12–15. Vigorous for this colour. Does not bud-up as freely as some as a young plant. Mildew resistant. Easy to root. Autumn colour. *PNW, SE U.S.A., GL.* Girard.

NABUCCO Vivid- to strong-reddish-orange, shaded and edged deeper, unspotted and unfading. An impressive very 'orange' orange. Hachmann.

NIFTY FIFTY Large, bright-yellow, frilled flowers in a full balled truss. Named for the fiftieth anniversary of American Rhododendron Society. An impressive large truss. *PNW.* Arneson.

OLD GOLD Light orange-yellow, flushed pink, with an orange blotch. *PV.* Exbury.

ORANGE HIT Light orange, with orange-red midveins, outside darker-orange. Hachmann.

ORANGE JOLLY (syn. GIRARD ORANGE JOLLY) Double, light orange flushed deeper-orange, in a full rounded truss. **'PINK JOLLY'** fragrant pink. Copper-orange autumn-colour. Tough. Girard.

ORANGE SPLENDOR Large, round bright-red-orange trusses with frilled margins, in a balled truss. Upright and spreading habit. Arneson.

ORANGEADE

ORANGEADE Orange with a lighter centre, some flowers semi-double, early. Leaves glossy. Mildew resistant. *AZ.* Knaphill.

OTTO HAHN Salmon-pink with an orange flare, mid–late. New growth tinged bronze. Fleischmann.

OXYDOL Pure white, with yellow spotting. Bushy upright plant. Leaves pale. *PNW.* Exbury.

PARAMOUNT Double, yellow, very late. Knaphill.

PARKFEUER Orange-red with red tones, unmarked. Hachmann.

PAVLOVA® Double, soft-apricot in rounded trusses. A new double-flowered hybrid from New Zealand. (PBR in New Zealand.) Blue Mountain.

PERSIL Large pure-white with a prominent deep-yellow flare in the throat, in a rounded truss. Foliage ribbed, pale greenish-yellow. The most popular white Knaphill. Tall. Mildew resistant. *AGM.* Slocock.

PERSIL

PETROUCHKA Strong-orange and yellow, mid. Knaphill.

PINK DELIGHT Deep-pink with orange-flushed throat. *AGM.* Exbury.

PINK FRILLS Bright frilly pink, scented. Ilam/Hughes.

POMPADOUR Mid-pink with a golden eye, fragrant. Knaphill.

PRINCESS MARGARET OF WINDSOR Large, deep-yellow, flushed orange. Exbury.

RAIMUNDE Single to semi-double, pale pink, striped and edged deeper, with an orange flare. Leaves bronzy when young. Hachmann.

RED SUNSET (syn. ARNESON'S RED) Vivid-red in a balled truss of 7–11, mid. Compact. Mildew resistant. *PNW.* Arneson.

RAIMUNDE

STRAWBERRY ICE

UMPQUA QUEEN

■ SPIEGELEI White with a bold-orange flare. Meltzer.

■ STRAWBERRY ICE Deep-pink buds open to flattish-pink with deeper veins and a yellow flare. Bushy and compact with pale green leaves, bronzy young growth. *AGM, PNW.* Exbury.

■ RENNIE (syn. RENNE) Vivid-red suffused yellow. *Cal.* Exbury.

■ ROSE RUFFLES Strong-pink, to yellowish pink, deeper on margins, single, in a rounded truss. A rather hot colour. *PNW.* Arneson.

■ ROYAL COMMAND Deep reddish-orange with no blotch, late. Tall but bushy habit. Resistant to mildew. *PNW.* Exbury.

■ ROYAL LODGE Deep vermilion-red, fading to crimson, long protruding stamens, very late. *TZ.* Exbury.

■ RUMBA Vivid-orange, red tube. Knaphill.

■ SARINA Moderate- to deep-red, blotch vivid-orange, some petaloid stamens, 9–10cm. Hachmann.

■ SATAN Deep-red buds opening deep orange-red, late. Mildew resistant. **'DEVON'** is very similar. *AGM, MD.* Slocock.

■ SAULE Yellow with an orange blotch, in balled trusses. A hybrid of *R. luteum*. *Latv.* Kondratovičs.

■ SCHNEEGOLD White with orange-yellow markings, often several trusses together. Hachmann.

■ SHAM'S YELLOW Deep-yellow buds open lemon-yellow, fragrant. *MD.* Shamarello.

■ SILVER SLIPPER Pink buds open to large white, with a prominent yellow-orange flare, late. Coppery autumn-colour. Compact. *AGM, AZ.* Waterer.

■ SUN CHARIOT Vivid-yellow with an orange-yellow blotch, late. Upright habit. Exbury.

■ SUNRAY Scented double, apricot fading to near-white, in full rounded trusses. A new double-flowered hybrid from New Zealand. Lower-growing than sister 'Pavlova'. Blue Mountain.

■ SUNSET PINK Pink with a yellow blotch. Exbury.

■ SUNTE NECTARINE Red buds open to yellow, flushed deep-orange. *AGM.* Exbury.

■ SWEET CHRISTIE Flower pale-lemon-yellow, very frilled, with a deeper-yellow flare, strongly fragrant. Pink-and-yellow autumn-colour. de Wilde/MagRuder.

■ SWORD OF STATE Pale purplish-pink, flushed deeper, with an orange-yellow flare. Solent Group. *PNW.*

■ SYLPHIDES White flushed pink with yellow throat, tube pink-apricot. Tall. *TZ.* Knaphill.

■ UMPQUA QUEEN Large semi-double yellow flowers, tinged orange in bud and on reverse, in a rounded truss. Leaves bullate, yellow-bronze in autumn. *PNW.* Schoneman.

■ WALLOWA RED (syn. RED HOT) Strong-red, unblotched, in a rounded truss. Open habit with arching branches. Lacking in vigour at Glendoick (maybe due to tissue culture). Yates/Wright/Slonecker.

■ WHITE SWAN White with a yellow blotch. Exbury?

■ WHITETHROAT Small, double, pure-white, funnel-shaped, mid–late, in a one-sided truss. Silvery light-green leaves. Neat compact spreading habit. Best in light or dappled shade. *AGM.* Waterer.

WHITETHROAT

■ WILHELM RÖNTGEN Carmine-rose blotched orange-and-red, late. Upright habit. Fleischmann.

SILVER SLIPPER

■ SILVERWOOD Creamy in bud, opening to white with a prominent golden-yellow flare, fragrant. Compact with good autumn-colour. Millais.

■ SOFT LIGHTS Soft creamy-pastel pink-peach, double, in full trusses. A new double-flowered hybrid from New Zealand. Flowers hold colour best in part shade. **'BABY GIRL'** is similar. Blue Mountain.

SYLPHIDES

■ TOTALLY AWESOME Red buds open yellow, with vivid reddish-orange edges and a bright-yellow blotch. Good autumn-colour. *CC.* Bunnell.

■ TOUCAN Pale yellow with deeper-yellow flare, pink-tinged margins, late. Tall. Resistant to mildew. *MA.* Knaphill.

■ TUNIS Dark red with a reddish-orange blotch, late. Said to be fragrant. Good autumn-colour. *PNW, NG.* Slocock.

■ UGUNS Frilled fiery-red with an orange blotch. A well-branched plant. *Latv.* Kondratovičs.

WILHELM RÖNTGEN

WINDSOR SUNBEAM

■ **WINDSOR SUNBEAM** Dark golden-yellow. Windsor.
■ **WRYNECK** Yellow with a deeper-yellow flash and pink edging, scented, mid. Vigorous. *AGM*. Knaphill.
■ **YELLOW CLOUD** Light yellow, deepening to brilliant yellow, with a deep-yellow blotch, slightly fragrant, in a truss of 12. Free-flowering and said to be tough. Upright habit, not very well branched. Not very vigorous in Scotland. Hyatt.

YELLOW CLOUD

OCCIDENTALE

Low–Medium/Tall (some to 3m in time) H4–5 (USDA 6a–6b) ML–L. Bred from the species *R. occidentale*, these hybrids have relatively large (to 7.5cm) pale-coloured flowers and most are scented. The least hardy of the older hybrid groups, most are suitable for moderate climates only. Most are susceptible to azalea mildew and some are rust prone. The oldest hybrids in this category date back to around 1895.

BRIDESMAID

■ **ADVANCE** Deep-pink, yellow blotch. Koster.
■ **BRIDESMAID** White with a yellow blotch, buds pale greenish-yellow. Tall but dense habit. Koster/Waterer.
■ **CENTENNIAL** Pale-yellow/white with yellow flare, lightly scented. Handsome ribbed, deep-green leaves, fairly compact and slow-growing. Said to be resistant to mildew. The flower looks to me rather like a fried egg. *PNW*. Mossman.

CENTENNIAL

■ **DELICATISSIMA (syn. DELICATISSIMUM)** Cream, tinged pink, yellow flare, scented. Koster.

DELICATISSIMA

■ **EXQUISITA (syn. EXQUISITUM)** Pale pink-apricot with orange centre, scented. Leaves retained through part of winter. Sometimes suffers rust fungus. One of the most popular scented pale-azaleas for moderate climates. Koster.

EXQUISITA

■ **GRACIOSUM (syn. GRACIOSA)** Pale orange-yellow, suffused strong-pink, blotched orange. Best in part-day shade. Koster/Waterer.
■ **IRENE KOSTER** Rose-pink with deeper markings, a yellow flare, sweetly scented. Probably the most popular of the *R. occidentale* hybrids with fine flowers. Foliage is retained till late winter. *AGM*.

IRENE KOSTER

■ **JOCK BRYDON** White, suffused pink, with a reddish-orange blotch and ruffled edges, scented. One of the most striking of this group. Leaves retained late into autumn. Very vigorous as a young plant with arching branches. (*molle × occidentale*). Clausen.

JOCK BRYDON

■ **MAGNIFICUM** Pink buds open creamy-white flushed pink with an orange flare, fragrant. Koster.
■ **SUPERBA (syn. SUPERBUM)** White flushed pink, fading to white with a large yellow flare, scented. Less popular than sisters 'Exquisita' and 'Delicatissima'. Koster.
■ **WESTMINSTER** Fine almond-pink, with a faint-orange flare, fragrant, late. Tall. Waterer.

MODERN 'SPECIES' HYBRIDS

For much of the twentieth century, the main aim in deciduous azalea hybridizing was to produce the largest possible flowers, especially in the Exbury and Knaphill types, by crossing hybrids with hybrids generation after generation. More recently, many breeders have returned to the smaller-flowered American species, some of which were previously ignored by hybridizers, in order to impart late-flowering, heat-tolerance and scent into an exciting range of new hybrids. With

an increase in interest in native plants, these have become particularly popular in recent years in eastern North America. Those bred from more northerly occurring species are suitable for areas with cool summers. Those bred from species from S.E. U.S.A. need heat to ripen their wood and are best in milder areas with hot summers. I have divided the new 'species azalea hybrids' into three subgroups, with the hardiest first.

NORTHERN LIGHTS SERIES

H8–H9 (USDA 4a–4b) ML–L. Bred in Minnesota for severest climates, the Northern Lights series are hardy to –34 to –40°C (–30 to –40°F) and are amongst the hardiest plants in the genus *Rhododendron*. They have small flowers and I'm not convinced that many of them are really worth growing in milder climates, where more flamboyant, but less hardy, varieties are suitable. Some have a light fragrance. They do seem to make a very strong root-system.

■ **CANDY LIGHTS** Clear light-pink, with pale-yellow streaks on the upper corolla lobe, of heavy substance, strongly fragrant. Ht 1.5–2m. The latest of the Northern Lights series and a replacement for 'Pink Lights', which was hard to propagate. (*atlanticum* × Mollis).

■ **GOLDEN LIGHTS** Small pale-yellow with orangey blotch, fragrant. Very hardy (–40°C). Mildew resistant. One of the best of this series. *GL, ME, S. Fin.*

■ **LEMON LIGHTS** Vivid-yellow with an orange-yellow blotch, lightly scented. A vigorous grower. Small flowered.

■ **LILAC LIGHTS** Medium pinkish-purple with darker speckles on upper lobes. Similar to 'Orchid Lights' but said to be an improvement. Fairly low-growing, maturing at about 1m high and 1–2m wide.

■ **MANDARIN LIGHTS** Ruffled, bright red-orange, small, with a light fragrance. Very floriferous. *S. Fin.* (*calendulaceum* × Orangeade). Said to be hardy to –37°C (–35°F), which is USDA zone 3b. One of the best of this series.

■ **NORTHERN HI-LIGHTS** Yellow fading to creamy-white, with a bright-yellow flare, with a moderate scent, 7–10 per truss. Mildew-resistant foliage emerges with a bronzy tone. *MS, S. Fin.*

NORTHERN HI-LIGHTS

■ **ORCHID LIGHTS** Small lilac-pink, in a truss of about 7. Low growing. Needs no dead-heading. Flowers are small and the colour is poor. Not worth growing unless your climate is extremely severe. *S. Fin.*

ROSY LIGHTS

■ **ROSY LIGHTS** Dark rose-pink, with deeper-rose-red shadings, lightly scented. A bit of a harsh colour. Not worth growing in mild climates. *PNW, S. Fin.*

■ **SPICY LIGHTS** Small strong-yellowish pink, blotched orange-yellow.

■ **TRI-LIGHTS** White, with purplish-pink marbling and pink spots, frilled, in a domed truss of 10–15. Vigorous and like all of this group, very tough.

■ **WESTERN LIGHTS** Reddish purple, outside pinkish-purple, small, slightly scented, in a dense, balled truss. A polyploid form of 'Orchid Lights' with thicker, glaucous foliage and larger flowers. I would grow 'Fraseri' in preference, as flowers are finer. Briggs.

■ **WHITE LIGHTS** Small pale-pink flowers fading to white, with faint golden markings, lightly scented. Rounded habit, Very hardy. Bud hardy to –37°C (–35°F), a best seller in America. *AGM, PNW, MW, AT, S. Fin.* (*prinophyllum* × Exbury).

WHITE LIGHTS

NORTHERN SPECIES HYBRIDS

(Bred from northerly American species parents.) H(4)5–7/8 (USDA 6a–4b) M–VL. Most of these are very tough, though not all do well in areas such as Scotland with cool summers. Many of the best were bred at Weston nurseries in Massachusetts. Quite a large number of this group are natural hybrids, selected from wild populations or wild-collected seed. The very late flowering ones are particularly useful for extending the season into mid- and late summer.

■ **A HEAVENLY THING** White flushed deeper pink, light-yellow flare. Very late, sometimes well into August. Carlson.

■ **ANNA'S SMILE** Pink to peach-pink with a yellow throat, fragrant. Glossy dark-green foliage. (Ghent × *arborescens*). Weston.

ANTILOPE

■ **ANTILOPE** Pink with faint-yellow blotch, small, scented, 10 per truss. Compact. (*viscosum* ×). Felix and Dijkhuis.

■ **APRICOT GLOW** Orange, very late, said to have some fragrance. Dark green leaves. (Seedling of *prunifolium*). The name is illegal so it will probably be registered as 'Weston's Apricot Glow'. Weston.

■ **APRICOT SURPRISE** Small, deep-yellow flushed orange, scented, 10–12 per flat truss. Compact grower, free-flowering. (? *calendulaceum* × ? *prinophyllum*). U. of Minnesota.

APRICOT SURPRISE

■ **APRIL SHOWERS** Large pale-yellow, with a deeper orange-yellow centre and slight blotch. Early, compact. J. Waterer.

■ **ARPEGE** Vivid-yellow, tinged yellow-pink on the tube, fragrant, small, 10 per truss. Tough, upright but compact. *PNW, TO.* (*viscosum* ×). Felix and Dijkhuis.

ARPEGE

■ **ASTRA** Yellow-orange with pink-red reverse. Good autumn-colour. (*molle* ssp. *japonicum* × *prinophyllum*). *Latv.* Kondratovičs.

■ **BALTIC AMBER** Golden yellow, with orange highlights, with a slight scent. Upright habit with striking blue-green leaves. A very attractive combination of flowers and foliage. Needs a sheltered, sunny site in Scotland. Good autumn-colour. Weston.

BALTIC AMBER

■ **BONBON** Fragrant pink, mid–late. Foliage blue-green. ([*viscosum* × *cumberlandense*] × *arborescens*). Weston.

■ **BUTTERCRUNCH** Peach-pink with golden-yellow flare, long pink stamens. Carlson.

■ **CAMILLA'S BLUSH** Fragrant soft-pink flowers. *R. canescens* seedling or form. USDA zone 6, so not as hardy as most of this group. Beasley.

■ **CARLSON'S CORAL FLAMEBOYANT** Vivid salmon-pink, early. (*calendulaceum* seedling). There is also a 'Golden Flameboyant'. Carlson.

■ **CARLSON'S POSTCRIPT** Seedling azaleas in pink, yellow, cream or coral. Small-flowered late-blooming seedlings. (*cumberlandense* × *arborescens*). Sold to colour; better to buy a named hybrid. **'CARLSON'S PINK POSTCRIPT'** shades of pink, **'CARLSON'S WHITE POSTCRIPT'** white, scented. Carlson.

■ **CASILLE** Pink, white with a yellow flare. (Contains *flammeum*, *canescens* and *alabamense*). Woodlanders.

■ **CASSLEY** Small-flowered, pale-pink, scented, June–July. To 1.5m. (*viscosum* ×). Millais.

■ **CHANEL** Light yellow, tubular funnel-shaped, suffused pink, dark-yellow blotch, fragrant. Felix and Dijkhuis.

■ **CHAUNCY BEADLE** Deep-pink with a yellow blotch, very late flowering. A semi-dwarf with hairy stems. (*cumberlandense* × *viscosum*). Biltmore Estate.

CHAUNCY BEADLE

GAMECOCK

■ **CHICKASAW** Light pinkish-orange aging to dark salmon-rose, slight scent, early. Free-flowering with fine bullate foliage. **'GAMECOCK'** narrow, strap-like corolla lobes. (*calendulaceum* × *periclymenoides*). Towe.

■ **CHOCOLATE DROP** Fragrant white, early. A seedling of *R. canescens* with striking reddish-brown young growth. May have some breeding potential for good foliage. Koone/Lazy K.

■ **CHOPTANK RIVER HYBRIDS** Small pale-pink or white, sweetly scented flowers. Natural hybrids of *R. atlanticum* × *R. periclymenoides*. Several named forms: **'CHOPTANK C1'** white with purplish-pink blush, **'CHOPTANK RIVER SWEET'** yellow, flushed peach, and at least five more. *SE U.S.A.* Hill.

■ **CLYO RED** Cherry-pinkish-red. This is either an exceptionally dark *R. canescens*, or more likely a hybrid, probably with *R. flammeum*. USDA zone 6. McCartney/Woodlanders.

■ **DAWN AT THE RIVER** Yellow, aging to orange and then red, giving a multi-coloured effect. Early–mid. A striking wild-collected seedling of *R. calendulaceum*. A good name. Beasley.

■ **DEEP ROSE** Strong purplish-red with an orange flare, scented. Upright but dense growth habit. *MS*. (Ghent × *arborescens*). USDA zone 4, so one of the hardiest of this group. Mildew resistant. Weston.

■ **DIORAMA** Red, 9–12 per truss, with a light scent. (*viscosum* ×). Very hardy. Boskoop.

■ **EVENING SUN** Flowers red and orange. Selection or natural hybrid of *R. austrinum* collected in Georgia. Sommerville.

■ **FALL FLING** Bright-red flowers in clusters. Bred for extremely late flowering, lasting well into September. Upright and tall to 2.5m. (*prunifolium* × *arborescens*). Waldman/Roslyn.

FRAGRANT STAR

■ **FRAGRANT STAR** Small, very sweetly-scented white flowers. Tetraploid version of 'Snowbird' with thick leaves and a more upright and rigid habit. Slow growing. Mildew prone in Scotland. Heat tolerant. Briggs.

■ **FRAMINGHAM (syn. JULY PEACH)** Peach-pink fragrant, late. Glaucous dark-green foliage. Low growing. Mildew resistant. (*viscosum* ×). Weston.

■ **FRANK ABBOTT** Vivid purplish-red, (very deep pink), with a spicy fragrance. Vigorous. Reddish-orange autumn-colour. *ME*. (*prinophyllum* × Mollis). Abbott.

FRASERI

■ **FRASERI** Purplish pink, two-lipped flowers. One of the few purple deciduous-azalea varieties, little known but very tough and more impressive than the Northern Lights azaleas of this colour. Hardy in S. Finland so should be more widely grown. (*canadense* × *mollis*). Fraser.

■ **FRED GALLE (syn. MEMORY OF FRED GALLE)** Small yellow flowers, very late in the season, July to early August in most climates. Named after Fred Galle, author of the major book on azaleas. Tall. (*arborescens* × *prunifolium*). Kehr.

■ **FREDERICK O' DOUGLAS** Creamy flowers with yellow, fragrant. Best in S.E. U.S.A. and other hot areas. ('Hotspur Yellow' × *austrinum*). Dodd.

■ **GABLE'S YELLOW** Light yellow with some fragrance. Leaves glossy, slow-growing. (*arborescens* × *cumberlandense*). Gable.

■ **GARDEN RAINBOW (syn. RAINBOW)** Flowers bright yellow with an orange-yellow flare. Foliage is mildew-resistant. Weston.

■ **GOLDBRICK** Bright yellow with a darker blotch and red stamens, 5–7 per truss. Fairly low growing and compact. (*arborescens* × *cumberlandense*, natural hybrid). Towe/Anastos.

■ **GOLDEN LAKOTA** Large ruffled yellow. Vigorous and upright. Heat tolerant. *SC*. (Sandra Marie × *austrinum*). Maple Leaf Nursery.

■ **GOLDEN SHOWERS (syn. GOLDEN ANNIVERSARY)** Peach, yellow and white, lightly scented flowers, very late. Bronze autumn-colour. A little susceptible to mildew. Not sure that the name was a good idea! Weston.

■ **HEY LOVELY LADY** White, flushed pink, fragrant, late. One of what I would term the 'sexist wolf-whistle series' of Carlson azaleas. It seems to demand a rude response. Carlson.

■ **HOLY MOLY** Deep-pink with orange flare. Tall and vigorous to 2.5m. June–July. Carlson.

■ **HONEYMOON HONEY** Pale creamy-yellow with a yellow flare, orange stamens, fragrant. Carlson.

■ **I SURRENDER DEAR** Probably after being battered over the head for the names of his azaleas! Deep-coral to soft apricot-pink with a yellow flare. Carlson.

■ **I'M YOURS** Peach-pink with a yellow flare, pink stamens. Late. 2–3m. Carlson.

■ **JANE ABBOTT g.** Large rich-pink flowers, with a strong sweet fragrance. Upright, spreading habit, showy red-orange autumn-colour. Extremely hardy. Not very good in Scotland. *PNW, CC, ME.* (*R. prinophyllum* × Mollis). There were many seedlings released under this name.

JANE ABBOTT g.

■ **JOLIE MADAME** Pink with a faint orange blotch, 7–9 per truss. Upright habit. Boskoop.

JOLIE MADAME

■ **JULY JESTER** Vivid red-orange with an orange blotch. A hardy, low-growing plant. (*R. cumberlandense* × *prunifolium*). **'JULY JOY'** salmon-red with gold blotch. Leach.

JULY JOY

■ **JUNE FIRE** Deep-red, 4–5 per truss. An outstanding colour. Said to be a *R. prunifolium* hybrid, but it may simply be a selection of *R. cumberlandense*. Pratt.

■ **JUNIDUFT** Pale pink with a yellow flare, tube red, sweetly scented. Purple-bronze young foliage appears before the flowers. A fine combination of flower and foliage. (*viscosum* ×). Hachmann.

■ **KARMINDUFT** Strong red and purplish red with a faint-orange blotch, with a spicy scent, in a loose truss, mid. A very 'hot' colour. (*viscosum* ×). Hachmann.

■ **KELSEY'S FLAME** Orange and yellow bicolour. Tall and upright. (Seedling of *R. calendulaceum*). Beasley.

■ **LATE DATE** Extremely fragrant white flowers with contrasting red stamens. Glossy leaf, upright narrow growth habit. (*arborescens* × *prunifolium*). **'LATE LADY'** deep-pink fragrant flowers in July–August. Towe.

■ **LEMONADE** Pale greenish-yellow, late, to 2.5cm. Foliage glossy. Weston.

■ **LOVING YOU** Light pink, with paler veining and white flare, light fragrance. Carlson.

■ **MARIE HOFFMAN** Flowers much larger than the parent species (*prinophyllum*) with extremely fragrant and clear pink flowers. Tall and vigorous.

■ **MARYDEL** White flushed purple-pink, tubular, tube and buds purple-pink, fragrant. Slow-growing and compact. *SE U.S.A.* (Natural hybrid, *atlanticum* × *periclymenoides* or pink selection of *atlanticum*). A Choptank River hybrid. Said to be unpalatable to rabbits and deer. I like the contrast between the dark tube and white lobes. Hill.

■ **MAZAIS JEFIŅŠ** Vermillion, blotched pale-yellow. *Latv.* (*molle* ssp. *japonicum* × *prinophyllum*). Kondratovičs.

■ **MILLENIUM** Tubular, slightly fragrant red to deep-pink, late, in trusses of about 6. Upright habit. Foliage blue-green, silver beneath, mildew resistant. Flowers stand up well to the summer heat. Truss size is small, but it is a useful late-flowering choice. Weston.

MILLENIUM

■ **MODOC APPLE BLOSSOM** Flowers white, blotched lavender-pink. Compact. A Choptank River-type hybrid. *SC.* (*periclymenoides* × *atlanticum*). Maple Leaf Nursery.

■ **MOIDART** Apricot-pink, scented, late, in a many-flowered balled truss. Upright habit. (*viscosum* ×). Millais.

■ **NACOOCHEE** White with pink flushing, very fragrant, about 15 per ball-shaped truss. Stoloniferous (spreading by rooting and layering). Selected Choptank River hybrids F2. The name is the Cherokee word for 'evening star' and commemorates a lover's suicide! Beasley.

■ **NECTAR** Lightly fragrant light pink-orange, opening from darker buds with moderate fragrance. Leaves with silvery undersides. Slow-growing with an upright habit. Somewhat mildew susceptible. (Probably *cumberlandense* × *arborescens*). Name illegal, so probably will be 'Weston's Nectar'. Weston.

■ **PASACIŅA** Lightly scented pale-pink blotched yellow. Purple-red autumn-colour. *Latv.* (*molle* ssp. *japonicum* × *prinophyllum*). Kondratovičs.

■ **PENNSYLVANIA** Light-pink star-shaped, fragrant, with an orange flare, July–August. Slow growing, yellowish autumn-colour. Very late flowering. Weston.

PENNSYLVANIA

■ **PINK & SWEET** Purplish pink, semi-double, with a golden flare, sweet-spicy fragrance, in June. Narrow leaves turn purple-bronze in autumn. Mildew resistant. Lacking in vigour in Scotland. *MS, PB.* (*arborescens* ×) Weston.

■ **PINK PUFF** Strong yellowish-pink, blotched yellow, 6–8 per truss. A natural hybrid. (*cumberlandense* × *arborescens*). Leach.

■ **POLĀRZVAIGZNE** Lightly scented, frilly, pure-white. *Latv.* (*molle* ssp. *japonicum* × *prinophyllum*). Kondratovičs.

POLĀRZVAIGZNE

■ **PRISONER OF LOVE** Apricot, flushed pink, yellow flare. Late June–July. Carlson.

■ **QUIET THOUGHTS** Yellow and orange, fragrant, early–mid. Upright growth habit. (Ghent × *arborescens*). Weston.

■ **REVE D' AMOUR** Light purplish-pink, pale-orange blotch, lightly fragrant, like 'Rosata'. (Mollis × *viscosum*).

■ **RIBBON CANDY** Pink flowers, striped white, with a spicy or peppery fragrance. Widely upright growing, Reddish autumn-colour. (*viscosum* × *arborescens*). Slightly susceptible to mildew. Should be a good parent for late scented-hybrids. Weston.

■ **RIGA** Light purple-pink scented. *Latv.* (*arborescens* × *molle* ssp. *japonicum*). Kondratovičs.

■ **ROSATA** Lightly scented pink with darker veins. A tough compact plant with small leaves. Easy to root and free-flowering. *AGM, TO, Scot.* Felix and Dijkhuis.

ROSATA

■ **RUBĪNS** Bright-red in rounded trusses. *Latv.* (*molle* ssp. *japonicum* × *prinophyllum*). Kondratovičs.

■ **SALUTE (syn. RED SALUTE)** Strong-red buds open to small red flowers, very late. A vigorous upright grower. (*viscosum* × *prunifolium*). 'INDEPENDENCE' from same cross is fragrant pink. Weston.

■ **SANDY** Apricot-pink with a yellow flare, with a scent like violets, late. Glossy leaves with a blue underside. (*arborescens* × *cumberlandense*?). Low growing. Weston.

■ **SEA BREEZE** Bright light-yellow. Fine blue-green leaves. Similar to 'Baltic Amber'. Weston.

■ **SNOWBIRD** Flowers very small, tubular, white, very fragrant. Foliage blue-green. A natural hybrid. Flowers small and habit poor but scent is excellent. *See also* 'Fragrant Star'. *PNW.* Biltmore.

SNOWBIRD

■ **SOIR DE PARIS** Pink with orange throat, lightly scented, 7–9 per truss. Small leaves with a slight blue-grey cast. A fine plant. *U.K.* (*viscosum* x). Felix and Dijkhuis.

■ **SOMEDAY SOON** Light peach-apricot, orange-red stamens. Late June–July. Carlson.

■ **SOMMERDUFT** Small, tubular, pure-white flowers from pale-pink buds, scented, late. (*viscosum* × *arborescens*). Fairly low and compact. Hachmann.

SOIR DE PARIS

■ **STOPHAM LAD** Pinky white, striped and streaked reddish pink, with a yellow blotch, scented. Ht 1.2–1.5m. Pratt.

■ **SUMMER BOUQUET** Light pink with soft-yellow flare. Carlson.

■ **SUMMER LYRIC (syn. JEFF)** White, overlaid with pale- and strong-pink, darker border, scented, very late. Good autumn-colour. (*prunifolium* × *arborescens*). Beasley.

■ **SUMMER STARS** Ruby-red with a white stripe. 2–3m. July. Unusual. Carlson.

■ **SUNDANCE YELLOW** Yellow, deeper blotch, 5–7 per truss, early. Light-green leaves. Compact. 'SPRING RAINBOW' pink with yellow/orange blotch. (both *calendulaceum* × *periclymenoides*). Towe-Anastos.

■ **SWEET SEPTEMBER** Clear-pink flowers and red stamens, slightly fragrant. Dark foliage, tall, upright habit. Bred for very late flowering, into September. (*prunifolium* × *arborescens*).

■ **TORRIDON** Small shell-pink flowers with a faint-orange flare. (*viscosum* x). Millais.

■ **TOWER DRAGON** Delicate salmon-pink, sweetly scented, with prominent stamens. Stoloniferous habit. (*atlanticum* seedling). Named after a Tower Court dog. Stevenson.

■ **TOY** Small pale-pink flowers, fragrant. Blue-green leaves. Heat and cold tolerant. Low and slow-growing. (*arborescens* × *viscosum*). Hill.

■ **WESTON'S INNOCENCE** Flowers small, white, fragrant, mid–late. Bronze-green foliage turning red in autumn. Compact mounding habit. Fairly mildew resistant. One of the best performing azaleas in S. New Hampshire. *MS, ME.* Weston.

■ **WESTON'S LEMON DROP (syn. LEMON DROP)** Flowers small, pale-yellow with reddish markings, lightly scented, very late. Glaucous foliage. One of the best late-flowering varieties for Scotland. Very easy to root. *MS, ME.* (*viscosum* x). Weston.

WESTON'S LEMON DROP

■ **WESTON'S LOLLIPOP (syn. LOLLIPOP)** Sweetly fragrant, pink, with a yellow flare, mid–late. Hardy, wide, spreading. Red-orange in autumn. Resistant to mildew. *MS.* Weston.

■ **WESTON'S PARADE (syn. PARADE)** Dark-pink, with a prominent orange blotch, with a vanilla fragrance, late. Fairly mildew resistant. *MS, PB.* (Ghent × *arborescens*?). Not very vigorous in Scotland. Weston.

■ **WESTON'S POPCORN** White, fragrant, with a yellow flare and pink stamens. Foliage slightly glossy, underside blue-silver, turning burgundy-red in autumn. *MS, ME.* (*arborescens* x). Weston.

■ **WESTON'S POPSICLE** Large, dark violet-pink, with an orange flare, fragrant. Upright habit. Burgundy foliage in autumn. Mildew resistant. *MS.* Weston.

■ **WESTON'S SPARKLER (syn. SPARKLER)** Ruffled, small, pink, with a spicy-chocolate scent. Small dark-green leaves, undersides silvery. Mildew resistant. Red autumn-colour. One of the best of the Weston hybrids in Scotland, and excellent in New England. *MS.* (*viscosum* x). Weston.

WESTON'S SPARKLER

■ **WHITE LIGHTENING** Flowers white with a large yellow blotch, strongly fragrant. Dark-green leaves on a compact plant. (*arborescens* seedling). Towe.

■ **WHOSE HONEY ARE YOU?** Reflexed, light-pink with orange flare. Late June. It surely deserves the reply: 'not yours'. Carlson.

■ **WISE DECISION** Flowers deep golden-yellow, tube light-red, very fragrant. Vigorous to 2.5m. (*R. austrinum* seedling, ARS seed exchange). Cummins.

■ **WOOD NYMPH** Orange in large trusses. Medium–Tall. Transplant.

SOUTHERN SPECIES HYBRIDS

H3–5/6 (but need heat) M–VL. These varieties are suitable for gardens with moderate winters and hot summers. They will not survive in areas such as Scotland, Scandinavia and E. Canada. Some may do well in coastal New England. Excellent for S. Carolina, Georgia, Alabama and similar climates with hot summers. Major hybridizers are Aromi, Sommerville and Dodd.

■ **ADMIRAL SEMMES** Medium-yellow with a deeper flare, fragrant. Confederate series. Heat tolerant and mildew resistant. Named after the Confederate admiral who sank or captured a record eighty-seven ships and still ended up on the losing side. Dodd.

ADMIRAL SEMMES

EARL'S GOLD

MY MARY

■ **AROMI GOLDSTRIKE (syn. GOLDSTRIKE)** Deep-yellow, with an orange blotch. Aromi.

■ **AROMI SUNNY-SIDE-UP** Pale-yellow buds open to lemon-yellow, with a darker blotch, moderately scented. (*austrinum* × Golden Sunset). Bred for heat tolerance. Aromi.

■ **AROMI SUNRISE** Yellow-orange with darker shading. (Hiawatha × *austrinum*). Aromi.

■ **AROMI SUNSTRUCK** Pale-yellow buds open to vivid-yellow with an orange-yellow blotch. (*austrinum* × White Swan). Bred for heat tolerance. Aromi.

■ **CAROUSELLE** Apricot with a lighter throat. Aromi.

■ **CHOICE CREAM** Very fragrant lemon-yellow, fading to paler, with yellow flare and touch of pink in the tube. Buds young, very floriferous. Early blooming. Partially stoloniferous. (*R. austrinum* × *R. atlanticum*). Galle.

CHOICE CREAM

■ **COLONEL MOSBY** Large dark-pink to salmon, fragrant flowers. Confederate series. ('Hotspur Yellow' × *austrinum*). Best in hot areas of S.E. U.S.A. Dodd.

■ **COPPER CANYON** Coppery-orange. Best in S.E. U.S.A. and other hot areas. ('Hotspur Yellow' × *austrinum*). '**JEFFERSON DAVIS**' fragrant reddish orange. Dodd.

■ **EARL'S GOLD** Flowers light-yellow with reddish stamens, in a balled truss, with some fragrance. (*R. austrinum* x). Not suitable for Scotland. Sommerville.

■ **EMMA SANSOM** Large, fragrant pink. Confederate series. ('Hotspur Yellow' × *austrinum*). Best in hot areas of S.E. U.S.A. Dodd.

■ **FOUR KINGS** Red buds open to bright-yellow, flushed red, with a deep-yellow blotch, 5cm. (Golden Peace × *austrinum*). Aromi.

■ **FRONTIER GOLD** Buds reddish-orange, flowers yellow, shaded scarlet with a deep-yellow blotch. (*austrinum* ×). Aromi.

■ **GENE'S GOLD** Creamy yellow, margins flushed rose, with a faint blotch. Aromi.

■ **GLORY BE** Bright-yellow, fragrant, with a yellow blotch. Azalea of the year (ARS) 2004. Said to be one of the best Aromi hybrids. Aromi.

■ **GREAT BALLS OF FIRE** Orange in rounded trusses. Aromi.

■ **HAZEL HAMILTON** Pure-yellow flowers that all open at once, giving a balled truss. An impressive clear-yellow colour. Hard to root. *AZ, CH.* (*flammeum* × or selection). One of the hardiest hybrids of this species, good as far north as New England.

■ **HIGHTIDE** Flowers cream, margins pale-pink, flare yellow. Aromi.

■ **JEB STUART** Medium-pink with orange-yellow throat. Later flowering than other Confederate azaleas. Good in S.E. U.S.A. ('Hotspur Yellow' × *austrinum*). Dodd.

■ **LACE CAP** Light pink. (*viscosum* × Ilam red azalea). Aromi.

■ **LISA'S GOLD** Bright yellow with light-red tube, fragrant. Very vigorous to 3m. (*R. austrinum*). Beasley.

■ **LIZ COLBERT** Buds red, open white flushed peachy pink, with a yellow-orange flare. (*viscosum* Serrulatum Gp. × *austrinum*). Aromi.

■ **MILLIE MAC** Flowers yellow with a bold-white margin, fragrant, early. A very striking flower and a plant that should have breeding potential. (probably *austrinum* × *canescens*). McConnell.

MILLIE MAC

■ **MY MARY** Fragrant light-yellow flowers with long stamens, in ball-shaped trusses of about 25. Compact, with thickly-textured foliage. Insect resistant. Stoloniferous. One of the best newer species hybrids. Best in areas with hot summers. Some success in New England. *AZ, CH, CC.* (Choptank C1 × *R. austrinum*). '**KENNEL'S GOLD**' is similar but deeper in colour. Beasley.

■ **ORANGE CARPET** Flowers orange, early (May). A groundcover azalea, which only reaches about 30cm but spreads readily. The original plant is now 2–3m wide. (*R. calendulaceum* × *R. flammeum* natural hybrid). Sommerville.

ORANGE CARPET

■ **PATHFINDER** Orange buds open to brilliant orange-yellow, flushed red, with a deeper blotch, sweetly scented. (*austrinum* ×). Aromi.

PATHFINDER

■ **PINK CAROUSEL** Buds scarlet, flowers pale-pink flushed red, with a strong golden blotch. (*austrinum* × Red Letter). Aromi.

■ **RED PEPPER** Vivid orange-yellow, shaded and tube red, with a deeper blotch, slightly scented. (Gallipoli × *austrinum*). Aromi.

■ **ROBERT E. LEE** Ruffled red fragrant flowers. Best in S.E. U.S.A. and other hot areas. ('Hotspur Yellow' × *austrinum*). **'PVT. LAFAYETTE ACREE'** fragrant, ruffled, orange. Dodd.

■ **STONEWALL JACKSON** Large fragrant light-orange flowers. Confederate series. ('Hotspur Yellow' × *austrinum*). Best in hot areas of S.E. U.S.A. Dodd.

■ **SUMMER EYELET** Small, slightly scented, white with reflexed lobes. Glossy dark-green leaves. (*viscosum* × *viscosum* Serrulatum Gp.). Beasley.

■ **TIPSY TANGERINE** Buds scarlet, flowers various shades of orange with a yellow blotch. Aromi.

AZALEODENDRONS

1–2m H4–5 (USDA 6a–6b). It is relatively difficult to cross rhododendrons and azaleas, but if you try hard enough, you can get a few hybrid seedlings. The results are sometimes interesting, though, in my opinion, all these are more novelties or curiosities rather than must-have garden plants, as many are small-flowered, rather lacking in vigour or subject to disease. The first one was raised in around 1800 and Galle lists just over twenty in total. Most are elepidote crosses with deciduous azaleas, apart from the Hardijzer hybrids, which are R. racemosum × evergreen azalea.

■ **GLORY OF LITTLEWORTH** Flowers creamy-white with an orange blotch in a small rounded truss of 15–18. Leaves blue-grey. Lacking in vigour. Undoubtedly this has the most spectacular flowers of the Azaleodendrons, but it has a sickly constitution and I have rarely seen a good plant. *PNW*. Mangles.

GLORY OF LITTLEWORTH

■ **HARDIJZERS BEAUTY** Flower clear-pink, from axillary buds, in trusses of 2–4. Leaves tiny, glossy, medium-green, purplish green in winter. Upright, dense habit. Prone to rust. Not heat tolerant. **'MARTINE'** very similar. **'RIA HARDIJZER'** deeper pink than the others. Hardijzer.

■ **MARTHA ISAACSON** Flower fragrant, white with distinctive red-pink streaks from centre to outside. Maroon-tinted semi-deciduous leaves. Vigorous. This may be the best of the azaleodendrons but it is very susceptible to rust fungus. It should have its AGM removed. *AGM*. (*occidentale* × Mrs Donald Graham). Ostbo.

MARTHA ISAACSON

■ **ODORATUM** Flowers pale lilac, lobes reddish purple, scented, about 12 per truss. An open grower with small green leaves. A nineteenth-century cross. (*ponticum* × *periclymenoides*). Young/Thompson.

■ **OREGON QUEEN** Flower fragrant, light pink. Tough and hardy. (A natural hybrid of *occidentale* × *macrophyllum*).

■ **TRESSA McMURRY** Flower deep purplish-pink with strong reddish-brown spots, in flat trusses of 10–14. Leaves narrowly oblanceolate, dark green. Upright, dense and vigorous growing shrub. (said to be *occidentale* × *ponticum*).

■ **VALLEY SUNRISE** Flowers purplish pink with an orange flare. Upright habit to 1.2m. Quite striking, though not everyone's colour. Prone to rust. Ticknor.

VALLEY SUNRISE

SUBGENUS TSUTSUSI: THE EVERGREEN AZALEAS

SECTION BRACHYCALYX

Height to 5m, small to large, deciduous to semi-evergreen shrubs. Leaves in pseudowhorls of three leaves near the ends of branchlets, usually rhombic. Flowers funnel-shaped to funnel-campanulate, purple, mauve, lavender, magenta, red, rose, pink, orange to white. The Japanese species of this subsection perform best in areas of high or moderately high summer temperatures that ripen the wood and set flower buds. In areas with cool summers they are rather shy-flowering and lacking in vigour. The Chinese species are more tender and of limited garden merit.

AMAGIANUM

■ **AMAGIANUM** Low–Medium H4 L–VL. Flowers open campanulate, reddish orange, in a truss of 1–3. Leaves rhombic. Needs a hot sunny site. Broader leaves and later flowering than its relatives. Can reach 5m in favourable conditions but usually low-growing as cultivated.

■ **FARRERI** Semi-dwarf H1–2? VE–E. Flowers lavender to purplish pink, spotted, 1–2 per bud. Leaves deciduous or semi-evergreen, hairy. A tender, heat-tolerant azalea from Hong Kong and coastal China. **MARIESII** Low H2–3 EM. Rose to purple, spotted, larger than *R. farreri*, rarely cultivated.

■ **RETICULATUM** Low–Medium H4–5 EM–L. Flowers funnel-campanulate, lavender, magenta, reddish-purple or white, 1–2 per bud, usually before the leaves. Best forms are very fine in flower. There are many different forms of this species from different Japanese islands, which differ in tiny details: **DILATATUM** ovary glandular, **HIDAKANUM** ovary short-stalked glandular, **NUDIPES** stamens 8–10, ovary hairy, **WADANUM** style with stalked glands. *Mel*.

RETICULATUM

RETICULATUM WHITE FORM

■ **SANCTUM** Low–Medium H4–5 ML–L. Flowers before the leaves, rose-pink, 3–4 per rounded truss. Distinctive rhombic foliage. Needs a hot sunny site. **'ZEKE'** a crimson form raised by Polly Hill.

■ **WEYRICHII** Low–Medium H3–4 EM–L. Flowers open funnel-campanulate, rich salmon-pink to brick-red with darker spots, 2–4 per truss. Leaves rhombic, not shiny, smaller than those of *R. amagianum*. Needs warm summers to grow best.

WEYRICHII

SECTION TSUTSUSI

EVERGREEN OR JAPANESE AZALEAS

Usually compact shrubs in cultivation, mostly 1–2m, H1–6. Flowers purple, red, near-orange, pink to white. The hardy species in this large section and their many hybrids are generally known as 'Evergreen', 'Japanese' or 'Obtusum' azaleas. Those grown for the pot-plant industry and outdoors in warm climates are known as 'Indian' or 'Indica' azaleas. Huge numbers of the latter are grown in specialized nurseries for year-round decoration in the home and are perhaps the most widely grown part of the genus *Rhododendron* world-wide. The majority of species and hybrids in section Tsutsusi are not suitable for Scotland and parts of northern Europe or the far south of New Zealand, where lack of summer heat leads to poor ripening of wood and subsequent winter damage. The selection and breeding of azaleas goes back hundreds of years in Japan and hybridization began in the west as soon as numbers of varieties were introduced in the early 1900s. Evergreen azaleas are subject to azalea gall and petal blight (*see* page 27).

Many new species in section Tsutsusi have recently been described in China, but few are likely to prove hardy except in very mild areas. These are not included in this book, as they have not yet been introduced to cultivation outside Asia.

■ **ARUNACHALENSE** Low H1? Flowers pink or purplish pink. The most westerly occurring evergreen azalea species, we found this at very low (tropical) altitudes in Arunachal Pradesh, India and it may be the most heat tolerant species of azalea, though likely very tender. Probably not yet in cultivation and I'm not sure when it flowers.

■ **ERIOCARPUM** Low H2–3 L–VL. Red, purplish-pink or white flowers, 2–4 per truss. Leaves hairy. Probably a parent of the 'Gumpo' and Satsuki azaleas. Useful for its late flowering. Heat tolerant and needs summer heat to ripen wood.

INDICUM

■ **INDICUM** Semi-dwarf–Medium H3–4 ML–VL. Flower broadly funnel-shaped, rose-red to bright-scarlet, 1–2 per bud. A Japanese species much used in hybridizing. Not to be confused with 'Indian' azaleas sold as houseplants. *Mel.*

KAEMPFERI

■ **KAEMPFERI** Low–Medium H3–5 EM–L. Flowers funnel-shaped, salmon, rosy red, red, orange-red, pink or white. A very hardy plant from Japan that is semi-evergreen in hard winters. Much used as a parent. **VAR. POLYPETALUM** strap-like narrow flowers. **VAR. TUBIFLORUM** open-tubular flowers. **LATISEPALUM Group** Pale salmon. Many selected forms: **'INDIAN SUMMER'** autumn-flowering, **'WILLIAM TRITT'** one of the hardiest, **'EASTERN FIRE'** a good form, **'PINK JOY'** a hardy Canadian selection. *AGM, MA, MS, Mel.*

KAEMPFERI POLYPETALUM

KIUSIANUM PINK

■ **KIUSIANUM** Dwarf–Semi-dwarf H5 M–ML. Flowers funnel-shaped, small, red, orange-salmon, pink, purple, or white, 2–3 per truss. There are many fine selected forms in many colours. Semi-dwarf prostrate species from Japan. Semi-deciduous. Very hardy, probably second to *R. poukhanense*, the hardiest species. Much used as a parent of low-growing, small-flowered cultivars. **'MAIOGI'** pink, with paler centre. *AGM, CT, PNW, AT, TO.*

KIUSIANUM BONSAI

■ **MICROPHYTON** Semi-dwarf–Low H2–3 EM–M. Flowers funnel-campanulate with a long tube, small, rose-purple, pink or off-white, in trusses of 3–6. A spreading, dense shrub from dry low-parts of Burma and S.W. China. It has been introduced several times but is seldom cultivated. It might be useful for heat and drought tolerance.

NAKAHARAE MARIKO

■ **NAKAHARAE** Dwarf H4 L–VL. Flowers red, orange-red or rose-red, 2–3 per truss. Tiny hairy, dark-green leaves on a prostrate, often very slow-growing species from Taiwan, much used as a parent of hardy hybrids. Useful for its late-flowering. **'MARIKO'** (*see* photo previous page) rose-red and **'MT 7 STAR'** red, are two fine dwarf selections. **NORIAKIANUM** is similar with a more upright habit.

■ **OLDHAMII** Low–Medium H2–3. Flowers large, funnel-shaped, brick-red to coral-pink, 1–4 per truss. Leaves hairy on a vigorous, spreading plant. **'4TH OF JULY'** is a selected clone from Patrick seed that repeat blooms; used to produce the Encore series. Resistant to lacewing. *Mel.*

OLDHAMII

■ **RUBROPILOSUM** Low–Medium H2–4 ML–L. Flowers funnel-shaped, pink-lavender, spotted, in a truss of 2–4. Hairy leaves on a fairly compact, dense plant that grows well at Glendoick. Not all that exciting.

RUBROPILOSUM

■ **SCABRUM** Low H2 M. Flowers rose-red to brilliant scarlet, 2–6 per truss. The largest-flowered Japanese/evergreen azalea species, but rather tender. A popular garden plant in Japan, rare elsewhere. *Jap.*

■ **SERPYLLIFOLIUM** Semi-dwarf H4–5 EM–M. Flowers tiny, pale or deep rose-pink to white, usually in one-flowered trusses. Tiny leaves on a compact, spreading plant. Deciduous or semi-deciduous. A fine, tough and neat plant.

■ **SIMSII** Low–Medium H1–2 M–ML. Flowers broadly-funnel-shaped, red to pink, in trusses of 2–6. Leaves usually narrow on a spreading plant. Very heat-tolerant but tender. Used as a parent of the houseplant azaleas. Found in the wild over a huge area of China, Burma, Thailand and Vietnam. *Mel.*

SIMSII

■ **STENOPETALUM VAR. LINEARIFOLIUM.** Low H3–4 M–ML. Flowers reddish pink, very narrow strap-like corolla. Very narrow hairy leaves. Hardier than the type species and very distinctive, it does best in areas with hot summers. *PNW.*

■ **TASHIROI** Low–Medium H3–4 EM–L. Flowers off-white, pink to pale rose-purple, 2–5 per truss. An upright plant, tall in the wild, with attractive flowers. Heat tolerant and best in warm climates. Deserves to be better known. **KANEHIRAI** from Taiwan is very similar.

■ **TOSAENSE** Low H3–4 EM–M. Flowers funnel-shaped, pink, lilac-purple or white, 1–6 per truss. Almost totally deciduous, leaves hairy, on a compact or erect plant. Best in areas with hot summers. **KOMIYAMAE Group** differs in having double the number of stamens.

■ **TSCHONOSKII** Dwarf–Semi-dwarf H5–6 L. Flowers tiny, pure white, in trusses of 3–6. Tiny hairy leaves on a compact plant. The flowers are almost laughably small but it is one of the toughest azalea species.

■ **TSUSIOPHYLLUM** Dwarf H4–5 L. Flowers very small (less than 1cm long), white, in a truss of 1–4. Very small leaves on a compact, twiggy plant. Previously in its own genus, but now considered an azalea.

■ **YEDOENSE VAR. POUKHANENSE** Low H5–6 EM–M. Flowers rose to pale lilac-purple, slightly fragrant, in trusses of 2–3. Leaves deciduous, on a semi-upright shrub. One of the hardiest species and an important parent of most of the hardiest evergreen azalea hybrids, especially those of Joe Gable. **'ROSEA'** pinker forms. **'SHIZANKO'** a good form. VAR. **'YEDOENSE'** double, purple. *MA, SE, MW, AT, ME.*

YEDOENSE VAR. POUKHANENSE

Evergreen azaleas are very important garden plants throughout much of the world. Some of them can be grown where typical rhododendrons cannot, such as Mexico City and even at altitude near the equator in Medellin, Columbia. The evergreen azaleas and their hybrids flourish in light shade in warmer climates. The further from the equator you live, the more sun is required to ripen wood and set flower-buds. In Scotland we find that they need to be planted in full sun. Petal-blight fungus affects the flowers of these azaleas in many warmer areas and this is decreasing their popularity.

There has been an absurd number of evergreen azalea hybrids named, which has left a legacy of confusion and mislabelling. The Glenn Dales are an example where, instead of choosing, say, the best 60–100 cultivars, over 300 were named, many of which are more or less indistinguishable from one another. The Holy Grail is to breed a yellow evergreen azalea, so if you want to get rich, this is what you need to concentrate your hybridizing efforts on. Many have tried…

I have listed the cultivars in the traditional categories, such as Indica, Satsuki, Kurume and Glenn Dale, and invented some new categories. The two most important of these are the 'North American Hardy' group, which contains the toughest American hybrids, and 'Northern European Hardy', which lists most of the best newer European azaleas. Flowering times are hard to specify as, in very mild climates, many will flower in winter and early spring, while in cold climates the same varieties may not flower till May–June. It is very important to select the right azaleas for your area. Beware of Home Depot, B&Q, Walmart and the other 'sheds' or 'big-box' stores that sell the same plants from one end of the country to another. They almost never have the correct varieties for your area and those irresistibly cheap plants are probably going to be annuals!

Azalea Cultivar Flower Types
The breeding of evergreen azaleas goes back for hundreds of years and many of the cultivars are far evolved from wild material, with various 'fancy' flower types described below. In addition, many sports occur, some stable and others less so, which accounts for the often outrageous flower-colouring, especially amongst the Indica and Satsuki hybrids.

1. **Single:** A single corolla with a small calyx.
2. **Hose-in-hose:** The appearance of one corolla inside another (the calyx is enlarged and coloured).
3. **Semi-double or petalloid:** Some of the stamens are fused in the centre of the corolla.
4. **Double:** All or almost all the stamens have fused to form extra petals.
5. **Double, hose-in-hose:** a flower with both fused stamens and one corolla inside another.

INDICA, BELGIAN INDIAN & SOUTHERN INDICA

H1–2 (USDA 8a–10a). Using the tender species *R. simsii*, hybridization of the Indica azaleas began in the 1830s and 1840s. These became the first of the so-called Belgian azaleas, used for forcing and as houseplants, which is by far the most important commercial part of the rhododendron industry, with millions produced every year. The European azaleas were exported to North America where further breeding was done, producing the Southern Indian & Rutherfordiana groups. Indica azaleas have proven to be good outdoor garden-plants in mild regions such as S. Australia, Georgia and California. The Augusta Masters Golf tournament in Atlanta is famous for its azalea-lined fairways. The breeding of azaleas over generations has produced huge flowers, and many double and multicoloured forms, often the results of sports which have stabilized. Quite a number of these azaleas have been trademarked or patented in America or Europe. In recent years further work on Indica azaleas has been done in America by Nuccio nursery and Buck Clagett, amongst others, and in Europe by breeders such as van Oost and the Institute of Ornamental Plant Breeding in Belgium. Outdoors, Indicas flower in spring, which can be as early as February/March in mild climates. Indoors they can be forced into flower from autumn onwards.

■ **ABUNDANCE (syn. ABONDANCE)** Vivid-red, double, 7.5cm. *Aus.* Haerens.

■ **ADVENT BELLS (syns ADVENTEGLÖCKEN, CHIMES)** Strong purplish-red, about 10cm, semi-double, early. Upright habit. Rather sun-sensitive. *Aus, Mel.* Ambrosius.

■ **ALBA PERFECTA (syn. ALBUM PERFECTUM)** Single white. Fairly compact. '**ALBA MAGNIFICA**' white, fragrant. '**ALBA MAGNA**' white, green throat. The register has corrected these to masculine (Magnificum and Magnum), but no one seems to have paid much heed.

■ **ALBERT-ELIZABETH** White with pink edge, late. Similar to 'Vervaeneana'. *Aus.* Haerens and Wille.

ALBERT-ELIZABETH

■ **ALINE** White, double, unmarked. Leaves dark-green. An outstanding performer in Australia. Glaser.

■ **ANNIVERSARY JOY** Pale pink, flushed deep-pink, red blotch, freckled green, frilled semi-double. 1.2–1.5m. *SE Aus.* Taylor.

■ **ANTARTICA** Semi-double, lilac-purple, blue-lilac. A new Belgian Indica for the houseplant market, flowering from January onwards if forced. van Oost.

■ **AVENIR** Double, pink, 6.5cm. A favourite houseplant azalea. Haerens.

■ **BABY JILL** Hose-in-hose, semi-double, purplish pink, darker veining, frilled to 7.5cm. Mossholder-Bristow.

■ **BALLERINA (PP) (syn. DANCER)** Deep salmon-pink, double. There are two other evergreen and one deciduous azalea under this name. *Aus.* Kerrigan.

■ **BALSAMINAEFLORUM (ROSAFLORA)** Double, salmon-pink, resembling tiny roses. Very low and densely branched, forming a tight spreading groundcover. *PNW.*

■ **BERTINA (PP)** Single, salmon-pink, 12.5cm, early. *Aus.* Stahnke.

■ **BONNIE McKEE** Double, mauve. *Aus.* Greentree.

■ **CALIFORNIA PEACH** Deep salmon-pink. Has a long flowering season in Australia. *Cal.* Unknown.

■ **CALIFORNIA SNOW (syn. BEVERLY HAERENS)** Large double, white with occasional salmon flecks. Renamed in California for marketing reasons.

■ **CALIFORNIA SUNSET (syn. HAEREN'S SAUMONEUM)** Red flowers with a pale-pink to white margin, to 6cm. A sport of 'Avenir'. Other sports: '**CALIFORNIA PINK DAWN**' double, blush-pink, '**CALIFORNIA BEAUTY**' salmon-pink with a wide white border. *Aus, Cal.*

■ **CAPTAIN BLOOD** Single or semi-double, brilliant rich-red. In S. Australia opens a few flowers in winter, main flowering in spring. Kerrigan.

■ **CHA CHA** White, purplish-red margin, large double, mid-season. *Aus.* Mossholder-Bristow.

■ **CHARLY** Strong purplish-red. Leaves broadly ovate, dark green. *Aus.* Glaser.

■ **CHRISTINE MATTON** Double, strong-pink, 2–3 per truss. Selection of *R. simsii*.

■ **CLOUD NINE** Double, white. A white version of the well-known 'Rosebud'. *Cal.* Kerrigan.

■ **COMTESSE DE KERCHOVE** Deep-pink, double, 10cm, mid-season. There is also a Mollis azalea with this name. *Aus.* Haerens.

■ **CONSTANCE (PP)** Moderate purplish-pink, darker blotch, frilled, to 5cm, early–mid. *Aus.* Rutherford.

■ **CORAL WING** Semi-double, hose-in-hose, salmon (yellowish) pink. A sport of 'Redwings'. *Aus.*

■ **CRIMSON GLORY (syn. NATALIE COE VITETTI)** Strong purplish-red, with a brownish blotch, semi-double, to 7cm, late. *Aus.* Rutherford.

■ **DAVINA (PBR)** (applied) Deep-pink. van Oost.

■ **DENISE ANN** Ruffled, white double, hose-in-hose, with strong purplish-pink markings flushed green, to 8cm. Leaves large. Late May. Fairly compact. Clagett.

■ **DESERT ROSE** Strong-pink, lighter throat, red flecks, frilled, to 10cm. *Aus.* Mossholder-Bristow.

■ **DOGWOOD (PP)** White, often striped moderate-red. *Aus.* Roberts.

■ **DOROTHY GISH (PP)** Frilled hose-in-hose flowers strong reddish-orange with a darker blotch to 6cm. '**WHITE GISH**' is a white sport. *Aus.* Rutherford.

■ **DOTTY ANN** Two distinct bicolour patterns: Reddish-purple border with a light purple centre; Orange-red border with a pale-red centre, to 6.5cm. Very slow growing, leaves glossy. Very unusual but may be too slow to make a commercial plant. Clagett.

■ **DR ARNOLD** Deep-pink, with white centre, red blotch. *Aus.* Burbank.

■ **DR KOESTER (PP)** Vivid-red, double, mid. *Aus.* Stahnke.

■ **EASTER BONNET** Single, lavender with a white throat, frilled, to 7.5cm. Mossholder-Bristow.

■ **EASTER PARADE** Light-pink with white marbling, semi-double, hose-in-hose, wavy, 6.5cm. '**CAPRICE**' is a sport, double-pink bordered deeper pink. *SE U.S.A., AZ, PD.* Mossholder-Bristow.

■ **ELISA** Semi-double, white, can be forced as early as August. van Oost.

■ **ELIZABETH ANN ROWE** Double, strong-red with assorted variegations of light purplish-pink on mature plants, to 6.5cm, mid-season. Leaves dark and shiny on a fairly dense plant to 1m. Clagett.

■ **ELIZABETH LAURENCE** Light-purple (magenta), single. *Aus.*

■ **ELSA KARGA (syn. ELSA KÄRGER)** Double to 8cm wide, vivid-red. Spot-blooms in winter in Australia. Alan Leslie reports five different spellings for this plant. *Aus.* Ambrosius.

■ **ERI (syn. ERIC) SCHÄME** Deep-pink, double, with irregular white margins to 7.5cm. There are lots of variations as to how this is spelled and accented.

■ **EUREKA** Lilac-pink with white margin, double. Low and compact habit. Lace-bug resistant. *Aus.* Burbank.

■ **FIRELIGHT (PP)** Moderate purplish-red, hose-in-hose, 3.5cm, early–mid. *Aus.* Rutherford.

■ **FLAME CREEPER** Single 5cm flowers, brilliant orange-red. Very low groundcover with glossy dark-green leaves. *CT.*

FLAME CREEPER

■ **FLAMINGO** Deep-pink, hose-in-hose. There are at least five Flamingo azaleas, all are, as you might expect, in pink shades. *Aus.* L. Brooks.

■ **FRECKLES (syn. WHITE PRINCESS)** White with red spots in throat, hose-in-hose. *Aus.* Hines.

■ **FRED SANDER (syn. MME ALFRED SANDER)** Large-flowered double, red. '**ORANGE SANDER**' is an orange-red sport.

■ **FRIEDHELM SCHERRER** Vivid-red, some flowers semi-double. Stahnke.

■ **GAY PAREE (PP)** White with dark-red edges, hose-in-hose. Hardier than most Indica vars, to –15°C (5°F) (USDA 7b). Named for the flowers' resemblance to can-can skirts. *Cal.* Kerrigan.

GAY PAREE

■ **GENERAL WAVELL** Deep yellowish-pink, suffused yellow, red spotting, large (to 8cm). Ingram.

■ **GLASER NUMBER 10 (syn. MANNI LACHS, ELKAR)** Single deep-pink to almost red. Dark leaves. Glaser.

GLORIA

■ **GLORIA** Purplish red with a white edge, hose-in-hose. (Sport of 'Dorothy Gish'.) *MA*. California Camellia Grds/Rutherford.

■ **GOYET** Vivid-red, double, large to 12cm. Upright but compact. The flowers are almost obscenely large. *Aus*. Burbank.

■ **GRANNY CEE** Hose-in-hose, very ruffled, with occasional petaloid centres, white with moderate striping of deep purplish-pink, green throat, flowers sport to strong purplish-pink, to 7.5cm. Leaves narrow, light-green with pubescent hairs. Clagett.

■ **HELLMUT VOGEL** Vivid purplish-red, double, early. A very important houseplant azalea with many sports. **'AQUARELL'** white and pink, **'HECTOR'** double, red, **'HUELSTEN'** double, reddish purple, **'ILONA'** pink with white edging, **'JULIA'** Purplish pink, edges white. *Aus*. Stahnke.

■ **ICEBERG** White with a green throat, semi-double. Vigorous. Sport of 'Vervaeniana'. There is also a white Kurume with this name. *Aus*. Cheesman.

■ **INCH** Single, white, with an abundance of stripes, flakes, and sectors of bright-deep-purplish-pink and strong-purplish-pink, late. Foliage: light-green, small, narrow and slightly pubescent. Plant habit: mounding, dense. A free-flowering, late, 'Indica'. Clagett.

■ **INGA** Purplish pink with white edge. There is also a pure-white version. One of the 'Hellmut Vogel'

INGA

group of Belgian houseplant azaleas. **'TERRA NOVA'** double, pale pink. **'NORDLICHT'** red. *Aus*. Stahnke.

■ **JINDABYNE** Deep-purple, semi-double, mid-season. *Aus*. Greentree.

■ **KNUT ERWEN** Frilled, strong purplish-red. Sports include: **'DE WAELE'S FAVOURITE'** pink with white edge, **'KNUT ALBA'** white, **'KNUT ORANGE'** orange-red, **'MARIE CLAIRE RODRIQUE'**, **'MEVR. ROGER DE LOOZE'** deep-pink with white edge. These sports were created with radiation. de Meyer.

■ **KOSMOS** Double, purplish red with a few spots. Leaves dark green. *Aus*. Glaser.

■ **LACINIATUM** Strap-like, deep yellowish-pink with a darker blotch. Low, dense and compact to 30cm.

■ **LAYNE ASHLEE** Double, vivid reddish-orange, centres and blotches of light pink, with stripes and flecks of deeper colour on mature plants, to 7cm. Late-mid-season. Dense and slow-growing to 60cm. (Clagett)

■ **LITTLE GIRL** Pale pink, hose-in-hose, ruffled, large. *Aus*. Burbank.

■ **LOUISE J. BOBBINK (syn. L. J. BOBBINK)** Hose-in-hose, reddish purple with a lighter throat, some whitish flowers, to 5cm. Rutherford.

■ **LUCI (PP) (syn. LUCIE)** Pink to vivid purplish-red, spotted darker, very early. Patented. *Aus*. Glaser.

■ **MACRANTHA** Flowers deep purplish-pink or salmon-red – so there are obviously two different plants under this name. Compact, leaves reddish in winter. Much used as a parent. Lace-bug resistant. **'MACRANTHA PINK'** and **'MACRANTHA PINK DOUBLE'** (both pink). **'LITTLE MACRANTHA'** a dwarf sport to 60cm. *PNW*.

■ **MADAME CYRILLE VAN GELE** Double, deep-pink. Sport of Mme John Haerens, grown under at least four other names, too, just to confuse things.

■ **MADONNA (PP)** Semi-double, ruffled, white, 7.5cm. A florist-azalea now grown in mild gardens outdoors. L. Brooks.

■ **MAGNIFICUM (syn. MAGNIFICA)** Rosy violet. There are several other Magnificum azaleas. One white cultivar grown in Australia is similar to and may be a synonym of 'Sekidera' (q.v.). *Aus*. Knight & Perry.

■ **MARTHA GARDNER** Double, vivid reddish-orange, from dark buds, with no stamens, 5–6cm, early. Fairly compact to 2m. *Aus*. Nichols.

MEVROUW GERARD KINT

■ **MEVROUW GERARD KINT** Deep-pink with a white edge. Grown in Australia as 'Mrs G. Kint'. There is also a white version. Kint.

■ **MISSION BELLS** Vivid-red, double to semi-double, ruffled. *Aus*. Yosimura.

■ **MOMMA CEE** Semi-double, strong purplish-red, with petaloid stamens, marked with varying amounts of white to very pale pink, to 6.5cm, early–mid. Leaves oval, dark-green and shiny. Open and spreading. Clagett.

MONT BLANC

■ **MONT BLANC** Double white with occasional pink lines and flecks. van Houtte.

■ **NAZARENA** Single or semi-double, red. Streck.

■ **NICOLETTE KEESSEN** Strong purplish-red to reddish-purple with darker flakes and stripes, with purplish-pink edge. *Aus*. Keessen.

■ **NUCCIO'S BRIGHTSIDE** Hose-in-hose, orange-red, to 7.5cm, mid. Dark-green leaves. Vigorous upright habit. Nuccio.

NUCCIO'S CARNIVAL

■ **NUCCIO'S CARNIVAL** Yellowish pink with orange undertones, blotched red, semi-double, to 10cm. Upright and spreading to 1.2m. The Carnival series varieties have a long flowering-period and are sun-tolerant. The flowers are very large in this clone. *Aus*. Nuccio.

■ **NUCCIO'S CARNIVAL CANDY** Vivid-red, to 10cm. Tall, to 1.2m. Another very large flower. *Aus*. Nuccio.

■ **NUCCIO'S CARNIVAL CLOWN** Vivid-purple, ruffled, to 7.5cm, early–mid. Vigorous, upright habit. *Aus*. Nuccio.

■ **NUCCIO'S CARNIVAL FIRECRACKER** Vivid reddish-orange to 6cm. Ht to 75cm. *Aus*. Nuccio.

■ **NUCCIO'S CARNIVAL MAGIC** Single, rose-red to 7.5cm. Ht to 90cm. *Aus*. Nuccio.

■ **NUCCIO'S CARNIVAL PARADE** Medium-large, mauve-pink-purple, to 6.5cm. Ht to 75cm. *Aus*. Nuccio.

■ **NUCCIO'S CARNIVAL TIME** Single, vivid-purple, to 7.5cm. Ht to 90cm. *Aus.* Nuccio.

■ **NUCCIO'S DAYDREAM** Double, light pink, with deeper-pink edges, to 7.5cm, early–mid. Moderately compact. **'NUCCIO'S DELIGHTFUL'**, **'NUCCIO'S WONDERLAND'** are similar. Nuccio.

■ **NUCCIO'S DREAM CLOUDS** Large ruffled, double, hose-in-hose, white with a green throat, to 7.5cm. Other similar hybrids include **'NUCCIO'S DREAMLAND'**, **'NUCCIO'S IVORY PALACE'**, **'NUCCIO'S MAGNIFICENCE'**, **'NUCCIO'S MASTERPIECE'**. Nuccio.

■ **NUCCIO'S FIESTA** Hose-in-hose, deep-pink, to 10cm, early–mid. Upright compact habit. Long flowering-season and, in California, flowers in autumn too. **'NUCCIO'S SPRING ECHO'** single to hose-in-hose soft-pink. Nuccio.

■ **NUCCIO'S GARDEN MAGIC** Hose-in-hose, light rose-pink, with pointed lobes, to 5cm, mid. Vigorous, upright. Nuccio.

■ **NUCCIO'S GARDEN PARTY** Deep-pink, semi-double to 7.5cm. Some flowering in autumn and winter in California. *Aus.* Nuccio.

■ **NUCCIO'S HAPPY DAYS (syn. HAPPY DAYS)** Light purple, double/hose-in-hose, to 6cm. A ten-month blooming season in California. *Aus.* Nuccio.

■ **NUCCIO'S MASTERPIECE** Double, ruffled, white to 10cm. Ht to 1.2m. Very vigorous and inclined to be straggly. Flower are very large. *Aus.* Nuccio.

■ **NUCCIO'S PINK BUBBLES** Double, coral-pink, to 7.5cm. Leaves large, on a vigorous grower. Nuccio.

■ **NUCCIO'S PINK CHAMPAGNE** Double, hose-in-hose, light pink, to 7.5cm. **'NUCCIO'S WHITE CHAMPAGNE'** a white sport with a red throat, double, hose-in-hose. Nuccio.

■ **NUCCIO'S WONDERLAND** Double or hose-in-hose, light salmon-pink, to 9.5cm, early–mid. Medium-compact habit. Nuccio.

■ **ONLY ONE EARTH** Deep purplish-pink, ruffled, semi-double, hose-in-hose. *Aus.* Burbank.

■ **ORANGE CHIMES** Deep reddish-orange, semi-double. Upright habit. *Aus.* Marshall.

■ **ORCHIDIPHILLUM (syn. ORCHIDFLORA, ORCHIDFLORUM)** Semi-double, moderate pink. Ht to 0.5m. **'SPELLBOUND'** a sport, rich-pink, edged white. Haerens.

■ **OSTA** Large, white with a burgundy throat. Dense, to 1.5m. Sport of 'Bertina'. *Aus.* Stahnke and Dettmer.

■ **OSTALETT** Reddish purple, double. Stahnke and Dettmer.

■ **OTTO** Double, red. Stahnke and Dettmer.

■ **PALOMA** Blush pink-white, semi-double. Sport of 'Hellmut Vogel'. *Aus.*

■ **PATRICK WILLIAM** Hose-in-hose, very ruffled, creamy white with a bold-chartreuse blotch, to 7cm. Very dense habit to 90cm × 90cm. An outstanding white for mild climates. Clagett.

■ **PEACE** Delicate-pale-pink to white with a dark throat, double. There is also a double, white, Kerrigan hybrid of this name. *Aus.*

■ **PERICAT PINK** Hose-in-hose, light phlox-pink, to 5cm. Similar to 'Dawn' but later and deeper in colour. Pericat.

■ **PERICAT SALMON** Light salmon-pink, hose-in-hose. Pericat.

■ **PERICAT WHITE** White, hose-in-hose. Pericat.

■ **PHOENICUM (syn. PHOENICEA)** Purplish red with darker blotch, said to have some fragrance, to 7cm. **'PHOENICUM ROSEA'** violet-pink. Vigorous, growing as wide as high. *Aus.*

■ **PINK DREAM** Large-flowered pale-pink with faint spotting, mid. There is another azalea under this name in Australia. *Aus.* van Houtte.

■ **PINK RUFFLES (PP)** Deep-pink, semi-double, hose-in-hose, to 5cm. Said to be hardy to −18°C (0°F). *AZ.* Rutherford.

PINK RUFFLES

■ **PRINCESSE MAUD** Single, purplish red, mid-season. Grown in Australia as 'Princess Maud'.

■ **PRINSESSE MATHILDE** Semi-double, pale pink with darker spotting. Compact, disease resistant and with a long flowering-period. Vervaene.

PRINSESSE MATHILDE

■ **PROFESSOR WOLTERS** Strong-red to pink with white edge, to 10cm. Belgian.

■ **PURITY** Hose-in-hose, white, to 6cm, early–mid. **'TICKLED PINK'** a sport, pink with a white edge. Rutherford.

■ **RED POPPY** Purplish red, occasional semi-double. Parent of Nuccio Carnival hybrids. *Aus.*

■ **REDWINGS (syn. RED RUFFLES, RED BIRD, RED WING) (PP)** Strong-red, hose-in-hose-double, ruffled, to 10cm. The most popular of the Brooks Indica hybrids, with huge flowers. Confusingly, it has been sold under lots of different names. Resistant to root rot and lace bug. *Cal, Mel.* L. Brooks.

■ **RIPPLES** Full double, ruffled, rose-pink, early. Foliage tinged purple in autumn and winter. *Cal.* Kerrigan.

■ **ROBIJN** Bright purplish-pink. An azalea with a pyramid habit. Dark-green leaves. Usually forced for December–Jan flowering. van Oost.

■ **ROSA BELTON** White or pale lavender, with a purple margin, ruffled, hose-in-hose. There is also a double form. A striking colour. Part-shade is best in Australia, where it has a long flowering-season. *Aus.*

■ **ROSALIE** Rose-red with speckled throat. *Aus.* Liebig.

■ **ROSE KING** Hose-in-hose, deep rose-pink. A long flowering-season. **'ROSE QUEEN'** a sport with semi-double bright-pink flowers. *Aus.*

■ **ROSE OF HEAVEN** Pale pink, semi-double. *Aus.* Hallam.

■ **ROSE QUEEN (PP)** Deep purplish-pink, white throat, to 4.5cm, early–mid. Low, spreading habit. **'ROSE QUEEN VARIEGATED'**, leaves with white edging, **'WHITE PRINCE'** a sport, white with red spots. *Mel, Cal.* Rutherford.

■ **RUTH MARION** Semi-double, hose-in-hose, purplish red, white throat, some selfs. *Aus.* Bell.

■ **SACHERSTERN (PBR)** White with narrow red edging. A late-flowering houseplant azalea becoming popular in Europe. Very attractive. **'TAGGI'** is similar.

SACHERSTERN

■ **SAMANTHA MICHELLE** Double, hose-in-hose, ruffled, deep purplish-pink, with very pale purple centres of varying size, some flowers with light-pink edges, to 7cm. Late. Small oval very dark green leaves. Dense habit. Clagett.

■ **SARA** Double, red. Disease-resistant cultivar for indoor/houseplant culture. van Oost.

■ **SAYONARA** Lilac-purple with a red flare.

■ **SEARCH LIGHT** White, occasional pink flecks, greenish throat, double. *Aus.* Lovegrove.

■ **SEDUCTION** Mauve-pink. Ht to 50cm. This is one of a series of azaleas with enticing names from Australia. None is registered, so I'm not sure who raised them.

■ **SHEILA** Red. Variegated leaf. Not hardy in Scotland. There is also a Glenn Dale of this name with purplish-pink flowers. Unknown.

■ **SILVER ANNIVERSARY** Light-pink, fading to white tips, semi-double, hose-in-hose. Burbank.

■ **SILVER SWORD** Hose-in-hose, deep reddish-purple. Variegated foliage with white margins. Inclined to revert and needs reverted shoots cut out. A witches broom has been named **'STILETTO'**. *PNW.* Meivogel.

■ **SISTER JO (PBR)** Semi-double, pale pink with a red flare. Manten.

■ **SNOW PRINCE** White semi-double to double, some flowers with central pink flush. Good sun tolerance. Flowers all winter in mild climates. *Aus.* Camellia Grove.

■ **SOUTHERN AURORA (syn. EVONNE)** Light reddish-orange, shading to white in centre and base, double. *Aus.* Huntingdale.

■ **SPLENDENS** Salmon-pink, fading. Tall. Although flowers fade in sun, they are quite long-lasting. There is also a pink Kurume with this name. *Aus, Mel.*

■ **SPREEPERLE** Double, bright pink. Manten.

■ **STARLIGHT (PP)** Light yellowish-pink, semi-double, to 6.5cm. A popular choice in California. *Aus, Cal*. Kerrigan.

■ **STELLA MARIS** White with moderate red-purple spotting. *Aus*. van der Meer.

■ **SUN VALLEY** Hose-in-hose creamy white to 7.5cm, late, buds are yellowish. Mossholder-Bristow.

■ **SWEET NELLIE (NELLIE)** Vivid purplish-pink, semi-double–double, hose-in-hose. *Aus*. Burbank.

■ **SWEETHART SUPREME** Semi-double, hose-in-hose, blush-pink, frilled, with a deeper blotch, to 4.5cm, late-mid. Medium height, dense, not very hardy: (Zone 8a). Root-rot resistant. *SC*. Pericat/Craig.

■ **TAMIRA** Semi-double, reddish purple with deep-red markings. Glaser.

■ **TEENA MAREE** Yellowish pink, hose-in-hose with partially petaloid stamens. *Aus*. Greentree.

■ **THE ROBE** Large, bright rose-pink. Variegated leaves, vigorous upright habit. Buds and Blooms.

■ **THELMA BRAY** Purplish pink, white throat, semi-double. *Aus*. Greentree.

■ **THESLA (PBR)** Deep- to strong-pink, with red spotting, double. Boone.

■ **TICKLED PINK** Light pink, white margins, hose-in-hose, 7.5cm. *Aus, Cal*. Rutherford.

■ **TIGRA (PBR)** Bright red, semi-double to petaloid.

■ **TINAS WHORLED** Strong reddish purple, lobes elliptic, not touching, giving a whorled effect to the flower. Leaves to 5cm. Foliage the same shape as the flowers giving an unusual effect. A distinctive azalea, which may well become very popular. Clagett.

TINAS WHORLED

■ **TWILIGHT** Single, rose-mauve. There are also two Kurumes with this name, one white flushed pink, the other hose-in-hose pink. *Aus*. Coolidge.

■ **VAN STRAELEN** White with a greenish-yellow throat.

■ **VERVAENEANA (syn. VERVAENEANUM)** Deep purplish-pink with a broad white margin and large reddish-brown blotch. A very old but still popular houseplant azalea. '**V. ALBA**' double, white with a green throat. '**PINK PEARL**' a sport with rich-pink flowers. *Aus*. Vervaene.

■ **VIOLACEA (syn. VIOLACEUM)** Vivid reddish-purple, double, mid. Weak wood and habit. *Aus*. Schultz?

■ **WHITE BOUQUET** Large, double to semi-double, white with a green throat, early. Dense habit to 1m. Long flowering-season in mild parts of Australia. *Aus*. Unknown.

■ **WHITE ORCHID (syn. WHITE ORCHIDS)** White with red flecks, single or petaloid. Ht 1.2–1.8m. Mossholder-Bristow.

■ **WHITE PRINCE** White with red spots, some flowers flushed pink, hose-in-hose, large. *Aus*. Rutherford/Camellia Grove.

SOUTHERN INDICA

■ **BRILLIANTINA (syn. BRILLIANT)** Deep-pink, blotch purplish-red, to 5.5cm, late. Spreading, of dense habit. Vervaene.

■ **DAPHNE SALMON (syn. PRIDE OF SOMMERVILLE)** Strong yellowish-pink, blotch darker, 5–6cm across. Tall and rangy. *SE*.

■ **DELAWARE VALLEY WHITE** White, to 6cm, similar to but smaller than those of parent 'Mucronatum'. Mounding, light-green foliage, leaves curl up in cold weather. One of the best of the hardier whites. It tends to hold on to its flowers when they have gone over. Resistant to phomopsis die-back. *PNW, CT, MD, SE, MS*.

DELAWARE VALLEY WHITE

■ **DUC DE ROHAN** Deep salmon-pink, blotch purplish-red, to 5.5cm. Early mid-season. Medium height.

■ **FIELDER'S WHITE** White, single 5–6cm. Very similar to 'Mucronatum' but more tender. Can reach 3m in height. A very old azalea, dating back at least to the 1840s. *Aus, Mel*. Fielder.

■ **FISCHER PINK (syn. DODD'S PINK, PERFECTION)** Light pink, mid-season.

■ **FORMOSA** Rose-purple, single, to 7.5cm. A very vigorous, rather coarse plant with large leaves. Heat tolerant, root-rot resistant, so popular in south U.S.A. Free-flowering. *SC, OZ*.

GEORGE L. TABER

■ **GEORGE L. TABER (syn. GEORGE LINDLEY TABOR, ALPHONSE ANDERSON)** White flushed light- to strong-pink, with a darker blotch, single, to 7.5cm. Sold as 'Alphonse Anderson' in Australia. Hardier than most Indica varieties, to –18°C (0°F). Very popular around Washington DC. *AZ, CH, OZ*. Hume.

■ **IMPERIAL PRINCESS (PP)** Purplish pink, darker blotch, semi-double, to 7.5cm. Compact. Hudson/Monrovia.

■ **IMPERIAL QUEEN (PP)** White shading to light-purplish-pink, darker blotch, hose-in-hose, occasionally semi-double, to 7.5cm. Compact and spreading. Hudson/Monrovia.

■ **IVERYANA** White with flecks of deep pink-red, occasional deep-pink selfs, or branch sports. The original hybrid dates back to the 1840s. What are grown now are sports of it. '**IVERYANA ROYAL**' dark purple, '**IVERYANA LAVENDER**' light lavender, '**IVERYANA SILVER**' white with some purple stripes. Ivery.

■ **JUDGE SOLOMON** Strong purplish-red, deeper blotch, to 6cm. Tall. Darker than the similar 'Pride of Mobile'. *AGM*.

JUDGE SOLOMON

■ **MOON MAIDEN** Creamy white with occasional pink markings, to 10cm. Very large flowers. Haworth-Booth.

■ **MRS G.G. GERBING** White, single, to 8cm. Sport of 'George L. Tabor'. Surprisingly, for an Indica, reported to be susceptible to root-rot in hot climates. *OZ*.

MRS G.G. GERBING

PRESIDENT CLAEYS

■ **PRESIDENT CLAEYS (syn. PRESIDENT CLAY)** Salmon edged white, with darker spotting, to 5.5cm, early–mid. Tall, upright habit. A plant with single, pinkish-red flowers is also grown under this name. *OZ*. van de Cruyssen.

■ **PRIDE OF DORKING** Large carmine-red (deep-pink), late. Medium. *Aus.*
■ **PRIDE OF MOBILE (syn. ELEGANS SUPERBA, WATERMELON)** Deep rose-pink, single 5.5cm. One of the most popular of the older Indica varieties. Flowers have good substance.

PRIDE OF MOBILE

■ **RED FORMOSA (syn. RED FORMOSUM)** Reddish purple, 6.5cm. Sport of 'Formosa'.
■ **SNOW HILL** Large white flowers with pale greenish-yellow eye, to 7cm. Low-spreading habit. Crown Estate.
■ **SOUTHERN BELLE** Strong purplish-pink with a darker blotch, hose-in-hose, to 6cm. Leaves variegated with whitish margins. Sport of 'Pink Ruffles'. *PNW.* Mitchell.
■ **SOUTHERN CHARM** Light-pink, darker blotch, to 6cm. There is also a variegated version with what looks like a bad virus. I would avoid it.
■ **WHITE GRANDEUR** Semi-double, white, mid-season. Dark-green leaves. Brooks.

KAEMPFERI

H4–5/6 (USDA 5b–9a) EM–M. This group of hybrids, derived from the species *R. kaempferi*, are often hardier and larger-growing than the Kurume azaleas. Many of them have been used to breed further hardy azaleas for severe climates. *R. kaempferi* was introduced to the west from Japan in the 1890s and many hybrids of it were made at Dutch nurseries, including Koster, van Nes and Vuyk, and at Exbury in England. Many of the hybrids have inherited their parents' semi-deciduous nature so they can look rather sparse in winter, and benefit from hard pruning, especially when young. Varieties such as 'Orange Beauty' and 'Johanna' are amongst the most popular evergreen azaleas in Europe. Most are relatively early flowering, in early May in the U.K.

■ **ALICE** Salmon (yellowish pink) with a darker flare. There are also two Indicas with this name with double rose and double white flowers. van Nes.
■ **ARABESK** Vivid-red with occasional petaloid stamens. Compact. van Nes.
■ **BEETHOVEN** Orchid-purple (strong purplish-red) with deeper blotch, petals fringed, 7cm. Vuyk.
■ **BENGAL FIRE** Vivid red to 6cm, late. A large and vigorous grower. A hybrid of *R. oldhamii*. Exbury.

BLUE DANUBE

■ **BLUE DANUBE (syn. BLAUE DONAU)** Strong purplish-red with deeper purple-red spotting, to 4cm. Upright spreading habit. Pretty tough but sometimes damaged by late frosts in Scotland. *AGM, Cal.* van Hecke.
■ **BRAZIER** Deep-pink tinged reddish orange, 5cm across, early–mid. van Hecke.
■ **CARMEN** Vivid-red with a darker throat, to 6.5cm. Tall and upright. There are also two Indica azaleas under this name, both with red flowers.
■ **CHARLOTTE** Dark orange-red. Two other evergreens with this name are a reddish purple.
■ **CHIPPEWA** Strong purplish-red with a darker blotch, frilled, to 6cm, very late. A useful hardy late-flowering azalea. Flowers tend to be rather hidden under new growth. Bobbink/Atkins.

CHIPPEWA

■ **CHRISTINA** Large, red, hose-in-hose or double. Quite a fine vigorous plant, but grown less than it used to be. There are also two Indica azaleas with this name. van Nes.
■ **DOUBLE BEAUTY** Strong purplish-red/pink, hose-in-hose, mid. Low and compact. *Cal.* van Nes.
■ **EARLY ON** Bright glowing-coral-pink. Galle.
■ **FEDORA** Deep purplish-pink with a darker flash, 5cm. Hardy in Scotland. Loses most of its leaves in winter. van Nes.
■ **FROSTBURG** White, spotted light yellowish green, hose-in-hose, 7cm. Said to have some fragrance. One of the 'yellowest' evergreen azaleas. *SE U.S.A.* Yates.

■ **GLEN'S ORANGE** Semi-double, orange-salmon, long-lasting. Compact with deep-mahogany winter-foliage. Unknown.
■ **GRETCHEN** Vivid reddish-purple with a darker blotch, to 5cm, late-mid. Upright habit. van Nes.
■ **HOLLAND (syn. HOLLAND RED)** Vivid-red, 4cm.

JOHANNA

■ **JOHANNA** Carmine-red, (turkey-red), mid. Dark shiny leaves turning dark red in autumn. Looks good all year. An outstanding commercial plant and a great parent both at Glendoick and for Hachmann. *AGM, PNW.* van Nes.

JOHN CAIRNS

■ **JOHN CAIRNS** Vivid or dark red to 4.5cm, 2–3 per truss. Small leaves. Hardy in Scotland. Endtz.
■ **KAEMPO** Deep purplish-pink with darker spots, to 4cm, mid. Low and compact. A cross between *R. kaempferi* and 'Gumpo'. Fowle.

KAEMPO

■ **KATHLEEN** Small-flowered, strong purplish-pink, mid. (*poukhanense* × *kaempferi*). van Nes.
■ **LEO** Vivid orange-red, to 4cm, late-mid. Low, spreading habit. Exbury.

LEO

■ **LILY MARLENE (syn. MARLENE VUYK)** Vivid purplish-pink, semi-double, hose-in-hose, frilled, to 4.5cm, early–mid. Broad, low spreading habit. Very hardy (to –23°C/–9.5°F) van Nes.

LILY MARLENE

■ **MADAME ALBERT VAN HECKE** Small-flowered, light salmon-pink. Vigorous. van Hecke.

MADAME ALBERT VAN HECKE

■ **MARIE** Purple-red, hose-in-hose, 7.5cm, early–mid. Upright to 1.2m. Exbury.

■ **NAOMI** Dawn-pink, overlaid empire-rose, flushed carmine, with light-orange spotting, 5cm. Leaves light green. Exbury.
■ **ORANGE BEAUTY** Salmon-orange with darker spotting, to 35cm. A neat grower with good autumn-colour. Almost pure *R. kaempferi*. Semi-deciduous. *AGM*. van Nes.

ORANGE BEAUTY

■ **ORANGE KING** Reddish orange, double. There is another similar Kurume under this name. Endtz.
■ **PEGGY ANN (syn. ROEHR'S PEGGY ANN)** White with a purplish-pink edge, hose-in-hose, to 5cm, late. Compact and dense. Hardy to –17°C (1.5°F). Roehr.
■ **PIPPA** Soft lilac-pink, large. Semi-dwarf, spreading habit. Exbury.
■ **PRINS BERNARD** Reddish orange (geranium-lake), with slight brown spotting. Low growing. There is also an orange Indica under this name. Vuyk.
■ **QUEEN WILHELMINA (syn. KONINGIN WILHELMINA)** Vermillion-red-orange, 5cm. Dwarf but with a loose habit. Best with some shade. Vuyk.
■ **RED PIMPERNEL** Reddish orange. Endtz.
■ **SANTA MARIA** Warm orange-red. Large dark shiny leaves. Upright habit. Not very hardy.
■ **SCHUBERT** Moderate purplish-pink, to 5cm. Vuyk.
■ **TIT-WILLOW** Very pale purple, speckled red, long white stamens. Popular in S. England. Stevenson.
■ **TOREADOR** Vivid purplish-red, 2.5cm, early. Wuyts.
■ **WILLY** Bright-pink with red spots and veins, early. Tough. Quite happy in Scotland. van Nes.

WILLY

H3–4 (USDA (6b)–7a–9a) EM–M. Kurume is a region of Kyushu Island, Japan, home of the Akashi nursery from where many of the early Kurume introductions to the west came. The Akashi nursery exhibited azaleas in San Francisco in 1915, selling many to the Domoto brothers in California, while plant hunter Ernest Wilson visited Japan in 1918 and introduced a selection of what he called Kurume azaleas (known as the Wilson 50). Kurume azaleas have masses of small flowers and are probably derived from *R. kaempferi* and *R. kiusianum*. The breeding and selection of these plants in Japan goes back hundreds of years and many new Kurume hybrids were also developed by hybridizers in Europe and America. Once very popular, these azaleas are now not so importantly commercially, as more adaptable home-grown hybrids have taken their place in most growing regions. Many Kurumes are far from evergreen, losing most of their leaves in winter in harsh climates, which is one of the reasons they are declining in popularity. Some are satisfactory in Scotland and similar northern climates but many do not grow well without considerable summer heat. Most are relatively early flowering, in late-April and May in the U.K., slightly later in colder climates.

■ **ADDY WERY** Deep-red (blood-red on orient-red) with an orange blotch, 4–5cm, early. Upright habit. Very popular in UK. *AGM*. den Ouden.
■ **ADONIS** White, hose-in-hose, frilled. Ht 60–80cm. There is also an Indica azalea of this name. Felix and Dijkhuis.
■ **ALADDIN** Geranium-lake. Hage.
■ **ALASKA** Yellowish pink. There is also a double, white Indica with this name. *PNW, SC*. Chisolm-Merritt.
■ **AMOENA (syn. AMOENUM)** Hose-in-hose, vivid purple-red, coloured calyx. A very old tough Japanese hybrid, still widely grown. Ht 60cm. **'AMOENA COCCINEA'** an unstable, redder sport that reverts to purple. *PNW, OZ*. Lindley/Fortune.
■ **APPLEBLOSSOM (syn. 'HO-O', 'DOMOTO')** Pale-pink with a white throat, with occasional red stripes.
■ **ASA-GASUMI (syn. ROSY MORN)** Vivid purplish-pink, hose-in-hose, to 3cm.
■ **AVALANCHE** Pure-white, very free-flowering. There is also a white Coolidge azalea of this name. Domoto.
■ **AYA KANMURI (syn. PINKIE)** Deep yellowish-pink, with dark spotting, 2.5cm.
■ **AZUMA-KAGAMI (syn. PINK PEARL)** Strong (phlox) pink, shaded darker, lighter centre, hose-in-hose to 4.5cm. Quite tall, best in semi-shade. Susceptible to root-rot in hot climates.
■ **BENI GIRI** Vivid purplish-red, to 3cm. Similar to Hinodegiri. Leaves matte.
■ **BETTY (syn. SUGA-NO-ITO, KUMO-NO-ITO)** Strong-pink, darker centre, hose-in-hose. There is also a *R. kaempferi* × with this name, flowers similar.
■ **BLAAUW'S PINK** (see photo next page) Salmon-pink, hose-in-hose, with paler shading, to 3cm. Popular in U.K. 'Salmon Spray' is a synonym. (Bill Steele.) *AGM, MD, SE, Mel*. Blaauw.
■ **CASABLANCA** White flowers to 5cm. Grows wider than high. **'CASABLANCA IMPROVED'** or **'C. TETRAPLOID'** with larger, thicker flowers and leaves. (Colchicine treated.) Beltsville.

BLAAUW'S PINK

GORBELLA

GUY YERKES

H.H. HUME

HAHN'S RED

■ **CHERRY DROPS** Cherry-red. Compact, densely-branched plant. Lustrous, deep-green leaves. Sport of 'Cherry Delight'. *PNW.*
■ **CHRISTMAS CHEER (syn. IMA-SHOJO)** Hose-in-hose, strong-red, to 2.5cm. Tall and upright to 2m or more. *OZ.*
■ **DAPHNE** White with strong reddish-purple edge, to 2.5cm. Upright and vigorous to 2m+. There is another purplish-pink cultivar with this name. *PNW.* Domoto.
■ **DEBUTANTE** Pale-salmon, speckled deeper, lighter centre, sometimes semi-double, to 3.5cm. *Aus.* Domoto.
■ **DELICATISSIMA** Single, white tinted pinkish-lavender at the edge, to 4.5cm. Slow growing and semi-deciduous. Tough. *NG.* Domoto.
■ **ELIZABETH BELTON** Deep-pink, paler margins, semi-double. Bred in Australia. *Aus.* Hazelwood.
■ **EXQUISITE** Hose-in-hose, deep purplish-pink, 3cm. Low, spreading habit. *Aus.* Domoto.
■ **FACE 'EM DOWN** A series of Mucronatum hybrids with scented white or pale-pink to lavender-pink flowers. Some sold as seedlings, white or pale pink, others named. Leaves hairy. White: **'SUPERSUDS'.** White flushed pink/lavender: **'I DOUBLE DARE YOU', 'MISSY', 'FOAMY', 'EARLY ERROL', 'BABY'S BLUSH'.** Pink: **'PINK PATOOTIE', 'STAR SCENT'.** Carlson.
■ **FAIRY QUEEN (syn. AIOI)** Pale yellowish-pink, blotched strong orange-red, hose-in-hose. There are also white and pink Indicas with the same name, which I suspect are what is grown in Australia under this name. *Aus.*
■ **FIREGLOW** Reddish orange to 3.5cm. Upright habit. A sport of and similar to 'Redwings'. Mayo.
■ **FLAME (syn. SUETSUMU)** Strong-red with a darker blotch. Several other azaleas have the same name. Domoto.
■ **FLANDER'S FIELD (syn. CORNELIA VAN HERDEN)** Single, vivid-red with a darker blotch, occasionally semi-double, to 5.5cm, late mid-season. Spreading, of medium height. Named after the red poppies that grow on the First World War battlefields. Pericat.
■ **GORBELLA (syn. CORBELLA)** Vivid purple-red with a white stripe, early. Ht to 1m. Wuyts.
■ **GUY YERKES** Salmon-pink fading to pale pink, hose-in-hose, spotted, 5cm. Well-branched. Named after the hybridizer of the Beltsville azaleas. *MS.* Beltsville.
■ **H.H. HUME** White, hose-in-hose, with faint yellow throat, 5cm. Erect but spreading habit. Very free-flowering. A favourite target for lace bugs. *MA, AZ.* Beltsville.

■ **HAHN'S RED** Bright scarlet (like 'Mother's Day'). Tall and upright, reaching 2m. Hahn.

HERSHEYS RED

HINO CRIMSON

■ **HAMPTON BEAUTY** Deep-pink with a darker blotch, partially petaloid sepals, to 5cm, early–mid. Spreading, low dense habit. Resistant to root-rot. Pericat/Le Mac.
■ **HANA ASOBI (syn. SULTAN)** Strong purplish-pink with white stamens, to 2.5cm.
■ **HATSU-GIRI** Bright crimson-purple, to 2.5cm, early. Compact and dwarf to 60cm. Semi-deciduous.
■ **HEATHER** Hose-in-hose, strong purplish-red (rose-lavender), to 3.5cm. *Aus.*

■ **HERSHEYS RED** Hose-in-hose, bright-red, 5cm, early. Dark-green glossy leaves. Compact to 60cm. A fine-looking plant. Susceptible to root-rot and lace bugs. Resistant to phomopsis die-back. *MA, AZ, ME.*
■ **HEXE** Deep-red, hose-in-hose, frilled. There are various other Indica azaleas called 'Hexe', usually with some designation such as Rosea or Grandiflora. *PNW.* Forster/Blaauw.
■ **HINO CRIMSON** Single, crimson-red, to 2.5cm, early. Very compact, glossy foliage red in winter. A widely grown commercial azalea. Susceptible to root-rot in hot climates. *AGM, PNW, MA, MS.*

■ **HINODEGIRI** Bright-crimson, with red anthers, to 2.5cm. There is also a hose-in-hose version. Once very popular but becoming less so, as it is semi-deciduous. *PNW, AZ.*
■ **HINOMAYO** Strong purplish-pink, speckled in the throat, to 2.5cm. More or less deciduous. One the most popular of the Japanese Kurumes in Europe. *Mel.*

■ **IROHAYAMA (syn. DAINTY)** White with margins of salmon-pink, to 4cm. One of the Wilson 50. *AGM.*

■ **IWATOKAGAMI** Vivid purplish-pink, single or hose-in-hose. There seems to be some disagreement about the flower form of this one. *SE U.S.A.* Domoto.

■ **JILL SEYMOUR** Pink, red stripes, hose-in-hose. *Aus.* Greentree.

■ **KARENS** Deep reddish-purple with darker spotting, slightly fragrant. Semi-evergreen. Very hardy. Ht to 1.2m. Said to tolerate neutral soil. Pedersen.

■ **KINTAIYO** Semi-double, white with margins and spotting of reddish pink. An *R. scabrum* hybrid. Wada.

■ **KOMO KULSHAN** Rosy pink with a lighter pink throat, to 2.5cm. Semi-deciduous. Often sold as a form of *R. kiusianum*, but obviously a hybrid. *PNW, SE, MW.*

KOMO KULSHAN

■ **KONOHANA** Salmon-pink with deeper-pink edging, and a darker blotch, to 4.5cm.

■ **KOROMO SHIKIBU** Lavender, with very narrow, strap-like flower lobes. Upright and spreading with hairy leaves. A curious and very attractive plant, which is probably a form of *R. macrosepalum*. There is also a fine white seedling: '**KOROMO SHIKIBU WHITE**'. *PV, CH.* K.S. White

KOROMO SHIKIBU WHITE

■ **KURI-NO-YUKI (syn. SNOWFLAKE)** White, hose-in-hose. Dwarf, compact and slow growing. Semi-deciduous.

■ **LAUGHING WATER** Large, white, single. Vigorous. Similar to 'Mucronatum'. Coolidge.

■ **LILLIPUT** Strong salmon-pink with wavy lobes and brown spotting. Compact with light glossy-green leaves.

KOROMO SHIKIBU

■ **MAYA-FUJIN** Single purplish-red, deeper blotch, 4cm.

■ **MISS SUZIE** Hose-in-hose orange-red to 5cm. Spreading to 60cm. Harris.

■ **MIZU-NO-YAMABUKI** Small, hose-in-hose, creamy-white flowers with a yellow flush. Expert breeder Augie Kehr thought that this would be a good parent for the Holy Grail of a yellow evergreen azalea.

■ **MOTHER'S DAY (syn. MUTTERTAG)** Bright-red with faint-brown spotting, hose-in-hose or semi-double. Very popular. Good glossy foliage. I have seen the name translated into several languages, such as Dutch and German. *AGM, PNW, MD.*

MOTHER'S DAY

MUCRONATUM

■ **MUCRONATUM (syn. LEDIFOLIA ALBA)** White with palest-pink flushing, to 2.5cm long, about 5cm across. Pale green-yellow, softly hairy leaves. A famous old azalea, widely grown and much used in hybridizing. Susceptible to whitefly.

■ **MULTIFLORUM (syn. MULTIFLORA)** Small dark-purple flowers. Spreading habit to 1m. A parent of the Geisha azalea hybrids. Unknown.

■ **NICOLA** Rose-bengal (rose-red). There is also Satsuki 'Nichola'. Waterer.

■ **NUCCIO'S ALL GLORY** Single vivid-pink, 4cm. Sisters: '**NUCCIO'S BIT O' SUNSHINE**' light-red, '**NUCCIO'S BLUE JAY**' deep-lavender, '**NUCCIO'S FASHION**' lavender, '**NUCCIO'S JEWEL BOX**' rose-pink, hose-in-hose, '**NUCCIO'S LILAC LADY**' light-lavender, '**NUCCIO'S RED GLITTERS**' rose-red. Nuccio.

■ **NUCCIO'S BLUE JAY (syn. BLUE JAY)** Single, deep lavender-purple flowers to 6.5cm. *Aus.* Nuccio.

■ **NUCCIO'S BUTTERFLY** Creamy white, hose-in-hose to 5cm. '**NUCCIO'S LIMELIGHT**' pale yellowish-white, '**NUCCIO'S POPCORN**' double yellowish-white. Nuccio.

■ **NUCCIO'S DANCING DOLL** Double, salmon-pink to 5cm. '**NUCCIO'S FIRST CALL**' small, hose-in-hose, light-salmon. Nuccio.

■ **NUCCIO'S IVORY TOWER** White to 5cm. Very vigorous and upright. Nuccio.

■ **NUCCIO'S LITTLE RED RIDINGHOOD** Small, brilliant orange-red, to 4cm. '**NUCCIO'S SHOWGIRL**' light salmon-orange. Nuccio.

■ **OLD MING** Small, single, purple. Vigorous and upright habit. Coolidge.

■ **ORANGE CUP** Orange-red, hose-in-hose. Seen in Philadelphia area. Unknown.

■ **ORCHID STAR** Small, star-shaped, lavender. Fairly compact.

■ **PARADISE PINK** Purplish pink (rose-madder). Compact low-spreading habit. Waterer.

■ **PHYLLIS MOORE** Hose-in-hose, white, to 45cm *NG, TO.* Unknown.

■ **PINOCCHIO** Deep-pink, double. There is also a 'Glenn Dale', with white flowers with reddish-orange stripes under this name. Pericat.

■ **POLAR BEAR** White, slight yellowish-green throat, serrated margins, hose-in-hose, 4–5cm. Erect habit. Good winter foliage for a white azalea. Beltsville.

■ **PRINCESS GWYNETH** White funnel-shaped hose-in-hose, with wavy edges, to 7cm, mid. Dense spreading. H4–5. There were at least seventeen named in the University of Maryland Princess series.

■ **PRINCESS LINDSAY** Deep purplish-pink. Other pinks in this series are: '**PRINCESS CONNIE**' pink with white edge, '**PRINCESS MARY LEE**' pink, '**PRINCESS MEGAN**' light pink, '**PRINCESS BARABRA**' double, pink, '**PRINCESS GINNETTE RENE**' double, deep-pink. U. of Maryland.

■ **PRINCESS SHARON** Clear-white semi-double with greenish throat, to 6.5cm, early–mid. Dense low-spreading habit. H4–5. Some drought resistance. Suitable for sun or shade. '**PRINCESS ALLISON**' white. U. of Maryland.

■ **PRINCESS TESSA** Deep-salmon, hose-in-hose and double, to 6cm, mid. Compact spreading habit. H4–5. '**PRINCESS DEBORAH**' is paler. U. of Maryland.

■ **RASHOMON (syn. METEOR)** Bright-salmon-red or strong-red. There may be two different plants under this name.

■ **ROEHR'S TRADITION (syn. TRADITION)** Hose-in-hose, carmine-pink, to 3cm, late. *MA.* Bauman.

■ **RUTH MAY** Small, pink flowers with white stripes and a lighter margin, to 6.5cm. Vigorous. Oliver & Simson.

■ **SAKATA RED (syn. KURUME RED)** Geranium-lake, margins of lobes reflexed, 4.5cm. Leaves glossy, mid-green. Ht to 30cm. **'SAKATA RUST'** single, orange-red. Koppeschaar.

■ **SALMON BEAUTY** Hose-in-hose, salmon-pink (rose-opal), with a darker throat.

■ **SALMON'S LEAP** Deep-pink. Variegated foliage. Best in sheltered position and protect from severe frosts. Useless in Scotland.

■ **SANTOI (syn. SHIN UTENA)** White flushed salmon-pink, deeper blotch, to 4cm.

■ **SCARLET GEM** Vivid orange-red, hose-in-hose. *Aus.* Huntingdale.

■ **SCHRYDERII** White spotted purplish-pink, throat pink, fragrant, to 2.5cm long, about 5cm across. Pale green-yellow, softly hairy leaves. A sport of 'Mucronatum', used in hybridizing in Australia. *Vic, NSW.*

■ **SEIKAI (syn. MADONNA)** White, hose-in-hose, to 3cm. *Aus.*

■ **SEKIDERA** Large, pure-white, fragrant flowers splashed and spotted rose. Clone of 'Mucronatum'. Low, spreading habit.

SEKIDERA

■ **SHERWOOD PINK** Single, strong-pink. **'SHERWOOD ORCHID'** reddish purple. *PNW.* Sherwood.

■ **SHERWOOD RED** Single, bright orange-red, to 4.5cm. Very free-flowering. Sherwood.

■ **SILVESTER** Purplish-red (solferino-purple) with paler margins. Early flowering. A popular commercial cultivar in the U.K. *U.K.*

SILVESTER

■ **SINGING FOUNTAIN** Single, light salmon-pink, edged deeper to 4cm. Coolidge.

SNOW

■ **SNOW** Hose-in-hose, pure white with a slight chartreuse blotch. The faded flowers hang on a long time. Not very hardy, subject to die-back in cold gardens. Susceptible to root-rot in warm climates. Resistant to phomopsis die-back. A sport, **'SNOWBALL'**, is better and it does not hang on to faded flowers. *SE, OZ, AZ.* Domoto.

■ **SPRING BEAUTY** Strong yellowish-pink with white throat and deep-pink blotch, 6cm across, late-mid. Upright medium-height, dense. Pericat/Mayo.

■ **SWEET BRIAR** Single, white, flushed purplish-red, with a darker blotch, less than 2cm.

■ **TAKASAGO (syn. CHERRYBLOSSOM)** White flushed deep-pink, dark spots, hose-in-hose. There is also a Satsuki with this name. Small-leaved, on a spreading plant.

■ **TANCHO (syn. SERAPHIM)** White flushed and edged pink, hose-in-hose, 2.5cm. There is also a Satsuki with this name with variegated leaves. *Aus.*

■ **TOKOHARU** Hose-in-hose, white with purple-red striping.

VIDA BROWN

■ **VIDA BROWN** Hose-in-hose deep purplish-pink (reddish-pink). Very compact and slow-growing with dark-green, dense foliage. A little too slow for a commercial plant. Brown.

■ **WAKAEBISU** Pale pink to white with deep pink-red margins, deeper blotch, 2.5cm. There is also a Satsuki under this name.

■ **WARD'S RUBY (syn. RUBY GLOW)** Dark ruby-red, spotted deeper, to 4cm. Dark green, glossy leaves turn bronze in winter. Less hardy than most Kurume azaleas, but a good colour. **'RUBY NUGGET'** a dwarf sport, tiny leaves turn maroon in cold weather. *AZ.*

■ **WHITE APRIL** Single, white. Coolidge.

■ **YOSHIMI-GATAKE** Purplish red (rose-madder), to 2cm. A second clone in U.S.A. has pink flowers with a white throat.

HYDE AZALEAS

H3? (USDA 7a?). A series of low and compact English azaleas raised by George Hyde, recently launched onto the market in England. It is unlikely that they will be successful in Scotland.

■ **DEAR GRANDAD** Vivid reddish-orange with deep-red markings, to 5cm. Height to 50cm, growing wider than high.

■ **FLOWER ARRANGER** Semi-double, frilled, strong-purple inside, light reddish-purple outside, with darker spotting, to 4cm, mid. Leaves glossy, ht to 60cm.

■ **FRED NUTBEAM** Orange-red, relatively large flowers. Ht 50–60cm in ten years.

■ **GEORGE HYDE** Semi-double deep purplish (orchid) pink with heavy darker spotting, early–mid. Ht to 60cm.

■ **HYDIE** Semi-double, deep-pink, marbled with white, with faint-red markings, to 3cm, early–mid. Ht to 50cm.

■ **MAGIC FLUTE** Hose-in-hose, moderate purplish-red with dark-red spotting, a few petaloid stamens, about 4cm, mid–late. Compact and neat habit to 1m.

■ **VALENTINE SURPRISE** Orange-red buds open to white centre with a red edge, anthers black, to 5cm. Leaves glossy, with good winter colour, on a compact plant to about 1m. A very showy plant, but probably not all that hardy.

MIXED PARENTAGE AMERICAN

H3–(4) (USDA 7a–8/9) Many breeders have combined varieties from many different categories, making their hybrids difficult to classify. Harris azaleas raised in Georgia are heat tolerant and large flowered. Few of the many Greenwood azaleas raised in Oregon are widely grown commercially. Linwood azaleas fall into more than one category: some are a mixture of indoor-forcing azaleas, while others are quite hardy. Some, such as 'Hardy Gardenia', are listed in the 'Eastern North America Hardy' category; a category which contains many Indica and Satsuki azaleas bred by Nuccio's nursery in California. The remainder grown by this nursery are here. The Nuccio azaleas are bred for and mainly grown in California and many have done well in Australia. Carlson azaleas are problematic: Carlson nursery has named an absurd number of cultivars, most of which are not commercially available at all. Most of the newer ones that the nursery currently sells have not been registered, despite the best efforts of the Rhododendron and Azalea Societies and, unlike every other major breeder, Carlson won't co-operate or share information, so I can't recommend any of them.

■ **ANNE LEE McPHAIL** Light pink, to 7.5cm. Harris.

■ **CAMISOLE ROSE** Hose-in-hose, deep pink-red, early. Ht to 1m. One of the 'Carlson Brave' group. Carlson.

■ **CARLSON'S ITSY BITSY** Coral-orange, hose-in-hose. Small glossy leaves. Ht 60cm–1m. Carlson.

■ **CONCHO** Vivid reddish-purple flowers, 5–6cm, late-mid. Low and spreading to about 50cm. Free-flowering. Guttormsen.

■ **ELLIE HARRIS** Light pink, hose-in-hose, to 5cm. Harris.

■ **EVELYN HART** Pale purplish-pink, double, hose-in-hose, 5–6cm. Linwood.

■ **FASCINATION** Large (10cm) pink flowers with a strong-reddish border, very showy. Broad spreading plant, to 1.2m. This is a really striking flower with a contrasting two-tone effect. *PNW*. Harris.

■ **FROSTED ORANGE** White with orange-red edge, to 10cm, very late. Broad spreading habit, densely branched, to about 1m. *PNW, AZ*. Harris.

■ **GREAT BIG DATE** Frilled, slightly petaloid, lavender-pink with darker spotting. May–June. 1m. Carlson.

■ **GREENWOOD ORANGE** Double, reddish orange, 5cm. Upright, open habit to 75cm. Greenwood.

■ **GREENWOOD ORCHID** Hose-in-hose, strong reddish-purple to 5.5cm. Rounded habit to 75cm. *PNW*. Greenwood.

■ **HARRIS FALL RED** Large, orange-red flowers in spring and autumn. Low and spreading habit. Harris.

■ **JAN** Hose-in-hose, purple red to 6cm, mid. Compact habit to 60cm. Greenwood.

■ **MIDNIGHT FLARE** Single, very dark-red to 7.5cm. Leaves large, bullate, turning red in winter. Hardy: H5. *CH*. Harris.

MIDNIGHT FLARE

■ **MONA LISA** Double, purplish pink to 7.5cm, mid. Ht to 90cm. Greenwood.

■ **NUCCIO'S ALLEGRO** Rich-red, semi-double to 6.5cm. *Aus*. Nuccio.

■ **NUCCIO'S CALIFORNIA DAWN** Single, moderate yellowish-pink, to 7.5cm. Vigorous. **'NUCCIO'S BREAK O' DAY'** light-salmon with red spots. Nuccio.

■ **NUCCIO'S CROWN JEWEL** Single to semi-double, tubular, white with salmon stripes, to 75cm. Very vigorous. Sister: **'NUCCIO'S SPRING CHARM'** pale salmon-pink with deeper edges. Nuccio.

■ **NUCCIO'S DEW DROP (syn. DEW DROP)** Single to semi-double, pale pink to white, heavily spotted throat, 4–5cm. Dark-green leaves. Vigorous but compact. Nuccio.

■ **NUCCIO'S EASTER DELIGHT** Tubular orchid-purple with pointed lobes, to 6.5cm, mid–late. Flowers are star-shaped. Nuccio.

■ **NUCCIO'S FASHION SHOW** Hose-in-hose, ruffled, salmon-pink, to 9cm. Vigorous with a rather open habit. Nuccio.

■ **NUCCIO'S GRAND WALTZ** Large single, white, tinted pale-purple, with green throat and pink stamens, to 10cm, mid. Vigorous and compact. Nuccio.

■ **NUCCIO'S HIGH NOON** Large single, salmon-orange. Large dark leaves. **'NUCCIO'S PUNKIN'** hose-in-hose, orange-salmon. Nuccio.

■ **NUCCIO'S HONEY BUNCH** Double hose-in-hose, white to off-white with deep salmon-pink edges. Erect habit, but fairly compact. *Aus*. Nuccio.

■ **NUCCIO'S MAMMA MIA** Large single to semi-double, white with green throat, mid–late. Vigorous but compact. Nuccio.

■ **NUCCIO'S MELODY LANE** Large single, pale pink, heavily spotted red, to 7.5cm. Vigorous and upright. Nuccio.

■ **NUCCIO'S MEXICO** Single, bright pink, tubular, 4–5cm. Long flowering-period. Nuccio.

■ **NUCCIO'S ORCHID QUEEN** Single, lavender. Similar to 'J.L. Bobbink', but with longer-lasting flowers. **'NUCCIO'S PALE MOONLIGHT'** is similar. Nuccio.

■ **NUCCIOS PINK SNOW** Single to semi-double, mid (flesh) pink, to 4cm. Nuccio.

■ **NUCCIO'S PRIMAVERA** Single to semi-double, white with a green throat, to 7.5cm. **'NUCCIO'S SNOWCAP'** single, white. Nuccio.

■ **NUCCIO'S PURPLE DRAGON** Narrow, spidery, single, purple, in clusters. Vigorous. **'NUCCIO'S DRAGONFLY'** similar, with lavender flowers. Nuccio.

■ **NUCCIO'S SKYROCKET** Single, deep orange-red, to 5cm, mid. Vigorous and upright. **'NUCCIO'S SUNBURST'** semi-double, bright orange-red. Nuccio.

■ **NUCCIO'S SPRING CHARM** Single, salmon-pink, deeper edge, 6.5–7.5cm. Very vigorous. Nuccio.

■ **NUCCIO'S SPRING FESTIVAL** Double, light salmon-pink, to 8.5cm, mid. Very vigorous. Nuccio.

■ **NUCCIO'S SPRING TRIUMPH** Single to semi-double, light pink, to 6cm, early–mid. Vigorous spreading habit. Nuccio.

■ **OPAL** Double, vivid purplish-red, to 6cm. Autumn blooming in some climates. Others from similar parentage include: **'LINWOOD PINK'** hose-in-hose, pink, **'LINWOOD WHITE'**, hose-in-hose, white, **'LINWOOD LAVENDER'** vivid purplish-red. All are H4. Linwood.

LINWOOD WHITE

■ **ORANGE SHERBERT** Vivid-red, double, to 7cm, mid. Low and spreading to 30cm. There is also a Pride azalea under this name with loose orange-pink flowers and orange-red new growth. *PNW*. Greenwood.

■ **OUR FULL MOON** Petaloid white. Mid-May. Autumn colour. 1–1.2m. Carlson.

■ **PINK CASCADE (PBR-EU)** Deep salmon-pink with a red blotch, to 5cm, late. Low-spreading habit to 1m. Good in hanging basket, as the branches will grow downwards at the edge of the container; it sometimes layers itself. A good commercial plant. Harris.

■ **PINK POCKETS** Hose-in-hose, bright pink, early. Carlson.

■ **PINKANDESCENT** Bright lavender-pink, early. 1m. Growing wider than high. Carlson.

■ **RAIN FIRE** Vivid orange-red, 5–6cm. Semi-dwarf to 60cm. Sun tolerant. Harris.

■ **ROYAL ROBE** Hose-in-hose, deep purplish-red, to 8cm. Broad and spreading, with a dense, compact habit to 45cm. Greenwood.

■ **TINA** Hose-in-hose, strong purplish-pink, to 2.5cm, early. Dwarf to 30cm, compact, rounded habit. There is also a Kurume under this name. Greenwood.

■ **TORCHLIGHT** Strong purplish-pink, hose-in-hose, 5–6cm. Compact and spreading to 45cm. Greenwood.

■ **WILD TIMES** Petaloid, lavender-pink. 60cm. Late-May–June. Carlson

NORTH TISBURY

H4–5 (USDA 6a–6b) L–VL. A group of late-flowering azaleas derived from the Taiwanese species *R. nakaharae*, raised by Polly Hill from Rokujo seed, on Martha's Vineyard, MA. They are mostly spreading in habit, forming a dense groundcover. Some will even grow downwards if grown in pots or baskets. This group of azaleas seem to be a particular favourite of rabbits and we find that many have flowers that don't last well. The Carlson 'Jeeper's Creepers' azaleas are bred from the North Tisburys. I'm not convinced they are any improvement and they are certainly far less popular.

■ **ALEXANDER** Bright reddish-orange, with a darker blotch, to 7cm, very late. Prostrate, spreading and cascading habit to 20cm × 1m. This may be the hardiest of the Polly Hill selections. *MS, AGM*.

■ **GABRIELLE HILL** Ruffled pink with a deep-pink blotch, to 6.5cm, very late. Low-spreading habit.

■ **JEFF HILL** Deep-pink with a red blotch, to 5cm, late. Spreading. One of the most free-flowering of this group.

■ **JOSEPH HILL** Single, vivid-red 5cm, late. Dark pointed leaves in a dense mound, groundcover. *U.K.*

JOSEPH HILL

■ **LATE LOVE** Strong-pink with a deep-red blotch, to 5.5cm, very late. Dwarf spreading creeping habit.

■ **LOUISA** Deep- to moderate-pink (salmon-pink), with a darker blotch, 5cm, late. Dense, low growing, spreading plant.

■ **MARILEE** Salmon-pink, with red blotch on three lobes, to 5cm, very late. Dense, very vigorous plant, purple leaves in winter. Rated the best North Tisbury for New England by Weston nursery.

■ **MICHAEL HILL** Bright pink, frilled/ruffled, more open than most of this group, to 7cm, late. Very low-growing, and the fastest spreader of this group. *SE, MS.*

■ **MT SEVEN STAR** Vivid reddish-orange, with darker spotting, to 5cm, very late. Forming tight little mounds with small dark leaves. Very slow-growing. A selection of *R. nakaharae*. Not always easy to please, but worth extra trouble. *PNW.*

MT SEVEN STAR

■ **PINK PANCAKE** Peachy pink, wavy-edged, with deeper centre and spotting, to 6cm, late. Dense, low-growing and spreading. *AGM.*

PINK PANCAKE

■ **RED FOUNTAIN** Deep reddish-orange with red spotting, to 4.5cm, late. A spreader that also sends up some vertical shoots, which is rather unusual. Occasional petalloid flowers. *PNW.*

■ **SUSANNAH HILL** Strong-red to 4.5cm, some flowers petaloid, late. Ht 15cm, spreading, almost prostrate habit.

■ **WINTERGREEN** Cherry-red, 5cm, late. Groundcover spreading to 2–3m, with excellent winter-foliage. There is also a Shammarello hybrid with this name. *SE, MS.*

■ **YUKA** Large, ruffled, white flowers blushed with pink, late. Low-growing and late-blooming, glossy leaves. '**LITTLE YUKA**' a dwarf sport.

CARLSON JEEPERS CREEPERS GROUP

■ **A LITTLE BIT MORE** Pure white with flecks of pink, very late. Low, spreading.

■ **COME TO BABY DO** Coral-pink with a deeper flare. Prostrate and spreading, June–July. One of the most nauseating names I have come across.

■ **FLAT OUT** White with green markings. Spreading to 30cm high.

■ **LADY JUDITH** Large, soft coral-pink with a deeper flare. Prostrate with cascading branches, late-June.

■ **LATE DATE** Light-pink with a deep flare. Very prostrate habit.

■ **L'IL DARLING** Large-flowered, lavender-pink. Low to 30cm. Mid–late-June.

■ **LITTLE PITCHERS** Light coral-pink with a deeper flare. Very low, spreading habit.

■ **SHORT SHEET** Clear-white with a green throat. Ht 30cm, spreading.

GLENN DALE AND BACK ACRES

H4–5 (USDA 6b–9a). Bred by Ben Morrison in Maryland, this was the most impressive breeding programme ever mounted for azaleas. From 1935–1950, 70,000 seedlings were tested and 440 clones named. The hardiest ones are suitable for much of coastal NE U.S.A. and they are popular in the Pacific Northwest. A few are popular in Europe, but most are not reliably hardy in Scotland and similar climates. Far too many were named, and, frankly, 100 would have been more than enough.

■ **ADVANCE** Vivid purplish-pink (tyrian-rose) to vivid-red, to 5cm across. Dense and twiggy to 1.5m.

■ **ALADDIN** Geranium-pink, white at the base, marked red.

■ **ALLURE** Light purplish-pink, 5–6cm across, early. Spreading and vigorous to 1.5m. *PV.*

■ **AMBROSIA** Deep rose-pink, to 5cm, 2–5 per truss. Hardy for a Glenn Dale. To 1m. Rated in top twenty Glenn Dale survey.

■ **ANCHORITE** Rose-pink with orange undertones, 5cm, early. Spreading habit to 1.2m. One of the earliest of this group.

■ **AZTEC** Salmon-pink to reddish orange, deeper spotting, to 7cm, late. Broad, spreading to 1m.

■ **BEN MORRISON** Orange-pink with a deep-scarlet blotch and white margins, to 7.5cm. Vigorous with twiggy habit to 1m. A very fine bicoloured azalea, one of the most striking of all, named after the hybridizer of the Glenn Dale azaleas. *PNW, SE, AZ.* Morrison/Creech.

BEN MORRISON

■ **BOLDFACE** White centre, deep purplish-pink margin, red blotch 7.5cm across, mid. Broad spreading habit to 1.2m. Tends to produce sports with less showy flowers that should be cut out. Top twenty Glenn Dale survey. *AZ, CH, PD.*

■ **BOUNTIFUL** Frilled phlox-purple (strong reddish-purple), to 7.5cm, mid–late. Bushy habit to 1.2m.

■ **BUCCANEER** Vivid orange-red, upper lobe darker, 5cm. Vigorous, erect, to 1.5m. One of the best Glenn Dale hybrids, in the top twenty listing 1980. Flowers need sun protection to avoid fading and bleaching. *AZ.*

■ **BURGUNDY** Deep yellowish-pink with strong-red margins and a purplish-red blotch, 5cm, early. Upright and spreading to 2m. '**CARMEL**' is similar but earlier.

■ **CADENZA** White, ruffled with magenta flakes, 5cm. Low, broad and spreading habit to 1.2m.

■ **CHANTICLEER** Deep purplish-red (Amaranth-purple), 5cm. Bushy, dense habit to 1.7m.

■ **COPPERMAN** Deep yellowish-pink (salmon), shaded orange, with a purplish-pink blotch, to 7.5cm. Dense and spreading to 1.3m. In top twenty Glenn Dale survey 1980.

■ **CRINOLINE** Strong reddish-purple, often with a white eye, ruffled, 7.5cm. Broad and spreading to 1.5m.

■ **DAYSPRING** White centre shading to light purplish-pink margin, blotch greenish yellow, 4–5cm, early. Broad, spreading habit to 2m. One of the top twenty Glenn Dale hybrids(1981). One of the hardiest of the Glenn Dales, good as far north as S. Ontario. *MD, PV.*

■ **DELOS** Double, light purplish-pink, to 6cm, sometimes flowers in autumn. Habit straggly and vigorous, often bent down with weight of flower. Ht to 2.2m. Top twenty Glenn Dale survey (1980). *PV.*

DELOS

■ **DIMITY** White, flecked and striped purplish-red. Tall upright habit to 2m. Semi-deciduous. A sport '**SOUTH GATE**' has light rosy-pink flowers, marked red. Good autumn-colour. *Aus.*

■ **DREAM** (*see* photo overleaf) Strong purplish-pink, deeper spotting, 6.5cm, early. Vigorous, spreading to 2m. Top twenty Glenn Dale 1980. Lace-bug resistant. *MA, PV.*

■ **DRIVEN SNOW** White, 8cm across. Erect, spreading habit to 2m. '**SNOWSCAPE**' is similar.

■ **ELIZABETH** Deep yellowish-pink with a bold purple-red blotch, 8cm, late. Spreading habit to 1.2m.

■ **EROS** Deep-pink, fading to lighter with small dark blotch, late. Low and spreading to 1m.

DREAM

■ **EVEREST** White with pale-green to yellow blotch, 5cm across. Broad-spreading to 1.5m. A parent of 'Panda'. Suffers in hard winters in Pacific Northwest. Not very reliable in Scotland. *PNW.*

■ **FASHION** Deep yellowish (salmon) pink with red-purple blotch and dark anthers, 5cm. Tall arching habit to 2m. Top twenty Glenn Dale survey 1980. *SE, AZ.*

FASHION

■ **FAVOURITE** Deep rose-pink, orange undertone, with heavy red blotch, irregular hose-in-hose, early. Erect habit to 1.5m. Hardy in Scotland. *U.K.*

FAVOURITE

■ **FESTIVE** White, striped and spotted purplish-red to 6cm, early. Erect and spreading to 2m. Top twenty Glenn Dale survey 1980.

■ **GAIETY** Light purplish-pink with a darker blotch, 5–6cm. Erect but spreading to 1.5m. Top twenty Glenn Dale survey 1980. Hardy in Scotland.

■ **GEISHA** Single white with a yellow-green eye, to 5cm, early. Tall and spreading to 1m. Not to be confused with the Arends Geisha hybrids. Top twenty Glenn Dale survey 1980.

■ **GLACIER** White with faint-green tone, 6–7cm, early. Leaves dark green. Erect and vigorous habit to 2m. Top twenty Glenn Dale survey 1980. Root-rot resistant. **'PAPINEAU'** is similar but more vigorous. *PNW, MA, AZ, CH.*

GLACIER

■ **GLAMOUR** Strong purplish-pink, 5–7.5cm, early. Leaves narrow. Vigorous to 1.5m. Top twenty Glenn Dale survey 1980 and seems to be one of the hardiest.

GLAMOUR

■ **HELEN CLOSE** White with a pale-yellow blotch that fades to white, 6–7cm, early. Dense and twiggy to 1.2m. Top twenty Glenn Dale survey 1980. *PNW.*

■ **JUBILEE** Deep purplish-pink with a few dark spots, to 6cm. Low and spreading to 1m.

■ **LOUISE DOWDLE** Large, rosy-purple flowers with deeper blotch, occasional pale centres, 7.5cm, late. Broad, wide spreading habit to 1.5m. Poor winter-foliage retention. Quite good in Scotland.

■ **MADRIGAL** Deep yellowish-pink, flushed red, blotched purple-red, 8–9cm, early. Narrow leaves on a spreading plant to 1.2m.

■ **MANHATTAN** Deep purplish-pink to reddish-purple, deeper blotch, to 6cm, late. Spreading and vigorous habit to 1.2m in height. One of the hardier Glenn Dales.

MARTHA HITCHCOCK

■ **MARTHA HITCHCOCK** Single white with magenta margins, 8cm, early–mid. An open spreading habit to 1.2m. Very striking with huge flowers. Sometimes reverts. Top twenty Glenn Dale survey 1980. Not always very free-flowering, but can be excellent. *PNW, TZ, MA, SE, AZ, PD.*

■ **MARY HELEN** Large, white flowers with wavy margins, yellow throat and dark anthers, 5cm. Broad and spreading to 1.5m. Not reliably hardy in Scotland.

■ **MEGAN** Deep purplish-pink, blotched purple, to 6.5cm. Straggly when young but improves with age. Needs pruning as a young plant. To 1.5m. Good in Scotland: the best large-flowered purple.

MEGAN

■ **MELANIE** Hose-in-hose, rose-pink with a deep-rose blotch, to 4cm. A vigorous upright and spreading grower to 1.5m.

■ **MERLIN** Light reddish-purple, to 7.5cm. One of the hardiest Glenn Dale hybrids, but almost deciduous in cold climates. Vigorous and spreading to 1.5m.

■ **MOONSTONE** Large, white with a green throat, 6–7.5cm, late. Spreading and vigorous to 1.5m. Good winter foliage for a white azalea.

■ **MORNING STAR** Deep purplish-pink, with a yellowish undertone, to 5cm, early. Erect, slightly spreading, to 2m. Probably *not* named after the Communist Party newspaper!

■ **NERISSA** Deep-pink, margins paler, blotched purple-pink, to 4.5cm, early–mid. Habit upright and arching, ht to 1.2m.

■ **NIAGARA** White, frilly flowers with faint yellow-green eye, 7.5cm. Dense twiggy upright habit to 1m. *AGM.*

■ **NOCTURNE** Deep red-purple with tube reddish-orange, 7.5cm, early–mid. Broad spreading habit to 1.5m.

■ **ORACLE** Strong purplish-pink with red spotting, to 7cm, early. Wide spreading habit, ht to 1.5m.

■ **PEARL BRADFORD** Strong purplish-pink, deeper blotch/spotting, 7.5cm, late. Broad and spreading habit to 1.2m. **'PEARL BRADFORD SPORT'** witches broom, tiny leaves, shy-flowering.

■ **PIRATE** Vivid reddish-orange with a red blotch, to 5cm. Leaves small, dark green. This looked impressive at Jenkins arboretum, PA, U.S.A.

PIRATE

■ **QUAKERESS** White with reddish-purple flakes, irregular flower colouring, 7–8cm. Erect to spreading, rather leggy, to 2m. Rather unstable, with spectacular and outrageous flowers. Not hardy in Scotland. *PV.*

■ **RED BIRD** Vivid red, blotch purplish red, 5–6cm, early. Semi-evergreen, upright, slow-growing to 1.5m. There are two other evergreen azaleas called 'Red Bird'. *SC.*

■ **REFRAIN** Margins white, suffused purplish pink, with a few stripes, hose-in-hose, to 5cm, early. Flowers are rather variable in colour. Tall but bushy, to 2.2m. Top twenty Glenn Dale survey 1980. *MD.*

■ **RHAPSODY** Frilled, light purplish-pink, with a darker blotch, to 7.5cm. Broad and spreading habit to 1.4m tall. There is also a salmon Indica with this name.

■ **ROSALIE** Strong reddish-purple with an undertone of salmon-pink, to 7.5cm, late. Leaves deep-green. Vigorous and spreading to 1.8m.

■ **SAGA** Deep purplish-pink with deeper blotch, frilled, to 7.5cm, late. Spreading habit, ht to 1m.

■ **SAGITTARIUS** Vivid-pink, orange undertone, white base, blotch darker, to 7.5cm across, late. Dense, broad and spreading to 1m. Top twenty Glenn Dale survey 1980. Flowers need sun protection.

■ **SCOUT** Light purplish-pink, 5cm across, early. Grows wider than tall, ht to 1.5m.

■ **SENECA** Strong-purple, with a bold flare of dark purple, to 8cm, early. Very erect with ascending branches, tall growing to 2m.

■ **SILVER LACE** Ruffled, white with a few purple stripes, green throat, to 7.5cm, late. Low and spreading, ht to 1m.

■ **SILVER MOON** Large, frilled white, with a pale-green throat, to 7.5cm. Broad, spreading habit to 1.5m.

■ **SURPRISE** Moderate-red, margins irregular, white, to 7.5cm. Upright with a dense twiggy habit, to 1m. *PD.*

■ **TANAGER** Vivid purplish-red, dark blotch, early–mid. Erect to broad spreading habit to 1.5m. 'PICADOR' is similar but flowers open a little earlier.

■ **TREASURE** White with pale-pink margins and blotch, 8–10cm, early. Vigorous and spreading to 1.5m. Top twenty Glenn Dale survey 1980. 'One of my favourite white azaleas,' says Bill Steele, Philadelphia azalea expert. Not very heat-tolerant in S.E. U.S.A. *PD, PV.*

TREASURE

■ **TROUPER** Strong-red with faint blotch, about 3cm, early. Dense and upright to 1.5m.

■ **VESPERS** Single to semi-double, white with green markings and occasional purple-pink stripes, to 7.5cm, mid-season. Broad, spreading habit to 1.5m.

VESPERS

■ **VIOLETTA** Light purplish-pink with a darker blotch, to 5.5cm, early. Vigorous and spreading, ht to 1.2m. Not to be confused with the German hybrid of the same name.

■ **ZULU** Vivid purplish-red, blotched deeper, to 10cm. Very vigorous and semi-deciduous, so not a very attractive plant out of flower. This is the last azalea in the Galle index, though there is one called 'Zyrnisa' in the register.

BACK ACRES

The Back Acres azaleas were Ben Morrison's retirement project. Cultivation information as for the Glenn Dales.

■ **DEBONAIRE** Vivid-pink with green centre, and deep-pink margin, to 7.5cm. Compact. One of the hardiest of this group.

■ **ELISE (syn. ELSIE) NORFLEET** Pastel-pink, edges vivid-red, blotched darker. Low growing, to 60cm.

■ **IVAN ANDERSON** White centre, margin deep purplish-red, double, 5–6cm. Ht 60cm–1m. Relatively tender for this group. *PNW.*

■ **KEEPSAKE** White, margin vivid purplish-red, deep blotch, 6–7cm. Height to 1.2m. One of the hardiest of this group. *MA.*

KEEPSAKE

■ **LARGESSE** Double, strong purplish-pink, to 6cm. Ht to 1.2m. One of the hardiest of this group.

■ **MARGARET DOUGLAS** Light pink, edged deeper-salmon-pink, to 6.5cm. Medium-sized, spreading habit to 1m. Heat tolerant. *AZ.*

MARGARET DOUGLAS

■ **MARIAN LEE (syn. MARION LEE)** White, with purple centre and a red border, to 7cm, Leaves narrow, fairly evergreen foliage, on a shrub to 1.4m. Susceptible to root-rot. *CH, AZ, PV.*

■ **RED SLIPPERS** Purplish red, blotched and spotted deeper, to 7.5cm. Tends to produce some autumn and winter flowers.

■ **TARGET** Deep salmon-pink with a red blotch, edged vivid-red, to 7.5cm. Spreading, of medium vigour. One of the hardiest of this group.

■ **WHITE JADE** White, ruffled, pale-green spotting, to 7.5cm. One of the hardiest of this group.

ROBIN HILL

H4–5 (USDA 6a–6b) M–L. This group of azaleas is the result of a breeding programme, begun in 1937 by Robert Gartrell from New Jersey, U.S.A., with the aim of imparting the flower colours and shapes of the Satsuki azaleas into hardier cultivars, more suited to colder parts of the eastern seaboard. Robert Gartrell named sixty-nine selections and others have named further seedlings. In New Jersey, the earlier cultivars flower in mid-May, while the later ones flower in the first half of June.

■ **BETTY ANN VOSS** Double, hose-in-hose, strong- to light-purplish-pink, with wavy margins, to 7.5cm. Fine dark-green foliage. Compact, growing broader than tall. Flowers are like rose buds. One of the hardiest of the group and very free-flowering. *PV.*

BETTY ANN VOSS

BETTY LAYMAN

■ **BETTY LAYMAN** Deep- to strong-yellowish-pink (salmon), to 8.5cm. Dark-green leaves, bronze winter foliage. Mounding, somewhat upright habit to 1m.

■ **CHANSON** Strong- to moderate-purplish-pink to light pink, occasional hairline edge of purplish red, double to semi-double, to 7.5cm. Mounding habit to about 1m.

■ **CHERIE** Double, deep reddish-orange, 5cm. Reddish winter foliage. Ht 60cm. One of the hardiest Robin Hills.

■ **CHRISTIE** Light- to pale-purplish-pink, to 7.5cm, 1 flower per bud. Low mounding habit to 60cm. Good winter-leaf retention. One of the hardiest Gartrells.

■ **CONVERSATION PIECE** Light pink with a lighter margin and prominent blotch, some flowers moderate purplish-pink, to 8cm, late. Low-mounding

habit to approx 75cm. Needs pruning and pinching as a young plant for best habit. This has amazing flowers of almost any shade. *TZ, AZ, CH, SE.*

CONVERSATION PIECE

■ **DOROTHY HAYDEN** White with pale yellow-green throat, to 8cm. Compact habit, height to 40cm.

■ **DOROTHY REES** White with pale-green throat, overlapping lobes, to 9cm. Low and spreading to 60cm, and can get very large.

■ **EARLY BENI** Semi-double, hose-in-hose, deep reddish-orange, to 6.5cm. Yellow-orange autumn-colour. Upright, semi-dwarf, 60cm–1m.

■ **GLAMORA** Pale purplish-pink with a slight pale-greenish/whitish throat, variably semi-double, 7.5cm, late for a Robin Hill. Habit very dense, low and spreading to 50cm.

■ **GLENCORA** Moderate-red, double, to 6.5cm, early. Low and spreading to 40cm.

GLENCORA

■ **GRESHAM** White with pink stripes, sectors and flecks, to 8cm, late. Very low and spreading to 60cm.

■ **GRETA** Strong purplish-red, to 7.5cm, mid–late. Low and spreading to 60cm.

■ **GWENDA** Light purplish-pink, slightly greenish-white throat, 7.5cm, mid–late. Mounding to 1m.

■ **HILDA NIBLETT** Delicate-pink, liberally marked with deeper rose-pink splashes, to 7cm, late-mid. A perfect dwarf mound. *SE.*

■ **JEANNE WEEKS** Mixed single, hose-in-hose and double, strong purplish-pink, to 5cm. Slow-growing and dense to 60cm. We tried this in Scotland, but it struggled. Thought to be one of the best Robin Hill selections. More than one clone has been distributed under this name.

GWENDA

HILDA NIBLETT

■ **LADY LOUISE** Strong-pink, blotched reddish, double or semi-double, to 7.5cm. Low, broad and spreading to 1m. Dark-green leaves turn orange-yellow in autumn. Much used as a parent for further Robin Hill hybrids. *TZ.*

■ **LADY ROBIN** White with pale-pink tinges and wedges and stripes of vivid purple-red. Low, broad and spreading to 1m.

■ **LAURA MORLAND** Moderate-pink with irregular dark striping or sectors, some semi-double flowers, to 6cm. Leaves glossy, tinged maroon, turn orange in autumn. Low, compact habit to 45cm.

LAURA MORLAND

■ **MARIA DERBY** Double, hose-in-hose, deep reddish-orange, to 6.5cm, mid–late. Dense, compact and spreading, ht to 1m.

■ **MRS EMIL HAGER** Semi-double or double, hose-in-hose, deep purple-pink to 6cm. Dwarf and compact to 40cm. Good orange-red autumn leaves. A very bright colour.

MARIA DERBY

■ **MRS VILLARS** Variable: ruffled, white with some salmon-pink flecks or spots, some whole flowers salmon-pink, mid–late. Glossy dark-green leaves. Ht to 1m. One of the hardiest Robin Hills.
■ **NANCY OF ROBIN HILL** Hose-in-hose with some double flowers, clear light-pink with an occasional light-red flare, 8cm, mid–late. Compact. Attractive flowers and pretty tough, one of the hardiest of this group. Bob Gartrell thought that this was his finest hybrid. *PNW, TZ, SE, CC.*

NANCY OF ROBIN HILL

■ **OLGA NIBLETT** White with faint-yellow throat, hose-in-hose, about 5cm. Upright habit. Two clones under this name, the second is hose-in-hose, white with red flecks. Not recommended for Scotland. *SE U.S.A.*

OLGA NIBLETT

■ **ORMSBY** Double, deep salmon-pink, to 6.5cm, mid–late. Dense and upright habit to 1m.
■ **PAT ERB** White shading to light yellowish- or purple-pink, with occasional deep sectors, double (like rosebuds). Glossy dark-green leaves. Tight and compact habit.
■ **REDMOND** Deep yellowish-pink, with reddish spotting. Large dark-green leaves. Tidy, with a very dense, bushy habit. The flowers are an unusual colour.
■ **ROBIN HILL CONGO (syn. CONGO)** Vivid reddish-purple, to 7.5cm. Ht 60cm–1m. Good red-to-orange autumn-colour. Spreading habit.

ROBIN HILL CONGO

■ **ROBIN HILL FROSTY (syn. FROSTY)** Strong purplish-pink with a narrow pale-pink margin and a purplish-red blotch, about 7cm. Semi-dwarf mounding to 60cm. The unusual flowers look like they have a ring of rime frost on them. Free-flowering.

ROBIN HILL FROSTY

■ **ROBIN HILL ROSANNE (syn. ROSANNE)** Ruffled, white, margined vivid purplish-red to deep-pink with occasional selfs, to 7cm. Spreading habit to 1m.
■ **SARA HOLDEN** White with ruffled margins and some flecks and sectors of salmon-pink, 6.5cm. Mounding to 1m.
■ **SCOTT GARTRELL** Double, hose-in-hose, deep- to strong-purplish-pink, to 7cm. *SE U.S.A.*
■ **SHERBROOK** Strong purplish-red, irregularly double, hose-in-hose, to 6.5cm. Some autumn flowering. Upright habit to 1m.

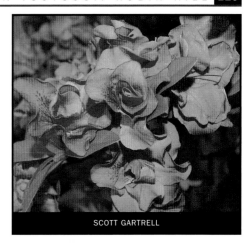

SCOTT GARTRELL

SHERBROOK

■ **SIR ROBERT** Pale purplish-pink with lighter throat, with very variable stripes and sections, late. A dense, compact semi-dwarf with good winter-foliage retention. In some climates, the flowers open over a period of several weeks. **'LITTLE SIR ROBERT'** a dwarf sport. *PNW, TZ.*
■ **SPINK** Strong purplish-pink, hose-in-hose, to 3.75cm, early. Ht 1.2m, upright habit.
■ **TALBOT** Light lavender-pink with a greenish-white throat, occasional white margin, to 7.5cm. Ht to 1m. Leaves tinged bronze.
■ **TURK'S CAP** Deep reddish-orange with some recurved lobes (lily-like), to 9cm. Growth habit loose and upright. The flowers only sometimes have recurved lobes.

TURK'S CAP

■ **WATCHET** (*see* photo overleaf) Ruffled, moderate-pink with a greenish-white throat, to 9cm. Dwarf, broad-spreading habit to 40–50cm, repeat flowering in some warmer climates. **'LITTLE WATCHET'**, a dwarf sport, ht to about 30cm.

WATCHET

■ **WEE WILLIE** Single, light purplish-pink with a lighter throat, ruffled, to 6cm. Compact with relatively large flowers. Dense habit but can eventually reach some size.

■ **WELMET** Strong purplish-pink, mature plants have bicolour flowers with white centres, to 8.5cm. Very small leaves. Somewhat loose, mounding habit to 1m.

■ **WHITE MOON** White with pale-green throat and occasional stripes and flecks of red, to 10cm, late. Ht to 1m. Leaves glossy. Habit rather loose and straggly. Flowers are very large.

WHITE MOON

■ **WHITEHEAD** White, occasionally with variable flecks and stripes of pink, to 7.5cm, late. Shiny leaves. Good winter-leaf retention. Spreading habit, ht to 1m.

SATSUKI

H3–4–(5) (USDA 7a–9b, a few are hardier) ML–L.
The Japanese have been selecting and naming Satsuki azaleas for hundreds of years: the classic treatise on Satsuki azaleas, translated as *The Brocade Pillow*, was published in 1692. The Satsuki azaleas are hybrids and selections of *R. indicum* and *R. eriocarpum*, natives of several of the Japanese islands. There are hundreds of named Satsuki hybrids. Many of them have different colours of flower on one plant, with dots, spots, rings and other effects. This makes naming some of them a nightmare – and a bit meaningless, as you never know what colour you'll get next. Added to this confusion is the fact that Japanese names are often transliterated or translated several ways, so a plant might be sold under several different names.

Satsukis are later flowering than most of the azalea groups, in late-May and well into June or even July and therefore are best in partial shade, to allow flowers to last. They make fine container-plants and are particularly popular for bonsai. Satsuki azaleas struggle in areas such as Scotland without summer heat to ripen the wood. Many Glenn Dale and Robin Hill azaleas contain Satsuki parents, usually crossed with hardier azaleas. Satsukis are the most beautiful of the evergreen azalea groups. I wish we could grow them in Scotland.

■ **AMAGASA** Vivid-red with darker spotting, overlapping lobes, 7–9cm across, late. Slow-growing and compact. *AZ*.

AMAGASA

■ **ARCADIA** Single, rose-pink border, pale centre, mid-season. There is also a deep-pink Glenn Dale under this name. Nuccio.

■ **BENI KIRISHIMA** Double, orange-red, 5cm diameter, late. Similar to 'Macrantha'. There is also a purplish-red Ito hybrid with this name. *MA*.

■ **BETH BULLARD** Yellowish pink, 10cm, late. Low and compact. *AZ, CH*. Pennington.

■ **BRUCE HANCOCK** White with pink border, to 9cm. Cascading habit. Rather tender. Claimed to be an azaleodendron, which it is obviously not, it is simply a 'Gumpo' seedling. Harris.

■ **CHINZAN** Vivid-pink with a darker blotch, to 5cm. Compact. Good for bonsai. *SC*.

■ **CHOJUHO** Narrow-lobed, star-like flowers open red, then fade to orange and to light green, long-lasting, with very long stamens, early–late. Name means 'treasure of longevity'. Very striking.

■ **EIKAN** White and salmon-pink, irregular stripes and blotches, 7.5–10cm, mid–late. Vigorous and spreading. Root-rot resistant. **'CHUGI BUNGWA'** similar but more compact. Chugei.

EIKAN

■ **EITEN** White with purple stripes or pale-purple over whole flower, lobes overlapping, to 8cm.

■ **FUJI-NO-MINE** Large, pink flowers with a darker centre, to 6.5cm, late. Leaves variegated with many flecks of yellow. This was originally described in Japan as pure-white.

■ **FUJI-ZAKURA** White with pink stripes and flecks, to 6cm, mid–late. Slow-growing, compact habit. Name means 'Mt Fuji Cherry Blossom'.

■ **GUMPO (syn. GUMPO WHITE)** White 7.5cm with small purple flakes and frilled margins, late. Low growing. **'DWARF GUMPO'** and **'MINI GUMPO'** are sports with smaller leaves and flowers. There are at least ten more Gumpo variations. *MA, AZ, CH*.

■ **GUMPO PINK (syn. PINK GUMPO)** Light pink, late. A sport of 'Gumpo' (white). Low, mounding and late-flowering. Root-rot and phomopsis die-back resistant. **'GUMPO ROSE'** a little darker. *MA*. A range of Olinda Nurseries (Australia) Gumpo seedlings include: **'TRANQUILITY'** single-pink, star-shaped, **'ADORATION'** lavender-pink, **'DEVOTION'** salmon-pink, **'INNOCENCE'** white, **'TEMPTATION'** pale-pink, **'INDULGENCE'** white with red margins, **'SEDUCTION'** mauve-pink, **'AFFECTION'** pink, **'ELUSIVE'** white with red flecks.

■ **GUNREI (syn. GUNBI)** Pale pink, with small pink flecks, occasional stripes, frilled, 5cm, very late.

GUNREI

■ **HAKATA-SHIRO (syn. HAKATA-JIRO)** White with pale-green spotting, 6–7.5cm. Low growing. *SC*.

■ **HIGASA** Deep rose-pink, with a darker blotch, single, lobes overlapping, 10–12.5cm. One of the most popular Satsuki varieties. The flowers are so big, the stems can't support them and they point downwards. Root-rot resistant. *Cal*.

HIGASA

■ **ISSHO-NO-HARU** Pale purplish-pink with purple stripes and flakes or solid reddish purple, 7.5–10cm. Compact.

■ **JOGA (syn. JOGHA)** White to light-pink or purple with occasional flecks of purplish red, red spotting, to 7cm.

■ **JUETSU** White, single, with coral-pink splashes.

■ **JUKO** Deep-pink, light pink, with white centres, striped or spotted, to 7.5cm.

■ **KAGETSU-MUJI** Deep purplish-pink, with occasional white centres. A second clone under this name is white with rose spots and stripes. As the name means 'unmarked flower', the second one is surely misnamed.

■ **KAZAN (syn. RUKIZON)** Lighter than strong-red, blotch dotted, to 5cm. Small dark glossy-green leaves. Known as 'Rubicon' in America and 'Kazan' elsewhere. There are several clones in the U.S.A. under this name. One has light- to dark-pink flowers. *AGM, PNW.*

■ **KIMIMARU** White with dark- and light-salmon-pink, sometimes white throat with pink border, 7–8cm.

■ **KINGETSU** Single 5–6.5cm, deep-pink with white centres on each corolla lobe, or white with occasional pink flecks and sectors, also claret-rose with a darker blotch, very late. Very striking, constantly sporting, so you can have almost any flower colour on one plant. Useful for its very late flowering. Chugai.

KINGETSU

■ **KINPAI** Single, white with an orange-red border and freckling, to 7.5cm, mid–late. Dense. Needs shade to avoid sunburn. The epithet 'kin' means 'gold'.

■ **KINSAI** Strap-like narrow petals of orange-red, some normal round-petalled flowers, 3–4cm. Low and spreading. A bonsai subject.

■ **KOHAN-NO-TSUKI** White to pale pink with orange-red margins, to 7.5cm. 'Moon of the Lake'.

■ **KOZAN** Pale salmon-pink to off-white, 2.5–3cm. Very slow growing with tight bushy growth.

■ **KOZAN-NO-TSUKI** Light salmon-pink speckled and striped deeper, to 5cm, mid–late. Slow growing with an open, spreading or cascading habit. Good for bonsai.

■ **MATSUYO** White, flecked, spotted and striped red, to 5cm. Low, compact and spreading. Ht to 50cm. Rokujo/Hill.

■ **MINATO** Single or semi-double, white centre with orchid-pink border, to 6cm, mid–late. Vigorous, open and upright habit. Good for bonsai.

■ **NACHI-NO-TSUKI** Small, single, white, speckled and striped reddish-purple, mid. Slow-growing, fairly compact.

■ **NASSAU** White with light-purple specks and flakes, green throat, double, 5–6cm, very late. Spreading habit to 45cm. Nelson.

■ **NUCCIO'S BLUE MOON (syn. BLUE MOON)** Single, lavender, some flowers with a white centre, to 5cm, late. Vigorous but compact. We tried this in Scotland without success. Nuccio.

■ **NUCCIO'S BUTTER BALL** Small, white, single, creamy white, mid–late. Bushy growth habit. Nuccio.

■ **NUCCIO'S DESERT DAWN** Single, coral-pink, early–mid. Compact and spreading. Nuccio.

NUCCIO'S DESERT DAWN

■ **NUCCIO'S FEATHERS 'N' STRING** Irregular, long, feathery, white/pink with irregular darker patches, some flowers with just stamens. Compact. Very unusual. **'NUCCIO'S SPIDER DANCE'** is similar with no petals at all, just stamens. Nuccio.

■ **NUCCIO'S JULY BREEZE** Soft pink-lavender, deeper in centre and margins, late. Fairly compact. Nuccio.

■ **NUCCIO'S JULY SUNRISE** Single, coral/salmon-pink, late. Dark-green curled leaves on a compact plant. Nuccio.

■ **NUCCIO'S LAVENDER ICE** Single, lavender, star-shaped, mid. Vigorous but compact. Nuccio.

■ **NUCCIO'S MAY SHOWERS** Light-lavender with a white centre, mid–late. Spreading. **'NUCCIO'S MAY QUEEN'** very similar. Nuccio.

■ **NUCCIO'S MOUNT BALDY** White with occasional red spotting in throat, to 5cm, early–mid. Compact with narrow recurved leaves. Nuccio.

■ **NUCCIO'S POLKA** Single, orange-red, to 6cm, early. Long flowering-season, compact habit. There is also a variegated form with a white border to the flower. Nuccio.

■ **NUCCIO'S RAZZLE DAZZLE** White with occasional rose-pink stripes, to 9.5cm, early–mid. Vigorous, bushy habit. Nuccio.

■ **NUCCIO'S RED SILK** Single, cherry-red, mid. Slow-growing and spreading. Nuccio.

■ **NUCCIO'S VOODOO** Semi-double, off-white centre, purple border, 6.5cm, early. Vigorous but compact. Nuccio.

■ **NUCCIO'S WARM HEART** Semi-double, medium-pink, early–mid. A white-edged sport is also available. Nuccio.

■ **NUCCIO'S WILD CHERRY** Vivid-red, to 7.5cm. Compact with dark narrow leaves. Nuccio.

■ **NUCCIO'S WILD MOON** Large single, white centre with purple border, late. Medium sized, spreading. Nuccio.

■ **ORCHID EMPERESS** Single, lavender to 6.5cm, mid–late.

NUCCIO'S WILD CHERRY

■ **OTOME NO MAI** White with pale-pink centres and irregular purple margins, 6–7.5cm.

■ **POLYPETALUM** Flowers reddish orange with narrow petals split to the base, to 5cm, late. Narrow linear leaves to 5cm long. Upright habit. *PNW.*

■ **SAKURAGATA (syn. AIDEN)** Soft-white flowers with a distinct lavender-pink border, very variable, to 6cm, late. Upright spreading habit to 1m. A very attractive colour combination.

SAKURAGATA

■ **SEIKA** White to light pink with random red stripes, to 6.5cm. Compact habit. There are two similar clones under this name.

■ **SETTYU-NO-MATSU (syn. SECCHU-NO-MATSU)** Single, tubular, white. Small, narrow, twisted and contorted leaves. Very slow-growing and compact.

■ **SHIKO** Light- to deep-lavender with occasional darker stripes, to 10cm, early–late. Medium vigour, spreading habit.

■ **SHIKO LAVENDER** Large, lavender-pink flowers. Sport of 'Shiko', mid. A neat and compact-growing plant.

■ **SHIKO PURPLE** Light pink/pink with occasional darker stripes. Large. **'SHIKO WHITE'** white, **'SHIKO PINK'** pink, large. May be the same as 'Shiko Lavender'. *Aus.*

■ **SHINKYO** Light salmon-pink, with deeper edges, with occasional white flowers, to 6cm, early–mid. Vigorous and upright habit.

■ **SHINNYO-NO-HIKARI** White, striped and flecked rose-red with occasional solid colours, to 7.5cm, late. Variegated leaves. Spreading habit.

SHINNYO-NO-TSUKI

■ **SHINNYO-NO-TSUKI** Large, single, white with a rose-red border, occasional flecks and solid flowers, to 11cm, late. Vigorous and spreading habit. Striking flowers.

■ **SHIRA FUJI** Variable: purple or white with purple flecks or purple border, irregular lobes, to 5cm. Variegated foliage of green, bordered with ivory-white. Suffers leaf-damage in cold weather.

■ **SHIRYU-NO-HOMARE** Single, medium-sized, purple with narrow 'spider' petals, very late. Leaves narrow and twisted. Vigorous with upright habit.

■ **YAMA-NO-HIKARE** Small, single, with pointed petals, white to light-salmon-pink, heavily striped and spotted deep-pink, some solid colours, to 6.5cm, mid. Vigorous, with upright growth habit.

■ **YAMATO-NO-HIKARE** Large single, white, speckled and striped rose-purple, to 10cm, very late. Slow-growing. There is also a sport known as #2.

■ **YATA-NO-KAGAMI** Single, blush-pink with deep-pink margins, to 6cm, early–mid. Low and spreading. 'Sacred Mirror'.

H3–4 (USDA 6b–8b). Bred in North Carolina and Louisiana for heat and drought tolerance and resistance to root-rot. In hardiness they are about equivalent to most Glenn Dale and Robin Hill cultivars. Little grown outside the U.S.A.

■ **ADELAIDE POPE** Strong-red with a darker blotch, 5–7.5cm. Dense, oval, upright habit to 1.5m. Susceptible to root-rot in hot climates.

ADELAIDE POPE

■ **AUTUMN SUN** Strong reddish-orange, hose-in-hose, to 4.5cm. Fairly compact and spreading, ht to 1m. Heat and root-rot resistant.

■ **BATON ROUGE** Deep reddish-orange with a white throat, hose-in-hose, 6cm, mid. Small leaves, bronze in autumn. Rounded habit to 1m.

■ **CARROR** Deep purplish-pink (rose), semi-double, about 5cm, mid–late. Low and spreading, ht to about 1m.

■ **COCHRAN'S LAVENDER** Moderate purplish-pink with a deeper blotch, to 8cm. Dense and spreading, ht to 1.2m.

■ **ELAINE** Light pink, fully double, rosebud type, 5–7cm. Ht to 1.2m. H2–3.

■ **EMILY** Deep rose-red, hose-in-hose, to 5cm. Leaves reddish in winter. Compact grower to 1m. Susceptible to root-rot in hot climates.

■ **JANE SPALDING** Strong purplish-pink, blotched darker, single, 5–7cm. Leaves reddish in winter. Habit irregular. Ht to 1.2m.

JANE SPALDING

■ **PINK CAMELLIA** Light purplish-pink, double, to 7cm, mid. Ht to 1.2m. Leaves slightly glossy.

PINK CAMELLIA

■ **PINK CLOUD** Light pink, predominately single, a few with petaloid stamens, 5–7cm. Spreading habit to 1.2m. *Cal, NC*.

■ **SUNGLOW** Strong purplish-red, 5–7cm. Leaves reddish in winter. Rounded habit to 1.5m.

■ **WOLFPACK RED** Strong-red, single, to 4cm, 1–4 flowers per bud. Semi-dwarf to 1m, spreading.

SUNGLOW

H2–3(4) (USDA 7–9) M–ML, VL (to frosts). Bred in Indiana, the 'Encore' azaleas are patented and being heavily marketed as the first repeat-flowering azaleas. They flower in spring and again, sporadically, from August until the first frosts in mild and southern areas of the U.S.A. Bred from *R. oldhamii* (a form called '4th of July') by Robert Lee, they are good in hot climates but do less well as you move further north in the U.S.A. I have sought information from all over and it appears that the azaleas are only reliably repeat-blooming in areas with long, hot, growing-seasons. I imagine they should also be good in Australia (where many azaleas are repeat-flowering) and northern New Zealand. I would not bother with them in the U.K., most of Europe (though France and Spain would be worth a try) or the Pacific Northwest.

■ **AUTUMN AMETHYST™ (PBR)** Strong purplish-red with red spotting. Purple winter-foliage. Probably the most cold-hardy of the group.

■ **AUTUMN ANGEL™ (PBR)** Pure-white, to 7cm. Dense and spreading to 1.2m.

■ **AUTUMN BRAVO™ (PBR)** Single to semi-double, red. Dark foliage, upright habit to 1m.

■ **AUTUMN CARNIVAL™ (PBR)** Bright pink. Low and spreading habit. The brightest pink of the Encores.

■ **AUTUMN CHEER™ (PBR)** Single, rose-pink. One of the lower growing of the Encore hybrids, reaching 60cm–1m.

■ **AUTUMN CHIFFON™ (PBR)** Light pink with a red-purple blotch. Compact to 80cm. Perhaps the most striking of the Encore azaleas in flower.

■ **AUTUMN CORAL™ (PBR)** Single, coral-pink with deeper spotting. Mounded, ht to about 1m.

AUTUMN CORAL

AUTUMN DEBUTANTE

AUTUMN TWIST

ANNA KEHR

■ **AUTUMN DEBUTANTE™ (PBR)** Soft-pink flowers 7–8cm across. Compact and mounding. The clearest pink Encore. 1.2m × 1.2m.

■ **AUTUMN EMBERS™ (PBR)** Deep orange-red, semi-double. Spreading habit. The best selling Encore. Habit can be rather rangy.

■ **AUTUMN EMPRESS™ (PBR)** Bright-pink, semi-double. Dark-green leaves, upright habit to 1.2m.

■ **AUTUMN MONARCH™ (PBR)** Semi-double, salmon-orange, spotted red. Light-green leaves, upright habit to 1.5m. Can be rather sparse at the base.

■ **AUTUMN PRINCESS™ (PBR)** Double, salmon-pink. Burgundy winter-foliage. Compact to about 1m.

■ **AUTUMN ROUGE™ (PBR)** Strong purplish-red with red spotting, 5cm across. Dark-green leaves. Upright habit to 1.2m.

■ **AUTUMN ROYALTY™ (PBR)** Strong purplish-red with strong purplish-red spotting. Dark-green foliage. A.R.S. Azalea of the Year 2004. (ARS).

■ **AUTUMN RUBY™ (PBR)** Ruby-red to 2.5cm. Dark-green leaves. Ht to 75cm.

■ **AUTUMN SANGRIA™ (PBR)** Bright pink, the largest flower of the Encore group, 8cm across. Dense habit to 1.2m.

■ **AUTUMN STARLITE™ (PBR)** White, with occasional pink stripes and flecks, 5cm. Narrow leaves. The most vigorous, reaching 1.5m × 1.2m.

■ **AUTUMN TWIST™ (PBR)** White and purple-striped, occasionally purple. Dark-green leaves, upright habit to 1.3m or more. This one has a very striking flower.

NORTH AMERICAN HARDY

H4–6 (USDA 5b/6a–7a). These azaleas have been bred in E. North America, mostly in New England and into the Midwest, with a few new ones from Nova Scotia. The earliest hardy azaleas were bred by J. Gable, T. Shammarello and O. Pride, who realized that the combination of the Korean *R. poukhanense* crossed with the Japanese *R. kaempferi* would produce really hardy plants. The only drawback is that the offspring of this cross tend to be almost deciduous and rather straggly. More recently, nurseries, such as Weston in Massachusetts, Girard in Ohio and Schroeder in Indiana, have bred some great, tough, compact and more-evergreen varieties, which can be grown widely in some of the colder parts of coastal E. North America. With testing in different areas and local breeding, there are now varieties suitable for climates, such as Indiana, Oklahoma and Kansas, not previously considered suitable for azaleas. Not all these azaleas do well in N. Europe, where we lack summer heat, but many are good.

■ **ABIGAIL ADAMS** Deep purplish-pink, to 7.5cm, mid. Vigorous, spreading and mounding habit to about 1m. Weston.

■ **AL'S PICOTEE** Hose-in-hose, bicolour, white, edged pink. Compact habit and good leaf retention. Said to withstand –30°C (–22°F) in Toronto area, which would make this one of the hardiest. (*kiusianum* × Elsie Lee). *NG*. Al Smith.

■ **ANNA KEHR** Double, strong purplish-pink, no stamens, to 4.5cm. Dark, glossy leaves on a compact plant to 60cm. H4. *PNW*. Kehr.

■ **BARBARA HILLE** Single, salmon-pink. Compact and slow-growing, 60cm–1m. Gable.

■ **BARRY JAY** Long-lasting, double, large, bright-rose. Dark-green leaves, upright. Roslyn.

■ **BIG JOE** Reddish violet with a brownish blotch, 5–6cm, early mid-season. (*poukhanense* × *kaempferi*). Loses most leaves in winter. Very hardy, one of the hardiest of all evergreen azalea-hybrids. Vigorous upright habit to 2–3m. Gable.

■ **BIXBY** Strong-red, to 3 per flat truss. Leaves dark green, turning red in autumn. Compact, low, spreading, semi-evergreen. *NG, MS*. Weston.

BIXBY

■ **BOUDOIR** Strong purplish-red, darker blotch, about 3.5cm. One of the hardiest and with good reports in E. Canada. *AT, NG, TO*. Gable.

■ **BRANFORD BEAUTY** Slightly fragrant lavender-pink, with a red flare. Vigorous, 1–1.5m. Nickou.

■ **BRIANNE** Deep-pink. Variegated leaves with white margin and pink-tinged autumn-colour. Sport of 'Girard's Rose'. There is also a dwarf sport of 'Brianne'. Sterling.

AUTUMN STARLITE

■ **AUTUMN SUNSET™ (PBR)** Single, orange-red. Deep-green leaves. Compact habit. 1.2m × 1.2m. There is also a Pericat hybrid with this name.

■ **AUTUMN SWEETHEART™ (PBR)** Soft-pink to off-white with purple spotting, 6–7cm. Compact to 1.2m × 1.2m. The flowers have a fine two-tone effect.

AL'S PICOTEE

BRIANNE

■ **BRICK RED** Orange-red. Best in part shade, low-growing and dense, with good winter foliage colour. Weston.

■ **CAMEO** Light pink, hose-in-hose, with some doubles, 3.5cm, late. *PNW*. Gable.

■ **CAMPFIRE** Strong-red, darker blotch, hose-in-hose. Tall and spreading. A good colour. There are two other azaleas with this name, a Kurume (syn. 'Hino Scarlet') and a red-purple Glenn Dale. Gable.

CAMPFIRE

■ **CAROL** Vivid purplish-red, hose-in-hose, late-mid. Low growing and very hardy. There is also a white Yerkes azalea with this name. Gable.

■ **CAROL KITTEL** Double, white flowers, edged light purple, to 7.5cm, mid. Leaves pale green. Dense habit. A second-generation 'Elsie Lee' hybrid from two Schroeder parents. Schroeder.

■ **CAROLINE GABLE** Brightest red with deeper blotch, 4.5cm, late-mid. Upright, medium-tall but spreading habit to 1.5m+. Very free-flowering. Red autumn-colour. *PNW*. Gable.

■ **CARRIE AMANDA** White with deep purplish-pink border to 6cm. Very compact, to 60cm × 60cm. Schroeder.

■ **CASCADE (syn. SHAM'S CASCADE)** White, 3cm. Very hardy and very fine in flower, one of the showiest hardy whites. Grows to 1m × 2m or more. There is also a less hardy pink Glenn Dale, 'Cascade'. *GL, AT, NG, TO*. Shammarello.

■ **CHIARA (syn. GIRARD'S CHIARA)** Deep purplish-pink with deep orange-red blotch, hose-in-hose, with ruffled edges, to 6cm. Ht 50–60cm. H6: one of the hardiest Girard hybrids. A good doer in most azalea growing areas. *PNW*. Girard.

■ **CLARA MARIE** White, ruffled, large, mid–late, 6–7cm. Ht 1.2m. Vigorous. H5. Girard.

■ **CORSAGE** Flowers orchid-purple-pink, lightly fragrant, about 6cm, late-mid. One of the best of this colour and useful for late flowering. Very tough, probably one of the hardiest of all. Semi-evergreen in cold climates. *AZ, CH, NG*. Gable.

■ **DAVID WALDMAN** Large, semi-double, with red centre, pink flare and contrasting white margin. Low and compact. Roslyn.

■ **DESIREE** Flowers white, frilled, 6cm. Ht to 1.5m. Shammarello.

■ **DR JAMES DIPPEL** Vivid reddish-orange with darker spotting, to 6cm. Compact, spreading habit to 50cm. May have potential in N. Europe. Schroeder.

■ **DR H.R. SCHROEDER** Clear pastel-pink flowers with darker-pink edging, to 6cm. Good foliage retention. Heat tolerant. **'MOBY DICK'** pale yellowish-white with green-yellow spotting. Schroeder.

DR H.R. SCHROEDER

■ **EDNA BEE (syn. EDNA B.)** Hose-in-hose sometimes double, deep purplish-pink, with a deeper blotch. A compact plant to 50–75cm. A tough seedling of 'Elizabeth Gable'. Yavorsky.

■ **ELIZABETH GABLE** Deep-red, frilled, with a darker blotch, 7.5cm. Medium-sized, spreading habit. One of the most evergreen of the hardy Gable azaleas. *MA*. Gable.

ELSIE LEE

■ **ELSIE LEE** Semi-double, light reddish-purple (lilac) to 6cm. Fairly compact but stiffly upright grower. Pale, semi-deciduous foliage. Very hardy. A very striking and unusual colour. The habit and leaf-retention could be better. Lace-bug resistant. Parent of many good hybrids. *AGM, SE, PNW, MD, CH, PD, TO, AT, PV, MA, U.K.* Shammarello.

FAIRFAX

■ **FAIRFAX** Huge petaloid, ruffled pink-and-white, variations include white centres. A broad, mounded, dense plant. **'I'LL BE DAMNED'** looks identical, is almost certainly the same as 'Fairfax', and should not have been patented (as it is not distinctive). **'ORCHIDO'** pale orchid-pink. Ring.

FAIRFAX

■ **FLORENCE WALDMAN** Large semi-double, hose-in-hose, white, spotted with red-purple flecks, stripes and sectors, with occasional pink selfs and pinks with white margins. Leaves glossy, dark green. Upright and spreading. Roslyn.

■ **FOREST FIRE** Deep-pink, small hose-in-hose flowers, 2.5cm. This is claimed to be a hybrid of *R. tschonoskii*, but there is no evidence that this species (with tiny white flowers) is involved. Gable.

FOREST FIRE

■ **GARDEN STATE GLOW** Hose-in-hose, strong purplish-red (china-rose), to 3cm. Leaves glossy, hairless. Linwood.

■ **GIRARD DWARF LAVENDER** Clear lavender-purple. Tough and very compact. Girard.

■ **GIRARD SANDRA ANN (syn. SANDRA ANN)** Large, ruffled, purple flowers to 7.5cm. Upright habit. H6: one of the hardier Girard hybrids. Girard.

■ **GIRARD SAYBROOK GLORY** Single and double, ruffled, vivid purplish-pink, to 7.5cm. Large dark-green leaves on a low, compact plant. Girard.

■ **GIRARD'S BORDER GEM (syn. BORDER GEM)** Deep-pink, to 3cm. Leaves small, on a dwarf plant with dense habit. Girard.

■ **GIRARD'S CAROLINE** Rose-red. Compact with excellent dark-green foliage, reddish in winter. Flowers are long-lasting. Girard.

■ **GIRARD'S CRIMSON** Strong purplish-red with a deeper blotch, 6cm. Growing wider than high, 50cm. Not one of the hardiest of this group. *SE*. Girard.

■ **GIRARD'S FUCHSIA** Deep reddish-purple with lighter spotting, ruffled, 6–7.5cm. Leaves dark and glossy, red in winter. Dense and spreading habit. The colour is unusual. *PNW, CT, MD.* Girard.

■ **GIRARD'S HOT SHOT** Dark reddish-orange with dark-red spotting, to 6cm. Handsome glossy dark-green leaves turn reddish in winter. One of the hardiest Girard azaleas, H6, but not completely reliable in Scotland. *PNW, MA, SE.* Girard.

■ **GIRARD'S JEREMIAH (syn. JEREMIAH)** Hose-in-hose, deep-pink, ruffled, about 6cm. Large dark-green leaves turn red in winter. Very free-flowering. H5. Heat tolerant. Girard.

■ **GIRARD'S NATIONAL BEAUTY** Ruffled, rose-pink, to 6cm. Leaves dark green, glossy, reddish in autumn. Compact to 1.2m. H5. Girard.

■ **GIRARD'S PINK** Strong pinkish-red with a deep purplish-red blotch, to 4.5cm. Spreading habit with glossy deep-green leaves, to 50cm. H5. Suitable for forcing. *SE.* Girard.

■ **GIRARD'S PINK DAWN (syn. PINK DAWN)** Hose-in-hose, deep-pink, 5–6cm. Dense upright habit. Deep-green leaves, reddish in winter. One of the hardier Girards: H6. Girard.

GIRARD'S PINK DAWN

■ **GIRARD'S PURPLE** Deep purplish-red with darker spotting with wavy lobes, to 6.5cm. Vigorous but quite tidy with dark-green leaves and flowers of a good shade of purple. Girard.

■ **GIRARD'S ROBERTA** Deep-pink, double, ruffled, to 7.5cm. Not one of the hardiest Girards, H4–5. Girard.

■ **GIRARD'S ROSE** Deep-pink, reverse deep yellowish-pink, 5–6cm. Leaves reddish-orange in winter. Ht 60cm–1m. Upright and vigorous. H5. **'GIRARD'S PETITE'** a more compact sport. *PNW, SE, GL.* Girard.

■ **GIRARD'S SALMON** Hose-in-hose, large, salmon-pink. Upright and tall growing, less compact than other Girard hybrids. Girard.

■ **GIRARD'S SCARLET** Strong-red with a deeper blotch, mid-season, 5cm. Low and compact with dark-green leaves. One of the hardiest azalea hybrids. 60cm. Girard.

■ **GIRARD'S VARIEGATED GEM** Bright rose-pink to 3cm. Leaves narrow with white variegation on the edges. Compact habit; potentially one of the best variegated azaleas. Girard.

■ **GIRARD'S VARIEGATED HOT SHOT (syn. HOTSHOT VARIEGATED)** Dark reddish-orange with darker spotting. Striking white edges to the leaves. The only variegated evergreen azalea we have found to be suitable for Scotland. The name appears in many variations. *Scot.* Girard.

GIRARD'S VARIEGATED HOT SHOT

■ **GREAT EXPECTATIONS** Double, orange-red, to 5cm, late. A fine *R. nakaharae* hybrid with spreading habit and bronzy autumn-colour. H4–5. This looks an excellent azalea as I saw it in Philadelphia area. *Cal.* Kehr.

■ **GREEN GLOW** Long-lasting hose-in-hose, white flushed green with green eye, like roses. Low and spreading. An unusual and striking flower. Hyatt/Roslyn.

■ **GROUND HOG** Vivid purplish-red with a large burgundy blotch, to 5cm, early–mid. Low and spreading, vigorous. Hardy, derived from *R. poukhanense.* Weston.

■ **HARDY GARDENIA (syn. LINWOOD HARDY GARDENIA)** Double, white, looks like an opening Gardenia flower. Dark-green leaves. Dwarf spreading-habit. Good winter-foliage. Often grown as a houseplant. *PNW, CT, SE.* Linwood.

HARDY GARDENIA

■ **HAROLD EPSTEIN** Fully double, hose-in-hose, white, unmarked, to 5cm, mid. Small leaves. A witches' broom of 'White Rosebud'. Roslyn.

■ **HELEN CURTIS (PP)** Semi-double, white, unmarked, 5–6cm. Very tough. New growth yellow-green. Size to approx 60cm × 1m. *SE U.S.A., NG, TO, MS.* Shammarello.

■ **HERBERT** Hose-in-hose, medium reddish-purple, with a darker-purple blotch and frilled edges, 4.5cm, early–mid. Low and dense with long, glossy, pointed leaves. Very hardy. Susceptible to root-rot in S.E. U.S.A. Often confused with 'Purple Splendor'. *MD, MA, SE, TO, MS.* Gable.

■ **HINO PINK** Strong purplish-pink, 5cm, early. Spreading habit, wider than high. Tough: H6. Shammarello.

HELEN CURTIS

■ **HINO-RED** Moderate-red, to 4.5cm, early. Compact and spreading to 70cm in ten to fifteen years. *AT, MW.* Shammarello.

■ **HINO-WHITE** White to 5cm, early. Spreading habit, ht to 40cm. *PNW.* Shammarello. **'HINO WHITE DWARF'** smaller sport of Hino-White.

■ **ISABEL** Bright-pink, hose-in-hose, 3.5cm. This selection was named in Boskoop, Holland. Gable.

■ **JAMES GABLE** Strong-red, hose-in-hose, darker blotch. Like 'Campfire' but lower growing. *TO.* Gable.

■ **JANET RHEA** Semi-double, hose-in-hose, pink and rose with white edges, to 6cm. Dwarf and spreading, probably only hardy to –18°C (0°F). Linwood.

■ **JANICE LYNN** Large, pink, hose-in-hose, with red flare and spotting, in spring, autumn and a few in summer. Low and spreading. (Nancy of Robinhill ×?). Roslyn.

■ **JOSEPHE GABLE (syn. JOE GABLE)** Single to hose-in-hose, large, white, tinged pink with a red flare. Very tough, light-green foliage. Fairly compact. Pride.

■ **KATHY ANN (syn. GIRARD'S KATHY)** White, slightly ruffled 6.5cm, mid. Semi-upright habit to 1m. Flowers can get lost in the foliage. *CT.* Girard.

■ **LAKE ERIE** Deep-pink, blotched/spotted reddish-orange, 75cm, mid. Very hardy. Sisters include: **'LAKE MICHIGAN'** purple-pink. **'LAKE SUPERIOR'** deep purplish-pink. (*poukhanense* × *kaempferi* F2). Stanton.

■ **LANNY'S PALE LILAC (syn. PALE LILAC)** Very pale purple. One of the hardiest evergreen azaleas, reputed to flower after –32°C (–25°F), so this would be a good starting point for breeding ironclad evergreen azaleas. (*kaempferi* × *pouhanense*). Pride.

■ **LA ROCHE** Magenta-purplish-pink, early May. Very bud-hardy. 1–1.5m. Gable.

■ **LESLIE'S PURPLE** Strong purplish-red with dark spotting, lobes wavy, to 6cm. Low and compact to 1m. H5. Girard.

■ **LINDA STUART** Hose-in-hose, pale-cream, edged salmon-pink, 5cm. Upright vase-shaped habit. One of the hardiest evergreen azalea hybrids of this colour. *PB, CT.* Yavorsky.

■ **LITTLE GARDENIA** Witches' broom sport of 'Hardy Gardenia': white double flowers. Tight-growing dwarf plant. Linwood.

■ **LORNA** Double, hose-in-hose, light purplish-pink. Like 'Rosebud', but less susceptible to azalea gall. Low dense habit with very light green leaves. *PNW.* Gable.

LOUISE GABLE

■ **LOUISE GABLE** Semi-double, deep-pink with a darker blotch, 5–6cm, late. Low, spreading and dense. Flowers need protection from strong sun. *CC*. Gable.

■ **MAJESTY** Strong reddish-purple, to 7.5cm, mid. Long, glossy, deep-green leaves turn burgundy in winter. Good winter-leaf retention. *MS*. Weston.

■ **MARY ANN** Semi-double lavender-pink, with a darker blotch. Low and spreading to 1m high. A magnet for rabbits. Colour is not that good. Gable.

■ **MARY DALTON** Reddish orange, hose-in-hose, 3cm, early–mid. Upright and quite tall. Flowers tend to hang down and they can burn in sun. Gable.

■ **MAY BELLE** Deep-pink to strong purplish-red, semi-double, 6cm. Compact and slow-growing. Very tough: H6. *GL, NG*. Shammarello.

■ **MILDRED MAE** Vivid reddish-purple, spotted deeper. Low, compact and spreading, lower than sister '**VIOLA**'. Semi-deciduous. Rated for its hardiness in Atlantic Canada. *PV*. Gable.

■ **MIRIAM** Deep rose-pink with deeper speckling, to 4.5cm, early. Red-orange autumn foliage. To 1.5m. Gable.

■ **MOHAWK** Red, ruffled, small. Small leaves, compact. Weston.

■ **MRS HENRY SCHROEDER** Fully double, strong purplish-pink, to 5cm. Leaves oval, on a compact plant to 60cm. (Elsie Lee × Frosty). Sisters include: '**ELIZA HYATT**' double, pale- to light-purple, '**MRS NANCY DIPPEL**' pale-pink with a darker stripe. Schroeder.

ELIZA HYATT

■ **NADINE** Light clear-pink. Used by Pride as his principal parent of very hardy azaleas. (*kaempferi* × *pouhanense*). Pride.

■ **OLD FAITHFUL** Large, orchid-pink (rhodomine-purple), with a dark blotch, 5–6cm, early–mid. Gable.

■ **PINK CLUSTERS** Ruffled, bright pink (strong purplish-red), to 3.5cm, mid. Small dark leaves on a slow-growing and compact plant. Red winter-foliage. '**TEXAS PINK**' is very similar. Weston.

■ **PINK DISCOVERY (syn. ED'S SILVER PINK)** Moderate purplish-pink, of good substance, to 6.5cm, early. An *R. poukhanense* seedling, and possibly the hardiest of the Weston evergreen azaleas. Weston.

■ **PINK ROSETTE** Double, deep rose-pink, very late. Gable.

■ **PLEASANT WHITE (syn. GIRARD'S PLEASANT WHITE)** White, rounded wavy lobes, to 6.5cm. Ht to 60cm–1m. A good tough plant. H5. *MD*. Girard.

PLEASANT WHITE

■ **PRIDE RED** Dark-red, late. Tough. Pride.

■ **PRIDE'S PINK** Good-sized pink, late. Very hardy plant, good red autumn-leaf colour. Pride.

■ **PRIDE'S WHITE** White. Tough. Pride.

■ **PURPLE PRIDE** Vivid reddish-purple with a deeper blotch, to 6cm. Compact habit to 60cm. Schroeder. '**SCARLET FROST**' deep-pink with a dark-red blotch.

■ **PURPLE SPLENDOR** Vivid reddish-purple (orchid-purple), with darker spotting. Spreading, vigorous, ht to 2m. Considered by some to be the best 'purple' for New England, but not good in hottest parts of S. U.S.A. due to root-rot susceptibility. *PNW, SE, NG*. Gable.

PURPLE SPLENDOR

■ **RED HEAD** Brick-red flower, to 4cm, early. Ht to 1.5m. Said to be hardy to –40°C (–40°F), which is highly unlikely, but it should be a tough plant. Martin.

■ **RED RED** Strong-red (crimson), 5cm. Compact, to 60cm, growing wider than high. This is a wonderful colour but not successful in Scotland or Nova Scotia. A good parent. Said to be very hardy as long as there is summer heat. *MW*. Shammarello.

■ **RENÉE MICHELLE (syn. GIRARD'S RENÉE MICHELLE)** Single, deep-pink, spotted red, ruffled, to 5cm. Ht to 1m. Impressive flowers. H5. Not hardy in Nova Scotia. *SE U.S.A., GL*. Girard.

■ **ROSE GREELY** Hose-in-hose, white with a yellow-green blotch, with a slight scent, about 6cm, early. Dense spreading habit. Fairly tough, but prone to bark-split in colder maritime climates, such as Nova Scotia. Gable's most complex hybrid. Resistant to root-rot. *MD, MA*. Gable.

■ **ROSEBUD** Deep purplish-pink double flowers like rosebuds, 4.5cm, mid–late. Slow, dense, spreading habit. Susceptible to galls. There are other plants masquerading under this name. Make sure you get the Gable hybrid, which is the toughest. *PNW, CC*. Gable.

ROSEBUD

■ **SCHROEDER'S WHITE GLORY** Hose-in-hose, white to pink with purplish-pink edging, 3.4–4cm. Compact to 60cm. Schroeder.

■ **SCOTIAN BREEZE** Cool pastel pink, mid–late. Compact, low and spreading habit. Bred for Nova Scotian climate. *AT*. Weagle.

■ **SCOTIAN CLOUDS** Pale red-purple (pink) edging, fading to white in the centre, giving bicolour effect, late. Spreading shrub to 50cm high. *AT*. Weagle.

■ **SCOTIAN FIRE** Orange-red. Compact and spreading. *AT*. Weagle.

■ **SCOTIAN MIRAGE** Single, palest lavender-white. '**SCOTIAN ROSEBUD**' soft-pink, full double and '**SCOTIAN PICOTEE**' white with brash rosy-pink petal-tips, like 'Komo Kulshan' but much later flowering. *AT*. Weagle.

SCOTIAN REEF

■ **SCOTIAN MIST** Pastel-pink. A spreading plant to 40cm. Good leaf-retention in the harsh Nova Scotian climate, where few evergreen azaleas do well. *AT*. Weagle. Sister **'SCOTIAN REEF'** white, pale rimmed pink.

■ **SHAPIRO PINCUSHION** Small lavender-pink. Small leaves on a compact mound. A seedling of *R. kiusianum*. Shapiro.

SHAPIRO PINCUSHION

■ **SPRINGTIME** Vivid purplish-red, darker blotch, 5cm, early–mid. Upright, tall. Extremely hardy, to –25°C (–13°F) or colder. There is also a salmon Indica hybrid and a white Kurume under this name. *AT, CC*. Gable.

■ **STEWARTSTONIAN** Vivid (rather harsh) red, 5cm. Upright and spreading to 1.5m × 2m, with glossy leaves, turning chocolate or reddish in winter. Very hardy. Sun tolerant. *PNW, TZ, MA, SE, AT, TO, CC*. Gable.

STEWARTSTONIAN

■ **SUSAN CAMILLE** Semi-double, hose-in-hose, very pale lavender-pink fading to off-white, to 6cm. Compact habit to 60cm. Schroeder.

■ **SWAN** Small, hose-in-hose, white. Slow growing and compact. Gable.

■ **UNSURPASSABLE (syn. GIRARD'S UNSURPASSABLE)** Single, deep-pink, 6–7cm. Dense and spreading. One of the hardier Girards: H6. Girard.

■ **WEIRDO** White strap-like petal is twisted or turned like a witch-hazel flower. Vigorous, upright habit. An oddity which appeals to some. Roslyn.

■ **WESTON'S VYKING** Rose-red (strong purplish-red), to 4cm, mid. Glossy leaves turn purple in autumn. Habit wider than high, good in full sun. *MS*. Weston.

WHITE ROSEBUD

■ **WHITE ROSEBUD (syn. KEHR'S WHITE ROSEBUD)** Double (rosebud-like), white with green throat, to 5cm. Not proving to be as hardy as the pink version, but said to take –23°C (–10°F) (H5). To 1m wide. *CH, SE, PD*. Kehr.

■ **WINTERGREEN** White, to 4cm, mid. Good winter-leaf retention for a hardy white azalea. Ht to about 40cm. There is also a North Tisbury azalea with this name. Shammarello.

NORTHERN EUROPEAN HYBRIDS

H4–6 (USDA 5b–6b). The dwarf species *R. kiusianum* and *R. nakaharae* have been crossed with larger-flowered but less hardy varieties to create selections satisfactory for Scotland, Scandinavia, Germany, E. Canada and other similar climates, where summer-sun strength is not reliable. Most are low-growing, tolerant of full exposure and most of the newer ones are relatively evergreen. Most of the best azaleas for Northern Europe are in this group. The most important hybridizers are Peter and Kenneth Cox (Scotland), G. Arends, C. Fleischmann and H. Hachmann (Germany).

■ **AGGER** Pale lilac with reddish markings. Upright and spreading to about 1.2m. Numerous sisters were named: **'BEVER'** light reddish-purple, **'WIPPER'** moderate reddish-purple, and so on. Huge plants can be found at Bremen Rhododendron Park. Arends.

■ **ALLOTRIA** Moderate to strong purple-red, 4–5cm. Ht 60cm. Impressive flowers. *Ger*. Hachmann.

■ **ARCTIC FOX** Pure-white with faint-green markings, to 6cm, early–mid. Leaves pale green, hairy. Fairly compact. **'GLENDOICK® ERMINE'** is a sister with smaller flowers. Hardier in Scotland than its parent 'Mucronatum'. Cox.

ARCTIC FOX

GLENDOICK® ERMINE

■ **BABUSCHKA** Double, vivid purplish-red fading to deep purplish-pink, about 4cm. Compact with good foliage. Ht to about 50cm. Hachmann.

■ **BABY DANE** Small-flowered pure-white. Very compact and semi-deciduous. ('Panda' × *kiusianum*). Should be very hardy. Birck.

■ **BETTY MUIR** Small lilac-pink. Small-leaved *R. kiusianum* × or selection. Very hardy. *Ger*.

■ **BLANICE** Pale purplish-pink to 2cm. 'A good doer': Holger Hachmann. (*poukhanense* hybrid). Semi-deciduous. Kavka.

■ **BLUE MONDAY** Small, lilac flowers. A low-spreading plant. **'BLASCHEK' (syn. SILVIA)** purple-red. Kerkhoff.

■ **CANZONETTA** Hose-in-hose, brightest-pink, 5–6cm. Very compact, to 30cm, and a fine commercial hybrid. Striking mahogany-red or darkest-green foliage in winter. Flowers are like tissue-paper. Extremely floriferous. *AGM*. Hachmann.

CANZONETTA

■ **CHIPMUNK** (*see* photo overleaf) Bright-pink hose-in-hose, to 5.5cm, mid–late. Compact slow-growing plant with neat glossy foliage. 'CHINCHILLA' is redder, but otherwise similar. 'MARMOT' deep purplish-pink. *Scot*. Cox.

■ **DIAMANT group (syn. DIAMOND)** (*see* photo overleaf) Small flowers in various colours: **LILAC, PINK, ROSY RED, WHITE (syn. LACHS, ROSA, ROT, WEIß)**. There were originally ten clones. Not all are in commerce. Free flowering and extremely hardy. Compact and low growing, 30–40cm. Inclined to have poor winter-foliage retention, so perhaps will become less popular. We have stopped growing them at Glendoick. *AT, GL, Ger*. Fleischmann.

CHIPMUNK

FRIDOLINE

GLENDOICK® DREAM

DIAMANT WHITE

■ **DIEMEL** Light yellowish-pink, with reddish-brown markings. A hybrid of *R. kaempferi*. Sisters include: **'ENNEPE'** strong purplish-pink, **'SORPE'** purple. Arends.

■ **DRAPA** Deep carmine-pink, late, 4.5–5.5cm. Compact. Sisters include: **'ELFIE'** bright pink, **'EVITA'** salmon-orange-red, **'TOOTSIE'** carmine-rose. (Chippewa × Squirrel). Hachmann.

DRAPA

■ **EISPRINZESSIN®** Hose-in-hose to semi-double, white with a greenish-yellow centre, to 6cm. Dark-green shiny oval leaves. Semi-deciduous. Impressive in flower but Hachmanns think 'Schneeperle' is a better plant. *Ger*. Hachmann.

■ **FALKENSTEIN** Hose-in-hose deep-pink, to 2.5cm. Ht to 30cm, spreading habit. Pillnitzer.

■ **FLORIDA** Deep-red hose-in-hose. A popular variety with deep glossy leaves turning reddish in autumn and winter. *AGM*. Vuyk.

■ **FRIDOLINE** Pure bright-red, 4–4.5cm. Dark-green leaves. Not a great commercial plant in Scotland, but its unfading flowers make it a good plant for Germany. *Ger*. Hachmann.

■ **GEISHA CARMINE/KARMIN (NORIKO)** Hose-in-hose, purplish pink to 3cm. Small leaves, very compact. Arends.

■ **GEISHA LILAC (syn. HANAKO)** Purplish pink. Very compact, dwarf habit. There were originally twelve Geisha hybrids: the names have been inconsistently translated into English and the clones are often confused in the trade. They are usually sold in Germany under the Japanese sounding names. *Ger, Hol, U.K.* Arends.

■ **GEISHA ORANGE/ORANGEROT (syn. SATSCHICO)** Bright reddish-orange, 2–2.5cm. Compact, mounded habit. The most popular azalea in this shade for U.K. *Ger, Scot.* Arends.

GEISHA ORANGE/ORANGEROT

■ **GEISHA PINK (syn. MOMOKO)** Pink, to 2cm. Small leaves, very compact. Arends.

■ **GEISHA PURPLE (syn. HARUKO)** Light reddish-purple, to 2cm. Dense and compact habit. Arends.

■ **GEISHA RED/DEEP PINK (syn. MICHIKO)** Small, deep purplish-red flowers, hose-in-hose, about 3cm. Compact to 30cm. Arends.

■ **GEISHA WHITE (syn. HISAKO)** Small white, early–mid-season. Compact. Arends.

■ **GEORG ARENDS** Reddish-purple, to 7.5cm. Ht to 1m. Originally claimed to be an azaleodendron but obviously not. Schumacher.

■ **GISLINDE** Bright rose-red, semi-double (with some petaloid stamens), 4.5–5cm. Ht 30cm. Leaves small. Hachmann.

■ **GLENDOICK® DREAM** Double, ruffled, red-purple, early to mid. Compact with dark-green leaves and good winter-leaf retention. *Scot.* Cox.

■ **GLENDOICK® GARNET** Deep-crimson, mid. Small pointed leaves, tidy upright habit. Hardier than its parent 'Red Red' in Scotland, and of similar colour. Cox.

GLENDOICK® GARNET

■ **GLENDOICK® GLACIER** Double, white, mid–late. The best double white for Scotland. Compact and spreading. *Scot.* Cox.

GLENDOICK® GLACIER

■ **GLENDOICK® GOBLIN** Carmine-red, unmarked, mid. Dark-green leaves turn reddish in winter. Fairly compact. A very striking colour. Cox.

GLENDOICK® GOBLIN

■ **GLENDOICK® SNOWFLAKES** White with a yellow throat. Handsome foliage, a little more evergreen than 'Panda'. Should be hardy as it is a cross of 'Diamant White'. Cox.
■ **GLENDOICK® CRIMSON** Dark crimson-red, waxy. Deep-green foliage turns reddish in winter. A bit straggly when young but better with age. A very good colour. Glendoick is a registered trademark. Cox.

GLENDOICK® CRIMSON

■ **HACHMANN'S ESTRELLA (syn. ESTRELLA)** Single, bright red, about 4.5cm. Ht to 30cm, spreading habit. *Ger*. Hachmann.

HACHMANN'S ESTRELLA

■ **HACHMANN'S GABRIELE (syn. GABRIELE)** Dark rose-red, (red-purple), 4.5–5cm. Ht to 60cm. *Ger*. Hachmann.

■ **HACHMANN'S GRANADA (syn. GRANADA)** Semi-double to double, vivid purplish-red, spotted deeper. Leaves glossy, olive in winter. Hachmann.
■ **HACHMANN'S ROKOKO (syn. ROKOKO)** Double, hose-in-hose, bright pink, 5cm. Compact with glossy leaves, ht to 40cm. *Scot, Ger*. Hachmann.

HACHMANN'S ROKOKO

■ **HACHMANN'S ROSALIND (syn. ROSALIND)** Star-shaped, bright pink, 4–5cm. Semi-deciduous. Ht to 1m. Hachmann.
■ **KERMESINA** Vivid purplish-red (hot-pink), to 2cm. Shiny leaves and compact habit. Very tough but flowers are small and a bit 'hot' coloured. *Ger, Scand, U.K.* Arends.

KERMESINA

KERMESINA ROSE

■ **KERMESINA ROSE** Rose-pink flowers with a white picotee edge. One of the toughest of the two-toned azaleas, excellent for U.K. & Northern Europe. Keeps around 50 per cent of its leaves in winter in Scotland. *Ger, Scand, U.K.*
■ **KERMESINA WHITE** Flowers small, pure-white. Compact and dwarf. Tends to sport sections of pink, but a good, hardy, compact white. *Ger, Scand, U.K.*

KERMESINA WHITE

■ **KIRSTIN** Bright pink, single, to 5.8cm. Ht to 40cm. Hachmann.
■ **LABE** Reddish pink, unmarked to 3.5cm. Compact and slow growing to 60cm. Rather prone to galls. Very hardy. Kavka.

LABE

■ **LEDIKANENSE** Pale purple-violet with a deeper-purple blotch. One of the hardiest azaleas, proving itself in S. Finland. More or less deciduous in winter. *Czech, Ger*. Kavka & Opatrnà.

LEDIKANENSE

■ **LEMUR** Deep-pink/light-red, 4cm, mid. Shiny leaves with attractive red buds. Low-growing with good winter-foliage retention. *Scot*. Cox.

■ **MAISCHNEE**® Pure white with a yellow throat, to 7.5cm. Ht to 50cm, spreading. The largest-flowered of Hachmann's compact white-azaleas with very fine flowers. Hachmann.

■ **MARUSCHKA** Carmine-red, 4–5.5cm. Excellent dark shiny winter foliage, one of the best we have seen for Scotland. Ht to 50cm or more. *Ger, Scot*. Hachmann.

MARUSCHKA

■ **MELINA** Hose-in-hose, dark purplish-pink, 4.5–5.5cm. Compact and tough. Ht to 30cm, spreading to 1m. Hachmann.

■ **MOZART** Deep purplish-pink to 6cm. Ht to 1.2m. There is also a white Indica with this name. Vuyk.

■ **NICO (syn. NICO RED)** Cherry-red, large flower. Dark-green leaves turn bronzy-red in autumn. One of the hardiest European evergreen azaleas. *PNW*. Vuyk, van Nes.

■ **OCTAVA** Pinkish-purple, to 5cm. Ht to 80cm. Semi-deciduous. 'OSLAVA' rose-pink. *Ger*. Jelinch.

OCTAVA

■ **PALESTRINA** Single, white with yellow-green flare, a soft fragrance. Upright grower, popular in Europe and U.S.A. A fine large-flowered white. *AGM, MA, CC*. Vuyk.

■ **PANDA** Pure white, with greenish-yellow throat, 3cm, mid. The most popular Glendoick azalea and now one of the most-grown white azaleas in the UK. Semi-deciduous with pale-green leaves. Very hardy in Scotland. *AGM, PNW*. Cox.

PANDA

■ **PEPPINA**® Light purple with midveins tinged strong purplish-pink, with a deep purplish-red blotch, to 5.5cm. Leaves glossy, mid-green. Ht to 30cm. Spreading habit. More compact than most of this shade and with reasonable leaf-retention, it looks like a winner for Scotland too. *Ger*. Hachmann.

■ **PETTICOAT**® Double, deep purplish-pink, edges deeper, to 6cm. Leaves ovate, glossy, hairy, with good winter-leaf retention. Rather straggly compared to other Hachmann double-pinks. Hachmann.

■ **PRINSES JULIANA** Light orange-red. Leaves to 4cm. Ht to 40cm. Vuyk.

■ **PURPLE TRIUMPH** Large, deep-purple flowers with deeper speckling. A broad spreading bush to 1m. Vuyk.

■ **PURPURKISSEN**® Single, vivid purplish-red, tinged strong-red, 5–6cm. Leaves ovate, dark, slightly glossy, bronzy in winter. Flower colour holds well in the sun. Ht to 40cm, spreading to 1.2m or more. Hachmann.

PURPURTRAUM

■ **PURPURTRAUM** Deep reddish-purple, to 3.5cm. Compact with small dark-green leaves. One of the best dark-purples for northern climates. *AGM*. Wemken.

■ **RACOON** Vivid- to strong-red, to 4cm, very late. Compact, spreading plant to 30cm. The latest-flowering of the Cox hybrids. *AGM*. Cox.

■ **ROSINETTA**® Flowers double (rosebud-like), strong purplish-pink with light reddish-purple markings, mid–late. Leaves glossy on a compact plant to about 1.5m. Sister of 'Petticoat'. Hachmann.

■ **RUBINETTA** Strong purplish-red with red markings, 4–5cm. Size to 1m × 1m or more. *Ger*. Hachmann.

RACOON

■ **RUBINSTERN** Deep rose-red, with small darker markings, to 5cm. Ht to 90cm, spreading habit. Hachmann.

■ **SCHNEEGLANZ** Pure white with a yellow throat, 4.5–5cm. Ht to 1m. Semi-deciduous. Being discontinued by Hachmann nursery. Hachmann.

■ **SCHNEEPERLE**® Double, creamy-white buds open to pure white, with yellow-green spotting, to 4.5cm. Leaves glossy, dark green, with fairly good leaf-retention in winter for a hardy white. Ht to 40cm. *Ger*. Hachmann.

■ **SCHNEESTURM** Flowers white with a faint-yellow throat, 5.5–6.5cm. Ht to about 70cm. Hachmann.

■ **SCHNEEWITTCHEN (syn. SNOW WHITE)** White, unmarked, 3–4cm. Ht to 40cm, spreading. *Ger*. Hachmann.

■ **SIGNALGLÜHEN** Light red with deeper markings, some petaloid stamens, 4.5–5.5cm. Ht to 30cm. No longer grown by Hachmann but still commercially available. Hachmann.

SIGNALGLÜHEN

SQUIRREL

■ **SQUIRREL** Bright-scarlet, long-lasting, hold their colour well, to 3cm, late. Dark-green small leaves, on a dense low-growing plant. The most popular of the Glendoick red azaleas and a commercial standard in the UK. *Scot, Ger*. Cox.

■ **STOAT** Deep purplish-pink, unmarked, to 3cm, early–mid. Fairly neat habit. We found it was a bit shy-flowering in Scotland, but it does better further south. Cox.

■ **STOPLIGHT (STOPPLICHT)** Brilliant-red, to 6.5cm. Low growing. Schumacher.

■ **THEKLA** Medium lilac-purple with some petaloid stamens, to 5.5cm. Ht to 50cm. A hybrid of 'Elsie Lee' × 'Purpurkissen'. A sister, **'MARINJA'**®, has lighter pinkish-purple flowers and is semi-double. Several other sisters have also been named. Hachmann.

■ **TORNELLA** Double, deep purplish-pink with deeper spots, to 6cm. Ht to 50cm, spreading. Leaves dark green and glossy, bronzed in winter. Hachmann.

■ **ULTAVA** Small, vivid-pink flowers to 2.5cm. A low and compact, tough Czech hybrid to 60cm. Jelinch.

■ **VIOLETTA** Light purplish with purple-red throat. Mid-season. Compact with small leaves. (*kiusianum* ×). There is also a Glenn Dale, a Kurume and an Indica with this name. Kerkhoff.

■ **VUYK'S ROSY RED** Rosy red, to 7cm, with darker flash, mid-season. Good glossy foliage that colours in autumn. Long a very popular commercial azalea in Europe. *AGM, PNW*. Vuyk.

■ **VUYK'S SCARLET** Crimson with wavy lobes, spotted darker, to 5.5cm, mid. Glossy foliage that colours in autumn and dense-mounding habit. A common UK commercial hybrid. *AGM*. Vuyk.

VUYK'S SCARLET

WOMBAT

■ **WOMBAT** Vivid purplish-red (deep-pink), to 5cm, late. Low and spreading, almost prostrate. The best low groundcover azalea for Scotland. (*nakaharae* hybrid). *AGM*. Cox.

TSUTSUSI THERORHODION

The two species described here have been included in the genus *Rhododendron* by some authorities and excluded by others. At the moment the consensus seems to be for exclusion, but as *R. camtschaticum* has so long been considered a rhododendron, I have included these two species in this book.

■ **CAMTSCHATICUM** Dwarf H5 L–VL. Flowers rotate, purple on short stalks, 1–3 per truss.

CAMTSCHATICUM RED

CAMTSCHATICUM PURPLE

Selected forms have red or white flowers. Native to Alaska and N.E. Asia. Does best in cool climates. A deciduous creeper that often flowers on and off through the summer. *S. Fin, Swe, Den, Ger, Scot.*

CAMTSCHATICUM WHITE

■ **REDOWSKIANUM** Essentially a regional variation from N.E. Asia. Almost impossible to cultivate so far.

RHODODENDRON AND AZALEA BEST LISTS

These lists are very deliberately my choice, very subjective and bound to provoke disagreement. You can let me know what you think for the next edition.

■ **The best white rhododendrons and azaleas:** R. decorum white, R. griffithianum, 'Loderi King George', 'Alena', 'Helen Everett', 'Dexter's Spice', 'Senator Henry Jackson', 'Helene Schiffner', R. atlanticum, R. occidentale, 'Persil', 'Panda', plus dozens of other evergreen azaleas, and many Vireya species.

■ **The best yellow rhododendrons and azaleas:** 'Crest', Goldkrone, 'Nancy Evans', 'Capistrano' (for severe climates), 'Curlew', 'Gold Topaz', R. wardii, R. luteum, R. macabeanum, R. lacteum, R. laetum.

■ **The best red rhododendrons and azaleas:** R. barbatum, 'Francesca', 'Captain Jack', 'Kilimanjaro', 'Grace Seabrook', 'Taurus', 'Squirrel', R. cumberlandense, 'Camp's Red', 'June Fire', 'St Valentine' and other Vireyas.

■ **The best purple rhododendrons:** R. niveum, R. russatum, 'Glendoick Velvet', 'Azurro' and other Hachmann purples, 'Edith Bosely'.

■ **The best orange rhododendrons and azaleas:** R. cinnabarinum (orange forms), R. citriniflorum var. horaeum orange, R. dichroanthum, 'September Song', 'Fabia', 'Gibraltar', 'Fireball', 'Arneson's Gem' and other Knaphill/Exbury hybrids, R. calendulaceum, many Vireyas such as R. javanicum, 'Kiandra' and 'Simbu Sunset'.

■ **The best hardy (H4–8) scented rhododendrons and azaleas:** 'Tinkerbird', 'Loderi', R. decorum, R. auriculatum, R. fortunei, 'Dexter's Spice', 'Barnstable', 'Snowbird', R. arborescens, R. atlanticum.

■ **The best tender (H1–2) scented rhododendrons:** R. jasminiflorum, R. formosum var. inaequale, R. edgeworthii, R. lindleyi, R. cuffeanum (as cultivated in California), R. nuttallii, plus hybrids of it such as 'Mi Amor'.

■ **Smallest growing rhododendrons and azaleas:** R. keiskei, 'Yaku Fairy', R. calostotum ssp. keleticum Radicans Group, R. lowndesii, R. nakaharae (some forms), R rubineiflorum.

■ **Best late flowering:** (July–August in N. Hemisphere): R. auriculatum, R. hemsleyanum, R. kasoense, 'Aladdin', 'Polar Bear', 'Maximum Roseum', R. viscosum, R. prunifolium, 'Lemon Drop', 'Sparkler', R. nakaharae, 'Racoon', R. kawakamii, plus many Vireyas.

■ **Best very early flowering:** (Dec–Feb in N. Hemisphere): R. moupinense, R. dauricum, R. sichotense, R. lapponicum, R. lanigerum, R. ririei, 'Nobleanum', 'Christmas Cheer',

■ **Rhododendron species with the best foliage:** R. bureavii, R. pachysanthum, R. falconeri ssp. eximium, R. campanulatum ssp. aeruginosum, R. proteoides, R. sinogrande, R. roxieanum, Vireyas such as R. taxifolium, R. stenophyllum.

■ **Cultivars with the best foliage:** 'Golfer', 'Viking Silver', 'Sir Charles Lemon', 'Graziela', R. oreotrephes, 'Bluecalyptus', 'Everred™', 'Wine & Roses ™'.

■ **The hardiest rhododendrons and azaleas:** R. brachycarpum Tigerstedtii Group. Finnish hybrids: 'Hellikki', 'Hellsinki University', 'Mikkeli'. Northern Lights azaleas: 'White Lights', 'Lemon Lights' and so on.

■ **Best evergreen azaleas:** 'Ben Morrison', 'Panda', 'Marushka', 'Girard's Variegated Hot Shot', 'Squirrel', 'Mother's Day', 'Komo Kulshan', 'Palestrina', 'Betty Ann Voss', 'Elsie Lee', 'Higasa', 'Nancy of Robin Hill', 'Koromo Shikibu'.

■ **Best deciduous azalea hybrids:** 'Arneson's Gem', 'Gibraltar', 'Gold Topaz', 'June Fire', 'Homebush', 'Irene Koster', 'Strawberry Ice'.

■ **Best Vireya Species:** R. acrophilum, R. rousiae, R. jasminiflorum, R. christii, R. zoelleri, R. laetum, R. nervulosum.

■ **Best Vireya hybrids:** 'Coral Seas', 'Java Light', 'Saxon Glow', 'Simbu Sunset', 'St Valentine' or 'Cape Cod Valentine', 'Strawberry Parfait', 'Gwenevere', 'Tropic Glow', 'Just Peachy'.

THE NAMING OF RHODODENDRON AND AZALEA HYBRIDS

All new hybrids and species selections should be registered. In Europe the registration is at RHS Wisley in England, some other countries, including the U.S.A. & Canada and Australia, have their own registrars. A name is only allowed to be used once but, prior to 1958 (the first published register), many names were used again and again, which has made life confusing. The worst examples I know are the eight plants named 'Violetta' and nine called 'Pink Delight'. What you name your hybrid is very important for sales and credibility. The lists that follow are just my personal choice of great and horrible names. I make no judgement here on plant quality.

■ **The best hybrid names:** 'Ashes of Roses' (it just makes me laugh), 'Bluecalyptus' (it really looks like one), 'Dream of Kings', 'Ghost', 'Hot Ginger and Dynamite' (the best-ever name in my opinion: I have to have this plant), 'Jurassic Fantasy', 'Red Red' and 'Pink, Pink, Pink' (if you've got it, flaunt it), 'Copper Kettles', 'Excaliber', 'Fuju-kaku-nu-

matsu' (and lots of other beautiful Japanese names). Ironically hybridizers Carlson, Delp and Lofthouse, all of whom named far too many untested hybrids, came up with some of the best names.

■ **The worst hybrid names:** (reasons: ugly, unpronounceable, sentimental, obscene, political, weird, or I just hate them). 'Dad's Killer' (why??), 'Cutie' (yuck!), 'Johnny Bender' (hmmm), 'Daffodilly' (childish, but not nice), 'Dixy Lee Ray' (next it will be 'George Bush' – which I'll set fire to), 'Oberburgermeister Janssen', 'Honeymoon Honey', 'Come to Baby Do', 'Whose Honey are You?' (these leave me speechless), 'Butkew', 'Dichdiap', 'Dichrofab' (and almost all Magor hybrids made of part of the names of the parents – no wonder no one grows any of them), 'Gay Divorcee', 'Gee Whiz', 'Geh Reg Rath Professor Doktor Wittmack' (oh come on!) …

THE UNOFFICIAL KEN COX AWARDS FOR THE BEST TEN RHODODENDRON HYBRIDS

■ 'Loderi'	(for scent and flowers)
■ 'Lem's Monarch'	(outstanding flower)
■ 'Taurus'	(perfect early red and good foliage)
■ 'Viking Silver'	(best silver foliage)
■ 'Nancy Evans'	(free-flowering deep-yellow)
■ 'Fantastica'	(best 'yak')
■ 'Lem's Cameo'	(so influential in breeding and very fine)
■ 'Wee Bee'	(one of the best dwarfs)
■ 'Glendoick® Mystique'	(the finest Glendoick elepidote hybrid)
■ 'Wine & Roses'	(red-purple leaf underside)

AND THE WORST/LEAST FAVOURITE TEN LIST

■ 'Barry Rogers'
■ 'Brigadoon'
■ 'Cranberry Swirl'
■ 'Elsie Straver'
■ 'Hong Kong'
■ 'Moerheim'
■ 'Pink Drift'
■ 'Pink Petticoats'
■ 'Rocket'
■ 'Sunup-Sundown'
(Purely personal of course, terrible flowers, poor foliage, bad habit, just not worth growing – they're dogs.)

GLOSSARY

axillary (Bud) coming from an axil, which is the angle between a leaf and a stem. Species such as *R. racemosum* produce flowers from axillary buds.

bark-split A physical injury; the sap in the stem is frozen while the plant is in growth, causing the bark to split. It can be fatal in severe cases.

chlorosis A yellowing of the leaves caused by mineral imbalance, too much or too little water, or climatic or genetic problems.

clone A genetically uniform assemblage of individuals derived from a single individual by asexual propagation (that is, not grown from seed). The finest forms of species are often given clonal names, for example, *R. calostrotum* 'Gigha'.

corolla The tube and lobes (petals) of the flower.

elepidote (opposite of *lepidote*) Without *scales* on the foliage. This distinction is of fundamental importance in the classification of rhododendrons.

epiphyte A plant that grows on another plant (a fallen log for example), but which does not derive any nutrient from it.

Ericaceae The plant family that includes rhododendrons, heathers, *Kalmia, Gaultheria* and several other genera. Hence Ericaceous, belonging the family Ericaceae.

glabrous Without hairs or glands of any kind.

glaucous (Leaf) green, strongly tinged with bluish grey; with a greyish waxy bloom, for example in *R. campanulatum* ssp. *aeruginosum, R. lepidostylum, R. oreotrephes.*

hose-in-hose (flower) A second corolla within the first; very common in azaleas.

indumentum A covering of hairs found on leaves, which can be thick and woolly or thin. The different types are very important for species identification.

lax or *loose* (*truss*) One in which the flowers hang downwards, often between the foliage.

lepidote 1. Scaly. 2. Part of the genus *Rhododendron*, in subgenus *Rhododendron*, the members of which have scales on the leaves. The opposite of *elepidote* (without scales). This distinction is of fundamental importance in the classification of rhododendrons. The scales are best viewed on the leaf underside with a microscope.

Maddenia (*subsection*) This group of species are rather tender, often grown indoors, and many of them and their hybrids are sweetly scented.

nectar pouches or *nectaries* Sac-like vessels in the base of the *corolla* of some species containing a sweet substance, in most species of subsections Irrorata and Thomsonia, for example.

petal blight A fungal disease that destroys flowers, turning them brown and limp.

Phytophthora A genus containing many serious pathogenic fungus diseases, especially root-rot, *Phytophthora cinnamoni.*

pinching A method of preventative pruning, where the terminal bud or growth is removed, to encourage branching and a denser growth habit.

powdery mildew A disease that attacks rhododendrons, causing leaf discoloration or leaf drop and which can be fatal in severe infections. Can be controlled with fungicides.

root-rot (*see* under *Phytophthora*)

rust A fungal disease that causes black spotting on the leaf upper-surface, with corresponding reddish-brown patches of spores on the leaf lower-surface.

scales Found on the leaves of *lepidote* rhododendrons; these can sometimes be seen with the naked eye but, magnified, their form can be used to aid identification.

self In evergreen azaleas, especially Satsukis, the pale flowers are often striped and spotted a deeper colour. When a whole flower is the deeper colour, it is known as a 'self'. Selfing also means the self-pollinating of a flower.

shrub A woody plant with several stems or branches from near the base; of smaller stature than a tree.

stamen The male part of the flower, which bears the pollen.

stigma The female part of the flower, at the end of the style, where the pollen is deposited.

subgenus The genus *Rhododendron* is divided into six subgenera, each containing related species. These are further broken down into sections and subsections.

subsection In the taxonomy of rhododendrons, the genus is divided up into subsections which contain one to thirty, or more, related species. For instance, subsection Triflora contains mostly tall and upright-growing scaly-leaved species with masses of small flowers.

suckering Producing shoots from near or below ground level (suckers). These should be removed if from rootstocks below the grafted union.

taxonomy The science of the identification, nomenclature and classification of plants.

truss A cluster of flowers on a single stalk, or from a single bud. This is not a technical scientific term: 'inflorescence' or 'umbel' are usually used in botanical texts.

vine weevil A pernicious insect pest, which notches foliage and whose grubs eat roots and bark.

Vireya Part of the genus *Rhododendron* is section Vireya, which contains several hundred flamboyant tropical species that need frost-free conditions to grow. Many hybrids have also been raised.

BIBLIOGRAPHY

Argent, Dr G., Bond, J., Chamberlain, Dr D., Cox, P., Hardy, A., *The Rhododendron Handbook 1998* (R.H.S., 1997)

Bean, W.J., *Trees and Shrubs Hardy in the British Isles*, Vol. III, 8th Revised Edition (John Murray, 1976)

Cox, K.N.E., *A Plantsman's Guide to Rhododendrons* (Ward Lock, 1989, 1993)

Cox, K.N.E., *Rhododendrons, A Hamlyn Care Manual* (Hamlyn, 1998) (Also in Dutch, French, Danish.)

Cox, P.A., *The Smaller Rhododendrons* (Batsford, 1985)

Cox, P.A., *The Larger Rhododendron Species* (Batsford, 1990)

Cox, P.A., *The Cultivation of Rhododendrons* (Batsford, 1993)

Cox. P.A. & Cox, K.N.E., *Cox's Guide to Choosing Rhododendrons* (Batsford, 1990)

Cox, P.A. & Cox, K.N.E., *The Encyclopedia of Rhododendron Hybrids* (Batsford, 1988)

Cox, P.A. & Cox, K.N.E., *The Encyclopedia of Rhododendron Species* (Glendoick Publishing, 1997 and 2001)

Fairweather, C., *Vireyas* (NCCPG Booklet, 2004)

Galle, Fred C., *Azaleas*, 2nd Edition (Timber Press, 1985)

Greer H., *Greer's Guidebook to Available Rhododendrons* (Offshoot Publications, 1982, 1996)

Kenyon, J. & Walker J., *Vireyas, a Practical Gardening Guide* (Timber Press, 1977)

Leslie, Dr Alan, *The Rhododendron Register* (RHS, 2004)

Leach, D.G., *Rhododendrons of the World* (Allen & Unwin, 1962)

Coker, B. & Miller, K. (eds), *Crossing the Rubicon* (The Canterbury Rhododendron Society, New Zealand)

Postan, C. (ed.), *The Rhododendron Story* (RHS, 1996)

Reiley, H. Edward, *Success with Rhododendrons and Azaleas*, Revised Edition (Timber Press, 2004)

Salley, H., & Greer, H., *Rhododendron Hybrids*, 3rd Edition (CD-ROM)

Towe, L. Clarence, *American Azaleas* (Timber Press, 2004)

Van Veen Nursery, *Rhododendrons You Should Meet*

White-Smith, E. & Sorenson-Smith, L. (eds), *Vireya Rhododendrons, An Anthology*

The Flora of China, Ericaceae
Journal of the American Rhododendron Society
Rhododendrons with Magnolias and Camellias, RHS Yearbook
The Azalean, Journal of the Azalea Society of America

INDEX

PHOTOGRAPHIC CREDITS

TL	TM	TR
UL	UM	UR
LL	LM	LR
BL	BM	BR

KEY

All photographs supplied by the author, with the exception of the following:

J. Barlup
   p152 UR
   p174 TM
J. Birck
   p42 UR
J. Coleman
   p199 LR & LL
   p200 LR
   p201 UM
   p202 UR, LR & BR
   p203 UL & BR
   p207 LL
   p211 UR
   p212 UL, UM, LM, TR & UR
   p213 BL & LM

   p214 TL, BM, LR & BR
   p215 UM, TR & LR
   p216 TL, UM, LM, TR & LR
M. Creel
   p192 TM
   p195 BM
   p195 LR
Richard Currie
   p76 TM & LM
   p77 TR
   p78 TM & TL
M. van der Giessen
   p195 BR
J. Hammond
   p146 BM
Matt Heasman
   p96 UM
   p98 BR
H. Helm
   p26 TL
DFE-CLO
   p200 TL, BL, BM & LM
   p205 TM
Don Hyatt
   p201 LR
   p215 LL
   p218 BM & TR

L. Jonsson
   p116 LM
Paul Molinari
   P50 LL
   p51 LL
PDSI
   p217 TL, LL & UM
Ron Rabideau
   p61 TM
   p178 BM
   p192 BL
Keith Rushforth
   p76 TL
Peter Schick
   p50 BR
   p51 LR
   p52 TM
Earl Sommerville
   p181 UL
   p195 TM & LL
Don Voss
   p205 LL
   p212 LL, LR
   p213 LL, UM, TR
   p220 BM
J. Weagle
   p220 BR